OS/2 Applications on the Companion Disks

WITHDRAWN

Desktop Applications

AV (Archive Viewer)	Displays and manages compressed-file archives
Blackjack	Plays the game of Blackjack
Chron	Launches applications at specific times
ClipEdit	Clipboard management program
DiskStat	Displays disk statistics
Galleria	Bitmap viewer, editor, and screen capture program
INIMaint	Manages OS/2 INI files
Lst/PM	Displays file contents in ASCII, EBCDIC or hexadecimal
Mah Jongg Solitaire	Plays the game of Mah Jongg
Numerical Assistant	An advanced calculator
Syscols (PM Color Configuration)	Configures all 41 desktop colors
SDPlus (Shut Down Plus)	Rapid system shut down from the desktop

Command-Line Utilities

DELPATH	Deletes directories and all files in those directories
FSHL	A command-line shell
LH/2	Compresses and decompresses files
KILLEM	Kills OS/2 processes
OS2SCAN	Detects and identifies computer viruses
OS2CLEAN	Removes computer viruses
TE/2	Communications and terminal emulation program
WHEREIS	Finds files

For every kind of computer user, there is a SYBEX book.

All computer users learn in their own way. Some need straightforward and methodical explanations. Others are just too busy for this approach. But no matter what camp you fall into, SYBEX has a book that can help you get the most out of your computer and computer software while learning at your own pace.

Beginners generally want to start at the beginning. The **ABC's** series, with its step-by-step lessons in plain language, helps you build basic skills quickly. Or you might try our **Quick & Easy** series, the friendly, full-color guide.

The **Mastering** and **Understanding** series will tell you everything you need to know about a subject. They're perfect for intermediate and advanced computer users, yet they don't make the mistake of leaving beginners behind.

If you're a busy person and are already comfortable with computers, you can choose from two SYBEX series—**Up & Running** and **Running Start**. The **Up & Running** series gets you started in just 20 lessons. Or you can get two books in one, a step-by-step tutorial and an alphabetical reference, with our **Running Start** series.

Everyone who uses computer software can also use a computer software reference. SYBEX offers the gamut—from portable **Instant References** to comprehensive **Encyclopedias, Desktop References,** and **Bibles.**

SYBEX even offers special titles on subjects that don't neatly fit a category—like **Tips & Tricks,** the **Shareware Treasure Chests,** and a wide range of books for Macintosh computers and software.

SYBEX books are written by authors who are expert in their subjects. In fact, many make their living as professionals, consultants or teachers in the field of computer software. And their manuscripts are thoroughly reviewed by our technical and editorial staff for accuracy and ease-of-use.

So when you want answers about computers or any popular software package, just help yourself to SYBEX.

For a complete catalog of our publications, please write:

SYBEX Inc.
2021 Challenger Drive
Alameda, CA 94501
Tel: (510) 523-8233/(800) 227-2346 Telex: 336311
Fax: (510) 523-2373

SYBEX is committed to using natural resources wisely to preserve and improve our environment. As a leader in the computer book publishing industry, we are aware that over 40% of America's solid waste is paper. This is why we have been printing the text of books like this one on recycled paper since 1982.

This year our use of recycled paper will result in the saving of more than 15,300 trees. We will lower air pollution effluents by 54,000 pounds, save 6,300,000 gallons of water, and reduce landfill by 2,700 cubic yards.

In choosing a SYBEX book you are not only making a choice for the best in skills and information, you are also choosing to enhance the quality of life for all of us.

OS/2 Secrets & Solutions

OS/2® Secrets & Solutions

PETER DYSON

San Francisco • Paris • Düsseldorf • Soest

SYBEX®

ACQUISITIONS EDITOR: Dianne King
DEVELOPMENTAL EDITOR: Gary Masters
EDITOR: James A. Compton
TECHNICAL EDITOR: David Farquharson
SERIES DESIGNER: Suzanne Albertson
PRODUCTION ARTIST: Helen Bruno
SCREEN GRAPHICS: Cuong Le
DESKTOP PUBLISHING: Stephanie Hollier
PROOFREADER/PRODUCTION ASSISTANT: Kristin Amlie
INDEXER: Nancy Guenther
COVER DESIGNER: Archer Design
COVER ILLUSTRATOR: Richard Miller

All screen images are reprinted by permission from IBM's OS/2 2.1, copyright © 1981, 1987, 1991, 1992, 1993 International Business Machines Corporation.

Copyrights for the shareware programs on the accompanying disks are as follows: AV (Archive Viewer) copyright © Mark Kimes; BlackJack copyright © Jon Cepale; Chron copyright © Hilbert Computing; ClipEdit copyright © Solaris Precision Software; DELPATH copyright © James M. Sauber; DiskStat, FSHL, Lst/PM, and TE/2 copyright © Oberon Software; Galleria copyright © Bitware; INIMaint copyright © Carry Associates; Killem and Whereis copyright © Code Blazers, Inc.; LH/2 copyright © A:WARE; MahJongg copyright © SynchroSoft; NA (Numerical Assistant) copyright © Snow Storm Software; OS2Clean and OS2Scan copyright © McAfee Associates; SDPLUS copyright © A.R. Scheicher; Syscols copyright © Donna Campanella.

Screen reproductions produced with Collage Plus.

Collage Plus is a trademark of Inner Media.

SYBEX is a registered trademark of SYBEX, Inc.

TRADEMARKS: SYBEX has attempted throughout this book to distinguish proprietary trademarks from descriptive terms by following the capitalization style used by the manufacturer.

SYBEX is not affiliated with any manufacturer.

Every effort has been made to supply complete and accurate information. However, SYBEX assumes no responsibility for its use, nor for any infringement of the intellectual property rights of third parties which would result from such use.

Copyright ©1993 SYBEX Inc., 2021 Challenger Drive, Alameda, CA 94501. World rights reserved. No part of this publication may be stored in a retrieval system, transmitted, or reproduced in any way, including but not limited to photocopy, photograph, magnetic or other record, without the prior agreement and written permission of the publisher.

Library of Congress Card Number: 93-83693
ISBN: 0-7821-1281-1

Warranty

SYBEX warrants the enclosed disks to be free of physical defects for a period of ninety (90) days after purchase. If you discover a defect in either of the disks during this warranty period, you can obtain a replacement disk at no charge by sending the defective disk, postage prepaid, with proof of purchase to:

SYBEX Inc.
Customer Service Department
2021 Challenger Drive
Alameda, CA 94501
(800)227-2346
Fax: (510) 523-2373

After the 90-day period, you can obtain a replacement disk by sending us the defective disk, proof of purchase, and a check or money order for $10, payable to SYBEX.

Disclaimer

SYBEX makes no warranty or representation, either express or implied, with respect to this software, its quality performance, merchantability, or fitness for a particular purpose. In no event will SYBEX, its distributors, or dealers be liable for direct, indirect, special, incidental, or consequential damages arising out of the use or inability to use the software even if advised of the possibility of such damage.

The exclusion of implied warranties is not permitted by some states. Therefore, the above exclusion may not apply to you. This warranty provides you with specific legal rights; there may be other rights that you may have that vary from state to state.

Copy Protection

None of the programs on the disks are copy-protected. However, in all cases, reselling these programs without authorization is expressly forbidden.

For NRD

ACKNOWLEDGMENTS

WHEN you read the acknowledgments in some books, you can almost hear the surly tone used as the author grudgingly gives thanks to the other people involved with the book. You know the sort of thing I mean, something like "Thanks to Snort, my wonderful copy editor, without whom none of this would have been possible." Many times you can almost hear the author's additional parenthetical remarks, such as, "Snort, who almost totally wrecked the book because he don't know no grammar and can't understand the comma rule!"

Well, this book was nothing like that. It really was a lot of fun to research and to write (honest), and as usual, I had a lot of help and good advice from many different people. This is my chance to say thanks to them.

At SYBEX, thanks go to the following: Dianne King, Acquisitions Manager, for all her encouragement and good humor; Gary Masters, the best Developmental Editor I have ever worked with, for his excellent advice, technical assistance, and his ability to keep the distant goal in careful focus at all times; Jim Compton, Editor, for his quiet and careful edit and dry sense of humor; Kristin Amlie, proofreader; Stephanie Hollier, desktop publishing specialist; Helen Bruno, production artist; and Cuong Le, screen graphics wizard.

At IBM, thanks to Melissa Robertson and Gail Ostrow, both Assistant Program Managers for OS/2 2.1 Independent Vendor Marketing, for all their help in providing a road map into the IBM organization, and for tracking down information from all those technical requests. Thanks also to all those IBMers who called to answer my questions directly; I couldn't have done it without you.

And finally, on a personal note, thanks to Nancy for her constant support; to Tom Charlesworth for his software developer's viewpoint of OS/2 and lunch at the Japanese place; to Gene Weisskopf for all that author talk and lunch at Vic's, and to David Farquharson for his excellent technical edit and lunch at Vic's; I'll pay next time, guys, I promise.

Contents

AT A GLANCE

CONTENTS

PART II   RUNNING OS/2, DOS, AND WINDOWS PROGRAMS

Requirements 338

CONTENTS

PART III OS/2 AND COMPUTER HARDWARE

PART IV   **BECOMING AN OS/2 POWER USER**

12   **Working from the Command Line**   493

CONTENTS

PART V   **ADVANCED OS/2 TOPICS**

15 Networking and OS/2   659

INTRODUCTION

OS/2 is a brilliant technical achievement, produced by a talented and dedicated group of individuals, and using it can change forever the way you think about computing on the desktop. OS/2 version 2.0 was released in the Spring of 1992 and version 2.1 in 1993. To date, millions of copies have been sold, and well over 1000 32-bit applications are now available for all kinds of computing tasks from the general to the highly specific.

In this book, I've tried to focus on the whys of OS/2, without losing sight of the hows. Too many OS/2 books only tell you how to perform a task, without sharing any of the reasoning behind their instructions, or discussing ways of applying this information to your everyday work. This book gives you that information.

Whom This Book Is For

This book is for you if you are an intermediate to advanced OS/2 user, or you have migrated to OS/2 from an MS-DOS or Windows environment. If you are an advanced user, you will learn lots of unique tips and tricks to get the most out of your system. If you are an intermediate user, there is plenty here for you too, by way of background information that will help you better understand how your OS/2 system works. You will find information on installing, optimizing, upgrading, and troubleshooting OS/2, as well as descriptions of how to get the most out of the desktop and the built-in Productivity applications.

If you are a curious OS/2 beginner making the transition from DOS or Windows, don't be put off; you too will gain many insights into why and how OS/2 does what it does. Start with Chapter 1 and work though Chapter 4, for a fast-paced introduction to the OS/2 graphical user interface, and then consult specific chapters for more information. With most topics in this book, I present a certain amount of background material before beginning the technical discussions.

Parts of this book deal with the issues faced by corporate users in a typical business environment; chapters are devoted to running MS-DOS, Windows, and OS/2 applications, and networking is covered in a special chapter.

How This Book Is Organized

This book is divided into the following parts:

Part I: Essential OS/2 (Chapters 1–4) introduces OS/2, showing you how to get the most from the graphical user interface, and how to perform common, everyday tasks from the desktop and from the OS/2 command line. Finally, you will learn about the Productivity applications bundles with OS/2.

Part II: Running OS/2, DOS, and Windows Programs (Chapters 5–7) describes the three operating environments available in OS/2—OS/2 itself, DOS, and WIN-OS/2—and shows how to tailor these environments to your applications. You will find information on how to start and configure a DOS session, and how you can load and run a stand-alone version of MS-DOS inside OS/2. Each chapter in this section also lists applications known to have problems running under OS/2 and briefly describes what you can do to solve some of those problems.

Part III: OS/2 and Computer Hardware (Chapters 8–11) concentrates on the many important hardware issues in the OS/2 world, including computers, hard disks, CD-ROMs, SCSI adapters, printers, plotters, tape drives, modem, mice, as well as the latest developments in multimedia.

Part IV: Becoming an OS/2 Power User (Chapters 12–14) covers how to use the OS/2 command line, and details many of the powerful commands you can use. Two chapters cover how to optimize OS/2's performance, and how to diagnose and resolve OS/2 problems.

Part V: Advanced OS/2 Topics (Chapters 15 and 16) includes information on using OS/2 with networks, as well as the Communications Manager, LAN Server, and Extended Services. Chapter 16 serves as an introduction to the powerful REXX programming language.

Part VI: The Best of OS/2 Shareware covers how to install and use the programs contained on the two companion disks accompanying this book. These disks, attached inside the back cover, contain many programs to increase your productivity, and also add a little fun to your OS/2 computing.

Appendix A: Installing OS/2 describes the issues involved in setting up OS/2 on your system, and covers all of the installation options.

Appendix B: OS/2 Resources is a complete resource list for OS/2, and contains information on technical support, bulletin boards, IBM and non-IBM publications, magazines, newsletters and periodicals.

Conventions Used in This Book

Throughout this book you will find many secrets and solutions, notes and warnings. Some are incorporated into the text, while others are set apart in boxes. The following headings indicate the subject matter of each type of boxed note:

- **Secret:** Secrets describe OS/2 features that are not generally known, or are undocumented in the normal manuals. Sometimes they may present a topic in a new way.

- **Solution:** Solutions are practical techniques you can use to help smooth out the rough patches in your day-to-day computing.

- **Note:** Notes contain information pertinent to the topic or procedure under discussion.

- **Warning:** Warnings alert you to potentially dangerous operations. They inform you about problems you might encounter if you use a procedure incorrectly, or without some forethought.

MS-DOS versus OS/2's DOS Emulation

Part of OS/2's universal appeal is that you can run all your existing MS-DOS and Windows programs in special OS/2 sessions. OS/2 does not actually contain MS-DOS or Windows, but it does contain programs that *emulate* or mimic these environments. This immediately poses the problem of what to call these different environments, and how to tell them apart.

Throughout this book I refer to the stand-alone, single-tasking operating system, whether developed by Microsoft or by IBM, as MS-DOS, and I describe the special OS/2 sessions that mimic this environment as DOS or as OS/2's DOS emulation. Similarly, I refer to Windows as the program from Microsoft that runs on top of MS-DOS, and I describe the Windows emulation that runs inside OS/2 as WIN-OS/2.

Syntax Conventions

Syntax descriptions are used in many chapters in this book to show just how to use a particular command. OS/2 commands are shown in UPPERCASE letters, and may be followed by any optional parameters or switches, shown in the usual order of entry. Any required parameters are shown in **bold lowercase italic**, while optional parameters are shown in *standard lowercase italic*. Any optional switches are shown as */switches*, and are described in full in the text that follows the command.

The Screen Captures

The screen captures used in this book were made with the intention of providing the clearest possible representation of the OS/2 desktop. Because you can change and configure the desktop in many different ways, do not be concerned if you detect small differences between the figures in this book and what you see on your own screen, particularly in the number and placement of icons.

PART I

Essential OS/2

CHAPTERS

OS/2 OS/2 OS/2

OS/2 OS/2 OS/2 OS/2 OS/2 OS/2 OS/2

OS/2 OS/2 OS/2 OS/2 (

1

Getting Started
with OS/2

OS/2 is IBM's advanced, multitasking operating system for personal computers. This beginning chapter describes the major features of the operating system, and the reasons why you would want to use OS/2. I'll describe some of the decisions you will have to make before you can install OS/2, and then we'll take a quick tour of the graphical user interface. The chapter ends with a description of the extensive help system available in OS/2.

This book covers OS/2 Versions 2.1 and 2.0, so we'll start with a brief history and comparison of these two releases.

OS/2 Version 2.1 and Version 2.0

OS/2 Version 2.0 was released in March of 1992, and was the first 32-bit release of the operating system; previous versions had been based on 16-bit architecture. OS/2 2.0 contained the object-oriented workplace shell known as the desktop, several small but powerful productivity applications, greatly improved DOS compatibility, and support for Microsoft Windows 3.0 programs.

OS/2 2.1 was released in early 1993, and contains many significant improvements and upgrades to OS/2 2.0; if you have not upgraded yet, you should do so as quickly as possible to take advantage of these new features.

Version 2.1 now supports Windows 3.1 programs, including programs that require Windows Enhanced mode. Programs that would not run under OS/2 2.0 now run without hesitation. Some users report that the Windows emulator, WIN-OS/2, runs as fast as native Windows, if not faster. WIN-OS/2 also includes many of the Windows 3.1 accessories, including the File Manager, Write, Paint Brush, Sound Recorder, and Media Player.

Support for hardware devices is much better in 2.1, and setting up and installing SCSI interface cards and CD-ROMs is a more straightforward process.

Other new features include a desktop fax productivity application, support for 256-color SVGA boards, Personal Computer Memory Card International Association (PCMCIA) input/output devices, enhanced support for pen-based systems and multimedia applications, support for the Advanced Power Management (APM) specification for battery-powered computers, and better support for OS/2 as an AS/400 client with a PCSupport program.

The Fundamentals of OS/2

There are many compelling reasons to use OS/2, and in this section we'll look at some of the more important parts of the operating system. All of the topics discussed here will be expanded in later chapters, but it is important that we establish a broad understanding of OS/2's capabilities early on, so we can build on that firm foundation.

Multitasking

For many people the most important aspect of OS/2 is that it was designed to be a multitasking operating system right from the very beginning; multitasking was not grafted on to an existing operating system as an afterthought. This has made it much easier for the programmers who wrote OS/2 to implement and maintain the system, and to add or expand features as needed.

Multitasking is the ability to run several programs on the same computer at the same time. Anyone who has ever had to wait for a computer to complete a time-consuming task will understand the potential benefits of being able to do several things at once. Imagine being able to word process a memo while your spreadsheet program is running a complex recalculation. At the other end of the scale, imagine playing Solitaire while you format a disk in the background. Another aspect of multitasking in OS/2, called *threads*, allows several different processes to run at the same time inside the same program. This means that one part of the program can be performing calculations while another part of the same program is drawing a graph or a chart.

The program that you are currently interacting with is known as the *foreground* application, and all the other programs running at the same time are known as *background* tasks.

See Chapter 13 for information on how multitasking in OS/2 works, and how you can use multitasking to your advantage by starting several programs running at the same time.

The Graphical User Interface

OS/2 provides an object-oriented graphical user interface known as the *Workplace Shell*, the first commercial product to be designed using a new user interface standard developed by IBM, known as Common User Access, or CUA for short. CUA is a part of a wider collection of definitions known as Systems Application Architecture (SAA) from IBM. SAA guidelines can be applied to software running on all kinds of computers, from PCs to mini-computers to mainframes. Products designed according to these standards are easier to use than earlier products because SAA provides for a much more consistent look and feel. For example, once you understand how the options in the File menu work in one application program, you will know how to use the same options when you encounter them in other programs, even though those other programs perform wildly different functions.

NOTE　The phrase "object-oriented" has become a common buzzword among software companies, and is in danger of being overused to the point of becoming meaningless. However, the user interface found in OS/2 is truly object-oriented, as it treats programs, files, folders, and peripherals as objects that the user can manipulate.

Another way the OS/2 Workplace Shell differs from other graphical user interfaces is that it uses both mouse buttons. The left mouse button is used as a selection device, and the right mouse button is used for drag-and-drop operations; occasionally, both mouse buttons are used together to perform special actions.

OS/2 also includes the traditional command-line prompt; see Chapter 12 for details.

Compatibility with OS/2 Version 1.X Programs

The 16-bit applications developed for OS/2 Version 1.X can run without change under the 32-bit OS/2 Version 2.X, although they cannot take advantage of all the features and performance of later versions of the operating system.

N O T E

The terms *16-bit* and *32-bit* are worth examining in more detail. They refer to the size of the basic unit of information used by a computer and its software, either 16 or 32 bits "wide." A 16-bit computer or operating system works with information 16 bits at a time, while a 32-bit system works with information 32 bits at a time. The IBM PC/AT and similar machines based on the Intel 80286 are 16-bit computers, while several of the IBM PS/2 computers and similar 80386/80486 clones based on the Intel 80386/80486 are 32-bit computers. What are the advantages? Plenty.

To provide this level of support for the older applications, the designers of OS/2 Version 2.X had to create an architecture in which both 16- and 32-bit program modules could exist, and find a way to convert 16-bit segmented addresses to the 32-bit flat address model used in Version 2.X. To solve this problem, they created the *thunk layer*, a part of the operating system that converts 32-bit parameters to 16-bit form, and maps linear address space to segmented addresses. The operation of this thunk layer is completely transparent to users and application developers.

Running MS-DOS Programs under OS/2

Changing to OS/2 doesn't mean you have to abandon all your DOS programs. One of the most critical benefits of OS/2 is that most of the estimated 30,000+ DOS applications currently available will run unchanged on OS/2, in *DOS sessions*. This allows users migrating to OS/2 from DOS to continue running their current application software.

A DOS session is an OS/2 software emulation of the familiar MS-DOS environment, and you can run your MS-DOS programs in an OS/2 window, in full-screen mode, or iconized in the background. DOS programs run in this way have access to more memory space than usual (approximately 630K), and you have the added benefit of being able to run many DOS sessions side-by-side at the same time.

NOTE

Certain DOS games and programs that talk directly to the PC hardware may not run, or may not run as you expect them to under OS/2. See Chapter 6 for more information on running and optimizing your DOS programs under OS/2.

Using Multiple DOS Sessions

OS/2 takes full advantage of many advanced features of the Intel 80386 and 80486 processors, and one such major innovation is the support for executing multiple 8086 (or 8088) tasks within the 80386 protected mode environment. These tasks are known as Virtual 8086 tasks, and OS/2 has the capability of encapsulating the whole DOS environment in a *virtual DOS machine* or VDM. This VDM gives the operating system far better protection from errant applications programs than is available in MS-DOS or Windows. Also, the DOS environment in OS/2 allows specific versions of MS-DOS to be loaded into a VDM (more on this in Chapter 6), to allow version-specific applications to run. The actual number of separate DOS sessions you can start in OS/2 depends on the space you have available in your swap file; if you have enough space available, you can create up to 240 simultaneous DOS sessions. OS/2 controls DOS sessions in the same way that it handles application programs, by swapping them to disk if necessary, so starting multiple DOS sessions does not increase system memory requirements.

OS/2 Does Windows!

In addition to DOS programs, you can also run Windows application programs under OS/2, without needing Windows itself. OS/2 2.1 is compatible with Windows 2.11, 3.0 and 3.1. Most of the estimated 5000+ available Windows applications will run unchanged under OS/2, although some programs will benefit from the simple tuning techniques described in detail in Chapter 7.

An agreement with Microsoft lets IBM include Windows code inside OS/2, and a Windows program cannot tell which platform it is running on. In this way, a user's investment in Windows software is preserved. Windows programs run on the same desktop as the DOS and OS/2 programs, and can run alongside other programs. Object Linking and Embedding (OLE) is also available between Windows applications.

OS/2 Crash Protection

In OS/2 the entire DOS session environment is contained in what is called a virtual DOS machine (VDM), and this VDM gives OS/2 much better crash protection than either MS-DOS or Windows can provide alone.

In MS-DOS or Windows, it is possible for an application to hang up the entire operating system. OS/2 provides each protected mode process with its own independent address space for code and data, and this protects the code and data from other applications. In OS/2, an errant application can only hang up its own session, either DOS or Windows, and cannot affect the whole operating system. A hung session can easily be terminated from the OS/2 desktop without affecting any of the other applications running in other sessions. This high level of protection, which is a major feature of OS/2, is not available in MS-DOS or in Windows, and it greatly improves the reliability and integrity of the operating system, particularly for mission-critical applications.

Moreover, a DOS or Windows program cannot corrupt any OS/2 operating system code or data, or any application program's code or data; protection is guaranteed by the 80386 processor. You'll find more about how OS/2 takes advantage of the processor architecture in Chapter 8.

The DOS environment under OS/2 also allows specific versions of MS-DOS to be booted into a VDM, allowing version-specific DOS application programs to run without any difficulties; more on this in Chapter 6.

Multimedia

OS/2 supports applications that use OS/2 and Windows multimedia extensions, allowing users to integrate multimedia into their desktop environment. See Chapter 11 for more information on the Multimedia Presentation Manager/2 now included with OS/2 version 2.

More Memory for OS/2

OS/2 takes advantage of the fact that the Intel 80386 can address a very large amount of memory, up to 4GB (1GB is equivalent to 1024MB) in a single contiguous unit. In doing so, it blows away the 640K memory boundary that MS-DOS users have spent so long fighting.

The basic allocation unit of memory is a 4K page, and memory is not divided into segments, but into *memory objects* that consist of one or more 4K pages. OS/2 also eliminates the need for the memory-consuming memory management programs so common in MS-DOS. OS/2 protects memory from unauthorized use; the process that allocates memory owns that memory, and no other application can access the same space. Authorized memory sharing is supported in OS/2, and there are several interprocess communications systems available to the programmer, including semaphores, pipes, and queues.

OS/2 can also use *virtual memory*, which is hard disk space used and managed as though it were RAM space. The use of virtual memory means that you can run an OS/2 program that requires more memory than you actually have installed in your computer.

Chapter 13 contains more information on how memory is managed in OS/2.

OS/2's File Systems

OS/2 has always supported installable file systems for hard disks or for CD-ROM systems. OS/2 offers the choice of two different hard-disk file systems; the *file allocation table* (FAT) file system, and the *High Performance File System* (HPFS). The FAT system is an enhanced version of the MS-DOS file system and is installed by default; the HPFS is loaded and installed during system initialization, and can only be used on hard disks; you cannot use the HPFS on a floppy disk.

The FAT system continues with the traditional MS-DOS "8.3" file-naming convention, with up to eight characters before the period, and up to three characters after the period. Also, FAT file names are always uppercase. The HPFS supports long file names, up to a maximum of 254 characters, and allows mixed-case file names as well.

The HPFS also supports up to 64K of *extended attributes* for each file. Extended attributes are not at all like the MS-DOS file attributes, and can be anything that an application chooses to attach to a file, including text, graphics, icons, even other files.

The HPFS places file-control information close to the actual file itself, rather than in a table structure like the FAT system. This goes some way towards minimizing hard disk head movement when reading files.

Both file systems use a similar hierarchical structure of directories and subdirectories, beginning at the root directory.

Chapter 13 provides a complete introduction to the HPFS.

OS/2 Extended Services

IBM's OS/2 Extended Services include the Communications Manager and the Database Manager. The Communications Manager includes three categories of functions: Systems Network Architecture (SNA) support, local area network (LAN) support, and Transmission Control Protocol/Internet Protocol (TCP/IP) support. Chapter 15 includes more information on OS/2 and networking. The Database Manager provides a relational database with an application development and run-time environment that follows the IBM Systems Application Architecture (SAA) standards, and it also supports Structured Query Language (SQL) for database access. For more information on OS/2 Extended Services, see Chapter 15.

OS/2 LAN Server

OS/2 LAN Server offers multivendor network support, as well as support for networking standards such as SNA, TCP/IP, the OSI model, Token-Ring, Ethernet, and the wide-area network standard, X.25. See Chapter 15 for more information about networking.

OS/2 has also been used by Microsoft's LAN Manager.

Adobe Type Manager

When you install OS/2, you install a set of bit-mapped fonts, and 13 Adobe Type 1 outline fonts. The Adobe Type Manager (ATM) is integrated into the OS/2 operating system, and it works with programs on the desktop, as well as with Microsoft Windows programs run in an OS/2 Windows session. With ATM, a single copy of a font can be used by many different applications. For more on working with Adobe Type Manager fonts, see Chapter 9.

Dynamic Linking

Dynamic linking gives a program running in OS/2 access to functions that are not part of its original executable code. *Dynamic link libraries* (DLL) are program modules that contain executable code but cannot be run as stand-alone applications. Modules from these libraries are loaded only when they are needed, decreasing the amount of memory space required for an application. Once a DLL is loaded, the operating system shares it with any other application that needs access to the function the DLL contains. This means that only one copy of the DLL is loaded into memory at any given time. A major portion of the OS/2 operating system consists of DLLs; see Chapter 5 for more information on how OS/2 uses DLLs.

Dynamic Data Exchange

There are two ways of exchanging information between programs in OS/2. A user-generated request is handled through the clipboard using cut, copy, and paste operations. An application-generated request to exchange data with another application is called *dynamic data exchange* (DDE). See Chapter 5 for more information on using DDE with OS/2.

Intel 80386 Features

OS/2 2.X takes advantage of several features of the 80386 and 80486 processors, in a way that earlier versions of the operating system did not. For example, OS/2 implements a flat memory model that allows OS/2 to escape from the confines of the segment:offset memory model used in earlier versions of OS/2 and in MS-DOS. Unlike the segment:offset model, which is tied to the Intel processors, the flat memory model is an architecture that is easily portable to many other processors. The flat model effectively hides all segmentation from the programmer, giving a portable programming model with a much higher performance than a segmented system can provide.

OS/2 applications view memory as a large, linear, addressable space addressed by 32-bit offsets from the beginning of memory. Paged virtual memory on the 80386 allows memory management to be more efficient, and the 80386 enhanced instruction set lets an application handle 32-bit values in single instructions. See Chapter 13 for more information on how OS/2 handles memory.

Program Portability and OS/2

One of the many benefits of the flat memory model is that it makes applications and the operating system itself more *portable*; that is, easier to move onto a different microprocessor, or *hardware platform*. Programs written for other operating systems that use a flat memory model can easily be moved to OS/2, and applications written for OS/2 will be portable to future versions of OS/2 running under different microprocessors or even to different operating systems.

While OS/2 was not designed to be an 80386-specific operating system, it is a portable 32-bit operating system implemented on the Intel 80386 and 80486.

The REXX Programming Language

OS/2 contains REXX (REstructured eXtended eXecutor), a fully featured structured-programming language that offers much greater capability than the batch processor found in MS-DOS. REXX is straightforward enough to be a good language for beginning programmers, but it is powerful enough for experienced programmers.

The REXX language, which originated on mainframe computers, but is now found on many computer systems, both large and small, includes extensive mathematical, text formatting, processing and searching functions. It also uses many English-like words, rather than the overly terse syntax used by languages such as C and C++. Chapter 16 describes how to use REXX and provides complete listings of several useful REXX programs.

Preparing to Install OS/2

There are many ways you can install OS/2: from 3.5" or 5.25" disks, from a local area network, or from a CD-ROM. You can also automate the installation process if you use a *response file*. Appendix A describes the methods you can use to install OS/2 on your system.

Many computer vendors, including IBM and several of the larger mail-order companies, are installing OS/2 before they sell you the computer, and this is by far the easiest way to get your copy of OS/2. If you want to install it yourself there are a couple of important decisions you must make before you start.

Choosing a File System

When you install OS/2 you can choose to use a file system on your hard disk that is compatible with MS-DOS called the *File Allocation Table* (FAT), or you can elect to use the OS/2 *High Performance File System* (HPFS). MS-DOS cannot recognize files created by HPFS, but OS/2 can recognize MS-DOS files as well as files created under its own FAT and by HPFS.

If you want to share files between OS/2 and a version of MS-DOS that is independent of the OS/2 DOS sessions, choose the FAT option so that you will be able to swap files backward and forward or between different computers without any problems.

If you will only use OS/2 and OS/2 applications, will never swap files with an MS-DOS system, and have a hard disk larger than 60MB, choose the HPFS instead. HPFS is optimized for accessing large hard disks quickly, it supports file names as long as 254 characters, and it allows for additional extended file attributes. HPFS can only be used on hard disks; you cannot format a floppy disk with HPFS.

S O L U T I O N

To use the HPFS you will have to format the hard disk or hard disk partition, and this process will destroy any information that is already on the disk. The answer to this conflict is to make a backup of your hard disk before you start the OS/2 installation process, then restore the files from the backup when the installation is complete.

Installing OS/2 as a Single Operating System

When you install OS/2 as the only operating system on your hard disk, you can install it either on a new, unused hard disk or as an upgrade to an earlier version of OS/2. If you are making an upgrade the installation program will update the appropriate OS/2 system files, but will not affect your application programs or data files. With OS/2 as the only operating system on your hard disk, you can run OS/2 applications, Microsoft Windows applications, and DOS applications.

Installing OS/2 Alongside MS-DOS

Another installation option is to add OS/2 to a system that already has a version of MS-DOS installed on it. This gives you the option of switching between MS-DOS and OS/2 should you need to; some poorly written

DOS programs do not run well under OS/2. With this option, you can run OS/2 applications, DOS and Windows applications under OS/2 software emulation, as well as MS-DOS applications in their own environment.

The disadvantage of this flexibility is that you have to reboot the computer when you change from OS/2 to MS-DOS. An OS/2 feature known as Dual Boot handles this; you can switch between operating systems from either the DOS or the OS/2 command line by using the BOOT command (see Chapter 6 for more information on this command), or from the OS/2 desktop by selecting the Dual Boot icon from the Command Prompts folder.

Installing Several Operating Systems

If you want to install several operating systems on your computer and switch between them easily, consider using the OS/2 Boot Manager option. When you install the Boot Manager, every time you start your computer a menu appears asking you to choose the operating system you want to use. You make your choice, and that operating system is started. This kind of setup is particularly useful for programmers and application developers who have to use several different operating environments.

To install the Boot Manager, you must establish several partitions on your hard disk, and specify which operating system will run from which partition. When the OS/2 installation is complete, you can install the other operating systems. Again, if you decide to use the Boot Manager option, make a complete backup of all the files on your hard disk before you start the OS/2 installation process, and reload them when the installation is complete.

OS/2 Hardware Requirements

To run OS/2 version 2.X you must have at least an 80386 (or better) 32-bit processor in your computer, and a 60MB hard disk. A partial installation of OS/2 occupies approximately 16MB of hard disk space, while a full installation takes about 30MB of free space. You will also need a megabyte or two for the OS/2 swap file.

NOTE OS/2 Version 1.X ran on the Intel 80286 processor as well as the 80386 and 80486; however, Version 2.X runs only on a 80386 or better processor.

Remember that these space requirements are for just the operating system; if you add application programs, as you surely will, or if you want to install other operating systems, you will have to factor in the space that these programs and their data files will take. You should also factor in a large amount of disk space to handle your plans for future expansion.

You need a minimum of 4MB of memory for OS/2, but add more memory if you can; 6MB or 8MB will give much better performance. Chapter 8 covers the hard disk and memory requirements of OS/2 in more detail. Finally, to take advantage of OS/2's graphical user interface, you also need a two-button mouse or a trackball.

IBM ships a single "universal" version of OS/2; it does not require every system manufacturer to create a custom version of the operating system specifically for their hardware. OS/2 runs on literally hundreds of qualified, non-IBM systems, from scores of different manufacturers (as well as IBM systems). Chapter 8 describes the qualification process, and other chapters in Part III cover the complete range of OS/2-supported hardware.

The second half of this chapter provides a quick tour of the user interface.

The OS/2 User Interface

OS/2 is not just an operating system. It also contains a complete, object-oriented graphical user interface known as the *workplace shell* that supports full drag-and-drop capabilities.

NOTE For users who prefer working at the command line, OS/2 also gives access to the OS/2 system prompt and a DOS session system prompt. You can find out more about working with these prompts in Chapter 12.

The workplace shell ensures consistency between applications, which is what makes it so valuable. Once you've learned a task in one application, you can perform that same task everywhere else without having to learn a new technique. The workplace shell is a collection of different *objects* that all work in a similar way. Objects can be grouped together in *folders*, and folders can be grouped inside other folders for convenience. The most familiar part of the workplace shell is the *desktop*, the place where users spend most of their time when not using specific applications.

The desktop is the first complete application designed according to IBM's Common User Interface definition, which itself is a part of the larger System Application Architecture (SAA) definition. This is all rather a long-winded way of saying that the desktop is designed according to precise rules for application design, formulated to make the user interface consistent and easy to use. The CUA definition is independent of operating systems; therefore, applications running on personal computers, minicomputers, and mainframes can all look and work in the same way.

The Elements of the Workplace Shell

When you work with the workplace shell, you are working with four main kinds of objects:

- **Program objects,** representing applications such as word processors, spreadsheets, and so on.

- **Folder objects,** representing collections of other objects. A folder may represent a directory and contain a collection of files, or it may represent a group of programs. Folders can also contain other folders. The OS/2 desktop is itself a folder and behaves just like other folders, except that it is always open.

- **Data-file objects,** including information such as text, database tables, spreadsheets, video, and sound.

- **Device objects,** such as printers, plotters, modems, CD-ROMs and facsimile machines.

Many of the objects seen on the desktop are represented by icons, or small pictures. Some of these icons resemble the device they represent, such as the Drive A icon; others represent folders and application programs and may look rather more exotic.

Using the OS/2 Desktop

The desktop fills the entire screen, and contains other objects, including (usually) the following folders and device objects:

- **OS/2 System folder:** This folder contains other folders, including the Startup folder, Productivity folder, Games folder, Command Prompts folder, System Setup folder, and the Drives folder.

- **Information folder:** This folder contains the README text file, REXX Information, the OS/2 Command Reference and Tutorial, and the Glossary. The first time OS/2 starts after the installation is complete, the tutorial opens on the desktop. You can view it then, or at any other convenient time.

- **Start Here object:** This object contains a set of topics and related help information.

- **Master Help Index object:** This contains the main OS/2 help information.

- **Templates folder:** This folder contains examples of different kinds of objects you can use to help you create a new object of that type on the desktop. Just drag a copy of the object to another place on the desktop.

- **Drive A object:** This object displays the contents of the floppy disk in drive A.

- **Shredder object:** When you drop an object onto the Shredder, it asks you to confirm that you want to delete the object. If you answer yes, the Shredder immediately deletes the object.

- **Printer object:** You can drag objects to the printer icon and print their contents.

Your desktop may also show folders containing OS/2, DOS, and Windows programs.

Figure 1.1 shows a typical arrangement with the OS/2 System folder open on the desktop.

FIGURE 1.1

The OS/2 System folder open on the desktop

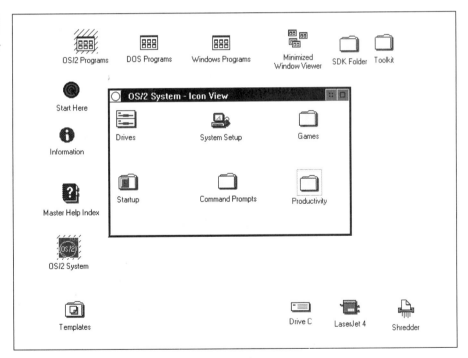

Using a Mouse

The OS/2 graphical user interface is designed for use with a mouse, or a similar pointing device such as a track ball. There are several ways you can use the mouse:

- Clicking the left mouse button (button 1) selects an object or an item from a menu.

- Clicking the right mouse button (button 2) on an object opens the object's pop-up menu.

- Double-clicking the left mouse button (pressing the mouse button twice in quick succession when the mouse pointer is over an object) opens the object.

- Dragging is a way to move an object. Place the mouse pointer on the object, then press and hold down the right mouse button. Now move the mouse to the object's new location while continuing to hold down the button, and release the mouse button.

The OS/2 help information refers to the mouse buttons as button 1 and button 2, rather than left and right, because you can configure the mouse to work left- or right-handed. Throughout the rest of this book, I refer to button 1 as the left mouse button, and button 2 as the right mouse button.

You can also use the mouse in combination with the Ctrl key; see the heading "Copying Files, Folders, and Disks" in Chapter 3 for more information.

Clicking the right mouse button on an object (*right-clicking* the object) opens that object's pop-up menu, which contains the operations you can perform with it. The basic selections in this menu are Open, Help, Create Another, Copy, Move, Create Shadow, and Find. Depending on the type of object you are working with, you may see other selections in the pop-up menu, including Select, Sort, Arrange, Window, Close, or Delete. You can even add your own entries into this menu; see "Using the Settings Notebooks" later in this section for more information.

To open the pop-up menu for the desktop, just click the right mouse button on a blank part of the desktop not occupied by an object or a window. There are two special entries in the desktop pop-up menu: Lockup Now and Shut Down. See "Securing Your Desktop" and "Shutting Down Your

Computer" later in this section for more information on these important topics.

S E C R E T

Many programs have hidden screens; screens that only appear when a special undocumented key sequence is used, and the OS/2 desktop is no exception. Place the mouse pointer on an empty part of the desktop, and press Shift+Ctrl+Alt+O from the keyboard. The desktop changes into a Florida beach scene, complete with palm tree, flamingo, and the S.S. Boca sailing by in the background. A scrolling window in the foreground lists all the people who worked on this version of OS/2. Press the Esc key to return to the desktop.

Some menu selections show an arrow pointing to the right. When you click on this arrow, you open a secondary, or *cascading* menu. If the arrow looks like a button, one of the selections in the cascading menu will be checked as a default. If the arrow is not a button but is flat, you have to make a choice from the items in the cascaded menu.

Using Windows

When you work with the desktop, objects are often displayed in a window. These windows may display other objects, folders, files or directories, but the individual elements found in all windows are essentially the same. As an example, Figure 1.2 shows the System Setup folder with the following elements:

- **Window border:** When two or more windows are open, the border of the active window is shown highlighted in a different color. You can drag the window borders to resize the window.

- **Title bar:** The bar across the top of the window contains the window title, the title-bar icon, and the minimize and maximize buttons. You can drag the title bar if you want to move the entire window rather than just resize it.

▶ S O L U T I O N

If you want to change the size of one of the windows on your desktop, just drag one of the window borders to resize the window. To change the size of a window permanently, press and hold down the Shift key as you drag the window border to its new location.

FIGURE 1.2

The many parts of a window

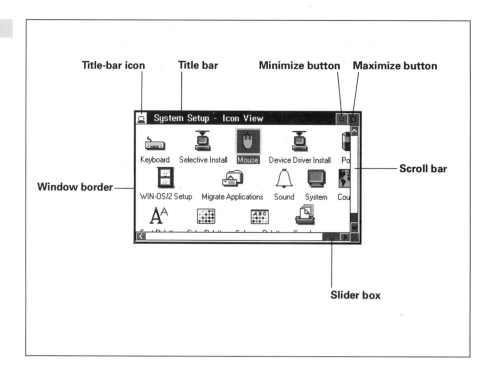

- **Title-bar icon**: The title-bar icon at the left end of the title bar shows a reduced icon for the object displayed in the window. Click on this icon to open the pop-up menu, or double-click on it to close the window. You can also right-click on any empty area inside the window to open the pop-up menu.

- **Minimize button:** Click on this button to minimize the window; that is, to reduce it to an icon. The minimized window is moved into the Minimized Window Viewer object to avoid cluttering up your desktop.

- **Maximize button:** Click on this button to expand the window to the largest possible size, usually the whole screen.

- **Scroll bar:** When a window is too small to display all the information it contains, scroll bars appear across the bottom and down the right side of the window. Click the arrowheads on the scroll bar to move through the information one line at a time, or hold down the mouse button to scroll through the information until you find what you are looking for.

- **Slider box:** You can use the slider box to move one page at a time through the information in a window. Click above, below, to the right, or to the left of the slider bar to move to the next or previous page.

Application programs may add many more elements to a window, including a menu bar containing pull-down menus, a tool bar for access to graphical controls, dialog boxes for parameter selection, and command or push buttons for additional options.

Selecting Objects

To select an object, move the mouse cursor onto the object and click left. This highlights the object to confirm that you have selected it. To select several objects, point onto the first object and click left as before; then hold down the mouse button as you point to other objects. You will see each object highlighted in turn as it is selected. Release the mouse button when you have completed your selections.

Use this method to select one or more items in a folder when you want to perform the same operation on a group of objects.

To select several noncontiguous objects, use the Ctrl key as well as the mouse button. Hold down the Ctrl key and click on each object you want to select; each will be highlighted in turn. Click a second time to deselect an object. When you have completed your choices, release the Ctrl key.

Using the Window List

The Window List shows the names of all the objects you are using and all the programs you are running. Hidden and minimized windows are also shown in the Window List. To switch from one object to another using the Window List, move the mouse cursor to an empty area of the desktop and click *both* mouse buttons together; an operation sometimes described as *chording*. This opens the Window List as a small window that contains an entry for each running application and active OS/2, WIN-OS/2, and DOS session on your system. Double-click the object you want to make current, or the minimized window you want to maximize. The titles of hidden windows are also shown in the Window List; see "Hiding Windows" later in this section for more information.

Keyboard Shortcuts

You can also use the keyboard with the workplace shell; there are keyboard equivalents for all the mouse-based operations. To help in this, each menu selection has one letter underlined. Just type that letter to select the option. Because several menu selections may start with the same letter, the choice of letters for some of the keyboard shortcuts may be less than intuitive. Table 1.1 lists all the OS/2 system functions you can perform from the keyboard. Table 1.2 lists all the keys you can use when you are working with objects. Table 1.3 shows the keys for working with windows. Table 1.4 lists the keys you can use within a help window. Finally, Table 1.5 shows the keys you can use when you are working with the Master Help Index. A plus sign, as in Ctrl+Alt+Del, means that you must hold down the specified keys together.

TABLE 1.1: Shortcut keys for System Tasks

KEY	FUNCTION
Ctrl+Alt+Del	Restarts the operating system
Alt+Tab	Switches to the next window
Alt+Esc	Switches to the next window or full-screen session
Ctrl+Esc	Opens the Window List
F1	Opens help

TABLE 1.2: Shortcut keys used with objects

KEY	FUNCTION
Arrow keys	Moves between objects
Spacebar	Selects an object
Enter	Opens an object or accepts a menu selection
Esc	Closes a pop-up menu, or cancels a mouse selection
Shift+F10	Opens the selected object's pop-up menu
Home	Selects the first option in a pop-up menu
End	Selects the last option in a pop-up menu
Underlined letter	Selects a specific choice from a menu

TABLE 1.3: Shortcut keys for a help window

KEY	FUNCTION
Alt+Spacebar	Opens the pop-up menu for a window
Alt+F4	Closes a window
Alt+F7	Lets you move a window using the arrow keys
Alt+F8	Lets you size a window using the arrow keys
Alt+F9	Minimizes a window
Alt+F10	Maximizes a window
Alt+F11	Hides a window
Pg Up, Pg Dn	Moves through the contents of a window one page at a time

TABLE 1.4: Shortcut keys used with Windows

KEY	FUNCTION
F2	Displays general help information
F9	Displays information for help keys, system keys, windows keys, object keys, and selection keys
F11	Displays Help index
Shift+F10	Displays the help topic "Help for Using the Help Facility"
Tab	Moves to the next highlighted help topic. Press the Enter key to display the associated help information
Esc	Displays the previous help information

TABLE 1.5: Shortcut keys used with the Master Help Index

KEY	FUNCTION
Enter	Opens the Master Help Index
Arrow keys	Moves through the help topics, one at a time
Pg Up, Pg Dn	Moves through the help topics one page at a time
Any letter	Moves to the first topic beginning with that letter
Alt+F6	Switches between an entry and the Master Help Index
Tab	Moves to the next highlighted help topic. Press the Enter key to display the associated help information.
Esc	Closes the help window

Using the Settings Notebooks

Every object has an associated settings notebook, opened from the object's pop-up menu. These notebooks let you look at and change the settings that control how the object behaves. They are called *notebooks* because that's what they look like on the screen. Figure 1.3 shows the Drive C Settings

FIGURE 1.3

The Drive C Settings notebook

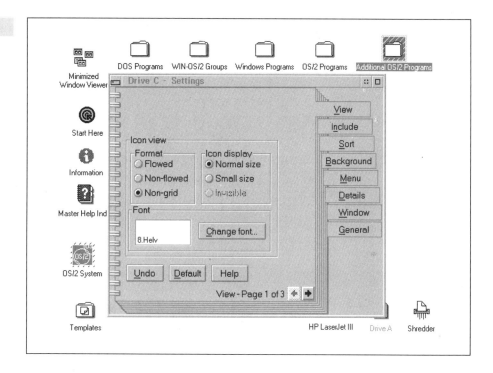

notebook as an example. Tabs on the right side of the notebook divide the different settings into functional groups, and each group may contain several pages of information. The number and the names of these tabs depend on the type of object you are working with.

You open the Settings notebook for the desktop by right-clicking anywhere that is not in use on the desktop. This opens the desktop pop-up menu. Then click on the arrow next to Open and choose the Settings option. To open the Settings notebook for any other object, right-click on the object, then choose Open, followed by Settings.

Each Settings notebook contains tabs specific to the object you are working with; similar objects usually have similar settings. For example, program objects have the following tabs, or groups, of settings:

- **Program** contains the path, file name, and directory name for the object.

- **Session** defines the type of session the program can run in: OS/2 full screen, OS/2 Window, DOS full screen, DOS Window, WIN-OS/2 full screen, or WIN-OS/2 window. A WIN-OS/2 program can also run in a separate WIN-OS/2 session.

- **Association** defines the types or names of data-file objects linked to the program. See "Associating Objects" in Chapter 2 for more on how to establish associations.

- **Window** controls the behavior of minimized windows.

- **General** contains the program title and icon information.

> # SOLUTION
>
> Normally, when you have several windows open on your desktop, you can click on the desktop, or select it from the window list, but the desktop does not "pop" to the front of the other windows. However, because the desktop is just another folder (albeit a rather special folder) there is a setting you can use to make the desktop do this. Open the Settings folder at the Window tab, check the Create New Window check box, then close the Settings notebook. Next time you want to pop the desktop to the front, right-click on any visible part of the desktop to open the pop-up menu, and choose one of the three views listed there; the Icon View being the most like the existing desktop. You can even keep two views of the desktop open all the time, one showing the tree view so you can find folders quickly, and the other in the icon view.

A disk drive object may contain all of the tabs described above, and may add several more, including the following:

- **View** controls the icon display and font type used.

- **Include** specifies the kinds of objects included in a view.

- **Sort** specifies a sort order of the objects contained in a view.

- **Background** specifies an image to display in the background of any folder, including the desktop folder.

- **Menu** controls the user-defined additions to an object's pop-up menu; more on this in a moment.

- **Details** displays the current information for the selected hard or floppy disk.

If a tab contains more than one page, you will see a page count just above the left- and right-facing arrow buttons at the bottom right of the page. Use the arrow buttons to move from one page to another, or from one tab to the next.

When you make a change in a Settings notebook, that change takes effect immediately; you do not have to save the change. If you decide to remove a change, click on the Undo button. To return to the original value for that item, click on the Default button.

You can easily add, delete, and change the menu items in an object's pop-up menu. Right-click on the object whose pop-up menu you want to change, and open the Settings notebook. Then select the menu you want to work with from those listed in the Available Menus field, and click on the Create Another button to create or change a menu. You can now change the name and the menu type for the item displayed in the Menu Name field. Menu Type can be either Cascade Menu (the item in the Menu Name field will be a cascaded-menu item), or Conditional Cascade (the item in the Menu Name field will show an arrow button to display the cascaded menu). Select an action from the Default Action field to change the default action for the current conditional cascade. A check mark indicates the default. Select a menu item from those listed in the Actions On Menu box if you want to change an individual item in a cascaded menu.

You can make as many experimental changes as you wish because the Undo button will change the settings back to those in effect before you opened the Settings window.

Using the Desktop

Now that I have described the individual elements found on the desktop, how do you use them? The following sections describe how you can perform everyday file-, disk-, and program-management tasks from the desktop.

Starting and Closing Applications

To start an OS/2 application, just double-click the appropriate program icon and the program will start running in its own window. If you want the application to use the whole screen, click on the maximize button in the top-right corner of the original window.

You can also select the object you want, then use the Open selection from the pop-up menu to start the program running.

Another way to start an application is to double-click on a data object; this opens the data object (letter, memo, or data file) and simultaneously starts the program associated with that data object. OS/2 automatically creates an icon for each new file or folder when you create it. See the heading "Associating Objects" in Chapter 2 for more information on how this works.

You can also start an application by typing its file name at the OS/2 command prompt.

To close an application, click the title-bar icon to open the menu, then choose Close. You can also type Alt+F4 or double-click the title-bar icon to close the application.

For more information on working with MS-DOS and Microsoft Windows application programs, see Chapters 6 and 7.

Hiding Windows

Some windows have a *hide button* to the left of the maximize button on the title bar, shaped like a plus sign (+). Click this button to hide the window. Other applications may have a Hide entry in the title-bar icon menu that you can access by pressing Alt+F11. In either case, the name of the window is added to the Window List so that you can still access the window, even though it is hidden.

Tiling and Cascading Windows

You can arrange open windows by hand if you wish, dragging them into place with the mouse, but it is easier and faster to use the Tile or Cascade commands.

When you tile windows, they are arranged side by side on the desktop with the active window placed at the top left corner of the desktop. Figure 1.4 shows several tiled windows on the desktop.

To tile several windows, first open the Window List, then select all the windows you want to tile. Point to one of the window titles in the Window List, and right-click to open the pop-up menu for that window. Choose Tile from the pop-up menu, and the selected windows will be redrawn on the desktop.

When you cascade windows, they appear arranged one behind the next, with only their title bars showing. The active window is always displayed at the front of the stack. To cascade a set of windows, follow the directions given above for tiling windows, but choose the Cascade option instead of Tile. Figure 1.5 shows several cascaded windows on the desktop.

To tile or cascade all windows open on the desktop, use the Select All option from the Window List, rather than selecting each window individually.

FIGURE 1.4

Tiled Windows on the
Desktop

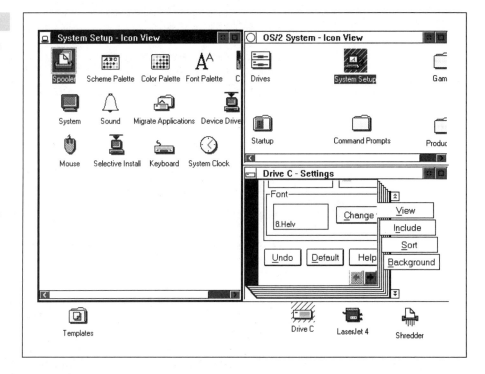

FIGURE 1.4

Tiled Windows on the
Desktop

Arranging Icons

You can also arrange the icons on the desktop or in an open folder by hand, dragging them one by one then dropping them at the new location, or you can make the system place the icons in a default arrangement for you.

To arrange all the icons on the desktop, open the desktop pop-up menu by right-clicking on an empty area of the desktop, and then select the Arrange option from the pop-up menu.

To arrange the icons in an open window, move the mouse pointer into the window and right-click the mouse, then select the Arrange option from the menu.

You can also use the Sort menu option to arrange the icons by name, date, time, and so on.

FIGURE 1.5

Cascaded Windows on
the Desktop

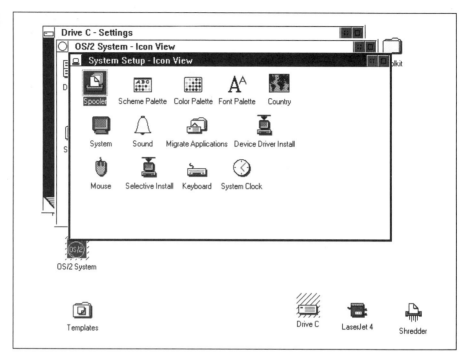

Shutting Down Your Computer

Before you turn your computer off, you *must* make sure that OS/2 is
closed down in a logical way, and you do that with the Shut Down command. Because OS/2 is a multitasking operating system, turning it off is
a more complex organizational task than turning off a simple operating
system such as MS-DOS or Windows. If you do not use Shut Down every
time before turning off your computer, sooner or later you will lose data,
and the operating system may not be able to start properly when you turn
your computer back on.

Shut Down makes sure that any information currently in the hard disk
cache buffer is saved on the hard disk, and that all open windows are
closed. Shut Down also checks all sessions for unsaved data before starting the actual shut down process. All of this status information is saved,
so that the next time you start OS/2, all objects that were open can reopen
and appear in the same view. Many OS/2 application programs can also
save their own state, and therefore can resume exactly where they left off.

To shut down your computer before you turn it off, click the right mouse button on any blank part of the desktop to open the desktop pop-up menu. Select Shut Down from this menu, and respond to any messages displayed on the screen as shut-down proceeds, closing any open applications. When you see the final message telling you that shut-down has completed, and it is now safe to turn off your computer, turn it off or press Ctrl+Alt+Del to restart it.

WARNING

If you don't see this final message, but see just a blank screen, you may be very nearly out of memory; wait until all hard-disk activity stops before turning off or restarting your computer. You should also carefully reevaluate your memory configuration; 4MB is the minimum required by OS/2, but installing more memory gives better performance. Chapter 8 has more on this.

You can also shut down OS/2 using the keyboard instead of the mouse. Press Ctrl+Esc to display the Window List, then use an arrow key to highlight the OS/2 Desktop—Icon View entry, and press the Enter key. Press Shift and the Space Bar to deselect any selected icons on the desktop, and press Shift+F10 to open the desktop pop-up menu. Use the down arrow key to move the highlight to Shut Down, then press the Enter key.

Securing Your Desktop

You can use the Lockup Now command from the desktop pop-up menu to make your computer screen go blank and lock the keyboard. You can also use this command to establish a desktop password if you wish.

To use Lockup Now, open the desktop pop-up menu by right-clicking an empty part of the desktop. Click the arrow button next to the Open selection, then choose Settings from the cascaded menu. Click the Lockup tab on the right side of the Desktop Settings notebook. This tab has three pages. On the first page, enable or disable the automatic lockup, then specify a timeout period—the number of minutes the system will wait after your last interaction before automatically locking. On the next page, specify the picture or *bit map* you want to display on the screen after the timeout expires. The file called OS2LOGO.BMP contains the OS/2 logo. On page 3 of the notebook, enter the password you want to use to unlock the desktop. If you forget this password, you will have to restart your computer, then enter a new password before the timeout expires. Double-click on the title-bar icon to close the Desktop Settings notebook.

Now when the timeout expires, or when you use Lockup Now from the desktop pop-up menu, the bit map you chose is shown on the screen, along with a small padlock icon and a Help button. Click on the Help button to open a small help box on the screen containing instructions on how to enter your password. If you wait long enough, eventually the bitmap will disappear from the screen to avoid burning in the image on the screen, and all you will see will be the padlock icon moving about the screen. Press any key on the keyboard to redisplay the bitmap and the Help button.

Printing from the Desktop

There are several methods you can use to print a file. If you have a printer (or plotter) installed on your system, you will see a printer icon on the desktop. If you use a network printer, you may find this icon in the Network folder rather than on the desktop.

The simplest way of printing a file is to drag it to the printer icon, but there are several other methods you can use:

- Select the Print option from the object's pop-up menu
- Use the Print command from an application program's File menu
- Use the PRINT or COPY commands in an OS/2 session
- Select the Print Topic button in a help window
- Press the Print Screen key on the keyboard

Each of these methods creates a *print job*, and if you open the printer object, you will see a window displaying the status of all the jobs waiting to be printed on your system. To delete one or more pending print jobs, open the pop-up menu for the job, and choose the Delete option.

Select the Delete All Jobs option if you want to delete all of the pending print jobs. You can create one or more copies of a print job if you use the Copy command from the object's pop-up menu. Finally, if you want to print to a file rather than to the usual printer, open the object's pop-up menu, click on the arrow to the right of Open, and choose Settings. Select the Output tab, then choose Output to File. Double-click on the title-bar icon to close the settings notebook. Chapter 9 contains much more information on printing.

Changing to the Command Prompt

OS/2 also features a command prompt as well as its graphical user interface. To change from the desktop to the OS/2 command line, double-click on the OS/2 System folder on the desktop. Then double-click on the Command Prompts folder, and choose one of the objects presented in this folder:

- **Dual Boot** lets you switch from OS/2 to the version of MS-DOS installed on your hard disk. You can only select this object if both MS-DOS and OS/2 operating systems are installed in the same primary partition.

- **DOS from Drive A:** lets you start a specific version of MS-DOS from a floppy disk in drive A. See Chapter 6 for more on this topic.

- **WIN-OS/2 Full Screen** displays the WIN-OS/2 program in a full-screen session with more than one program running.

- **DOS Window** opens a window containing a DOS-session prompt.

- **DOS Full Screen** displays the DOS prompt in a full-screen session.

- **OS/2 Window** displays the OS/2 command prompt in a window.

- **OS/2 Full Screen** displays the OS/2 command prompt in a full-screen session.

To return to the desktop, press the Ctrl and Escape keys together to open the Window List, and choose the OS/2 Desktop—Icon View, or double click on the title-bar icon of a windowed session.

How to Get Help in OS/2

There are many ways you can access OS/2's abundant online help information. Many of the pop-up menus and dialog boxes have a Help entry containing immediate information. You can also access specific help information on a pop-up menu selection by pressing (but not releasing) the left mouse button, then pressing the F1 function key. If you want to look up a topic alphabetically, you can turn to the Master Help Index on the desktop.

Using the Master Help Index

Double-click on the Master Help Index icon on the desktop to open the Master Help Index, which contains thousands of help topics arranged in alphabetical order. These topics are displayed in the form of a notepad with tabs down the right side. Click on a tab to go directly to the group of entries that begin with that letter. If the letter you want is not currently displayed, select the double-arrow tabs at the top and bottom of the notepad to bring the right letter into view. To search the Master Help Index for an entry, click on the Search Topics button. Enter the text you want to search for into the Search String box, then click on the Search button. When matches are found, they are listed in the Matched Items box; double-click on one of these matches to display its help information. When you have located the right topic, you can print the entry by clicking on the Print Topic button. Information for the entry is shown in a window that opens to the right of the Master Help Index, as illustrated in Figure 1.6.

FIGURE 1.6

The Master Help Index

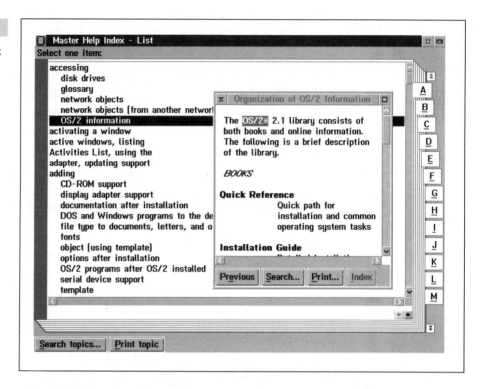

Use the scroll bars or the Pg Up and Pg Dn keys to move through the information. At the end of the help text, you will see several topic headings listed under Related Information. Double-click one of these items to open the associated help entry. Use the Previous button to return to the previous help topic you viewed, the Search button to search for specific text in this section or in all sections of the master Help Index, and the Print button to print the text contained in the current section, in all sections, the help index, or the help contents.

Using the Information Folder

The Information folder on the desktop contains the following:

- The **Tutorial** gives an overview of the OS/2 operating system, divided into the following topics; Using a Mouse, Using Objects, Using Window Parts, Getting Help, and OS/2 System Overview.

- The **Glossary** lists and explains commonly used computer-related terms.

- The **Command Reference** contains information about all the commands you can use at the OS/2 and DOS-session system prompts. If you are at an OS/2 system prompt in a full-screen or windowed session, you can type **Help command**, where *command* is the name of one of the OS/2 system commands, and the OS/2 Command Reference will automatically open at the correct entry.

- **REXX Information** describes the REXX programming language.

- The **README** file is a text file that contains late-breaking news that became available after the manuals were printed.

Start Here

The Start Here Object on the desktop contains general information about using OS/2, and describes how to install programs, customize your desktop, and perform simple tasks on the desktop. Start Here is similar in operation to the Master Help Index, although its scope is more limited. The Previous, Search, Print, and Index buttons all work here just as they do in the Master Help Index. Double-click the title-bar icon to return to the desktop when you have finished with Start Here.

OS/2 OS/2 OS/2

OS/2 OS/2 OS/2 OS/2 OS/2 OS/2 OS/2 OS/2 OS/2

OS/2 OS/2 OS/2 O

Customizing and Configuring Your Desktop

NOW that we have looked in some detail at the OS/2 graphical user interface and how you can use the desktop, it is time to look at some of the configuration choices you can make for the OS/2 desktop. First I'll cover the items in the System Setup folder, then take a look at some of the other ways you can customize your desktop.

Using System Setup

You can use System setup to change the way that something looks or works on the desktop, or to add an OS/2 feature that you originally chose not to install. Double-click the OS/2 System icon on the desktop, then choose System Setup from inside this folder, and you will see the icons shown in Figure 2.1.

To start any one of these program objects, double-click on the appropriate icon, and a window opens containing choices you can make. When you are done, double-click on the small title-bar icon in the top-left corner of the window, or select the Close option for the pop-up menu to end the program. Any settings you changed will take effect and will remain in effect for subsequent OS/2 sessions.

Let's look at each of the items contained in the System Setup folder in turn.

Color Palette

Color Palette lets you choose the colors used for any one of the 26 different elements of a desktop window. First select a color from the palette, then drag it to the object that you want to color and release the mouse button.

FIGURE 2.1

System Setup—
Icon View

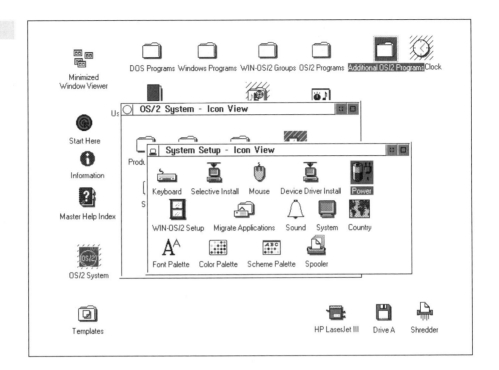

> ► **S O L U T I O N**
>
> Don't try to make all your color selections in a single session. Use the Color Palette to change just a few colors and then work with the desktop for a while to get used to them. You can always change more colors later. Choose your color combinations carefully; some combinations can be visually distressing, to say the least, while others can be completely unreadable.

To change the foreground color of a window, press and hold down the Ctrl key as you drag the color from the palette; to change the background color, press and hold down the Alt key as you drag the color. You can create several color palettes if you wish, each with as many as 30 colors.

> ## SOLUTION
>
> The only way to change the color of the title text of all the icons in a window is to press and hold the Ctrl key, drag the selected color to the folder, then release the Ctrl key. You cannot change the color of individual icon-title text.

To invent your own colors, rather than use those initially presented in the palette, select the Edit Color button. This opens a new window that contains a color wheel you can use to change the colors. Click the Values button, then check the RGB box if you want to select color by blending red, blue, and green (the RGB color model), or check the HSB box if you would rather work with hue, saturation, and brightness (the HSB color model).

The black crosshairs on the color wheel intersect at the current color and act like a pointer. As you move the crosshairs with the mouse, you change the properties of the color you selected. The slider, at the right side of the window, shows the range of brightness from bottom to top for the currently selected color. As you create new colors on the color wheel, you will see the range of colors on the slider also change. Select the Solid Color check box to change the slider to a few areas of solid color rather than a continuous gradation of brightness.

Select the Values button if you would rather specify numerical values for the color. In the RGB color model, values can range from 0, indicating that the color is not present, to 255, indicating that the maximum amount of color is in use. In the HSB color model, the values represent the position of a color along the circumference of the color wheel, and can range from 0 to 359.

If you don't like the color you've invented, just use the Undo button to restore the colors to their original values.

Scheme Palette

Use the Scheme Palette if you want to change colors and fonts for any of the 26 different elements of a window, including window text, menu bars, screen backgrounds. You can even change the width of the horizontal or vertical window borders.

The Palette window displays several preconfigured color schemes you can use, including:

- Spring
- Summer
- Autumn
- Winter
- Monochrome
- Windows
- Default
- New Scheme

To use one of these preconfigured color schemes, first select it in the Scheme Palette window, then drag it to the window you want to change. To change all windows system-wide to the new color scheme, press and hold down the Alt key as you drag the preconfigured color scheme to the desktop.

If you would rather choose your own color scheme, a good way to start is to select the preconfigured scheme closest to what you want, and then change some of the colors. Select the color scheme you want to begin with from the main Scheme Palette window, then click on the Edit Scheme button to open the window shown in Figure 2.2.

This window helps you decide which elements you want to change, and it lets you look at the changes as you make them. You work with the following fields:

- **Scheme Title** lets you change the name of the currently selected color scheme.
- **Window Area** lists all the choices you can use to change screen and window parts:
  3D Highlight Bright
  3D Highlight Dark
  Active Border
  Active Title Background

FIGURE 2.2

Use the Edit Scheme
window in the Scheme
Palette to choose colors
for all the elements of a
window

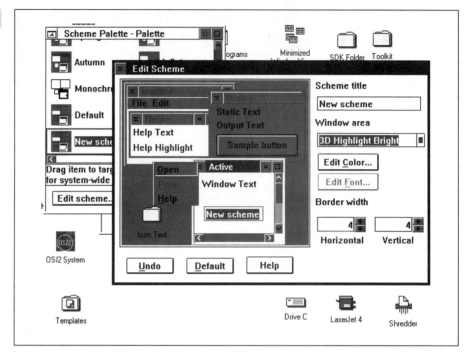

Active Title Text
Active Title Text Background
Application Workspace
Dialog Background
Drop Shadow
Entryfield/Listbox Background
Frame
Help Background
Help Highlight Text
Help Text
Icon Text
Inactive Area
Inactive Border
Inactive Title Background

Inactive Title Text

Inactive Title Text Background

Menu Background

Menu Disabled Text

Menu Highlight Background

Menu Highlight

Text Menu Text

Notebook Page Background

Output text

Pushbutton Background

Pushbutton Default Border

Screen Background

Scroll Bar Background

Selection Background

Selection Foreground

Shadow Highlight Background

Shadow Highlight Text

Shadow Text

Static Text

Title Bottom

Window Background

Window Text

- **Edit Color** displays the Color Palette window, so you can change the color of any of the window parts. To do this, move the mouse pointer to the color you want to use, then drag the color to the window part you want to change and release the mouse button. The sample window shows the result of any color changes.

- **Edit Font** lets you change the font name, style, point size, style, and emphasis.

- **Border Width** lets you change the width of either the horizontal or the vertical window borders; the higher the number, the wider the border.

S O L U T I O N

Wider window borders are easier to manipulate using a mouse than narrow borders, but they do take up more space on the screen. Different display adapter resolutions require different border sizes; higher resolution screens may present thinner window borders (for the same border width settings), and these thinner borders may prove harder to grab. You should experiment with these settings until you find the best window border combination for the way that you work.

If you decide that you don't like the color scheme you have developed, use the Undo button to change the colors back to those that were active before this window was displayed, or use the Default button to go back to the settings that were active when you installed OS/2.

Font Palette

The Font Palette displays examples of some of the fonts available on your system. You can drag a font sample from this window and drop it onto any text on the desktop, and that text will change into the chosen font. Hold down the Alt key as you drag if you want to make a system-wide change. Select the Edit Font button to add, delete, or edit fonts. In the Edit Font window, the Name list box displays the names of all the fonts installed on your system. This list will include some or all of the following:

- Courier
- Helv
- Helvetica
- Roman
- Swiss
- Symbol Set
- System Monospaced
- System VIO

- System Proportional
- Times New Roman
- Tms Rmn

The Size field contains the point size of the currently selected font; the higher the number, the larger the characters. The Style field displays the style of the current font; normal, italic, bold, or bold italic, while the Emphasis field changes the way a font is presented—outlined, underlined, or with a horizontal strikeout line through each character. All these font changes are shown, as they are made, in the Sample field at the lower-right.

To add a new font, use the Add button and specify the floppy disk drive that contains the font disk, or select a different drive and directory. To remove a font, choose the Delete button to open the Delete Font window, select the font or fonts you no longer need from the list, and click Delete.

► S O L U T I O N

If you are running short of hard disk space, consider deleting any fonts that you don't use; you could save over 1MB of disk space. You can use the Delete button in the Edit Font window to delete a font. This not only removes the font from the Font Palette, it also deletes the font file from your hard disk. Alternatively, you could manually move the font file you don't need onto a floppy disk for safe keeping. Font files are located in the OS2\DLL directory, and have names like COURIER.FON (for monospaced fonts) or TIMESNRM.PSF (for proportionally-spaced fonts). Use the Move option from the C drive's pop-up menu, or open drive windows on both the source and destination disks, and then use the mouse to drag and drop the font file onto the floppy disk. See Chapter 3 for detailed information on copying, moving, and deleting files.

And once again, the Undo button can be your savior; use it to change the settings back to those in effect before you opened this window.

Country

The Country icon lets you change the way that the time, date, number and currency formats are shown in OS/2. Just click on one of the tabs down the right side of the window to open the appropriate item:

- Country
- Time
- Date
- Numbers
- General

You can choose from the following countries (see Chapter 11 for more information on how to internationalize OS/2).

Arabic Speaking	Korea
Asian English	Latin America
Australia	Netherlands
Belgium	Norway
Brazil	Other Country
Canada (French Speaking)	People's Republic of China
Czechoslovakia	Poland
Denmark	Portugal
Finland	Spain
France	Sweden
Germany	Switzerland (French Speaking)
Hebrew Speaking	Switzerland (German Speaking)
Hungary	Taiwan
Iceland	Turkey
Italy	United Kingdom
Japan	USA
	Yugoslavia

Mouse

Use the Mouse icon to change the following settings:

- **Timing** sets the double-click speed; the amount of time between consecutive clicks that can pass and still be recognized as one single operation, and the tracking speed; the speed that mouse movement is reflected on the screen. You can drag the sliders in this window to vary these settings, and you can test the double-click setting in the Test Here box on the right side of the window. If the double-click is within the rate you have set, the Test Here box will change color.

- **Setup** lets you choose between a right- or a left-handed mouse. The mouse is initially set up for right-handed use, and the left mouse button is called button 1. If you change to left-handed use, the right mouse button becomes button 1. Any changes you make here are effective immediately.

- **Mappings** lets you reassign mouse buttons to specific operations, such as dragging objects, displaying pop-up menus, and editing title text. Again, any changes you make here are effective immediately.

- **General** contains the current name and icon of the mouse object.

Keyboard

Use the Keyboard icon to change the following settings:

- **Timing** lets you change the keyboard repeat rate, the keyboard repeat delay rate, and the cursor blink rate. The keyboard repeat rate adjusts the speed at which a key, when held down on the keyboard, repeats its function. The repeat delay rate controls the time that the key must be held down before the keyboard repeat rate takes effect. Radically changing either of these settings can have a profound effect on your typing, either increasing or decreasing your error rate. You can test the effects by typing some sample text into the Test Here field at the lower-left of this window. Adjust the settings until you feel you can type at a comfortable rate.

- **Mappings** lets you customize the way that certain keys on your keyboard work on the desktop. To change the key that displays a pop-up menu, or the key that lets you edit the names of objects or title bars, select a key from the Primary Key list. You can also add one of the Shift, Ctrl, or Alt keys to make a key combination if you wish.

- **Special Needs** lets people with additional requirements tailor the keyboard response to their individual needs. The *sticky keys* method lets you press a series of keys in sequence rather than all at the same time. For example, instead of pressing and holding down the Ctrl and the Alt and the Del keys all at the same time, sticky keys lets you press each key in turn.

- **To enable sticky keys,** choose the Settings Activation On radio button. For every key that you want to use in this way, press the Shift key three times, then press the key you want to stay stuck down; you will hear a beep to acknowledge that the key has been accepted. To turn off a sticky key, press and release it once.

► S O L U T I O N

By using Special Needs in the Keyboard notebook and by sizing text using settings in the Font Palette, visually-challenged users can customize the desktop to their own individual needs. Having this kind of facility built right into the operating system, instead of grafting it on as an afterthought, represents a significant step forward in thinking on the part of the operating-system planners.

- **General** contains the current name and icon of the keyboard object.

Spooler

The Spooler lets you specify a new path and directory for the spool files stored on your hard disk waiting to print. The default path used for storing print spool files is SPOOL.

To change this path, either wait until all the print tasks in the print queue finish printing, or delete any pending print jobs, then select Change Status, and Hold from each printer object's pop-up menu to prevent any application programs from printing. Then open the Spooler and type in the new path information into the Spool Path field. When you are done, close the Spooler, select Change Status, and then Release from each printer object's pop-up menu to allow the printer to print again. Any changes you make to the path become effective immediately.

S O L U T I O N

Use the Hold command from the printer or the fax object's pop-up menu when you need to load more paper or change a toner cartridge in a laser printer during a print job. Remember to use the Release command when you are finished so that your print jobs can continue to print.

You can also adjust the speed with which spooled print jobs are printed by setting a print priority using the slider. Valid values range from 1 (sets the lowest priority) to 189 (sets the highest priority), and the default is 125. Setting the print priority higher than 125 will certainly give your print jobs a higher priority, but may also slow down the overall response time of your system due to this overhead.

System

Use System to change the OS/2 default settings for any of the following:

- **Confirmations** lets you control confirmation messages on file or folder deletions, file renaming, and related operations.
- **Title** lets you select what happens when an item is added to a folder that already contains an object of the same name.
- **Window** controls settings for animation, window and object behavior.

- **Print Screen** enables or disables the Print Screen function invoked when you press the Print Scrn key from the keyboard.

SECRET

To print the contents of an open window, position the mouse pointer inside the window, then press the Print Scrn key on the keyboard; to print the whole screen, place the mouse pointer somewhere on the desktop away from any open windows, and press the Print Scrn key.

- **Logo** controls the length of time that logos are displayed on your screen.
- **General** contains the current name and icon of the System object.

SECRET

If you use an XGA display adapter, you will see an additional choice called Screen. If you change from a higher screen resolution to a lower resolution, some applications may open windows that now appear to be partially off your screen. To fix this, press Ctrl+Esc to open the window list, and right-click on the name of the application to open the pop-up menu. Now select Tile or Cascade, and the window will appear on the screen correctly.

System Clock

Open the System Clock Settings notebook to look at or change any of the following:

- **View** lets you specify that the time, the date or both are displayed, and also lets you choose between a digital and an analog display.
- **Alarm** lets you set the time and date when you want the alarm to go off. You can also select a message box option to emphasize the alarm.

- **Date/Time** lets you set or reset the current date and time settings.
- **Window** allows you to choose several window characteristics for the System Clock window.
- **General** contains the current name and icon of the System Clock object.

Check the Show Title Bar check box if you want to show the clock with the typical window title, including title-bar icon, name, and minimize and maximize buttons. Clear the check box if you don't want to see these elements.

Sound

After you install the MMPW/2 package using OS/2 version 2.1, you can use the Sound object to associate sound files with system events such as opening or closing windows, or starting up or closing down the system. Once you have made a sound association, your system will play the sound file whenever the associated system event occurs. If you have an audio adapter, the Sound object plays the associated WAV file; if you don't have an audio adapter, the Sound object plays a tune file created with the OS/2 Tune Editor.

You can associate sound files with the following events:

N O T E

If you use OS/2 version 2.0, or you have not yet installed MMPM/2 onto OS/2 version 2.1, you can use the Sound object to turn a warning beep on or off, but you cannot assign sound files to system events.

- Begin Drag
- End Drag
- Error
- Information
- Shred

- System Shutdown
- System Startup
- Warning
- Window Open
- Window Close

Several sound files are provided as part of the MMPM/2 package, but you can use WAV files from other sources too, if you have them. Use the Sound File list to find the file you want to use, then click on the Speaker button to play the sound now, so you know you have chosen the correct file. After the association is established, you will hear the sound whenever you perform that particular system operation.

Use the Volume Control to set the sound level to your liking, and if you check the Apply Volume to All Sounds check box, you can set the same volume level for all system sounds.

If you want to temporarily turn these sounds off, remove the check mark from the Enable System Sounds check box; now you will only hear the normal PC warning beep for Information, Warning and Error events.

To use sound files located in other directories or on other hard disks, scroll to the end of the Sound File list, and you will see a list of drive letters. Double-click on a letter to access that drive, then choose the directory you want. If the directory does not contain any suitable sound files, you will see the entry <None> in the Sound File list.

Selective Install

You can use Selective Install to change or modify your original OS/2 installation choices. When you double-click Selective Install, a System Configuration window opens offering the same choices you saw during installation:

- Mouse
- Serial Device Support
- Primary Display

- Secondary Display
- Keyboard
- Country
- CD-ROM Device Support
- SCSI (Small Computer System Interface) Adapter Support
- Printer

Place a check mark in the box next to any of the settings you want to change, then click the OK button.

Mouse

If you click on the Mouse check box, you can choose one option from the following list:

- PS/2 (™) Style Pointing Device
- Bus Style Mouse
- InPort Style Mouse
- Serial Pointing Device
- Logitech (™) Serial Mouse
- IBM Touch Device
- Other Pointing Device for Mouse Port
- No Pointing Device Support

If your mouse is attached to the system mouse port, and is not explicitly listed here, select Other Pointing Device for Mouse Port. If you don't plan to use a mouse, choose No Pointing Device Support. Choose an option, then click on OK to select the serial port that your mouse is attached to.

Serial Device Support

Under the Serial Device Support heading, check either the Install Support or the Do Not Install Support check box. If you plan to use the new

OS/2 version 2.1 Fax/PM application for sending or receiving one-page faxes, be sure to check the Install Support check box.

Primary Display

When you select the Primary Display option, you can choose from the following:

- Color Graphics Adapter (CGA)
- Enhanced Graphics Adapter (EGA)
- PS/2 Display Adapter
- Video Graphics Display (VGA)
- Display Adapter 8514/A (8514)
- Extended Graphics Array (XGA)
- Super Video Graphics Array (SVGA)
- Other

Although technically, OS/2 does support the Color Graphics Adapter (CGA), using OS/2 in CGA mode would be very difficult and is definitely not recommended.

If you have two displays connected to your computer, select the display with the higher resolution as the primary display.

> ## SOLUTION
>
> If the display adapter you use is not listed, select Other. When the Advanced Options window is displayed toward the end of the installation process, make sure that the Install Device Support Disk check box is checked. When prompted, insert the disk containing the device driver for your display adapter (provided by the manufacturer), and select OK to open the OS/2 Device Driver Installation window. Follow the instructions on the screen to install the device driver.

Secondary Display

If you choose Secondary Display, you have two more choices in addition to those shown above:

- Monochrome/Printer Adapter (MPA)
- None

Country

If you select Country, you can select a code page, or character set, from 32 different options. A code page contains all the language characters, letters, numbers, and symbols that the computer uses on the screen and when printing. The Country options in Selective Install are the same as those listed for the Country icon earlier in this chapter, and those determine the symbol used for currency, the decimal separator, and the date and time format used by the system.

Keyboard

When you choose Keyboard, you can select a keyboard layout from 29 different options. When you choose a keyboard layout, you are in effect telling OS/2 which character to expect when you type a key on the keyboard.

CD-ROM Device Support

Extensive support for CD-ROMs is built into OS/2 version 2.1. When you check the CD-ROM Device Support box, you can choose from the following CD-ROM drives:

- CD Technology T3301
- Hitachi CDR-1650, 1750, 3650
- Hitachi CDR-3750
- IBM CD-ROM I
- IBM CD-ROM II
- NEC CDR-36, 37, 72, 73, 74, 82, 83, 84

- Panasonic CR-501, LK-MC501S
- Sony CDU-541, 561, 6211, 7211
- Sony CDU-6111
- Texel DM-3021, 5021
- Texel DM-3024, 5024
- Toshiba 3201
- Toshiba 3301
- Other

Highlight the CD-ROM of your choice, and click on OK to return to the System Configuration window.

SCSI Adapter Support

OS/2 also provides extensive support for SCSI adapter cards. Check the SCSI Adapter Support check box, then click on OK to see a window containing the following SCSI adapters:

- IBM PS/2 SCSI Adapters
- Adaptec 1510, 1512, 1520, 1522
- Adaptec 1540, 1542, 1544
- Adaptec 1640, 1642, 1644
- Adaptec 1740, 1742, 1744
- DPT PM2011, PM2012
- Future Domain 1660, 1670, 1680, MCS 700
- Future Domain 850IBM
- Future Domain 860, 870, 880
- Future Domain 7000EX

Confirm the name and number of your SCSI adapter card, then highlight your choice, and click OK to return to the system Configuration window.

Printer

When you select the Printer check box, a window opens listing over 200 supported printers and plotters by name, as well as the option Do Not Install Default Printer. Choose the printer you want to install as the default printer from the list, and click OK to return to the System Configuration window. See Chapter 9 for more information on printers and printing under OS/2.

Finally, when you have completed your choices from the System Configuration window, click the OK button to open the next window, shown in Figure 2.3.

If you are changing your OS/2 installation, select an option by clicking on the appropriate check box; to deselect an option, click on the check box a second time.

FIGURE 2.3

OS/2 Setup and Installation Optional Features

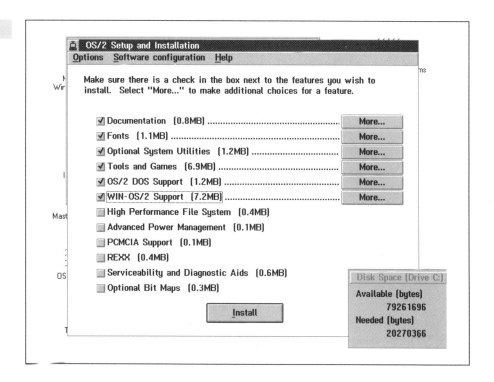

Each option shows the amount of disk space it will occupy if you choose to make the installation, and the first few selections in the list have More buttons, indicating that further settings or choices are available:

- **Documentation** allows you to choose to install the OS/2 Tutorial, the OS/2 Command Reference, or REXX Information.

- **Fonts** lets you select fonts for installation by name. If you decide not to install any of these fonts, only the System Proportional, Courier, and Helvetica fonts will be available on your system.

- **Optional System Utilities** lets you choose which of the utilities to install. If you install all of them, they occupy just over 1MB of hard disk space.

- **Tools and Games** lets you select the productivity applications and games you want to install.

> ## ▶ S O L U T I O N
>
> If you originally installed all of the OS/2 Productivity tools and games, and later find that you only want to use a small number of them, delete all the files in the directories OS2\APPS and OS2\APPS\DLL, and then use the Tools and Games option to selectively install those that you do use. By deleting all the files in these two directories, you can be sure that you have removed all the files associated with each application and game, including all executable files, dynamic link library (DLL) files, and help files, *but you will also delete any data files you have created using these programs, so proceed carefully.* Data files usually have one or more $ characters in their file-name extensions so you can tell them apart from the program files. Chapter 3 contains detailed information on copying, moving, and deleting files.

- **OS/2 DOS Support** lets you install support files for DOS Protected Mode Interface, Virtual Expanded Memory Management, or Virtual Extended Memory.

- **WIN-OS/2 Support** allows you to select the drive on which WIN-OS/2 support files will be installed, and lets you individually specify whether to install the WIN-OS/2 Readme files, Accessories, Screen-savers, and Sound applications.

The Options menu contains selections you can use to start the installation process, format a disk, or go directly to the OS/2 command prompt. The Software Configuration menu contains two advanced items for experienced users who want to fine-tune OS/2 or DOS system parameters. These options are described in detail in Chapter 6.

When you have completed your selections, use Install from the Options menu, or click on the Install button to start adding the system options that you chose. You will be asked to insert the appropriate OS/2 installation disks throughout the process.

Migrate Applications

Use this special System Setup option to search your hard disk for MS-DOS, Windows, or OS/2 programs that you want to see represented in a folder on the desktop. The Drives list includes all your hard disks and hard disk partitions; all the highlighted drives will be searched for applications. A program can migrate to the desktop if an entry for it appears in a file called DATABASE.DAT in the OS2\INSTALL directory.

Click on the Find button when you are ready to start looking for programs to migrate. As OS/2 recognizes major applications on your hard disk, it lists their names in alphabetical order in the Applications window. To see a list of all the individual program files found by Migrate Applications, click on the Add button below this window. Now you can use the Add or Remove buttons in the Add Programs window to select or deselect individual applications for migration. Click the OK button when your selection is complete, and you will return to the Migrate Programs window. Remove the highlighting from any programs shown in the Applications list that you do not want to migrate, and then click on the Migrate button to start the process running. Migrate Applications creates an OS/2 folder, a DOS folder, and a WIN-OS/2 Program Manager folder. A program object is created in the appropriate folder on the OS/2 desktop for each

➤ **S E C R E T**

If you are a knowledgeable OS/2 user or system administrator, and you have unique or proprietary DOS or Windows applications that the main migration database DATABASE.DAT cannot know about, you can create your own migration database using the PARSEDB utility from the OS/2 command prompt.

To create a custom migration database, you must first create a database of the relevant information as a text file, then run PARSEDB using this file to create the binary database file.

PARSEDB has three parameters:

- Tag_File is the name of the file that contains the definitions of the information used to migrate a program.
- Text Database contains the application settings for the OS/2, MS-DOS, or Windows programs.
- Binary Database specifies the name of the resulting binary database file; this prevents the default file, DATABASE.DAT, from being destroyed by the creation of a new file.

The syntax for PARSEDB is:

PARSEDB Tag_File Text_Database Binary_Database

When you create the Text_Database file, each program must have the following migration information:

- **Name** The name of the executable file that starts the program.
- **Title** The program object name that you want to see underneath the program's icon on the desktop.
- **Type** The program type; OS/2, DOS, or Windows.
- **Assoc-file** The file name associated with the file name specified in the Name field above.
- **Def-dir** Specifies the directory where the program is located.

PARSEDB does not check for duplicate entries in the Text_Database file, it does not require that entries be arranged in any particular order, and it is not case-sensitive.

program highlighted in the Applications list. If you used the Add Programs button, you will find that Migrate Applications also created an Additional DOS Programs folder and an Additional Windows Programs folder.

Device Driver Install

This selection guides you though adding a device driver to OS/2 from a Device Support Disk provided by the manufacturer of a particular piece of hardware. You can also start this program directly from the OS/2 command line if you type **DDINSTALL**.

In the Device Driver Installation window, specify the Source Directory and Destination Directory, insert the Device Support Disk in the correct disk drive, and click on the Install button. When the installation is complete, select Shut Down from the desktop pop-up menu, shut down your system and then start it back up again to make sure that the new device driver is loaded properly.

Do not use this window to install device drivers that are a part of the OS/2 operating system or are supplied on the OS/2 Printer Driver Disks; these drivers are handled by the Selective Install program.

Device Driver Install uses a device-driver profile file from the floppy disk to control the installation process, to add the appropriate support statements to your CONFIG.SYS file, and to copy the appropriate files into the correct directory or directories on your hard disk.

WIN-OS/2 Setup

WIN-OS/2 Setup, new in OS/2 version 2.1, lets you configure your WIN-OS/2 sessions, as well as the system clipboard and the dynamic data exchange facilities available in OS/2. Double-click on the WIN-OS/2 Setup icon inside the System Setup folder to open the three-page settings notebook.

On the first page, choose the session type you want to use for your Windows programs running under WIN-OS/2 version 3.1. Check the WIN-OS/2 Full Screen box if you want to run WIN-OS/2 as a full-screen session. Remember that if you choose this option, you cannot see other windows or program icons. Select WIN-OS/2 Window to run your Windows program in a window rather than full screen. If you want to run just one Windows program in a WIN-OS/2 window session, select Separate Session. The default is set to run Windows programs in a shared WIN-OS/2 window.

You can also look at or change the WIN-OS/2 settings. The Settings field contains a list of all the system settings that relate to either DOS or Windows programs. Each is preset by OS/2, but you can change these values if you wish; sometimes there are very good reasons for changing these settings, and I'll describe when and why in more detail in Chapters 6 and 7. If you do change the value of one of these settings in an open session, only the programs running in that session are affected. To make sure that changed settings are used every time you use a particular program or session, be sure to use the Save button. As I say, more on this in Chapters 6 and 7.

Click on the Data Exchange tab to open the second page of the WIN-OS/2 Setup Settings, where you can control DDE and the OS/2 clipboard. You can make DDE public so that data can be shared between OS/2 and WIN-OS/2 programs (the default setting), or private, so that information is not shared with WIN-OS/2 programs. You can use similar check boxes to control how the clipboard works in OS/2 and WIN-OS/2.

The third page of settings, opened with the General tab, contains the usual object name and icon information.

Power

The Power object is also new in OS.2 version 2.1, and you use it to manage and track power consumption in a laptop or other battery-powered computer that supports the Advanced Power Management (APM) standard. The APM standard defines several ways that your computer can go into a suspended mode and save power without actually turning the computer off. When you go into this suspended mode, the display dims, and certain devices, not in use, are turned off. The way you return to normal operation depends on the computer; some computers have a resume button, others return to normal operation when you open the lid.

Open the Power object's Settings notebook, and you will see the following tabs:

- **Power**. Use this page to turn power management features on or off, and to make the Power object display a window so you can confirm that you want to start suspended mode.

- **View**. Use this page to specify how you want the battery-status information displayed, and whether you want this information updated automatically, or refreshed periodically.

- **General**. This page contains the usual entries for icon, and icon title, as well as the Create Another, Edit, and Find buttons.

The Power object is a welcome addition to the System Setup options and will make life easier for anyone using a battery-powered computer. See Chapter 8 for information on support for PCMCIA Type II adapters, which will also be of interest to laptop and other portable-computer users.

Customizing Your Desktop

The second part of this chapter looks at some of the techniques you can use to make your desktop even easier to use, by grouping programs and their data files together in a special folder known as the startup folder, and it shows how you can use a special kind of program link known as an *association*.

Using a Startup Folder

You can drag programs or batch files that you want to execute every time you start OS/2 into a special folder on the desktop called the *Startup* folder. This folder is intended for use with programs that you want to start running during system initialization, but that may not need to run throughout an OS/2 session. For example, if you always need to log onto a network, rather than a large application program, you could include a batch file that does so.

Think carefully before you place programs or batch files in the Startup folder, because there is no way to specify the order in which these programs are started; OS/2 makes that choice for you.

Disabling the Startup Folder

If you decide that you want to prevent the programs in the Startup folder from running when the computer is restarted, press the Ctrl+Shift+F1 keys on the keyboard when the mouse pointer and the zooming boxes first appear. Hold these keys down for about 15 seconds, or until the first desktop icons appear on your screen. If the hard disk light on your computer stops during this step, quickly release the keys, and press and hold them again until the desktop icons appear.

Creating a Custom Startup

If you want to customize the startup of your desktop, you can use the OS/2 Enhanced Editor, described in Chapter 4, to add the following statements to your CONFIG.SYS file.

SET RESTARTOBJECTS = There are several different ways you can use SET RESTARTOBJECTS =, as follows:

YES	This is the default setting, and it restarts all the objects that were running when the operating system was last shut down.
NO	Does not restart the applications that were running when the operating system was last shut down.
STARTUP FOLDERS ONLY	Starts only those objects in the Startup folder.

S O L U T I O N

If you shut down OS/2 when you have lots of windows open on the desktop, all these windows will be reopened next time you start the operating system, and this can take time. If you don't want this to happen, but would rather have OS/2 just open the objects you place in the Startup folder, use the Enhanced Editor to add this line to your CONFIG.SYS file:

SET RESTARTOBJECTS = STARTUPFOLDERSONLY

See Chapter 13 for more CONFIG.SYS secrets.

REBOOTONLY   Starts objects only if the desktop is started after turning the computer on or resetting with Ctrl+Alt+Del.

SET AUTOSTART = The SET AUTOSTART statement is used to start parts of the OS/2 Workplace shell. If you remove one or more of the options in this list, you effectively restrict users from accessing that portion of the shell and thus allow them access only to certain programs.

You can use one or more of the following with SET AUTOSTART:

FOLDERS   Opens folders, including the desktop folder.

TASKLIST   Opens the Window List.

PROGRAMS   Starts program objects running.

CONNECTIONS   Reestablishes the network connections that were in effect when the operating system was last shut down.

A typical, non-networked CONFIG.SYS file might contain the following statement:

SET AUTOSTART=PROGRAMS,TASKLIST,FOLDERS

to open programs, the Window List, and folders on the desktop.

Associating Objects

You can create a special kind of link, known as an *association*, between a program and one or more data files. This association lets you open both the program and the data file simply by double-clicking on the data file. For example, you can associate a single document or all your documents with your word processing program. Most of the time, you will associate a file with the original application program that created the file in the first place. To associate a program object to all data-file objects that have one or more specific file types, open the pop-up menu for the program object, select Settings, then choose the Associations tab. Select one or more file types from the Available Types list and then click on the Add button; the association is complete.

To associate a program object to all data-file objects with similar names, open the Settings note book, then type the file-name extension you want to associate into the New Name field, and click on the Add button. You can use global wildcard characters if you wish. For example, to associate all text files with a program, use *.TXT. Repeat this process to associate more than one file-name extension with the same program object.

▶ S O L U T I O N

By default, all data files are initially associated with the OS/2 System Editor, but you can easily change that to the Enhanced Editor, or any other editor of your choice. The Enhanced Editor is a much more capable editor than the OS/2 System Editor, so making this change is a good idea. Both editors are described in Chapter 4.

Right-click on the Enhanced Editor in the Productivity folder inside the OS/2 System folder, then click on the arrow next to the Open selection, and choose Settings from the cascaded menu. When the Settings notebook opens, click on the Association tab to display the list of file types that will be displayed using the Enhanced Editor. Select one or more types from the Available Types list:

- Assembler Code
- BASIC Code
- Binary Data
- Bitmap
- C Code
- COBOL Code
- Digital Audio
- Digital Video
- DOS Command File
- Dynamic Link Library
- Executable
- FORTRAN Code
- Icon
- Metafile
- Microformatic Fax
- Midi
- OS/2 Command File
- Pascal Code
- PIF File
- Plain Text
- Pointer
- Printer Specific
- Resource File

Alternatively, you can type the file name of the data-file object you want to associate with the program into the New Name field, then click on the Add button. Or, to associate all data-file objects that share a common file-name extension, enter that extension and click on Add. For example, enter *.DOC to associate all data-file objects whose names end in .DOC. Repeat this step as many times as you like to add all the file-name extensions you want to associate. Finally, you can choose one or more of the object types from the Available Types list, and then select the Add button. Close the folder when you have completed your choices. Next, locate the icon for the original OS/2 System Editor in the Productivity folder on the desktop, open the Settings notebook at the Associations page, and click on the Remove button to remove Available Types from the Current Types list that you want to use with the new editor. That's all there is to it.

Creating Work-Area Folders

A slightly different kind of association, one that allows you to group objects related to a specific task, is known as a *work-area folder*. For example, you can create a work-area folder to hold everything associated with a particular project, including data-file objects containing early versions of your report, the actual report itself, the word processing program you used, and a specially configured printer.

Work-area folders have several important features that makes working with them very easy:

- When you close the folder, all the windows that belong to the objects contained within the folder are also closed automatically.

- When you next open the folder, all the windows are reopened just as they were when you closed the folder.

- If you hide the work-area folder window, all other windows belonging to objects within the work-area folder are also hidden automatically.

- If you minimize a work-area folder, only the icon for the folder is displayed; the windows that belong to the objects inside the folder are not displayed.

- A work-area folder is considered to be a single object in the Window List, so that you can manage all the objects in the folder with a single action.

To create a new work-area folder, or convert an existing folder into a work-area folder, open the pop-up menu for the folder you want to convert, or drag a new template folder onto the desktop. Select the arrow to the right of the Open selection, choose Settings, and then click on the File tab. Check the Work Area check box on page one, then double-click on the title-bar icon to close the notebook.

Creating a New Object from the Templates Folder

If you want to create a new desktop object, the fastest way of doing this is usually to make a duplicate of one of the objects in the Template folder. The folder contains at least the following templates:

- Data File
- Folder
- Program
- Printer
- Network Printer

You may also see templates for Color Palette, Font Palette, and Scheme Palette, used to create additional sets of colors, fonts, and color schemes on your system. Additional types of data file templates are often added by specific applications. For example, if you install a drawing program that is supplied with sample files, you will find templates for these file in this folder.

To move a template to the desktop or into another folder, just drag and drop the template using the right mouse button.

S E C R E T

You can also reverse this process and create your own template from an existing object. The new object will have the same content and settings as the original. Use the right mouse button to open the pop-up menu for the object you want to make into a template, and open the Settings notebook using the General tab. Select the Template check box, and close the settings notebook. Your selected object is now displayed as a template, and you can drag it to the Templates folder for safekeeping.

Changing the View

You can look at the information contained in a folder in three different ways by using Icon View, Tree View, or Details View.

- **Icon View** shows the objects in the folder as different icons. Programs have their own special icons; files are assigned generic icons depending on the file type; text files, program files, and so on all have different icons; and directories are shown as folders. The Icon View makes it very easy to move or rearrange the objects inside a folder.

- **Tree View** shows the objects in the folder arranged in a hierarchical fashion. It is most useful for displaying the contents of directories because it gives a good indication of how things are organized. Tree View is described in more detail in Chapter 3 under the heading "Listing Files and Folders."

- **Details View** gives you all the information about each of the objects in the folder, including a tiny replica icon, the icon title, the real name (usually the file name), size, the last write time, the last access date and time, the create date and time, and the file attributes or flags.

To change the view, open the pop-up menu, select the arrow next to Open, then choose either Icon View, Tree View, or Details View from the menu.

S E C R E T

If you want to change a folder's default view permanently, open the Settings notebook at the Menu tab, and click on the Open menu in the Available Menus box to enable the Settings button. Click on this Settings button to open the Menu Settings dialog box. Now select the view you want to use as the default from the selections offered in the Default Action list; click on OK when you have made your choice, and then double-click on the title-bar icon to close the folder's settings notebook. Next time you double-click on this folder, you will see the contents displayed using the view you just selected.

If no default view has been set for a folder, it inherits the default view from its parent folder. If you set the default view for subdirectories starting at the root directory, all subfolders of that folder, or in other words, all the folders on the drive will inherit the default view. While drive objects look like folders, they do not inherit the default view.

Adding Productivity Applications to the Desktop Pop-Up Menu

The OS/2 desktop lets you group common items together in folders to preserve desktop space, but at some point your desktop is going to look cluttered and full. One way of preventing further clutter is to add items that you use on a regular basis to the desktop's pop-up menu. This way you can access programs quickly, without the need for extra icons on the desktop, and without searching through folders. Before you can add a program to the desktop pop-up menu, you must know the name of the executable file used to start the program, and the name of the directory or folder where the file is located. All the OS/2 Productivity applications and games, described in detail in Chapter 4, are located in the OS2\APPS directory, and their file names are listed in Table 2.1.

TABLE 2.1: OS/2 Productivity Applications and Games Files Names

PROGRAM NAME	PROGRAM FILENAME
Activities List	PMDLIST.EXE
Alarms	PMALARM.EXE
Calculator	PMDCALC.EXE
Calendar	PMDCALEN.EXE
Cat and Mouse	NEKO.EXE
Clipboard Viewer	CLIPOS2.EXE
Daily Planner	PMDDIARY.EXE
Database	PMMBASE.EXE
Data Update	PMDDE.EXE
Enhanced Editor	EPM.EXE
Fax/PM Scheduler	FAXPM.EXE
Fax/PM Viewer	FAXVIEW.EXE
Fax/PM DDE	FAXDDE.EXE
Icon Editor	ICONEDIT.EXE
Jigsaw	JIGSAW.EXE
Monthly Calendar	PMDMONTH.EXE
Notepad	PMDNOTE.EXE
OS/2 Chess	OS2CHESS.EXE
OS/2 System Editor	E.EXE
Picture Viewer	PICVIEW.EXE
Planner Archive	PMDDARC.EXE
PM Chart	PMCHART.EXE
Pulse	PULSE.EXE
Reversi	REVERSI.EXE
Scramble	SCRAMBLE.EXE
Seek and Scan Files	PMSEEK.EXE

TABLE 2.1: OS/2 Productivity Applications and Games File Names (Continued)

PROGRAM NAME	PROGRAM FILENAME
SoftTerm	SOFTTERM.EXE
Solitaire-Klondike	KLONDIKE.EXE
Spreadsheet	PMSPREAD.EXE
Sticky Pad	PMSTICKY.EXE
To-Do List	PMDTODO.EXE
To-Do List Archive	PMDTARC.EXE
Tune Editor	PMDTUNE.EXE

When you have decided which program or programs to add to the desktop pop-up menu, open the desktop Settings notebook, and click on the Menu tab to open the menu settings window. Now click on the lower of the two Create Another buttons to open the Menu Item Settings dialog box. Enter the name you want to use with this program into the Menu Item Name field, and enter the complete path name for the program into the Name field. For example, to add the OS/2 spreadsheet program into the desktop pop-up menu, type Spreadsheet into the Menu Item Name field, and the path name C:\OS2\APPS\PMSPREAD.EXE into the name box. Finally, click on the OK button to save this new menu item. Repeat this operation for each of the programs you want to add to the pop-up menu, then double-click on the title-bar icon to close the Settings notebook. Now when you right-click on an empty area of the desktop, you will see a new section at the bottom of the menu containing your additions. With these new entries in your desktop pop-up menu, you can now run favorite applications with just two mouse clicks.

S E C R E T

If you find that you use an OS/2 window on a regular basis, you can save yourself lots of time by adding the OS/2 window to the desktop pop-up menu. Follow the procedure I just described for Productivity applications, but type **OS/2 Window** into the Menu Item Name field, and **CMD.EXE** into the Program Name field. Double-click on the title-bar icon to close the Settings notebook when you are done. Now when you next open the desktop pop-up menu, you will see this new entry at the end of the menu. Click on it and an OS/2 window will open on the desktop. To close the window again, either type EXIT at the command prompt, or choose CMD.EXE from the Window List, and use Close from its pop-up menu.

If you decide you want to remove an item from the desktop pop-up menu, just open the desktop Settings notebook and select the Menu tab. Your additions appear in the Actions On Menu list box. Highlight an item, and then click on the Delete button. When you next open the desktop pop-up menu, the item will not be there.

OS/2 OS/2 OS/2

OS/2 OS/2 OS/2 OS/2 OS/2 OS/2 OS/2 OS/2

OS/2 OS/2 OS/2 O

Managing Disks and Files under OS/2

THE first part of this chapter describes the file systems available in OS/2; the File Allocation Table (FAT) file system, and the High Performance File System (HPFS), as well as other installable file systems used with CD-ROMs and other devices.

The second part of this chapter describes how you can use either the desktop or the OS/2 command line to perform routine file-maintenance tasks like moving or copying files, creating and removing directories, and formatting floppy disks.

An Introduction to the OS/2 File Systems

The file system is that part of the operating system that gives you access to files and programs stored on a disk. OS/2 offers two file systems, the File Allocation Table or FAT system, and the High Performance File System, abbreviated to HPFS.

The file system organizes disks into volumes, directories, and files. Each volume must have a root directory, containing file and directory entries, and these directories can also contain further subdirectories.

You can also use another kind of file system, known as an installable file system, if you add a special command, IFS, into your CONFIG.SYS file to load it when needed. An installable file is one that is loaded every time the operating system is started. If you use any file system other than the FAT, you must have the appropriate IFS command in your CONFIG.SYS file. The HPFS itself is considered to be an installable file system, and so requires the appropriate statements in CONFIG.SYS. OS/2 loads the appropriate device driver and dynamic link libraries, and initializes a specific drive for use with the installable file system.

In OS/2 you can have multiple file systems active at the same time; for example, you can have a FAT file system on one hard disk, the HPFS active on another, and a third type of file system active on a CD-ROM.

What follows is an introduction to the file systems available in OS/2. A more complete discussion of their differences and similarities appears in Chapter 13, where you'll learn how to optimize OS/2 performance by setting up appropriate CONFIG.SYS entries for each file system.

Using the File Allocation Table (FAT) File System

MS-DOS users migrating to OS/2 will recognize most of the elements of the FAT from similar structures found in DOS. The FAT uses a table structure to assign units of disk storage to files. When the operating system requests a file, information in this table is used to locate the file on disk and read it into memory. Using this scheme, the file may be divided into several parts stored in different areas of the hard disk. This effect is known as *file fragmentation*, and in extreme cases can impair system performance. You should be careful when using the traditional MS-DOS file-defragmentation programs because these programs may not know about OS/2's extended attributes; make sure that the program can run with the OS/2 file systems. Files created under the HPFS do not suffer from fragmentation.

The OS/2 FAT is compatible with MS-DOS file structures, so you might want to use the FAT if maintaining compatibility with your MS-DOS systems is an important issue. MS-DOS cannot read files created with the HPFS, but DOS applications running in a DOS session under OS/2 *can* recognize files and directories on both FAT and HPFS disks. Also, the HPFS can read files created by the FAT and by MS-DOS.

The FAT uses the familiar but limited "8.3" naming convention, where a file or directory name can have up to eight letters, followed by a period, and then an optional three-letter extension.

S O L U T I O N

If you plan to send files to or receive them from other countries, you and your correspondent should agree not to use any special or accented characters in the file names, as these special characters may not be available on all keyboards.

You cannot use the following symbols in an OS/2 file or directory name:

    & – > < | ? * : / \ " . ,

and don't use the @ symbol as the last character of a file name; the @ usually designates the file as a packed file.

Several special names are reserved, and you cannot use them for files or directories: COM1, COM2, COM3, COM4, CON, KBD$, LPT1, LPT2, LPT3, NUL, PRN, CLOCK$, MOUSE$, POINTER$, and SCREEN$. Nor can you use any of the operating system command names for the names of your files or directories.

Three more reserved names are already in use by OS/2, and you should avoid them when naming directories: PIPE, SEM, and QUEUE. For example, the C:\SPOOL directory is used by the OS/2 print spooler to hold print jobs waiting to be printed. SPOOL contains a subdirectory for each printer queue you install. These names are reserved for OS/2 as long as there is no filename extension in use, so you can create a file called SPOOL.JIM, but not a file just called SPOOL.

The FAT system is a good system to use if maintaining MS-DOS compatibility is an important consideration, or if your hard disk (or disk partition) is smaller than about 60MB. If MS-DOS compatibility is not important and you have more than about 60MB, consider using the HPFS instead.

Using the High Performance File System (HPFS)

The HPFS includes the following features that contribute to its increased performance:

- Caching of directories, data, and files; this gives faster access on large hard disks, and computers with more than 6MB of memory.
- Multi-threaded input/output operations.
- Strategic allocation of directory structures.
- Highly contiguous file allocation; files and extended attributes are kept together, and file fragmentation is eliminated.
- Support for large storage devices, up to 64GB.
- Long file names, up to 254 characters, including path information.

N O T E   You cannot use the HPFS on a floppy disk. All floppy disks are formatted using the FAT system.

In the HPFS, many of the MS-DOS-style file system restrictions have been removed. For example, files can have names of up to 254 characters long, and can combine characters that are illegal in the FAT system. Also, file names can combine upper- and lower-case letters and may include several periods.

N O T E   MS-DOS cannot recognize the structure created by HPFS, so if you start your computer by booting MS-DOS from a floppy disk, or from a partition formatted by MS-DOS, you will not be able to access or recognize any of your HPFS files.

The HPFS allows fast access to very large disk volumes, using a disk cache divided into 2K blocks. All data read from or written to the disk passes through this cache. Frequently used data will be read from the cache rather than from the disk, thus saving the time that another disk read would take. When an application requests data that is not in the cache, OS/2 writes out the information contained in the least used block, and reads the new data into that space. Data in the cache may not be written to disk immediately, but may be written out in the background as system load allows. This is known as *lazy writing* and is covered in detail in Chapter 13.

Application programs can attach additional information to files in the form of *extended attributes*. These extended attributes can describe the file to another application, or to the operating system, and can be used for a variety of purposes, including:

- Appending extra information to the file.
- Describing the format used to store data in the file.
- Storing notes on the file, such as the name of the creator.
- Categorizing the contents of files: icons, bitmaps, text, and so on.

NOTE Both HPFS and the OS/2 FAT system support extended attributes, but MS-DOS does not. Extended attributes are used by application programs; they are not manipulated by users.

Extended attributes are associated with the file object, but are not part of the file or the file's data. They are stored as separate files, but linked together by the file system. A file may have more than one extended attribute, whose contents can be text, graphics, icons, binary data—anything that an application wants to associate with the file. So that applications can understand the kind of information that is stored in an extended attribute, the first word of the extended attribute must specify the data type, as follows:

- Binary (non-text) data
- ASCII text data

- Bit map data

- Metafile data

- Icon data

- ASCII name of another EA associated with the file

- Multi-valued, multi-typed data

- Multi-valued, single-typed data

- ASN.1 field data

The maximum size of an extended attribute is 64K. The description of the DIR command later in this chapter shows how you can find out how much disk space extended attributes occupy on your system.

OS/2 Files and Directories

During installation, OS/2 places files in several new directories on your system, as well as in the root directory. OS/2 keeps the root directory clear of files except for the OS/2 configuration file CONFIG.SYS, and the DOS-session startup file AUTOEXEC.BAT. The following directories are created during installation:

- C:\DESKTOP (known in OS/2 version 2.0 as C:\OS!2 2.0 Desktop (HPFS) or C:\OS!2_2.0_D (FAT)). This directory contains information on the desktop, and includes subdirectories used for documentation, icons, and network information.

- C:\OS2. This directory contains the OS/2 executable programs, including the OS/2 Productivity applications and the OS/2 games.

- C:\NOWHERE. This directory is used for internal OS/2 purposes, and you will not see any files listed in this directory.

- C:\SPOOL. This directory is used by OS/2 to hold spool files being sent to the printer. It contains a subdirectory for each installed printer queue.

- C:\PSFONTS. This directory contains files that relate to proportionally-spaced fonts, and will contain any additional Adobe Type Manager fonts you add later.

NOTE   Do not delete *any* files from these directories unless you know exactly what you are doing, because most of them are crucial to the proper operation of OS/2.

Managing Files and Folders from the Desktop

The most common objects in either file system are files and directories. Directories contain files and other directories, often called subdirectories, and are arranged in an hierarchical structure, with the so-called *root* directory at the top of the whole structure.

On the object-oriented OS/2 desktop, directories are usually referred to as folders, and they behave just like all the other objects on the desktop. By using an object's pop-up menu you can look at and change the settings, and by taking advantage of the desktop's drag-and-drop features, you can move or copy files and folders with your mouse without knowing all the details of the underlying structure.

If you have migrated to OS/2 from Windows, the seamless integration of file-management tasks on the desktop will come as a very pleasant surprise; there is no artificial distinction made in OS/2 between managing file and program functions.

In the next few sections, I'll describe how you can perform common file- and folder-management tasks from the desktop, then go on to explain how you can perform these and other functions using the OS/2 command prompt.

Listing Files and Folders

To look at the file structure on a disk, open the Drives folder in the OS/2 System folder. You will find icons for each of the drives on your system inside the Drives folder.

Note that a shadow of drive A is always available directly from the desktop; you can drag other drives from the Drives folder to the desktop too, if you wish. A *shadow* is just a copy of an object that is linked back to the original object; this means that the same object can appear to be in two places at the same time. In this case, drive A is available both in the Drives folder and on the desktop. You will find more on shadows later in this chapter.

By default, files and folders (or directories) are displayed on the desktop in the Tree view to show off their hierarchical structure. Figure 3.1 shows part of the structure on drive C.

At the top of the drive window, you will see a short summary of the free and total space available on the drive. The rest of the window is occupied by the display of folders and files inside those folders. A plus sign to the left of a folder indicates that there are other objects inside this folder; click on the icon to display the contents. A minus sign means that all the objects in the folder are displayed; click on this icon to collapse the structure. As

FIGURE 3.1

Part of the drive C tree structure

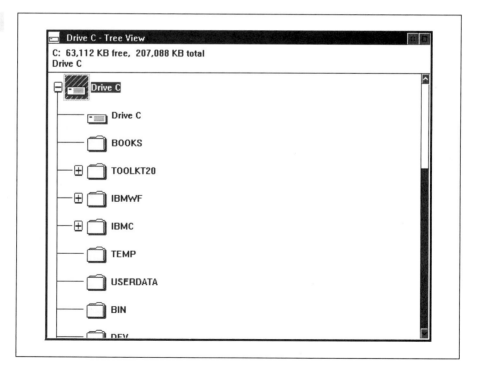

you expand and contract this display, remember that nothing is happening to the files and folders on your disk; only the display in the drive window is changing.

Sometimes, you might want to see more detail on the individual files in a folder, and you can do this using the Details view instead of the Tree view. Figure 3.2 shows a Details view for drive C.

FIGURE 3.2

Details view of the files and folders on drive C

Icon	Title	Real name	Size	Last write date	Last write time	Last access date	Last acc
	TEST	TEST	0	10-19-92	12:59:24 pm	0-0-80	1
	TIPS	TIPS	0	10-27-92	4:08:36 pm	0-0-80	1
	SHARE	SHARE	0	11-3-92	11:41:12 am	0-0-80	1
	DEV	DEV	0	11-24-92	3:22:30 pm	0-0-80	1
	BIN	BIN	0	11-24-92	3:22:30 pm	0-0-80	1
	USERDATA	USERDATA	0	11-24-92	4:47:22 pm	0-0-80	1
	TEMP	TEMP	0	11-24-92	4:47:22 pm	0-0-80	1
	IBMC	IBMC	0	11-24-92	5:23:40 pm	0-0-80	1
	IBMWF	IBMWF	0	11-24-92	5:27:20 pm	0-0-80	1
	TOOLKT20	TOOLKT20	0	11-24-92	5:25:30 pm	0-0-80	1
	BOOKS	BOOKS	0	11-29-92	2:30:58 pm	0-0-80	1
	AUTOEXEC.BAK	AUTOEXEC.BAK	228	8-31-92	3:49:20 pm	0-0-80	1
	AUTOEXEC.BAT	AUTOEXEC.BAT	249	8-31-92	5:37:10 pm	0-0-80	1
	AUTOEXEC.ND0	AUTOEXEC.ND0	228	8-31-92	3:49:20 pm	0-0-80	1
	AUTOEXEC.NDW	AUTOEXEC.NDW	228	8-31-92	3:49:20 pm	0-0-80	1
	AUTOEXEC.OLD	AUTOEXEC.OLD	243	9-9-92	10:19:30 am	0-0-80	1
	COMMAND.COM	COMMAND.COM	47,845	4-9-91	5:00:00 am	0-0-80	1
	CONFIG.ND0	CONFIG.ND0	104	8-31-92	3:40:38 pm	0-0-80	1
	CONFIG.NDW	CONFIG.NDW	104	8-31-92	3:40:38 pm	0-0-80	1
	CONFIG.OLD	CONFIG.OLD	104	8-31-92	4:40:42 pm	0-0-80	1
	CONFIG.SYS	CONFIG.SYS	2,126	11-30-92	4:17:16 pm	0-0-80	1
	DOS	DOS	0	8-28-92	2:40:26 pm	0-0-80	1
	KLONDIKE.INI	KLONDIKE.INI	1,213	9-7-92	1:26:40 pm	0-0-80	1

Drive C - Details View

From left to right, for each file and folder object, the Details view shows:

- An outline of the object's icon
- The object's title on the desktop
- The object's real name
- Size, in bytes
- Last write date

- Last write time
- Last access date
- Last access time
- Creation date
- Creation time
- Flags

 S E C R E T

The left and right portions of the Details view scroll independently, and you can drag the double vertical bar between the Title and the Real Name columns to change the relative proportions of the two parts of the window.

The flags are exactly equivalent to the file *attributes* used in MS-DOS. See the headings "Looking at Simple File Attributes," and "Looking at File Attributes with ATTRIB" later in this chapter for more information on these flags.

You can change the order in which files and folders appear in the Details view by using the Sort option from the pop-up menu. You can sort according to the following criteria:

- Name
- Type
- Real Name
- Size
- Last write date
- Last write time
- Last access date
- Last access time

- Creation date
- Creation time

S O L U T I O N

There is a check box in the Settings notebook Sort tab called Always Maintain Sort Order. Check this box if you want the desktop to present information sorted this way whenever you open the view.

As soon as you make a choice from the list, you will see your files and folders rearranged immediately. You can also use the Sort tab in the Settings notebook to specify these sort options.

The third view you can use when looking at files and folders is the Icon view. Open the pop-up menu and select Open, followed by Icon View, and you will see each element of the file system represented by a different icon.

Finding Files and Folders

If you cannot see the file or folder you are looking for, you can use Find to help locate it. If you are not sure where to begin your search for a file, remember that all folder and drive objects contain the Find selection in their pop-up menus. Open the pop-up menu, then click on Find to open the Find notebook, shown in Figure 3.3, and enter the information needed to find your folder.

In the Folder text field, type the name of the folder that contains the folder you are searching for. Then click on the Locate button to open the Locate Folder notebook so you can specify where to start the search. Choose from:

- **Opened**. Displays all open folders.
- **Related**. Displays the folders near the current position in the directory tree structure.
- **Desktop**. Shows all folders on your desktop.

FIGURE 3.3

The Find Notebook

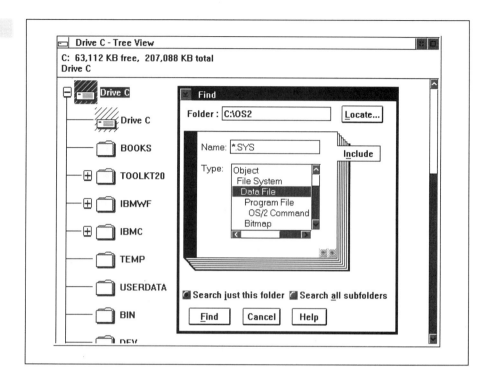

- **Drives**. Lets you select another folder or another drive.
- **Path**. Allows you to enter the path statement of the folder you want to access.

SOLUTION

File searches on computers with large hard disks can take a long time to complete, so anything you can do to make the search more specific will shorten the search time. Use the wildcard characters ? and * in the Name field, along with a selection from the Type field to help narrow the search. For example, use *.DOC to narrow the search to just .DOC files, or 12*.TXT to limit the search to text files created in December.

Click on OK when you have specified where you want the search to begin, then back on the Find page, enter the name of the file or folder you are looking for into the Name field.

Specify the type of object you are looking for in the Type field. The default setting for Type is Object, which will match any file. Use the radio buttons at the bottom of this page to specify that you want to search just this folder or to include all subfolders in your search. Finally, click on the Find button to start the search process running.

If you search only the current folder, Find automatically creates a Find Results folder on the desktop; if you search all subfolders, the Find Results folder displays the names of the folders that contain the objects you were looking for.

WARNING

If you change the title of an object in the Find Results folder, the name of the original object will also be changed.

Creating Files and Folders

There are two ways you can create a new file or folder:

- Right-click on a folder to open the pop-up menu, then select the Create Another option. This creates a new folder with the same settings as the original.

- Open the Templates folder and drag the example folder to a new location. This creates an empty folder that you can customize as you wish using the pop-up menu and the Settings notebook.

Both of these operations work in the same way for creating new data-file objects; in the Templates folder, choose the example data-file object rather than the example folder.

Copying and Moving Files and Folders

When you copy an object, you create an exact replica of the original object in a new location; when you move an object, you transfer the object from the original location to a new location. Copying or moving on the desktop is easiest using the mouse; here's how.

Open an icon view on the disk that contains the file objects or folders you want to move or copy, then select the appropriate objects with the left mouse button. To move the data file or folder, press and hold down the right mouse button while you drag the object to the target object. If you want to copy the object (and keep the original), hold down the Ctrl key on the keyboard as you drag the object to the new location. Release the right mouse button, and the data-file object will be copied or moved to the new location.

You can also move or copy an object using its pop-up menu. Right-click the folder or file to open its pop-up menu, then click Move or Copy in this menu, depending on the operation you want to perform. Figure 3.4 shows the Copy Notebook; the Move Notebook is very similar. Select a tab on the notebook that corresponds to the destination object for this move or copy operation. The selections are the same as described above for Find:

- Opened
- Related
- Desktop
- Drives
- Path

When you have specified a destination, click either the Move button or the Copy button at the bottom of the notebook to complete the operation.

FIGURE 3.4

Use the Copy notebook to specify the destination for a copy operation

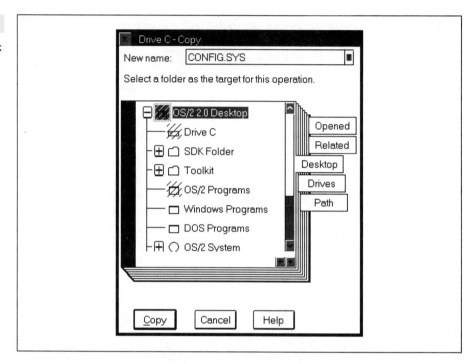

Creating a Shadow of an Object

Sometimes it is useful to have two copies of the same object available on the desktop at the same time. The OS/2 mechanism that makes this possible is called a *shadow*. The data in a shadow is always the same as the data contained in the original, and any operation you perform on a shadow also occurs in the original. If you delete an object, you automatically delete its shadow. You can think of a shadow as being an alias for the original object. If you just copy an object, the new version of the object has no automatic attachment to the original object; they are completely separate versions of the same object, and you can modify, change, or delete the copy without affecting the original.

NOTE OS\2 will not let you copy the system Clock, so if you want to have two clocks on different parts of the decktop, just create a shadow of the system clock.

To create a shadow copy of an object and its contents, select the object you want to shadow, and hold down the Ctrl and Shift keys while you press and hold down the right mouse button. Now drag the shadow of the object into any folder, and release the right mouse button. Alternatively, you can use the Create Shadow selection from the object's pop-up menu.

The pop-up menu of a shadow object contains an Original option, which you can use to return to the original object. Click the arrow next to Original to open a submenu and then click Locate to open the folder that contains the original of the shadowed object. There is no Create Shadow option in the pop-up menu of a shadow object; you cannot make a shadow of a shadow. You can delete a shadow, however, without affecting the original object.

Deleting Files and Folders

When you want to delete an object, you can drag it to the Shredder on the desktop or you can use the Delete selection in the pop-up menu. If you delete a folder (using either method), you also delete all of the folder's contents, including files and other folders.

To use the Shredder, select the object using the left mouse button, then drag the object and drop it onto the Shredder. A confirmation window opens to check that you really do want to delete this object; click on the Delete button and the object is history. If you are deleting a folder, an additional confirmation window opens, to make sure that you want to delete the folder *and all the files contained in the folder*. Click Yes to continue, No to end this task, or Cancel to return to the desktop. Remember, however, that the Shredder is not a folder; you cannot recover objects from the Shredder.

Deleting with the pop-up menu takes just a few more steps. First right-click on the object you want to delete to open its pop-up menu, and choose the Delete selection. Confirm your determination to delete this object with the Delete button. If the object you are deleting is a folder, you will see an additional message asking if you are sure you want to delete the folder *and all of its contents*; click Yes to proceed.

Renaming Objects

If you want to change an object's name, there are two methods you can use. If the object is a newly created copy, you can use this fast method of name editing. Press and hold down the Alt key on the keyboard, then click on the object whose name you want to change. Release the Alt key, and use the Backspace and Delete keys on the keyboard to remove the old name. Then enter the new name. Finally, click the object a second time to complete the renaming process.

Alternatively, you can select the object, then right-click to open its pop-up menu. Click on the arrow next to Open and then choose Settings to open the Settings notebook. Click on the General tab and enter a new name or edit the existing name in the Title box at the top of the page. Double-click on the title-bar icon to close the Settings notebook, and you will see that the object's name has changed.

Copying Floppy Disks

If you want to make an exact copy of a disk, you can use the Copy Disk command from a drive's pop-up menu. This command requires that both of the disks and the disk drives used in this operation be identical in both size (3.5" or 5.25") and capacity. If they are not identical, OS/2 halts the copy and displays an error message.

If you want to copy the disk in drive A onto the disk in drive B, use the Copy Disk command in drive A's pop-up menu; use drive B's pop-up menu if you want to go the other way.

When you start this command, an OS/2 window opens on the screen to guide you through the duplication operation; when you are finished, you return to the desktop.

Formatting a New Disk

To format a new floppy disk, open the OS/2 System folder on the desktop, then open the Drives folder and select the disk drive containing the disk you want to format. Right-click on the drive icon to open its pop-up menu, and select Format Disk. Using the Format Disk dialog box, enter any text you want to use as an optional volume label, and select the appropriate capacity for the disk. If you are formatting a hard disk, choose between the FAT or the HPFS. When you are ready, click on the Format button to start the formatting process. A graphic shows the progress made by the format, and lists the total and free space on the disk when the format is complete.

Because the Drive A icon is always available on the desktop, you can cut out several of the steps listed above if you want to format a disk in this drive; just right-click on the drive icon to open its pop-up menu and choose Format Disk.

Checking a Disk

If you are about to install a large application, it is useful to be able to check a disk for problems and to determine the amount of disk space free for use before you start the installation process. Open the OS/2 System folder on the desktop, and open the Drives folder to select the appropriate disk drive. If you want to check a floppy disk, insert it into the drive before you select the drive. Right-click on the drive icon to open its pop-up menu, click on Check Disk, then click on the Check button. If you want to correct any disk problems that this process might find, check the Write Corrections to Disk check box.

The Check Disk-Results report shown in Figure 3.5 displays the following information:

- Type of file system in use on the disk.

- Total amount of disk space, in bytes.

- Free space remaining on the disk, in bytes.

FIGURE 3.5

The Check Disk-Results display

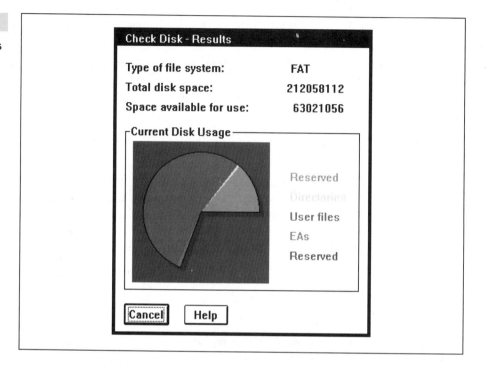

- A pie chart showing the amount of space on the disk reserved for system files and the amount of space occupied by folders, user files, unusable areas on the disk, and extended attributes.

Click the Cancel button to dismiss this report.

Looking at Simple File Attributes

In the Details view of files and folders, the last column of the window lists the flags, or attributes, for each file. Flags are used by the operating system as follows:

- The *archive* flag indicates whether a file has changed since it was last backed up. If the file has changed, or has just been created, the archive flag is set. However, if you use the BACKUP command to copy the file, as described later in this chapter, the archive flag is turned off. This is how the BACKUP command keeps track of the files it has already copied and those it has not.

- The *read-only* flag indicates that the file can be read, printed, or copied, as normal, but cannot be written to or changed in any way.

- The *hidden* flag hides a file from view in a Tree or Details view window.

- The *system* flag indicates that the file is a part of the operating system. System files are also read-only and hidden, so they do not appear in Tree or Detail windows either.

Changing the settings of these flags is best left to the operating system, but if you want to look at all the settings for a particular file, select the file and open its pop-up menu. Choose Settings, and click on the File tab. Click the arrows at the bottom of the page until you can see page 2 of the three pages of file settings. This page is shown in Figure 3.6. Click on the check box for the flag you want to change. Once again, the Undo button will restore the settings that were in effect before you opened the current window. Click the title-bar icon to close this notebook when you have finished.

WARNING   If you set a read-only, system, or hidden flag for a folder, that folder will not be displayed next time you start the system after performing a shut down.

FIGURE 3.6

The Date/Time, Size, and Flags settings shown in the File Settings notebook

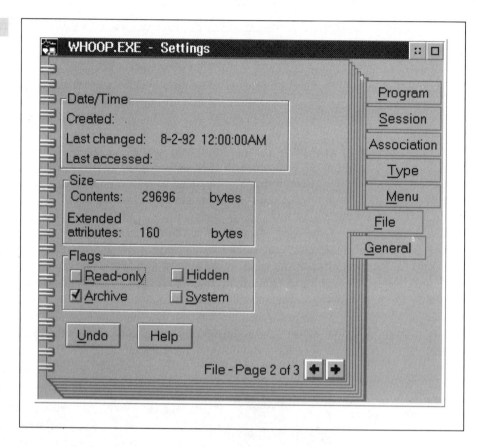

Managing Files and Directories from the OS/2 Command Line

If you have migrated to OS/2 from MS-DOS, the object-oriented desktop will be a pleasure to use. However, for some users, the command line represents the real power, speed, and convenience of OS/2. In the second part of this chapter, I'll describe how you can use the OS/2 command line to perform all the file and folder management tasks that you can do from the desktop, and then go on to cover a few that you can't.

To gain access to the OS/2 command line, open the OS/2 System icon, double-click the Command Prompts folder, then double-click on either the OS/2 Window icon or the OS/2 Full Screen icon. You can work at the OS/2 command line from either of these system prompts, but remember that when working in a window, you may not be able to see the complete display at all times; the window boundaries may obscure some information.

You can also use all the commands described in the rest of this chapter from the command prompt in a DOS session, and many of the commands will be familiar to users of the MS-DOS command line. In fact, because OS/2 is a multitasking operating system, you can run as many DOS sessions as you need. To start a DOS session, double-click the DOS Window icon or the DOS Full Screen icon in the System Prompts folder.

Using DIR to Look at File Structure

The DIR command lists the contents of a directory, along with additional information about the disk. If you use the DIR command by itself with no parameters, the command displays the contents of the current directory, both files and subdirectories. You can use the wildcard characters * or ? with the DIR command to display only those files that match the wildcard specification. If you are working from the OS/2 command prompt, you can also specify multiple file names or path statements at the same time, and the DIR command will list them one after the other.

The DIR command usually lists the following information:

- disk volume label
- disk volume serial number
- directory name
- file names and extensions
- subdirectory names
- file sizes in bytes

- date and time of file creation or last modification
- total number of files in the directory
- amount of disk space used, in bytes
- amount of disk space remaining, in bytes

If the disk you are looking at was created using the FAT, you will see the file and directory names listed on the left side of this display; if the disk was created using the HPFS you will see the file and directory names on the right side instead. (HPFS file names can be much longer than FAT file names, and so they need the extra space.) A DIR listing in an OS/2 window for drive D is shown in Figure 3.7.

FIGURE 3.7

HPFS file and directory
information for a
hard disk

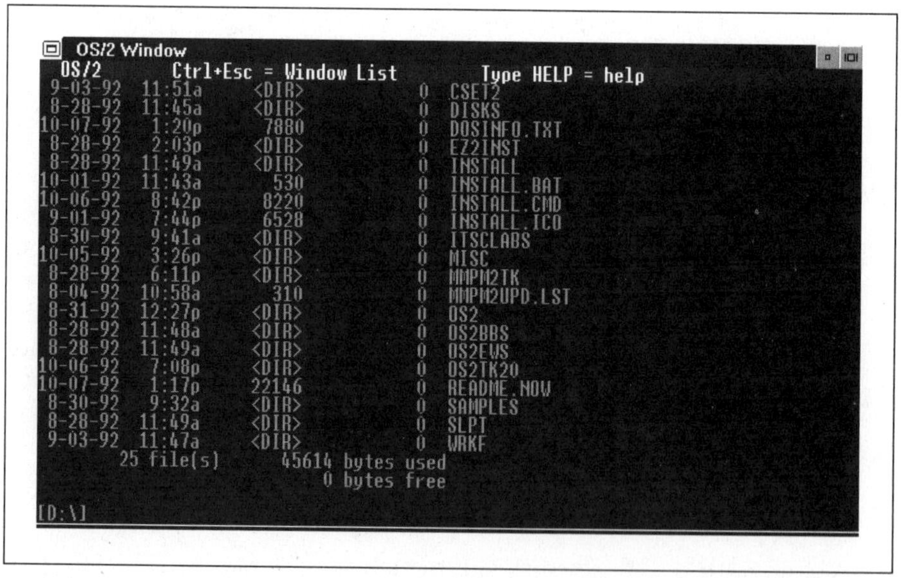

```
▣  OS/2 Window                                                         □ ▣◨
   OS/2          Ctrl+Esc = Window List         Type HELP = help
   9-03-92   11:51a    <DIR>           0  CSET2
   8-28-92   11:45a    <DIR>           0  DISKS
  10-07-92    1:20p     7880           0  DOSINFO.TXT
   8-28-92    2:03p    <DIR>           0  EZ2INST
   8-28-92   11:49a    <DIR>           0  INSTALL
  10-01-92   11:43a      530           0  INSTALL.BAT
  10-06-92    8:42p     8220           0  INSTALL.CMD
   9-01-92    7:44p     6528           0  INSTALL.ICO
   8-30-92    9:41a    <DIR>           0  ITSCLABS
  10-05-92    3:26p    <DIR>           0  MISC
   8-28-92    6:11p    <DIR>           0  MMPM2TK
   8-04-92   10:58a      310           0  MMPM2UPD.LST
   8-31-92   12:27p    <DIR>           0  OS2
   8-28-92   11:48a    <DIR>           0  OS2BBS
   8-28-92   11:49a    <DIR>           0  OS2EWS
  10-06-92    7:08p    <DIR>           0  OS2TK20
  10-07-92    1:17p    22146           0  README.NOW
   8-30-92    9:32a    <DIR>           0  SAMPLES
   8-28-92   11:49a    <DIR>           0  SLPT
   9-03-92   11:47a    <DIR>           0  WRKF
             25 file(s)       45614 bytes used
                                  0 bytes free

  [D:\]
```

There are several options or *switches* you can use to modify the basic listing made by DIR, including:

/W	Selects a wide display format capable of listing five columns of file names on an 80 character display.
/F	Displays just the drive letter, directory name, and file name for each entry. This is known as the *fully qualified file name*. The special directory entries . and .. are not shown.
/A	Displays only those files and directories that possess the attributes or flags that you specify. You can use any combination of these attributes you like but do not separate them with spaces. You can use the following:

A	files ready to backup or archive
-A	files unchanged since the last backup
D	directories, but not files
-D	files, but not directories
H	hidden files
-H	files that are not hidden
R	read-only files
-R	files that are not read-only
S	system files
-S	files that are not system files

/B	Removes the heading information from the directory listing
/L	Displays information in lowercase.

/N   Displays files created using the FAT file system in the format used for the HPFS directory listings. This includes: the date and time the file was created or modified; the size of the file in bytes, or <DIR> if the entry is a directory; the size of the file's extended attributes, in bytes; and the file name.

When you use the HPFS, the extended attribute information is always shown in a directory listing, regardless of whether you use the /N switch.

/O   Displays the files and directories in the sort order you specify, from the following options:

D	date and time, earliest first
–D	date and time, latest first
E	alphabetical order of filename extension
–E	reverse alphabetical order of filename extension
G	directories listed first, before files
–G	files listed first, before directories
N	alphabetical order of file name
–N	reverse alphabetical order of file name
S	size, smallest first
–S	size, largest first

/P   Displays one screenful of entries and then pauses. To see the next screen, press any key.

/R   Displays long file names in an OS/2 session, even when you use the FAT file system. For example, you will see the name OS/2 2.0 Desktop opposite the OS!2_2.0_D directory entry.

/S Lists all occurrences of the specified file in the current directory, and in all subdirectories of the current directory.

If you use the /P or /W switches in a window, you may not be able to see all the entries. Maximize the window before using the command, or open the session in full-screen mode.

➤ S E C R E T

You can use any of the DIR command switches with a little-known OS/2 environment variable called DIRCMD. By setting DIRCMD in CONFIG.SYS, you force OS/2 to check this variable every time you use the DIR command, and to present the directory information in the format specified by the DIR switches. An example will make this clearer. If you add the following command into your OS/2 CONFIG.SYS file using the Enhanced Editor:

  SET DIRCMD= /OGN /A /N /P

and then use Shut Down to restart your system, any time you type the DIR command (without switches) at the OS/2 command prompt, you will see a list of your directories, followed by a list of your files (including all hidden and system files), all sorted into alphabetical order by name, displayed in the HPFS format. This list is displayed one screen at a time; just press the Enter key to see the next screen.

If you have a favorite way of displaying or ordering your files and directories, create your own SET DIRCMD settings in CONFIG.SYS so that you don't have to remember how to type all the DIR command switches. It's that easy!

The TREE command takes the file-listing concept a little further. TREE lists all the directories in the current directory, and if you add the optional switch /F, TREE lists all the directory paths and names of all the files in all the directories on the current drive.

You can use the standard redirection methods to send the TREE output command to a printer (TREE>PRN) or a file (TREE>MYFILE), so that you can read or process the listing at your leisure.

Using CD to Move Around the File Structure

The CD command changes the current directory. CD is an abbreviation for CHDIR; you can type either command because they both do the same thing.

You can use the CD command to change to a different directory on the current drive, change to a subdirectory of your current directory, go straight to the root directory, or change to the parent directory of your current directory.

If you use CD with no options, the name of the current directory is displayed.

S E C R E T

If you are using the HPFS, and some of your directory names include spaces, you must enclose the complete directory name in quotes when using the CD command.

To change from your current directory to the OS2 directory, type:

    CD \OS2

To change to the SYSTEM subdirectory within the OS2 directory, type:

    CD SYSTEM

If you want to retrace your way back up your directory structure one directory at a time, type the following command several times; you change to the parent directory of your current directory every time you type it:

    CD ..

The .. option is a shorthand way to specify the name of the parent of your current directory. To go straight from your current directory to the root directory, type this shorthand sequence:

CD \

Creating New Directories with MD

OS/2 supports multiple levels of directories, with the root directory at the top of the whole structure, and directories leading to other directories from the root.

NOTE The terms *folder, directory,* and *subdirectory* are often used interchangeably.

The MD command, an abbreviation of MKDIR, creates a new directory or subdirectory on a disk, and requires that you specify the directory name on the command line. For example, type:

MD NEWNAME

to create a directory called NEWNAME as a subdirectory of the current directory. If you add a backslash before the new name, the directory will be created in the root directory, or if you specify complete drive and path information, you can create the new directory on another drive.

In the FAT, directories must observe the "8.3" naming convention of eight character name, a period, and a three character extension, but under the HPFS, you can use up to 254 characters in a directory name.

► S E C R E T

Because the HPFS supports spaces, long file names, and upper- and lower-case file names, the same directory or file name can appear in a slightly different form on a FAT system. The change is made automatically by OS/2 when the file system is created during installation.

Two subdirectories can have the same name, as long as they exist in separate directories. For example, the \LOTUS123 directory can have a subdirectory called \DATA (\LOTUS123\DATA), and so can the \WP directory (\WP\DATA).

Copying Files

There are two commands you can use to copy files, COPY and XCOPY. The XCOPY command is rather more powerful in that it can copy parts of your directory structure as well as files.

Using COPY

You can use COPY to rename, combine, append, or output files. Because there are several different ways that you can use the COPY command, the syntax varies slightly in each case. The most common use of the COPY command is to duplicate a file by typing:

COPY **source filename** target filename /switches

The COPY command requires as a minimum, a *source filename*, which can include wildcard characters, as well as drive and path information. You can also use a *target filename* which is usually another file name, and may contain a drive letter and path information. If the target file specification contains only a directory name, the files are copied without changing their names. If there is not sufficient room on the target disk for all the files you are trying to copy, you will see the message:

There is not enough space on the disk.

The source and target cannot be the same file name in the same location on disk; in other words, COPY will not copy a file onto itself.

You can use a plus sign to append one file to another, or to join several files together. In this case, the syntax becomes:

COPY *source filename*+*source filename*+*etc...***target filename**

You can still use wildcard characters when joining files in this way.

Finally, you can use COPY to update the date and time associated with a file to the current date and time, if you use the following syntax:

COPY *source filename +,,*

There are several switches you can use with COPY, as follows:

/A   Indicates that the file is an ASCII file. When this switch is used with the source file, the data in the file is copied up to but not including the first end-of-file character (Ctrl+Z) found in the file; the rest of the file is not copied. When used with the target file, it adds an end-of-file character as the final character in the file.

/B   Indicates that the file is a binary file. When this switch is used with the source file, the whole file is copied, based on information contained in the file's directory entries. When used with the target file, no end-of-file character is added as the last character in the file.

/F   Halts the COPY operation if you attempt to copy a file with OS/2 extended attributes onto a system that does not support these extended attributes. (If you do not use the /F switch in this situation, OS/2 stores the extended attributes in a special file called EA DATA. SF on the target system, and so they are not lost.)

/V   Makes the operating system check that all the sectors written on the destination disk are recorded
correctly and without error. This switch slows down
the COPY operation slightly, but you should use it
when copying critical data.

To copy a file called MYFILE.TXT from drive C to drive B, for example,
you would type:

    COPY C:\MYFILE.TXT B:

To copy OLDFILE.DOC from drive C to drive B and rename the file
NEWFILE.DOC at the same time, you would type:

    COPY C:\OLDFILE.DOC B:\NEWFILE.DOC

To join three ASCII files together and create a new file containing the
result, you would type:

    COPY START.TXT + MIDDLE.TXT + END.TXT /A WHOLE.TXT

To append or add one file to the end of another, you would type:

    COPY FIRST.TXT + SECOND.TXT

In this example, the file SECOND.TXT is added to the end of
FIRST.TXT. Note that you do not have to specify a target file name.

Be careful that you understand what happens when you specify wildcard
characters in file names with the COPY command. In this next example:

    COPY *.BAK + *.DOC *.FIL

suppose that there are three files called ONE.BAK, TWO.BAK, and THREE.
BAK, and three more files called ONE.DOC, TWO.DOC, and
THREE.DOC. The results would be as follows. The file ONE.FIL would
contain the combination of ONE.BAK and ONE.DOC, TWO.FIL
would contain TWO. BAK and TWO.DOC, and THREE.FIL would
contain THREE.BAK combined with THREE.DOC.

To change the time and date on all the files on the default drive to the
current system time and date, type:

    COPY *.* /B +,,

If you want to use the COPY command to send a file to a peripheral device such as the printer, make sure that the printer is on-line and ready to receive the information, and then type:

COPY README.TXT PRN

where PRN is the device name for the printer.

Finally, you can use the COPY command to copy characters from the standard input device, the console (which for our purposes we will consider to be the keyboard) and store them in an ASCII file. This technique is especially useful when you want to write a very short batch file from the command line, and you don't want to wait for the Enhanced Editor to load. When you issue the COPY command, the screen waits for you to type characters from the keyboard.

COPY CON MYFILE

End each line of text with the Enter key, and when you have entered all the information, press function key F6 (or Ctrl+Z) to place and end-of-file character at the end of the file, followed by the Enter key.

Using XCOPY

The XCOPY command copies groups of files or subdirectories, and the general syntax is:

XCOPY *source destination* /switches

In the XCOPY command *source* specifies the file or files to copy, and may include a directory name, and *destination* specifies the location and name of the copied files. You can use the wildcard characters * and ? if you wish.

XCOPY is almost always faster than the COPY command when copying groups of files because of its more efficient use of available memory.

There are several important switches you can use with XCOPY:

/A   Copies files that have the archive
                      attribute set, but docs not change the
                      attribute.

/M	Copies files that have the archive attribute set, but turns off the archive attribute. You can use the ATTRIB command to reset this attribute if you wish.
/D:*mm-dd-yy*	Copies files created or changed on or after the specified date.
/P	Prompts you before copying each file.
/S	Copies directories and subdirectories; does not copy empty subdirectories.
/E	Copies directories and subdirectories, even empty subdirectories.
/V	Performs a verification check to make sure that the data has been written to disk correctly.
/F	Halts the XCOPY operation if the destination file system does not support HPFS extended attributes.

► S O L U T I O N

You can use XCOPY to make a backup of the files on your hard disk, but there are distinct advantages and disadvantages in using XCOPY when compared with the BACKUP command. The advantages are:

- XCOPY is faster than BACKUP.
- You can use the backed up files directly from the floppy disks; there is no need to reprocess your files with the RESTORE command before you can use them.

The disadvantages of using XCOPY are:

- You will need more floppy disks with XCOPY because it does not compress the files.
- Files larger than the floppy disk capacity cannot be backed up. This could be a major problem if you have lots of graphics files, or use a lot of scanned images, as these files can be huge.

- Target floppy disks must be formatted and empty.
- XCOPY stops when a disk is full, so if you want to back up lots of files, you will have to write a small batch file such as the one shown below.

If the advantages of XCOPY outweigh the disadvantages, you can use this batch file:

```
:BACKUP
ECHO Insert a target disk into drive A:
PAUSE
XCOPY C:\*.* A: /M /E
IF ERRORLEVEL 4 GOTO :BACKUP
ECHO The Backup is Complete
```

As this batch file runs, you will see the file names and path information for the copied files listed on the screen. Next time the batch file runs, different files will be copied because the /M switch clears the archive bit of previously saved files. Many commands use return codes that indicate a successful or unsuccessful completion, and by using an IF statement, you can make a decision in your batch file based on that code. XCOPY returns the following codes:

- 0 Normal completion
- 1 No files found to XCOPY
- 2 Some files or directories were not copied due to file or directory errors
- 3 XCOPY was ended by the user
- 4 XCOPY ended due to error, usually *insufficient disk space*

To copy all the files in the current directory to a floppy disk in drive B:, for example, you would type:

```
XCOPY *.* B:
```

To duplicate the entire directory structure of drive A: onto drive C:, you would type:

```
XCOPY A:\ C:\ /S /E
```

If you do not use the /F switch when copying files that may possess extended attributes to a disk that does not support them, you will see the message:

> The extended attributes for the file or directory
>
> were discarded because the target file system does not
>
> support extended attributes.

on the screen as XCOPY processes the files. So that the extended attributes are not lost in the FAT copy, OS/2 stores them in a hidden system file called EA DATA. SF located in the root directory of each FAT partition on the destination disk. The spaces in this file name, and the fact that it is a hidden, read-only, system file, make it extremely difficult to erase by accident. See the section later in this chapter called "Looking at File Attributes with ATTRIB" for more information on hidden, read-only, and system files.

S E C R E T

The Workplace Shell also uses extended attributes to store information about the current configuration of your desktop. In the FAT system, these extended attributes are stored in a hidden system file called WP ROOT. SF located in the root directory.

Moving Files

Sometimes you may not want to copy a file; you may want to move it instead; the MOVE command moves files from one directory to another on the same drive. The general form of this command is:

> MOVE **drive:\path1\filename1** path2\filename2

where *path1\filename1* specifies the file you want to move, and *path2\file name2* specifies the new file name and location.

The MOVE command works only when both the source and the target directories are on the same disk. If you don't specify a target directory, the file or files will be moved into the current directory. You can use the asterisk and question mark wildcard characters (* and ?) in either the source or the target file specification. Also, if you specify a new file name and extension you can move the file and rename it at the same time. To move MYFILE.TXT into the WP directory, type:

    MOVE MYFILE.TXT \WP

To move all the files with the filename extension .DOC into the WP directory, use:

    MOVE *.DOC \WP

To move a file called CHAPTER1 into a directory called BOOK and rename the file CHAPTER2, type:

    MOVE CHAPTER1 \BOOK\CHAPTER2

Replacing Files

The REPLACE command replaces files on the target drive with files of the same name copied from the source drive. REPLACE can also selectively copy files from the source drive to the target drive.

The syntax is:

    REPLACE *sourcedrive:\path***filename targetdrive:***\path /switches*

In the REPLACE command, filename specifies the file to be copied from the source drive that will replace a file of the same name on the target.

You can use the wildcard characters * and ? in file names or extensions, however, hidden and system files are not copied if you use the *.* method of specifying all files.

There are several switches you can use with REPLACE:

/A	Copies all the files from the source drive that do not exist on the target drive.
/S	Updates those files that already exist on the target with new copies from the source.

/P	Prompts you as each file is found on the target drive, allowing you to control the process and selectively add or not add files as you wish.
/R	Replaces read-only files on the target drive.
/W	Waits for you to insert a floppy disk before starting to search for the source files.
/U	Updates only the files on the target drive that are older than those on the source drive.
/F	Halts the REPLACE command if the source file contains extended attributes and the target disk cannot support extended attributes.

WARNING   You cannot use the REPLACE /A switch (prevents the overwriting of existing files) in combination with the REPLACE /S or REPLACE /U switches (require the overwriting of existing files), because they are mutually exclusive.

To replace the MEMO file on drive B with a copy of MEMO from drive C, for example, you would type:

    REPLACE C:MEMO B:

To copy all the files from the current directory that do not exist on drive A without overwriting existing files, you would type:

    REPLACE C:*.* A: /A

Looking Inside Files

There are several commands you can use to look at the contents of a file, especially text files, OS/2 online documents, and picture files. There are also several special commands you can use to help manage and search your text files.

Using TYPE and FIND

The TYPE command displays the contents of one or more files on the screen, but is best suited to displaying ASCII text files; other file types may be unreadable. In an OS/2 session, you can TYPE multiple files; you can even use the wildcard characters * and ? if you wish.

S O L U T I O N

The TYPE command lets you look at a file's contents, but you cannot change these contents with TYPE; use the OS/2 Enhanced Editor for this task instead.

To display the contents of the file MYFILE.TXT in the C:\DATA directory, for example, you would type:

    TYPE C:\DATA\MYFILE.TXT

In an OS/2 session, to display the contents of the files CHAPTER1.DOC, CHAPTER2.DOC, and CHAPTER3.DOC in the current directory, you would use:

    TYPE CHAPTER1.DOC CHAPTER2.DOC CHAPTER3.DOC

The files are displayed in sequence, and each file name is displayed before the contents are displayed.

The TYPE command can write the contents of a file to the screen a lot faster than you can read it, so OS/2 provides several commands you can use as alternatives. The FIND command searches a file or files for a specified text string, while the MORE and SORT commands are special commands that filter text.

FIND searches through the file or files you specify, looking for the characters contained in a search string. The general syntax is:

    FIND /switches "string" drive\path\filename

The search characters must be contained within quotes and must be in the same case (uppercase or lowercase) as the text in the file. For example, the string "OS/2" is not the same as "os/2". If the text you are looking for is already contained within quotes inside the file, then you must use two sets of quotes with the FIND command.

S E C R E T

When you use the FIND command, you must explicitly state all the file names you want to search; you cannot use the wildcard characters * or ? in file names.

There are several switches you can use with FIND, but remember to place the switches you want to use *before* the search string. In most OS/2 commands, the switches are placed at the end of the command line entry.

/C	Counts the lines that contain the search string. If you use /C in combination with /V, FIND counts the lines that do not contain the search string.
/I	Tells FIND to ignore case differences when looking for the search string. When you use the /I switch, OS/2 and os/2 *are* considered to be equivalent.
/N	Adds a line number before the display of each match. This switch cannot be used with /C.
/V	Displays all the lines that do not contain the search string.

To count the number of times that the word *Elvis* appears in the file ROCKSTAR, for example, you would type:

    FIND /C "Elvis" ROCKSTAR

To display the line number in the file where the text *Elvis* appears, you would use:

FIND /N "Elvis" ROCKSTAR

To locate the text contained in quotes *"Go west, young man"*, in the file BOOK.TXT, you would use the following FIND command:

FIND ""Go west, young man"" BOOK.TXT

Using MORE and SORT

The MORE command displays text information in a file one screen at a time, instead of scrolling continuously until the whole contents of the file have been displayed. MORE is one of a group of special commands known as *filters*, because MORE always acts on the output produced by another command:

command | MORE

Where *command* is the command (including parameters if appropriate), whose output you want to display one screen at a time. When the screen is full, you will see the prompt

— MORE —

on the last screen line. Press any key to see the next 24 lines of output. The | symbol above represents a pipe.

The MORE command can also take input from a file, as in the following syntax:

MORE <*path\filename*

where the < character is a redirection symbol.

To pause the output when typing the OS/2 README file, use:

TYPE README | MORE

An alternative way of producing the same result is to type:

MORE < README

You can use Ctrl+Break at the —More— prompt to cancel the MORE command and return to the command processor.

Be careful when using the MORE command in a window, as you may not be able to see all the output, depending on the size of your window.

The SORT command rearranges the contents of ASCII text files. It can also take input from a command, or a device, and output sorted lines of text to a file or a device. The syntax is:

SORT /R /+column

The SORT command usually sorts from A to Z, then from 0 through 9, although you can reverse this order with the /R switch if you wish. SORT does not differentiate between uppercase and lowercase letters, and it sorts characters above ASCII 127 based on rules derived from the currently active COUNTRY code.

SORT is a filter command and usually takes its input from a pipe, a redirected file, or a device, and then sorts that input.

WARNING The OS/2 SORT command does not work with files larger than 63K (64,512 bytes).

There are two ways to use SORT:

- To sort the contents of a data file, type **SORT**, the redirection symbol for input (<), and then the name of the file you want to sort. Do not use any wildcard characters in the file name. SORT will read the file you specified, sort the contents, and display the result. This command might look like this:

SORT < MYFILE.TXT

- To sort the output of a command, type the command along with any parameters or switches, then the redirection symbol for a pipe (|), and then the SORT command. For example, a DIR command redirected to SORT might look like this:

DIR | SORT

There are two switches you can use with the SORT command:

/R	Reverses the normal sort order to sort from Z to A, then from 9 to 0.
/+*column*	SORT usually takes the character in column 1 as the basis for sorting, however, you can specify that the character in column number *column* be used instead.

To sort the contents of a file called CHAPTER.ONE into reverse order and store the result in a file called REVISE.ONE, for example, you would type the following:

```
SORT /R < CHAPTER.ONE > REVISE.ONE
```

To sort the contents of the current directory into alphabetical file name order, and display the resulting list on the screen one screen at a time, you can combine the SORT and the MORE filters, as follows:

```
DIR | SORT | MORE
```

To sort the output of the DIR command starting with the 20th column of the displayed output, you would type:

```
DIR | SORT /+20
```

Using VIEW and PICVIEW

The VIEW command displays the contents of online help documents such as the OS/2 Command Reference. The syntax for VIEW is as follows:

```
VIEW filename topic
```

VIEW displays document files with the file-name extension of .INF, such as CMDREF.INF (Command Reference) or REXX.INF (REXX Information). You do not have to specify the file-name extension of the document file. If you know the name of the topic you are interested in, you can add that name to the command line also.

To open the OS/2 Command Reference file on the COPY command, you would type:

```
VIEW C:\OS2\BOOK\CMDREF COPY
```

To look in the REXX.INF file at the CALL instruction, type:

VIEW C:\OS2\BOOK\REXX CALL

The PICVIEW command lets you display a picture file. To start PIC-VIEW from the OS/2 command prompt, use the following:

PICVIEW *path\filename /switches*

where *path\filename* specifies the path and filename information for the picture file you want to display.

S O L U T I O N

You can also start PICVIEW by double-clicking on the Picture Viewer icon inside the OS/2 Productivity Folder, as described in Chapter 4.

If you type PICVIEW with no parameters, the Picture Viewer window opens; select a file to view using the Open selection from the File menu. If you type PICVIEW followed by a filename, the Picture Viewer window opens displaying the specified file. You can look at graphics metafiles or picture interchange format (PIF) files with PICVIEW.

A metafile is a special kind of graphics file that contains not only the image, but also instructions on how the image should be displayed. This allows the image to be output to a variety of different output devices. Metafiles always have the filename extension .MET.

A PIF file is a type of file format used in exchanging images between applications. Picture interchange files always have the filename extension .PIF.

PICVIEW switches are as follows:

/P   Tells PICVIEW to print the selected file

/S   Specifies that the Picture Viewer should return to its default screen position

To view a metafile called ELVIS.MET, for example, you would type:

PICVIEW ELVIS.MET

If you wanted to print the file, you would add:

PICVIEW ELVIS.MET /P

You can also display spool files using PICVIEW. OS/2 spool files always have the filename extension .SPL.

Printing Files

The PRINT command prints or cancels the printing of one or more files. You can use the wildcard characters * and ? to specify the printing of several files in a directory, and the files are queued for printing in the order that you specify them. The syntax is as follows:

PRINT *drive:\path***filename** */switches*

There are several optional switches you can use with this command:

/D:*device*	Specifies the printing device name; the default is LPT1. Acceptable names are PRN, LPT1 through LPT3, and if you are using a network printer, LPT4 through LPT9. This switch must be the first switch on the command line.
/B	Prevents Ctrl+Z characters being interpreted as end-of-file markers and interrupting printing. The entire file is printed.
/C	Cancels the file now printing if spooling is active. This switch is only available in OS/2 sessions.
/T	Cancels all printing if spooling is active. This switch is only available in OS/2 sessions.

To print the file in the current directory called MYFILE.TXT on the default printer, LPT1, for example, you would type:

PRINT MYFILE.TXT

To cancel the printing of the current file, you would use:

    PRINT /C

and to cancel the file currently being printed and all the other files in the print queue, type:

    PRINT /T

To print MYFILE.TXT on the LPT2 device, use:

    PRINT /D:LPT2 MYFILE.TXT

and to prevent Ctrl+Z characters from being interpreted as end-of-file markers as MYFILE.TXT prints, you would use:

    PRINT /B MYFILE.TXT

Comparing Files and Disks

From time to time, it can be useful to determine whether one file or disk is an exact copy of another. For example, you might have two files in different directories with the same name and the same size; are their contents identical? Or you might have a copy of a distribution disk; is it exactly the same as the original? OS/2 offers commands for both comparisons, COMP and DISKCOMP.

Using COMP

The COMP command compares the contents of two files, or two groups of files, to determine if the files are identical. The syntax for COMP is:

    COMP *filename1 filename2*

where *filename1* and *filename2* specify the names of the files to be compared. You can use wildcard characters if you wish.

If you type this command with no parameters, you will be prompted to enter the file names you want to compare. If the files are not the same length, COMP informs you of this and asks if you want to continue with the comparison. If you answer yes, the comparison proceeds based on the length of the smaller of the two files. Results are displayed in hexadecimal on the screen, and an error is displayed for any information that does not match. After 10 such mismatches, the comparison is automatically terminated, because it is obvious by this time that the two files are anything but identical.

If you want to compare two files in your current directory, type:

COMP MYFILE1.TXT MYFILE2.TXT

Using DISKCOMP

The DISKCOMP command compares the contents of two disks. The disks must be of the same type, with the same size and density.

WARNING
DISKCOMP does not work in a DOS session when ASSIGN, JOIN, or SUBST commands are in effect. Also, DISKCOMP does not work on network drives.

To use DISKCOMP, type:

DISKCOMP *source-drive target-drive*

The parameters *source-drive* and *target-drive* specify the drives that contain the disks to be compared. DISKCOMP compares the contents of two floppy disks, track by track, to determine whether they are identical. Both disks must be of the same size and density; you cannot use DISKCOMP to compare 3.5" and 5.25" disks. However, you can compare two different disks using the same drive, and the DISKCOMP command prompts you when it is time to swap disks.

To compare the contents of a 3.5" floppy disk in drive A with the contents of another 3.5" floppy disk in drive B, type:

DISKCOMP A: B:

If you want to compare two 5.25" disks using drive A, your only 5.25" drive, type:

DISKCOMP A: A:

and the DISKCOMP command will guide you through the comparison, prompting you to swap the disks when necessary.

Renaming Files

The REN command (short for RENAME) changes a file's name or extension. In an OS/2 session, you can also change the name of a directory. The syntax for REN is as follows:

REN *drive:\path***oldname newname**

where *oldname* specifies the file to be renamed, and *newname* specifies the new filename. The name may also be the name of a directory that you want to change.

You cannot specify a drive and path name in *newname*; therefore the file stays in the same directory after the name is changed.

To change the name of a file in the current directory called BUDGET92 to BUDGET93, for example, you would type:

REN BUDGET92 BUDGET93

To change all the file name extensions in the current directory from .LVS to .ELL, you would type:

REN *.LVS *.ELL

S E C R E T

To save time, you can use the wildcard characters * or ? when renaming files, however, you cannot use these wildcard characters if you are renaming directories.

Deleting Files

The DEL command erases one or more files, and is used interchangeably with the ERASE command. The syntax is:

DEL *drive:\path***filename** */switches*

where *drive:\path\filename* specifies the name of the file you want to delete; it may contain wildcard characters if you want to erase a group of files all at the same time.

If you use the global wildcard specification *.* with the DEL command, it means that you want to delete all the files in the current directory. Because this is a potentially dangerous command, OS/2 responds with the prompt:

Are you sure (Y/N)?

Type Y (yes) if you are sure you want to proceed, or type N (no) to cancel the command.

> ## ► S E C R E T
>
> Using a directory name with the DEL command has the same effect as specifying that you want to delete all the files in that directory. For example, typing:
>
> DEL MYDIR
>
> deletes all the normal files from inside the MYDIR directory, just as if you had changed to the directory and typed:
>
> DEL *.*
>
> To erase a directory once it is empty, you must use the RD command, as described in the next section.

Two switches are available for use with DEL:

/N   Tells the DEL command not to display the *Are you sure (Y/N)?* message when you are deleting the entire contents of a directory. Most people find this message a useful reminder that they are about to perform a potentially dangerous delete operation; others find it annoying. If you are in this latter category, you can turn the message off by using this switch.

/P   Tells the DEL command to ask you whether to delete each file individually when you issue a DEL *.* command.

The DEL command cannot erase files that have the read-only or hidden attribute set, such as certain of the operating system files.

To delete a single file called SUNDAY from the current directory, you would type:

    DEL SUNDAY

To delete all the files in the current directory with the filename extension .BAK, use:

    DEL *.BAK

If you want to erase all the files in the current directory, type:

    DEL *.*

OS/2 responds with the message *Are you sure (Y/N)?*. Type Y to continue the delete operation and erase all the files in the directory; type N to cancel the command.

You can also delete all the files in a directory if you use the directory name in a DEL command. For example, if the current directory contains a sub-directory called \DAILY, you can delete all the files in this directory if you type:

    DEL DAILY

You will also see the *Are you sure (Y/N)?* message here, too, unless you use the /N switch, as follows:

    DEL DAILY /N

To review each file name in a directory before deciding whether to delete it, use:

    DEL *.* /P

This switch is very useful if you want to delete some of the files from a directory but keep others, particularly when the files do not share common filename extensions and so wildcards are of little use in differentiating between groups of files.

You may be able to recover files that you erase by accident if you use the UNDELETE command immediately after you discover the mistake. Do not use the computer for any other operation until you have recovered any accidentally deleted files; there is always the chance that you might over-write the deleted files before you can recover them. See Chapter 14 for more information on troubleshooting.

Removing Directories with RD

The RD or RMDIR command removes the specified directory as long as the directory is empty.

RD *drive:\path*

You must delete all files from a directory before you can remove the directory from your system. If a directory contains subdirectories, you must first delete all the files in the subdirectories, then the subdirectories, and finally the parent directory.

In an OS/2 session you can remove several directories with just one RD command. To remove the empty PROGRAMS subdirectory from the CLIB directory and the empty ELVIS directory from the ROCKSTAR directory, type:

RD \CLIB\PROGRAMS \ROCKSTAR\ELVIS

There are several logical restrictions on the RD command. For example, you cannot remove the root directory or the current directory. In a DOS session you cannot remove directories affected by a JOIN or a SUBST command.

Formatting a Disk with FORMAT

The FORMAT command prepares the disk in the specified drive for use by the operating system, and checks the disk for defects. The syntax for the FORMAT command is as follows:

FORMAT *drive* /switches

The FORMAT command performs several tasks in preparing a disk for use:

- It creates a set of sectors and tracks that the operating system can use when storing data.

- It checks the disk media for physical defects, and marks defective areas so that they will not be used.

- It creates the system area on the disk that includes the root directory and file allocation tables.

- It assigns a volume serial number to a newly formatted disk.

- It lets you add a volume label to describe the contents of the disk.

WARNING

If you format a floppy or hard disk that already contains information, all of the original information will be obliterated and lost. This is in sharp contrast to the current MS-DOS FORMAT command, which, by default, performs a *safe* format—that is, the actual data on your disk is not destroyed during the format process. If you do format a disk by accident using MS-DOS, you can use the UNFORMAT program to recover most of the files on the disk. This feature is unfortunately not yet available in OS/2.

If you format a drive for use with the HPFS, the FORMAT command checks the IFS statement in your CONFIG.SYS file to see if there is an /AUTOCHECK parameter for the drive. If the drive is listed, FORMAT does not update the IFS statement; if not, FORMAT adds the drive letter.

Make sure that you use the FDISK or FDISKPM commands to establish an OS/2 partition on a hard disk before you format it. If no DOS or OS/2 partition exists, FORMAT will not recognize the disk as being an OS/2 disk, and will not format the disk but will skip over it to the next disk.

There are several switches you can use to customize the FORMAT command:

/ONCE   Tells the FORMAT command that you
                 intend to format only one disk; and so when
                 FORMAT has finished, it does not ask if
                 you want to format another.

/4   Formats a 360K floppy disk in a 1.2MB disk
                 drive. Not all 360KB disk drives will be able
                 to read this disk, so use this switch with
                 caution.

/F:*nnn*   Specifies the capacity to which the disk
                 will be formatted; FORMAT creates the
                 appropriate number of tracks and sectors.
                 The FORMAT command is very flexible,
                 and you can specify the capacity for the disk
                 in a variety of different ways, as follows:

360KB 5.25"	360, 360K, 360KB
720KB 3.5"	720, 720K, 720KB
1.2MB 5.25"	1200, 1200K, 1200KB, 1.2, 1.2M, 1.2MB
1.44MB 3.5"	1440, 1440K, 1440KB, 1.44, 1.44M, 1.44MB
2.88MB 3.5"	2880, 2880K, 2880KB, 2.88, 2.88M, 2.88MB

/FS:*name*   Specifies that the FORMAT command
                 should execute another file system's format
                 program *name*.

/L   Specifies the long format procedure for use
                 with IBM's read/write optical disk which
                 takes about 20 minutes. This switch also
                 installs a file system on the optical disk.

/N:*sectors*   Formats a floppy disk to the specified
                 number of sectors

/T:*nnn*   Formats a floppy disk to the specified number of tracks. If /T is not specified, the default value of 80 tracks is used.

/V:*label*   Specifies a volume label for the disk.

Use the following values for /N (sectors) and /T (tracks) according to the floppy disk size:

360KB 5.25"	/T:40 /N:9
720KB 3.5"	/T:80 /N:9
1.2MB 5.25"	/T:80 /N:15
1.44MB 3.5"	/T:80 /N:18
2.88MB 3.5"	/T:80 /N:36

For example, to format one 3.5" high density floppy disk in drive B, type:

FORMAT B: /ONCE

If you want to format a 720K 3.5" disk in a 1.44MB floppy disk drive in drive A, use the following:

FORMAT A: /T:80 /N:9

Alternatively, you could use:

FORMAT A: /F:720

instead.

To add the text Budgets as a volume label to a disk formatted in drive B, you would type:

FORMAT B: /V:"Budgets"

To format a partition on drive D with the HPFS, type the following:

FORMAT D: /FS:HPFS

or to format the partition as a FAT partition, use:

FORMAT D: /FS:FAT

WARNING The FORMAT command does not work on network drives or on drives with ASSIGN, JOIN, or SUBST commands in effect.

Creating a Volume Label

The LABEL command lets you attach or change the short text description of a disk known as the volume label. The syntax is:

LABEL *drive: text*

where the *drive* parameter specifies the drive letter that contains the disk you want to label; if you don't specify a drive letter, the LABEL command defaults to the current drive.

The *text* specifies the text label you want to attach to this disk, up to a total of 11 characters. You can use spaces between words in the label text, but leading spaces will be ignored. You cannot use punctuation characters in a volume label.

For example, if you want to look at the volume label on drive C, type:

LABEL C:

The operating system will then prompt you to enter a new volume label, or to press the Enter key to leave the volume label unchanged.

To change the volume label on drive C to the text BIG_DISK, you would type:

LABEL C: BIG_DISK

The LABEL command does not work on drives that have an ASSIGN, JOIN, or SUBST command in effect, and LABEL does not work on network drives.

Backing Up and Restoring Files

A *backup* is an up-to-date copy of all your files that you can use to reload your system in the event of an accident. It is an insurance policy against hard disk failure and the resulting loss of information. Back up your system regularly; be prepared.

The most important reasons for making regular, planned backups are:

- To guard against hard-disk failure. A hard disk can fail at almost any time, but it is *always* at the most inconvenient moment.

- Protection against accidental deletion of files and directories. If you backed up your system, you can retrieve the file from the backup.

- Moving very large files, that will not fit onto a single floppy disk, from one computer to another.

- To make a permanent archive at the end of a project, or at the end of a financial reporting period.

Once you have decided you should back up your hard disk, the next question is, how often should you back up? To arrive at a conclusion that fits the kind of work you do, ask yourself the following questions:

- How frequently do the data in your files change: every minute, hour, day, week, or month?

- How important to your day-to-day operations are these data? Can you work without them, and how long would it take to recreate them?

- How much will it cost to recreate the lost data in terms of time spent and business lost?

It all comes down to a single rule: back up all the files that you cannot afford to lose. It may take hours or days of work to create a file, but it can be lost in milliseconds. A hard disk failure, a mistaken Delete command, overwriting a long file with a short one of the same name—these can destroy a file just as completely as fire or flood. You just have to lose one file to become a convert to regular, planned, backups.

Using BACKUP

The BACKUP command runs in an OS/2 session and copies files from one disk to another using a special file format to optimize the use of space on the backup disk. You can also use BACKUP and the companion command, RESTORE, to move a file or set of files from one computer to another. BACKUP has the following syntax:

BACKUP *source: target: /switches*

You must specify both *source* and *target*; the source is the drive that contains the files that you want to back up, usually a hard disk, while the target is the drive to which all the files will be copied, usually a floppy disk. As a minimum, *source* and *target* must specify unique drive letters (you cannot use the same drive letter for both), and *source* can also include path information, file names, or wildcard characters.

When the BACKUP command fills a floppy disk but there are still files waiting to be backed up, BACKUP asks you to insert another disk. Label and number the floppy disks with the date and the disk number in sequence as they are created by the BACKUP command. If you have to use the RESTORE command later, you will be asked to load the disks in the same order.

BACKUP does not back up the OS/2 system files (COMMAND.COM and CMD.EXE), hidden system files, or any open dynamic data link (DLL) files; you will see an error message from BACKUP if you try to back up these files.

The OS/2 HPFS allows up to 64K of extended attributes to be associated with each file or directory. These extended attributes are maintained by application programs and can include notes, comments, and information about icons. The BACKUP command will automatically back up all extended attributes associated with a file.

Use the following switches with BACKUP:

/A	Adds the new files to the end of an existing backup disk. When you use BACKUP with this switch, existing backup files are not erased or overwritten by the new files.

/D:*mm-dd-yy*   Backs up only those files created or
modified after the specified date. This
switch is usually used with the /T switch.
The date must be entered in the appropriate form specified by the COUNTRY
command in your CONFIG.SYS file.

/F:*nnn*   Formats an unformatted target floppy
disk before backing files up to the disk.
This switch cannot be used on hard disks
and will not format a previously formatted
floppy disk. When you specify this switch,
you can begin a backup without worrying
about the exact number of diskettes that
will be needed; you'll be able to format
new disks as required.

Specify *nnn* to define the size of the floppy
disk in kilobytes, as follows:

360 = 360K double-sided 5.25"
720 = 720K double-sided 3.5"
1200 = 1.2MB double-sided 5.25"
1440 = 1.44MB high-density 3.5"
2880 = 2.88MB high-density 3.5"

/L:*filename*   Creates a backup log file with the
specified filename. If no filename is
specified, the default file BACKUP.LOG
is created in the root directory of the
source drive. This log file contains
information about all the files backed up
during the current backup.

/M   Backs up only the files that have been
created or changed since the last backup
operation was performed.

/S   Includes files contained in subdirectories
below the current directory in the backup.

/T:*hh:mm:ss*   Backs up only those files created or
                     modified after the specified time. You can
                     use the /D and the /T switches together to
                     define exactly the files you want to back up.

To back up all the files in the root directory of drive C to a floppy disk in
drive A, for example, you would type:

    BACKUP C: A:

and to make sure any files in subdirectories are also included in the backup, type:

    BACKUP C: A: /S

If you just want to back up a single file, type:

    BACKUP C:\MYSTUFF\MYFILE.TXT A:

If you want to back up files created on or after January, 1993, type

    BACKUP C: A: /D:01-01-93

To back up all the files and subdirectories on drive C to drive A without
overwriting any previous backup, and formatting any new 1.44MB 3.5"
disks as needed, type:

    BACKUP C:*.* A: /A /S /F:1440

Using RESTORE

The RESTORE command runs in an OS/2 session and reloads files that
were made using the BACKUP command. You can use the RESTORE
command to reload backed up files after a hard-disk problem; you can
also use BACKUP and RESTORE to move a file or set of files from one
computer to another. The syntax is as follows:

    RESTORE *source drive: target drive:**path**filename* /*switches*

In the RESTORE command *source drive* indicates the drive letter containing the files that you previously backed up, and *target drive* specifies the
location to which you want to restore those files. RESTORE works only
with files originally created using the BACKUP command, and restores
files to the directories in which they were originally located. If you have
several floppy disks to restore, you must load them in the same order that

they were created. You can use the wildcard characters * and ? with RE-STORE if you wish.

The following switches are available for RESTORE:

/P	Asks your permission before restoring read-only files, or files that have changed since the last backup was made.
/M	Restores only those files on the target disk that have changed since the last backup was made.
/B:*mm-dd-yy*	Restores only those files on the target disk that were modified on or before the specified date.
/A:*mm-dd-yy*	Restores only those files on the target disk that were modified on or after the specified date.
/E:*hh:mm:ss*	Restores only those files on the target disk that were modified before the specified time.
/L:*hh:mm:ss*	Restores only those files on the target disk that were modified at or after the specified time.
/S	Restores files and subdirectories. If you do not specify this switch, the RESTORE command only works within the source directory.
/N	Restores files that do not exist on the target disk.
/F	Stops the RESTORE command if the target disk cannot support the HPFS extended attributes present on the source disk.
/D	Lists all the files on the backup disk that match file names on the target disk, but without restoring any files.

For example, to rebuild all the files on drive C using a set of backup disks loaded using drive A, you would type:

    RESTORE A: C:*.* /S

If you just want to restore a single file, MYFILE.TXT, from drive A, type:

    RESTORE A: C:MYFILE.TXT

To list the files on the backup disk that match files on the target disk, but not restore any files, type:

    RESTORE A: /D

The RESTORE command does not restore COMMAND.COM and CMD.EXE, or any of the OS/2 or DOS hidden files normally found in the root directory. This means that you cannot use RESTORE to create a bootable hard or floppy disk.

Using CHKDSK to Monitor Free Disk Space

The CHKDSK command produces a status report on your files and directories, and also reports the amount of disk space occupied by extended attributes.

N O T E   When used with the appropriate switches, CHKDSK can fix certain file-related problems. See Chapter 14 for more information on troubleshooting OS/2.

CHKDSK also displays the disk volume label and volume serial number. If you use CHKDSK without parameters, you will analyze your current drive; specify a drive letter if you want to analyze a different drive. For a FAT disk, CHKDSK reports the following:

- the type of file system in use
- the disk volume label
- the disk volume serial number

- the total formatted disk space, in bytes
- the amount of space occupied by hidden files, in bytes
- the number of hidden files
- the amount of space occupied by directories
- the number of directories
- the amount of space occupied by user files, in bytes
- the number of user files
- the amount of space occupied by extended attributes, in bytes
- the remaining available disk space, in bytes
- the size of the disk allocation unit, in bytes
- the total number of disk allocation units on the disk
- the number of available disk allocation units

For an HPFS disk, there is no volume label or serial number, and all totals are given in K rather than in bytes. For a CD-ROM, the report is very brief. You will see the following:

The type of file system for the disk is CDFS.

The CDFS file system program has been started.

541728 kilobytes total disk space.

0 kilobytes are available for use.

The amount of total disk space will vary from CD-ROM to CD-ROM; it represents not the absolute capacity of the CD, but the space occupied by files.

NOTE

CHKDSK cannot be used on network drives; if you use a Novell network, use the Novell CHKVOL command instead.

If you run CHKDSK in a DOS session, you will also see:

- the total amount of conventional memory available to the DOS session, in bytes
- the conventional memory available for application programs, in bytes

To determine whether a file consists of one single contiguous area of disk space or is *fragmented* into several separate pieces, specify a filename with CHKDSK. You can also include drive and path information if you wish. There is no harm in files becoming fragmented, although extreme fragmentation with the FAT system may slow down your hard disk performance.

The following switches are available for use on both FAT and HPFS disks.

/F   Tells CHKDSK to fix any errors found. See Chapter 14 for more information on this switch.

/V   Displays all files along with appropriate path information for the specified drive. This switch creates a very long file listing that is usually only of interest to system managers or people concerned with software inventories.

Several CHKDSK switches are available only when using the HPFS. See Chapter 14 for more information.

Remember that CHKDSK can give accurate results only when the disk being analyzed is not being used or actively written to by another session or application program.

Looking at File Flags with ATTRIB

The ATTRIB command displays or changes the simple attributes, or flags, associated with a file. A file can have one or more flags or attributes set at any given time; alternatively, it may have none of its flags set.

The syntax is as follows:

ATTRIB *mode filename(s) /switches*

With the ATTRIB command, *filename(s)* specifies the file or files whose flags will be changed. The file specification may include drive and path information, as well as wildcard characters; all the file names matching the specification will be changed.

ATTRIB lets you look at or change four attributes, or flags:

Read-Only (R) A read-only file cannot be modified or deleted by the normal file-management commands.

Archive (A) This attribute tells the BACKUP or XCOPY command that the file has been changed, and so should be included in the next backup operation. This attribute is set and cleared, as appropriate, automatically by the operating system.

System (S) This attribute indicates that this file is a system file. It is also hidden, and cannot be accessed by most other operating system commands.

Hidden (H) When this attribute is set, the file becomes invisible to most of the file manipulation commands.

The following switches are available with the ATTRIB command:

mode Tells the ATTRIB command whether to set or reset each attribute, as follows:

+A Turns on the archive attribute.

–A Turns off the archive attribute.

+H Turns on the hidden attribute, making the file into a hidden file that is not shown in directory listings.

-H   Turns off the hidden attribute, making the file appear in directory listings once again.

+R   Sets the read-only bit.

-R   Turns off, or resets, the read-only bit.

+S   Turns on the system attribute.

-S   Resets the system attribute.

/S   Includes all files that match the filename parameter in subdirectories. This is especially useful if the same file exists in several different directories, and you want to change an attribute on all copies of the file.

To turn on the archive attribute of a file called MEMO.TXT, for example,

S E C R E T

In OS/2 version 2.0, there is an interesting hidden file in the OS2\BITMAP directory. From the OS/2 command prompt, type ATTRIB *.* to see a list of all the attributes assigned to all the files in this directory, then type **AT-TRIB –H AAAAA.*** to remove the hidden attribute for two of the files there. Now type **AAAAA** for a surprise display. Press any key to end the display and return to the command prompt.

you would type the following:

    ATTRIB +A MEMO.TXT

To turn off the archive attribute on MEMO.TXT, type:

    ATTRIB –A MEMO.TXT

To make MEMO.TXT into a read-only file, type:

    ATTRIB +R MEMO.TXT

and to turn it back into a normal file, type:

```
ATTRIB –R MEMO.TXT
```

If you use the ATTRIB command without a *mode* parameter, ATTRIB displays the attributes of all the files matching the *filename* parameter. Use:

```
ATTRIB ATTRIB.EXE
```

to see a list of the attribute settings for this particular file, or type:

```
ATTRIB C:*.* /S
```

if you want to see a list of the current attributes for all files on drive C.

OS/2 OS/2 OS/2

OS/2 OS/2 OS/2 OS/2 OS/2 OS/2 OS/2 OS/2 OS/2

OS/2 OS/2 OS/2

Using the OS/2 Productivity Applications

THIS chapter describes each of the productivity and games programs supplied with OS/2 2.1. Many of these are extremely powerful applications in their own right; and as a package, they considerably enhance your ability to do useful work with OS/2 from the very first moment. All the Productivity applications and games use the OS/2 graphical user interface, and if you wish, you can run them all simultaneously in separate windows on the desktop.

To locate these applications, open the OS/2 System folder on the desktop, then double-click either the Productivity folder or the Games folder. The icons contained in the Productivity folder are shown in Figure 4.1; just double-click an icon to open the application you want to use.

In this chapter, we'll look first at the Productivity applications, then at the OS/2 Games programs.

OS/2 Productivity Applications

The OS/2 Productivity applications fall into two main groups; the general-purpose applications, such as the Database, Spreadsheet, or PM Chart, and the time-management applications, such as the Daily Planner, the Monthly Planner, and the To-Do List. We'll look at the general-purpose applications first.

FIGURE 4.1

Application icons in the Productivity folder

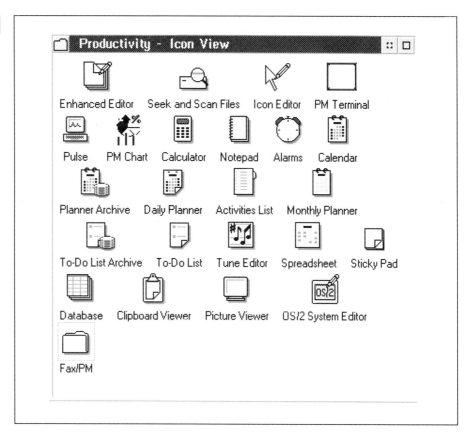

Calculator

The Calculator mimics a hand-held calculator on the screen. You can enter numbers directly from the keyboard, or by clicking on the calculator keys on the screen. The results of your calculations are shown on the paper tape or *tally roll*. If you use the memory register, its contents are displayed above the tally roll in a separate memory display.

S O L U T I O N

The Calculator automatically turns on Num Lock, so you can enter numbers from the keypad at the right side of your keyboard. If you make a different window active, OS/2 turns Num Lock off again for you.

The Tally menu contains options for clearing and printing the tally roll, while the Customize menu contains options for configuring the calculator. With the Floating Point option, you can make the Calculator display as many digits after the decimal point as necessary, and if you choose the Fixed selection, you can make the Calculator round numbers in the display to two decimal places. If you like to enter numbers using the keyboard, you can control the status of the Num Lock key (above the numerical keypad) from the Customize menu by using the Num Lock toggle. You can also change colors and font sizes from this menu.

Clipboard Viewer

The Clipboard Viewer lets you look at the contents of the OS/2 clipboard, the area of memory where information is held temporarily while being moved between applications (or within an application) by a cut, copy, or paste operation.

In OS.2 Version 2.1, the Clipboard Viewer has File, Display, and Help menus, and to view the contents of the OS/2 clipboard, select Display, followed by Render, then choose a format from the Available formats field, and click on the OK button.

 S O L U T I O N

If you are using OS/2 Version 2.0, the Clipboard Viewer has several additional functions that in version 2.1 have been moved into the WIN-OS/2 Setup program. In OS/2 2.0, when you double-click on the Clipboard Viewer icon, you open the viewer minimized. To use it to examine the contents of the clipboard, you must first restore it. Press Ctrl+Esc or press both mouse buttons together to open the window list, and then double-click on the Clipboard Viewer entry. Alternatively, you can open the Minimized Window Viewer folder, and double-click on the Clipboard Viewer icon.

By using the Options menu, you can designate the Clipboard as private or as public. When Private Clipboard is selected, the information on the clipboard is available only to other OS/2 Presentation Manager applications. If you have to exchange information between the OS/2 and WIN-OS/2 clipboards, you must use the Import and Export options in your application program's File menu instead.

However, when Public Clipboard is selected from the Options menu, information *can* be shared between the OS/2 clipboard and the WIN-OS/2 clipboard. The Public Clipboard choice must be selected in both clipboards for this to work.

To close the Clipboard Viewer, use the Exit option in the File menu, or double-click on the title-bar icon. Refer to the section headed "WIN-OS/2 Setup" in Chapter 2 for more information on the OS/2 clipboard, and see Chapters 6 and 7 for information on how you can use the clipboard with your DOS and Windows programs.

Database

The Database application supports a small, easy-to-use database, designed to be used as an electronic address book or similar application.

A Database file can hold up to 5000 records containing up to eight fields, and each field can contain up to 30 characters. In other words, the database can hold up to eight separate pieces of information on as many as 5000 people, as long as each piece of information is smaller than 30 letters or numbers. The Database also contains an *autodialer*, a feature that can dial a telephone number contained in the database.

To create a database from scratch, first choose New from the File menu, then use Edit Line Headings from the Edit menu to enter the names of the eight fields in the database. In an address-book database, these fields might be Name, Address, City, State, Zip, Title, Phone, and Fax. Remember to save this information using the Save option from the File menu, then use Add a New Record from the Edit menu to add the appropriate entry information for each person you want to keep in the database. Figure 4.2 shows a typical example of this kind of database.

FIGURE 4.2

A typical address-book database

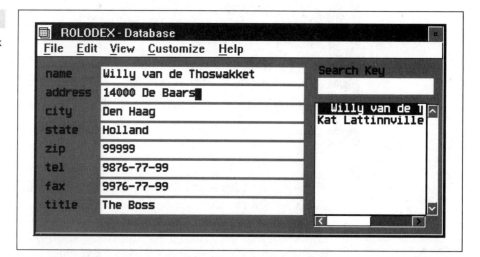

NOTE

The Database automatically assigns the file-name extension .$$F to database files.

As you enter information into the database, the entry in the first field, "Name" in this example, is shown in the window to the right. If you want to review the information contained in a previously entered record, just double-click the entry in this window. All the information will be displayed in the window on the left. Use the selections in the View menu to change from one field to another and to display database statistics.

You can use Search Key to find information in your database. As you type characters into this text box, the program attempts to find a match with information already in your database. When you enter a character, the database displays the first entry that begins with that character. If no entry begins with that character, the database will display the entry that it considers comes closest to matching.

You may not want to search your database always using the first line of a record. The options in the View menu reflect the headings you used to set up your database. Use these entries to specify the line in the database that you would like to use as your Search Key. Now, when you type into Search Key, the database matches records having that information in the selected line of the record.

If you find you have made a mistake in entering your data into the database, you can change it quite easily. Select the record you want to edit using the Search Key selection list, and when the right record is displayed, use the normal text editing keys to make your changes. When all the changes are complete, use Save to save the changes.

To use the autodialer feature of the Database you must have a modem attached to your computer. To set up the modem, use Dial Setup from the Customize menu. First select the serial port you will use with the modem (from COM1 through COM4), then enter any special characters your modem needs for dialing or hanging up and click Set. See your modem manual for more information on dialing and hanging up. To dial a number, locate the appropriate record in the database, then choose the Dialing Function selection from the File menu. This collects all the numbers found in the record (these numbers might include the address and the zip code, as well as a fax number and the telephone number) and displays them in a window.

> **S E C R E T**
>
> When entering telephone numbers into the database, add any dialing prefixes you might need, because you cannot add them when you dial the number. For example, if you always dial out through an office switchboard or private branch exchange (pbx), add a 9 at the beginning of the number. For long distance numbers, be sure to start the number with a 1. Valid entries for a telephone number are 0 through 9, W, and a comma. The W and the comma are "wait" characters. You can use spaces, periods, and hyphens to delimit the telephone numbers because these characters are always ignored.

You choose the number that you want to dial and click the Select button; after you know that the phone is ringing, you should press Enter and switch over to the telephone handset to complete the call.

Choose Print List Format from the File menu to set up a tabular printout of the information in your database. You can print up to four columns of information across the report. Use the spin buttons to select the arrangement of the data in the report. You can choose to have no separating characters between records, or you can use blanks or hyphens. The report can be sent to a printer for immediate printing, or it can be output to a spool file (called PMDSPOOL.$$$) for printing later. Click the Save button to save the report format you just generated in this dialog box as the default format for this database. In the future, when you want to recreate this report, just click File, then select Print, and this format will be used for the report.

Data Update (OS/2 Version 2.0)

In OS/2 Version 2.0, the Data Update application is the mechanism used to exchange information between programs that support Dynamic Data Exchange (DDE). DDE ensures that when data is changed in one session, the same information is updated in other sessions, either automatically or on demand.

In OS/2 Version 2.1, these DDE functions are controlled using WIN-OS/2 Setup in the System Setup folder. This is described in Chapter 2. For more on using the OS/2 clipboard and DDE, see Chapters 5, 6 and 7.

The initial default setting for DDE is *public*, which means that you can exchange information between suitable programs running in OS/2, WIN-OS/2, and DOS sessions. If you just want to exchange information between programs running in the same WIN-OS/2 session, you can make the DDE *private*. See the description of WIN-OS/2 Setup in Chapter 2 for more information on these settings.

 S E C R E T

How do you find out if your applications support Dynamic Data Exchange (DDE)? Look in the application's Edit menu for a selection called Paste Special or Paste Link. These options not only allow you to paste information from one program into another, but Paste Link also establishes a DDE link, so that when you change the original information in one program, it will be updated in the other, either automatically or on demand. If these menu selections are not present, then your application probably does not support DDE; check your program documentation or help system for more information.

Enhanced Editor

The Enhanced Editor is a full-featured ASCII text editor, offering more features and capability than the OS/2 System Editor (which is described in the next section). There are several ways you can open a file using the Enhanced Editor:

- Double-click the Enhanced Editor icon in the Productivity folder, then use the Open command in the File menu.

- Drag and drop a text file onto the Enhanced Editor icon.

- Double-click a file name in a drive window once the appropriate association has been established. Chapter 2 contains a Secret that tells you how to associate your text files with the Enhanced Editor.

- Type **EPM** at an OS/2 command prompt, and use Open in the File menu.

S O L U T I O N

One small quirk of the Enhanced Editor is that pressing the Alt key with a lowercase letter that corresponds to the name of a menu does not open that menu as you might expect. You must also hold down the Shift key along with Alt and the menu letter. For example, Alt+f does not open the File menu. Using Alt+Shift+f does open the File menu.

Figure 4.3 shows the CONFIG.SYS file open in the Enhanced Editor.

The File menu contains the usual options for opening, saving, and printing files as well as a text file import and a rename file selection. The New option in the File menu clears everything from the Editor (after giving you the option of saving anything you might want to save), so that you can start a new file in an empty window. The Open .Untitled option starts a second Enhanced Editor session, but with no file loaded into the Editor window.

S O L U T I O N

The Open .Untitled selection can be useful if you want to create a new file which is based on information contained in an existing file. You can open the original file in the Enhanced Editor, mark the text you want to transfer, and use the Copy command to pass the information to the clipboard. Now use Open .Untitled to bring up a second window, into which you can paste the text. Make the appropriate modifications to the file, then use Save As to store the changed file under a new name so as not to destroy the original.

FIGURE 4.3

The Enhanced Editor open on a CONFIG.SYS File

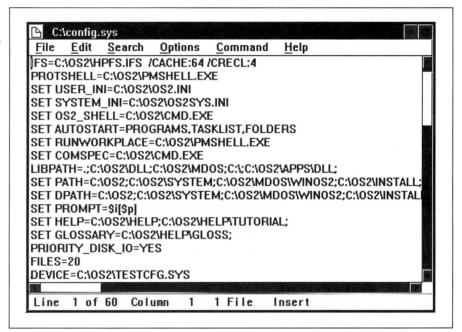

The Edit menu supports cut, copy, and paste operations to and from the clipboard, as well as block or mark operations such as Copy Mark, Move Mark, and Delete Mark.

The Search menu offers Search, Find Next and Change Next options, and a mechanism to set both temporary and permanent bookmarks. When you select Search, the window shown in Figure 4.4 opens.

To search for specific text, enter the text you want to look for into the Search field, and click the Find button. To look for the next occurrence of the same text, click Find again. If you want to find a specific text string and then replace it with another, the steps are just a little more complicated. First enter the text you want to search for into the Search field, enter the replacement text into the Replace field, and choose one of the following options:

- **Find** to locate the next occurrence of the search string

- **Change** to change the found text to the text contained in the replacement string

FIGURE 4.4

Searching for text in the
Enhanced Editor

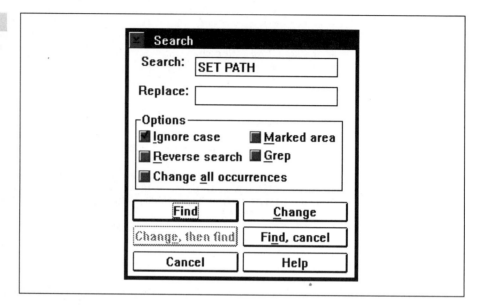

- **Change, then find** to perform the same operation as **Change**
  but to continue the search for another match when the change has
  been made

- **Find, cancel** to locate the next occurrence of the search text,
  then exit the search window

All searches start at the current cursor position, so be careful to place the
cursor at the beginning of the first line if you want to search the whole file.
The more specific you can make the search, the less time it will take to
find a match. There are several options you can use to make the search
more specific:

- **Ignore case** treats upper- and lower-case letters the same, so that
  OS/2, Os/2, and os/2 are all treated the same.

- **Reverse search** searches from the current cursor position
  towards the beginning of the file, rather than from the current
  cursor location to the end of the file.

- **Change all occurrences** replaces all occurrences of the search
  string with the text contained in the replacement field.

- **Marked area** limits the search to the current marked area in the file.
- **Grep** lets you use special pattern-matching characters in the search string. Table 4.1 lists these special characters.

 S E C R E T

Grep is also the name of a Unix program used to locate specific text in a file. The term comes from the ed editor, whose command for searching through a text file looking for lines that match a regular expression and then printing the matches is *g*lobal *r*egular *e*xpression *p*rint, where r*egular expression* is a special string of characters, created to locate matching strings of text. See Table 4.1 for more information.

TABLE 4.1: Characters Available for Use in a Grep Search

CHARACTER	MEANING
.	Matches any character.
^	Matches the beginning of a line.
$	Matches the end of a line when following the search text.
\character	Matches *character*. Used to override or ignore any special meaning the character posesses.
[characters]	Matches any of the characters contained in the list. Use a hyphen to indicate a range of characters; for example **[a-z]** matches with any alphabetic character. Use a caret (^) as the first character inside the braces to negate the set.
*	Matches a sequence of 0 or more of the following expression.
+	Matches a sequence of 1 or more of the following expression.

You can also use an option in the Search menu to set a *bookmark* in your text file. A bookmark attaches a unique name (that you specify) to the character at the current cursor location in your text file. If you choose the Set button, the bookmark will be available only for the duration of your Enhanced Editor session. If you choose Set Permanent, you create a permanent bookmark that is saved as an extended attribute when you save the file, and is available again the next time you load the same file. See Chapter 1 for more information on extended attributes. If you move the marked character, the bookmark moves too, but if you delete the character, you also delete the bookmark. If you subsequently edit a file that contains permanent bookmarks with an editor that does not support extended attributes, your bookmarks will be lost.

Use the List option in the Search menu to list all the bookmarks in your file by bookmark name, and to change from one to another.

The Options menu lets you configure the operating details of the editor, so you can tailor it to your needs. Select Preferences to change the following editor configuration options:

- **Settings** lets you look at or change the tabs setting, the positions of the margins, dialog box color use, the autosave and temporary path names, the number of modifications that can be made to a file before it is automatically saved, font and point size information, and key configurations for when the Enhanced Editor is in normal mode and stream editing is turned off.

- **Advanced Marking** is a toggle that lets you choose the way in which text is marked using the mouse. You can switch between CUA marking mode and the Enhanced Editor marking mode.

- **Stream Editing** is another toggle that switches between stream editing and normal editing. In stream mode, the Enhanced Editor treats a file as one long continuous stream of text, and new-line characters are treated just like any other text. In normal mode, a file is treated as a set of individual lines of text, each separated by a new-line character. Normal mode is the default.

- **Ring Enabled** is a toggle that when enabled lets you load and edit multiple text files. When Ring Mode is active, two new icons appear at the right end of the title bar to let you move quickly from file to file. Click the clockwise arrow to move to the next file in the ring, or click the counter-clockwise arrow to move to the previous file.

S E C R E T

Two new options are added to the Enhanced Editor menus when you use Ring Enabled; the Add File command, which lets you add files into the editing ring, appears in the File menu, and List Ring, a shortcut alternative to using the two arrow icons when you are working with a large number of files, appears in the Options menu.

- **Stack Commands** enables or disables the stack-related commands on the Edit menu. These commands are Push Mark, Pop Mark, Swap Mark, Push Cursor, Pop Cursor, and Swap Cursor.

Many of the Preferences are toggles: when they are enabled, you will see a check mark to the left of the menu entry. If there is no check mark, the option is not currently selected.

Select Autosave to control the number of modifications made to a file before it is automatically saved. Set this value to 0 to disable autosaving. To see a display of the Enhanced Editor error and status information, select Messages from the Options menu. You can also mark any of these error messages and copy them to the clipboard if you wish.

Choose Frame Controls from the Options menu to turn the following toggles on or off:

- Status Line
- Message Line
- Scroll Bars
- Rotate Buttons
- Info at Top
- Prompting

When you have finished adjusting the Enhanced Editor configuration settings, don't forget to use the last choice in the Options menu, Save Options, to preserve these settings for your next Enhanced Editor session.

The Command menu (F6) gives you access to a command dialog so you can enter OS/2 or DOS commands, macros, or editor commands, as well as a Halt command you can use to stop them again. The Enhanced Editor supports a wide range of general-purpose editing commands, including ASCII-to-character and character-to-ASCII conversions, evaluation of mathematical expressions in decimal, hexadecimal, or octal, case conversion, and file locking and unlocking. The most important Enhanced Editor commands are summarized in Table 4.2.

TABLE 4.2: Enhanced Editor Command Summary

COMMAND	MEANING
nnn	Moves to line *nnn*. You can use +*nnn* to move forward *nnn* lines, or −*nnn* to move back *nnn* lines.
ADD	Sums the currently marked numeric expressions, and displays the result on the next line after the mark.
ALL /*search string* /C	Creates a temporary file containing all occurrences of the text specified in *search string*. /C makes the search case-insensitive.
APPEND *filename*	Adds marked text to the file specified in *filename*. Use APPEND LPT*n* to print a marked block of text.
ASC*character*	Displays the ASCII value of *character*.
AUTOSAVE	Displays or sets the current autosave values. AUTOSAVE *nnn* sets the autosave count to the number specified by *nnn*; AUTOSAVE ON resets the current autosave count to the default; AUTOSAVE OFF turns off autosaves; AUTOSAVE ? displays the current values in a window, along with a button that lets you list all the files in the autosave directory; AUTOSAVE DIR lists all the files in the autosave directory.
BOTTOM	Moves the cursor to the last line of the file.

TABLE 4.2: Enhanced Editor Command Summary (Continued)

COMMAND	MEANING
BOX	Draws a box around the current marked block; the box type depends on the specified option:

	1	Single line
	2	Double line
	3	Dotted line
	4	Thick line
	5	Double horizontal line, single vertical line
	6	Single horizontal line, double vertical line
	A	Assembler-language comment box
	C	C-language comment box
	P	Pascal-language comment box
	B	Box of blanks
	/*character*	Box of specified *character*

COMMAND	MEANING
	If you want to see characters lined up on the screen, use a monospaced font such as System Monospaced or Courier. If you use a proportional font, the lines may not always line up, even though they are in the correct columns.
BROWSE	Determines if a file can be updated. BROWSE ON allows the file to be read, but not updated; BROWSE OFF allows the file to be read and updated. BROWSE ? displays the current browse mode.
CD *path*	Changes to the specified directory.
CENTER	Centers text within the current mark.

TABLE 4.2: Enhanced Editor Command Summary (Continued)

COMMAND	MEANING
CHANGE /search-string/ replace-string/options	Finds *search-string* and replaces it with *replace-string*. The options are as follows:
	– Searches backward from the current cursor position.
	+ Searches forward from the current cursor position.
	★ Replaces all occurrences of *search-string* with *replace-string*.
	A Searches the entire file.
	C Ignores case while searching for *search-string*.
	E Considers case when searching for *search-string*.
	F Searches forward, left to right, within each line.
	M Searches only inside the marked area.
	R Search is reversed, right to left, within each line.
	The default options are + A E F.
CHR *code*	Displays the character associated with the specified ASCII *code*.
CLOSE	Closes all files in the current edit ring.
COPY2CLIP	Copies the marked text to the clipboard.
CUT	Cuts the marked text to the clipboard.
DIR *path*	Opens a temporary file containing the directory listing for the current directory, if no path is specified.

TABLE 4.2: Enhanced Editor Command Summary (Continued)

COMMAND	MEANING
DOLINES	Processes the marked text as though they were typed at the command prompt.
DPATH	Opens a temporary file containing the DPATH environment setting.
DRAW *options*	Draws lines in a document. See the BOX command above for information on options.
ECHO	Turns echo mode on and off.
EDIT *filename*	Loads the specified files into the edit ring.
EPATH *filename*	Searches the environment for the specified file, then loads the file.
ESCAPEKEY *mode*	Turns the escape key mode on or off. When on, the escape key brings up the command-line dialog box.
EXPAND *mode*	Turns syntax expansion on or off.
FILE *filename*	Saves the file specified by *filename*.
FILL *character*	Fills the current mark with the specified character.
GET	Retrieves a file and inserts it at the line following the current cursor location.
KEY *nnnn character*	Repeats the *character* the number of times specified by *nnn*, on the same row.
LIST *filespec*	Loads a list of file names that match *filespec*.
LOCATE *search-string*	Finds *search-string*.
LOCK *filespec*	In a local area network (LAN), locks the file that matches *filespec*. A locked file is automatically unlocked by the FILE or QUIT commands, and can be manually unlocked with the UNLOCK command.

TABLE 4.2: Enhanced Editor Command Summary (Continued)

COMMAND	MEANING
LONGNAMES *mode*	Toggles the long filename option on or off.
LOOPKEY *nnnn character*	Repeats the *character* the number of times specified by *nnn*, in the same vertical column.
LOWERCASE	Converts all uppercase text in the marked block to lowercase.
MARGINS *left right paragraph*	Sets the margins according to *left, right,* and *paragraph.*
MATCHTAB *mode*	When set to on, Tab uses the previous line's setting for a tab stop.
MATH *expression*	Calculates the value of *expression*, in decimal. Use MATHX to see the value in hexadecimal, or use MATHO to see the value in octal.
MESSAGEBOX *message*	Displays *message* in the editor message box.
MULT	Multiplies the numeric expressions in the current marked block, and displays the result on the next line.
NAME *filename*	Renames the file in the editor, but not the original file name on disk. The new name will be used the next time the file is saved.
OPATH *filespec*	Searches the environment setting for the specified file, and loads it into a new window.
OPEN *filespec*	Loads the specified file or files into a new edit window.
OS2 *command*	Runs the OS/2 command processor, and starts the *command.*
PASTE	Pastes text from the Clipboard into the Enhanced Editor.

TABLE 4.2: Enhanced Editor Command Summary (Continued)

COMMAND	MEANING
PATH	Opens a temporary file containing the path environment settings.
PRINT	Prints the marked block if one exists, otherwise prints the whole file.
PROFILE *mode*	Sets the profile setting on or off; the default is off.
QUIT	Exits the current file.
QD	Displays the current system date.
QT	Displays the current system time.
RC *command*	Displays a command's return code in the information window.
SAVE	Saves the current file.
SET	Opens a temporary file containing the environment settings.
SHELL	Creates an Enhanced Editor command shell session. Adds two new entries to the Command menu; Create Command Shell creates a new shell window, and Write to Shell allows you to write a string to the shell window.
SORT	Sorts the lines in the current marked block, or sorts the entire file if no marked block exists. SORT R reverses the sort order, SORT C sorts into collating order, as indicated by the code page and country settings in effect, and SORT I ignores case when sorting.
STAY *mode*	Controls the position of the cursor after a CHANGE command. With STAY ON, the cursor remains in its original position, and with STAY OFF, the cursor moves to the last changed string.
SUBJECT	Displays, sets, or changes the file subject field.

TABLE 4.2: Enhanced Editor Command Summary (Continued)

COMMAND	MEANING
TABKEY *mode*	Turns the tab key mode on or off. When on, the tab key enters a tab character; when off (the default), the tab key moves the cursor to the next tab stop, without entering a tab character.
TABS *tab1 tab2...tabn*	Sets the position of the tab stops according to *tab1 tab2...tabn*.
TOP	Moves the cursor to the first line in the file.
TRIM	Resizes the window so that no partial characters are shown at the right and bottom edges of the window.
TYPE	Displays, sets or changes the file type.
UNLOCK	Unlocks a previously locked file.
UPPERCASE	Converts all the lowercase characters in the marked block to uppercase characters.
VER	Shows the Enhanced Editor version number.
VOL	Shows volume label.

S E C R E T

Many of the commands in Table 4.2 can be abbreviated to just one or two letters:

APPEND	APP
BOTTOM	BOT
CHANGE	C
EDIT	E
EPATH	EP

LOCATE	L
MARGINS	MA
OPATH	OP
QUIT	Q
QDATE	QD
QTIME	QT
SAVE	S

The Quick Reference option in the Enhanced Editor Help menu lists all the editing keystrokes and commands available in the Enhanced Editor, and also describes how to copy, move, or delete text, and how to configure certain software development tools to use the Enhanced Editor. It also contains an ASCII reference chart, showing decimal and hexadecimal codes for all the ASCII characters.

S E C R E T

You can add your own information, comments, or specific help instructions into this quick reference section; doing so will give you access to your own information directly from the Help menu. Use the Enhanced Editor to add your information to the quick reference file, EPMHELP.QHL, located in the C:\OS2\APPS directory.

OS/2 System Editor

The OS/2 System Editor is the text editor that was included with previous versions of OS/2. It offers basic text manipulation features, along with clipboard support, font and color selections, a find and replace option, and word wrap. It is easy to learn, works quickly, can be used to review or change OS/2 system text files, such as CONFIG.SYS or README, and it is the default editor used by the Seek and Scan Files application. If you need more from a text editor, use the much more capable Enhanced Editor instead.

S E C R E T

You can also start the OS/2 System Editor by dragging and dropping a text file onto its icon in the Productivity folder, or by typing its program name, **E**, along with the name of the file you want to open, at the OS/2 command prompt. To open the editor on the CONFIG.SYS file, for example, type **E CONFIG.SYS** at the OS/2 command prompt, and you will see the desktop appear, quickly followed by the OS/2 System Editor containing a copy of your CONFIG.SYS file. Double-click on the title-bar icon to return to the command prompt when you have finished with the editor.

Icon Editor

Desktop icons are one of the most useful and attractive elements in the OS/2 graphical user interface. Icons can represent application programs, groups of programs, or file folders. The Icon Editor lets you look at or change an icon, a bit map, or the pointer that follows mouse movement across your screen.

If you have used any of the popular paint programs, using the Icon Editor will be a breeze. Even if you haven't, it won't take you long to learn.

When you first open the Icon Editor, the workspace in the center of the window is blank. You can begin to create a new icon right away or you can load the icon file that you want to modify using the commands in the File menu. Figure 4.5 shows the Icon Editor ready to start work on an icon.

Icon files have the file-name extension .ICO. Each icon is defined as a square element, 32 pixels (picture elements) wide by 32 pixels high. Each pixel is equivalent to one spot of color in an icon. The small square at the top left of the Icon Editor window displays the icon at its actual size. You can also assign a color to each of the two mouse buttons, and these colors are displayed on the replica mouse next to the icon display.

FIGURE 4.5

The Icon Editor

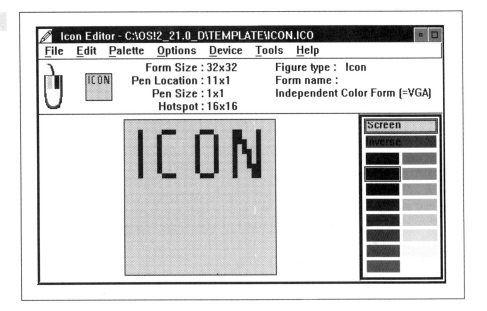

The File menu contains the usual options for opening and closing files, and the Edit menu contains the Cut, Copy, and Paste commands, as well as commands to flip a shape horizontally or vertically. The Palette menu helps you work with different color sets, and the Options menu controls Editor-wide settings, as well as pen-size selections. The Device menu contains advanced display device selections. The Tools menu helps you to identify the colors in an icon; and its Color Fill option will flood a shape with the color assigned to a mouse button.

➤ S O L U T I O N

If you want to create an icon for an application that does not have one, but has graphics that could be used for that purpose, you can turn that graphic into an icon. Run the program in a window session, and when you see an icon-sized graphic you like, size the window to the approximate size of an icon, then click on the window's title-bar icon, and select Mark to mark the graphic. Next, use the Copy command to move the graphic to the clipboard. Open the pop-up menu for the object you want to add this icon to, and open the Settings notebook at the General page to display the default icon. Select Create Another to open the Icon Editor, then in the Icon Editor's File menu, select New, followed by Icon, then select OK. Next, select the Edit menu, and then the Paste command to move the graphic from the clipboard into the Icon Editor. Make any changes you want using the tools available in the Icon Editor. Open the File menu and select Save or Save As to store the icon file in the same directory as the program executable file. Remember to use the same file name as the executable file, and the file-name extension .ICO, then double-click on the Icon Editor title-bar icon to close the Icon Editor. Back in the Settings notebook again, click on the Find button to locate the ICO file you just saved. Click on the icon, then save the file. Finally, exit the Settings notebook; the original icon has been replaced with the graphic from the application.

Notepad

The Notepad contains a set of five pages you can use to collect short notes and reminders for yourself. The Notepad is not a word processor, but it is useful for jotting down ideas you don't want to forget.

Each page can contain up to 25 lines of information, and each line can be up to 180 characters long. The usual menu selections in the File menu help you to open and save Notepad files; Notepad files have the file-name extension .N.

The five pages of the Notepad are shown cascaded across the screen; the first line of each page is always visible to help you move through your notes, page by page. To switch between pages, just click the page you want to bring to the front. You can also use the selections in the View menu to manage the pages. The selections in the Edit menu help you manage the Notepad and provide a way of adding graphical characters to your notes, while the Customize menu controls colors and font sizes.

Picture Viewer

The Picture Viewer lets you look at three different kinds of files: metafiles, picture interchange files, and spool files.

S E C R E T

You can also open the Picture Viewer directly from the OS/2 command line if you type PICVIEW, followed by the name of the file you want to view.

A *metafile* is a special kind of graphics file that contains not only the image, but also instructions on how the image should be displayed. This allows the image to be output to a variety of different display devices. Metafiles always have the file-name extension .MET.

A *picture interchange file* is a special file format used in exchanging images between applications. Picture interchange files always have the file-name extension .PIC. Use the Code Page selection from the Options menu to select a code page for the country of origin of the file, if the file was created abroad. A code page is just a collection of letters and numbers, but you need the right one to make sense of the displayed information.

A *spool file* contains information that is waiting to be printed. Spool files have the file-name extension .SPL. You can display some of the information in a spool file, as long as the file contains a picture in the standard OS/2 format.

Use the Open option from the File menu to specify the type of file you want to view. The Edit menu contains the normal Cut, Copy, and Paste selections, so you can transfer information to and from the clipboard.

The Page menu helps you to move through the information you display, page by page. You can also zoom into or out of a picture once it is displayed. Just move the mouse pointer to the part of the image you are interested in, and double-click the left mouse button; the image can be zoomed up to five times. Scroll bars are available so you can move to different parts of the image once it is zoomed. To zoom out again, press the Shift key and double-click the left mouse button.

The Options menu contains Viewer-wide control selections, while the Sequence menu works to show information as part of a series of images.

PM Chart

PM Chart is a powerful business-graphics application you can use to create charts, graphs, and illustrations. This program can open and display files created by Micrografx Charisma either as graphics (.GRF) or as data (.DAT), and it can open and display Micrografx Draw files (DRW).

As shown in Figure 4.6, PM Chart can also import data from files using the following formats: data interchange format (.DIF), space-delimited ASCII (.SPC), Microsoft symbolic link (.SLK), Lotus 1-2-3 (.WK1 and .WKS), and Microsoft Excel (.XLS), but it cannot load files created by the OS/2 Spreadsheet productivity application. You can also create a brand new file using PM Chart. Choose the appropriate file type in the Open selection in the File menu. PM Chart can save files in either .GRF or .DRW file format.

The tool bar at the left of the PM Chart work area contains the following tools, from top to bottom:

- **Select arrow.** This option turns off the previous mode.

FIGURE 4.6

Work Area in PM Chart

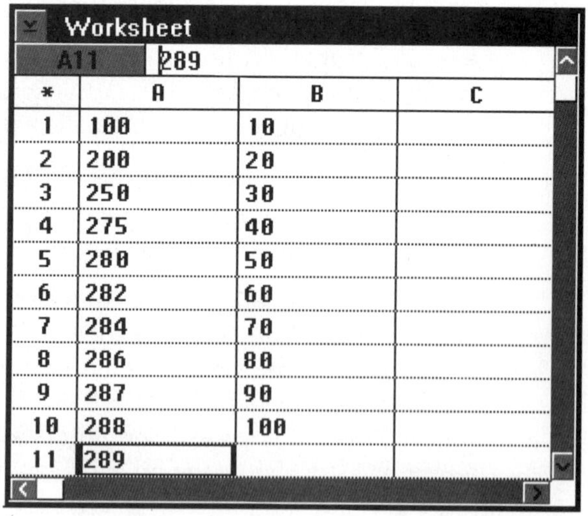

*	A	B	C
1	100	10	
2	200	20	
3	250	30	
4	275	40	
5	280	50	
6	282	60	
7	284	70	
8	286	80	
9	287	90	
10	288	100	
11	289		

Worksheet — A11 = 289

- **Use a worksheet.** The worksheet can hold up to 100 rows and 75 columns of information. When you are in worksheet mode, you can use the Data menu to sort the worksheet or to apply simple arithmetic functions. You can also specify a constant for use with these functions.

- **View a symbol.** Choose the view level or zoom mode.

- **Draw a symbol.** Select one of the drawing functions to create a rectangle, curve, ellipse, straight line, and so on.

- **Create a chart.** Choose from area, bar, column, line, pie, exploded pie, or table chart. Three-dimensional effects are also supported.

- **Type text.** Create a text object to annotate a chart, select the font and type style, and choose the text-justification options you want to use.

- **Change colors** and style of fill, line, and text.

The Edit menu provides options for cut-and-paste operations, and for clearing and removing objects from the workspace.

You can enter information directly into PM Chart if you open the worksheet by clicking on the right mouse button anywhere in the PM Chart work space, or if you click the worksheet icon in the tool bar. The worksheet has 75 columns from A to CV, and rows from 1 to 100; it is large enough for most charting jobs you are likely to encounter. Click the right mouse button a second time to put away the worksheet. The Change and Preferences menus appear and disappear automatically as you move in and out of worksheet mode. The Change menu lets you modify a selected symbol or group of symbols, and the Preferences menu lets you specify the default values to use when drawing figures.

To create a chart from scratch, first enter the data into the worksheet, either by hand or by loading one of the approved file types. Then select the data in the worksheet that you want to include in the chart by pressing and holding down the left mouse button and dragging the pointer over the desired area. Choose the chart type you want to use from the selections available from the tool bar, and use New to create the selected chart. You can also use Overlay to combine charts, Replace to delete the selected chart and replace it with a new one, or Cancel to return to the workspace.

You can also choose among several optional items: 3D creates a three-dimensional image, Legend adds a small legend to the chart, and New positions the chart in the center of the workspace.

After creating the chart, you can change its shape by dragging one of the black handles, or *control points*, to a new location. You can also add text labels or titles to your chart in a variety of fonts or type styles. Use the options in the File menu to save your chart when it is complete.

PM Chart can also use clip art (copyright-free line art) in your presentations. Select the ClipArt option from the File menu to load a clip art file in either .GRF or .DRW format. A few example clip art files in .GRF format are available with PM Chart, but if you want to use more, you will have to buy a separate add-on clip art package.

There are many more tricks in the PM Chart arsenal, including the ability to flip or rotate an image, manipulate the background color, and combine or duplicate images.

PM Terminal

PM Terminal (also known as Softerm Custom Version 1.00) is a full-featured asynchronous-communications and terminal-emulation program for use with a modem over telephone lines. PM Terminal has two main modes, the Session Manager used to establish your configuration, and the Session Window to manage your online transactions.

Using the Session Manager

The Session Manager establishes and maintains communications information and collects all this information into *profiles,* which are saved on disk in a file called CUSTOM.MDB; PM Terminal supports only one configuration database. A backup copy of this information is kept in the file CUSTOM.BAK. Each profile contains all the information needed to start and then manage a communications session with one specific target system; it includes terminal emulation information, environment information, connection and modem information, file-transfer protocol selections, and telephone numbers. Templates for several online services are shown in the opening PM Terminal screen, including CompuServe, MCI Mail, the IBM Public bulletin board, and a generic template you can use to log on to any bulletin board. Before you can use PM Terminal, you must be a registered user of the service, and you should have an account ID, a user ID, and a password. Double-click one of these templates to enter your own local configuration data for the service.

Choose Setup Profiles from the Session menu to open the window shown in Figure 4.7.

FIGURE 4.7

The Setup profiles window in PM Terminal

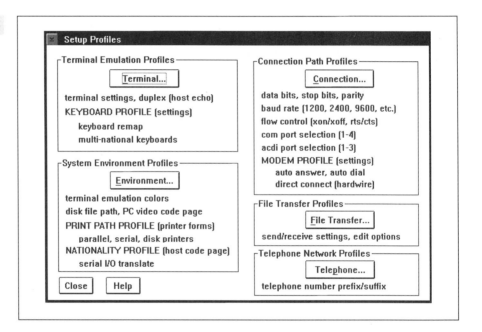

Using the buttons in this window, you can look at and change many of the PM Terminal settings. You can also change many of these parameters from the Settings menu in the Session Window. These settings are described in the following sections; if you don't need this technical information, skip ahead to "Using the Session Window."

Terminal The Terminal button lets you look at or change the terminal emulation settings and keyboard profile in use. In terminal emulation, a computer uses software to mimic whatever kind of display device the on-line service's remote mainframe computer expects to work with, so that information transmitted by the service can be interpreted and displayed properly.

PM Terminal can emulate the following types of terminal:

ANSI 3.64

DEC VT100

DEC VT52

GEnie Terminal

IBM 3103 - 10

IBM 3101 - 20

IGM ANSI

IGM INVT100

TTY

You will probably never need to change or tune any of these emulation configurations, but if you do, you can add a new or change an existing emulation by using the Add or Change buttons. First select an emulation from the Terminal Emulation Profiles list, then click the Change button to make your changes. You can look at or change settings under the following headings (depending on the selection you made from the Terminal Emulation Profiles):

- Transmit/Delay Trigger String
- Buffer Definitions
- Video Definitions
- Duplex (Echo) Setting
- Line Turnaround Character
- Operating Mode
- Printer Definitions
- Status Line Definition

- Answerback Message
- Keypad Mode
- Tab Stops

You can also change to a different keyboard profile if you need to remap the functions of certain keys, or if you are not using a 101-key keyboard.

Environment The Environment button lets you examine system environment settings such as color use, the code page in use, or the system path information.

You can set up a Nationality Profile, although in most cases you won't need one unless you routinely communicate with computers that do not use the US character set. A Nationality profile filters and changes the characters transmitted or received between computers, but it does not affect what appears on your screen in terminal emulation mode during a communications session; this is controlled by the Video Code Page setting in the System Environment profile.

WARNING

Because a Nationality Profile translates characters during the transmission, and can cause havoc if used incorrectly in communications, proceed very carefully if you decide to use one. In almost every case, the best and safest choice is to use one of the PM Terminal predefined translations. Be sure to test your choice of Nationality Profile on several different types of non-essential files to make sure that it is not introducing any unexpected results before you use the profile as part of your routine communications.

By using the Print Path setting, you can define the default printer as either a serial printer, a parallel printer, a disk file, or the print spooler.

The System Environment Settings control color usage, the default path used in file transfer and printing operations, and the Video Code Page being used. The Video Code Page determines the appearance of characters (particularly the high-order "extended" ASCII characters) on the screen. The US code page is 437, and the multinational code page is 850.

Connection   The Connection button gives you access to settings used by PM Terminal when talking to your modem. For each of the connection types shown in the Connection Paths window, you can look at or change the modem information, the communications parameters, or the method of flow control. Select a connection type in the window, then click Change. Alternatively, you can just double-click directly on the connection type in the window. Select the COM port that your modem is attached to, then click Setup to change the modem settings. You can look at or change any of the following:

- Dialing Strings
- Device Initialization String
- Response Strings
- Device Carrier Exchange Timeout
- Call Failure type and Response String
- Hangup String
- Voice-to-Data Strings
- Auto-answer Strings

See your modem manual for suggestions on how to use these settings.

To change the parameters used during communications, select Communications Parameters in the Connection Path Settings window, and click Change. You can choose a baud rate from the following: 110, 150, 300, 600, 1200, 2400, 4800, 9600, and 19200; and the data bits, stop bits, and parity settings choices are shown in Table 4.3. Many bulletin boards use 8 data bits, 1 stop bit, and no parity for their communications.

If you want to look at the parameters that govern data synchronization between sending and receiving computers, choose Flow Control from the Connection Path Settings window, and click the Change button. The flow control parameters should be set to match the requirements of the host or remote computer.

TABLE 4.3: PM Terminal Data Bits, Stop Bits, and Parity Settings

DATA BITS	STOP BITS	PARITY
8	2	Odd
8	2	Even
8	2	Mark
8	2	Space
8	2	None
8	1	Odd
8	1	Even
8	1	Mark
8	1	Space
8	1	None
7	1	Odd
7	1	Even
7	1	Mark
7	1	Space
7	1	None
7	2	Odd
7	2	Even
7	2	Mark
7	2	Space
7	2	None

File Transfer The File Transfer button allows you to look at the file transfer protocols available in PM Terminal. You will find the following protocols available:

- Character (also sometimes called ASCII)
- Kermit
- Kermit Server
- Softtrans
- Xmodem
- Xmodem 1K
- Ymodem
- Ymodem 1K
- Ymodem-G
- Ymodem-G 1K

Again, you must choose a protocol that is supported by the sending or receiving computer. Many PC bulletin boards support Xmodem and Ymodem file transfers, and larger computers, especially in universities, support Kermit.

Telephone The Telephone button lets you add or change telephone number prefix and suffix information. In addition to the digits 0–9 and the special touchtone characters * and #, you can use any of the predefined dial modifiers listed in Table 4.4. The first 32 ASCII characters can be used as control codes if you type the appropriate acronym in square brackets; for example use [CR] for carriage return, or [LF] for line feed.

Dial modifiers are processed in the order in which they appear in the Telephone Network Prefix or Telephone Network Suffix fields.

TABLE 4.4: Predefined Dial Modifiers

MODIFIER	MEANING
[DIALTONE]	Waits for a dial tone, up to a maximum of three seconds.
[PAUSE_n]	Sends a command string to pause the modem for up to n seconds, where n can be a positive number from 1 to 9.
[PULSE]	Selects pulse dialing.
[TONE]	Selects touchtone dialing.
[VOICE]	Switches over to voice after dialing the number.
[WAIT_n]	Invokes an internal program pause for n seconds, where n is a positive number from 1 to 9.

▶ S O L U T I O N

If you usually dial out through an office switchboard or private branch exchange (pbx), add 9,, into the Telephone Network Prefix field to dial an outside line (the ,, adds a two-second delay). You can also use this setting to cancel call waiting, if available, otherwise your online session may be interrupted by the noise that signals an incoming call.

Using the Session Window

The PM Terminal Session Window, also known as the Runtime window, Terminal Emulation window, or Online window, orchestrates your online transactions using information from one of the profiles you established in the Session Manager.

To dial a remote computer, just double-click the correct entry in the Session Phonebook, shown as the opening PM Terminal screen. Using the Session Window, you can perform the following functions:

- Dial a remote computer
- Send files to a remote computer
- Receive files from a remote computer
- Capture data displayed on the screen in a disk file or on a printer
- Send command strings to a printer
- Hang up and break the connection

When you are online, you will be in one of the following modes of operation:

- **Terminal Emulation mode.** As discussed in "Using the Session Manager," this mode turns your computer into a terminal and is most often used for communications with a large remote computer. PM Terminal supports all the popular terminal types you are ever likely to need.

- **File Transfer mode.** In this mode you can exchange files with a remote computer using a file-transfer protocol you've agreed upon. PM Terminal supports all the popular file-transfer protocols, including Xmodem, Ymodem, and Kermit.

The functions available in the menus change in the Session Window to reflect the current operation. The File menu, for example, has options for file transfer or display, dialing a number, hanging up the modem, and transferring files to disk or to a printer. Selections from the Options menu let you display the current keyboard layout, and start and stop keyboard macro mode.

SOLUTION

A macro is a collection of keystrokes, saved in a file, that you can use to automate complex or repetitive tasks.

To create a macro, choose Begin Keyboard Macro Record Function from the Options menu, and select the identification number you want to use with the macro. The very next key you type will be the first keystroke stored in the macro. Type all the characters you want to include in the macro (mouse movements cannot be stored), and when the macro is complete, choose End Keyboard Macro Record Mode. To run this macro, use the Perform Keyboard Function and enter the appropriate macro number.

The macro file is called KBPLAYBK, and the file-name extension starts at 000 for the first macro, and increases sequentially to the maximum of 025. PM Terminal limits you to storing 25 macros in a directory; if you need more than 25, just save the extra macros in a different directory.

A status line at the bottom of the Session Window indicates whether you are online and contains other status information, depending on which mode you are using. Any information in the center of the window is either being sent from the remote computer or bulletin board, or represents information you have entered in response to prompts received from the remote computer.

PM Terminal is a complex and flexible application capable of meeting all your computer-to-computer communications needs.

Pulse

The Pulse application shows a small graph of the activity of your computer's microprocessor. The higher the graph, the more work your computer is doing. The graph is updated continuously, so you can see the effects of opening and closing applications, changing operating parameters, or even just moving the mouse.

The Selections in the Options menu let you control the display colors and the nature of the graph. You can even freeze the graph to capture an important event if you wish.

S O L U T I O N

You can also use Pulse to monitor the activity level of a program or system utility running in the background. As a demonstration, start formatting a floppy disk, then return to the desktop and double-click on Pulse. You might be surprised at the low level of activity; you can see that your computer is not doing very much work as it formats the disk.

Seek and Scan Files

The Seek and Scan Files application (also known as PMSeek) can find a lost or misplaced file anywhere in your directory structure on any drive. It can also find specific text inside the files you are looking for.

S O L U T I O N

You can also launch the Seek and Scan Files application directly from the OS/2 command prompt by typing **PMSEEK** followed by the name of the file you want to look for. For example, to search for the file CONFIG.SYS, type **PMSEEK CONFIG.SYS** at the OS/2 command prompt. If you start the PMSEEK program from the command prompt, you will return to the command prompt when you leave the PMSEEK program, rather than to the desktop.

There are just a few steps involved in using Seek and Scan Files. First, tell the program *what* to look for by entering a file name in the File Name to Search For box. Then tell it *where* to look using the Drives to Search check boxes. Enter any text you are looking for, and finally, start the search by selecting the Search button.

When Seek and Scan Files locates files that match your specified settings, they are listed in the Files Found box in the lower half of the window. The information displayed for each file includes its complete path, the file date and time, and the file size. Figure 4.8 shows a search for files on drive C called CONFIG.SYS that contain the text SET. Two are found, and the total time to search this 200MB drive was 9 seconds.

Use Stop if you want to halt the search, and use the Open button to open the default text editor on the file so you can review its contents. The Editor Filespec field contains the name of the default editor program, usually the OS/2 System Editor, but you can use any editor program you like. If the Enhanced Editor is iconized on the desktop, you can drag and drop a file onto its icon, and the Enhanced Editor will open the file.

FIGURE 4.8

Seek and Scan Files found two files called CONFIG.SYS on this 200MB hard disk in 9 seconds

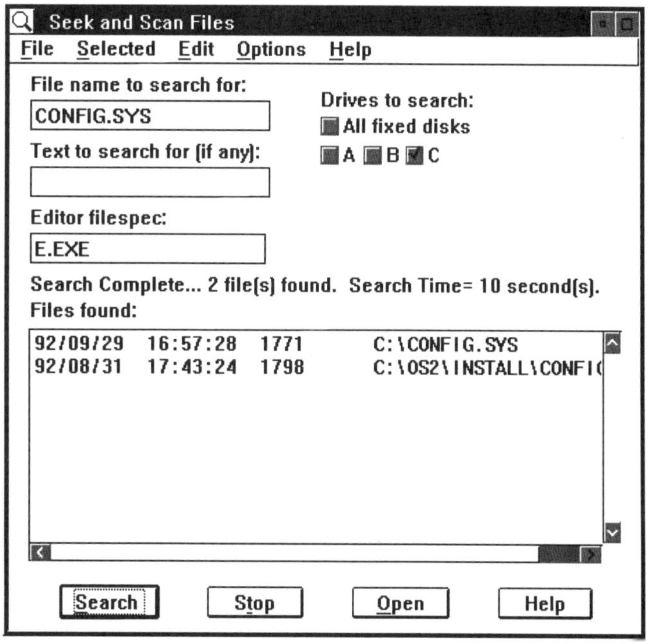

After selecting a file in the Files Found box, you can use the Open command from the Selected menu to open the default editor on the file, the Process command to run a program file once it's found, or the Command option to execute an operating system command such as REN or DEL on the found file.

With settings from the Options menu, you can extend the search as follows:

- **Search Subdirectories** extends the search to include all subdirectories.

- **Display Found Text** displays the search string when it is located.

- **Ignore Case** is a toggle you can use to make the text search case sensitive or case insensitive.

- **Clear on Search** clears the Files Found box when you initiate a new search.

Once you have collected a list of found files, you can save this list if you select Save from the File menu. A dialog box opens so you can enter the file name you want to use, and then an information box opens to remind you of the number of entries saved in that file.

Spreadsheet

The Spreadsheet application creates a simple 26-column by 80-row spreadsheet you can use to keep track of expenses, sales figures, or other numbers. Spreadsheet is no match for the high-powered spreadsheets from the major software companies, but how often do you need all that power? You will be surprised how well Spreadsheet performs.

To create a new spreadsheet, select New from the File menu, and enter the numbers into the Spreadsheet. Then use Save or Save As from the File menu to save the contents of the Spreadsheet.

NOTE The OS/2 Spreadsheet application uses its own special file format and cannot import or export data in Lotus 1-2-3 or any other file formats. It automatically assigns the .$$$ file-name extension to spreadsheet data files.

You can use all the major operators—addition (+), subtraction (–), multiplication (*), and division (/)—to add simple formulas to your spreadsheet. You can sum or add all the cells in a range of cells with the area summation (@), and you can use parentheses to change the order in which a calculation is performed. Each cell can contain either an alphanumeric or a numeric value up to 8 characters long, or a formula of up to 30 characters. Adding titles above your entries is a good way to make the spreadsheet more readable.

S E C R E T

You can total a rectangular set of cells, as well as rows and columns. For example, C5@D6 sums the contents of all four cells in this part of the spreadsheet, C5, C6, D5, and D6.

If your spreadsheet is large, it may be faster to recalculate only those cells that have changed, rather than the whole worksheet. Use the options in the Recalculate menu to establish just when and how you want the spreadsheet recalculated:

- Recalc Current Cell Only
- Recalc Top->Bottom, Left->Right
- Recalc Left->Right, Top->Bottom

When it is time to print your spreadsheet, use the Print selection from the File menu. To see the formulas in your spreadsheet, use the Print Formula/Cell Data option instead.

Sticky Pad

The Sticky Pad application lets you stick notes on your desktop. Figure 4.9 shows my desktop with two notes containing reminder messages. You can create up to ten notes, and each one can contain up to eight lines of 29 characters. They can even contain graphical elements. As soon as you type a character into a note, a timestamp appears on the first line of the note. You can use the Reset Timestamp option from the Edit menu to change this if you wish.

To create a new note, select the Sticky Pad icon, and position the sticky note in the window. Type the note, and when you minimize the window, the sticky note will be attached to that window. When the window is displayed, the note will appear in one of the corners.

FIGURE 4.9

Sticky Pads on the desktop

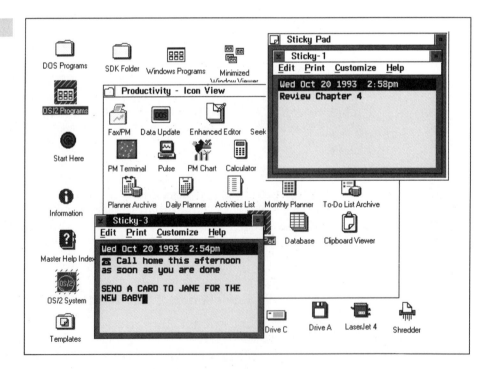

The selections in the Customize menu help you to place the note in the correct position; choose from:

- Bottom Left of Frame
- Top Left of Frame
- Top Right of Frame
- Bottom Right of Frame
- Set Default Attach Position

You can also drag the note to a new location using the mouse.

Use the Print selection from the Print menu to print a note. You can send the output to your printer directly, or to a spool file for printing at a later time.

Tune Editor

The Tune Editor can display, create, or change the tunes used with the Alarms application. Each tune file can contain up to 36 individual tunes, and each tune within this file can contain up to 20 different notes. Use the Open option in the File menu to open the default tune file PMDIARY.$$A; this file contains the tunes used by the Alarm application. Now use the Open Tune selection to choose the tune you want to display in the Tune Editor window. The Play menu lets you play the current tune or cycle through all the tunes contained in the current tune file.

If you want to edit the current tune, use the selections from the Edit menu to add sharps or flats, or change the timing value of a note in the tune. You can also use the value, note, pitch, and tempo sliders to make changes in a tune.

These tunes do not require any additional computer hardware; they use the built-in computer speaker to generate their tones.

Fax/PM

Fax/PM is a set of fax management utilities, new with OS/2 Version 2.1, that you can use to send and receive single-page faxes directly from your desktop. Figure 4.10 shows the Fax/PM folder and the Fax/PM Scheduler open on the desktop. Fax/PM works with Group III Class 2 fax modems, and even contains a modem-simulation mode you can use to simulate fax transmission and reception. See Chapter 11 for details on configuring your fax modem hardware with OS/2.

FIGURE 4.10

The Fax/PM folder and the Fax/PM Scheduler open on the desktop

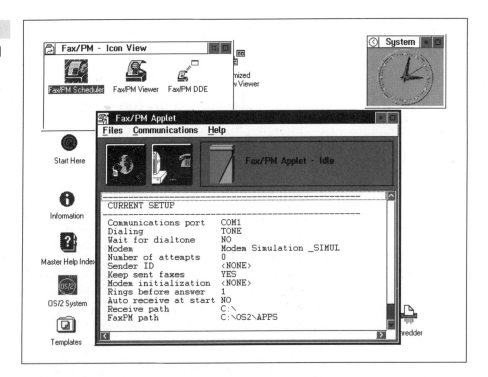

When you double-click Fax/PM inside the Productivity folder, you will see three objects:

- **Fax/PM Scheduler** lets you transmit and receive faxes, and set up communications parameters. The main window contains two large iconized buttons for initiating a fax and for setting up communications parameters. The rest of the main window shows the fax status area and the real-time activity log for fax processing.

- **Fax/PM Viewer** allows you to look at faxes that have been sent or received using Fax/PM; you can also copy all or part of a fax to the clipboard.

- **Fax/PM DDE** is a Fax/PM dynamic data exchange (DDE) server for Win-OS/2. You must start Fax/PM DDE before you try to send a fax from a WIN OS/2 program.

To configure Fax/PM, double-click the Fax/PM Scheduler, then select Setup from the Communications menu, or click the setup icon at the top of the main window. This opens the four-page Fax/PM settings notebook:

- **Communications** lets you select the communications port, dialing method, and modem for use with your fax. Fax/PM only supports local communications ports; it does not support remote ports. Select the name of your Group III Class 2 modem from the list; if your modem does not appear in this list, select the generic Modems Class 2.

- **Miscellaneous** allows you to enter sender identification information that will be added to the printed information on the destination fax, select whether faxes are kept or deleted after they have been sent, set the number of times a fax connection should be attempted (limited to one in this version of the program) and specify any special modem initialization commands that might be necessary.

- **Receive** lets you specify fax receive options, including Auto Receive to make Fax/PM wait for incoming fax transmissions, the number of rings to wait before the modem answers, and path information used for storing incoming faxes. If you decide not to use Auto Receive, you can use the Receive a Fax option from the Communications menu instead; the only drawback is that this option is not automatic, and you have to know when you are about to receive the fax to use it.

- **Modem Tuning** allows you to set the scan time, specify that a fax transmission begins with the first received XON character, or reverse the bit order used in the transmission.

Click OK when you have completed any changes in the settings notebook, use Undo to reset changed values back to their original settings, or use Cancel or press the Escape key to exit without saving your changes.

When you are ready to send a fax, double-click the Fax/PM Scheduler, then select Requests from the Files menu, or click the globe icon at the top left of the window. When the Send Requests window opens, double-click the New field to enable the Create button. Now you can enter all the information relevant to this new fax, including:

- The name of the document or file you want to fax.
- The format of this document.
- The destination fax number.
- The Request State; choose between Ready (R) or Held (H). All the other Request Status selections are dimmed out and unavailable in this version of the program.

You will also see information in the Request Selection List for faxes currently being processed by Fax/PM; including:

- A Request sequence number.
- The destination fax number.
- The fax status, either R (Ready) for a fax that is waiting to be sent, or H (Held) for a fax that has been placed on hold.
- Full path information for the document to be faxed.

To change any of this information for an existing fax, double-click the entry in the Request Selection List, then use the Modify or Delete buttons as appropriate. You can always edit fax information unless the fax is in the process of being sent, in which case you will see its status listed as In Progress. To abort a fax while it is being sent, use the Stop Transmission option from the Communications menu.

► S O L U T I O N

There is another, much faster, way you can send a fax, this time without leaving your application program. The Fax/PM icon on the desktop works just like a printer object. You can create your fax using any application you like, then drag and drop the fax onto Fax/PM on the desktop to send it. A dialog box opens for you to enter the telephone number of the destination fax machine, and that's all there is to it.

Fax/PM Viewer lets you look at faxes you have sent or received with Fax/PM. The Open command in the File menu lets you specify the fax file you want to work with, and the selections in the Views menu help you specify a reduced view, a large view, or a full-screen view of the fax. Use Flip to rotate the fax if it was sent upside down. If you know that you will always use the same view for every fax, make this choice in the Setup window. Options in the Edit menu allow you to copy the fax to the clipboard if you want to paste the fax into another document. You must use the large view when you select part of a fax for copying to the clipboard; the Select command in the Edit menu is not available in the other views.

Daily Planner

Several of the time-management applications on the OS/2 desktop are closely related, and can give you different views of the same information. The Daily Planner is the central application, and so we'll look at that first, but a file created by the Daily Planner can be used by all the other time-management applications on the desktop, including the Calendar, the Monthly Planner, and the Activities List. The only independent time-management application not tied into the Daily Planner data file is the To-Do List application.

NOTE   The Daily Planner application automatically assigns the file-name extension .D to planner files.

You can use the Daily Planner to keep track of your activities, and you can store this information in a Daily Planner File. The fields in the main Daily Planner window, shown in Figure 4.11, are:

- **Start** is the beginning time of the activity.

- **End** is the ending time for the activity.

- **Alarm Time** represents the number of minutes *before* the Start that you want an alarm to sound; enter a number between 0 and 59.

- **Alarm Tune** represents the number of the tune you want to play as the alarm.

- **Description of the Activity** contains up to 180 text characters describing the activity.

FIGURE 4.11

The Daily Planner main window

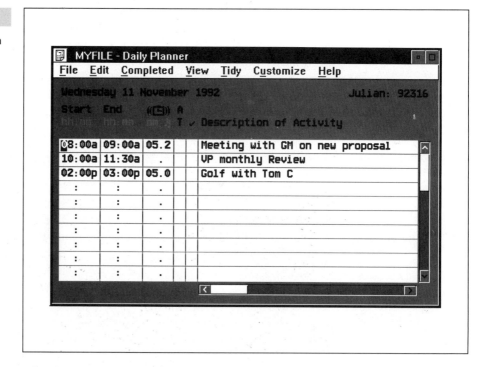

Activities can be grouped by using Activity Type from the Edit menu; choose from Out-of-Office, Personal Holiday, or National Holiday. You can also add a graphic to the Activity Description box to jog your memory, or choose an alarm tune from the selection of built-in tunes. If you have a regularly occurring activity, use the Propagate/Delete Lines option from the Edit menu to automatically schedule the activity for you, rather than entering the event manually every time you want to schedule it. This feature is good for regularly scheduled events like softball games or department meetings. If you fill up the Daily Planner window, use the scroll bars to move among the entries; the Description of Activity window is also scrollable.

You can use the entries in the View menu to display the next or previous day's entries, or to return to today's entries.

If you mark Daily Planner events as completed using commands from the Completed menu, you can add these events to your own personal archive, accessible to the Planner Archive application; any previously archived activity can be retrieved and restored to your Daily Planner schedule. The Tidy menu contains options you can use to delete and archive Daily Planner activities.

Planner Archive

The Planner Archive maintains the information you saved from the Daily Planner using the options in the Completed and Tidy menus. Archiving your Daily Planner information enables you to restore events deleted by accident or review past activities. This information is stored in a separate file you can open and review with the Planner Archive application.

NOTE The Planner Archive automatically uses the file-name extension .$DA for Planner Archive data files.

The Statistics option from the File menu lets you review your activities with a time breakdown over a specific month. You can also sort archived activities using up to three different sort fields.

Note that activities erased from the Daily Planner are not available to the Planner Archive; only those activities you specifically archived are available.

Alarms

The Alarms application lets you set or cancel a built-in alarm system. You can set an alarm for a specific day, hour, and minute, and then select a graphic element for display in a pop-up window and a tune fragment that will be played when the alarm goes off.

S E C R E T

You can use the Set Alarm option in the Alarms menu to run a command or batch file at a specific time, if you check the Execute Comment as Command at Alarm Time check box. This makes the Alarms application work as a scheduler you can use to start a process running at a specific time. Simple, but effective. For example, to run a REXX procedure at the same time each day, add the name of the REXX batch file into this field. Be sure to enter the file name and extension, as well as any required path information. You can also use this feature to schedule other application programs that you run on a regular basis.

Use the Customize menu to specify the number of times the tune will be played and the length of time you want to use as the *snooze* period. You can also tie the alarms into a master planner file, so that the alarms in this file can be activated too.

When you schedule an activity using the Daily Planner, you can enter an alarm time from 0 to 59 minutes. This is the number of minutes before the activity start time you want the alarm to sound.

Activities List

The Activities List lets you look at, but not change, all your Daily Planner entries. The only information you can't see is the empty time slots. You can copy or find entries, and you can sort activities by Planner Date or by Description.

Monthly Planner

The Monthly Planner gives you a monthly perspective on your activities. You can open a file created with the Daily Planner and show the information in the Monthly Planner format.

Available time is shown in white, and scheduled activities are shown in contrasting colors. Weekends are shown in gray, and any days displayed from the previous or following months are shown in a different shade of gray.

An alarm is represented by a red dot in the lower corner of the activity. The first two letters of the activity description are also shown, so if you can establish a set of two-letter codes to represent the different activities you want to track, you will be able to see them in this monthly view. If you use a graphic as the first character of an activity, it will be displayed instead.

Use the selections from the View menu to display information for a specific month, for the previous month, for next month, for the previous year, for next year, and to return to today.

To see all the details of an activity, double-click anywhere on the bar representing the day you are interested in, and the Daily Planner will open so you can review, edit, or delete the information.

Calendar

The Calendar presents a concise view of your month. If you open a file created by the Daily Planner, those days containing activities are displayed in the Calendar with a red border, and free days are shown with no border. Double-click a date to open the Daily Planner so you can enter new information or review existing information.

The menu selections in the View and Customize menus are the same as those in the Monthly Planner.

To-Do List

The To-Do List lets you organize the things you have to do, assign them a priority, and store them in a file.

N O T E   The To-Do List uses the file-name extension .T for its data files.

You can enter a two-character priority into the Priority column, a date into the Date column, and a brief description into the Task-Description column. Using the Sort option from the View menu, you can sort by priority, date, or description to arrange your tasks into the order you want.

Tasks that were due to be done earlier today appear in red, while tasks that are due to be done later are shown in black. If you use a graphic element as the priority indicator, note that graphics are sorted to the end of the list, after numbers and letters.

Use the selections from the Mark menu to show that tasks are complete. The word *Done* appears in the Priority column opposite the appropriate entry.

The To-Do List has its own archive, called the To-Do List Archive, because the To-Do List is not one of the group of applications that use Daily Planner information. Use the options from the Mark menu to archive or delete completed tasks.

To-Do List Archive

The To-Do List Archive maintains the information you saved from the To-Do List using the options in the Mark menu. This information is stored in a separate file you can open and review. The To-Do List Archive file-name extension is .$TA.

You can sort archived activities using up to four different sort fields, including priority, date, description, or archive date.

Note that activities erased from the To-Do List are not available in the To-Do List Archive; only those activities you specifically archived are available.

OS/2 Games

There are several games provided as part of the OS/2 operating system. They range from simple programs suitable for children such as the Cat and Mouse game, to a full-featured chess game that will challenge the most skillful players.

Cat and Mouse

In the Cat and Mouse game, a cat chases your mouse around the screen; when you move your mouse, the cat follows until you stop. When you stop moving the mouse, the cat stops, sits, and finally goes to sleep until you move it again. If you open other windows, you will see the cat peer out at you from behind these windows from time to time. You can change the Play Time, Speed, and Step sliders to change how the cat reacts on the screen, and the Hide button clears all the other open windows from your desktop so you can concentrate on the cat; press the Alt key to bring the other windows back again. You can use the Register button to save your current settings for future use.

> # S E C R E T
>
> For real fun, start several copies of this program running at the same time, and watch a whole litter of cats chase your mouse. Start one version of the program from the desktop, another from an OS/2 window, and the third from the OS/2 full-screen prompt. To start the program running from one of these command prompts, change to the OS2\APPS directory and type
>
> NEKO
>
> to start the program running. Set up some of the cats to run at a slow speed and others at a fast speed, and then watch them all respond to mouse-cursor movements. When you stop moving the mouse, they will all eventually fall asleep in a big heap on your desktop, just as real cats do.

Jigsaw

The Jigsaw game makes a jigsaw puzzle from a graphical image. Select the image you want to use in the Open option in the File menu, then choose how large you want to make the pieces using Size from the Options menu. When you are ready to play, select Jumble! from the Options menu. Now use the mouse to put the pieces back together again, by dragging them one at a time. One small final hint; you will never have to rotate a piece to make it fit.

S O L U T I O N

To make new pictures available to the Jigsaw, just copy your favorite bitmap file into the OS2\BITMAP directory, then use the Open selection in the Jigsaw File menu to create the jigsaw. Once bitmaps are in the OS2\BITMAP directory, you can also select them for use as a window or desktop background. Right-click on the desktop to open the pop-up menu, choose Open and Settings, then click on the Background tab. Choose Image as the Background Type, and select the file you want to use from the selections in the File list box. Double-click on the Settings notebook title-bar icon to close the notebook when you have made your choice.

OS/2 Chess

The chess game uses a realistic-looking chess set, and you can play against the computer, against a human sitting at your computer, or against other human players on your network. Use drag-and-drop with either mouse button to move the pieces. You can take advantage of a surprising number of options, including a move timer, sounds, and warning messages. You can even turn the board around when it is time for your move.

You can use the Set Position selection in the Options menu to set up the pieces on the board in order to follow famous games from the past or games from books or magazines; you don't have to start every game from the beginning. If you run out of time, use Save from the Game menu to store the game status, then use Load when you return to the game at a more convenient time in the future.

The selections in the View menu let you look at the current game, as well as change the current setup. Move Status shows the number of moves completed by each player, as well as a count of the elapsed time. Game Record lists the history of the current game in algebraic chess notation, move by move, while the Valid Moves option lists all the available legal moves for the current player; just click the move you want to make next. Analysis is the computer's suggestion for the best move to make, and Captured Pieces shows a graphical representation of all the pieces captured so far in the current game.

Reversi

Reversi works just like the board game of the same name. The objective is for you to have more red pieces on the board at the end of the game than the computer has blue pieces. The game is over when all the squares on the board are filled, or when no more legal moves can be made.

The game calls for both offensive and defensive thinking; a move that changes many blue pieces into red pieces may not be the best move in the long run. There is often an advantage to occupying the locations along the edges of the board, or the four corners, because these positions cannot be outflanked.

You can always ask the computer for advice by clicking on Hint in the Moves menu. A cross-hair appears in the best location; just click the mouse button to use this as your next move.

Scramble

The Scramble game is the same as the hand-held version of this game; the objective is to unscramble all the tiles and arrange them back into the correct order.

There are several different games to choose from; numbers, the OS/2 logo, or Frisky Cats from the cat and mouse game. Use the Open selection in the Games menu to choose the one you want to play.

S E C R E T

If the task of rearranging the tiles proves to be too much of a challenge, use the Reset command from the Game menu to make Scramble automatically finish the game for you.

As you place the mouse pointer on a tile, an arrow indicates the direction you can move that tile in; just click the mouse button to move it. You can also use the keyboard arrow keys to move tiles if you wish.

Klondike Solitaire

The OS/2 version of the Solitaire game is just like the card game. And yes, you can still cheat; see the selections in the Moves menu.

S E C R E T

Each time you click on Cheat you get one move, but you can click on Cheat as many times as you like.

If you cheat and win, however, not only you will see the usual winner's fireworks display, but also a count of the number of times you cheated during the game!

PART II

Running OS/2, DOS, and Windows Programs

CHAPTERS

OS/2 OS/2 OS/2

OS/2 OS/2 OS/2 OS/2 OS/2 OS/2 OS/2 OS/2

OS/2 OS/2 OS/2 O

Running OS/2 Programs

IN many ways, OS/2 offers the best of all possible worlds: you can run tens of thousands of OS/2, DOS, and Microsoft Windows applications, all without changing anything in your computer system.

You can run these applications in side-by-side windows on the desktop, or as full-screen sessions. In this chapter I'll look at running OS/2 programs, and then in the next two chapters I will cover running DOS and Windows programs respectively.

Running OS/2 Programs

Applications running on OS/2 can take advantage of many important operating system features, including:

- **Multitasking.** This is the ability to run several programs on your computer at the same time. Multitasking allows you to format a floppy disk, download a file from an online information service such as CompuServe, or update a large database, all at the same time that you are working on a letter in your word processor.

  A *task* is very strictly defined by the Intel 80386 processor architecture, and so in OS/2, each running program is actually described as a *process* rather than a task to avoid confusing the two terms. In OS/2, there really are no programs; they are all called processes. You can think of an EXE file or a COM file as being a process, and as you will see in Chapter 13, a process can run one or more other processes.

- **Multithreading.** Individual operations inside the same application program can be programmed as separate *threads* to optimize program performance. A thread is either the *primary* thread, created when the process starts, or a *secondary* thread, created by the primary thread to handle a particular operation. This means that a single program can run several threads at the same time and thus perform several operations simultaneously.

- **Interprocess communications.** OS/2 offers several different levels of interprocess communications, including semaphores, shared memory, signals, pipes, and queues. These terms are explained in detail in Chapter 13.

- **Crash protection.** OS/2 protects applications from each other, so that if one program has a problem it does not bring down the whole operating system. You just have to restart the application that had the problem.

- **Larger memory.** OS/2 removes the 640K memory limitation so familiar to MS-DOS users, as well as removing the need for a separate memory-management program. OS/2 takes care of everything.

- **Dynamic Data Exchange.** DDE allows applications to exchange data between running OS/2 programs, or even between OS/2 and Windows programs.

- **Object Linking and Embedding.** OLE allows a WIN-OS2 application to update information managed by another program either manually or automatically.

- **Graphical User Interface (GUI).** The graphical user interface, or workplace shell, has a strong object-oriented design where almost everything is treated as an object, including icons, folders, applications, and files. Applications programs can take advantage of the graphical user interface in presenting their own interface.

- **High Performance File System (HPFS).** The HPFS is a file-management system unique to OS/2. It offers better file-naming features, faster disk access, and up to 64K of extended attributes per file.

- **32-Bit APIs.** New Application Programming Interfaces (APIs) support 32-bit applications; while many APIs are essentially the same as their 16-bit equivalents, comprehensive changes have been made in others.

S E C R E T

Some calculation-intensive programs will not run if they cannot detect the presence of a floating-point coprocessor. OS/2 contains a virtual math coprocessor in the form of code that emulates, or mimics, the performance of an 80387 math (or floating-point) coprocessor. This emulation software is not as fast as that provided by a real 80387, but is certainly appropriate for occasional or experimental use in either an OS/2 or in a DOS session. However, if the application program explicitly asks whether a coprocessor is present, OS/2 tells the truth, and returns a "no" value to the program.

All OS/2 applications execute as protected-mode processes, and are provided with preemptive multitasking and full memory protection; this means that all applications are isolated from each other and also from the operating system itself.

Starting OS/2 Programs from the Desktop

Starting OS/2 programs is easy once you understand how to use the desktop. Just double-click the appropriate program object, and the program will start running in its own window. If you want the application to use the whole screen, click the maximize button in the top-right corner of the original window.

The exact procedure depends on the currently active view. Figure 5.1 shows all three views, Icon View, Tree View, and Details View, for drive C.

FIGURE 5.1

The contents of drive C shown as an icon view, a tree view, and a details view

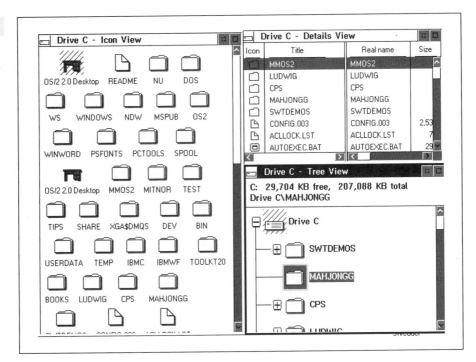

Using the Icon View is straightforward enough; it is usually the default view, and works like the desktop. Just double-click the icon to start the program. If you use the Tree or Details View for a drive folder, you must first use the scroll bars to find the folder that contains the program you want. Then, double-click the folder to open its window, and choose the program object you want to start. In the Details View, you can double-click on any of the columns to open this window.

You can also select the object you want, then use the Open selection from the pop-up menu followed by the Program option to start the program running. Right-click the object to open its pop-up menu.

Another way to start an application is by double-clicking a data object you've associated with the application; this opens the data object (letter, memo, or data file) and simultaneously starts the associated program. You can associate a single data object, all data objects of a specific type, or all data objects with a specific extension with an application program. See the heading "Associating Objects" in Chapter 2 for more information on how this works.

You can also start an application by typing its file name at the OS/2 command prompt. Open the OS/2 System folder on the desktop, then open the Command Prompts folder. Now you can choose between the OS/2 Window icon or the OS/2 Full Screen icon to start your command-line session. More on using the command line in a moment.

To close an application, click its title-bar icon to open the menu, then choose the Close selection. You can also type Alt+F4 or double-click the title-bar icon to close the application.

You can switch from window to window by using the selections in the Window List, by pressing Alt+Tab, or by using the Minimized Window Viewer, described in Chapter 2. To switch to the next window or full-screen session, press Alt+Esc, and to switch between a window and a help window, press Alt+F6.

If you work with a Local Area Network (LAN), you will see a Network folder on your desktop. This folder contains all the network objects that you can access. To log in to the network, right-click to open the object's pop-up menu and select Login. Then enter the password information assigned to you by your network administrator. If you plan to leave your system unattended for a period of time, do not stay logged in to the network; open the Network folder pop-up menu and select Logout to leave the network.

Starting OS/2 Programs from the OS/2 Command Line

To access the OS/2 command line from the desktop, open the OS/2 System folder, then open the Command Prompts folder. Double-click either the OS/2 Window icon or the OS/2 Full Screen icon, depending on the type of session you want to start.

To start a program running from the OS/2 command prompt, you usually have to change to the appropriate directory, unless this directory is already specified by the current PATH statement, and then just type the name of the executable file. The program runs, and when you exit from the program, you return to the OS/2 system prompt again.

N O T E

If you try to start an OS/2 application from a DOS session command prompt, the program will politely refuse to start, and you will see an error message such as *This program requires OS/2 Presentation Manager.*

Customizing an OS/2 Session Environment

There are a couple of tricks you can use to customize the environment of an individual OS/2 session for a particular application. The system settings established by CONFIG.SYS are used as default settings for all sessions, but you can change these setting if you wish. You can change them individually from the command line, or you can use a batch (CMD) file that contains special SET commands tailored exactly to the needs of your application. You can also use the same batch file to start the application program running if you wish.

For example, to add a new directory to the existing PATH statement, use:

```
SET PATH=E:\MYPROG;%PATH%
```

in your batch file or from the command prompt.

> ## SECRET

In OS/2, the dot (.) can be used in a SET PATH, SET DPATH, SET HELP, or SET BOOKSHELF statement to indicate the current directory. For example, if you use:

SET PATH=.\MYPROG;C:.;%PATH%

OS/2 first searches for an executable file in the current directory of the session. If the file is not found, the search continues through the subdirectory MYPROG, then the current directory of drive C, and finally all the other directories specified in the previous value of the PATH variable for that session.

The dot should also be used with the LIBPATH command in CONFIG.SYS, but because this command does not establish an environment variable, it cannot be set from the command line.

The LIBPATH statement in CONFIG.SYS tells OS/2 where to look for the system and application DLLs (more on DLLs in a moment), and the dot tells OS/2 to search the current directory first. If the dot is left out, OS/2 will not search there for a DLL, and you will see an error message if it can't find the correct DLL in any of the other directories in the LIBPATH statement.

A typical batch file used to set specific environment variables and then start an application program could have the following general structure:

Establish current directories

SET any required environment variables

Start the application running. Use the name of the executable file, followed by any command-line parameters you want to pass to the program

EXIT

Listing 5.1 shows a batch file that uses this kind of structure to change its environment and then start an application program running.

LISTING 5.1

A batch file that uses
SET commands

```
:REM CHANGE TO DRIVE D

D:
CD D:\MYPROGS

:REM ADD THIS DIRECTORY TO THE CURRENT PATH
SET PATH=D:\MYPROGS;%PATH%

:REM SET THE HELP
SET HELP=.\APPLIC\HELP;

:REM SET THE BOOKSHELF
SET BOOKSHELF=.\APPLIC\BOOK;

:REM START THE PROGRAM
PROGEXE
EXIT
```

> ## S E C R E T

If you want to start OS/2 in text mode at the OS/2 system prompt, rather than at the desktop, use the Enhanced Editor to change the line in your CONFIG.SYS file that reads:

　　SET RUNWORKPLACE=C:\OS2\PMSHELL.EXE

to read

　　SET RUNWORKPLACE=C:\OS2\CMD.EXE

and then shut down and restart your system. When OS/2 restarts after this change, you will find yourself at the OS/2 command prompt rather than the desktop. The only problem with using this technique is that you cannot shut down your system from the command line.

To get back to the desktop so that you can shut down OS/2, type:

　　PMSHELL

at the OS/2 system prompt, and shut down in the usual way using the desktop pop-up menu Shut Down selection.

OS/2 and Dynamic Link Libraries (DLLs)

In Chapter 1, I said that OS/2 uses Dynamic Link Libraries for optimization and to save space, but what are DLLs, exactly? There are two kinds of executable files in OS/2: the familiar EXE modules for programs, and DLL modules, which contain shared libraries. Dynamic linking allows the linking of code to be delayed until the program is loaded, or until the program asks to be linked to a specific DLL.

In this way, code that is common to several programs can be removed from an EXE file, where it can only be accessed by a single program, and placed in a DLL, where it can be loaded and unloaded by all the applications that need access to that code. By contrast, in conventional *static linking*, all libraries are bound into the executable file as a part of the compilation stage of software development; and so several applications may need to contain the same code.

Using DLLs means that executable files can be smaller and can load faster, because common code is removed from EXE files and is placed in DLL files instead.

In many operating systems, most of the code is contained in the kernel, the central core of the operating system, but one of the design goals of the OS/2 development team was to make OS/2 easily extensible. They accomplished this goal by using DLLs; these units can be added, removed, or updated very easily, without affecting any of the code in the kernel, and without requiring the kernel to be recompiled or relinked.

Dynamic Data Exchange and Object Linking and Embedding in OS/2

Dynamic Data Exchange (DDE) is a mechanism in OS/2 that allows two independent application programs to exchange information. This allows you to set up a *link* between different data files, and as the information in one file is updated or changed, the other linked file will be updated automatically, without any intervention or action on your part. For example, if you link a spreadsheet file to a word processor file using DDE, any changes you make to the spreadsheet file automatically appear in the word processor file. DDE exchanges work with any combination of OS/2 and Windows programs, and can increase productivity tremendously; now you don't have to remember to make your changes in all your files, just leave it up to DDE.

Microsoft has taken this concept further, and created a new specification called Object Linking and Embedding (OLE). OLE extends DDE, and allows you to embed an *object* and its associated source application information in the linked document. When you select an embedded object, the application originally used to create the object starts, and the object is loaded ready for editing. For example, a drawing program using OLE can exchange text with a word processor, and can use the word processor's editing features on text embedded in a drawing.

The only limitation to OLE would arise when, for example, the drawing is moved to a computer that does not have the word processor used to create the embedded text object. You could still look at the embedded object, but not edit or change it.

OS/2 supports OLE between Windows programs running in a single WIN-OS/2 session, but does not support OLE between Windows programs running in individual WIN-OS/2 sessions, or between OS/2 programs and Windows programs. Full OLE support has been promised for future versions of OS/2.

Making OS/2 Version 2.X Look Like Version 1.3

The designers of OS/2 version 2.1 have made the operating system so flexible that you can even make it look like an earlier version of OS/2 if you are particularly attached to the version 1.3 user interface. Version 2.0 or 2.1 must already be installed on your system before you try this transformation.

The OS/2 2.X desktop does not include a Desktop Manager, a File Manager, a Print Manager, or a Control Panel as in earlier versions; these elements all disappeared with the arrival of OS/2 2.0. Now everything you need is displayed in one convenient location, the desktop, and there is no need to switch between these managers to perform tasks. However, if you want to give your version of OS/2 2.1 an OS/2 1.3 look, you can, but remember, this process does not change version 2.1 into version 1.3, so there will undoubtedly be some confusing inconsistencies. Back up your current INI files before you try this procedure, just in case things go wrong.

► S O L U T I O N

To make OS/2 version 2.1 look like OS/2 version 1.3, put your OS/2 Installation Disk into drive A, and turn on or restart your computer. When the logo screen appears, remove the Installation Disk and insert Disk 1 into drive A. When you see the Welcome screen, press the Escape key to jump to the OS/2 command prompt; then remove Disk 1 from the drive.

Change to the hard disk that contains OS/2, often drive C, and then change to the OS/2 directory by typing:

```
CD\OS2
```

Modify the current user INI file by typing:

    MAKEINI OS2.INI OS2_13.RC

and press Enter. Wait for a successful completion message, then restart the operating system.

If you want to return to the 2.1 desktop look, follow the steps described above, but change the last command as follows:

    MAKEINI OS2.INI OS2_20.RC

press Enter, and restart the system once again.

When the transformation to OS/2 1.3 is complete, you will see the Desktop Manager and the Main group window both displaying icons in a menu list. The DOS compatibility box, used to run DOS applications, is available on the desktop, as is an icon for the OS/2 2.1 desktop. You can switch to the 2.1 desktop by selecting this icon.

After you change back to the real 2.1 desktop using the MAKEINI command again, you will now find you have one more icon on the desktop than you had before. This new icon represents the OS/2 1.3 desktop, and you can use this icon to switch to the 1.3 look. After you have done this, right-click on an empty part of the desktop and choose Close when you are ready to return to the 2.1 desktop.

Guidelines for Installing New OS/2 Programs

At some point, the time will come when you will want to install new OS/2 application programs on your system. This section offers some general guidelines on how best to approach this apparently simple task.

Maintaining CONFIG.SYS

The CONFIG.SYS file sets default environment values for every session running under OS/2. These environment values include system and user variables such as PATH, DPATH, HELP, PROMPT and BOOKSHELF, drive and directory information, and even information on remote Local Area Network (LAN) drives.

You establish user variables with a SET command. It may be placed inside CONFIG.SYS, to set the value for all sessions, or in a batch (.CMD) file, or issued from the OS/2 command prompt. To see the present value of all system and user environment variables, type SET from the OS/2 system prompt.

Most applications' installation programs suggest modifying your CONFIG.SYS file to include their specific requirements; this allows the application to be used in any session, because CONFIG.SYS sets the system-wide defaults. The downside is that CONFIG.SYS can become overburdened with unnecessarily long PATH statements containing many directories. If you remove a program because you no longer use it, or have decided to recover that disk space for some other purpose, you also have to remember to remove the corresponding statements from CONFIG.SYS. Finally, different installation programs use different methods of changing CONFIG.SYS. Some programs copy the current version of the file to a new name, CONFIG.OLD, or CONFIG.BAK perhaps, but if that file already exists, it gets overwritten and therefore disappears.

► S O L U T I O N

Before you install a program, create a directory called BACKUP or ROOT; the name doesn't matter, just as long as you remember it. Now copy your current CONFIG.SYS file into this directory, and rename the file CONFIG.*nnn*, where *nnn* is a simple sequence number. Repeat this operation before you install each new program. The first copy will be CONFIG.001, the second CONFIG.002, and so on. This will give you a complete history of CONFIG.SYS files, and you can organize them by this sequence number.

It also makes good sense to copy all your INI files and the file STARTUP.CMD into this directory as a safety measure.

Organizing Your Hard Disks

Installation of OS/2 is fully covered in Appendix A, but a few remarks about system organization are appropriate at this point.

There are several classes of file connected with any application; the system files that comprise the operating system, the files that make up the application program package, and the data files created by that application. Here's how to organize them:

- **OS/2 System Files.** Keep all the operating system files on drive C; it does not matter if drive C is a physical or a logical drive. Grouping these files together makes upgrading easier. Also, if you want to install more than one operating system on your computer, you can isolate the files from each one on a different drive, or on a different partition, if you are using the OS/2 Boot Manager. See Appendix A for a complete discussion of how to install more than one operating system on your computer.

- **Application Files.** Each application should be located in its own separate directory. Again, this makes upgrading or removing the package easy. The only exception to this rule might be a small utility program that consists of a single executable file. Place this kind of program in a directory close to the beginning of the PATH statement, rather than in its own directory.

- **Data Files.** Data files and application configuration files should likewise be placed in their own directory, usually immediately below their parent application directory.

By following these simple recommendations, you will minimize any maintenance or program-removal problems you might encounter in the future.

Figure 5.2 shows part of a well-ordered hard disk, where each application is contained in its own directory. Some applications, such as Galleria, have additional subdirectories specifically for user-created and temporary information.

FIGURE 5.2

Part of the directory
structure of a
well-organized
Hard Disk

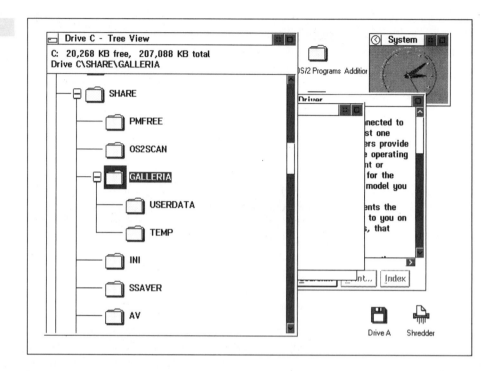

OS/2 Compared to Other Personal Computer Operating Systems

OS/2 is just one of the operating systems available to run on Intel-based computer systems. This brief section discusses some of the other operating systems available, and shows how they compare with OS/2.

MS-DOS

MS-DOS is a single-tasking, single-threaded operating system that runs on Intel processors in real mode. It provides no protection, so that errant programs can corrupt important structures such as the file allocation table, or the boot track on the hard disk, as well as interfere with the running of the operating system itself. MS-DOS does not enforce or require user interface standards, so all application programs have to manage this function themselves. This has led to a huge number of variations in interface design, as well as some notable lawsuits where one company claims that another has illegally taken advantage of the "look and feel" of an application interface.

MS-DOS's major advantage is that it is ubiquitous; it is available everywhere in the world, in English and in many different foreign languages. Over 100 million IBM and compatible systems in use today run a version of MS-DOS, or IBM's own version, PC-DOS. In the 12 years or so that it has been available, tens of thousands of applications have been developed. This all adds up to a very compelling reason why OS/2 must provide complete DOS compatibility.

Windows 3.1

Microsoft Windows is not really an operating system, it is an application program running on top of MS-DOS; however, it is fair to call the combination of MS-DOS and Windows an *operating environment*. Initial versions of Windows were slow and unwieldy, and very few applications were available in the early days. All that changed with the release of Windows 3.0.

Windows 3.0 and later versions attempt to correct some of the weaknesses of MS-DOS; chiefly they provide a standardized graphical user interface, and the ability to cooperatively multitask Windows programs. See Chapter 13 for a full discussion of multitasking in OS/2.

Windows unfortunately cannot escape many of the original MS-DOS limitations, such as the 8.3 file-naming convention, poor application protection, and the often complex tuning of EMS, XMS, and DPMI memory when switching between operating environments.

Windows NT

Microsoft Windows NT (for New Technology) is a full-featured operating system that can be compared with OS/2 in terms of power and features for certain applications. Windows NT is aimed at large network file servers and engineering workstations rather than the more traditional desktop users. Like OS/2, Windows NT is designed to be a portable operating system and is initially targeted at three very different microprocessor architectures; Intel-based, MIPS R4000-based, and DEC Alpha-based.

Many of the advanced features of Windows NT are of little interest to most OS/2 users. For example, it is certifiable at the U. S. Government C-2 level, and it adds another file system, NTFS, along with FAT and HPFS. NTFS allows for *transaction rollback*, which allows incomplete transactions to be removed or undone in the event of a system failure. NT also contains peer-to-peer networking, and supports Symmetric Multi-Processing (SMP), which allows individual threads in a program to execute on different processors in a multi-processor computer.

As Windows NT is so new, hardware requirements in terms of memory and hard disk space are still evolving, but they are likely to be large, and to grow even larger as the operating system matures.

Unix

The Unix operating system has been available for many years and in certain market sectors it is very well understood and well liked. Unix is a multiuser, multitasking operating system, originally developed by a small group of programmers working at Bell Labs in the early 1970s. Some users complain that the traditional user interface, a command line known as a shell, is bleak and unforgiving; others delight in the fast and cryptic commands. More recently, two sets of graphical user interfaces, Motif and Open Look, have emerged as standards.

Many slightly different versions of Unix are available, and in many ways this has slowed its acceptance. However, Unix is available from the Santa Cruz Operation for Intel-based systems, and several other major companies have Intel-based versions of Unix in the pipeline, including Sun, NeXT, and Novell.

Macintosh

The Macintosh was the first commercially-available computer to offer a version of the graphical user interface developed by researchers working at Xerox's Palo Alto Research Center (PARC). The current version of the operating system, System 7, offers a consistent user interface (there is no equivalent of the OS/2 command line) across applications, as well as cooperative multitasking. The major drawback to the operating system is that it is only available on specific Apple-licensed hardware.

Pink

In 1991 Apple and IBM began a joint agreement to develop an object-oriented operating system that has become known as "Pink". This project is under development at a company called Taligent, owned by both Apple and IBM, and is aimed at the new PowerPC made by both companies. Pink is currently expected sometime during 1994.

The design of Pink is said to encompass:

- A high degree of portability to other hardware
- Support for multiple Application Programming Interfaces (API's) so that you can run MS-DOS, Windows NT, Unix, Macintosh, and OS/2 applications on the same system, all at the same time.
- Advanced object-oriented design

How Pink and OS/2 fit together into IBM's future operating system strategy has not yet been made public.

The Future of OS/2

A future version of OS/2 might include a microkernel based on the Mach kernel developed at Carnegie-Mellon University. It might also include Symmetric Multi-Processing support, add C-2 level security, and perhaps include some component of Pink. Future versions of OS/2 will be available for Intel- and IBM-based architectures.

OS/2 Applications

Applications specifically written for OS/2 can exploit all the advanced features of the operating system, and OS/2 version 2.X 32-bit applications will almost certainly be faster than their 16-bit counterparts.

Most of the popular MS-DOS and Windows applications are available in 32-bit OS/2 versions, including Lotus 1-2-3, cc:Mail, Notes, and AmiPro from Lotus Development Corporation; WordPerfect from WordPerfect Corporation; PageMaker from Aldus Corporation and all the applications from Micrografx Inc.

SOLUTION

The IBM NSC Bulletin Board at 404-835-6600 maintains an on-line product database of OS/2 software. A directory of OS/2 applications, IBM document G362-0029-02, is also available from Graphics Plus, Inc, at 640 Knowlton Street, Bridgeport, CT 06608 or 800-786-PLUS. Over 1000 new 32-bit OS/2 applications were available by the end of 1992.

Programming languages and application generators available for OS/2 include Assembler, BASIC, C, C++, Cobol, Forth, Fortran, LISP, Modula-2, ObjectVision, Pascal, Smalltalk, as well as REXX, which is included with every copy of OS/2. Language translators such as f2c (Fortran to C) and p2c (Pascal to C), and Computer Assisted Software Engineering (CASE) systems are also available. These computer language products are available from companies such as IBM, Borland International, Clarion, WATCOM Products, Inc, Zortech, Microway, and many others.

OS/2-specific versions of popular file compression programs such as PKZIP/PKUNZIP, ARC, and LHA are also available from many of the OS/2 bulletin boards listed in Appendix B.

Finally, a large number of Unix utilities have been translated or *ported* to OS/2; many of them are available from bulletin boards. Also, the Hamilton C Shell is available from Hamilton Labs at 508-358-5715 as an alternative to the usual OS/2 command processor; and a Bourne shell and awk (a programming language designed to manipulate text files named after its developers Aho, Weinberger and Kernighan) are both available from Thompson Automation at 206-224-1639.

Notes on OS/2 Application Compatibility

Following are some notes about the compatibility of certain programs with OS/2. The information is version-specific; later versions of these programs may work with no problems. Fixes or workarounds are noted when available.

Aldus PageMaker

When in SVGA mode, pasting a bit map into this program can produce a blank screen or an incorrect black-and-white bit map.

Arts & Letters Composer

If you copy a portion of an image as a metafile, it may not be visible when you view the clipboard in both VGA and Tseng ET4000 SVGA. However, this works correctly for XGA mode.

In SVGA mode, if you stretch or flip a bit map pasted from the clipboard, you may get a program trap in the Tseng ET4000 and XGA display resolution.

AutoCAD

Some of the background colors can be set to very pale colors that may not show up well on XGA displays.

CorelDRAW 2.0

If you do a large amount of printing while using CorelDRAW, you may run out of memory. You should save your work and exit CorelDRAW from time to time to avoid this problem.

In SVGA mode, you may see that status words and coordinate text under the action bar menus of client windows are blacked out.

Describe

If you use the hollow attribute for a letter when in SVGA mode, the letter will not display.

If you insert text at the end of a document using SVGA mode, the text at the end of the input line may be corrupted. This is easy to fix; just scroll up and down to force the screen to be repainted.

When printing TIF graphics image files using SVGA mode, you may find that the printout is skewed.

Designer

Install the Designer file MIRRORS.DLL in the Designer program directory, not in the C:\OS2\DLL directory, and start the program from this directory. This conflict arises because both OS/2 and Designer use a dynamic link library with the same name but radically different functions.

DynaComm Asynchronous OS/2

The dynamic link library (DLL) files included with this program must be installed in a different directory than the one used by the program executable file. Add this new directory to the end of the LIBPATH statement in your CONFIG.SYS file before using the program.

Lotus Freelance Graphics for OS/2

If you have installation problems with this program, contact Lotus Development Corporation for a fix. Alternatively, you can download the file FLGOS2.ZIP from the IBM bulletin board or from the IBMFILES section on CompuServe, or download INSTAL.ZIP from the LOTUS section of CompuServe.

If you have problems with the colors used in the program, change the palette using the program menus. A set of new default palettes is also available from the OS2 Support forum (library 17, IBMFILES) on CompuServe as PALETT.ZIP, or from the IBM bulletin board as the same file name. See Appendix B for information on CompuServe, and other bulletin boards.

Lotus Notes

To use Lotus Notes Version 2.X, you must delete the file QNC.EXE from the Notes program directory.

Microsoft Excel for OS/2 3.0

You should avoid using the Help index and the Keyboard Help windows as they do not operate correctly.

Microsoft Word

There are occasional problems when selecting items from the application menu, and the application appears to freeze. There is a fix for this, available if you call the Microsoft support number.

Sidekick

A printer must be installed and present on the desktop to use the Notepad in Sidekick.

Soft Term

The first time that a drive is changed in the Send or Receive windows, the Directory window does not update properly; after the first time, the Directory window works fine.

OS/2 OS/2 OS/2

OS/2 OS/2 OS/2 OS/2 OS/2 OS/2 OS/2 OS/2 OS/2

OS/2 OS/2 OS/2 O

6

Running DOS Programs under OS/2

THERE are more DOS applications in use throughout the world than any other type of application. Complete and thorough support for these applications has always been a high priority for the OS/2 designers, because DOS support was absolutely necessary for OS/2's continuing commercial success. In fact, many users may begin using OS/2 as a way to multitask their DOS applications.

OS/2 runs DOS programs by *emulating* DOS; in other words, a part of the OS/2 operating system software looks and works just like MS-DOS. (In order to keep this distinction clear, this book refers to Microsoft's standalone operating system as *MS-DOS* and the emulation that you run under OS/2 as *DOS*.) For most purposes, this emulation is complete, but there are some programs that may not run as you expect them to, or even refuse to run altogether. OS/2 contains over 40 DOS Settings you can use to tune your DOS session. You must set the following settings before you begin the DOS session; the other settings you can change at any time.

> COM_HOLD
>
> DOS_AUTOEXEC
>
> DOS_BREAK
>
> DOS_DEVICE
>
> DOS_FCBS
>
> DOS_FCBS_KEEP
>
> DOS_HIGH
>
> DOS_LASTDRIVE
>
> DOS_RMSIZE
>
> DOS_SHELL
>
> DOS_STARTUP_DRIVE

DOS_UMB

DPMI_DOS_API

DMPI_MEMORY_LIMIT

DMPI_NETWORK_BUFF_SIZE

EMS_FRAME_LOCATION

EMS_HIGH_OS_MAP_REGION

EMS_LOW_OS_MAP_REGION

EMS_MEMORY_LIMIT

HW_ROM_TO_RAM

INT_DURING_IO

MEM_EXCLUDE_REGIONS

MEM_INCLUDE_REGIONS

VIDEO_MODE_RESTRICTION

VIDEO_8514_XGA_IOTRAP

XMS_HANDLES

XMS_MEMORY_LIMIT

XMS_MINIMUM_HMA

You might need a specific version of MS-DOS to run a particular program that does not run well under OS/2's DOS emulation. If you have a bootable floppy disk containing the right version of MS-DOS, you can use the object called DOS from Drive A in the Command Prompts folder on the desktop to start this version as a separate DOS session. Alternatively, you can run the program from what is called an image file.

This chapter looks at all these topics. It describes how you can use the DOS settings to customize your DOS sessions, and includes some notes on problems that DOS programs may experience under OS/2.

Is OS/2 a Better DOS than DOS?

OS/2 is designed to exploit all the capabilities of the Intel 80386 (and later) processors. A major innovation in the 80386 is support for the execution of multiple 8086 tasks in the 80386 protected mode environment. An 8086 task in this environment is known as a virtual 8086 (V86) task. In OS/2, V86 tasks are implemented as *virtual DOS machines*, or VDMs. Each VDM runs as a single-threaded, protected mode process, and OS/2 controls switching between VDMs in the same way that it controls switching between other OS/2 applications.

DOS applications running in a VDM can:

- Run in full-screen mode or in a window
- Run in a background session and not be suspended
- Use the clipboard to copy text, or copy graphics as a bitmap
- Run graphics in full-screen mode
- Switch between full-screen and window mode

The DOS emulation in OS/2 supports all documented DOS interrupts and features, as well as some lesser-known or undocumented aspects of these functions that popular DOS applications have come to rely on.

Because OS/2 controls this DOS emulation, the system can be optimized for the OS/2 environment. As a result, much more memory is available to DOS applications running under OS/2 than to applications running on native MS-DOS.

DOS emulation in OS/2 provides the following features and support:

- Up to 240 concurrent DOS sessions, either full screen or windowed, with preemptive multitasking.
- Support for other MS-DOS versions, including DOS 3.3, 4.0, 5.0, 6.0, DR DOS, Concurrent DOS, and other 8086 operating systems.

- Customized DOS version numbers.

- Full protection between applications and operating system. An errant DOS application cannot bring down the whole OS/2 operating system.

- Increased conventional memory space, in excess of 630K, to a maximum of 730K.

- LIM EMS 4.0 support for up to 32MB memory.

- XMS 2.0 support for up to 16MB memory.

- DPMI support for up to 512MB memory.

- Individual AUTOEXEC.BAT files for specific sessions.

- Session-by-session loading of device drivers.

Installing New DOS Programs

Many of the caveats in Chapter 5 on installing OS/2 programs also apply to installing DOS programs. Programs modify CONFIG.SYS or AUTO-EXEC.BAT, often to change the PATH statement to include newly created directories; and sometimes they do this without even telling you what they are doing. It makes good sense to implement some kind of systemized backup of these two files, as described in Chapter 5, so that you can recover or rebuild them if they are changed in a way that causes problems.

Also, if a new device driver is installed in CONFIG.SYS, this driver will be made available to all DOS sessions, and this may not be what you want. See the section on the DOS_DEVICE setting later in this chapter for information on how you can customize a session's device drivers.

To install a new program, first read its installation documentation, then open a DOS Full Screen session. Insert the first floppy disk, and type the appropriate installation instructions at the command prompt. When the installation is complete, close the session, and use the Migrate Applications program (discussed in Chapter 2) to install this new program on the desktop.

Starting DOS Applications

To run an MS-DOS program from the desktop, open the folder that contains your MS-DOS programs, and double-click on the icon that represents the program you want to run. The icon can be on the desktop, or in a folder.

If you open a drive window, you can also double-click an icon that represents an executable DOS file name. OS/2 will start a DOS session, then start the program you chose inside that session.

When you quit the program, you will automatically return to the desktop. You can also return to the desktop by opening the Window List with Ctrl+Esc. If you do this, you will notice that the name of the application you were working with is shown as an entry in the Window List. You can double-click the entry to return to the session.

If you want to work at the DOS system prompt, you can either select an existing session from the Window List or open a new session. You can also use these steps to start a DOS application for which there is no OS/2 desktop icon.

NOTE An OS/2 application can start a DOS application if it includes a DosExecPgm() function call in its code. The DOS application can be started as an independent or a dependent child process of the original OS/2 application.

To start a new DOS session, open the OS/2 System icon on the desktop, and then open the Command Prompts folder. You can choose to run DOS as a window on the desktop by selecting the DOS Window icon, or as a full-screen session by selecting the DOS Full Screen icon. Now you can type the DOS commands or executable file names directly at the DOS command prompt. When you quit the application, you will return to the DOS command prompt rather than directly to the OS/2 desktop. You can use Ctrl+Esc to return to the desktop, and you can use the Window List to go from the desktop back to the DOS session. Depending on the kind of session you originally opened, the entries in the Window List will be DOS Window and DOS Full Screen, respectively. For example, if WordStar is running in a DOS full-screen session, the Window List entry will be DOS Full Screen—WS.EXE.

To close the DOS window, double-click on the icon in the top left corner of the title bar, or type EXIT at the command prompt.

You can also run an OS/2 batch file containing the START command, and any appropriate switches.

Understanding DOS Session Settings

There are many settings you can use to "tune" your DOS or Windows sessions, and they fall into the following groups:

- Keyboard settings
- Memory settings
- Mouse and touch-screen support
- Printer settings
- Video settings
- Other DOS settings
- WIN-OS/2 settings

The sections that follow cover all these groups of settings except those in the final category, WIN-OS/2 settings, which is described in Chapter 7.

To look at or change any of these settings, display the pop-up menu for the object whose setting you want to change by clicking the right mouse button on its icon.

Usually, this will be either the DOS Window or the DOS Full Screen icon in the Command Prompts folder. Click on the arrow to the right of the Open command, select Settings, then click on the Sessions tab, and you will see the window shown in Figure 6.1.

FIGURE 6.1

The Session Page of the DOS Settings Notebook

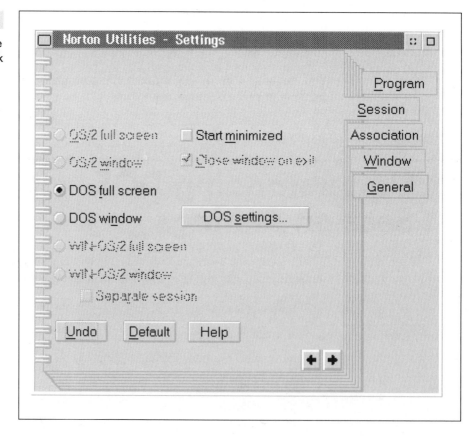

The left side of the window contains three pairs of settings for OS/2, DOS, and WIN-OS/2 sessions, and whether a WIN-OS/2 session is run as a separate session. (This figure is specific to a particular DOS object; other screens will show different defaults and disabled options.) On the right, you will see the following options:

- Start Minimized selects whether a session begins in the foreground or in the background. By default, this option is not set.

- Close Window on Exit determines whether the session terminates when the application exits to DOS; this option is set by default.

The DOS Settings button is used to access a list of the current values of the settings for the type of DOS session you selected. This list is displayed in the window shown in Figure 6.2.

FIGURE 6.2

DOS Session Settings

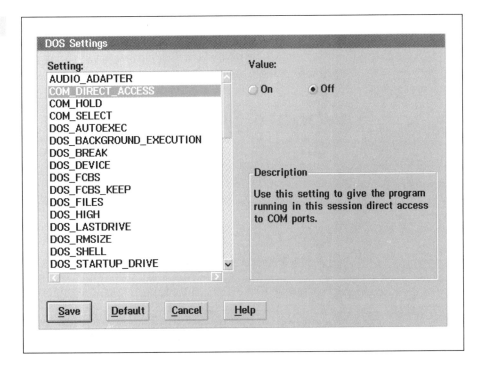

Even though many of these settings have text descriptions associated with them, many are poorly understood, and in the sections that follow I will list the various options or permissible range of values available for each setting. To make a change, first choose the setting from the list on the left side of the window, then make the appropriate selection from the options shown on the right. These choices may include a radio button, a slider, or text input depending on the setting you choose. Many DOS and WIN-OS/2 settings should be changed before you start a session; if you change them during a session, the changes will affect only the programs that you run in that session. Exceptions to this rule will be noted as we go though the list.

Information on DOS settings is stored in a database in the OS/2 kernel, and includes information such as the name of the setting, a "standard" value for the setting, the setting type (Boolean, integer, or string), and the name of the help file and help ID number for the setting. This database is managed by OS/2 and is not accessible by the user.

Any settings you change for an open session are *not* saved when you close the session, or when you turn your computer off, even if you use the shut-down procedure.

Keyboard Settings

The following settings control how the keyboard reacts in a DOS session. You can enable or disable certain keystroke combinations and control the type-ahead buffer. You can change any of these settings during an active DOS session.

KBD_ALTHOME_BYPASS
(Alt+Home bypass)

Normally, OS/2 lets you change your session from a full- screen session to a windowed session, and back again, by using the Alt+Home key combination. However, sometimes you may encounter an application program that uses this combination for its own purposes. The default setting is Off, but set KBD_ALTHOME_BYPASS to On if you want OS/2 to ignore this key sequence, and to pass it through to your application program.

KBD_BUFFER_EXTEND (Buffer extension)

DOS stores up to 16 keystrokes in a type-ahead buffer, but by default OS/2 increases the size of this buffer to 128 keystrokes. Not all programs can take advantage of this increase, but for those that can, it improves performance at only a small memory cost. By default, the KBD_BUFFER_EXTEND setting is On. Ctrl+Break will flush the entire buffer, just as it does with the standard buffer.

KBD_CTRL_BYPASS (Ctrl key bypass)

When you press Ctrl+Esc in OS/2, the Window List appears, and when you press Alt+Esc you switch between sessions. Use KBD_CTRL_BYPASS to make OS/2 ignore one of the key sequences so that a DOS or Windows program can use it; the settings are NONE (the default), ALT_ESC, or CTRL_ESC.

The default value for this setting in a WIN-OS/2 full-screen session is CTRL_ESC, which allows the WIN-OS/2 Task List to appear rather than the OS/2 Window List.

KBD_RATE_LOCK (repeat rate lock)

The 8042 keyboard-controller chip, used in the PC/AT and later computers, accepts software instructions to modify the repeat rate (the rate at which a keystroke repeats if you hold down that key) and the delay time of keystrokes. The Keyboard object in the System Setup folder on the desktop lets you adjust these timing features.

Some DOS programs can change the key repeat rate. As the result may not be what you want, you can turn on KBD_RATE_LOCK to stop these applications from changing the repeat rate.

Memory Settings

The settings in this group control how DOS accesses conventional, expanded, and extended memory.

DOS_HIGH (load DOS high)

Use this setting if you want to load the DOS kernel above the 640K memory address, leaving more memory space available for DOS application programs.

Occasionally, a DOS application may need access to DOS internal control structures that require DOS be loaded into low memory, but this is fairly rare.

DOS_RMSIZE (DOS memory size)

This setting determines the amount of conventional memory available for each DOS session. Its initial value is derived from the RMSIZE= entry in your CONFIG.SYS file. If you routinely run many simultaneous DOS sessions, there could be some benefit in reducing this number, especially if you have problems because of memory limitations or swap file size. Also, if your video adapter requires some of the 640K usually available for application programs, you will have to reduce this number. See your hardware manual for more information. The valid range of entries for DOS_RMSIZE is from 128 to 640, in increments of 16.

DOS_UMB
(DOS upper memory blocks)

The range of memory addresses from 640K to 1024K can be divided into upper memory blocks (UMBs). When device drivers and terminate-and-stay-resident programs are loaded into these UMBs, more conventional memory becomes available for application programs. Normally, DOS manages UMBs with DEVICEHIGH and LOADHIGH statements in CONFIG.SYS, but some programs must own UMBs for successful operation; in this case, change this setting to Off.

DPMI_DOS_API

This setting determines whether DOS Protected Mode Interface (DPMI) is available, and if so, whether it is managed automatically. DPMI allows applications to access memory above the normal DOS 640K barrier.

There are three selections available:

- Select AUTO if some of your programs can take advantage of DPMI. OS/2 monitors these programs and selects the appropriate mode.
- Select ENABLED if you use programs that expect the operating system to handle the translation. In this context, *translating* means changing the initial request for memory access from above to below 1MB. Once it is below 1MB, DOS can access and meet the request.
- Select DISABLED if your programs do not use DPMI.

Windows programs expect OS/2 to manage DPMI requests.

DPMI_MEMORY_LIMIT

The DPMI_MEMORY_LIMIT setting specifies the amount of DPMI memory, in MB, available to the session. OS/2 actually reserves this memory, so specifying more memory than a session needs can lead to unexpected swapping and can increase the size of the swap file.

Permissible values range from 0 to 512MB in one megabyte intervals, and the default is 4MB; set the limit to zero if you want to disable DPMI altogether. This setting cannot be changed once the session has started.

DPMI_NETWORK_BUFF_SIZE

This setting specifies the size of the network translation buffer, in K, for DPMI programs in this session. The range of values is from 1 to 64K, and the default is 8K.

If you find that a network-specific Windows program does not run correctly under OS/2, increase this setting, and then restart the Windows session.

EMS_FRAME_LOCATION

You can use this setting to change the location of the 64K memory area used as the Lotus/Intel/Microsoft expanded memory specification (LIM EMS) frame; however, most users will never need to change this setting.

LIM EMS uses a 64K address region known as an *EMS page frame*, through which programs can access expanded memory. You may have to move the frame if your current setting interferes with device drivers or TSR programs. The best option for EMS_FRAME_LOCATION is AUTO, but there are several other alternatives available. These are a series of memory locations shown as hexadecimal addresses, and you should try to find one that is not in use by a hardware adapter, a device driver, or a TSR program.

If the problem is caused by a hardware conflict, you can also use two other DOS settings, MEM_EXCLUDE_REGIONS and MEM_INCLUDE_ REGIONS to specify the addresses that the hardware uses, rather than use EMS_FRAME_LOCATION.

EMS_HIGH_OS_MAP_REGION

Use this setting to adjust the size of an additional expanded memory specification (EMS) region. This setting applies to software that uses the Lotus/Intel/Microsoft expanded memory specification (LIM EMS).

You may notice conflicts between programs that need LIM and device drivers or TRS programs. To solve an expanded-memory address conflict with a device, set EMS_HIGH_OS_MAP_REGION to zero. The field for this setting ranges from 0 to 96K, in increments of 16K; the default is 32K.

EMS_LOW_OS_MAP_REGION

Use this setting if your programs can map additional frame space into conventional memory, and you want to specify the size of the remappable memory available to a session. The default is 384K, and the range of values is from 0 to 576K.

EMS_MEMORY_LIMIT

The EMS_MEMORY_LIMIT specifies the amount of EMS available to the session. Select zero if your program cannot use EMS, otherwise select a value from 0 to 32768K; increments are of 16K at a time, and the default is 2048K. OS/2 does not reserve EMS until a program specifically asks for EMS.

MEM_EXCLUDE_REGIONS

Use this setting to specify regions of memory that EMS/XMS should not use because they are needed for device drivers or other uses. You can specify a starting memory address, in which case a 4K section is excluded, or you can exclude a range of memory addresses if you specify a starting and ending memory address. Enter the addresses as hexadecimal numbers, and if you want to exclude several regions, separate them using commas. By default, this field is empty.

MEM_INCLUDE_REGIONS

This setting is the opposite of the previous setting, and lets you specify memory areas that EMS/XMS can use between 640K and 1MB. You specify the starting address, or one or more address ranges, in the same way as for MEM_EXCLUDE_REGIONS, described above. By default, this setting has the value of RMSIZE.

XMS_HANDLES

Extended memory is allocated in blocks, and each block has a *handle* or unique number associated with it. Use this setting to change the number of handles needed to identify blocks of XMS. Reserving space for a large number of handles may slow down your system.

Values range from 0 to 128 handles, and the default value is 32.

XMS_MEMORY_LIMIT

Use this setting to specify the amount of XMS memory available to the session. The default value of 2048K is appropriate for many programs, but you can increase it to 16,384K (16MB) if necessary. Specifying an unreasonably large amount of memory for XMS_MEMORY_LIMIT can noticeably slow down your system. Check the documentation or the help information that came with your application program for advice on this limit.

XMS_MINIMUM_HMA

Memory between 640K and 1MB—the high memory area (HMA)—can be allocated to a program for use as conventional memory. Only one program can control HMA at a time, and you can use this setting to adjust the minimum allocation size of the HMA. This prevents a small program from reserving HMA and wasting the space that remains between the program size and the total HMA area of slightly less than 64K. The default is 0K, no minimum, which causes OS/2 to assign the whole HMA area to the first program requesting access, and the maximum is 63K.

Only real-mode programs use HMA as conventional memory. If your programs can run in the protected mode specified by DPMI, you do not need this setting.

Mouse and Touch Screen Settings

The following settings determine how the mouse or a touch-sensitive screen will behave.

MOUSE_EXCLUSIVE_ACCESS

OS/2 provides the mouse pointer for both OS/2 and DOS sessions. Occasionally, you will encounter a DOS program that tries to manage the mouse directly, and when this happens, you may see two mouse pointers at the same time. If that happens, turn MOUSE_EXCLUSIVE_AC-CESS on. Then, when you click a mouse button in the DOS session or window, the pointer provided by OS/2 will disappear. Press Alt, Ctrl+Esc, or Shift+Esc to turn the OS/2 pointer on again.

WordPerfect 5.1 provides its own block-shaped mouse pointer, which can appear along with the OS/2 system mouse pointer. Turning MOUSE_EXCLUSIVE_ACCESS on lets you remove the system mouse pointer when using WordPerfect.

TOUCH_EXCLUSIVE_ACCESS

Turn this setting on if you use a touch-sensitive display, such as the IBM PS/2 8516 Touch Display, and a program running in a DOS window does not respond as you expect when you touch the display. This setting is not needed for a program running in a full-screen session.

Printer Settings

The following settings determine how your system prints.

PRINT_SEPARATE_OUTPUT

This setting, new in OS/2 version 2.1, lets you separate the printer output coming from two or more DOS programs running in the same session into individual spool files so that their output is not mixed together. The separation of data into individual spool files occurs when:

- The DOS session ends.
- The DOS application ends.
- You press the Ctrl+Alt+PrtScrn keys all at the same time.
- The time limit set by PRINT_TIMEOUT expires.

The default setting for PRINT_SEPARATE_OUTPUT is On, which separates the printer output into distinct spool files.

PRINT_TIMEOUT

PRINT_TIMEOUT specifies the number of seconds you want to elapse before information is sent from a DOS program to a print spool file.

Because MS-DOS is a single-tasking operating system, information to be printed can go directly to the printer. OS/2, however, can multitask several programs, and therefore must manage printing very carefully to avoid collisions. The OS/2 print spooler handles this chore, and coordinates all the print jobs from all applications. After some specified period of time, during which the spool file does not grow any larger, OS/2 sends the information to the printer as a single, complete, print job. Some

MS-DOS programs may neglect to tell the spooler that they have finished printing until you exit from the program; this means that output from two or more programs may be mingled together.

If your DOS session print jobs are being divided into more than one print file, increase the value for PRINT_TIMEOUT. The default is 15 seconds, and the valid range is from 0 to 3600 seconds. OS/2 will close the spool file if nothing has been added to the file for the number of seconds specified by PRINT_TIMEOUT.

A value of 1 to 2 seconds is usually appropriate for small print jobs, such as printing the screen. When printing large files, formatting complex documents with desktop publishing programs, or running calculations, however, the value must be big enough to allow all print information to reach the spooler before the timeout expires. If the timeout does expire, you will see your information output through two or three separate spool files; increase PRINT_TIMEOUT further to avoid this.

Video Settings

The following settings manage video resources and determine the behavior of the video hardware on your system.

VIDEO_8514A_XGA_IOTRAP

NOTE   This setting applies only to 8514/A or extended graphics array (XGA) adapters.

Set VIDEO_8514A_XGA_IOTRAP to Off if you want your DOS program to access the 8514/A or XGA video directly. The program may run faster, and you can reuse the 1 MB of memory reserved for storing video information for a DOS session. However, when VIDEO_8514A_XGA_IOTRAP is turned off, you cannot copy information from that session to the OS/2 clipboard, nor can you view the program from a window.

If you have this setting Off, and then leave and return to your program, the screen image may not be correct. To fix this problem, set

VIDEO_SWITCH_NOTIFICATION to On; this tells your DOS application to redraw the screen when you return to the program.

When you're using Windows with the 8514/A display driver, certain operations such as painting dithered backgrounds will run significantly faster with VIDEO_8514A_XGA_IOTRAP set to On.

VIDEO_FASTPASTE

Unlike the other video-related settings, VIDEO_FASTPACE has to do with character transfer rather than setting a video parameter.

Use this setting to speed up input from devices other than the keyboard, such as text pasted to or from the clipboard. Unfortunately, doing so can cause problems for programs that cannot handle the fast delivery of a large number of pasted characters. If you think that characters are being lost in the transfer, make sure this setting is Off.

This setting can be changed at any time, so you can easily experiment with different applications. The default value is Off.

VIDEO_MODE_RESTRICTION

This setting restricts your video adapter to monochrome or CGA-level performance, and frees up memory for application use.

If your program can run at a CGA-equivalent level, with 640 × 200 monochrome graphics, 320 × 200 4-color graphics, and 80 × 25 16-color text, select CGA from the list, and your program will have an additional 64K of conventional memory.

If your program does not use graphics, and can run entirely in monochrome, select MONO and the program will gain 96K of conventional memory.

WARNING

If you choose one of these settings, do not enable a higher-resolution video mode, because the program might write video information all over your data, destroying the data in the process.

OS/2 supports both of these modes, but they are pretty grim to use for any length of time, and are not really recommended for extended use.

VIDEO_ONDEMAND_MEMORY (On-demand memory allocation)

This setting tells OS/2 to use memory space to store a video image only when it becomes necessary, and not before. This frees memory for other applications and allows applications to load faster.

When you switch a DOS application into the background, OS/2 stores the current video image in memory, so that it can restore the image to the screen when you switch the program into the foreground again. Table 6.1 lists the amount of memory needed to store an image from each of the commonly used video modes.

OS/2 does not allocate the free RAM needed to save a copy of the full-screen video image until you switch away from the application. If you end the session rather than switch out of it, that memory won't be needed.

TABLE 6.1: Memory Requirements for Different Video Modes

MODE	REQUIRED MEMORY(K)
80 × 25 text	4
80 × 43 text (EGA only)	7
80 × 50 text (VGA only)	8
CGA graphics	16
EGA graphics	56
VGA graphics	256
super VGA graphics	256 to 1024
XGA graphics	1024

VIDEO_RETRACE_EMULATION

OS/2 keeps track of all the current sessions running simultaneously on the system; these sessions may be running in different video modes, and may be using different color palettes, but OS/2 manages all these differences as you switch between sessions.

Keeping track of all the video modes in use does add a slight performance penalty, and if you turn the setting for VIDEO_RETRACE_EMULA-TION Off, you can speed up certain programs. VIDEO_RETRACE_EMULATION, when set to On, simulates the retrace signals originally generated by your monitor hardware. The downside is that turning the emulation off can cause some sessions to be improperly restored; you may see a blank screen, or the color palette may be altered.

You can change this setting at any time, so if you see a blank screen on a DOS application in full-screen mode, experiment with this setting.

VIDEO_ROM_EMULATION

In many cases, the functions contained in video read-only memory (ROM) can be performed faster from RAM, and OS/2 contains several 32-bit video functions to take advantage of this. You will probably see a dramatic performance boost if you run a windowed session with VIDEO_ROM_EMULATION turned on. However, if you use special software that takes advantage of proprietary functions built into your video hardware, make sure this setting is Off.

This setting can be changed at any time during a session.

VIDEO_SWITCH_NOTIFICATION
(Screen-switch notification)

When this setting is turned On, applications are told when they switch to or from full-screen mode, and this causes them to redraw their screens. WIN-OS/2 sessions can use this notification, as can applications written to the MS-DOS Task Switcher API. Select On if the OS/2 video driver cannot support all the features on your video adapter that are used by your DOS programs.

You should also set VIDEO_SWITCH_NOTIFICATION to On if you use VIDEO_ONDEMAND_MEMORY, because concurrent buffer allocation and screen switching can blank the screen.

This setting can be changed at any time.

VIDEO_WINDOW_REFRESH (Window refresh interval)

VIDEO_WINDOW_REFRESH is relevant only to a windowed DOS session. This parameter sets the window update rate, in tenths of seconds, from the default of 0.1 seconds to 60.0 seconds. Slowing the refresh rate can provide more time to the operating system and other tasks, but slowing it down too much can render the application virtually useless; menus open sluggishly, and the screen looks jerky.

This setting can be changed at any time, so you can test the impact on your session as you tune the setting value. Try using the DIR command or the TYPE command on a text file to see the effects of changing this setting.

Other DOS Settings

This section covers communications settings as well as several other miscellaneous DOS-session settings.

AUDIO_ADAPTER

This setting controls how DOS and WIN-OS/2 sessions use your audio adapter or sound card. There are three self-explanatory choices in the Value field for this setting:

- Use only if hardware is free
- Compete for access
- Never access audio adapter

COM_DIRECT_ACCESS

Use this OS/2 2.1 setting to allow a program direct access to COM ports. Select On to track which COM port is in use by the DOS session. The default setting is Off, and this disables direct COM port access.

COM_HOLD (Hold COM resource)

When this setting is Off, OS/2 releases a COM port as soon as the application using the port ends, even if the DOS session is still active. This can cause problems for certain communications programs or batch files that use several programs in quick succession. If you change this setting to On, OS/2 keeps the port assigned for as long as the DOS session is active.

COM_SELECT

Some DOS applications take control of all available COM ports, even if they use only one of them. Once such a program starts, the other COM ports cannot be accessed by other programs. The OS/2 2.1 COM_SELECT setting prevents the DOS program from taking control of resources that it cannot use. You can select the COM port you want to use in this session from ALL, COM1, COM2, COM3, or COM4. The default is ALL.

DOS_AUTOEXEC

This option allows you to specify the path and filename of a batch file you want to use instead of the default AUTOEXEC.BAT usually used to initiate environment variables for the current DOS session. With careful use of this option, you can tailor specific environments for separate sessions, each in a different batch file.

The default is blank, which means that the AUTOEXEC.BAT file in the root directory of the startup drive will be used.

S O L U T I O N

The combination of DOS_AUTOEXEC and DOS_DEVICE is a very powerful one; these two settings used together allow you to tailor the DOS-session environment to your exact needs. For example, the best way of using an Intel SatisFAXtion fax modem is in a separate DOS session. You can use DOS_DEVICE to load the fax device driver into the session, and then use DOS_AUTOEXEC as a batch file to load the fax application program. What you have as a result is a custom DOS session dedicated to fax support.

DOS_BACKGROUND_EXECUTION

This setting specifies whether a DOS application will continue to run when it is switched into the background. When set to Off, the program will stop when it is not in the foreground. Since most DOS programs cannot do anything when they are not interacting with the user, this is a reasonable assumption. However, if you do want the program to continue running when it is switched into the background, as you work on other things in the foreground, DOS_BACKGROUND_EXECUTION must be set to On.

Make sure that you turn this setting on for all communications programs and for WIN-OS/2 DDE.

WordPerfect 5.1 and Lotus 1-2-3 Release 2.2 are examples of programs that will continue to check for keyboard input even when switched into the background. In a multitasking environment, this can have an important impact on performance, especially if more that one such program is running at a time. Set DOS_BACKGROUND_EXECUTION to Off to minimize this impact.

You can change this setting at any time.

DOS_BREAK

This setting lets certain DOS applications halt when you press the Ctrl+C or Ctrl+Break key combination, however, not all applications will respond to this key combination.

Unless you specify otherwise during the installation of OS/2, the system adds a BREAK = OFF statement to your CONFIG.SYS file. This means that OS/2 checks only for the Ctrl+C during standard input and output operations, but does not check while the program is processing information. Programs will run more slowly if you set DOS_BREAK to ON, as OS/2 has to constantly check for these keystrokes.

This setting is not particularly important in OS/2, because if a program in a DOS session does get into trouble, you can always open the Window List and close the session.

DOS_DEVICE

Device drivers are programs that allow applications to work with specialized hardware, such as graphics tablets, digitizers, and some printers. In order to run DOS applications effectively, OS/2 must also understand DOS device drivers. All device drivers are loaded using a DEVICE = statement in CONFIG.SYS, and then OS/2 decides which ones are for OS/2 and which ones are DOS device drivers. Drivers loaded through CONFIG.SYS become available to all DOS sessions. Even though OS/2 makes more conventional memory available than MS-DOS can, you may not want all device drivers loaded into all DOS sessions, especially if a session will never use the hardware supported by the device driver. DOS_DEVICE is the answer; it lets you load a specific device driver into the selected DOS session.

Clicking on DOS_DEVICE opens the window shown in Figure 6.3.

Enter the path and filename information of the device driver you want to load into this session. Put each device driver on a new line in the Value window.

NOTE When specifying the path and filename for the device driver that you want to add to the selected session, you do not need the DEVICE = statement that is normally used in CONFIG.SYS.

FIGURE 6.3

DOS_DEVICE Setting

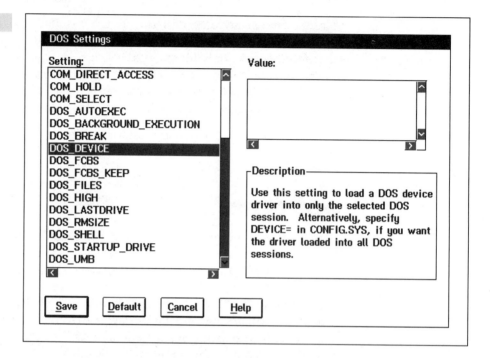

To stop a device driver from loading into a session, just delete the whole entry from the Value field; you can also add, remove, or change any of the parameters associated with the device driver using this field.

DOS_FCBS

This setting specifies the maximum number of file control blocks (FCBs) that the current DOS session can access. This setting only affects file-sharing modules, for example, when files are shared across a network. The default is 16, and the range is from 0 to 255.

Setting DOS_FCBS too high can depress the performance of the whole system, and if you notice poor performance in a networked environment, use this setting to limit the number of FCBs. If the session tries to open another FCB after the maximum has been reached, the least recently used FCB is closed first. You can also use the next setting, DOS_FCBS_KEEP, to prevent DOS from closing one or more of the first FCBs that it opens.

DOS_FCBS_KEEP

Use this setting to specify the number of FCBs that the operating system cannot close to make room for opening another file. This setting is only seldom changed; see your application software documentation for more information on how many FCBs it needs.

The default is 16, and values can range from 0 to 255. Changing the FCBS statement in your CONFIG.SYS file also changes the default for this setting.

DOS_FILES

This setting is equivalent to the FILES = setting in CONFIG.SYS and specifies the number of files that the DOS session can open at one time. A small amount of memory is reserved for tracking each file, so don't set DOS_FILES higher than necessary. For a DOS session, the default is 20, and for a WIN-OS/2 session, the default is 48. Database and other file-intensive applications such as inventory control, accounting, and materials resource planning (MRP) may need a higher value; dBASE IV requires a setting of at least 40.

You can change this setting at any time, and the change will take effect immediately.

DOS_LAST_DRIVE

The DOS_LAST_DRIVE setting lets you specify the highest drive letter that can be accessed from the DOS session. This setting is similar to the LASTDRIVE = statement in a DOS CONFIG.SYS file.

The default is drive Z, so the only reason to change this setting is to recover the small amount of memory that it uses (100 bytes per drive letter), or to restrict access to certain drives such as network drives.

DOS_SHELL

Use this setting to specify path and file name information for the DOS command processor you want to use in the current session. The default is C:\OS2\MDOS\COMMAND.COM C:\OS2\MDOS /P. If you decide to use a replacement shell, check the program documentation to make sure that it will work in the OS/2 environment. Because this field is quite long, and entries are not always visible all the time, you should take care to clear this field before you change it; characters left over from a previous entry could cause chaos.

DOS_STARTUP_DRIVE

This is the setting you use to tell OS/2 to boot another version of MS-DOS or a version of DR-DOS, and is described in the section headed "Running Specific Versions of MS-DOS" later in this chapter. System performance with a specific version of MS-DOS will not be as good as in an OS/2 DOS session, which is optimized for use in the OS/2 environment. This setting must be changed before starting the session.

DOS_VERSION

This is a rather complex setting that you can use when you have to run a program that needs a version of MS-DOS other than the DOS emulation offered by OS/2, and is an alternative to booting that version of MS-DOS from a floppy disk.

NOTE The DOS_VERSION setting is analogous to the MS-DOS command SETVER, but is a great deal more flexible in how it works.

Some programs are version-sensitive; they look at the version of MS-DOS they are running on, and if they don't like what they see, they just stop running. OS/2 provides a great deal of flexibility here, and this is one of the ways that OS/2 provides more DOS-compatibility than many other versions of MS-DOS. Figure 6.4 shows the DOS_VERSION window.

FIGURE 6.4

The DOS_VERSION
Window

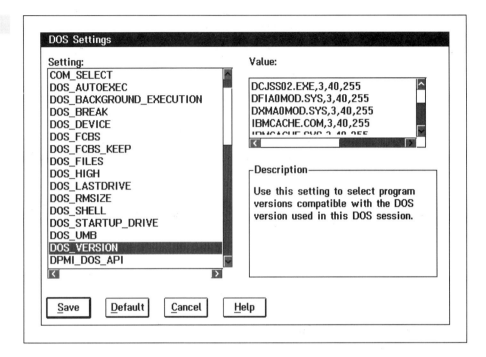

To use this setting, you must know the name of the executable file used
to start the application program, and the major and minor version numbers of the operating system that the program requires. An entry in the
DOS_VERSION Value field looks like this:

program name, version number, sub-version number, count

These parameters are always separated by commas, and are defined as follows:

- *program name* is the name of the executable file that starts the
  program running.

- *version number* is the number before the decimal for the version of
  MS-DOS you want to emulate. For MS-DOS version 4.01, this
  number would be 4.

- *sub-version number* is the number after the decimal for the version
  of MS-DOS you want to emulate; always use both digits. For
  MS-DOS version 4.01, this entry would be 01.

- *count* is the number of times you want the operating system to report this version of MS-DOS to the program. A value of 255 is equivalent to specifying no limit to the number of times this simulated information is reported.

Type your entry directly into the DOS_VERSION Value field. If the list of applications in this field is long, use the horizontal or vertical scroll bars to move through the entries.

You can also specify the OS/2 version for an OS/2 session, by typing two digits for both parts of the operating system version number identifier. For example, if the program LVIS.EXE requires OS/2 version 1.1, enter:

```
LVIS.EXE,10,10,255
```

HW_NOSOUND (Sound inhibit)

This setting, when set to Off, disables sounds produced through the computer speaker in a DOS session; select On to restore the sound.

Using this setting, you can silence your normally noisy games, and thus play them undetected, and you can turn off those annoying chirps and beeps that some programs produce. Mercifully, you can change this setting at any time, and the change takes effect immediately.

HW_ROM_TO_RAM

The Basic Input/Output System (BIOS) is the low-level software that allows the operating system access to the underlying hardware. The BIOS is stored in nonvolatile Read-Only Memory (RAM), so that it is not lost when power is turned off. Unfortunately, code stored in ROM executes more slowly than code stored in Random-Access Memory (RAM). Use this setting to copy BIOS code from ROM into RAM to improve system performance. A similar feature, known as *shadow RAM*, is offered by some PC manufacturers as a part of the system setup.

The designers of OS/2 decided to make as much memory as possible available to applications running in the DOS session, so they made the default for the HW_ROM_TO_RAM setting Off. The trade-off between using that memory and the speed increase seen when BIOS operates from RAM, however, is such that you should change this setting to On.

HW_TIMER

This setting, when On, gives a program running in the current session direct access to hardware (8253) timer ports. For some timing-critical programs, this access may be vital; some programs will run erratically or not at all without direct access to the 8253.

If you turn this setting Off, OS/2 provides an emulation of the 8253.

Changing this setting in a session that contains a running program may produce unexpected results.

IDLE_SECONDS

Application programs spend most of their time waiting for us to do something (and that's the way it should be, too), but as they wait, they also consume system resources. This setting lets you specify how long the operating system should wait before cutting the program's priority, and therefore reduces its load on the system. Values range from 0 to 60 seconds; the default is 0 seconds.

IDLE_SENSITIVITY

This setting lets you establish a threshold for judging when a program is idle, and is waiting for input. This value is a percentage of the maximum frequency with which a program checks for input. The default is 75 percent, which means that OS/2 will not consider a program to be idle until it is spending 75 percent of its time waiting for input from the keyboard.

Increasing IDLE_SENSITIVITY to 100 effectively turns idle detection off, which can help performance in programs like games.

For some communications applications, such as ProComm Plus, it is better to set this value low, to around 30, rather than 75. You can also experiment with the TIMESLICE parameter in CONFIG.SYS if performance is still slow. Start with values like TIMESLICE = 64,128 and experiment. See Chapter 13 for more on TIMESLICE.

INT_DURING_IO
(Interrupt during input/output)

You can use this setting to enable or disable interrupts during disk read and write operations, and allow programs to receive interrupts as they wait for a disk operation to finish. This setting should be set to On for multimedia applications, as many such applications require access to interrupts during these operations.

This setting is new in OS/2 version 2.1. It is a significant addition, because it allows a virtual DOS machine to run dual threads; one thread services any interrupt that may occur while the other thread performs the file read/write operation. In OS/2 version 2.0, each virtual DOS machine operated as a single thread. If that thread was busy with a long file operation, it could not see an interrupt until that operation completed. With a second thread, interrupts can be serviced while disk operations continue.

Running Multiple DOS Sessions

To start multiple DOS sessions from the desktop, open the OS/2 System folder, then open the Command Prompts folder. Copy one of the DOS objects—for example, the DOS Window—by holding down the Ctrl key and dragging the object using the right mouse button. You can copy the object into the same folder, into a new folder, or onto the desktop if you wish. Release the mouse button and the Ctrl key when you reach your destination. If you already have a DOS object on the desktop, a window may open to remind you that you now have two objects on the desktop with identical names; use the Rename Object To text box to enter a new name for the copied object. Now, just double-click on the icon to open a new DOS session with that name. Once you start this session running, you will also see its name in the Window List. Repeat these steps to create more icons for more sessions as you need them.

If you plan to use multiple command prompts very often, you can make a template of the command prompt object. Open the command prompt's Settings notebook at the General tab, and check the Template checkbox.

Running multiple DOS sessions can sometimes lead to apparently strange results, when programs that work flawlessly in a single session behave strangely when run in multiple sessions. The reason for this lies in the way that OS/2 tries to detect whether the DOS applications are idle or working. Since MS-DOS is a single-tasking operating system and can only do one thing at a time, most applications go into an endless loop when waiting for something to happen. This loop often includes polling the keyboard waiting for input. OS/2 is designed to detect when a program is waiting, but because there are as many different ways to implement this detection as there are DOS applications, it is not possible to detect an idle program with 100 percent accuracy. Multiply this uncertainty by the number of different DOS applications you run, and the problem will be magnified.

One possible solution is to tune the DOS settings for IDLE_SENSITIVITY and IDLE_SECONDS to see if you can get a better overall result. By adjusting one program at a time while running the Pulse productivity application to displays CPU activity, you should be able to see the results of any changes you make.

Running Specific Versions of MS-DOS

One of the most important goals for the designers of OS/2 was to create an operating system that would run past, present, and future DOS application programs; and most available DOS applications do indeed run without any problems in an OS/2 DOS session.

The DOS emulation provided by OS/2 is highly optimized for and specific to OS/2. It was designed to be as complete as possible, but there are certain DOS control structures, such as block device drivers, or undocumented features, that are not available to DOS applications running in a virtual DOS machine (VDM). Application programs that access these structures cannot run in a VDM, so the designers of OS/2 added another feature, the virtual machine boot, or VMB for short, to solve this problem.

 S O L U T I O N

You can use the BOOT command to switch back and forth between OS/2 and the version of MS-DOS that was installed on your system before you loaded OS/2, but you cannot multitask these two operating systems using BOOT. You *can* multitask OS/2 and a specific version of MS-DOS, if you use a virtual machine boot in a virtual DOS machine.

These two terms sound very similar, but their meanings are quite different. A virtual DOS machine is the official OS/2 name for a DOS session, where OS/2 provides the DOS emulation, and the virtual machine boot is a specific version of MS-DOS booted up inside a virtual DOS machine.

 S O L U T I O N

Another use for the Virtual Machine Boot, in a multilingual or training environment, is to run several different national-language versions of DOS, and have them all controlled and loaded by OS/2. This means that you don't have to reload and reconfigure your hard disk for a different version of DOS each time the nationality of your students changes.

The Virtual Machine Boot (VMB)

The virtual machine boot allows you to load a "real" version of MS-DOS into a virtual DOS machine, either from a bootable floppy disk, or from an image file stored on your hard disk. Since this means that a real version of MS-DOS is running in the VDM, *all* features and internal code structures of that version are now available to the application.

N O T E

The software that supports the IBM 3363 Optical disk drive must be run in a specific DOS session started from drive A. Also, you should only run a small number of other applications when using this device.

As the virtual machine boot starts, control is passed to the boot record, the first sector of the DOS system disk, which in turn loads and starts the DOS kernel, in just the same way as when starting a real PC.

The virtual DOS machine environment is so complete that a virtual machine boot can actually load *any* 8086 operating system, such as Novell's DR DOS, Concurrent DOS, and CP/M, and MS-DOS from Microsoft. Since the point of the virtual machine boot is to run DOS applications, support is provided for IBM PC DOS 3.X, 4.0, and 5.0. Table 6.2 shows the amount of conventional memory available for a DOS session, for MS-DOS in a virtual machine boot, and for several versions of native MS-DOS.

TABLE 6.2: Free Conventional Memory for Different DOS Environments

CONFIGURATION	VDM DOS EMULATION	MS-DOS 3.3	MS-DOS 4.0	MS-DOS 5.0
DOS low	610K	545K	588K	566K
DOS high	633K	N/A	N/A	612K
CGA Mode Restriction	728K	670K	653K	707K

A virtual DOS machine using virtual machine boot is similar in function to any other virtual DOS machine. You can start and operate multiple virtual DOS machines using virtual machine boot, and each one runs in its own virtual 8086 machine. Access to hardware and other system resources is managed by OS/2; applications that run using VMB can take advantage of the EMS, XMS, and mouse support provided to all DOS sessions by OS/2.

Configuring the VMB

You can load a version of MS-DOS into a virtual machine boot from:

- An MS-DOS system floppy disk
- An image of an MS-DOS system floppy disk saved on your hard disk
- An MS-DOS partition on your hard disk

For all of these alternatives, copies of CONFIG.SYS and AUTOEXEC.BAT must be available, along with the real MS-DOS to boot. Table 6.3 shows where these configuration files must be located.

TABLE 6.3: Location of CONFIG.SYS and AUTOEXEC.BAT Files

VIRTUAL DOS MACHINE TYPE	FILE LOCATION
Virtual Machine Boot from drive A	Drive A
Virtual Machine Boot from image file	Embedded in the image file
Virtual Machine Boot from DOS partition	Root directory of OS/2 boot drive

To prepare a bootable MS-DOS disk, either shut down OS/2 and boot the version of MS-DOS you want to use, or find a system that already runs this version. Place a fresh floppy disk in the appropriate drive and enter the following at the command prompt:

```
FORMAT A: /S
```

The /S switch tells the FORMAT command to prepare the floppy disk with the system files needed to boot MS-DOS. Next, copy CONFIG.SYS and AUTOEXEC.BAT onto this floppy disk. Because the booted DOS session in a virtual machine boot will receive memory management (including extended, expanded, and DPMI), and mouse, disk cache, print spooler, and RAM disk support from the virtual DOS machine provided by OS/2, it should not load its own device drivers for these services, but load stub drivers from the OS2\MDOS directory instead. (These stub drivers allow the DOS application to detect and address the device driver. They operate in V86 mode inside the virtual DOS machine, while the main part of the driver executes in protected mode. We'll get back to these stub drivers in a moment.) Check through CONFIG.SYS and AUTOEXEC.BAT using your favorite editor for these device drivers. You can also place a REM statement at the beginning of each line that you don't need; this will keep the line intact, but prevent it from being invoked.

How can MS-DOS, which only understands the FAT file system, access HPFS volumes, and how can older version of MS-DOS read today's larger drives? OS/2 provides two files that help provide complete access to the OS/2 system; the device driver FSFILTER.SYS, and the program FSACCESS.EXE. FSFILTER.SYS is an OS/2 device driver that handles MS-DOS access to OS/2 file systems. Copy this device driver from the OS2\MDOS directory onto the bootable floppy disk, and add the following statements to the CONFIG.SYS file there:

    REM load the fsfilter.sys device driver

    DEVICE=A:FSFILTER.SYS

    REM load the stub XMS and EMS memory drivers from OS/2

    DEVICE=C:\OS2\MDOS\HIMEM.SYS

    DEVICE=C:\OS2\MDOS\EMM386.SYS

The line containing the FSFILTER.SYS statement should be added before any other DEVICE statements in the file. This driver can also be loaded using DEVICEHIGH if you are using MS-DOS 5 or later.

FSFILTER.SYS gives MS-DOS access to all OS/2 partitions, regardless of the file system type or partition size. For example, even MS-DOS 3.3 can easily access a 300MB hard disk once FSFILTER.SYS is loaded. However, there are still several important restrictions:

- A virtual machine boot session cannot access HPFS files with long file names, multiple dot separators or other characters that are illegal in a FAT file name. Lowercase letters are translated into uppercase letters.

- MS-DOS commands that require low-level disk access will fail. This includes CHKDSK, FORMAT, MIRROR, UNFORMAT, UNDELETE, and SYS.

You must also add a statement to AUTOEXEC.BAT to load the OS/2 mouse driver, as follows:

REM load the stub mouse driver from os/2

C:\OS2\MDOS\MOUSE

The OS/2 FSACCESS command is designed to run in a virtual machine boot session, and it works with FSFILTER to manage drive letters in the virtual machine boot session.

▶ S O L U T I O N

Once FSFILTER is installed, there are three main ways you can use FS-ACCESS, as follows:

FSACCESS *DOSdriveletter*

where *DOSdriveletter* specifies a particular local drive letter. The following colon is optional.

FSACCESS *DOSdriveletter – DOSdriveletter*

The minus sign and second drive letter indicate an inclusive range of drive letters.

FSACCESS *DOSdriveletter = OS/2driveletter*

In this case the equal sign maps a local DOS drive letter to an OS/2 drive letter. Again the following colon is optional.

In most circumstances, your DOS drive letters are assigned the same drive letters for OS/2 drives. To check the current mappings, use the FSACCESS command with no parameters. To change the mapping, use the FS-ACCESS command and the appropriate drive letter. To indicate that a drive should not be mapped, use an exclamation point before the drive letter.

The startup disk is now ready. To boot this disk, open the OS/2 System folder on the desktop, then open the Command Prompts folder. Insert the bootable floppy disk into drive A: and double-click on DOS from Drive A:. By default, the DOS session will occupy a full screen session. If you would rather use a windowed session, open the DOS from Drive A: icon's pop-up menu before you start the session, select the Session tab, and click the DOS Window button to make the change. The EXIT command does not work from a virtual machine boot, so to close the session, open the Window List, select the session (it will be called "DOS from Drive A:"), and use Close. You can also use the Close option from the title-bar icon in a windowed session.

WARNING

Remember that the Ctrl+Alt+Del keystroke sequence will reboot the entire OS/2 operating system, not just the foreground virtual DOS session.

Making an IMAGE File on the Hard Disk

If you plan on regularly using MS-DOS in a virtual machine boot, you can load from your hard disk rather than from a floppy disk. First create a floppy disk, as described above, then use the OS/2 VMDISK command to create an image of this disk.

VMDISK has the following syntax:

> VMDISK *sourcedrive: targetdrive:\path\filename*

In the VMDISK command, *sourcedrive:* specifies the floppy disk drive where the DOS startup disk is located; *targetdrive:\path\filename* represents the image file. You must specify a file name for the image file. Also, the target drive must have more available space than the source drive.

For example, to create an image file of an MS-DOS 6 startup disk in the root directory of drive C, place the startup disk in drive A, and type:

> VMDISK A: C:\MSDOS60.IMG

A progress display shows the percentage complete as VMDISK creates the image file.

To start this session, open the Settings notebook for DOS from Drive A at the Session page, and click on the DOS Settings button. Next, click on DOS_STARTUP_DRIVE, and enter the complete path and file name information for the image file you just created into the Value field. Click on the Save button to store this change. You can also go to the General tab, and change the icon title to something more meaningful than *DOS from Drive A:*. In the case of this example, using a name like MS-DOS 6 makes much more sense. To start the session from the image file, double-click on the icon, and the session will start.

N O T E

You can always tell when you are working with a virtual machine boot DOS session by the response given by the VER command. In native MS-DOS, the VER command will always give the MS-DOS version number; in OS/2 or in an OS/2 virtual DOS session, the VER command always gives the OS/2 version number.

When you start a DOS session from the image file, all subsequent references to drive A actually access the image file rather than the real A drive.

Use FSACCESS to close the image file and map drive letter A to the real floppy disk drive. Change to the OS2/MSDOS directory on drive C and type:

FSACCESS A:

at the DOS command prompt.

Booting from a DOS Partition

To load DOS from a DOS partition, make sure the following requirements are satisfied:

- The OS/2 Boot Manager must be installed

- DOS must be installed on a primary partition on the first hard disk.

- OS/2 must be installed on an extended partition on the first hard disk.

Then specify drive C as the value for DOS_STARTUP_DRIVE in the DOS settings.

You might think that you would have to keep separate sets of configuration files handy, depending on whether the partition is being booted into a virtual machine boot and needs access to the stub drivers or is starting directly from the Boot Manager and needs the real device drivers. The answer is to specify *both* sets of drivers, in CONFIG.SYS and in AUTOEXEC.BAT, but in the following order:

```
DEVICE=C:\DOS\SETVER.EXE

DEVICE=C:\DOS\HIMEM.SYS

DEVICE=C:\DOS\EMM386.EXE NOEMS

DEVICE=E:\OS2\MDOS\HIMEM.SYS

DEVICE=E:\OS2\MDOS\EMM386.SYS

DOS=HIGH,UMB
```

assuming DOS 5 is installed on the C: primary partition, and OS/2 is installed on the E: extended partition.

When this file is processed in a VMB session, the HIMEM load fails because it cannot see any available extended memory, and the EMM386 cannot load because protected-mode software is already running. Then the OS/2 drivers load as normal.

When the file is processed as a normal DOS boot, the DOS drivers load, but the OS/2 drivers do not, because they detect that they are not running under OS/2.

In AUTOEXEC.BAT, the mouse driver is managed in a similar way, except that the drivers are loaded the other way round:

```
LH E:\OS2\MDOS\MOUSE
LH C:\DOS\MOUSE
```

Using the Clipboard with DOS

One of the benefits of using DOS in a VDM is access to the OS/2 clipboard. You can use the copy and paste features of the VDM to transfer text and graphical information between the DOS application, the clipboard, and any other application that supports the clipboard.

WARNING Some graphical applications suffer a severe performance penalty when in windowed mode. Use a full-screen session for these programs. You will find that there can be a significant performance difference between running a DOS application full screen and running it in a full-screen window (a window that fills the entire screen).

Open DOS sessions have functions that you can select from the title-bar icon menu, including:

- **Full-Screen** switches from a window to a full-screen session.
- **Font Size** lets you change the size of the text shown in the window.
- **Scroll** turns window scrolling on and off.
- **Mark** lets you mark text or graphics for copying to the OS/2 clipboard.
- **Copy** lets you copy the marked material to the clipboard.
- **Copy All** lets you copy the entire contents of the window to the clipboard.
- **Paste** lets you copy the contents of the clipboard, text or graphics, to the active window.
- **DOS Settings** lets you change the settings for the programs that run in the currently active DOS window.

To copy text or graphics to the clipboard, first use the Mark command, then drag the mouse (using the special mouse pointer) to mark the material you want to send to the clipboard. A check mark appears next to the Mark option name in the menu to remind you that the Mark function is enabled. Then use the Copy command to copy the material to the clipboard.

WARNING

Remember that the clipboard can hold only one thing at a time; if you copy new information to the clipboard, you automatically delete the information that was there before.

To go the other way, use the Paste command to copy the contents of the clipboard into the currently active window.

The clipboard function Copy All is also available to full-screen sessions. This lets you copy the contents of the whole screen to the clipboard; you cannot use Copy, as there is no mechanism available to mark the text or graphics on the screen. To use Copy All, press the Ctrl+Esc keys to return to the desktop, then right-click on the application icon, and select Copy All from the menu.

Notes on DOS Application Compatibility

Some DOS programs assume that they are the only application ever to run on the operating system, and that they have complete and uninterrupted access to all system resources. This assumption is no longer true, of course, when running an application in a DOS session under OS/2. Programs that fall into one or more of the following categories may not work properly with OS/2:

- Programs that write directly to physical disk sectors when performing disk-write operations. Many of the popular DOS UnDelete or UnErase programs fall into this category.

- Programs that manipulate the 80386 processor control registers, such as program language debuggers used in software development.

- Certain game programs that use out-of-date copy protection schemes.

- Some MS-DOS communications programs.

- MS-DOS extenders that require exclusive access to the 80386 control registers, such as the Virtual Control Program Interface (VCPI) are not supported.

- Fax boards and programs that issue more than 1000 interrupts per second. The following fax packages may contain timing sensitivities that could prevent reliable operation:

    ATI ETC

    Cardinal FAX

Practical Peripherals
Smartfax
Twincomm 24/96

The following list includes information on the compatibility of certain MS-DOS programs and OS/2. These programs either cannot run under OS/2 because they violate system integrity, or require special tuning. Much of this information is version specific, and later versions of the same software may well operate flawlessly.

> ## S E C R E T

Some DOS games that use the PC speaker to create complex sounds can sound very slow and hard to understand when run in an OS/2 DOS session. These programs were written with no consideration of a multitasking environment, and they attempt to take control of the processor, issuing from 16,000 to 32,000 interrupts per second. This might work in a single-tasking operating system such as MS-DOS, but is definitely not appropriate in a preemptive multitasking operating system such as OS/2. OS/2 delivers only 1000 interrupts per second to a DOS session. The solution is to turn off the sound option in the offending program, or to use a sound board like Ad-Lib or the SoundBlaster card instead. You might also experiment with the DOS setting HW_NOSOUND, or change the following settings:

```
HW_TIMER=ON
IDLE_SECONDS=60
IDLE_SENSITIVITY=100
```

These settings allow the DOS session to take more system resources, and not be as affected by OS/2's multitasking. Of course, then multitasking suffers as a result, and other programs, particularly communications programs, may fail.

AutoCAD Version 10

Always close this program from the desktop.

AutoManager 4.0

Use the real-mode version of this program because the extended-memory version uses an unsupported DOS memory extender.

This program expects to find COMMAND.COM in the root directory of drive C. To fix this, copy COMMAND.COM from the C:\OS2\MDOS directory to the root directory.

Borland C++ 2.0 and 3.0

Set the DOS setting DPMI_DOS_API to Enabled.

Borland Turbo C++ 2.0

Use the standard-mode version of this program because the extended-memory version uses an unsupported MS-DOS memory extender.

Borland Turbo Debugger 2.01

Use the standard-mode version of this program because the extended-memory version uses an unsupported MS-DOS memory extender.

The 80386 version of the debugger, TD386, directly manipulates the 80386 control registers, and this is not supported.

Borland Turbo Pascal

Use the standard-mode version of this program because the extended-memory version uses an unsupported MS-DOS memory extender.

Central Point Backup for DOS 7.1

Run this program in a DOS full-screen session to avoid the garbage characters displayed when the program runs in a DOS window.

Commander Keen

Set the DOS setting VIDEO_RETRACE_EMULATION to Off.

Control Room 1.0

Use this program in a DOS full-screen session if you want to use the screen blanking feature.

dBASE IV 1.1

Set the DOS setting DOS_FILES to 30 to avoid a "too many open files" error message, and set the DOS_VERSION setting to DBASE-.EXE,5,0,255.

When using Hyperdisk, you may have to adjust the EMS and XMS memory limits, and set the DOS_VERSION setting to DBASE1-.EXE,5,0,255.

This program must be run in a specific DOS session when used in multi-user mode.

F-117A Stealth Fighter 2.0

If this program stops with a blank screen just after you start it running, press the Escape key and the program will continue without further problems.

Set the DOS setting VIDEO_RETRACE_EMULATION to Off.

F19

Set the DOS setting VIDEO_RETRACE_EMULATION to Off, and the HW_ROM_TO_RAM setting to On.

Fastback Plus 2.1 and 3.04

If you have problems backing up files to a floppy disk, back up to a network disk drive or to a tape instead.

FastLynx 1.1

Remove the DEVICE = C:\OS2\MDOS\VCOM.SYS statement from CONFIG.SYS and restart the system if you want to use a serial port with this program. The parallel port works fine.

If you experience other problems, try the following DOS settings:

    HW_TIMER = On
    IDLE_SENSITIVITY = 100
    IDLE_SECONDS = 10

Framework III 1.1

Disable this program's print spooler to avoid printing errors.

This program expects to find COMMAND.COM in the root directory of drive C. To fix this, copy COMMAND.COM from the C:\OS2\MDOS directory to the root directory.

IBM PC LAN Support Program

After you close the DOS session running this program, you must reset the token-ring adapter card before restarting the session. There is a fix for this problem; download the file RSTTOK.ZIP from the IBM bulletin board or from CompuServe. See Appendix B for details on both these services.

IBM PC/3270 2.0

Set the DOS setting VIDEO_MODE_RESTRICTION to CGA, and add DXMA0MOD.SYS and DXMC0MOD.SYS to the DOS_DEVICE setting, including the appropriate path information. Finally, on the Program page of the settings notebook, set the Path and File Name to *, set the Parameters to /K PC3270.BAT, and set the Working Directory to the appropriate path statement.

Intel SatisFAXtion

This program must be run in a specific DOS session.

Do not load the SatisFAXtion software or device drivers into all DOS sessions, because the fax might be reset when another session opens. Reserve one session for faxing, and load the appropriate software and drivers into that session only.

King's Quest

Remove the DOS=HIGH from the CONFIG.SYS file or from the DOS setting DOS_DEVICE.

LAN Support Program Device Drivers

To avoid conflicts, you should only use the IBM Token-Ring adapter in one session at a time.

After you close the DOS session running the LAN Support Program (LSP) device drivers, you must reset the Token-Ring adapter card before using the LAN again from another DOS session. To make sure that the adapter is reset, download RESTKN.ZIP from the IBM National Support Center bulletin board, or from CompuServe. See Appendix B for more information on these services.

LANtastic 4.0

Problems are known to exist with this version of LANtastic; use version 4.1 instead. For more information, contact the Artisoft bulletin board at 602-293-0065.

LANtastic 4.1

When using Artisoft AE-2 or AE-3 adapters, make sure they are in 8-bit mode. See the documentation for details.

Run this program from a specific DOS session. Use the DOS setting DOS_STARTUP_DRIVE to specify the drive you want to boot from.

LapLink Pro

Before you run this program, type the following from the DOS session command prompt:

```
MODE COMx IDSR=Off ODSR=Off OCTS=Off
```

where x is the number of the serial port you want to use.

LapLink III 3.0

To use a serial port with this program, set the DOS setting COM_DIRECT ACCESS to On. It may just be easier to use the parallel port instead.

Lotus 1-2-3 Release 3.1+

The Lotus 1-2-3 Release 3.1+ installation program checks the DOS version number, so to fool it, select the DOS setting DOS_VERSION, and enter:

```
INSTALL.EXE,3,40,255
```

Lotus 1-2-3 Release 3.1+ is usually started in DOS with the program 123.EXE, however, this program has characteristics that allow it to start both the DOS version and the OS/2 version. As a result, OS/2 detects that this program can be started as an OS/2 program and will gray out the option to run it in a DOS session in the settings notebook. The Migrate Applications program will not work either, because 123.EXE will be identified as an OS/2 program. If you start Lotus 1-2-3 from a batch file, all these problems go away. The batch file should contain the following as the last two lines in the file:

```
SET 123MEMSIZE=2048

123.EXE
```

Add the batch file name to the Path and File Name field of the Program page of the settings notebook. Finally, select or add the following DOS settings:

```
DOS_UMB = On

DOS_HIGH = On

DOS_VERSION = INSTALL.EXE,3,40,255

                123.EXE,3,40,255

                LOTUS.EXE,3,40,255

                123DOS.EXE,3,40,255

                ZAP.EXE,3,40,255

                INS.EXE,3,40,255
```

Also set DPMI_MEMORY_LIMIT to 4MB or more.

Lotus Magellan 2.0

The Undelete function in this program uses physical-sector addressing which is not supported in OS/2. Use the OS/2 UNDELETE command (described in Chapter 14) instead.

MicroProse Civilization

Set the DOS setting HW_TIMER to On, and the VIDEO_ RETRACE_ EMULATION setting to Off.

Microsoft Chart 3.0

Install this program's mouse driver, and then set the DOS setting MOUSE_EXCLUSIVE_ACCESS to On.

MS Excel 2.1

Set the DOS setting XMS_MEMORY_LIMIT to 0.

MS Windows

Run Windows and Windows programs in a WIN-OS/2 session rather than in native Windows.

Mirrors III

Type the following at the command prompt before you run this program:

```
MODE COMx BUFFER=Off
```

where x represents the number of the serial port you want to use with the program.

National Geographic Mammals

Run this program with the DOS setting INT_DURING_IO turned On.

National Geographic Presidents

Run this program with the DOS setting INT_DURING_IO turned On.

Norton Utilities 5.0

The deleted file recovery program UnDelete requires physical-sector addressing not supported in OS/2.

Several of the hard-disk utilities, including UnDelete, DiskTool, UnFormat, the Norton Disk Doctor, the Disk Editor, and Calibrate can cause a system halt.

PaintShow Plus 2.21

Load the version of MOUSE.COM that comes with this program before starting to use PaintShow Plus.

Paradox 3.5

Use the standard-mode version of this program because the extended-memory version uses an unsupported DOS memory extender.

Peachtree Complete III 5.0

Set the DOS setting DOS_FILES to 60.

The Lookup function displays meaningless characters rather than the expected list of companies.

PFS First Choice

When this program is run in a DOS window, the mouse pointer does not reflect tool selection.

When using the communications feature, set the baud rate to 2400 baud or lower.

Quattro Pro 3.0

When installing printers, do so from inside the program rather than during program installation.

Quicken

Remove the DOS=HIGH statement from CONFIG.SYS or from the DOS_HIGH setting.

SantaFe Media Manager

To install this program, start a DOS session, run FFIX /find (find must be in lower-case), install the program, then run FFIX /u.

Signmaster 5.11

The Plot/Preview feature causes an illegal instruction to be issued.

SoundBlaster

The SBTEST utility program reports an incorrect direct memory access (DMA) level during installation; ignore this message and continue with the installation. The program will be installed properly.

The PARROT program does not run in a DOS session.

Space Quest IV

To suspend this program when switched into the background set the DOS setting DOS_BACKGROUND_EXECUTION to Off.

For best performance, start the program in a full-screen session.

If your computer has a SoundBlaster card, type SQ4FIX at the command prompt in the directory that contains the Space Quest IV files.

N O T E   Stac Electronics now ships Stacker for OS/2 and DOS. This program contains both MS-DOS and OS/2 device drivers, understands OS/2 extended attributes, and can compress OS/2 FAT system and MS-DOS hard disks so that they provide twice their original storage capacity. It does not work with OS/2's HPFS, although this could be a future goal for the developers. The program is compatible with OS/2 versions 2.0 and 2.1, as well as MS-DOS 5 and 6; this means that it can read compressed volumes created under MS-DOS or under OS/2. Contact Stac Electronics at 619-431-7474 for more information.

Stacker 2.0

The DOS version of this program does not work under OS/2.

Wing Commander I and II

Make sure that the DOS setting HW_TIMER is turned On.

WordPerfect Office 3.0

Install the keyboard-enhancement program manually by adding it to CONFIG.SYS when program installation is complete.

Xtree Pro Gold 2.0

The Zip Manager cannot locate the ZIP file, so avoid using this feature.

Ways to Improve Program Compatibility

There are several techniques you can use to improve program compatibility with OS/2, depending on the type of program being used:

- The performance of DOS communications programs will be improved by using a serial board that uses the 16550 universal asynchronous receive/transmit (UART) chip.

- On slower systems, the combined baud rate should never exceed 9600 for one or more concurrent DOS applications for reliable communications.

- Some DOS applications must be run from a specific version of DOS started by booting a version of MS-DOS.

- Some programs are designed to run in a DOS or OS/2 session, but must be installed from DOS.

- Some older MS-DOS programs use a hardware security device, called a "dongle," connected to the parallel port as protection against software piracy. As the program starts, it checks a code number in the dongle. If the dongle sends back the wrong number, or no number at all, the program assumes that it is an illegal copy, and stops running. If more than one DOS session is running one of these programs, you may see a SYS1799 error telling you more than one application is trying to use the same port. You can avoid this error if you open the Settings notebook at the Output tab, and open the port in question. Now check the Shared Access checkbox to share the port between sessions.

- If you run a DOS communications program, and see a lot of time-out errors, you can change several of the DOS settings to try and fix the problem. Change these settings in sequence; make the first change, and if that does not correct the problem, make the second change, and so on through the list:

- Set HW_TIMER to On
- Set IDLE_SECONDS to 60, and IDLE_SENSITIVITY to 100
- Set COM_HOLD to On
- Set HW_ROM_TO_RAM to On

If these combined settings do not fix the problem, you'll need to change the PRIORITY_DISK_IO setting in your CONFIG.SYS file to NO.

OS/2 OS/2 OS/2

OS/2 OS/2 OS/2 OS/2 OS/2 OS/2 OS/2 OS/2

OS/2 OS/2 OS/2 O

Running Microsoft Windows Programs under OS/2

ALONG with support for DOS programs, support for Microsoft Windows programs was a very high priority for the designers of OS/2. Windows programs are supported by that part of OS/2 known as WIN-OS/2. Under an agreement with Microsoft, IBM included a rewritten version of Windows 3.1 in OS/2, and called it WIN-OS/2. Like the DOS emulation we looked at in the last chapter, WIN-OS/2 isn't native Windows, but is an OS/2 software emulation of Windows. WIN-OS/2 supports Windows applications, but does not attempt to clone Windows; indeed WIN-OS/2 is far more complex, internally, than native Windows. All of this means that WIN-OS/2 can do everything that Windows can do, as well as several very important things that native Windows cannot do, like run Windows Version 2.X applications, provide complete application protection, allow access to the HPFS, and allow preemptive multitasking.

With this support, Windows 2.X and 3.X applications can multitask with applications running on native MS-DOS or in a DOS session, and with OS/2 applications, all on the same computer, and all at the same time.

This chapter looks at many aspects of running, configuring, and optimizing your Windows programs under OS/2, and it ends with a look at some of the Windows programs that may not work correctly.

Is OS/2 a Better Windows than Windows?

Just as native Windows runs on top of a version of MS-DOS, Windows applications in OS/2 run in a virtual DOS machine (VDM), and so have access to the same system resources described in Chapter 6 for a VDM.

Windows applications receive the application protection provided by running in a VDM; they are protected from other Windows applications, as well as from DOS and OS/2 programs running at the same time. By contrast, in the native Windows environment, protection is limited to DOS applications (Windows programs share access to a common address space), and is only available when Windows is running in standard or 386 enhanced mode. Because Windows programs share the same address space, the potential is always present for one application to corrupt another's memory area, which is certainly the cause of some of the unrecoverable application errors (UAE) seen so often in Windows. After a UAE, native Windows must be restarted; OS/2 has no such restrictions.

OS/2's preemptive multitasking extends to Windows, DOS, and OS/2 applications, again in contrast to the native Windows environment, where multitasking is distinctly limited.

The WIN-OS/2 component of OS/2 can also run programs that the current version of Windows cannot, including applications written for Windows 2.X, 3.0, and 3.1. Native Windows 3.1 has occasional compatibility problems with certain applications written for Windows 3.0 that actually run well under OS/2's WIN-OS/2.

N O T E Not all Windows programs will run on all versions of OS/2. Version 2.0 of OS/2 supports Windows programs running in standard and real mode, while version 2.1 adds support for Windows programs running in enhanced mode.

In OS/2 version 2.1, the 32-bit graphics engine and the changes to the WIN-OS/2 kernel make most Windows applications run faster than they do under native Windows.

What's New in WIN-OS/2 3.1?

OS/2 version 2.0 included WIN-OS/2 3.0, which provided support for Microsoft Windows 3.0 applications running in real and standard modes. OS/2 version 2.1 contains a version of WIN-OS/2 upgraded to the 3.1 release of Windows, and applications can now run in standard and 386 enhanced modes. WIN-OS/2 also includes the following enhancements and upgrades:

- Enhanced-mode compatibility, allowing the small number of Windows 3.1 386 Enhanced mode applications, such as Mathematica, OmniPage Professional, and Vellum, to run in WIN-OS/2.

- Ability to start OS/2 or DOS applications from a Windows application.

- Seamless support for WIN-OS/2 sessions with VGA, SVGA, and XGA display adapters; full-screen sessions are still available.

- Support for Windows 3.1 printer drivers.

- Inclusion of Windows applications, including the following in the WIN-OS/2 Main Group:

  - File Manager
  - Print Manager
  - Control Panel
  - Clipboard Viewer
  - WIN-OS/2 Setup
  - ATM Control Panel and README file

  and in the WIN-OS/2 Accessories Group:

  - Calculator
  - Card File
  - Calender
  - Character Map

- Clock
- Media Player
- Midi Mapper
- Notepad
- Object Packager
- Paintbrush
- Sound Recorder
- Write

The Windows games are not included.

- Improved DDE, OLE, and clipboard support to allow these functions to run faster and consume fewer system resources. The Windows applets Write and Paintbrush both support OLE.

- Truetype font support is included in WIN-OS/2. ATM fonts are not installed in WIN-OS/2 by default, but you can install them from Printer Disk #5 using the ATM Control Panel.

These additions are all good news for users of Windows programs, and they illustrate IBM's commitment to maintaining OS/2's lead as the integrating platform. There are actually very few Windows programs that use the 386 Enhanced mode, so the addition of the enhanced compatibility mode to WIN-OS/2 illustrates the strength of IBM's commitment to maintaining the flexibility of the OS/2 operating system.

Installing Windows Programs

By far the easiest way of installing Windows programs on your system is to use WIN-OS/2. Start a full-screen WIN-OS/2 session from the Command Prompts folder, and when the Windows desktop appears, use the Run command from the File menu to start the installation program.

NOTE If you already have Microsoft Windows on your system, you can delete it (but not your Windows applications), to save hard disk space. With WIN-OS/2, you don't need Microsoft Windows installed on your system also.

You can do the same thing from a full-screen DOS prompt, if you type:

    WINOS2 A:\INSTALL

and in fact, you don't really need to type WINOS2. If you type:

    A:INSTALL

OS/2 examines the file, and, if it finds that the file is a Windows file, automatically launches WIN-OS/2 and starts the installation program for you. Some Windows installation programs are called SETUP rather than INSTALL.

Finally, you can also use the Drive A icon on the desktop to install Windows programs. Put the first disk into drive A and double-click on the icon, then scroll through the icons in this folder until you find the installation program. Double-click on this program to start installing.

Windows' Configuration Files

If you install Windows application support as part of your initial OS/2 installation (see Appendix A), the normal Windows initialization files are constructed. If a version of native Windows was installed prior to the OS/2 installation, the installation process locates the original .INI files and copies them into the C:\OS2\MDOS\WINOS2 directory.

OS/2 then modifies these files, as necessary, to adjust for the appropriate video, mouse, country, and keyboard settings. Windows group files (.GRP), and other Windows application-specific initialization (.INI) files are also copied. Printer definitions for the Windows environment reflect the OS/2 setup, rather than any other previously selected device driver. Finally, the PATH statement in CONFIG.SYS is modified to reflect the new location of these important files.

The following initialization files are either created from scratch, or modified, as necessary:

- WIN.INI
- PROGMAN.INI
- CONTROL.INI
- SYSTEM.INI

Let's look at each of these files in turn.

WIN.INI

This file contains several sections that the user can change and customize, and includes information about fonts, printers, communications, multimedia devices, import filters, and much more. Listing 7.1 shows the first part of a typical WIN.INI file.

Entries in this file will change as you change your Windows configuration, and as you add new Windows application programs. Many application programs insert their own private entries into WIN.INI, such as pointers to their own working directory; other programs include their entire configuration information, and so are extremely dependent on finding this file intact.

LISTING 7.1

The First Part of a
Typical WIN.INI File

```
[windows]
device=HP LaserJet III,HPPCL5A,LPT1.OS2
load=
run=
Beep=yes
Spooler=yes
NullPort=None
BorderWidth=3
KeyboardSpeed=31
CursorBlinkRate=530
DoubleClickSpeed=452
Programs=com exe bat pif
Documents=
DeviceNotSelectedTimeout=15
TransmissionRetryTimeout=45
swapdisk=
MouseThreshold1=10
MouseThreshold2=0
MouseSpeed=0

[Desktop]
Pattern=(None)
Wallpaper=(None)
TileWallpaper=0
GridGranularity=0
IconSpacing=120

[Extensions]
doc=winword.exe ^.doc
dot=winword.exe ^.dot
rtf=winword.exe ^.rtf

[intl]
sCountry=United States
iCountry=1
iDate=0
iTime=0
iTLZero=2
iCurrency=0
iCurrDigits=1
iNegCurr=1
iLzero=2
iDigits=0
iMeasure=0
s1159=AM
s2359=PM
```

LISTING 7.1

The First Part of a
Typical WIN.INI File
(Continued)

```
sCurrency=$
sThousand=,
sDecimal=.
sDate=/
sTime=:
sList=,
sShortDate=M/d/yy
sLongDate=dddd, MMMM dd, yyyy
sLanguage=ENU

[ports]
; A line with [filename].PRN followed by an equal sign causes
; [filename] to appear in the Control Panel's Printer Configuration dialog
; box. A printer connected to [filename] directs its output into this file.
LPT1.OS2=
LPT2.OS2=
FILE:=
EPT:=
LPT1:=
LPT2:=
LPT3:=
COM1:=9600,n,8,1
COM2:=9600,n,8,1
COM3:=9600,n,8,1
COM4:=9600,n,8,1

[fonts]
Arial (TrueType)=ARIAL.FOT
Arial Bold (TrueType)=ARIALBD.FOT
Arial Bold Italic (TrueType)=ARIALBI.FOT
Arial Italic (TrueType)=ARIALI.FOT
Times New Roman (TrueType)=TIMES.FOT
Times New Roman Bold (TrueType)=TIMESBD.FOT
Times New Roman Bold Italic (TrueType)=TIMESBI.FOT
Times New Roman Italic (TrueType)=TIMESI.FOT
WingDings (TrueType)=WINGDING.FOT
MS Sans Serif 8,10,12,14,18,24 (VGA res)=SSERIFE.FON
Courier 10,12,15 (VGA res)=COURE.FON
MS Serif 8,10,12,14,18,24 (VGA res)=SERIFE.FON
Symbol 8,10,12,14,18,24 (VGA res)=SYMBOLE.FON
Small Fonts (VGA res)=SMALLE.FON
Courier New (TrueType)=COUR.FOT
Courier New Bold (TrueType)=COURBD.FOT
Courier New Bold Italic (TrueType)=COURBI.FOT
Courier New Italic (TrueType)=COURI.FOT
Symbol (TrueType)=SYMBOL.FOT
```

LISTING 7.1

The First Part of a
Typical WIN.INI File
(Continued)

```
[PSCRIPT]
External Printers=6
Printer1=40291760
Printer2=40291730
Printer3=40293930
Printer4=40293960
Printer5=IBM17521
Printer6=IBM39521

[PrinterPorts]
HP LaserJet III=HPPCL5A,LPT1.OS2,45,15,LPT1.OS2,45,15
Generic / Text Only=TTY,LPT1.OS2,45,15,LPT1.OS2,45,15
FAXPM Driver=FAX,NONE,15,45

[devices]
HP LaserJet III=HPPCL5A,LPT1.OS2,LPT1.OS2
Generic / Text Only=TTY,LPT1.OS2,LPT1.OS2
FAXPM Driver=FAX,NONE

[HPPCL5A,LPT1.OS2]
FontSummary=C:\OS2\MDOS\WINOS2\SYSTEM\FSLPT1.PCL

[MSWord Text Converters]
Text with Layout=Text with Layout, C:\WINWORD\TXTWLYT.CNV,  ANS
DOS Text with Layout=DOS Text with Layout, C:\WINWORD\TXTWLYT.CNV,  ASC
WrdPrfctDos=WordPerfect 5.1, C:\WINWORD\WPFT5.CNV,  DOC
WrdPrfctDos50=WordPerfect 5.0, C:\WINWORD\WPFT5.CNV,  DOC
WordPerfect 4.2=WordPerfect 4.2, C:\WINWORD\WPFT4.CNV,  DOC
WordPerfect 4.1=WordPerfect 4.1, C:\WINWORD\WPFT4.CNV,  DOC
MSWordWin1=Word for Windows 1.x, C:\WINWORD\WORDWIN1.CNV,  doc
MSWordDos=Word for DOS, C:\WINWORD\WORDDOS.CNV,  doc
MSWordMac=Word for Macintosh 5.0, C:\WINWORD\WORDMAC.CNV,  mcw
MSWordMac4=Word for Macintosh 4.0, C:\WINWORD\WORDMAC.CNV,  mcw
RFTDCA=RFT-DCA, C:\WINWORD\RFTDCA.CNV,  rft
MSBiff=Excel Worksheet, C:\WINWORD\XLBIFF.CNV,  xls
ATdBase=Ashton-Tate dBase, C:\WINWORD\DBASE.CNV,  dbf
Lotus123=Lotus 1-2-3, C:\WINWORD\LOTUS123.CNV,  wk1
WordStar 5.5=WordStar 5.5, C:\WINWORD\WORDSTAR.CNV,  DOC
WordStar 5.0=WordStar 5.0, C:\WINWORD\WORDSTAR.CNV,  DOC
WordStar 4.0=WordStar 4.0, C:\WINWORD\WORDSTAR.CNV,  DOC
WordStar 3.45=WordStar 3.45, C:\WINWORD\WORDSTAR.CNV,  DOC
WordStar 3.3=WordStar 3.3, C:\WINWORD\WORDSTAR.CNV,  DOC
Windows Write=Windows Write, C:\WINWORD\WRITWIN.CNV,  wri

[Windows Help]
H_WindowPosition=[213,160,213,160,0]
```

LISTING 7.1

The First Part of a
Typical WIN.INI File
(Continued)

```
[Sounds]
SystemDefault=ding.wav, Default Beep
SystemExclamation=chord.wav, Exclamation
SystemStart=tada.wav, Windows Start
SystemExit=chimes.wav, Windows Exit
SystemHand=chord.wav, Critical Stop
SystemQuestion=chord.wav, Question
SystemAsterisk=chord.wav, Asterisk

[mci extensions]
wav=waveaudio
mid=sequencer
rmi=sequencer

[FontSubstitutes]
Helv=MS Sans Serif
Tms Rmn=MS Serif
Times=Times New Roman
Helvetica=Arial

[Microsoft Word 2.0]
HPDSKJET=+1

[Compatibility]
NOTSHELL=0x0001
WPWINFIL=0x0006
CCMAIL=0x0008
AMIPRO=0x0010
REM=0x8022
PIXIE=0x0040
CP=0x0040
JW=0x42080
TME=0x0100
VB=0x0200
WIN2WRS=0x1210
PACKRAT=0x0800
VISION=0x0040
MCOURIER=0x0800
_BNOTES=0x24000
MILESV3=0x1000
PM4=0x2000
DESIGNER=0x2000
PLANNER=0x2000
DRAW=0x2000
WINSIM=0x2000
CHARISMA=0x2000
```

LISTING 7.1

The First Part of a
Typical WIN.INI File
(Continued)

```
PR2=0x2000
PLUS=0x1000
ED=0x00010000
APORIA=0x0100
EXCEL=0x1000
GUIDE=0x1000
NETSET2=0x0100
W4GL=0x4000
W4GLR=0x4000
TURBOTAX=0x00080000

[spooler]
window=0 0 636 408
```

PROGMAN.INI

This file contains the Windows Program Manager settings and includes
the following sections:

- **Settings:** Describes the Program Manager settings, along with
  user preferences.

- **Groups:** Specifies the Program Groups that exist in the Program
  Manager, along with the PATH setting for the group (.GRP) files.

Listing 7.2 shows a typical PROGMAN.INI file.

LISTING 7.2

A Typical
PROGMAN.INI File

```
[Settings]
Window=38 24 581 363 1
SaveSettings=0
MinOnRun=0
AutoArrange=0
display.drv=wspdssf.drv
Order=1 2 3 4

[Groups]
Group1=C:\OS2\MDOS\WINOS2\WOS2ACCE.GRP
Group2=C:\OS2\MDOS\WINOS2\WOS2MAIN.GRP
Group3=C:\OS2\MDOS\WINOS2\APPLICAT.GRP
Group4=C:\OS2\MDOS\WINOS2\APPLICA0.GRP
```

CONTROL.INI

The CONTROL.INI file contains the color and desktop settings for the Windows Control Panel. The exact contents of this file depend on the installation choices made, but will include at least the following sections:

- **Current:** Specifies the window color settings.
- **Color Scheme:** Lists the available color options.
- **Custom Colors:** Lists up to 16 customization colors.
- **Patterns:** Specifies options for desktop patterns.

Listing 7.3 shows the first part of a typical CONTROL.INI file.

SYSTEM.INI

The SYSTEM.INI file contains the system-wide information used by Windows when it starts running. Any changes you make to SYSTEM.INI will not take effect until you restart Windows. You may find the following sections in SYSTEM.INI:

- **Boot:** Lists the device drivers and information about certain Windows modules.
- **Keyboard:** Contains information about the keyboard.
- **Boot.description:** Lists the names of the devices that the user can change using Windows Setup.
- **NonWindowsApp:** In a migrated Windows environment, this section might contain information, but it will be ignored by OS/2.
- **Standard:** Contains information used by Windows when run in standard mode.
- **386Enh:** Contains information used by Windows when run in enhanced mode.

Listing 7.4 shows part of a SYSTEM.INI file.

LISTING 7.3

Part of a Typical
CONTROL.INI file

```
[function]
settings=colors,fonts,ports,mouse,desktop,printers,sound,network, international

[Custom Colors]
ColorA=FFFFFF
ColorB=FFFFFF
ColorC=FFFFFF
ColorD=FFFFFF
ColorE=FFFFFF
ColorF=FFFFFF
ColorG=FFFFFF
ColorH=FFFFFF
ColorI=FFFFFF
ColorJ=FFFFFF
ColorK=FFFFFF
ColorL=FFFFFF
ColorM=FFFFFF
ColorN=FFFFFF
ColorO=FFFFFF
ColorP=FFFFFF

[Patterns]
(None)=(None)
Boxes=127 65 65 65 65 65 127 0
Paisley=2 7 7 2 32 80 80 32
Weave=136 84 34 69 136 21 34 81
Waffle=0 0 0 0 128 128 128 240
Tulip=0 0 84 124 124 56 146 124
Spinner=20 12 200 121 158 19 48 40
Scottie=64 192 200 120 120 72 0 0
Critters=0 80 114 32 0 5 39 2
50% Gray=170 85 170 85 170 85 170 85
Quilt=130 68 40 17 40 68 130 1
Diamonds=32 80 136 80 32 0 0 0
Thatches=248 116 34 71 143 23 34 113
Pattern=224 128 142 136 234 10 14 0

[MMCPL]
NumApps=11
X=0
Y=0
W=430
H=240
```

LISTING 7.4

Part of a Typical
SYSTEM.INI File

```
[boot]
useos2shield=1
os2shield=winsheld.exe
shell=progman.exe
network.drv=
comm.drv=comm.drv
sound.drv=sound.drv
mouse.drv=mouse.drv
keyboard.drv=keyboard.drv
system.drv=atmsys.drv
sdisplay.drv=wspdssf.drv
MAVDMApps=!printman
fonts.fon=vgasys.fon
fixedfon.fon=vgafix.fon
oemfonts.fon=vgaoem.fon
display.drv=wspdsf.drv
atm.system.drv=system.drv
language.dll=
os2gdi.exe=GDI.EXE

[keyboard]
; type 3 AT 84 or 86 keyboard
; type 4 101/102 enhance keyboard
subtype=
type=4
oemansi.bin=
keyboard.dll=

[boot.description]
network.drv=Network not installed
language.dll=English (American)
display.drv=640x480x256 Small fonts 512K Trident
sdisplay.drv=640x480x256 Small fonts 512K Trident

[386Enh]
keyboard=*vkd
device=*vpicd
device=*blockdev
device=*vdmad
device=*pagefile
device=vtdapi.386

[mci]
WaveAudio=mciwave.drv
Sequencer=mciseq.drv
CDAudio=mcicda.drv
```

LISTING 7.4

Part of a Typical SYSTEM.INI File (Continued)

```
[drivers]
timer=timer.drv
midimapper=midimap.drv

[NonWindowsApp]
localtsrs=dosedit,ced
```

Windows Sessions

During the installation of OS/2, your Windows programs were configured to run in a WIN-OS/2 window session, and if you start one or more Windows programs, they will run in this window. However, you can configure your programs to run full-screen or even in a separate WIN-OS/2 session.

Open the Settings notebook for a Windows object at the Sessions page, and you will see a window like the one shown in Figure 7.1.

Running Windows Programs in a Window Session

You can run Windows programs in a window on the desktop, just like OS/2 and DOS programs, and still have all the capability of the desktop available. This is known as the *seamless* mode, because it de-emphasizes the differences between the Windows world and the OS/2 world, letting you concentrate on using the application, rather than worrying about implementation details.

The first program started in the WIN-OS/2 windows session determines the WIN-OS/2 settings used for all the other programs running in that session, and you cannot change any of these settings while the session is active.

FIGURE 7.1

The Settings Note-
book open at the
Session page

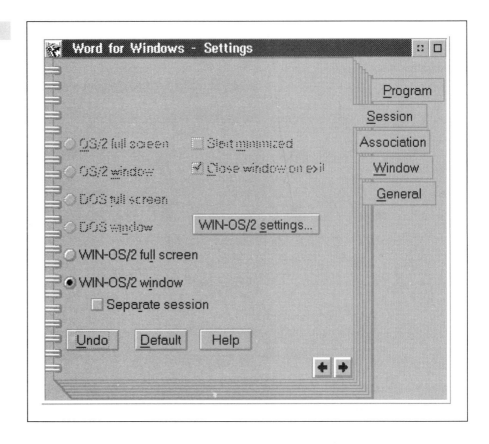

Figure 7.2 shows Microsoft Publisher for Windows open in a window on
the desktop, next to a drive window opened on drive C.

Running Windows Programs
in a Full-Screen Session

To start a WIN-OS/2 full-screen session, open the OS/2 System folder,
open the Command Prompts folder, then double-click on the WIN-OS/2
Full Screen icon.

FIGURE 7.2

Microsoft Publisher for Windows open on the desktop in a window session

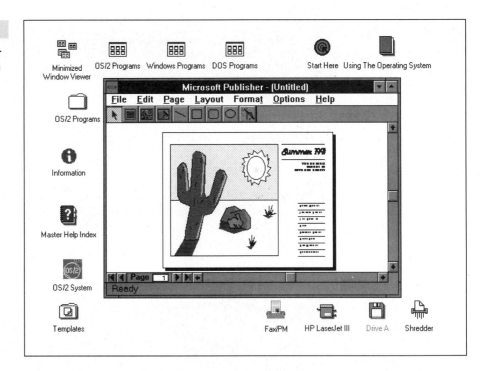

A full-screen session uses the WIN-OS/2 Program Manager to start programs; just start any program by selecting it from the appropriate OS/2 Program Manager group window. Once the program is running, use Ctrl+Esc or Ctrl+Alt to switch to any other session running on the desktop. This mode is probably the most familiar to long-time Windows users, as it closely approximates the way native Windows works. Use the icons at the bottom of the window to start other programs and to switch to the desktop.

To make a program run in a full-screen session every time it runs, open the settings notebook at the Session page, and change the type of session to a WIN-OS/2 Full Screen.

Running Windows Programs in a Separate WIN-OS/2 Session

Sometimes, you may decide that you want to use specific settings with a Windows program, and the easiest way to do this is to start the program in a separate WIN-OS/2 session. The next section of this chapter describes the settings that routinely affect Windows sessions.

To make a separate WIN-OS/2 session the default for a program, display the pop-up menu for the program, open the Settings notepad at the Session page, and check the Separate Session box.

Changing WIN-OS/2 Settings

Most of the DOS settings we looked at in Chapter 6 apply equally well to a Windows session because the WIN-OS/2 kernel is a DOS application. However, there are three special settings dedicated to controlling the Windows environment. Also, several of the DOS settings described in Chapter 6 are set to specific values when using Windows.

WIN-OS/2 Settings

Open the Settings notebook of a Windows object, and choose the Session tab, then click on the WIN-OS/2 Settings button to open the WIN-OS/2 Settings window shown in Figure 7.3.

WIN_RUN_MODE

This setting specifies the mode that WIN-OS/2 runs in, either 3.1 Standard or 3.1 Enhanced. Choose Enhanced mode for programs that require Microsoft Windows Version 3.1 Enhanced mode.

FIGURE 7.3

The WIN-OS/2 Settings window

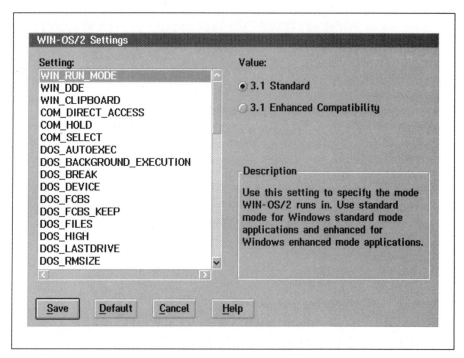

Another way to specify either Standard or Enhanced mode is to open the Settings notebook at the Program tab, and in the Parameters files, enter /S for Standard, or /3 for Enhanced mode.

You must change this setting before starting your Windows session.

WIN_DDE

New in OS/2 version 2.1, this setting lets WIN-OS/2 share DDE information between public and private WIN-OS/2 and OS/2 sessions. You can change this setting at any time.

WIN_CLIPBOARD

Also new for OS/2 2.1, this setting lets WIN-OS/2 share clipboard information between public and private WIN-OS/2 and OS/2 sessions. You can change this setting at any time.

DOS Settings

Several of the DOS settings can be tuned for your Windows sessions; good choices for DOS applications are not always good for Windows programs.

KBD_CTRL_BYPASS

This setting is automatically set to CTRL_ESC by WIN-OS/2 so that the Ctrl+Esc key combination brings up the Window List.

MOUSE_EXCLUSIVE_ACCESS

Set this to On if you want to run your single- or multiple-application VDM in a window on the desktop.

DPMI_MEMORY_LIMIT

This is automatically set to 2MB. You can always increase this value to 4MB or higher, but decreasing it is not recommended.

IDLE_SENSITIVITY

This is set to a default value of 75. If the mouse pointer seems jumpy or jerky in your Windows application, set IDLE_SENSITIVITY to 100, effectively disabling the setting.

DOS_FILES

The value for this setting should be around 35 or 40, or even higher if you run multiple applications that access many files.

VIDEO_FASTPASTE

If you plan to use the clipboard for extensive cut-and-paste functions, you can speed operations considerably by changing this setting to On.

Starting Windows Applications under OS/2

There are several ways to start your Windows applications:

- **From the OS/2 desktop:** As with all applications, this is the preferred method. Double-click on the folder that contains your Windows applications, then double-click on the icon for the program you want to run. The type of session that starts is determined by the settings in the Settings notebook. When you quit the program, you return to the desktop.

- **From the Windows desktop:** Double-click on the OS/2 System icon on the desktop, then double-click on the Command Prompts folder, and finally, double-click on the WIN-OS/2 Full Screen icon. The Program Manager window opens, and you can use all of the usual Windows features. To return to the OS/2 desktop, choose Exit WIN- OS/2 selection from the Program Manager File menu, select Close from the system menu, or double-click on the close box to return to the OS/2 desktop when you are done. Closing the session automatically exits each running Windows program.

- **From the OS/2 or DOS command prompt:** Type WINOS2 followed by path and file-name information at the command prompt. For example, to run Microsoft Word for Windows from the OS/2 session prompt, type

  WINOS2 C:\WINWORD\WINWORD.EXE

  When you quit the program, you return to the command prompt, not the desktop.

To return to the OS/2 desktop without closing your Windows session, select the OS/2 Desktop icon at the bottom of the WIN-OS/2 session screen, then select the program or session name from the Window List to return to your WIN-OS/2 session.

Starting Windows Programs Automatically

You can set up a WIN-OS/2 session so that it automatically starts one or more Windows programs when you double-click on the session's icon on the desktop. Select the Command Prompts folder from the OS/2 System icon, open the pop-up menu for WIN-OS/2 Full Screen, then select the arrow to the right of the Open command. Select Settings, then select Program. In the Parameters field, type the path and file-name information for each program you want to start automatically, separating each one with commas. Add an exclamation point (!) before a file name if you want the application to appear as an icon when the session begins. Then close the Program Settings window.

Next time you start this Windows session, your chosen application will start automatically. When you close the application, you return directly to the OS/2 desktop.

Starting DOS or OS/2 Programs from WIN-OS/2

You can start a DOS or OS/2 program from a WIN-OS/2 session if you select Run from the WIN-OS/2 Program Manager menu bar, and type the path and file name information at the Command Line field.

Alternatively, you can select the WIN-OS/2 Main group from the WIN-OS/2 Program Manager, select the File Manager, and choose the program name from the directory tree.

If you use either of these methods to start programs, you return to the WIN-OS/2 session when you quit, not to the command line or to the OS/2 desktop.

Exchanging Data in Win-OS/2

There are three different levels of interprogram data exchange available in OS/2. They are, in order of increasing automation and ease of use:

- The clipboard, a completely manual method that can be used to move data between any combination of DOS, OS/2, and WIN-OS/2 programs.

- DDE, an automatic linking system available to move information between two OS/2 applications, two WIN-OS/2 applications, or an OS/2 and a WIN-OS/2 application. All must support DDE.

- OLE, a fully automatic linking and embedding mechanism for use between WIN-OS/2 applications only. It is not available anywhere outside WIN-OS/2.

Using the Clipboard

OS/2 provides clipboard support between Windows programs, DOS programs, and OS/2 programs. In Chapter 6 we looked at using the clipboard with DOS applications; this section will deal with Windows and OS/2 applications.

The clipboard lets you exchange formatted text or graphical information between programs.

NOTE   Objects in the clipboard can be any size and format.

OS/2 supports the following clipboard formats, as well as several private formats:

- **Text:** Text terminated with a nul character.

- **OEMTEXT:** Null-terminated text using an OEM (original equipment manufacturer) character set.

- **Picture:** A metafile.

- **Bitmap:** A device-dependent bitmap.

- **DIB Bitmap:** A device-independent bitmap.

- **SYLK:** Short for symbolic link, a proprietary data interchange format used by Microsoft when transferring spreadsheet data.

- **DIF:** Standard data interchange format, used for spreadsheet and database information.

- **TIFF:** Tagged image file format, used for graphical images.

- **Any Private Format:** For information that falls into this "other" category, the clipboard just passes the information through; it is up to the sending and receiving programs to make sense and impose order on the data.

Also, WIN-OS/2 will convert some of the data formats on their way to the clipboard, to handle differences in format:

- **Windows DIB Bitmaps:** Windows device-independent bitmaps are converted to or from OS/2 bitmaps.

- **Windows Bitmaps:** Pre-Windows 3.0 bitmaps are converted into OS/2 bitmaps.

- **Windows Metafiles:** Windows metafiles are converted into the Windows DIB format.

- **OS/2 Metafiles:** OS/2 metafiles are converted into a bitmap.

- **Text:** ASCII text can be converted in either direction. If the sending and receiving environments use different code pages, the appropriate translation will take place.

To cut or copy information to the clipboard, first use the mouse to mark the information, then use either the Cut or the Copy command from the application's Edit menu to place the information on the clipboard. Now open the data file in which you want to place the information, and point to the spot in the file where you want to place the information from the clipboard. Use the Paste command from the Edit menu to insert the information.

Using Dynamic Data Exchange

Dynamic Data Exchange (DDE) is a more automatic method of exchanging information between two programs that both support it. This method creates a link between the source and destination files, so that any changes you make to the information in its source (for example, a range of cells in a spreadsheet) can be automatically reflected in its destination (perhaps a formatted table in a word processed document). You no longer need to remember to change information in two places; DDE does it for you.

To create a link, first start the source application (in our example, the spreadsheet). In the appropriate file, select the information you want to link. Choose Copy from this program's Edit menu. Now use the word processor to open the destination document, and place the mouse pointer where you want to insert the linked information. Choose the Paste Link option from the Edit menu in this application, and select the type of information you want to add to your document. The Paste Link command not only copies the marked information from the spreadsheet, but also creates a link between these two applications and data files. Now that a link is established, your document will be updated automatically whenever you update the information in the original spreadsheet document.

Configuring the Clipboard and DDE

The clipboard and the DDE function can be set to public or to private. When they are set to public, information can be shared with programs running in other sessions; for example, an OS/2 application can exchange information with a Windows program. The default setting for both the clipboard and for DDE is public. When the clipboard or DDE is set to private, data sharing between sessions (but not inside the same session) is restricted.

S O L U T I O N

The main reason you might want to make the clipboard private is to improve performance. The clipboard uses a technique called *delayed rendering,* which means that only the name of the data format is passed to the clipboard when you Cut or Copy; the actual data is loaded into the clipboard when you invoke the Paste command. With this technique, the data is passed to the clipboard at the last possible moment. However, when you use the clipboard to share information between OS/2 and WIN-OS/2 sessions, the clipboard receives all the information and then sends it to the other sessions, which can be time-consuming.

To change the Clipboard or DDE to private, double-click on the WIN-OS/2 Setup icon in the System Setup folder, and select Data Exchange. Select the Private button for either the clipboard or DDE, and close the Settings notebook.

When the WIN-OS/2 clipboard is private, you cannot use programs running in an OS/2 session to cut, copy or paste information to or from the WIN/OS2 clipboard. In other words, you can only cut, copy and paste within the WIN-OS/2 session. When DDE is set to private, similar restrictions on data transfer apply; you can only share information with other Windows programs.

To make DDE and the clipboard public or private for a WIN-OS/2 separate session, open the Windows Programs folder, display the pop-up menu for the program object, and open the Settings notebook at the Session page. Select the WIN-OS/2 Settings button, then choose either the WIN_CLIPBOARD or the WIN_DDE settings from the list, and check either the On or Off radio buttons; then close the Settings notebook. Now restart the program by double-clicking on the program icon.

Using Object Linking and Embedding

Object Linking and Embedding (OLE) offers the most efficient methods of exchanging information between Windows applications that support the feature. Like DDE, OLE also lets you automatically update information in a destination (or *client*) document to reflect changes made in the source (or *server*) file. But OLE goes a step further by allowing you to call up the source application from within the destination document. For example, suppose you've created a drawing in a paint program and copied it into a word processor document. If you select the drawing in the word processor file, WIN-OS/2 will call up the paint program to let you edit it as needed. If you've *linked* the copy back to its source, you are actually editing the original drawing, and your changes will appear in both places. If you've *embedded* the drawing, you are editing only the copy; the original remains unchanged. You link an object by choosing Paste Link on the destination application's Edit menu; you embed an object by choosing Paste. Windows appliations may support OLE as client, server, both, or neither.

Making OS/2 Look Like Windows 3

If you are in charge of a number of Windows users migrating to OS/2, you can make OS/2 look more Windows-like, and so ease the transition to the new operating system. The setup for this is somewhat involved, and should be performed by someone already familiar with Windows, the OS/2 desktop, and the OS/2 command line.

Place the original OS/2 Installation disk in drive A, and boot or reboot your computer. When the OS/2 logo screen appears, remove this disk and insert Disk #1 in drive A. When you see the Welcome screen, press the Escape key. Change to the C drive and to the OS2 directory, then type:

MAKEINI OS2.INI WIN_30.RC

When you see a message indicating a successful completion, remove the floppy disk from drive A, and reboot your computer as normal. Rebuilding the desktop takes quite a while, but when it opens, you will see a strong resemblance to Windows.

Once your users are comfortable with this in-between version, you can turn the option off and turn them loose on the real OS/2, by repeating the steps described above and this time typing:

        MAKEINI OS2.INI OS_20.RC

at the command prompt. Restart your system, and it will rebuild the OS/2 desktop.

Notes on Windows Application Compatibility

The following list contains information about the OS/2 compatibility of various Windows programs, and how you can use some of the DOS and WIN-OS/2 settings to tune the environment in which they run. The information that follows is, of course, version-specific; later versions of these programs may well work without any problems at all. This list also assumes you are using OS/2 2.1, which includes support for Windows Enhanced mode.

Action! Sampler 1.0

Set DPMI_MEMORY_LIMIT to 5 or more for this application to run.

Adobe Type Manager

If you use an IBM 4029 printer with Adobe Type Manager, some Windows applications may not function correctly. This can be avoided by not using the printer's resident fonts. To do this, open the ATM Control Panel in WIN-OS/2 and disable the Use Pre-built or Resident Fonts option.

After Dark

To run After Dark in a WIN-OS/2 window, you must change the object's settings to hide or minimize the program icon on the desktop.

Also, After Dark adds a TSR to AUTOEXEC.BAT when it is installed; to run in a WIN-OS/2 window, remove this reference.

Aldus PageMaker 4.0

In PageMaker 4.0, the spelling checker cannot find the dictionary, and you also have to deselect the Public setting to use the clipboard.

If you have problems when spooling Standard format files to the printer, set printing to Raw mode by opening the printer object's Settings notebook at the Queue Options tab and checking the Printer-Specific Format check box.

Aldus Persuasion 2.0

You must use the parallel printer ports for printing from Persuasion, and you must also deselect the Public setting if you want to use the clipboard.

Arts & Letters Graphics Editor 3.1

The DECIPHS utility program requires that a DOS session is started from the Windows environment, and this is not supported in OS/2 version 2.0; to run this program in a WIN-OS/2 window, change the object's settings so that it is minimized on the desktop.

Arts & Letters creates a directory called A&L. Unfortunately, the & character is reserved for indicating multiple commands on the OS/2 command line. The easiest way of changing to this directory is to enclose the whole directory name in quotes:

```
CD "A&L"
```

NOTES ON WINDOWS APPLICATION COMPATIBILITY

but you could also add a caret (^) prefix before the & and achieve the same result. In this case the command becomes:

```
CD A^&L
```

If you see a system error when running Arts & Letters, you must restart the operating system before running the program again. A portion of the program continues to run after the error, and you cannot start a new version of the program while that portion is running. When you restart the computer, this part of the program will also restart automatically. Close this copy of the program after the system restarts, and start a new copy from the program icon.

Borland Turbo Debugger for Windows

Run this program in a WIN-OS/2 full-screen session. When the debugger is called from Turbo C++, the screen may be temporarily corrupted, but it is restored correctly after the first screen repaint. You can force a repaint by clicking on several different windows.

Central Point PC Tools Deluxe 7.1

PC Tools 7.1 is mainly a DOS product, but also contains several Windows utilities too. Many of these utilities require starting a DOS session from the Windows environment, and that technique is not supported in OS/2 version 2.0. Instead, start these programs from a separate DOS session.

The backup program in this package works like Central Point Backup for Windows, which is in the list of programs that do not work correctly with OS/2.

Commute

When you install this program under WIN-OS/2, the statement:

```
KEYBOARD.DRV=COMMKBD.DRV
```

is added to the SYSTEM.INI file. This reference should be changed to:

```
KEYBOARD.DRV=KEYBOARD.DRV
```

CorelDRAW 2.0 for Windows

Install this program in a DOS session, and run it in a WIN-OS/2 full-screen session.

CorelDRAW 2.1 for Windows

To install this program, start a DOS session. Run FIXX /date (date must be lowercase). Run WIN-OS/2 from the command line, install the program, then exit WIN-OS/2. Now run FIXX /u.

Run the program in a WIN-OS/2 full-screen session.

Crosstalk

Before you run this program, type the following at the command prompt:

```
MODE COMx BUFFER=OFF
```

where *x* represents the number of the communications port you want to use.

Drafix CAD Version 1.11 for Windows

This program must be run in a WIN-OS/2 full-screen session.

Drafix CAD Version 3.0 for Windows

This program must be run in a WIN-OS/2 full-screen session.

Fastback for Windows

Use Version 1.01 of Fastback for Windows. It is available to registered users at no charge from Fifth Generation Systems at 800-873-4384.

In the Options menu, make sure that the Media setting is set to the system default. The other Media settings write to direct memory access (DMA) device drivers, which have compatibility problems.

FormBase 1.2

If you use this program and Lotus 1-2-3 in the same WIN-OS/2 session, make sure you always start FormBase first.

The installation program adds a SHARE statement to the AUTO-EXEC.BAT file; use one of the OS/2 editors to remove this statement before running the program.

Form Publisher

Make sure that the program's printer driver is installed before running the program.

FotoMan

Run this program in a WIN-OS/2 full-screen session.

Guide

For best results, run this program in a WIN-OS/2 full-screen session. If you don't, you may have problems using the program's pop-up boxes.

Harvard Draw for Windows

During installation of this program using WIN-OS/2, you will see an error dialog box. Just select the OK button, and the installation will finish normally.

Harvard Graphics for Windows

During installation of this program using WIN-OS/2, you will see an error dialog box. Just select the OK button, and the installation will finish normally.

Run this program in a WIN-OS/2 full-screen session. If you run it in a WIN-OS/2 window, the Color Selection windows do not show the Color Selection grid.

hDC FileApps 1.0 for Windows

This program opens the Windows Notepad on the README text file during installation. Just indicate that you don't want to read the file and the installation will complete normally.

HP New Wave 3.0 for Windows

Install this program from a DOS session. If you have problems with program or session termination, use an editor to set UseOS2shield=0 in the SYSTEM.INI file in the OS2\MDOS\WINOS2 directory. If that doesn't help matters, run the program in a WIN-OS/2 full-screen session.

IBM PC/3270 2.0

Use the Migrate Applications object to move this program to the desktop, then select the WIN-OS/2 Settings button on the Session page of the notebook, and add:

- /C PC3270WO.BAT to the DOS_SHELL setting
- D:/*path*DXMA0MOD.SYS, D:/*path*DXMC0MOD.SYS, and D:*path*PCS802.SYS V=N to the DOS_DEVICE setting

Run this program as a WIN-OS/2 separate session or as a WIN-OS/2 full-screen session.

Icon Author

Animations and graphics shipped with this program should be run on a VGA system or in a low-resolution XGA WIN-OS/2 full-screen session. If you use XGA in high-resolution, the graphics will be scaled to only a part of the screen and the text drawn in normal size.

Lotus Freelance Graphics for Windows

The pointer to printer objects points to Screen Show instead of to the printer.

MagiCorp for Windows

Running this program along with other programs in the same WIN-OS/2 session could cause a system halt, so run the program by itself in a WIN-OS/2 full-screen session.

Mathcad 3.0 for Windows

Start a DOS session to install this program, then run FIXX /date (date must be in lowercase), and install the program. Finally, run FIXX /u.

Mathcad 3.1 for Windows

Use the following WIN-OS/2 settings for this program:

- Set DPMI_MEMORY_LIMIT to 64 or more
- Set XMS_MEMORY_LIMIT to 0
- Set EMS_MEMORY_LIMIT to 0

Media Player and Recorder

Run this software in a WIN-OS/2 full-screen session. If you use a window, the session will end when you open a file with a .WAV filename extension.

Microsoft Bookshelf—CD-ROM Reference Library

This program needs version 6.14 of the mouse driver, MOUSE.COM, installed with the product.

To avoid audio and video problems, set INT_DURING_IO to On.

The program will not install if the path statement in your AUTO-EXEC. BAT file is longer than 254 characters. First make a backup of your AUTOEXEC.BAT, then edit the file and add the appropriate path statement. Finally, save AUTOEXEC.BAT and start a WIN-OS/2 session to install the program.

Microsoft CodeView for Windows

You should run this program in a WIN-OS/2 full-screen session.

Microsoft Excel for Windows

You must first deselect the Public setting if you want to use the clipboard.

When using dynamic data exchange (DDE), run the program in the same WIN-OS/2 session as the Windows program Excel is communicating with.

Microsoft Money 1.0

This program calls the Windows Calculator program. Use the OS/2 Calculator from the Productivity folder instead.

Microsoft Project for Windows 1.0

Install this program in a DOS session.

Microsoft QuickC

Run this program in a WIN-OS/2 full-screen session.

More Windows

Avoid the Full-Page Paper White or Full-Screen Color modes, because the screens may appear corrupted.

Norton Desktop for Windows

The Norton Desktop assumes that if it is not the first program loaded, then another desktop is running. Include the UseOS2shield=0 in your SYSTEM.INI file in the OS2\MDOS\WINOS2 directory on your startup disk.

If you have difficulty formatting floppy disks, use the OS/2 FORMAT command.

You should run the Norton Desktop in a WIN-OS/2 full-screen session.

Perform Pro 1.0 for Windows

Run this program in a WIN-OS/2 full-screen session.

PFS WindowWorks 1.75

Run this program in a WIN-OS/2 full-screen session.

Photostyler for Windows

Run this program in a WIN-OS/2 full-screen session.

When an image is scanned or input into a WIN-OS/2 window session when using SVGA mode, and a pull-down menu covers the image, if you then open a second pull-down menu, the first menu is not repainted properly.

Publisher's PowerPak 2.1 for Windows

You should create the directory C:\OS2\MDOS\WINOS2\POWERPAK before you run the installation batch file.

Quicken for Windows

This program calls the Windows Calculator program. Use the OS/2 Calculator from the Productivity folder instead.

SQLWindows 3.0 for Windows

This program occasionally accesses drive A. It is a good idea to keep a blank formatted disk in drive A to avoid "The A device is not ready" error messages.

Tetris for Windows

If you run Tetris in a WIN-OS/2 window session, you may see icon corruption on the desktop. If you do, use the Refresh command from the desktop pop-up menu to make the desktop repaint itself.

The Way You Work (Windows/DOS)

You should install this program from a DOS session. When installation is complete, you can run the program in a DOS session or in a WIN-OS/2 session.

Windows Multimedia Extensions

If you run this program with another program that accesses your audio adapter at the same time, you may get rather unpredictable results. You can avoid this by using the OS/2 Multimedia Presentation Manager.

Winfax Pro for Windows

You should only run this program in a WIN-OS/2 full-screen session.

When using dynamic data exchange (DDE), avoid switching out of the current WIN-OS/2 full-screen session, as the DDE link may fail if you do.

WordPerfect for Windows

If you have problems running WordPerfect, change to the directory that holds the WordPerfect files, and type:

    FIXWP WPWINFIL.EXE

To allow WordPerfect to run under DOS or native Windows 3.0, type:

    UNFIX WPWINFIL.EXE

Sometimes, button bar icons do not appear correctly; however, they operate correctly, and the button bar text is correct.

PART III

OS/2 and Computer Hardware

CHAPTERS

OS/2 OS/2 OS/2

OS/2
OS/2
OS/2
OS/2
OS/2
OS/2
OS/2
OS/2
OS/2

OS/2 OS/2 OS/2 O

OS/2 and Computer Systems

OS/2 OS/2 OS/2 OS/2 OS/2 OS/2 OS/2 OS/2 OS/2 OS

IBM has created one universal version of OS/2, designed to run on all qualified hardware, rather than building several versions of the operating system all tailored to different hardware.

To confirm compatibility, IBM puts each computer system provided by an OEM through a series of 18 tests.

OS/2 Hardware Requirements

OS/2 is a large operating system that is more capable and more complex than MS-DOS (alone or with Windows) and, as such, needs access to more hardware resources.

The basic hardware requirements for running OS/2 are usually quoted as:

- Intel 80386 (or higher) processor
- 4MB or more memory
- Two-button mouse or other pointing device
- 60MB hard disk with 15 to 30MB of free space, depending on the options you install
- High capacity floppy disk drive configured as drive A

You should consider these requirements to be the absolute minimum; OS/2 will run reliably, but will seem very slow for most applications. This chapter will help you determine more realistic requirements for your system.

You will need a high-capacity floppy disk drive to install OS/2, and because the PC architecture only allows an operating system to boot from drive A, and not from drive B, make sure that you have the appropriate configuration. If you use 5.25" disks, the drive must be a 1.2MB drive, and if you use 3.5" disks, the drive capacity can be either 1.44MB or 2.88MB. After OS/2 is installed you can read from or write to lower density floppy disks, such as 360K 5.25" disks, and the 720K 3.5" disks.

NOTE   IBM has set up OS/2 to install from drive A, but if the OS/2 installation disks you have are the wrong size for your A drive, call 800-3IBMOS2, and IBM will send you two disks that will let you boot the installation from drive A and then continue with the rest of the installation using drive B. This utility is also available on CompuServe and other bulletin boards.

When to Add Memory

You may have installed 4MB of memory in your computer, but if OS/2 still does not run satisfactorily, your computer may be using some of that memory for its own purposes. Some computers use 128K as shadow RAM, remapping ROM firmware into RAM to make the system execute faster. If this is the case, your computer no longer has 4MB available. One of the most common signs of tight memory is that the final screen of the desktop Shut Down operation is never displayed. This screen tells you that Shut Down is complete, and that it is now safe to turn off or restart your computer. If you don't see this message, consider adding more memory.

Most OS/2 systems have the following hardware installed:

- Intel 80386 processor running at 25MHz, or higher
- 6 to 8MB of RAM
- 100MB hard disk with 60MB of free space

This system will run most normal applications, providing a reasonable response time. With 6MB of memory, you can run an OS/2 application, a couple of DOS applications, or a couple of Windows applications. If you use lots of Windows applications, plan on adding 1MB for every additional Windows application you want to run concurrently with the others.

To multitask full-featured OS/2 applications, you need 1MB to 3MB per concurrent application. Check the documentation that comes with your application programs for more on this; system memory requirements will increase and decrease as applications invoke the print spooler, or when applications are started or stopped.

▶ SOLUTION

The easiest and most cost-effective way to improve OS/2 performance is to add more memory. If you are concerned about the length of time your system takes to load programs, switch between tasks, or start new sessions, you can improve performance by adding more memory. The greatest increase in speed occurs by increasing RAM from 4MB to 8MB or 16MB.

If you make unusual demands of your OS/2 system—for example, if you use CADD or engineering applications, or if you are a software developer —consider upgrading your whole system:

- 80486 running at 33MHz, or better
- 16MB memory
- 200MB hard disk with at least 125MB free space

Application Memory Use

Graphical applications can consume large amounts of memory, and if you want to multitask several such applications, you will need lots of it. Table 8.1 shows the approximate memory used by different parts of the OS/2 environment, and Table 8.2 shows the memory used by different kinds of applications.

TABLE 8.1: OS/2 Memory Usage—Operating System Components

OPERATING SYSTEM COMPONENT	MEMORY USED (MB)
OS/2 Operating System	3.0
HPFS	0.5
DOS Full-Screen Session	0.3
Each Additional Full-Screen Session	0.2
DOS Window Session	0.3
Each Additional Window Session	1.0
First WIN-OS/2 Session	2.0
Each additional WIN-OS/2 Session	1.0
Active Spooling	0.5
DDE	0.4
Clipboard	0.2

The figures for application programs in Table 8.2 are given as approximate guidelines only; consult your reseller for specific information on specific applications.

Some programs are capable of generating huge data files, and so we'll look at hard disk space requirements next.

Planning OS/2 Disk Space Requirements

OS/2's disk space requirements call for 15 to 30MB of free disk space, depending on the operating-system features you install. You need 15MB for the minimum OS/2 installation and 30MB for a complete installation; a partial installation will fall somewhere between these two figures.

TABLE 8.2: OS/2 Memory Usage—Application Categories

APPLICATION CATEGORY	MEMORY USED (MB)
Communications	0.5
Language Compilers	0.8
Database	1.0
Engineering or Scientific	2.0
Games	0.2
Graphics	1.0
Spreadsheets	1.0
Utility Programs	0.5
Word Processors	0.5

Remember, these figures are just for the operating system; they take no account of the space you will need for application programs and the data files that you will create, nor do they include OS/2 add-ons like the Extended Services or Database or Communications Manager.

If you plan to partition your hard disk to support different operating systems, Table 8.3 will help you decide on the minimum partition size for various versions of MS-DOS and OS/2.

When you install OS/2, you can choose which of the optional features you want to install, and when the installation is complete, you can run the Selective Install program to change these options at any time. Table 8.4 lists the hard disk space requirements for each of the optional features for OS/2 version 2.1. You can use this table to decide which features to install.

TABLE 8.3: Planning Table for Hard Disk Partitions

OPERATING SYSTEM	SPACE REQUIRED (MB)	COMMENTS
MS DOS 3.3	2	Must be in a primary partition within the first 32MB on the first hard disk.
MS DOS 4.0	3	Must be in a primary partition on the first hard disk.
MS DOS 5.0	4	Must be in a primary partition on the first hard disk.
OS/2 1.X Standard Edition	20	Must be in a primary partition on the first hard disk.
OS/2 1.X Extended Edition	30	Must be in a primary partition on the first hard disk.
OS/2 2.X	15–30	Can be in either a primary partition or on a logical drive.

TABLE 8.4: Hard Disk Space Requirements for Optional Features

CATEGORY	OPTION	SPACE REQUIRED(K)
CD_ROM DEVICE SUPPORT (OS/2 2.0)	CD-ROM Installable File System	51
	IBM CD-ROM Device Drivers	33
DOCUMENTATION	OS/2 Tutorial	168
	OS/2 Command Reference	391

TABLE 8.4: Hard Disk Space Requirements for Optional Features (Continued)

CATEGORY	OPTION	SPACE REQUIRED(K)
DOCUMENTATION (continued)	REXX Information	195
FONTS	Courier	87
	Helvetica	222
	System Monospaced	34
	Times Roman	205
	Courier (outline)	200
	Helvetica (outline)	160
	Times Roman (outline)	172
OPTIONAL SYSTEM UTILITIES	Backup Hard Disk	82
	Change File Attributes	35
	Display Directory Tree	33
	Manage Partitions	217
	Label Disks	33
	Link Object Modules	284
	Picture Viewer	33
	PMREXX	83
	Recover Files	45
	Restore Backed Up Files	29
	Sort Filter	30
	Installation Aid	265
PRODUCTIVITY TOOLS AND GAMES	Enhanced Editor	882
	Search and Scan Tool	69
	PM Terminal	1501
	Fax/PM	1205

TABLE 8.4: Hard Disk Space Requirements for Optional Features (Continued)

CATEGORY	OPTION	SPACE REQUIRED(K)
PRODUCTIVITY TOOLS AND GAMES (continued)	PM Chart	1159
	Personal Productivity	1344
	Solitaire—Klondike	371
	Reversi	33
	Scramble	59
	Cat & Mouse	51
	Pulse	29
	Jigsaw	68
	Chess	251
OS/2 DOS & WIN-OS/2 SUPPORT	DOS Protect Mode Interface	20
	Virtual Expanded Memory Management	18
	Virtual Extended Memory Support	8
	OS/2 DOS Support	1200
	WIN-OS/2 Support	7200
OTHER OPTIONS	HPFS	400
	Advanced Power Management (OS/2 2.1 only)	100
	PCMCIA Support (OS/2 2.1 only)	100
	REXX	400
	Service & Diagnostic Aids	600
	Optional Bit Maps	300

A Quick Look Inside the 80386/80486 Processors

Intel manufactures a whole series of CPU chips, including the various models of the 80386, and its matched math coprocessor the 80387, the 80486, and now the Pentium, also known as the P5 or 80586 chip. Each chip builds on the speed and capabilities of its predecessor. For example, the 80486 also contains an on-board math coprocessor. With earlier systems such as the 80386, you had to add the math coprocessor as a separate chip.

N O T E

For the purposes of this discussion, we can consider the Pentium to be a faster and more capable version of the 80486, and the 80486 to be a faster and more capable version of the 80386. While some might argue that this is a gross oversimplification, it is essentially correct in terms of the software they can run.

The speed of each chip is expressed in MHz (megahertz)—20MHz, 25MHz, 33MHz, and so on. The clock speed is the rate at which the clock oscillates, generating a stream of digital timing pulses used to synchronize every operation inside the computer. The clock speed of the processor is one of the major factors determining overall system performance (the others being issues such as bus speed, bus size, and hard disk speed). The general rule is that the higher the clock speed, the faster the processor, although this is not always true, and the relationship is often difficult to quantify precisely. Some more recent chips run at one speed internally, so that they can make maximum advantage of technological advances, and a lower speed "externally," when communicating with slower devices inside the computer.

There are many other chip designations besides clock speed, including 80386DX (a full 32-bit processor), 80386SX (a low-cost 80386 with a

16-bit data bus), 80486DX (a full 32-bit 80486 processor), 80486 (a lower-cost 80486 without the built-in cache or math coprocessor), and 80486DX-2 (a double-speed 80486DX). For the purposes of this book, we can think of all these chips as being the same thing because they can all run the same software.

The 80386 has three modes of operation:

- **Real Mode**. The simplest of the three modes, real mode allows the 80386 to operate as a very fast version of the older 8086 chip. If you use MS-DOS on an 80386, you will operate in real mode, and be able to address 1MB memory.

- **Protected Mode**. Protected mode increases the possible address space to 4GB, and allows for the running of virtual memory programs of almost unlimited size. In addition, protected mode provides a sophisticated memory management and hardware-assisted protection mechanism, designed to support multitasking operating systems like OS/2.

- **Virtual 8086 Mode**. Virtual 8086 mode allows the execution of 8086 applications, while still offering the protection methods and advantages of protected mode. This mode gives OS/2 access to multiple virtual DOS machines for DOS and WIN-OS/2 sessions.

IBM has an Intel license to make CPU chips. Some of the IBM computers contain chips made by Intel, while others contain chips made by IBM. Several other companies, most notably AMD (Advanced Micro Devices) have agreements with Intel, many of which await clarification in the US court system.

Using OS/2 with IBM Hardware

OS/2 was originally developed on IBM hardware, and it runs on the following IBM systems (as IBM continues to release new hardware as part of its aggressive new marketing campaign, this list will also grow):

PS/1 2133 386SX/25
PS/1 2133 486SX/20
PS/1 2133 486DX/20
PS/1 2133 486DX/40
PS/1 2155 386SX/25
PS/1 2155 486SX/20
PS/1 2155 486DX/20
PS/1 2155 486DX/33
PS/1 2155 486DX/40
PS/2 8540 386SX/20
PS/2 8543 386SX/20
PS/2 8555 386SX/16
PS/2 8556 386SX/20
PS/2 8556 386SLC/20
PS/2 8557 386SX/20
PS/2 8557 386SLC/20
PS/2 8565 386SX/16
PS/2 8570 386DX/16-25
PS/2 8570 486DX/25
PS/2 8573 386DX/16
PS/2 8575 486DX/33
PS/2 8580 386DX/20
PS/2 8590 486SX/25
PS/2 8590 486DX/25-33
PS/2 8590 486DX2/50-66

PS/2 8595 486SX/25

PS/2 8595 486DX/25-33

PS/2 8595 486DX2/50-66

PS/2 9556 486SLC2

PS/2 9557 486SLC2

PS/2 9576 486SX

PS/2 9576 486DX2

PS/2 9577 486SX

PS/2 9577 486DX2

PS/2 9585 486SX

PS/2 9585 486DX2

PS/2 9595 486DX

PS/2 9595 486DX2

PS/2 295 486DX

PS/ThinkPad N45SL 386SL

PS/ThinkPad N51SX 386SX

PS/ThinkPad N51SLC 386SLC

PS/ThinkPad CL57SX 386SX

PS/ThinkPad 300 386SL

PS/ThinkPad 700 486SLC

PS/ThinkPad 700C 486SLC

PS/ValuePoint 325T

PS/ValuePoint 425SX

PS/ValuePoint 433DX

PS/ValuePoint 466DX2

Using OS/2 with Non-IBM Hardware

Because of fears that OS/2 might not run on a large number of different computers, IBM has tested, and continues to test, a large number of personal computer manufacturer (PCM) systems for OS/2 compatibility.

These tests verify 18 key areas of OS/2 operation and are based on systems provided by the original manufacturers. Because testing continues, the list of qualified machines continues to grow. Table 8.5 lists the computers qualified as of this writing, and includes over 500 computers from 95 different manufacturers from around the world. You can update this information by downloading the file PCMTAB.TXT from Library 17 of the CompuServe OS/2 Support Forum (GO OS2SUP), or from the IBM National Support Center bulletin board. See Appendix B for more information on how to contact both of these services.

TABLE 8.5: Non-IBM Computers Qualified to Run OS/2

MANUFACTURER	MODEL
ACER	1125E
	AcerFrame 300 486DX/33
	AcerFrame 1000
	AcerFrame 3000 MP/33
	AcerMate 386/33
	AcerMate 386SX/20N
	AcerPower 386SX
	AcerPower 425s
	AcerPower 433e
	AcerPower 486SX
	AcerPower 500

TABLE 8.5: Non-IBM Computers Qualified to Run OS/2 (Continued)

MANUFACTURER	MODEL
AEG OLYMPIA	Olystar 70V
	Olystar 80S
ALR	BusinessSTATION 386DX Model 1
	BusinessSTATION 486SX/20 Model 101
	BusinessVEISA 386/33 Model 1
	BusinessVEISA 486/33 Model 101
	MPS Modular 386/33 Model 1
	MPS Modular 486/33 Model 101
	PowerFlex 20SX Model 80
	PowerFlex FLYER Model 60
	PowerPro 33/486 Model SMP 128/150
AMAX	PC/486
AMBRA	Enterprise Full Desktop 4865X/25
	Enterprise Full Desktop 486DX/33
	Enterprise MAX 486DX/33
	Enterprise MAX 486DX/50
	Enterprise MAX 486DX2/50
	Enterprise MAX486DX2/66
	Enterprise Slim Profile 386SX/33
	Enterprise Slim Profile 486SX/25
	Hurdla 386SX/33
	Hurdla 486SX/25
	Hurdla 486SX/25
	Hurdla 486DX/33
	Hurdla 486DX/50
	Hurdla 486DX2/50

TABLE 8.5: Non-IBM Computers Qualified to Run OS/2 (Continued)

MANUFACTURER	MODEL
AMBRA (continued)	Hurdla 486DX2/66
	Sprinta 386SX/33
	Sprinta 486SX/25
AMI	EZ-Flex
AMSTRAD	PC3386 SX
AOX	Micromaster 386 in PS2 Model 60
	Micromaster 486 in PS2 Model 55
APD	Series/40
APRICOT	LS 386SX-20
	LS PRO 386SX
	Qi 386-25
	Qi 486-25
ARCHE	Legacy 486
ARES	TP 386/33 SONIC
	TP 486/33 SONIC
ASEM	DS 486/33
ASI COMPUTER	Easyline 486 SX 25
	Megaline 486/33
AST	Bravo 3/25s
	Bravo 386SX/20
	Bravo 486/25 83V
	Power Premium 4/33
	Premium 386/33
	Premium 486/33E
	Premium 486/33TE
	Premium II 386SX/20

TABLE 8.5: Non-IBM Computers Qualified to Run OS/2 (Continued)

MANUFACTURER	MODEL
AST (continued)	Premium II 386/33
	Premium II 486SX/20
	Premium EXEC 386SX/20
	Premium EXEC 386SX/25 Color
	Premium SE 4/33
	Premium SE 4/50
ATOMSTYLE	APC 386-33
AT&T	Safari
	StarServer S
	6386/25 WGS
	6386SX/EL20 WGS
CAS	386SX-20
C & C COMPUTERS	MT 450/256
CHEM CORP	386DX-40 Opti
CLUB AMERICA	FALCON 433
COMMODORE	386-33C
	386SX-20
	486-33C
COMPAQ	386/20
	LTE-386s/20
	DeskPro 386/25e
	DeskPro 386/25M
	DeskPro 386/33L
	DeskPro 386/N
	DeskPro 386/s
	DeskPro 386S/20

TABLE 8.5: Non-IBM Computers Qualified to Run OS/2 (Continued)

MANUFACTURER	MODEL
COMPAQ (continued)	DeskPro 486/16M
	DeskPro 486/50L
	SystemPro 386
	SystemPro 486
COMPUADD	320sc
	325
	333T
	433E
COPAM PC	486B/33
CRITIKON	8600
CUBE COMPUTER	340 ATX
	433 ATX
	450 ATX
CUMULUS	486SX/20
	GLC 386SX/20
	GLC 386DX/25
	GLC 386DX/33
	GLC 486DX/33
	WORKBOX 16
	WORKBOX 20
DAILY COMPUTER	Daly 386-40
	Daly 486-33
	Daly 486E-50
DEC	DECpc 316SX
	DECPC 320
	DECpc 325

TABLE 8.5: Non-IBM Computers Qualified to Run OS/2 (Continued)

MANUFACTURER	MODEL
DEC (continued)	DECpc 325sxLP
	DECpc 333
	DECpc 420SX
	DECpc 425
	DECpc 425ST
	DECpc 433dxLP
	DECpc 433dxMP
	DECpc 433ST
	DECpc 433T
	DECpc 433 Workstation
	DECpc 450d2MP
	DECpc 450D2LP
	DECpc 450ST
	DECpc 452ST
	DECpc 466d2MT
	DECpc 466ST
	DECstation 320
	DECstation 320+
	DECstation 333c
DELL	320N+
	320SX
	325P
	333D
	433DE
	433/L
	433s/ME
	450/M

TABLE 8.5: Non-IBM Computers Qualified to Run OS/2 (Continued)

MANUFACTURER	MODEL
DELL (continued)	450SE
	466/T
	486D/25
	486P/33
DTK COMPUTER	Grafika - 4A
	Grafika - 4C
	Grafika - 4D
	Grafika - 4E
	Grafika - 4F
	Grafika - 4G
	Grafika - 4H
	Grafika - 4I
	Grafika - 4J
DYNEX	386-25
EPSON	T0341U
	T2331U
	EISA Series T2331C
	EISA Series T2331U
	EISA Series 4s/25Te
	EISA Series 4/33Te
	EISA Series 4/50De
	EISA Series 4/50Te
	Equity 320SX Plus
	Equity 386/33 Plus
	Equity 486DX2/50 Plus
	ExpressStation 4s/25

TABLE 8.5: Non-IBM Computers Qualified to Run OS/2 (Continued)

MANUFACTURER	MODEL
EPSON (continued)	ExpressStation 4/33
	386/33 EX0-2804D-000L
	486SX/20 EX0-2904A-010L
	486SX/25
	486/33 EX0-2904D-B1
	486/33e EX0-2904D-01EL
	486/33e EX0-2908D-01EC
	486DX2
	486DX2/50 EX0-2804P-E1ET
	DX2/50
	Step MegaCube DX/50e
	Tempo 386/33 EX0-4408M-00HL
	Tempo 386/33c EX0-4404M-00HS
	Tempo 486/20 EX0-4504J-00HL
	Tempo 486SX/20c EX0-4504J-00HS
	Tempo 486/33 EX0-4608M-00HL
	Tempo 486/33c EX0-4608M-00HS
	Tempo 486DX2/50 M
	Tempo Standard 386/25
	Tempo Standard 386SX/16
	Tempo Standard 386SX/20
	Tempo Standard 386SX/25
GATEWAY 2000	386SX/20C
	386/33C
	486/33C
	486/33E

TABLE 8.5: Non-IBM Computers Qualified to Run OS/2 (Continued)

MANUFACTURER	MODEL
GRID	386is-25
	386sx-MFP20
	4020SX
	4025LS
	4025LX
	GRiDCASE 1550sx
	APT/425se
	APT/450e
	MFP/420s
	MFP/425s
	MFP 425s+
	MFP 433+
	MFP 433s+
	MFP/450
	MFP 450+
	MFP 466+
	MFP/540
G2 COMPUTER SYSTEMS	S1-SX
HERTZ	486/33
HEWLETT PACKARD	QS/20
	Vectra 386/16N
	Vectra 386/25
	Vectra 486/25T
	Vectra 486s/20
	Vectra RS/25C
	Vectra 486/33T

TABLE 8.5: Non-IBM Computers Qualified to Run OS/2 (Continued)

MANUFACTURER	MODEL
HEWLETT PACKARD (continued)	Vectra 486/50U
HYPERTEC	386SX/25—PS/2 Mod 50Z
	386SX/33—PS/2 Mod 50Z
	486/33—PS/2 Mod 80
HYUNDAI ELECTRONICS AMERICA	425SP
	433DP
	433SP
	450D2P
ICL	Personal Computer CL386S
	Personal Computer CL386s/25
	Personal Computer CL486
	Personal Computer CL486s/25
	Personal Computer CS386s
	Personal Computer CS386s/25
	Personal Computer CX386s
	Personal Computer CX386s/25
	Personal Computer CX486
	Personal Computer CX486s/25
	Personal Computer CXe486
	Personal Computer CXe486s
	Personal Computer CXe486/66
	Personal Computer FX486
	Personal Computer FX486s
	Personal Computer FX486/66

TABLE 8.5: Non-IBM Computers Qualified to Run OS/2 (Continued)

MANUFACTURER	MODEL
ICL (continued)	Personal Computer NB386L
	Personal Computer NB386LC
INACOM	386/33
INTEL	SnapIn/386 - IBM PC/AT
	SnapIn/386 - PS2 Model 50Z
	SnapIn/386 - PS2 Model 60
	DT386-33H
	LP486SX25E
	Professional GX
	XPRESS Desktop 50mhz i486DX2
INTERCOMP	Digit 486SLC-25
	Master 486DX-50
	Master 486DX2-66
	Planet 486DX-50 EISA
	Target 486SLC-25
	Target 486DX-33
INVESTRONICA	WS-900 SX
	WS-600 CACHE
ITAUTEC	IS 486 D33E (IDE)
	IS 486 D33E (SCSI)
JEN ELETIRONICA S.R.L.	PR 466E/256
	ST 386SX33/32
	ST 486/66
KINGSTON	SX/Now! 50Z
	SX/Now! 60
	SX/Now SX25/GAM-PS/2 Mod 50

TABLE 8.5: Non-IBM Computers Qualified to Run OS/2 (Continued)

MANUFACTURER	MODEL
KINGSTON (continued)	SX/Now SX25/LCM-PS/2 Mod 50Z
	SX/Now SX25/GAM-PS/2 Mod 60
	SX/Now SX33/LCM-PS/2 Mod 50Z
KONTRON ELEKTRONIK	IP Lite Color 486
KREX COMPUTERS	Krex 486
LEADING EDGE	MT33
	D4/SX20
LOCLAND	486-SX Convertible
	486-33 Convertible
	486-50 Convertible
	486-50 EISA Convertible
MEMOREX	TELEX Model 8090-50
	TELEX Model 8257
	TELEX Model 8267
	TELEX Model 8280
	TELEX Model 8290
MIND COMPUTER PRODUCTS	486SX-25 OuC3
	486-DX-33
MINI-MICRO	386
	486
MITAC	MiStation 3052E
	Personal Computer 3060F
MONYDATA	386 SX
	Modula 60
NCR	System 3220/3220 Model 0100

TABLE 8.5: Non-IBM Computers Qualified to Run OS/2 (Continued)

MANUFACTURER	MODEL
NCR (continued)	System C3314
	System 3320/3421 Model 2014
	System 3335/3432 Model 1000
	System 3335/C3432 Model 5000
	System 3340/C3314 Model 1000
	System 3345/C3433 Model 5000
	System 3345/3433 Model 2000
	System 3350 Model 1000
	System 3355/C3355 Model 4100
	System 3445/C3434 Model 3000
	System 3445/C3434 Model 5000
	System C3420
	System 3447/3437 Model 3000
NEC	PowerMate SX/20i
	PowerMate SX/20vi
	PowerMate 386/33E
	PowerMate 386/33i
	PowerMate 425
	PowerMate 433
	PowerMate 486SX/25i
	PowerMate 486/25E
	PowerMate 486/33e
	PowerMate 486/33i
	PowerMate 486/50e
	PowerMate 486/50i
	PowerMate 486/66i

TABLE 8.5: Non-IBM Computers Qualified to Run OS/2 (Continued)

MANUFACTURER	MODEL
NEC (continued)	PowerMate DX2/66e
	Ready 325
	Ready 425
	Ready 433
	Ready 466
	Ultralite SL/20
	PWS 45/50 SCSI
NIXDORF	PWS M45
	PWS M50
NORMEREL	NS 48
	NS 78
NORTHGATE	Elegance 433E
	Elegance ZXP
NOTESTAR	NP-925
	NP-933
OCCIDENTAL SYSTEMS	Executive 486DX-33
	Upgradeable 486DX-33
OLIVETTI	LSX5010
	LSX5020
	LSX5025
	M300-08
	M300-10
	M300-15
	M300-25
	M380-40
	M400-10

TABLE 8.5: Non-IBM Computers Qualified to Run OS/2 (Continued)

MANUFACTURER	MODEL
OLIVETTI (continued)	M480-30
	P750
PACKARD-BELL	486-33
PANATEK	486DX-33
PHILIPS	P3348
	P3371
	P3448
PHOCUS	PD340-240
	PS333-105
	PST433-425
	PT433-670
	PW325-105
PROFESSIONAL COMPUTER MFG	Emerald Flexi 3486
	Emerald Flexi 486V
PROLOGICA	ATSP 386DX
	ATSP 486
REEVES	386SX-25
	386SX-25C
	386-33C
	486SX-20C
	486-33C
REPLY	Turbo Upgrade Planar / 50-50Z
	Turbo Upgrade Planar/2-55
	D16 3SX-160 Model 16 MCA
	D32 386-20C Model 32 MCA

TABLE 8.5: Non-IBM Computers Qualified to Run OS/2 (Continued)

MANUFACTURER	MODEL
REPLY (continued)	D32 386-25C Model 32 MCA
	D32 386-33C Model 32 MCA
	D32 4SX-200 Model 32 MCA
	D32 486-250 Model 32 MCA
	D32 486-330 Model 32 MCA
	D32 486-50C Model 32 MCA
	D32 486-50D Model 32 MCA
RESEARCH MACHINES	QE 486 33c
SCANDIC PRODUCTS	1-34201i
	1-45201i
	3-43201E
	3-45201E
SEC	DeskMaster 386S/25
	DeskMaster 486C/25
	DeskMaster 486S/25N
	DeskMaster 486/33E
	NoteMaster 386S/25
	NoteMaster 486c/25
	NoteMaster 486s/25
	SD760 Desktop PC
	SD925 Desktop PC
	SD940 Desktop PC
	S3800 Notebook PC
	S3900 Notebook PC
SIDUS SYSTEMS	Formula 386-33/DT
	Formula 486sx-25/LP

OS/2 AND COMPUTER SYSTEMS

TABLE 8.5: Non-IBM Computers Qualified to Run OS/2 (Continued)

MANUFACTURER	MODEL
SIDUS SYSTEMS (continued)	SCI925Dsx/LP
SIEMENS NIXDORF	PCD-3Bsx
	PCD-3Msx/20
	PCD-4H
	PCD-4T/33
	PCE-4C
	PCM-3Dsx/16
	PCM-4T
SPEAR TECHNOLOGY	Shuttle HOT 307-40
STAVER COMPUTER	386SX40
	PC386SX-33
	PC386SX40-80
	PC486DLC-80
	PC486DLC33-720
SWAN	386/33M
TANDON	OPTIoN T30000
	OPTIoN PRO T30050
	PAC II 486/33
TANDY	425 sx
	433 sx
	433 DX
	450 DX2
	466 DX2
	2500 sx/33
	4020 SX/386
	4025 LX/386

TABLE 8.5: Non-IBM Computers Qualified to Run OS/2 (Continued)

MANUFACTURER	MODEL
TANDY (continued)	4825 sx
	4833 LX/T
	4850 EP
	4866 LX/T
TATUNG	TCS-8160S
	TCS-8460S
	TCS-8800D
	TCS-8960S
	TCS-9600T
TEXAS INSTRUMENTS	386SX/20
	386SX/25
	386SXP
	386/33
	386/33P
	486/33E
	486/33TE
	486/50TE
	TravelMate 3000 Series
TEXAS MICRO SYSTEMS	C-486SE/33 3014A
THONNES DATENSYSTEME	DX386-33
	DX486-33
TI'KO	PS325
	PS325C
	PS340C
	PS420C
	PS433C

TABLE 8.5: Non-IBM Computers Qualified to Run OS/2 (Continued)

MANUFACTURER	MODEL
TI'KO (continued)	PS450C
TOSHIBA	T1800
	T1850
	T1850C
	T2000SX
	T2000SXe
	T2200SX
	T3100SX
	T3200SX
	T3200SXC
	T3300SL
	T4400SX
	T4400SXC
	T5200
	T5200/100
	T6400SX
	T6400SXC
	T6400DX
	T6400DXC
	T8500 Model 25
TOUCH	TD333
	TD433
TRIGEM COMPUTERS	TG SX 486 MM
TULIP	cd486 sx
	de486 dx/e
	de486 dx/50

TABLE 8.5: Non-IBM Computers Qualified to Run OS/2 (Continued)

MANUFACTURER	MODEL
TULIP (continued)	de486 dx/66
	Vision Line dt-486sx
	Vision Line dt-486dx/e
	Vision Line de-486sx/e
TWINHEAD	Slimnote 425sx
	SS 600/425 C
	Superpro 900E
ULTRA-COMP	486DX - 33 I
	486DX - 50 I
	486DX2 - 66 I
UNISYS	PC1-32532
	PW2-4163-SX
	PW2-Advantage 4336DX
VICTOR	V386M/33
	V386MX/20
	V486M/33
	V486MX/20
VIGLEN	Genie Executive 4DX33
	Genie Micro 4SX20
WANG MICROSYSTEMS	DTE33
	DTI250
	DTI66
	EC 480/33C
	PC-350-40C
WEARNES	Boldline 385SX-25
WYSE TECHNOLOGY	6000i 645

TABLE 8.5: Non-IBM Computers Qualified to Run OS/2 (Continued)

MANUFACTURER	MODEL
WYSE TECHNOLOGY (continued)	7000i 740MP-INT
	7000I 760MP-INT
	Decision 486SE-25SX
	Decision 486SI-25SX
	Decision 486/33E
	Decision 486SE-33SX
	Decision 486SI-33SX
	Decision 486SE-33DX
	Decision 486SI-33DX
	Decision 496SE-50DX2
	Decision 486SI-50DDX2
	Decision 486SI-66DX2
XTEND	Renaissance System Upgrade 386SX/20 PS/2 50
	Renaissance System Upgrade 386SX/20 PS/2 50Z
	Renaissance System Upgrade 386SX/20 PS/2 60
ZENITH DATA SYSTEMS	MastersPORT 386SL
	MastersPORT 386SLe
	Z-325/SX
	Z-386/25
	Z-386/33E
	Z-425SX
	Z-486SX/20E
	Z-486SX/25E
	Z-486/25E
	Z-486/33E

TABLE 8.5: Non-IBM Computers Qualified to Run OS/2 (Continued)

MANUFACTURER	MODEL
ZENITH DATA SYSTEMS **(continued)**	Z-486/33ET
	Z-NOTE 325L
	Z-NOTE 425 Ln
	Z-SERVER
	Z-STATION 420Sn
	Z-STATION 425Sh
	Z-STATION 433DEh
	Z-STATION 450XEn
ZEOS	386SX-208DT
	386DX-33CT
	486-33/8
	486SLC
	486DX-33T
	486DX-33U
	486DX-50C
	486DX2-50U
	486DX2-66E
	486DX2-66U
	Upgradeable 486-33C
	Upgradeable 486DX2-66
	Upgradeable Local Bus - i486DX2-66
	Upgradeable Local Bus - IDE
	Upgradeable Local Bus - SCSI

NOTE If you install OS/2 on a computer that's not on this compatibility list, and you have problems, are you out of luck? Not at all. Just call the IBM Defect Support Center at 800-237-5511 and explain the problem. If IBM technicians cannot provide a workaround, or develop a patch in 90 days, they will offer to refund you the purchase price of OS/2 as a gesture of goodwill.

If your computer is not in this list, that does not mean it will not run OS/2; most computers will. It just means the computer has not completed IBM's compatibility confirmation process. Also, most of the computers in this list will also run OS/2 LAN Server and OS/2 Extended Services, as long as they have enough expansion slots for the appropriate peripherals. See Chapter 15 for more information on these two products.

➤ S E C R E T

On non-IBM systems, using BASIC.COM and BASICA.COM commands can cause serious system problems, including the SYS3176 error, *A program in this session encountered a problem and cannot continue.* This is because BASIC and BASICA are tied to code installed in a ROM that is only found on IBM systems; it is not available on non-IBM systems. OS/2 includes a copy of IBM QBasic, so use it instead; your programs will run without changes. QBasic also has several other advantages, including a built-in debugger you can use to track down problems, a full-screen editor, and a built-in syntax checker. You can delete BASIC.COM and BASICA.COM from your machine to save space.

OS/2 and BIOS Upgrades

The Basic Input\Output System (BIOS) is a layer of software that lives in read-only memory (ROM) on the motherboard of your computer. The BIOS is the low-level interface between the operating system and the PC hardware, which allows the operating system software to remain hardware-independent. This layer of insulation is very useful when an engineering change is made to the hardware components of the computer; if a controller needs a slightly different interface, the BIOS is changed to support the new interface, and the operating system continues to run, completely unaware of the changes.

> ## ▶ S O L U T I O N
>
> If you want to find out the release date of your BIOS, you can use the DEBUG utility. Choose either the DOS or the OS/2 command prompt, and type:
>
> ```
> DEBUG
> ```
>
> and press the Enter key. You will see a single hyphen (-) on the screen; this is the DEBUG command prompt. Now type:
>
> ```
> D F000:FFF0
> ```
>
> This tells DEBUG to dump the 16 bytes of memory starting at the hexadecimal memory address FFFF0. A line resembling the following should appear on your screen:
>
> ```
> F000:FFF0  CD 19 E0 00 F0 30 37 2F-30 37 2F 39 31 00 FC 00  ..07/07/91
> -
> ```
>
> The two-letter codes are hexadecimal numbers representing the contents of these memory locations. On the right of the screen, you will see these same characters in ASCII, and you should see the date of the BIOS in month/day/year format. Type Q for Quit at the DEBUG command prompt to return to OS/2 or to DOS.

In IBM hardware, the BIOS consists of two separate sets of BIOS code. The ABIOS is compatible with and is used by DOS, and CBIOS was created especially for OS/2.

There are many manufacturers of PC hardware, but fortunately, there are relatively few manufacturers of BIOS chips; Phoenix Technologies, and AMI (American Megatrends, Inc), are two of the largest. For each BIOS that it supports, OS\2 requires a particalar version, and in some cases converting to OS/2 may require a later version of your computer's BIOS than you've used with MS-DOS. See the hardware manual that came with your computer for more information.

Phoenix   Phoenix BIOS chips are used in many PCs, including those sold by Dell, Gateway, NEC, Swan, and many others. You must have a level 1.02.05D or later BIOS from Phoenix to run OS/2. Phoenix states that because there are so many different implementations of their BIOS chips for different manufacturers, you should contact the vendor who sold you the PC to obtain an upgrade.

AMI   AMI BIOS chips are used in many popular direct-sales PCs from companies such as Hyundai, Everex, Northgate, and others. AMI provides a screen ID code, visible at the lower left part of the screen as the computer boots, which, for AMI BIOS and AMI BIOS Plus, has the form:

    aaaa-bbbb-mmddyy-Kc

For the AMI Hi-Flex BIOS, it has the form:

    ee-ffff-bbbbbb-gggggggg-mmddyy-hhhhhhhh-c

If the code is in a different form, there are two possibilites. You may have an early version, in which case you should contact Washburn & Co, distributors of AMI motherboards and BIOS products, at 3800 Monroe Avenue, Pittsford, NY 14534, phone 716-248-3627, fax 716-381-7549. Or the BIOS may have been produced by a company with a source-code license, in which case you should contact the system board manufacturer or distributor. All versions of the Everex 386 BIOS are in the latter category.

If an IDE hard disk is installed, the date *mmddyy* must be later than 040990 for use with any operating system, because of the special timing requirements of IDE drives. With any other type of drive, including

MFM, RLL, ESDI, or SCSI, OS/2 might install and work correctly if *mmddyy* is 092588, or later, as long as the keyboard controller revision level is correct for OS/2.

The keyboard controller revision level, *c* in the above examples, must be F for correct OS/2 operation. If the revision level shows a 0, 9, or M, the chip is not an AMI chip; contact the motherboard manufacturer for information.

If a replacement for your AMI BIOS is in order:

- AMI BIOS and BIOS Plus for cached system boards are customized to specific board designs, and so upgrades must be purchased from the system board OEM, except BIOS's with *aaaa* of E307, which can often be replaced by a standard BIOS. BIOS's with *aaaa* of DAMI, DAMX, or EDAMI are for cached boards built by AMI, and so can be replaced. Mylex or Leading Technology boards with these prefixes can only be upgraded by the original board manufacturers. The BIOS on a Northgate or Motherboard Factory system board can also be replaced by a standard type, except for the Northgate Slimline, which has VGA BIOS in the same chip. The Slimline can be updated to the 040990 release as long as the clock speed of the processor is specified as 20, 25, or 33MHz.

- In the case of a Hi-Flex BIOS, the complete three-line screen code is needed; if this code is not immediately visible, press the Insert key as the system boots. This will probably generate a keyboard error, but you will be able to read all three lines of the code. To dismiss the keyboard error, press F1, or reboot your computer.

Micronics   If you see errors such as divide underflow errors, you may have revision E of the Micronics system board. If you bought the computer from Gateway, call 800-523-2000 for an upgrade to revision F.

Gateway   If you have a Gateway 486 with a revision E system board, there is a chance you will see errors when running software that takes advantage of the math coprocessor built into the 486. If this occurs, contact Gateway about upgrading to a revision F system board. Trap 2 errors on installation or on boot of a Gateway computer may be caused by a bad read-ahead cache (press Ctrl+Alt+Esc to disable caching) on the motherboard, or by bad memory. On a Gateway Nomad, if you see a "COUNTRY.SYS not found" message, you will need a BIOS upgrade.

ZEOS If you attempt to install OS/2 on a ZEOS Notebook, and the installation fails, call the OS/2 Technical Support Center at 800-237-5511 and ask them to send you a patched Installation Disk.

S O L U T I O N

If you find that you need to upgrade your BIOS, and you can't get help from the original manufacturer, you can get Phoenix and AMI upgrades from a company called Upgrades, Etc, at 2432 Palma Drive, Ventura, CA, 93003. Call 800-541-1943, or fax 805-650- 6515.

If you need an upgraded BIOS for an IBM machine, contact Komputerwerk of Virginia, Inc, at 8133 Forest Hill Avenue, Richmond, Virginia, VA 23235. Call 804-320-8835.

Adding Another Hard Disk

Everyone runs out of disk space at some point, and adding another hard disk is a good way out, as long as your hard-disk controller can support two hard disks. OS/2 supports controllers that conform to the Western Digital (now owned by Future Domain) chipset interface standard, and this includes almost all of the MFM, RLL, IDE, and ESDI adapters you are likely to encounter, as well as Adaptec, Future Domain, and IBM SCSI controllers. MFM, RLL, IDE, and ESDI controllers all use the same bus interface, and all use the same IBM1S506.ADD device driver.

On ISA machines, it is worth checking that the disk controller is ST-506 compatible, and that the system bus speed is held at 8MHz, and is not allowed to run faster or to float. You can configure bus speed either in the system setup as the computer boots, or by setting hardware jumpers or switches on the motherboard itself.

NOTE

If you use a Seagate SCSI controller ST-01 or ST-02, it must be the only drive controller present on the system, as there are conflicts between this controller and MFM and RLL hard disk controllers.

OS/2 also offers INT 13 device driver support (the device driver file is called IBMINT13.I13) for all other hard disk controllers, including Iomega's Bernoulli drives and Syquest's removable media, but this device driver cannot be used with a CD-ROM. For more on CD-ROMs, see the heading "CD-ROM and SCSI Adapter Support in OS/2" later in this chapter.

SOLUTION

If you are replacing a system drive, first make a complete backup of your current hard disk, preferably to a tape drive or to a spare volume on a network file server drive. Then follow the usual instructions for installing OS/2 on a hard disk; you must install OS/2 before you can run the backup software in restore mode to reload the backup you just made.

Installing a New Hard Disk

Turn the computer off, ground yourself to the chassis, and install the new hard disk in one of the spare drive bays. Turn the computer on again, and adjust the system's CMOS settings to reflect this new drive. You can often access the setup screen used to change CMOS if you press a certain sequence of keys as the computer boots up; press the Del key if you have an AMI BIOS, or press Ctrl+Alt+Esc if you have an Award BIOS.

MFM and RLL drives need a low-level format, but IDE, ESDI, and SCSI drives do not. Use the low-level format contained in your computer's setup menu, or use Disk Manager or SpeedStor to low-level format the drive.

WARNING When you format the new drive, make *absolutely certain* that you do not format your startup drive; if you do, the FORMAT command will wipe out everything on the hard disk.

Now use FDISK or FDISKPM to partition the drive, and use the FOR-MAT command to format the drive. To format a disk for the HPFS, use this syntax:

    FORMAT n: /FS:HPFS

where *n* is the drive letter. To use the FAT file system, type:

    FORMAT n: /FS:FAT

To format and install the file system on a read\write optical disk, you would type:

    FORMAT n: /L

See Chapter 3 for more information on FDISK, FDISKPM, and FORMAT.

CD-ROM and SCSI Adapter Support in OS/2

CD-ROMs are widely used in multimedia applications, where their huge storage capacity is of tremendous benefit, but as they become better supported and more common, CD-ROMs are also being used more often for software distribution. IBM distributes beta copies of OS/2 to software developers on CD-ROM, and currently ships a Professional Developer's

Toolkit, as well as OS/2 version 2.1 on CD-ROM. One CD-ROM is much easier to manufacture, manage, transport, and store than a whole box of floppy disks.

Some level of CD-ROM support was available in OS/2 version 2.0, but the device driver certainly did not work with all available CD-ROM devices. Many users had to manually edit their CONFIG.SYS files, inserting the appropriate statements to include the OS/2 Adapter Device Driver (ADD) files provided by individual CD-ROM manufacturers.

For example, to add support for a CD Technology CD-ROM drive with a Future Domain SCSI adapter card, I added the following statements to CONFIG.SYS:

```
BASEDEV = FD8XX.ADD
BASEDEV = OS2SCSI.DMD
IFS = C:\OS2\CDFS.IFS /Q
DEVICE = C:\OS2\CDROM.SYS /Q /N:4
```

CD-ROM Support

OS/2 version 2.1, however, adds much more support for CD-ROMs as part of the operating system. The installation program (or Selective Install in the System Setup folder), lets you choose the CD-ROM model and the SCSI adapter separately. OS/2 version 2.1 supports the drives listed in Table 8.6. All of these CD-ROMs need the OS2CDROM.DMD device driver, and some of them also need an additional filter driver to work correctly. A filter driver is needed by CD-ROMs that adhere to the SCSI-1 standard, rather than to the SCSI-2 standard. The filter converts the SCSI-2 commands generated by the OS2CDROM.DMD driver into the vendor-specific SCSI-1 required by the drive. Table 8.6 also lists these filter drivers, where appropriate.

The SCSI controller used for your CD-ROM does not have to control your hard disks as well; OS/2 allows you to use a different type of controller for your hard disks. You can use SCSI adapters in the same machine as IDE, MFM, or RLL hard disks.

TABLE 8.6: CD-ROMs Supported by OS/2 2.1

MANUFACTURER	CD-ROM MODEL	REQUIRED DEVICE DRIVERS
CD TECHNOLOGY	T3301	OS2CDROM.DMD
HITACHI	CDR-1650S	OS2CDROM.DMD & HITCDS1.FLT
	CDR-1750S	OS2CDROM.DMD & HITCDS1.FLT
	CDR-3650	OS2CDROM.DMD & HITCDS1.FLT
	CDR-3750	OS2CDROM.DMD
IBM	CD-ROM I	OS2CDROM.DMD & TOSHCDS1.FLT
	CD-ROM II	OS2CDROM.DMD & TOSHCDS1.FLT
NEC	CDR-36	OS2CDROM.DMD & NECCDS1.FLT
	CDR-37	OS2CDROM.DMD & NECCDS1.FLT
	CDR-72	OS2CDROM.DMD & NECCDS1.FLT
	CDR-73	OS2CDROM.DMD & NECCDS1.FLT
	CDR-74	OS2CDROM.DMD & NECCDS1.FLT
	CDR-82	OS2CDROM.DMD & NECCDS1.FLT
	CDR-83	OS2CDROM.DMD & NECCDS1.FLT
	CDR-84	OS2CDROM.DMD & NECCDS1.FLT
PANASONIC	CD-501	OS2CDROM.DMD
	LK-MC501S	OS2CDROM.DMD

TABLE 8.6: CD-ROMs Supported by OS/2 2.1 (Continued)

MANUFACTURER	CD-ROM MODEL	REQUIRED DEVICE DRIVERS
SONY	CDU-541	OS2CDROM.DMD
	CDU-561	OS2CDROM.DMD
	CDU-6111	OS2CDROM.DMD & SONYCDS1.FLT
	CDU6211	OS2CDROM.DMD
	CDU-7211	OS2CDROM.DMD
TEXEL	DM-3021	OS2CDROM.DMD & SONYCDS1.FLT
	DM-3024	OS2CDROM.DMD
	DM-5021	OS2CDROM.DMD & SONYCDS1.FLT
	DM-5024	OS2CDROM.DMD
TOSHIBA	XM-3201	OS2CDROM.DMD & TOSHCDS1.FLT
	XM-3301	OS2CDROM.DMD

► S O L U T I O N

Single-session Kodak Photo CD disks are supported with the following CD-ROM drives: CD Technology Porta-Drive T3301, Hitachi CDR-3750, IBM CD-ROM II, Sony CDU-541, CDU-6211, CDU-7211, Texel DM-3024, DM-5024, and the Toshiba XM3301.

In most cases, OS/2 supports CD-ROM drives that use a SCSI adapter rather than a proprietary system; you will probably find that proprietary systems do not have IBM-supported OS/2 device drivers. If that is the case, you may be able to access the drive from inside a DOS session, or from a DOS session running as a virtual boot machine. See Chapter 6 for more on how to use a virtual boot machine.

OS/2 version 2.1 also includes updated device drivers (ADDs) for the IBM, Future Domain, and Adaptec SCSI adapters. ProCom+ Micro Channel SCSI adapters are not supported by OS/2 version 2.1; contact the manufacturers for support information.

SCSI Adapter Support

Support for Adaptec, DPT, and Future Domain SCSI adapters is built into OS/2 version 2.1, and if you have one of these adapters in your system when you install OS/2 version 2.1, the operating system will detect its presence, and automatically install the correct device driver. If you install one later, use the Selective Install program found in the System Setup folder.

Table 8.7 lists the SCSI adapters supported by OS/2 version 2.1 and their associated device driver files.

> ## ▶ S E C R E T
>
> These drivers are found on OS/2 version 2.1 floppy disk #8 in a file called DASDDRVS. You can manually unpack this file with the following command:
>
> UNPACK A: DASDDRVS OS2 /N:*xxxxxxxx*.ADD
>
> where *xxxxxxxx* is the name of the file. Then place the appropriate BASEDEV = statement in your CONFIG.SYS file, and shut down and restart your computer.

TABLE 8.7: SCSI Adapters Supported in OS/2 2.1

SCSI ADAPTER	DEVICE DRIVER FILE NAME
Adaptec A/C 6260	AHA152X.ADD Adaptec
AHA 1510/1512/1520/1522	AHA152X.ADD
Adaptec 1540/1542/1544	AHA154X.ADD (For the 1542B, set the default data rate to 5)
Adaptec AHA 1640/1642/1644	AHA164X.ADD
Adaptec AHA1740/1742/1744	AHA154X.ADD (Standard mode operation)
	AHA174X.ADD (Enhanced mode operation)
Distributed Processing Technology PM-2011/PM-2012	DPT20XX.ADD
Future Domain TMC-850/860/875/885	FD8XX.ADD
Future Domain TMC-1660/1670/1680	FD16-700.ADD
Future Domain MCS-600/700	FD16-700.ADD
Future Domain TMC-850IBM	FD850IBM.ADD
Future Domain FD7000EX	FD7000EX.ADD

The Adaptec SCSI Programming Interface (ASPI) is available for OS/2 device drivers (but not for DOS), and can be found in the file OS2ASPI.DMD in the OS2 directory. To enable this support, add the following statement to CONFIG.SYS:

```
BASEDEV = OS2ASPI.DMD
```

The OS/2 ASPI device driver manages host adapter resources, and makes the hardware-independent ASPI to SCSI applications and drivers. The ASPI device manager does not have to control all of the SCSI devices attached to the host adapter.

> ### S O L U T I O N

> If you are using an IBM non-cached SCSI adapter in a Model 80, check the FRU number on the card. If the number is FRU 15F6561, it should be replaced. Call IBM at 800-IBM-SERV and ask for hardware change ECA-032. If the adapter is cached FRU 64F0124, ask for ECA-027. In most cases there is no charge for this change. You might also check the number on the replacement card too, just in case.

The AMI Fast Disk, the AMI Fast Disk II, and the CEI Cumulus C5640B SCSI Micro Channel adapters are all incorrectly recognized as Adaptec adapters. If you have one of these adapters in your system, once the restart after installation is complete, delete the following line from your CONFIG.SYS file:

    BASEDEV = AHA1xxx.ADD

where *xxx* can be any character, and make sure that the following line is present in the file:

    BASEDEV = IBMINT13.I13

This device driver provides generic hard-disk support.

If you use an Always Technology IN-2000 SCSI adapter, and you experience problems during or after installation, the BIOS on the adapter itself may be the problem. If your BIOS is revision 3.06A or 3.20 (as seen during the system self-test), you need an upgrade. The current revision for OS/2 is VCN:1-02. If you do need to make this upgrade, you may also have to upgrade a companion PROM (programmable read-only memory). Contact Always Technology at 818-597-9595 for more information.

Unsupported CD-ROM and SCSI Adapter Combinations

The combinations of CD-ROM and SCSI adapters listed in Table 8.8 are not supported in OS/2 version 2.1. This table reflects current knowledge, and may change as testing continues.

TABLE 8.8: Unsupported CD-ROM and SCSI Adapter Combinations

CD-ROM TYPE AND MODEL	SCSI ADAPTER
NEC CDR-36 AND CDR-37	IBM SCSI adapter without cache
	IBM SCSI adapter with cache
	Future Domain TMC-7000EX
	Adaptec, all adapters[1]
PANASONIC, ALL MODELS[2]	IBM SCSI adapter without cache
	IBM SCSI adapter with cache
SONY CDU-541, 6211, 7211	Future Domain TMC-7000EX
TEXEL, ALL MODELS	IBM SCSI adapter without cache
TEXEL DM-3121, DM5021	Future Domain TMC-7000EX

[1]Parity must be disabled by on-card jumper.

[2]On a PS/2, a Panasonic CD-ROM will identify itself as 8 separate drives during setup. Use the "Set and View SCSI Device Configuration" choice on the PS/2 setup disk to turn off this error reporting.

Support for Removable Media

OS/2 does not completely support removable SCSI hard disks, such as the Bernoulli drives from Iomega Corporation or the removable drives made by SyQuest. Although OS/2 recognizes these drives, and you can certainly use them, it treats them like large floppy disks. You can only format them as FAT disks, not as HPFS disks, and you cannot partition them into smaller units, or boot up from these drives.

N O T E

If you use the OS/2 generic hard disk driver IBMINT13.I13 with these removable disks, the drive will be treated as a hard disk, but the cartridge must be in the drive at startup time. Use the Shut Down command from the desktop pop-up menu before you remove the cartridge from the drive.

Bernoulli 44MB and 89MB drives work when connected to Adaptec, Future Domain, or IBM SCSI adapters, but not when connected to the Bernoulli adapter. Bernoulli users should call Iomega at 800-456-5522 for information on an upgrade for their adapter.

Tape Drive Support

SCSI tape drives from IBM have been tested and found to work with programs like PMTAPE or PS2TAPE. If you only have one device, the tape drive, attached to the SCSI interface, you may be able to make the system work using a virtual machine boot DOS session as described in Chapter 6. For example, if you use a Colorado Jumbo connected to a floppy disk controller, you can start a virtual machine boot DOS session from a floppy disk image file on your hard disk, and run the tape backup from that session.

S O L U T I O N

If you use the Colorado Jumbo tape backup program, make sure you set the Concurrent Disk/Tape Operation to No. To change this option, start the Colorado program in a virtual machine boot session, and select the Utilities menu (F3). Then select Software Setups (F6), and change this option to N.

Several companies, including Colorado (at 800-346-9881) and Mountain (at 800-458-0300) are working on an OS/2 version of their backup programs, so watch for announcements.

If you do run the backup program from a virtual machine boot, remember that you will not be able to back up your HPFS volumes, because DOS cannot access them. The answer is to upgrade your backup system so that it is completely OS/2 compatible as soon as you can.

Advanced Power Management Support for Portable Computers

OS/2 version 2.1 adds two important new features for users of battery-powered computers. In this section we'll look at Advanced Power management support, and in the next section we'll look at PCMCIA support.

Advanced Power Management (APM) was originally defined by Microsoft and Intel as a method of prolonging battery life in a portable computer by communications between the operating system and the computer hardware. To date, almost 40 companies have endorsed the specification. Longer battery life translates directly into more usable time for users of battery-powered computers.

APM places a device driver between the operating system and the hardware that monitors and manages power consumption so that battery life can be prolonged. If your computer supports APM, the Power object is installed on your system automatically; you can also install it manually using the Selective Install object described in Chapter 2. You control this device driver using the Power object also described in Chapter 2. Power provides information on the current power source in use (AC line or battery), battery life, and battery status. Battery status can be high, low, critical, charging, or unknown. Power also lets you put the computer into a suspended mode, where power consumption is as low as it can be without actually turning the computer off. When you select Suspend, the display is dimmed, and any peripherals not in use are turned off. The way you resume normal operations depends on the computer you are using; with some computers you just open the lid, with others you may have to press a special key sequence.

PCMCIA Support for Portable Computers

Another advance for users of portable computers in OS/2 version 2.1 is support for Personal Computer cards (PC cards) as defined by the Personal Computer Memory Card International Association (PCMCIA). PC cards are small adapters about the size of a credit card that fit into a PCMCIA slot in the computer. There are two types of card: Type I cards can provide many different functions including additional RAM, flash memory, one-time programmable (OTP) memory, as well as other kinds of ROMS, while Type II cards can be modems, LAN connections, or host communications. PCMCIA cards can be use with notebooks, laptops, and other portable computer systems.

OS/2 OS/2 OS/2

OS/2 OS/2 OS/2 OS/2 OS/2 OS/2 OS/2 OS/2 OS/2

OS/2 OS/2 OS/2 O

Printers and
Printing in OS/2

OS/2 supports over 250 printers of many types, including dot-matrix, laser, PostScript, and PaintJet printers, as well as many HP and IBM pen plotters. In addition, some manufacturers provide device drivers for printers that OS/2 does not support directly, and you can install that support yourself.

Because OS/2 is a multitasking operating system and can run several programs at the same time, all of which might need access to printer resources, controlling the printing process is rather more complex than in simple systems like MS-DOS.

In this chapter, we'll look at all aspects of the printing process, including installing and configuring printer device drivers, controlling the print spooler, working with fonts, and solving OS/2, WIN-OS/2, DOS, and network printing problems.

Understanding Printing in OS/2

In the MS-DOS world, printing seemed straightforward enough. You created a document using an application program, and when you were done, you selected a font and printed the document. In OS/2, several programs may be running at the same time, and they may require access to one or more printers attached to your computer. Left to their own devices, these programs could all output to the printer at the same time, and produce totally meaningless output.

OS/2's Print Management System

To solve the problem of simultaneous access, OS/2 controls the printing process by using three different elements: a print spooler, a queue driver, and a printer device driver:

- **Print Spooler:** The spooler takes output from an application and directs it to a file. The word *spooler* is an acronym for *s*imultaneous *p*rint *o*perations *on* *l*ine. By diverting the whole print job to a file, the print spooler frees the user from waiting for the printer to finish before moving on to another task. There are in fact two spoolers, one for OS/2 programs, and one for WIN-OS/2 programs, but the OS/2 spooler is the overall coordinating spooler for the whole system.

- **Queue Driver:** After the print output has been spooled to a file, the queue driver keeps track of which file goes to which output port, and sends them, one-by-one, to the printer device driver.

- **Printer Device Driver:** Up until this point in the printing sequence, the output from the application has been printer-independent, but because different printers require different control codes for underlining or bold printing, each also requires its own printer device driver. The printer device driver frees the application program from having to generate output customized for different printers.

Printer Device Drivers

In OS/2, all printer device drivers are DLLs with the filename extension .DRV, and they provide the following functions:

- Convert the commands in a spool file to the printer-specific commands that will produce the appropriate output on the printer.

- Reply to queries from the application about the printer's capabilities, including the use of color, and available resolution.

- Display a dialog box to allow you to specify job properties such as print orientation.

- Display a dialog box to allow you to describe the printer's physical configuration, including information on installed hardware fonts and paper tray sizes.

Table 9.1 lists all the printers supported by OS/2, along with the name of the appropriate OS/2 device driver.

TABLE 9.1: Printers and Plotters Supported in OS\2

CATEGORY	OS/2 PRINTER DRIVER	MANUFACTURER/MODEL
DOT-MATRIX PRINTERS	EPSON.DRV	Citizen PN48
		Epson 24-pin
		Epson 9-pin
		Epson AP-2550
		Epson AP-3250
		Epson AP-5000
		Epson AP-5500
		Epson DFX-5000
		Epson DFX-8000
		Epson EPL-6000
		Epson EX-1000
		Epson EX-800
		Epson FX-1050
		Epson FX-1170
		Epson FX-286e
		Epson FX-850
		Epson FX-870
		Epson JX-80
		Epson LQ-1010

TABLE 9.1: Printers and Plotters Supported in OS\2 (Continued)

CATEGORY	OS/2 PRINTER DRIVER	MANUFACTURER/MODEL
DOT MATRIX PRINTERS (continued)	EPSON.DRV (continued)	Epson LQ-1050 (N9)
		Epson LQ-1050
		Epson LQ-1070
		Epson LQ-1170
		Epson LQ-2500
		Epson LQ-2550
		Epson LQ-500
		Epson LQ-510
		Epson LQ-570
		Epson LQ-850 (N9)
		Epson LQ-850
		Epson LQ-860
		Epson LQ-870
		Epson LQ-950 (N9)
		Epson LX-800
		Epson LX-810
		HP DeskJet 500 (in Epson EPL-6000 mode)
		IBM 5183 Portable Printer
		Panasonic KX-P1123 (in Epson LQ-850 mode)
		Panasonic KX-P1124 (in Epson LQ-2500 mode)
		Panasonic KX-P1124i (in Epson LQ-850 mode)

TABLE 9.1: Printers and Plotters Supported in OS\2 (Continued)

CATEGORY	OS/2 PRINTER DRIVER	MANUFACTURER/MODEL
DOT MATRIX PRINTERS (continued)	EPSON.DRV (continued)	Panasonic KX-P1180 (in Epson FX-86e mode)
		Panasonic KX-P1191 (in Epson FX-86e mode)
		Panasonic KX-P1624 (in Epson LQ-2550 mode)
		Panasonic KX-P1654 (in Epson LQ-1050 mode)
		Panasonic KX-P1659 (in Epson FX-1050 mode)
		Panasonic KX-P2123 (in Epson LQ-860 mode)
		Panasonic KX-P2124 (in Epson LQ-860 mode)
		Panasonic KX-P2180 (in Epson LX-850 mode)
		Panasonic KX-P2624 (in Epson LQ-1050 mode)
HP LASERJET AND COMPATIBLE PRINTERS	LASERJET.DRV	Epson ActionLaser II
		Epson EPL-7000
		Epson EPS-8000
		HP LaserJet 2000
		HP LaserJet 4
		HP LaserJet 4M
		HP LaserJet 500 Plus

TABLE 9.1: Printers and Plotters Supported in OS\2 (Continued)

CATEGORY	OS/2 PRINTER DRIVER	MANUFACTURER/MODEL
HP LASERJET AND COMPATIBLE PRINTERS (continued)	LASERJET.DRV (continued)	HP LaserJet Classic
		HP LaserJet IID
		HP LaserJet III
		HP LaserJet IIID
		HP LaserJet IIIP
		HP LaserJet IIISi
		HP LaserJet IIP Plus
		HP LaserJet IIP
		HP LaserJet Plus
		HP LaserJet Series II
		IBM 4019 Laserprinter E
		IBM 4019 Laserprinter
		IBM 4029 Laserprinter 10
		IBM 4029 Laserprinter 10L
		IBM 4029 Laserprinter 5E
		IBM 4029 Laserprinter 6
		Kyocera F-1000A/F-1000
		Kyocera F-1800A/F-1800
		Kyocera F-2000A/F-2200S
		Kyocera F-3000A/F-3300
		Kyocera F-5000A/F-5000
		Kyoccra F-800A/F-800

TABLE 9.1: Printers and Plotters Supported in OS\2 (Continued)

CATEGORY	OS/2 PRINTER DRIVER	MANUFACTURER/MODEL
HP LASERJET AND COMPATIBLE PRINTERS (continued)	LASERJET.DRV (continued)	Kyocera F-820
		Kyocera FS-1500A/FS-1500
		Kyocera FS-850A/FS-850
		Panasonic KX-P4410
		Panasonic KX-P4420
		Panasonic KX-P4430
		Panasonic KX-P4450
		Panasonic KX-P4450i
POSTSCRIPT PRINTERS	PSCRIPT.DRV	AST TurboLaser
		Agfa Matrix ChromaScript v51_8
		Agfa-Compugraphic 9400PS v49_3
		Agfa-Compugraphic 400PS
		Apple LaserWriter II NT
		Apple LaserWriter II NTX
		Apple LaserWriter Plus v42_2
		Apple LaserWriter Plus
		Apple LaserWriter
		COMPAQ PAGEMARQ 15
		COMPAQ PAGEMARQ 20
		Colormate PS v51_9
		Dataproducts LZR-1260 v47_0

TABLE 9.1: Printers and Plotters Supported in OS\2 (Continued)

CATEGORY	OS/2 PRINTER DRIVER	MANUFACTURER/MODEL
POSTSCRIPT PRINTERS (continued)	PSCRIPT.DRV (continued)	Dataproducts LZR-2665
		Digital LN03R ScriptPrinter
		Digital LPS PrintServer 40
		Epson EPL-7500 v52_3
		Epson EPL-8000 PS Card 82605
		Generic PostScript Printer
		HP LaserJet 4/4M PS v2011_110
		HP LaserJet IID v52_2
		HP LaserJet III Cartridge Plus
		HP LaserJet III v52_2
		HP LaserJet IIID Cartridge Plus
		HP LaserJet IIID v52_2
		HP LaserJet IIIP Cartridge Plus
		HP LaserJet IIIP PS v52_2
		HP LaserJet IIISi PS v52_3
		HP LaserJet IIp v52_2
		HP PaintJet XL300 PS v2011_112
		IBM 4019 v52_1 (17 fonts)
		IBM 4019 v52_1 (39 fonts)
		IBM 4029 (17 fonts 300 Dpi)
		IBM 4029 (17 fonts 600 Dpi)
		IBM 4029 (39 fonts 300 Dpi)

TABLE 9.1: Printers and Plotters Supported in OS\2 (Continued)

CATEGORY	OS/2 PRINTER DRIVER	MANUFACTURER/MODEL
POSTSCRIPT PRINTERS (continued)	PSCRIPT.DRV (continued)	IBM 4029 (39 fonts 600 Dpi)
		IBM 4079 Color Jetprinter PS
		IBM 4216-031 v51_4 SheetFeed
		IBM Personal Page Printer II-30
		IBM Personal Page Printer II-31
		IBM Personal PagePrinter
		Kyocera P-2000
		Kyocera Q-8010
		Linotronic 100 v38_0
		Linotronic 100 v42_5
		Linotronic 200 v47_1
		Linotronic 200 v49_3
		Linotronic 300 v47_0
		Linotronic 300 v47_1
		Linotronic 300 v49_3
		Linotronic 500 v49_3
		NEC LC-890
		Olivetti LP 5000
		Panasonic KX-P4455 v51_4
		Phaser Card v1_1
		QMS 860 Print System
		QMS ColorScript 100 Mod 10
		QMS ColorScript 100 Mod 30

TABLE 9.1: Printers and Plotters Supported in OS\2 (Continued)

CATEGORY	OS/2 PRINTER DRIVER	MANUFACTURER/MODEL
POSTSCRIPT PRINTERS (continued)	PSCRIPT.DRV (continued)	QMS ColorScript 100 Mod 30si
		QMS ColorScript 100
		QMS IS X320T
		QMS-PS 1500
		QMS-PS 1700
		QMS-PS 2000
		QMS-PS 2200
		QMS-PS 2210
		QMS-PS 2220
		QMS-PS 410
		QMS-PS 800 Plus
		QMS-PS 800
		QMS-PS 810 Turbo
		QMS-PS 810
		QMS-PS 815 MR
		QMS-PS 815
		QMS-PS 820 Turbo
		QMS-PS 820
		QMS-PS 825 MR
		QMS-PS 825
		Qume ScripTEN
		Seiko ColorPoint PS Model 04
		Seiko ColorPoint PS Model 14
		Seiko Personal ColorPoint PS

PRINTERS AND PRINTING IN OS/2

TABLE 9.1: Printers and Plotters Supported in OS\2 (Continued)

CATEGORY	OS/2 PRINTER DRIVER	MANUFACTURER/MODEL
POSTSCRIPT PRINTERS (continued)	PSCRIPT.DRV (continued)	Seiko Personal ColorPoint PSE
		Silentwriter LC 890XL v50_5
		Silentwriter2 290 v52_0
		Silentwriter2 Model 90 v52_2
		TI 2115 (13 fonts)
		TI OmniLaser 2108
		TI OmniLaser 2115
		TI microLaser PS17 v_52_1
		TI microLaser PS35 v_52_1
		Tektronix Phaser 200e (17 fonts)
		Tektronix Phaser 200e (39 fonts)
		Tektronix Phaser 200i v20011_108
		Tektronix Phaser II PX v2_02
		Tektronix Phaser II PXe (17 fonts)
		Tektronix Phaser II PXe (39 fonts)
		Tektronix Phaser II PXi v2010
		Tektronix Phaser III PXi v2010
		Tektronix Phaser IISD v2011
		Varityper VT-600
		Wang LCS15 FontPlus
		Wang LCS15

TABLE 9.1: Printers and Plotters Supported in OS\2 (Continued)

CATEGORY	OS/2 PRINTER DRIVER	MANUFACTURER/MODEL
PLOTTERS	PLOTTERS.DRV	HP 7470A
		HP 7475A
		HP 7550A
		HP 7580A
		HP 7580B
		HP 7585A
		HP 7585B
		HP 7586B
		HP ColorPro HP 7440A
		HP DraftMaster I HP 7595A
		HP DraftMaster II HP 7596A
		HP DraftPro HP 7570A
		IBM 6180 Plotter
		IBM 6182 Plotter
		IBM 6184 Plotter
		IBM 6186-1 Plotter
		IBM 6186-2 Plotter
		IBM 7371 Plotter
		IBM 7372 Plotter
		IBM 7374 Plotter
		IBM 7375-1 Plotter
		IBM 7375-2 Plotter

TABLE 9.1: Printers and Plotters Supported in OS\2 (Continued)

CATEGORY	OS/2 PRINTER DRIVER	MANUFACTURER/MODEL
MISCELLANEOUS PRINTERS AND PRINTER DRIVERS	SMGXPJET.DRV	Micrografx PaintJet Presentation Driver
	HPDJPM.DRV	HP DeskJet
		HP DeskJet 500
		HP DeskJet 500C
		HP DeskJet 550C
		HP DeskJet Plus
		HP DeskJet Portable
	IBM4019.DRV	IBM 4019 LaserPrinter E
		IBM 4019 LaserPrinter
		IBM 4029 LaserPrinter 10
		IBM 4029 LaserPrinter 10L
		IBM 4029 LaserPrinter 10P
		IBM 4029 LaserPrinter 5E
		IBM 4029 LaserPrinter 6
		IBM 4029 LaserPrinter 6P
	IBM42XX.DRV	IBM 2380 PPS II
		IBM 2381 PPS II
		IBM 2390 PPS II
		IBM 2390 PS/1
		IBM 2391 PPS II
		IBM 4070 IJ
		IBM 4072 ExecJet
		IBM 4201 Proprinter II

TABLE 9.1: Printers and Plotters Supported in OS\2 (Continued)

CATEGORY	OS/2 PRINTER DRIVER	MANUFACTURER/MODEL
MISCELLANEOUS PRINTERS AND PRINTER DRIVERS (continued)	IBM42XX.DRV (continued)	IBM 4201 Proprinter III
		IBM 4201 Proprinter
		IBM 4202 Proprinter II XL
		IBM 4202 Proprinter III XL
		IBM 4202 Proprinter XL
		IBM 4207 Proprinter X24
		IBM 4207 Proprinter X24E
		IBM 4208 Proprinter XL24
		IBM 4208 Proprinter XL24E
		IBM 4224 01
		IBM 4224 02
		IBM 4224 E3
		IBM 4224 C2
		IBM 4226 Model 302
	IBM52XX.DRV	IBM 3816 01D
		IBM 3816 01S
		IBM 5202 QuietWriter III
		IBM 5204 QuickWriter
	IBM52012.DRV	IBM 5201 QuietWriter II
	IBMNULL.DRV	IBM NULL Printer Driver

S O L U T I O N

Some printers let you select between several operating modes, in which they can emulate other standard printers, such as Epson, HP, IBM, or Post-Script printers. These modes may be selected via the printer front panel, or by internal hardware switches. If your printer is not listed in Table 9.1, consult your printer documentation to see if it can emulate one of the printers that is listed, or call the manufacturer's technical support number to see if an OS/2 device driver is available.

For example, if you use a Star NX-1000 or an NEC P3200 printer, you can use the Epson printer driver EPSON.DRV, because the Star NX-1000 emulates the Epson LX-800 printer, and the NEC P3200 emulates the Epson LQ-850 printer. The NEC P6200 and the Canon Bubble-Jet, which both emulate the Epson LQ-2550, can also use the same driver.

Different printers have different capabilities, and therefore require different device drivers, but device drivers are usually written to service a number of printers of the same type. For example, the single printer device driver EPSON.DRV supports all the dot-matrix printers listed in Table 9.1, including several non-Epson printers working in an Epson-emulation mode.

Printer device drivers are usually included as part of the OS/2 installation, but you can use Selective Install in the System Setup folder if you change your printer after the installation is complete.

Obtaining Printer Device Drivers

There are several ways you can obtain new or updated device drivers, including the following sources:

- **IBM:** Updated device drivers are available in a form suitable for downloading from the IBM National Support Center bulletin board, described in Appendix B. These drivers may be for both IBM and non-IBM printers.

- **Lexmark:** For new or updated device drivers for IBM printers, contact the Lexmark International bulletin board at 800-453-9223, and use either the XMODEM or the ZMODEM file transfer protocol to transfer the file. If you have problems logging on to the bulletin board, call Lexmark at 800-537-2540.

- **Printer Vendors:** Many hardware vendors place new or updated device drivers on their own bulletin boards, or in their forum on CompuServe. Also, many vendors provide a disk containing device drivers along with the printer itself.

- **Software Developers:** Major software developers often provide a set of device drivers with their product. Some small developers market specific device drivers independent from any application. You will find these drivers advertised in the computer press, and they also may be available via CompuServe or other bulletin boards.

If you use one of the older IBM printers, such as the IBM 3812, IBM 3852, IBM 5152, IBM 5182, IBM 5201-1, or IBM 5216, you will find that OS/2 version 2.1 printer drivers are not available. Instead, you can use OS/2 version 1.3 device drivers downloaded from Library 17 in the OS/2 Support Forum on CompuServe, or from the IBM National Support Center bulletin board.

Installing and Changing Printers

The easiest way to add a printer object to your desktop is to specify your current printer during the OS/2 installation process. After installation is complete, you can change printers using the Selective Install program from the System Setup folder, as described in Chapter 2.

NOTE Network printers are located inside the Network folder on the desktop.

There are other ways you can create a printer object:

- From a template
- By changing an existing printer object

We'll look at each of these methods in turn.

Using a Template to Create a Printer Object

Using a template is a very convenient way to create a printer object on the desktop; there are several steps involved:

- Drag a printer template to the desktop.
- Name the printer object.
- Locate and install the correct device driver for the printer.
- Establish the output port you want to use for printing.

If you are creating a new printer object, you may also be asked if you want to install the equivalent WIN-OS/2 printer driver, but this depends on the printer driver you are installing. See the heading "Looking at the DRV.INF File" later in this chapter for more on how this works.

To start this process, open the Template folder, and drag the printer template to the desktop. You will see the Create Printer window open on the desktop as Figure 9.1 shows.

Type a convenient name into the Name field. This name will appear along with the icon on your desktop, and the system will use it to create the name of the spool queue. Although the Name field can hold up to 47 characters, the spool queue name is limited to 8 characters, so that it can work with FAT systems. Thus, the first 8 characters in the name need to be unique. Once the system has created this name, you cannot change it except by deleting the printer object and creating a new one.

FIGURE 9.1

The Create a Printer window

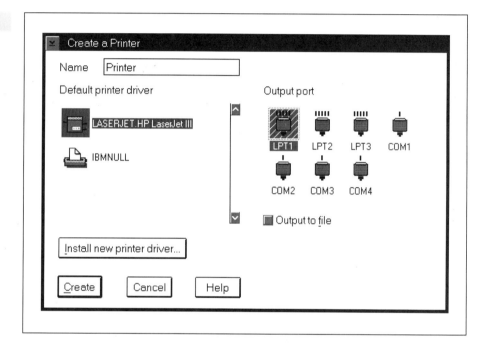

▶ **S O L U T I O N**

In both versions 2.0 and 2.1 of OS/2, you can also right-click on the printer icon in the Create a Printer window to open the icon's pop-up menu. This menu contains three entries: Help, Delete, and Install. Selecting Install also opens the same Install New Printer Driver window shown in Figure 9.2. You will only see the Delete option if more than one device driver is already installed; at least one printer driver must be present at all times.

The Default Printer Driver field will show the driver for whatever printer is currently installed. If you are adding a printer of the same type, just click the Create button at the bottom of this window now. In OS/2 version 2.1, if the right printer driver is not shown in this field, click on the Install New Printer Driver button to open the Install New Printer Driver window shown in Figure 9.2.

If your printer is supported by an OS/2 driver (as listed in Table 9.1), check the Printer Driver Shipped With OS/2 button, select the driver from the list in the central window, and click on the Install button. A dialog box opens asking you for the appropriate drive and file information. When you've identified the driver file's location, click on OK, then click on the Install button to load the driver.

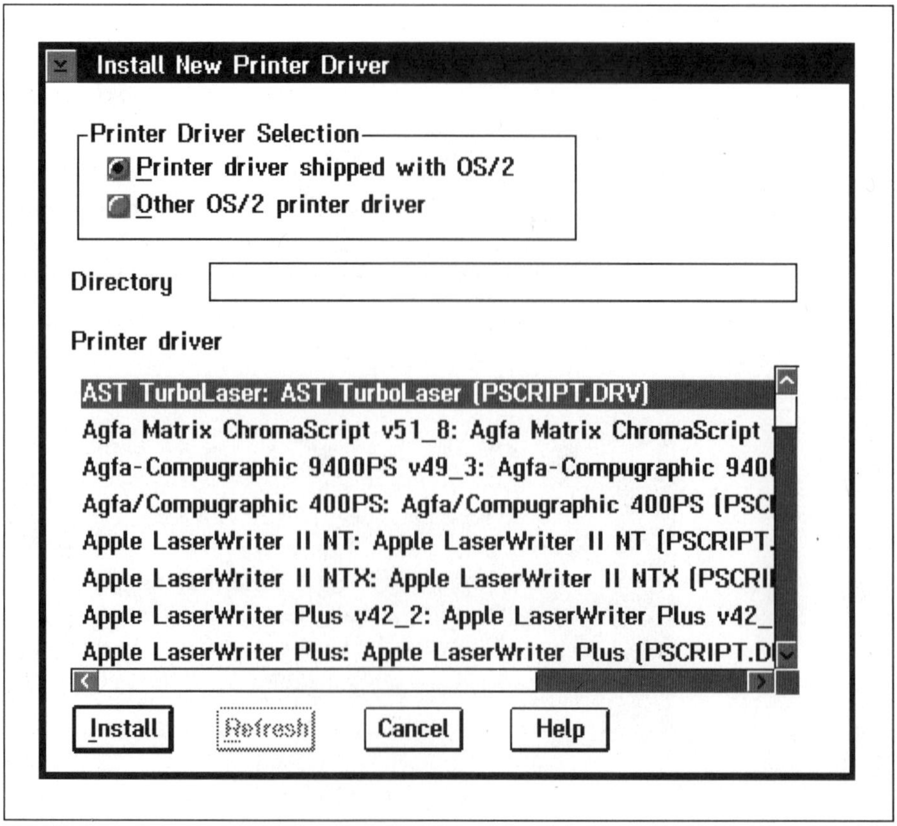

FIGURE 9.2

Use the Install New Printer Driver window to specify your printer

If your printer is not supported by OS/2 directly, you will have to load the device driver from a floppy disk supplied by the printer manufacturer. To start this process, click on the Other OS/2 Printer Driver button, and type the name and path information for the driver into the Directory field. You should find this information included with your printer documentation. You may find that there are drivers for several printers on the same floppy disk, or you may have to hunt through more than one disk to find the right driver. If you do change driver disks, you will also have to click on the Refresh button to display the contents of the new disk. If there are several drivers on the disk, scroll through the list until you find the one you are looking for; if you don't see it, insert a different disk into the drive, and click on the Refresh button again. When you find the right driver, select it from the list and click on Install.

Finally, choose the output port you want to use with this printer from the choices shown in the Output Port field on the right side of the Create a Printer window.

N O T E

The Output to File check box tells the selected printer to create a printable file rather than route it to a printer port. If you check this option and then create a print job, a window opens asking you to specify the file name for the print job. You can only use this feature with OS/2 programs.

Now click on the Create button in the Create a Printer window. When this new printer object is created, you may see a dialog box asking:

Do you want to install an equivalent Win-OS/2

3.1 printer configuration?

Click on the Yes button in the dialog box, and OS/2 will prompt you to load the appropriate device driver disk. If you are using an OS/2-supported printer, this will be the same driver disk you used for the OS/2 printer device driver; otherwise, load the disk provided by your printer manufacturer. Insert the disk, click on the OK button, and the printer object will appear on your desktop ready for use.

Modifying an Existing Printer Object

Once you have installed a printer object, you can use Create Another and then the Printer option from a printer object's pop-up menu to make more. This opens the desktop Create Another window. Type an appropriate name for this new printer into the New Name box; this name is also used for the spool queue as described above. Click on the folder (usually the desktop) in which you want to create this new object, then click on the Create button to open the Create a Printer window shown in Figure 9.1 above. The dialog from this point is the same as described above for creating a printer from a template.

S O L U T I O N

To find out which printer driver to select for a specific printer, open the file PRDESC.LST using the Enhanced Editor. In OS/2 version 2.0, you will find this file on the first printer driver floppy disk, and in later versions of OS/2, you will find the file in the OS2\INSTALL directory on the hard disk used to boot the system. PRDESC.LST contains an alphabetical list of the OS/2-supported printers and the device drivers each one uses. A similar file, PRDRV.LST, tells you which printer driver is on which OS/2 printer driver disk.

Configuring the Printer Object

After the printer object is created, you can use the Settings notebook to change the detailed printer setup. This notebook has the following tabs:

- **View:** The View page shows you the printer object's name, which is also the internal name of the queue and the queue folder in the spooler folder. You cannot change this name here.

  You can use the Default View selections to specify whether your print jobs are displayed as icons or in a more detailed text format that includes a description of their current status.

- **Printer Driver:** This page shows the installed printer drivers as well as the default printer driver. Right-click on the printer icon to open the pop-up menu with the following selections:

  - **Open:** Choose Open followed by Settings to see the Printer Properties window shown in Figure 9.3. You can also open this window if you double-click on the icon for the default printer driver.

    The information and choices available in this window will be different for all the different types and makes of printer that OS/2 supports. Figure 9.3 shows the properties for an HP LaserJet III printer. The most important piece of information in this window is the Driver Version number, usually shown in the lower part of the window. This number indicates the revision level of the printer driver and helps you keep track of different printer drivers.

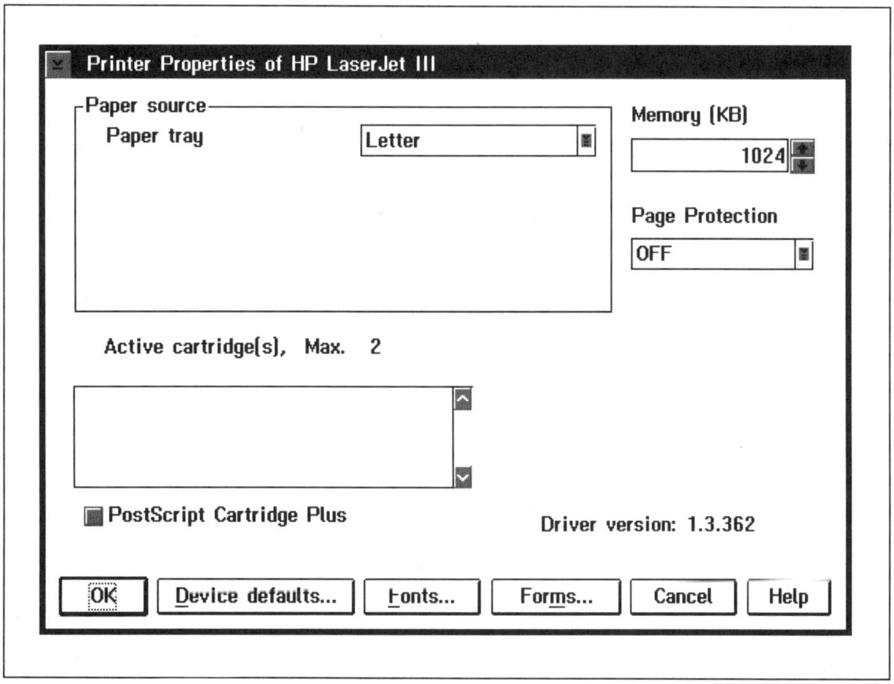

FIGURE 9.3

The Printer Properties window for the HP LaserJet III

- **Help:** Opens the normal OS/2 help system.
- **Delete:** Use this selection to delete a printer driver; you can also drag the printer object to the shredder on the desktop and achieve the same result.
- **Install:** Opens the Install New Printer Driver window described above.

Click on the Job Properties button to display the window shown in Figure 9.4. The information shown here is for an HP LaserJet III printer; you will see the window for your printer instead.

FIGURE 9.4

The Job Properties window for an HP LaserJet III printer

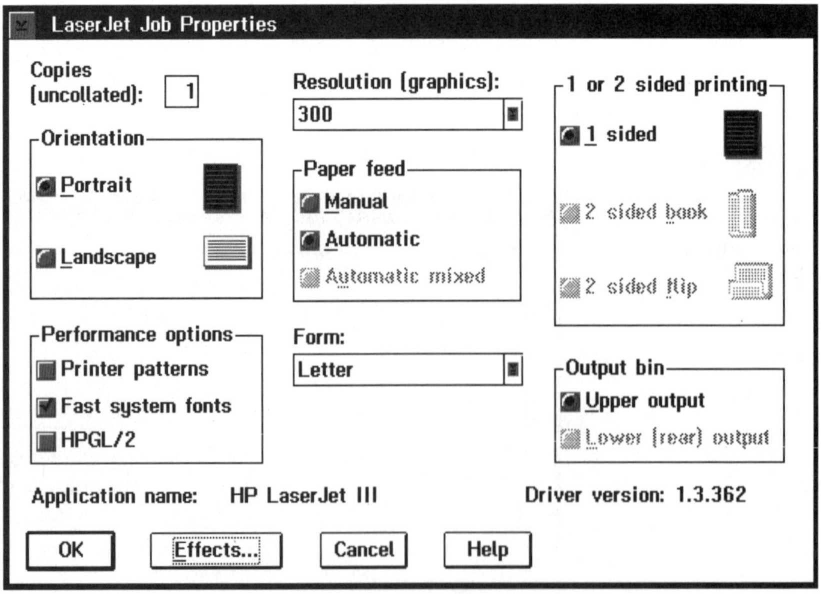

This window displays the default printer job settings that will be used unless they are modified by the application program creating the print job. Job Properties work in conjunction with Printer Properties and are specific to each printer type in just the same way.

S O L U T I O N

The Job Properties window contains an Uncollated Copies option. Collated copies are convenient, but they also require that each page be processed over and over again to produce the right number of copies. If you specify uncollated copies, particularly for graphics images, the printer can make all the required copies of each page all at the same time, before moving on to the next page. This can result in up to a *five-fold* increase in speed when compared with collated copies. With plain text, the time saving will be much less noticeable.

- **Output:** This page shows the available ports and the ports selected for use with this printer. If you select the Output to File check box, you will be prompted for a file name when you send output to this printer object. This file will be created in a printer-specific form based on the default printer driver, so that you can take this file to another system that has the same printer model and print it there.

- **Queue Options:** Use this page to choose a print queue driver. The normal choice is PMPRINT, but you may see another choice here, PMPLOT, if you use IBM or HP pen plotters. The Job Dialog Before Print check box will display the printer object's Job Properties if you initiate printing using drag and drop. At other times, you can control these Job Properties from inside your application program by using a menu selection or dialog box called Printer Setup.

    If you need to create printer-specific files for later printing on a non-OS/2 system, check the Printer-Specific Format check box. This also allows the printer driver to begin creating the file immediately. OS/2 automatically selects this option for a network printer if the network server does not support Presentation Manager drivers. Printer-Specific Format print jobs take up much more hard disk space than normal printer-independent print jobs.

- **Print Options**. On this page you can specify a separator file, used to divide up continuous printouts. Separator files are common in networked environments, and two example files called

SAMPLE.SEP and PSCRIPT.SEP are included in the OS2 directory. You can also set print start and stop times to limit the hours during which jobs can print. If you specify a Start Time, you must also specify a Stop Time.

NOTE Only the network administrator can change these settings on a networked printer.

- **Window**. Use the selections on this page to tell the printer object how you want it to behave when you minimize it.

- **General**. Use the settings on this page to change the desktop icon, or to clone this printer object. You can also make this printer object behave as a template by checking the Template box.

WARNING You cannot copy system templates to other computers, because they depend on system-specific settings in the OS2.INI file. Unfortunately, if you have many non-networked users with similar printers needing the same configuration, you must configure each one individually.

Changing the Default Printer Object

OS/2 uses the default printer for all print jobs and print screens. You can change to another printer by using the Set Default option from the printer object's pop-up menu. In many cases in OS/2 version 2.1 the other choice will be Fax/PM. The current default is always indicated by a check mark to the left of the printer name.

Holding and Releasing the Printer Object

If you need to halt the print queue temporarily while you perform routine maintenance such as changing the toner cartridge or adding more paper, use the Change Status option from the printer object's pop-up menu to go from Release to Hold. When you have finished the maintenance, remember to set the status to Release again so that printing can continue with the next job in the queue.

Controlling the OS/2 Spooler

The spooler stores all print jobs created by OS/2, DOS, and WIN-OS/2 applications, PRINT commands, and print screens as files in the SPOOL directory until the printer is available to print the job. The spooler (but not the contents of the spooler) is controlled by the Spooler object in the System setup folder, and was described in Chapter 2.

The spooler should always be left enabled, except when there is a solid reason to disable it. There may be rare programs, particularly older MS-DOS programs, that cannot print properly using the spooler, and you may have to turn the spooler off when you use such a program. To disable the spooler, right-click on the Spooler object, and choose Disable Spooler from the pop-up menu. You will now have to shut down and restart your system, because this change will not come into effect until you do so.

Once the spooler is disabled, OS/2 cannot separate your print jobs, so *you* must wait for one job to complete before starting another; otherwise, print jobs may collide and all your output will be meaningless rubbish.

To turn spooling back on again, open the pop-up menu for the Spooler object, and select Enable Spooler. This change takes effect immediately, so there is no need to shut down and restart your system.

Viewing the Spool Queue

If you want to look at the print jobs in the spool queue for a printer, double-click on the printer object icon on the desktop. You will see a window like the one shown in Figure 9.5.

Your print jobs will appear in either Icon View or Details View, depending on the printer object's default view setting. You can use the Change Status option from the pop-up menu to hold or release the entire queue. Held print jobs have a slightly different icon from released jobs, and jobs that are currently being printed show an arrow between the document and the printer on the print-job icon.

You can duplicate a print job if you use the Copy command from the print-job object's pop-up menu, or you can create multiple copies if you open the object's Settings notebook at the Printing Options page, and type in the number of copies you want.

Double-click on the print-job icon to view the actual contents of the print job. If the file is a text file, the System Editor opens on the file, and if it is a graphical image, the Picture Viewer program opens instead.

FIGURE 9.5

Icon View of print jobs waiting to print

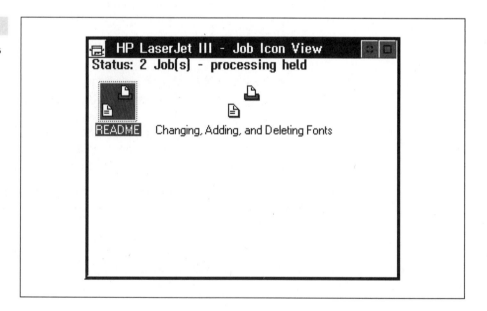

NOTE The PICVIEW command covered in Chapter 12 and the Picture Viewer object described in Chapter 3 both let you look at a spool file (a file with the file-name extension .SPL) as long as the file contains a picture in a standard OS/2 format.

Changing Print Job Status

There will inevitably come a time when you want to print a small file quickly, but find to your horror that it is queued up after a huge report with lots of graphics that will take an eon to print. Fortunately, you can change the priority of print jobs in the spool queue.

To make a specific print job print before any other queued job, double-click on the appropriate printer object, then right-click on the print-job icon, and select the Print Next option.

You can also change the priority of a print job so that it prints before or after other queued jobs. Open the print-job's pop-up menu by right-clicking on the print job icon, and open the Settings notebook at the Printing Options page. The number in the Job Position field indicates the number of this job in the queue. For example, if you see a 4 in this field, three other jobs must print before this one can print. You cannot change this value, but you can change the value shown in the Priority field. Priority ranges from 1 (the lowest value) to 99 (the highest value); the higher the number, the greater the chance that the job will print before other print jobs. Jobs with the same priority number print in the order in which they were submitted.

If you've interrupted a print job after it has started to print, you can restart it by using the Start Again option from the print job's pop-up menu. If the job is queued but not printing, the Start Again option is not available.

You can delete a single print job if you right-click on the print-job's icon, and select the Delete option. To delete all the print jobs for a specific printer object, click on the title-bar icon of the queue and then select Delete All Jobs.

WIN-OS/2 Printer Support

During the installation of an OS/2 printer driver, you may have been asked if you wanted to install the equivalent WIN-OS/2 printer driver at the same time. If you answered Yes to this question, the system prompted you to insert the appropriate floppy disk, and the driver was installed. If you replied No, you must install the printer using the WIN-OS/2 Control Panel.

Setting up a WIN-OS/2 Printer

To set up a WIN-OS/2 printer driver from one of the printer driver floppy disks, first open a WIN-OS/2 session, then double-click on the WIN-OS/2 Control Panel, and double-click on the Printers object. Select Add; if no printers are installed, WIN-OS/2 selects Add for you. Select the printer you want to install from the List of Printers, and click on the Install button. If your printer is not listed here, check your printer documentation to see if the printer can emulate one of the printers that is in the list.

If a printer driver for this printer is already on the system, WIN-OS/2 asks whether you want to use this driver or install a new version of the driver. Click on Current to use the existing driver, or click on New and insert the device driver floppy disk, then click on OK. After the driver loads from the floppy disk, you may also be asked to insert a disk containing font files for this printer.

Next, click on the printer in the Installed Printers list, then click on the Connect button to assign a printer port to the printer device driver. Choose a parallel or serial port, or choose FILE if you always want to send print output to a file. Select the ports with the .OS2 extension as they will provide improved support and spooled output.

> # SOLUTION

If you want to access LPT3.OS2, or the logical ports LPT4.OS2 through LPT9.OS2, edit the WIN.INI file located in the OS2\MDOS\WINOS2 directory. In the [ports] section, insert new lines for these ports, as follows, leaving the rest of the file unchanged:

```
[ports]
; A line with [filename].PRN followed by an equal sign causes
; [filename] to appear in the Control Panel's Printer Configuration dialog
; box. A printer connected to [filename] directs its output into this file.
LPT1.OS2=
LPT2.OS2=
LPT3.OS2=
LPT4.OS2=
LPT5.OS2=
LPT6.OS2=
LPT7.OS2=
LPT8.OS2=
LPT9.OS2=
FILE:=
```

After saving the WIN.INI file, you must restart the WIN-OS/2 session so that the new settings will be loaded. Select the Control Panel, and you will find that you can now select the new destinations.

If you use a COM port with a printer from both OS/2 and WIN-OS/2, you must set the port configuration in the WIN-OS/2 Control Panel to the same settings you used for the OS/2 desktop printer object.

Adding an Unlisted Printer

If you want to use a WIN-OS/2 printer driver supplied by the manufacturer, follow the procedure described above, but select Unlisted Printer from the list of printers, then select the Install button. The Add Unlisted or Updated Printer window opens so you can select the drive and directory where the driver is located, and also type the name into the Driver name field. Once the driver is loaded, continue with the printer installation process by selecting the port you want to use.

Looking at the DRVMAP.INF File

When you install an OS/2 printer object, OS/2 may not prompt you to install the equivalent WIN-OS/2 printer, especially if you have installed a printer not supported by OS/2 and have therefore used an OEM device driver. The reason for this is that the default printer driver may not be listed in the DRVMAP.INF file located in the OS2\MDOS\WINOS2\SYSTEM directory. Figure 9.6 shows the beginning of this text file, displayed in an OS/2 window.

The entries in this text file map the OS/2 printer device drivers to their WIN-OS/2 counterparts, and the file is referenced when you install a printer driver in OS/2. If the printer driver you installed is listed in DRVMAP.INF, the system asks whether to install the equivalent WIN-OS/2 driver. Once you know that a particular mapping is not present in DRVMAP.INF, you can edit the file. Then you, or your users, will be prompted as you install the OS/2 printer object, and the appropriate printer driver will be installed in WIN-OS/2 correctly and automatically. This can be a great help if you have to work with many computers, particularly if they are networked. You

FIGURE 9.6

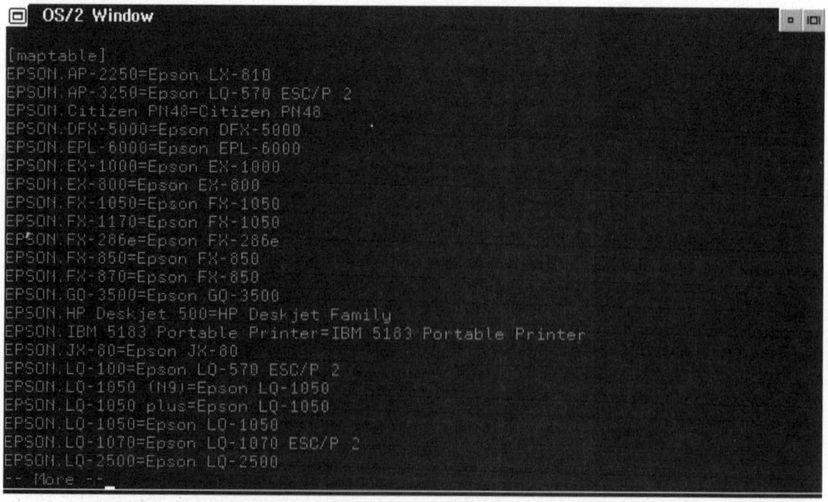

Part of the DRVMAP.INF file shown in an OS/2 window

```
[maptable]
EPSON.AP-2250=Epson LX-810
EPSON.AP-3250=Epson LQ-570 ESC/P 2
EPSON.Citizen PN48=Citizen PN48
EPSON.DFX-5000=Epson DFX-5000
EPSON.EPL-6000=Epson EPL-6000
EPSON.EX-1000=Epson EX-1000
EPSON.EX-800=Epson EX-800
EPSON.FX-1050=Epson FX-1050
EPSON.FX-1170=Epson FX-1050
EPSON.FX-286e=Epson FX-286e
EPSON.FX-850=Epson FX-850
EPSON.FX-870=Epson FX-850
EPSON.GQ-3500=Epson GQ-3500
EPSON.HP Deskjet 500=HP Deskjet Family
EPSON.IBM 5183 Portable Printer=IBM 5183 Portable Printer
EPSON.JX-80=Epson JX-80
EPSON.LQ-100=Epson LQ-570 ESC/P 2
EPSON.LQ-1050 (N9)=Epson LQ-1050
EPSON.LQ-1050 plus=Epson LQ-1050
EPSON.LQ-1050=Epson LQ-1050
EPSON.LQ-1070=Epson LQ-1070 ESC/P 2
EPSON.LQ-2500=Epson LQ-2500
-- More --
```

can copy the edited DRVMAP.INF from the network over the default file
that comes with OS/2.

S O L U T I O N

If your printer is supported by a WIN-OS/2 printer driver, but no OS/2
driver is available, set up the WIN-OS/2 printer driver using the WIN-OS/2
Control Panel, then set up the OS/2 printer using the IBMNULL.DRV
driver, and you will be able to print from a WIN-OS/2 session.

Entries in DRVMAP.INF are constructed as follows:

- The name of the OS/2 printer driver file, without the normal
  .DRV file-name extension. In the first entry shown in Figure 9.6,
  this is EPSON.

- The name of the OS/2 printer in the driver file. In Figure 9.6, this
  part of the entry is .AP-2550.

- The name of the WIN-OS/2 printer. In Figure 9.6, this part of the
  entry is =Epson LX-810.

Before you edit this file, make a backup copy first, so that you can restore
the original should anything go wrong during the editing process.

Using the WIN-OS/2 Print Manager

To get the benefit of OS/2 support when using WIN-OS/2, you should
leave the OS/2 spooler enabled. Print jobs from all sources will then be
managed and controlled by the spooler. However, if you leave the spooler
enabled, you will not see any print jobs sent by WIN-OS/2 applications to
a parallel attached printer in the WIN-OS/2 Print Manager. To look at the
status of these print jobs, you should use the OS/2 spooler, as described
above in the section "Controlling the OS/2 Spooler."

On the other hand, if you do all your printing work in WIN-OS/2 applications, and do not print from the desktop, from DOS, or from OS/2 applications, you can disable the OS/2 spooler. When you disable the OS/2 spooler, you *can* control all your WIN-OS/2 print jobs using the WIN-OS/2 Print Manager.

Disabling the WIN-OS/2 Print Manager has the same effect as disabling the OS/2 spooler, but it affects only WIN-OS/2 print jobs. If the OS/2 spooler is enabled, disabling the Print Manager will only affect WIN-OS/2 print jobs sent to a local serial printer.

NOTE   The following descriptions apply to all print jobs sent to serial printers, and they apply to print jobs sent to parallel printers *only when the OS/2 spooler has been disabled.*

The Print Manager can operate at any of three priority levels. Open the Options menu in Print Manager, and select from Low Priority, Medium Priority, or High Priority. If you select High Priority, print jobs will certainly print faster, but there may be other unanticipated effects such as application programs running slowly.

To look at the jobs in the print queue, double-click on the Print Manager icon in the WIN-OS/2 Main Group on the desktop. If you want to change the order of a print job in the queue, just drag the print job up or down the print queue to a new location.

In the WIN-OS/2 Print Manager, you can pause or resume the entire print queue, but you cannot pause or resume individual print jobs. To pause the queue, click on the information line for the queue in the Print Manager window, and select the Pause button. The selected queue status information changes to indicate the queue is now held or paused. To release or resume a queue, click on the information line, and select Resume.

Pooled and Shared Printer Connections

OS/2 adds another powerful dimension to printing in *pooled* and *shared* connections. *Pooling* is the ability to assign multiple ports to a single printer object, and *sharing* is the reverse; the ability to assign multiple printer objects to a single physical printer port.

Printer Pooling

It is more and more common to find several printers attached to the same workstation or network as demand for printing resources continues to grow. If all these printers are identical, you can set them up for printer pooling. You can create one printer object and assign it to all of the ports that have identical printers attached to them. OS/2 will then direct the print job to the next available printer for printing, and your days of waiting for a printout to appear are over!

S O L U T I O N

For pooling to work, the printers do not have to be absolutely identical, but they do have to use the same printer device driver with the same settings. For example, you could use an Epson printer along with a Panasonic printer configured for Epson emulation, or an IBM Proprinter XL III and an IBM 4072 ExecJet printer in Proprinter emulation mode.

To establish pooling, open the printer object's Settings notebook at the Output page. Then select all the ports you want to assign to this object by dragging the mouse pointer across the ports while holding down the left mouse button. You can also hold down the Ctrl key as you click on each port in turn; note that clicking on an already selected port deselects that port.

Printer Sharing

Printer sharing is the ability to assign several desktop printer objects to a single printer port. For example, you may have a laser printer with two paper trays, one for letter paper and the other for legal size paper. By creating two printer objects, you can print all your jobs without having to continually check or change the printer properties or settings to make sure you are using the correct paper.

To do this, create two printer objects on the desktop with different and appropriate names, and assign the same printer driver and the same output port to both objects. Then open the Settings notebook for one of these objects at the Printer Driver page, and click on the Job Properties button. Specify the appropriate paper size or paper bin location you want to use with this printer object, while leaving the other printer object assigned to the default paper size or paper bin location. Now when you want to print on normal-sized paper, you simply select the printer object for the paper size you want.

You can combine pooling and sharing in any combination you can think of, to provide as much printing flexibility as you need.

Network Printing Using OS/2

OS/2 lets you add a network printer object in order to configure and manage your network printer or printers.

If you are a network user, you will find there is a template in the Template folder on the desktop that you can use to define the network printer. To define this printer, make sure you are logged on to the network and know the server name and the printer name. Open the Template folder, and drag the network printer template to the desktop or to a convenient folder. The Access Another Network Printer dialog box opens, displaying three fields which may or may not contain names. These fields are Network, Server, and Resource, and you can either type in the appropriate information, or click on the button to the right of each field to see a list of available options. When you are happy with these entries, click on OK to return to the desktop.

The Settings notebook for a network printer object accessed by a normal user ID differs from the normal printer notebook in several ways:

- The View page adds additional network settings:

  - **Network Job View**: This setting lets you choose between seeing all printer jobs or just your own printer jobs when you display the network printer queue.

  - **Refresh Interval**: This setting displays the number of seconds your local system will wait before updating information on the network queue. Keep this number as high as possible, because any unnecessary network access will impact the performance of your computer. You can also set Refresh Interval to 0 so that there is no refresh interval.

- The Output and General pages do not exist.

- The Print Options page lets you look at but not change the settings.

- You cannot change, install, or delete printer drivers or printer ports.

- A new page called Network Status is added, containing information about the network printer as it relates to the server.

You cannot use a network printer until it has been initialized, and a device driver has been installed for it; all users on the network must do this on their own desktops. You can initialize the printer by:

- Dragging the network printer object to the desktop.

- Dragging and dropping a file onto the network printer object.

- Accessing the job properties, printer properties, or printer driver settings for the network printer object.

In each case, a dialog box opens asking you to install a printer driver. Click on the Install button, and the Install New Printer Driver window opens. Select the appropriate printer driver from the list, and continue with the installation as for a local printer.

You will now be able to print to this printer from your normal OS/2 applications, as well as use drag-and-drop to print files. If you select the network printer as the default printer object, you can also direct print screens from the desktop or from windowed sessions to this printer.

Solving Printing Problems

Printing problems usually fall into one of two categories:

- The print job did not print for some reason.
- The print job seemed to print, but you don't know where it went.

In the following sections we'll look at some of the causes for these problems, and describe solutions where possible.

Nothing Prints

The most common reason for a print job not to print is that the settings in the printer do not match the OS/2 printer or job settings used by the printer object when creating the print job. Here are some other reasons.

If nothing prints to a printer attached to a parallel port, you should:

- Check that the printer is turned on and is online. If you sent a print job to a printer that was offline, then put the printer online, and responded Yes to the Retry message on the screen, the job may not print as you expect. Cancel the job, place the printer online, and reissue the print job.
- Make sure that the correct printer device driver is installed. If several printer device drivers are installed on your system, check

the printer object's Printer Driver page in the Settings notebook to make sure that the right driver is selected.

- Confirm that the hardware printer ports are configured correctly.

- Make sure that the correct port is selected in the printer object's Settings notebook Output page.

- Make sure that the printer object is not set up to print to a file rather than to the output port.

If nothing prints on a printer attached to a serial port, you should also check that the serial cable you are using meets OS/2's specifications. A cable that worked fine under MS-DOS before you upgraded may not work under OS/2. See Chapter 11 for more on cables and cabling.

Printing is Slow

If you use an AT-bus computer, and printing seems slow, check the revision level of the port adapter you are using, and also check the port addresses and hardware interrupts. See Chapter 11 for more on this.

If you find that printing is slow from a WIN-OS/2 session, but is acceptable everywhere else, try increasing the print priority level in the Print Manager.

Selecting a high print resolution can slow laser printers down considerably; for example, changing from 75 dots per inch (dpi) to 600 will make the print job run much slower.

Printing Stops

If a DOS application that is sending PostScript output stops printing suddenly, cancel the print job that made the printer stop. Then open the printer object's Settings notebook at the Queue Options page, and turn off the Print While Spooling check box. Now you should be able to restart and resend the print job with no further problems.

Unfamiliar Printer Name

If you try to select a printer or plotter from inside an application program, but you don't see the printer object name that you expect to see, it may be that the application program is calling the printer by another name. Open the Settings notebook for the printer object at the View page, and check the entry in the Physical Name field. The Physical Name is often the first 8 characters of the printer object name. Now go back to the application program and see if you can find this Physical Name listed in the program's printer selections.

S O L U T I O N

If you use an IBM 4029 printer in Proprinter data stream (PPDS) mode with Adobe Type Manager, some Windows programs may not function as you expect. If this happens, do not use the printer's resident fonts. Open the ATM Control Panel and make sure that Use Pre-built or Resident Fonts is turned off.

The Print Job Spools but Nothing Prints

The OS/2 spooler will not print a job until the sending application closes the print-data stream. Unfortunately, several DOS applications keep this stream open longer than they should. If you look at the print jobs in the spool queue and notice that the arrow in the icon points from the printer to the document, rather than from the document to the printer as you would expect, the job will not print.

If the job does not print after 15 seconds, you may have to adjust the DOS setting PRINT_TIMEOUT for this application.

The Print Job is Broken Up into Several Print Jobs

If you find that your print job is split into many small spool files, you may have to disable the spooler to get the results you want. Some DOS applications open and close the printer data stream for every character, line, or page of output, which creates lots of small spool files. When these files print, the result looks nothing like the printout you expected.

Disabling the spooler with the Spooler object in the System Setup folder is one way to correct this problem. A better alternative is to contact the software company to see if an upgrade is available.

Printing Only Starts When You End a DOS Application

If your print job does not start printing until after you end the DOS application, the program has not closed the print data stream. You can use the DOS_DEVICE setting to load the device driver LPTDD.SYS from the OS2\MDOS directory. Once this driver is loaded, you can use the PRINT_TIMEOUT setting to close the print stream without having to exit from the program.

You may also have to use this driver if you want to print from a DOS session to an LPT port currently redirected to a network printer.

A DOS Application Prints OK, but Nothing Else Prints

If you can print from a DOS application, but you find that you cannot print anywhere else until you end this DOS application, it may be that the program is accessing the parallel printer port hardware directly. OS/2 prevents two (or more) applications from simultaneously accessing the same parallel port hardware. The second application must always wait for the first to end, even if the second application is the OS/2 spooler.

The Print Job Ran, but I Can't Find It

Losing a printout is a common problem in networked environments, where there may be several printers or printer servers available to all users. There are two easy steps you can take to make your printout more noticeable:

- Use a very obvious separator page between print jobs with a highly visible user name or user ID.

- Use the network's messenger service to display the server name, device name and, output port that the job was sent to.

Adobe Type Manager Fonts in OS/2

OS/2 uses two kinds of font to output to displays and to printers. These fonts were installed automatically as part of the OS/2 installation, and consist of both bit-map fonts and Adobe Type Manager (ATM) Type 1 outline fonts.

Bit-map fonts represent their characters as sets of dots, while ATM Type 1 outline fonts represent each character by a series of straight lines and Bezier curves defined in PostScript language. The main benefit to outline fonts is that they can be scaled to any size easily, and without the jagged edges often associated with bit-map fonts. ATM also allows even inexpensive printers to produce PostScript fonts that were previously the domain of high-end printers.

The Adobe Type Manager is integrated into the OS/2 operating system, and fonts are added or removed using the Font Palette in the System Setup folder. See Chapter 2 for information on the Font Palette. ATM for WIN-OS/2 is a separate program installed onto the WIN-OS/2 desktop, and fonts are added or removed using the ATM Control panel in the WIN-OS/2 main group.

Installing Additional ATM Fonts in OS/2

Many companies and individuals supply ATM Type 1 fonts, including Adobe, Bitstream, Agfa-Compugraphic, Autologic, and Linotype. You will also find Type 1 fonts on CompuServe in the IBM OS/2 forums, and they are also available from shareware distributors.

To add an additional ATM font to OS/2, use the Font Palette in the System Setup folder. Click on the Edit Font button, then click on the Add button. A window opens asking for the location of the font files. Insert the appropriate floppy disk. The Add New Font window opens, listing all the located font files. Click on the font files you want to add, and their font names will appear. Click on the Add button to start the installation. When installation is complete, you return to the Edit Font window. You must close this window and then open it again to access the new fonts you just installed.

ISO Fonts in OS/2 Version 2.1

The International Organization for Standardization (ISO) committee ISO 9241-3 has developed several font and display standards. Displays must be designed to reduce the amount of flicker, display sharp characters and stable images, increase brightness, and reduce glare.

ISO 9241-3 fonts must be legible, with consistent line width; and ascenders, descenders, and accented characters must not collide with one another. All characters within the font must be distinguishable from each other; for example, the number 0 and the capital letter O must be sufficiently different.

The ISO System Proportional font replaces the old System Proportional font; all other new ISO fonts are in addition to the previous fonts. The new fonts are called Courier ISO, Helv ISO, and TmsRmn ISO. By default, the desktop, and all full-screen and window OS/2 and DOS sessions use this System Proportional ISO font, but you can change this if you wish to use a different font in its place.

ATM and TrueType Fonts in WIN-OS/2

ATM font support is also automatically installed in WIN- OS/2, but remains inactive until you install at least one font. This is why the ATM icon shows a large red cross when you start a WIN-OS/2 full-screen session.

ATM is managed by the ATM Control Panel in WIN-OS/2, which you can use to turn ATM support on or off, to add new fonts or to remove existing fonts, and to change the size of the font cache. The font cache specifies the amount of memory available to store font information. The default setting is 96K, but you can use any value from 64K to 32,000K. If your applications seem slow when you scroll the display or change pages, experiment with different font cache settings. When you change any of the options in the ATM Control Panel (except the Use PreBuilt or Resident Fonts option), you must exit and restart your WIN-OS/2 session so that your changes can take effect.

OS/2 version 2.1, with its Windows 3.1 support, also includes TrueType font support. TrueType fonts use an advanced font technology similar to that used by ATM, which allows scalable fonts to be displayed and printed accurately.

You can select and manage TrueType fonts using the Fonts option in the WIN-OS/2 Control Panel. ATM fonts are not installed into WIN-OS/2 3.1 by default, but if you plan to use ATM fonts, use the ATM Control Panel to load and install them from Printer Driver floppy disk #5.

WIN-OS/2 INI Files

In addition to the conventional WIN-OS/2 .INI configuration files described in Chapter 7, ATM adds another called ATM.INI, as shown in Figure 9.7.

FIGURE 9.7

Part of the ATM.INI file
shown in an OS/2
window

```
┌──────────────────────────────────────────────────────────────┐
│ ▣  OS/2 Window                                         ▫ ▫▢    │
│                                                                │
│ [Fonts]                                                        │
│                                                                │
│ [Setup]                                                        │
│ PFM_Dir=C:\psfonts\pfm                                         │
│ PFB_Dir=C:\psfonts                                             │
│                                                                │
│ [Settings]                                                     │
│ FontCache=96                                                   │
│ BitmapFonts=On                                                 │
│ ATM=On                                                         │
│ SynonymPSBegin=9                                               │
│ QLCDir=C:\psfonts                                              │
│ Version=2.0                                                    │
│                                                                │
│ [Mono]                                                         │
│ Courier=Yes                                                    │
│ LetterGothic=Yes                                               │
│ PrestigeElite=Yes                                              │
│ Orator=Yes                                                     │
│                                                                │
│ [Aliases]                                                      │
│ Helv=Helvetica                                                 │
│ -- More --                                                     │
└──────────────────────────────────────────────────────────────┘
```

This file is located in the OS2\MDOS\WINOS2 directory and contains
details of the ATM fonts you have installed as well as details of your ATM
setup, including whether ATM is turned on or off, the size of the font
cache, and whether to use prebuilt or resident bit-map fonts.

OS/2 OS/2 OS/2

OS/2 OS/2 OS/2 OS/2 OS/2 OS/2 OS/2 OS/2 OS/2 OS/2

OS/2 OS/2 OS/2 O

10

Video Boards and Monitors in OS/2

A great deal of OS/2's appeal lies in its use of graphics. OS/2 supports programs written for OS/2, Windows, and DOS environments, running in windowed or in full-screen sessions, and also provides the graphical user interface known as the desktop. To be able to do this efficiently, OS/2 supports a wide range of display adapters, including the color graphics adapter (CGA), enhanced graphics adapter (EGA), video graphics array (VGA), super VGA (SVGA), extended graphics array (XGA), and the 8514/A adapter.

Video Boards and OS/2

Most of the video standards found on the PC have been developed by IBM, including CGA, EGA, VGA, 8514/A, and XGA. IBM is even part of the industry committee that supports the non-IBM standard SVGA. The screen resolution produced by these adapters is described in terms of the number of picture elements, or pixels, that can be displayed horizontally and vertically on the screen. The SVGA adapter, for example, is described as supporting 800 × 600 resolution, 800 pixels horizontally and 600 vertically.

Table 10.1 lists the video standards supported in OS/2.

OS/2 supports different display adapters in the same way that it supports different printers, by using specific display device drivers.

TABLE 10.1: Video Standards Supported by OS/2

STANDARD	HORIZONTAL RESOLUTION	VERTICAL RESOLUTION	MODE	NUMBER OF SIMUL- TANEOUS COLORS
CGA	640	200	text	16
	320	200	graphics	4
	640	200	graphics	2
EGA	640	350	text	16
	720	350	text	4
	640	350	graphics	16
	320	200	graphics	16
	640	200	graphics	16
	640	350	graphics	16
8514/A	1024	768	graphics	256
VGA	720	400	text	4
	360	400	text	2
	640	480	graphics	16
	320	200	graphics	256
SVGA	800	600	graphics	16
	1024	768	graphics	256
XGA	640	480	graphics	65,536
	1024	768	graphics	256
	1056	400	text	16

NOTE

The Color Graphics Adapter (CGA) and the Enhanced Graphics Adapter (EGA) are early video display standards, officially obsolete, but still supported by OS/2. Because of the graphical nature of the OS/2 desktop, using CGA mode graphics would be difficult and frustrating, and it is definitely not recommended.

OS/2 may have been designed with the VGA display adapter in mind, but version 2.1 brings integrated support for the higher-resolution SVGA adapter. In the next few sections we'll look at each of the popular adapter types, and then we'll close this chapter with a look at some common display problems and ways to fix them.

8514/A

The IBM 8514/A video standard offers a high-resolution display with 1024 pixels horizontally by 768 lines vertically. The 8514 was an early standard from IBM, but failed to generate much interest because of its cost and its use of interlacing technology to achieve its high resolution. Interlacing uses two screen passes to refresh the display; first the odd-numbered scan lines (the horizontal lines that make up the display) are drawn, followed by the even-numbered lines on the next pass. Interlacing also induces a flickering effect that most people find annoying. Vendors other than IBM, such as Paradise and ATI, make 8514/A-compatible adapters you can switch to provide a noninterlaced display. The Mitsubishi Diamond Scan and the NEC 4D monitors are both capable of displaying noninterlaced 1024 × 768 resolution.

To run a WIN-OS/2 full-screen session on your 8514 display, use the DOS settings to set VIDEO_8514A_XGA_IOTRAP to Off, and VIDEO_SWITCH_NOTIFICATION to On. In a full-screen WIN-OS/2 session, do not switch to another session when an application is updating the screen or when you see the hourglass icon.

S O L U T I O N

The 8514/ULTRA from ATI must be installed as the primary display when you install OS/2; it defaults to high-resolution mode. Change the following line in your CONFIG.SYS file:

    DEVICE=\OS2\MDOS\VVGA.SYS

to read

    DEVICE=\OS2\MDOS\SVGA.SYS

VGA

The Video Graphics Array standard was introduced by IBM in 1987 along with the PS/2 computer line. VGA adapters and analog monitors can display as many as 256 colors with a resolution of 640×480 pixels.

VGA is backward-compatible with the earlier video display standards in the sense that it can display output written to the EGA and CGA standards, and the specification has been available for long enough so that almost every display and monitor adapter manufacturer has a highly compatible product.

Super VGA

The Super VGA standard grew from the desire of several important video adapter manufacturers for a higher resolution than that provided by IBM's VGA standard. These companies formed the Video Electronics Standards Association (VESA) to define and promote SVGA.

N O T E   All SVGA adapters are supported in VGA mode with the VGA adapter driver provided with OS/2 version 2.1.

SVGA has become extremely popular in the PC marketplace. In OS/2 version 2.0, support for SVGA was provided mostly by the manufacturers of SVGA video adapters rather than by IBM, but OS/2 version 2.1 supports this display adapter directly, with the appropriate device drivers. Indeed, IBM has recently added SVGA adapters to several newer PCs, including PCs in the PS/ValuePoint Range. Table 10.2 lists the SVGA chip sets supported by version 2.1.

> ## ► S O L U T I O N

Many of the display adapter manufacturers provide updated device drivers and information on their own in-house bulletin boards:

- Trident's Technical Support number is 415-691-9211. You can reach their West Coast bulletin board at 415-691-1016, and their East Coast number is 203-483-0348.

- Orchid's 2400-baud number is 510-683-0327, and their 4800-baud number is 510-683-0555.

- ATI's 2400-baud bulletin board number is 416-756-4591.

One of the many reasons SVGA has grown in popularity is that most of the "multiscanning" monitors, beginning with the NEC Multisynch, are capable of 800 × 600 displays. As time passes, more manufacturers will provide OS/2 device drivers for their own SVGA display adapters, or will release adapters that use the chip sets listed in Table 10.2.

To run DOS or WIN-OS/2 programs that use SVGA on non-IBM PS/2 Micro Channel computers, you must first turn on the SVGA support. The installation program detects the SVGA chip set used on your system, but it cannot detect the adapter board that the chip set is installed upon. To enable SVGA support, type the following from a DOS command prompt:

    SVGA ON

and then shut down and restart the system.

TABLE 10.2: SVGA Display Adapter Support

ADAPTER	CHIP SET
Amdek Smartvision	Tseng ET4000
Boca Research SVGA	Tseng ET4000
Diamond Speedstar SVGA	Tseng ET4000
Everex ViewPort NI	Tseng ET4000
Sigma Legend II	Tseng ET4000
STB Powergraph VGA	Tseng ET4000
Orchid Prodesigner II-MC	Tseng ET4000
STB Ergo VGA	Tseng ET4000
Speedway	Tseng ET4000
VGAWonder XL	ATI-28800-5
Headland Technologies	Video 7-HT209/D
Western Digital	WD90C00
	WD90C11
	WD90C30
	WD90C31
VGA Graphic JAX-8212	Trident Microsystems TVGAA8900B
	Trident Microsystems TVGAA8900C
IBM	VGA256C
Cirrus Logic	CL-GD 5422, 5424

Because there are many different implementations of SVGA, OS/2 supports the following resolutions with 256 colors:

- 640 × 480—with 512K on-board memory
- 800 × 600—with 512K on-board memory
- 800 × 600—with 1MB on-board memory
- 1024 × 768—with 1MB on-board memory

You can use the Selective Install program, described in Chapter 2, to configure your SVGA adapter, or you can use a program called DSPINSTL. Attempting to configure your SVGA in any other way will probably not work, and may leave you staring at a blank screen.

Close any WIN-OS/2 applications running on your system before running DSPINSTL, or OS/2 will not be able to complete the SVGA installation. Type:

    DSPINSTL

at an OS/2 command prompt and press Enter to start the program. When the Display Driver Install window opens, select the Primary Display checkbox, and click on OK. If you are going to install two displays, be sure to configure the higher resolution display as the primary display. The Primary Display Adapter window (shown in Figure 10.1) opens, and OS/2 checks to determine the adapter type present on your system.

FIGURE 10.1

The Primary Display Adapter window

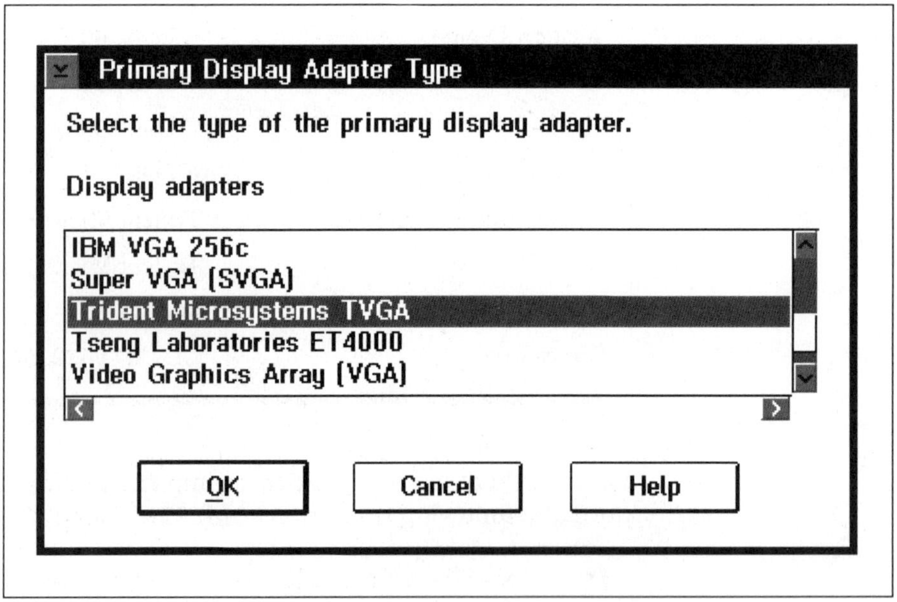

WARNING

Systems using an IBM 16-bit VGA may show the Primary Display as being SVGA. If you choose this default, you will see a warning message telling you not to continue with the installation. If you persist, the 256-color device driver is installed, and this may well cause what is euphemistically known as "unpredictable results."

Accept the preselected display adapter, or choose a different adapter from the list, and click on OK. OS/2 now checks to see which display resolutions your system can support and opens the Select Display Resolutions window. Choose the resolution you want to use. Normally, you would choose the highest resolution your system can support, but there may be times when you would want to use a lower resolution; for example, you may have an older application that does not support the highest resolution. Click on OK, and the Source Directory window opens for you to specify the name and location of the device driver. Click on the Install button, and OS/2 starts the installation. When the Display Driver Install window opens again, click on the Cancel button. A dialog box opens, reminding you that because system changes have been made, you should shut down your system and restart it so that the changes can be implemented. When the installation is complete, OS/2 automatically runs the command SVGA ON.

WARNING

If you want to remove SVGA support from your OS/2 version 2.1 system, do *not* run the SVGA OFF command, as this will erase the PMI file, which in turn will result in a blank screen when you next start your system. The only way to recover from this mishap is to *reinstall the entire operating system*. Instead, always use Selective Install or the DSPINSTL program when you need to reconfigure your system.

As part of the SVGA support in OS/2 version 2.1, a new text file called SVGADATA.PMI is created in the OS2 directory during installation.

This file contains configuration data for your system, including the name of the chip set used on your SVGA adapter, and the modes that your adapter can support. OS/2 also updates the CONFIG.SYS file and the WIN-OS/2 configuration files WIN.INI and SYSTEM.INI.

XGA

The Extended Graphics Array is a newer IBM video display standard that replaces the older 8514/A standard. XGA adapters with 1MB of memory can display 65,536 colors in the low-resolution 640 × 480 mode, and 256 colors in the high-resolution 1024 × 768 mode. The XGA is also backward-compatible with code written for the VGA standard.

When you installed OS/2, you had the choice of using a VGA or an XGA display driver. If you chose VGA at that time, but now you want to use XGA, use the Selective Install program to make the change.

WARNING   When you install XGA for the first time, you must also reinstall the system fonts, because OS/2 uses a different set of fonts for XGA.

Once you have installed the XGA drivers, you can easily change your display resolution by opening the Settings notebook for the System object in the Systems Setup folder at the Screen tab. The first page lets you change the display resolution, and the second lets you change the type of screen attached to the system. If you use an IBM screen, you won't have to change any of the settings on this second page, but if you use a non-IBM display, you may have to.

In most cases OS/2 recognizes the XGA display adapter and will load the correct driver. If you have a non-IBM display that OS/2 cannot recognize, the system defaults to an 8514/A. If this happens on your system, you can override the automatic selection process, called Display Mode Query and Set (DMQS), with the DMSQ Override setting on the second page of the Screen tab in the System settings notebook. DMQS Override creates the file XGASETUP.PRO in the XGA$DMQS directory. This file contains information on the display.

SOLUTION

If you choose the wrong settings for your display, your system may become unusable. To cancel the effect of the DMQS override, boot your system using the OS/2 boot disk described in Chapter 14, change to the C:\XGA$DMQS directory, and just delete the XGASETUP.PRO file. Remove the boot disk, restart the system again, and your display will now operate using the default settings.

Laptop Displays

If you use a laptop computer with an LCD or monochrome plasma display, use the Scheme Palette object in the System Setup folder to select the monochrome color scheme. This color scheme will be optimized for maximum legibility and will also provide a reasonable set of colors for a VGA desktop display.

Solving Video Problems

OS/2 makes extensive use of graphics, and because of this, it may be flushing out problems with video adapters that were just not seen in other environments. Video problems may arise when switching from one mode into another, or when trying to run an application in a window on the desktop. In other cases, problems may be caused by interactions between a video board and another device installed on your system. Another common source of problems between OS/2 and video adapters is the memory space that these adapters claim. Video adapters may contain 512K, 1MB, or more of video memory, which must be provided with its own address space.

There are many variations between different manufacturers' SVGA cards. In a full-screen DOS session, entering the command SVGA WHO checks the recognition of your SVGA card. The program will put your adapter through a short but colorful test, then return the name of the adapter type as well as the name of the chipset used on the board.

Video Corruption

If you see video corruption when returning to a WIN-OS/2 full-screen session from another session, change VIDEO_SWITCH_NOTIFICA-TION in the DOS settings to On.

Color Translation Problems

You may see some color corruption when running DOS applications in a window. This is a limitation of the VGA desktop. The color palette used in the DOS session has to be translated to OS/2, and sometimes the 640×480 sixteen-color desktop does not provide enough colors. A good solution to the problem is to run the program in a full-screen session instead of a window.

Graphics Problems

You may see that the graphics produced by some applications are corrupted when displayed in a window. These programs may be using a non-standard VGA mode that the adapter can support, but that OS/2 does not. Call the video adapter manufacturer to see whether an OS/2 display device driver is available.

BIOS Initialization

Some video adapters require that the PC's DOS BIOS initialize the video adapter. If you see corrupted information at the OS/2 full-screen command prompt, you may have one of these adapters. To fix this, open a DOS full-screen session, and type:

```
EXIT
```

at the DOS command prompt, then return to the OS/2 command prompt where the text should now appear as normal. You can automate this process by creating a DOS batch file that runs when you start your computer if you add the following to STARTUP.CMD:

```
START /FS /DOS DOSFILE.BAT
```

Then create a file called DOSFILE.BAT that contains the single command EXIT.

Desktop Redraws

If you use an SVGA, you may see display errors on the OS/2 desktop if you switch to the desktop when the screen is redrawing. Switch back to the SVGA screen to allow the redraw to finish, then switch to the desktop.

Video Mode Considerations

There are several limitations to using certain video modes in OS/2 that you should be aware of:

- CGA, EGA, and 8514/A resolution can only support full-screen WIN-OS/2 sessions. VGA, XGA, and SVGA all support WIN-OS/2 window and full-screen sessions.

- DOS programs may be suspended when they attempt to write to the following adapters when a program is in a background session and the desktop does not have control of the display:

  - EGA, VGA, or SVGA adapter using 256 colors with resolutions greater than 320×200, or 16 colors with resolutions greater than 640×480.
  - XGA adapter in XGA or VGA graphics modes with 256 colors and resolutions greater than 320×200, or any 16-color mode.
  - 8514/A adapter in 8514/A mode, or in VGA mode using 256 colors with resolutions greater than 320×200, or 16 colors with resolutions greater than 640×480. These programs cannot run in a window on the desktop.

NOTE   Certain Windows non-OS/2 full-screen display drivers may not suppress writing to the display when in the background, and this may cause the Windows program to suspend operations under conditions similar to those just described for DOS programs.

• All WIN-OS/2 full-screen display drivers shipped with OS/2 version 2.1 write to the display only when the full-screen session is in the foreground; they suppress all background operations that write to the display to allow the program to keep running while the program is in the background. When you switch the program back to the foreground, the screen is automatically redrawn.

Dual Display Problems

If you use two XGA displays, an 8514/ULTRA adapter and an OS/2-supported SVGA adapter, you will have to change the DEVICE= statement in your CONFIG.SYS file from:

    DEVICE=C:\OS2\MDOS\VVGA.SYS

to

    DEVICE=C:\OS2\MDOS\VSVGA.SYS

Slow SVGA Performance

SVGA gives you two benefits over the VGA standard—more colors and better resolution. Tests have shown that increasing the screen resolution impacts system performance slightly, but increasing the number of colors is the real killer. Using 256 colors can slow down graphics by a factor of three or more, so think very carefully before selecting a 256-color device driver; after all, very few OS/2 applications use more than 16 colors.

DOS Display Errors

If you see the error message SYS3176 when you try to open a DOS session or application, you can turn the DOS setting HW_ROM_TO_RAM to On, and in CONFIG.SYS, you can change the RMSIZE parameter from 640 to 624.

OS/2 OS/2 OS/2

OS/2 OS/2 OS/2 OS/2 OS/2 OS/2 OS/2

OS/2 OS/2 OS/2

11

Multimedia and Other Hardware Issues in OS/2

IN the previous chapters of Part III: OS/2 and Computer Hardware, we've looked at how the operating system supports different computers, printers, and video monitors. This chapter addresses the remaining major hardware topics: the Multimedia Presentation Manager/2 (MMPM/2) bundled with OS/2 2.1, internationalization of keyboards for foreign languages, and support for serial devices such as modems, fax modems, and pointing devices.

Multimedia Support in OS/2

Multimedia (or as IBM calls it, Ultimedia) has been defined many different ways, but it is best described as being the integration and synchronization of computer hardware and software with audio, video, and animation to provide interactive applications. However you want to describe it, the main components are:

- **Audio** refers to the computer's ability to add music, the human voice or other sounds, either digitized on disk or recorded on tape, to the image shown on the video display.

- **Video** refers to the computer's ability to add graphical images, either digitized or computer-generated, on the screen integrated with text where appropriate. Certain animation techniques may also be used, such as multiple-image display, and the capture of full-motion video images from an NTSC-compatible video-capture board.

N O T E

The NTSC (National Television Standards Committee) US standard specifies 525 horizontal lines per frame, displayed at a rate of 30 frames per second, using interlaced scan techniques.

- **Synchronization** refers to an often-neglected aspect of multimedia—making sure that the audio and video components are timed correctly, and so actually make sense.

- **Interaction** allows the user to take control of the content, nature, and sequencing of the audio and video components of the application.

When all these elements come together in a well-organized presentation, the effect can be stunning. Multimedia is well suited to interactive training and educational projects such as language teaching and online encyclopedias.

Multimedia Presentation Manager/2

Support for multimedia, in the form of the Multimedia Presentation Manager/2 (MMPM/2), is now bundled with OS/2 version 2.1. OS/2 is an ideal multimedia environment because of its protected multitasking environment, high-performance memory management and interprocess communications, and its high overall system integrity. Specifically, multimedia applications can take advantage of several important OS/2 operating system features, which are not available from the MS-DOS/Windows combination, including:

- Preemptive rather than cooperative multitasking.

- Multithreading to allow resource sharing and extremely responsive applications.

- Crash protection to avoid collisions between applications and provide a stable user environment.

- Fast or protected threads, which are reserved for time-critical processing such as streaming multimedia data objects.

- HPFS to manage multimedia's large data files.

- Interprocess communication mechanisms such as pipes, semaphores, and message channels.

N O T E   MMPM/2 has its own multivolume Technical Library entirely separate from the OS/2 Technical Library. See Appendix B for more details on these libraries.

OS/2 allows for fast application responsiveness, so that the program can react quickly to user's requests and interactions, while at the same time maintaining sufficient processing speed behind the scenes to avoid the kind of processing delays that can lead to audio or video breakup, where an application cannot send a digitized audio signal to the sound card at a fast enough rate.

MMPM/2 supports the following multimedia devices (the names that appear on your system depend on the installation choices you've made):

- **Compact Disc:** A device that plays compact discs, and is controlled by the CD Player.

- **Digital Audio:** A device that uses information converted to and stored in digital form, controlled by the Digital Audio Player, and the Digital Audio Recorder.

- **MIDI:** A device that uses MIDI (Musical Instrument Digital Interface) format files. Controlled by the MIDI Player and the MIDI Recorder.

- **Videodisc:** A device that uses a videodisc to store programs. Controlled by the Videodisc Player.

All hardware devices are controlled through a 32-bit, device-independent interface known as the Media Control Interface (MCI), developed as a joint venture between IBM and Microsoft. Each device has its own MCI driver to implement a standard set of functions, and each driver can also add specialized functions for a particular device. MCI also shields the application from the complexities of different file formats.

The MMPM/2 package includes device drivers, operating system support, utilities for MMPM/2 installation, setup, and data conversion, and several applications that allow you to use some of the capabilities of multimedia for simple tasks.

Installing Multimedia Presentation Manager/2

MMPM/2 is distributed as either a set of two floppy disks, or as part of the OS/2 version 2.1 package on CD-ROM. To install MMPM/2, open an OS/2 command-line session and run the MINSTALL program, which you will find on the first MMPM/2 floppy disk or on the CD-ROM. When you start MINSTALL, the MMPM/2 Installation window opens, as in Figure 11.1.

First make sure that the Source Drive and Path fields display the correct entries for your system; then, in the Target Drive field, select the drive on which you want to install MMPM/2. By default, all the MMPM/2 components are selected in the lower portion of this window; if you don't have a particular piece of hardware on your system, just click on that entry to deselect it. If you change your mind about these installation options, you can always come back and install a component later. All the MMPM/2 components you select for installation will be copied into the MMOS2 directory. Select the Install button to start the installation process.

As a part of the installation, various device drivers must be added to your CONFIG.SYS file; you can have the installation process do this for you, or, if you would rather not, the installation program will create a new file for you called CONFIGH.NEW. This file is a replica of the CONFIG.SYS file that the installation program would have created. You can look the file over, and if all looks well, use it to replace your existing CONFIG.SYS file. Use this option if you want to install MMPM/2 on your system before you install the specified multimedia hardware. You should not

FIGURE 11.1

The MMPM/2 Installation Window

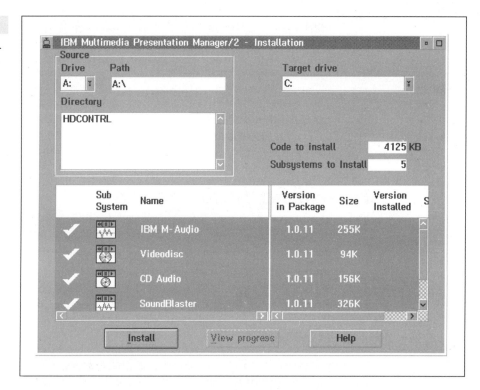

invoke this CONFIG.SYS file until *after* the hardware is installed and correctly configured.

As OS/2 copies the files to your hard disk, it will ask several questions about the multimedia hardware available on your system, including:

- **M-Audio Adapters:** The M-Audio Capture and Playback Adapter (M-ACPA) is a PS/2 adapter card with the ability to record and play back high-quality sound. The adapter converts analog audio input into a digital form, and then compresses and stores the data. You can use up to four adapters in the same machine.

- **Pioneer videodiscs:** MMPM/2 adds support for Pioneer laser-disc models LD-V4200, LD-V4300D (supports both the American NTSC and the European PAL TV standards for storing analog video signals), LD-4400, and LD-V8000, at baud rates of 4800 or 9600. You can install up to 10 videodiscs, and the number you select here must include those already installed on your system.

- **Sound Blaster:** Select the specific Sound Blaster card you have on your system, Sound Blaster, Sound Blaster Pro (ISA with OPL2), Sound Blaster Pro (ISA with OPL3), or Sound Blaster Pro MCV. Many audio cards made by other manufacturers also have a Sound Blaster mode or emulation available. You can install one or two Sound Blaster cards.

NOTE If you have an older Sound Blaster card, make sure you have version 2.0 or higher of the DSP module to take full advantage of MMPM/2. You can contact Creative Labs, Inc., at 800-998-5227.

- **Pro AudioSpectrum 16:** Adds support for a Media Vision Pro AudioSpectrum 16 sound card.

To start MMPM/2 once the device drivers are copied onto your hard disk, you must first remove any floppy disks, then close down and restart your system. Now you will see the MMPM/2 folder on the desktop, and if you open the folder, you will see the multimedia applications, as Figure 11.2 shows.

In the next section I'll describe how to configure the multimedia applications, and then look at using the applications.

Multimedia Setup

Double-click on the Multimedia Setup object in the MMPM/2 folder, and the Multimedia Setup notebook will open, as in Figure 11.3.

Down the right side of the notebook, you will see a tab for each of the hardware devices you chose when you installed MMPM/2; and in some cases, such as the MIDI device, you will also see one or more tabs at the

FIGURE 11.2

The MMPM/2 folder contains the Multimedia Applications

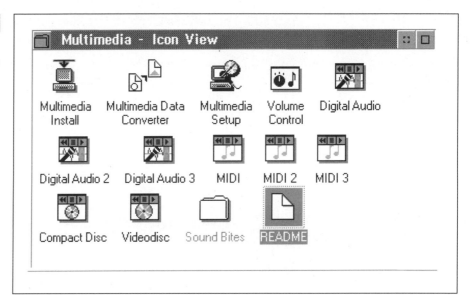

FIGURE 11.3

The Multimedia Setup Settings Notebook

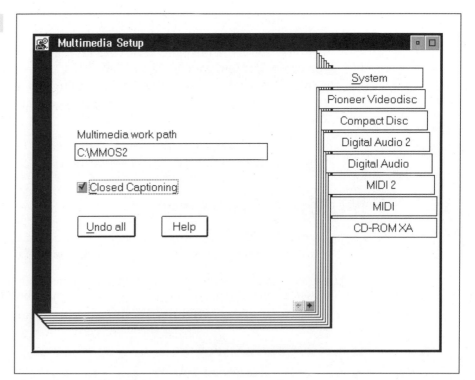

bottom of the notebook. (If you can't see any tabs at the bottom of the notebook, drag the whole notebook up the screen until they become visible.) You will see tabs for:

- **System:** Use the System page to specify the directory where you want applications to place any temporary work files they have to create. Select a disk that you can both read from and write to, and that has ample free space. One minute of recorded information requires at least 2.5MB of hard disk storage space.

  Use the Closed Captioning check box to enable closed captioning for those applications that support it. Closed captioning provides hearing-impaired users with a visual representation of audio sounds, usually in the form of text that accompanies spoken words. Many TV channels provide programming that includes closed captioning.

- **Pioneer Videodisc:** This page has additional tabs for Name and Communication. The Name page lets you change the name and description of the device, and also whether it is the default. The Communication page lets you look at or change the serial communications parameters used with the videodisc. Refer to the documentation that came with your videodisc for the appropriate values for these settings.

► S O L U T I O N

If you connect a Videodisc to your system, and have problems accessing information, make sure the communications settings for the Videodisc in the Multimedia Setup object match those on the videodisc hardware; if they don't, you must change one group of settings until they match the other.

- **Compact Disc:** This page lets you change the name and description of the Compact Disc, and also whether it is the default.

- **Digital Audio:** The Name page lets you change the name and description of the Digital Audio device, and also whether it is the default. The Association page lets you look at or change the file types associated with this multimedia device. The use of associations was described in detail in Chapter 2 under the heading "Associating Objects." The appropriate filename extensions are .WAV and ._AU. Support is provided for standard RIFF Wave audio files sampled at rates of 11.025, 22.050, or 44.100 kHz (more about RIFF files later in this chapter), and AVC audio files.

- **MIDI:** This page also has extra tabs for Name and Association, (the appropriate filename extension is .MID), and has a new tab called Mapper. The MIDI Mapper page, shown in Figure 11.4, lets you select the MIDI device type and the active MIDI channels. The MIDI Device Type entry is important, and must be correct, as this information is used to convert from the standard MIDI file format to the format needed by the hardware installed on your system. The Active Channels check boxes indicate which MIDI channels should be used. In standard MIDI, channels 1 through 9 are the extended melodic tracks, channel 10 is the extended percussion track, channels 11 and 12 are unused, channels 13 through 15 are the base-level melodic tracks, and channel 16 is the base-level percussion track.

  The specifications for MIDI and MIDI files can be obtained from:

  > International MIDI Association
  > 5316 West 57th Street
  > Los Angeles, CA 90056
  > 310-649-6434

- **CD-ROM XA:** This page also includes Name and Association tabs. The appropriate filename extension is .XA.

FIGURE 11.4

The MIDI Mapper
controls active channels

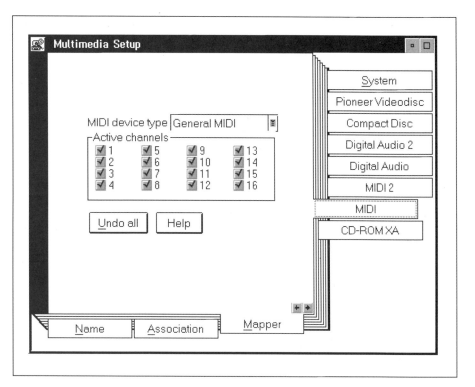

N O T E

CD-ROM XA is short for CD-ROM Extended Architecture, an extended format developed by Phillips, Sony, and Microsoft, which is consistent with the ISO 9660 (High Sierra) standard. CD-ROM XA adds ADPCM (adaptive differential pulse code modulation, a data compression technique that affords a 16:1 compression of audio data), audio, images, and interleaved data.

Once all the multimedia hardware devices are configured, you can use any of the MMPM/2 applications described in the next section.

Using the Multimedia Applications

Most of the multimedia applications in the MMPM/2 folder fall into two broad categories: the media players, which process data from a specific source; and the utility program used to convert data from one format to another. Two MMPM/2 applications that don't fall into these categories are Volume Control and Sound Bites:

- **Volume Control:** This small application controls the sound level on all active multimedia devices, independent of the application currently managing the hardware. When you double-click on this object, you will see that it uses a circular slider that looks remarkably like a volume control knob.

- **Sound Bites:** Sound Bites is a folder holding several sample MIDI or digital audio files that you can use to test whether your hardware is working as you expect.

Besides the control knob in the Volume Control application, the multi-media applications bring several new CUA elements to the OS/2 user interface to present a common look and feel to the user. These elements mimic the controls found on VCRs or cassette players, so if you can use a cassette player, you can use these applications.

Using the Media Players and Recorders

The media players are applications you can use with the multimedia devices installed on your system:

- **Compact Disc:** This application lets you play standard audio compact discs even without a sound adapter. Plug headphones with a standard jack into the socket on the CD drive to hear the music played back. If you load a CD-ROM or a CD-ROM XA instead of a compact disc, you will see the message "Wrong Media type."

- **Digital Audio:** This application allows you to record and play back digitally-recorded audio from a wave file through a sound card. You can record from a microphone connected to the appropriate input jack, or using the line-input jack on your audio adapter.

- **MIDI:** This application lets you record and play synthesized music through an audio adapter.

- **Videodisc:** This application lets you play videodiscs; you will also need a full-motion video adapter.

N O T E

MIDI and Digital Audio templates are automatically added to the Templates folder on the desktop when you run one of the MMPM/2 media players on your system. These templates allow you to create multiple instances of the media players.

When these applications are running, they all look very similar; Figure 11.5 shows MIDI in action.

The media player screens mimic the control panel of a VCR or similar device, with buttons to play, stop, pause, rewind, record, and mute, and a slider bar to control the volume. You can also type shortcut keystrokes from the keyboard.

The usual options are available in the application's File menu so you can select the file you want to work with.

Using the Multimedia Data Converter

The Multimedia Data Converter lets you convert from one image or audio file format to another. For example, you can convert an OS/2 bitmap image into a format suitable for display on an IBM M-Motion adapter.

FIGURE 11.5

The MMPM/2 MIDI window

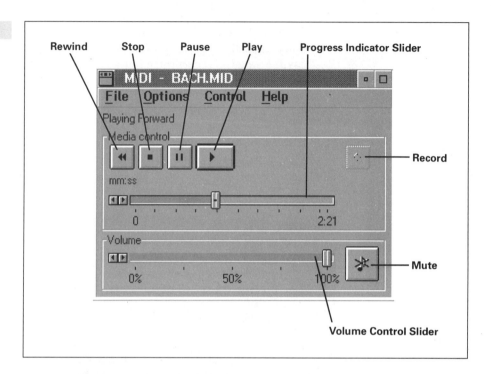

Rewind   Stop   Pause   Play   Progress Indicator Slider

MIDI - BACH.MID

File   Options   Control   Help

Playing Forward

Media control

Record

mm:ss

0   2:21

Volume

0%   50%   100%

Mute

Volume Control Slider

NOTE

The M-Motion environment consists of the M-Motion Video Adapter/A and the M-Control Program/2, and provides analog video in addition to high quality sound and images.

Double-click on the Multimedia Data Converter icon in the MMPM/2 folder, and you will see the window shown in Figure 11.6.

Specify the file or files you want to convert, then click on the Convert button. Alternatively, use the Include button to specify or restrict the image and audio file formats you want to use, then choose a file. You can use the Preview button to display a currently selected image file; Preview does not work for other file types.

Not all multimedia applications use standard filename extensions, but Table 11.1 lists the most common types and their filename extensions.

FIGURE 11.6

The Multimedia Data
Converter

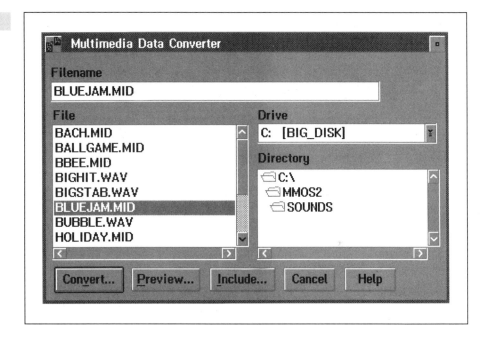

FIGURE 11.6

The Multimedia Data
Converter

TABLE 11.1: Common Multimedia File Types and Extensions

EXTENSION	TYPE	DESCRIPTION
_AD and _AU	Audio	IBM AudioVisual Connection
_IM and !IM	Image	IBM AudioVisual Connection
BMP	Bit map	General
MID	MIDI	MIDI and MIDI RIFF
VID	Image	IBM M-Audio
WAV	Audio	Digital

N O T E   The AudioVisual Connection (AVC) is an IBM product used
to develop and deliver professional-quality multimedia
presentations on a PS/2 computer.

The Resource Interchange File Format (RIFF) is the standard format used by multimedia applications; it allows audio, image, animation, and other multimedia elements to be combined into a common file format. A major advantage of the format is that it uses *chunks*, building blocks identified by unique tags. This means that a multimedia application can process the chunks that it understands, while ignoring those it does not. RIFF can also be expanded to include new tags without requiring that existing applications be rewritten; they will just ignore the tags that they don't understand.

Multimedia Support in WIN-OS/2

Microsoft Windows version 3.1 supports audio files and devices; WIN-OS/2 in OS/2 version 2.1 provides the same support. Just as with MMPM/2, special hardware is needed—for example, a CD-ROM drive or a sound card—for this audio. The following multimedia applets are included with WIN-OS/2:

- **Media Player:** This application lets you play multimedia data files on the appropriate hardware. In the case of a CD-ROM or video disk, commands are sent to the hardware to play back the sound. If the files are stored on your hard disk, such as MIDI control sequences, animation or sound files, the files are read and then passed to the appropriate hardware such as the sound board or the MIDI system.

- **Sound Recorder:** This application lets you record sounds from a microphone, and then edit them. You can also edit .WAV files with Sound Recorder.

- **MIDI Mapper:** If you have installed a sound driver that supports the MIDI protocol, this icon appears in the Control Panel. You can use it to establish MIDI settings such as channel assignments and key remappings. If you have a non-standard MIDI board, you can use a MIDI Mapper patch map to correct for the strange patch-numbering schemes that some synthesizers use.

- **Sound Settings:** This part of the Control Panel lets you assign specific sound files, stored in the .WAV format, to Windows events such as information dialog boxes, error messages, and starting and leaving Windows.

The Microsoft DOS CD-ROM device driver MSCDEX.EXE was partially supported in OS/2 version 2.0, but audio support was limited. In OS/2 version 2.1, support for MSCDEX is complete. This means that DOS and Windows multimedia applications that use the MSCDEX audio interface can run in a virtual DOS machine (VDM) with OS/2 version 2.1.

MMPM/2 Language Translations

MMPM/2 is available from IBM in several different languages, including Universal English, French, German, Italian, Japanese, Norwegian, and Spanish. In the next part of this chapter, we'll look at some of the wider issues involved in supporting different languages in OS/2.

OS/2 International Support

A major goal for the designers of OS/2 was that the operating system should be flexible in its approach to nationality. First, it had to be available in what is called Universal English, but it also had to be able to support as many foreign languages as possible. OS/2 is available in the following languages:

Chinese, People's Republic of China

Chinese, Taiwan

Danish

Finnish

French

German

Italian

Japanese

Korean

Dutch

Norwegian

Portuguese

Spanish

Swedish

In these translated versions, information on the screen and in the manuals is presented in the national language, but commands, device names, and file names stay in their original form. In the next few sections in this chapter, we'll look at how this national language support (NLS) is implemented and managed, as well as describe the configuration commands used.

Country Codes and Code Pages

As part of the national language support, each country has a unique country code, and each country code is assigned a primary code page and at least one alternative code page. A code page consists of characters that your keyboard can generate, your screen can display, and your printer can print. Only one code page can be in use at a time. In OS/2, there are two kinds of code page:

- **Single-byte character set (SBCS):** These code pages contain up to 256 characters, although some characters may be device control characters and therefore unprintable. These SBCSs make up the vast majority of the code pages that OS/2 supports.

- **Double-byte character set (DBCS):** Asian languages, such as Chinese, Korean, and Japanese, use many more than 256 characters, and so a two-byte code is used. IBM has defined the following character sets for OS/2 systems:

  - Japanese Graphic Character Set (7263 characters)
  - Korean Graphic Character Set (8877 characters)
  - Traditional Chinese Graphic Character Set (14,060 characters)

  Because most OS/2 applications accept only one code page at a time, special DCBSs were needed to support these languages.

► SOLUTION

The IBM PS/55 computer is designed to handle data entry, display, and printing in Asian languages, and has the following additional capabilities:

- **Display Resolution:** To display the very complex forms of ideographic characters, the special PS/55 is equipped with ROM fonts for either Japanese, Korean, or Traditional Chinese.
- **Keyboards:** Special keyboards are used to support one of the three languages.
- **Printers:** Printers contain specialized fonts, and are managed using unique control codes and escape sequences.

Along with this code page information, OS/2 provides installable keyboard translation tables, display and printer character sets, and country/language information for each of its code pages.

NOTE

A code page does not define how a specific character looks; it only defines what the characters are. The final appearance of a character is defined by the particular font being used.

OS/2 version 2.1 supports the country codes and code pages listed in Table 11.2.

TABLE 11.2: Country ID Codes and Code Pages for OS/2's National Language Support

COUNTRY OR LANGUAGE	COUNTRY ID CODE	CODE PAGE (PRIMARY/SECONDARY)
Arabic	785	864/437 or 850 *
Asian English	099	437/850
Australia	061	850/437
Belgium	032	850/437
Brazil	055	850/437
Canadian English	001	437/850
Canadian French	002	863/850
Czechoslovakia	042	852/850
Denmark	045	865/850
Finland	358	437/850
France	033	437/850
Germany	049	437/850
Hebrew	972	862/437 or 850 *
Hungary	036	852/850
Iceland	354	850/861
Italy	039	437/850
Japan	081	932 or 942/437 or 850 **
Korea	082	934 or 944/437 or 850 **
Latin America	003	437/850

TABLE 11.2: Country ID Codes and Code Pages for OS/2's National Language Support (Continued)

COUNTRY OR LANGUAGE	COUNTRY ID CODE	CODE PAGE (PRIMARY/SECONDARY)
Netherlands	031	437/850
Norway	047	865/850
People's Republic of China	088	938/948 or 437/850 **
Poland	048	852/850
Portugal	351	850/860
Spain	034	437/850
Sweden	046	437/850
Switzerland	041	437/850
Traditional Chinese (Republic of China)	088	938 or 948/437 or 850
Turkey	090	857/850
United Kingdom	044	437/850
USA	001	437/850
Yugoslavia	038	852/850

* Code pages 862 and 864 provide bidirectional support for Hebrew- and Arabic-speaking countries, and these code pages are installed as the defaults when OS/2 is installed for these countries. The secondary code page is 437, but you can select 850 as the alternate when you install the operating system.

** Code pages 932, 934, 938, 942, 944, and 948 are supported by the Asian version of OS/2 running on specialized Asian hardware.

Two of the code pages in Table 11.2, code page 850 and code page 437, are of particular interest, as they are by far the most commonly encountered code pages in OS/2:

- **Code Page 850**. Code page 850 is also called the Latin-1, or multilingual code page. It contains the characters required by 13 languages used in approximately 40 different countries.

- **Code Page 437**. Code page 437 is the standard PC code page. The lower 128 characters are based on the 7-bit ASCII code, while the upper half contains characters from several European languages and some graphics characters.

The following commands are used to manage code pages and national language support in OS/2:

- CHCP
- CODEPAGE
- COUNTRY
- DEVINFO
- GRAFTABL
- KEYB

Some of these commands can only be used in CONFIG.SYS, while others are designed to be used only at the command line. In the sections that follow, we'll look at each command in turn.

CHCP

The CHCP command lets you swap between two code-page character sets defined in your CONFIG.SYS file.

You can use CHCP from either the OS/2 or the DOS command prompt, with the following syntax:

CHCP *nnn*

The optional *nnn* parameter is the number of the code page you want to change to.

These code pages determine the characters produced when you use the keyboard corresponding to the COUNTRY statement in your CONFIG.SYS file.

In the United States, OS/2 defaults to the following code pages:

437   United States

850   Multilingual

Many other code pages are available, as Table 11.2 shows.

If you use the CHCP command with no options, you will see the number of the active code page displayed on the screen, along with the numbers of both the prepared system code pages.

CODEPAGE

The CODEPAGE command in CONFIG.SYS specifies the system code pages for code-page switching. You can set the code pages for keyboard, printer, and display independently, but not all printers and displays support code-page switching; see your hardware manuals for more information.

Here's the syntax:

CODEPAGE = *ppp, sss*

Use *ppp* to specify the number of the primary code page, and *sss* to specify the number of the alternate code page. (See Table 11.2 for these code pages.)

You must also include the appropriate DEVINFO statements for keyboard, printer and video for both pages in your CONFIG.SYS file.

Examples

To prepare the U.S. code page and the multilingual code page as the primary and alternate code pages, respectively, add the following line to your CONFIG.SYS file:

CODEPAGE = 437, 850

COUNTRY

The COUNTRY command in CONFIG.SYS prepares OS/2 for international use, and specifies date, time, and decimal separators, currency, and case conversions. Here's the syntax:

COUNTRY = **nnn**, *drive:\path\filename*

In the COUNTRY command nnn specifies a three-digit country-identification code, as listed in Table 11.2. This code is usually the same as the international telephone dialing code for the country; Germany is 049, the United Kingdom 044, and so on. The *drive:\path\filename* parameter specifies the file that contains the country information; normally C:\OS2\SYSTEM\COUNTRY.SYS.

N O T E The country setting is always the same for OS/2 and DOS sessions.

Examples

To establish the U.S. standards for dates, times, currencies, and other settings, add the following line to your CONFIG.SYS file:

COUNTRY = 001, C:\OS2\SYSTEM\COUNTRY.SYS

DEVINFO

The DEVINFO command in CONFIG.SYS prepares a device for code-page switching.

To prepare a keyboard, use the following syntax:

DEVINFO = **KBD,layout,**drive:\path**filename**

where *layout* specifies a keyboard country code, and *filename* is KEYBOARD.DCP, the device driver that translates keystrokes. Keyboard country codes are listed in Table 11.3, located in the KEYB entry later in this chapter.

To prepare a display, use the following syntax:

DEVINFO = **SCR,type,**drive:\path**filename**

In this variation of the DEVINFO command, *type* describes a reserved device name from the following: CGA, EGA, VGA, or BGA (an 8514/A adapter with memory option), and *filename* must be VIOTBL.DCP.

To prepare a printer, use the following:

DEVINFO = **LPT#,device,** drive:\path**filename, ROM=(xxx,yyy)**

Here *device* specifies the physical device number (for example, 4201 for an IBM Proprinter I or II, and 5202 for an IBM Quietwriter), and *filename* is the corresponding device driver (here, either 4201.DCP or 5202.DCP). *ROM* specifies that system code pages are contained in ROM, *xxx* represents the code page number, and *yyy* the font identification number associated with this code page. See your IBM printer handbook for more information.

Examples

To prepare a U.S. keyboard, use the following line in CONFIG.SYS:

DEVINFO=KBD,US,C:\OS2\KEYBOARD.DCP

To set a VGA display for a new code page, use the following:

DEVINFO=SCR,VGA,C:\OS2\VIOTBL.DCP

GRAFTABL

The GRAFTABL command allows a DOS session to display the characters in the extended ASCII character set (numbers 128 through 255). GRAFTABL works only for certain modes of the CGA, for the EGA and the VGA; it has no effect when used with other video display adapters, and because it is a DOS-session command, GRAFTABL has no effect in OS/2 sessions. Here's the syntax:

GRAFTABL *nnn /switches*

In the GRAFTABL command, *nnn* specifies a three-digit number to indicate the code page to use, from the following:

437	United States
850	Multilingual
860	Portuguese
863	French Canadian
865	Nordic

Switches

/?	Displays a short summary of code page options as well as the number of the graphics code page in use.
/STA	Displays the number of the graphics code page currently in use.

KEYB

The KEYB command loads a keyboard-translation table that allows your computer to generate country-specific characters in all OS/2 and DOS full-screen sessions. After you specify the translation table, pressing certain key combinations will now produce language-specific accented characters. Here's the syntax:

KEYB *layout layout ID*

The KEYB command is a quick way to change keyboard layout if you include a DEVINFO statement in your CONFIG.SYS file.

Type KEYB with no parameters to see the current settings for KEYB as well as information on the current code page.

NOTE

It is very easy to arrive at the point where the keyboard layout and code page in memory are out of synchronization. To avoid this, make sure that the KEYB command and the CODEPAGE command in CONFIG.SYS both specify the same country. You cannot use the KEYB command if there is no DEVINFO statement included in your CONFIG.SYS file.

If you want to change your keyboard layout, specify *layout* as one of the two-letter keyboard codes from Table 11.3, and add a *layout ID* code if necessary.

TABLE 11.3: Keyboard Layout Codes Supported by OS/2

LANGUAGE OR COUNTRY	KEYBOARD CODE	LAYOUT ID
Arabic	AR	238
Belgium	BE	120
Canada (French)	CF	058
Czechoslovakia (Czech)	CS 243	243
Czechoslovakia (Slovak)	CS 245	245
Danish	DK	159
Dutch	NL	143
Finnish	SU	153
French	FR 120	120
French	FR 189	189
German	GR	129
Hebrew	HE	212
Hungarian	HU	208
Icelandic	IS	197
Italian	IT 141	141
Italian	IT 142	142

TABLE 11.3: Keyboard Layout Codes Supported by OS/2 (Continued)

LANGUAGE OR COUNTRY	KEYBOARD CODE	LAYOUT ID
Latin American	LA	171
Norwegian	NO	155
Polish	PL	214
Portuguese	PO	163
Spanish	SP	172
Swedish	SV	153
Swiss (French)	SF	150F
Swiss (German)	SG	150G
Turkish	TR	179
United Kingdom	UK 166	166
United Kingdom	UK 168	168
United States	US	103P
Yugoslavia	YU	234

NOTE: Add a *subcountry* code, as shown in Table 11.4, for countries that have more than one layout.

For countries that have more than one keyboard layout code, you'll need to add a subcountry code from Table 11.4.

TABLE 11.4: Subcountry Codes for Counties with More Than One Keyboard Code

SUBCOUNTRY CODE	COUNTRY
243	Czechoslovakia, Czech
245	Czechoslovakia, Slovak
189, 120	France
141, 142	Italy
166, 168	United Kingdom

Example

To set up a United States system to handle Norwegian characters, you need the following statements in CONFIG.SYS:

    COUNTRY=047,865,C:\OS2\COUNTRY.SYS

    DEVINFO=KBD,NO,C:\OS2\KEYBOARD.DCP

    KEYB NO,865

Bidirectional Languages

OS/2 also supports bidirectional languages, such as Hebrew and Arabic. Such languages require that video and printer output is presented for reading from left-to-right or from right-to-left, and for the indentation of phrases or paragraphs from either direction. This support is only available in full-screen sessions.

 S O L U T I O N

The example that follows is typical of the OS/2 CONFIG.SYS commands used to support Arabic:

    COUNTRY=785,C:\OS2\SYSTEM\COUNTRY.SYS
    CODEPAGE=864,437
    DEVINFO=KBD,AR,C:\OS2\KEYBOARD.DCP
    RUN=C:\OS2\SYSTEM\BDPRTM.EXE

Similar commands are used to support Hebrew:

    COUNTRY=972,C:\OS2\SYSTEM\COUNTRY.SYS
    CODEPAGE=862,437
    DEVINFO=KBD,HE,C:\OS2\KEYBOARD.DCP
    RUN=C:\OS2\SYSTEM\BDPRTM.EXE

Configuring Other Hardware

In the final part of this chapter, I'll deal with OS/2 configuration issues for various device, including mice, modems, COM ports, touch screens, scanners, and faxes.

Serial, Bus, and PS/2 Mice

The OS/2 installation program and the Selective Install program in the System Setup folder both let you specify the name of the mouse you use. The program then detects the mouse attached to your system, and most of the time automatic detection avoids compatibility problems altogether. If you don't use a mouse or other pointing device, select the No Pointing Device Support option; however, using the OS/2 graphical interface is going to be difficult without a mouse, and some operations will just be impossible. If your mouse is attached to the System Mouse Port on a PS/2 computer, and is not listed by name in the Mouse window in the Selective Install program, choose the Other Pointing Device for Mouse Port option.

Many mice, including several from Logitech, can emulate the Microsoft mouse, so you should choose the Serial Pointing Device option for these models; use the Logitec Serial Mouse option only if you use a Mouse Systems PC Mouse or a Logitech C7 or C9 serial mouse.

The Logitech 3-button mouse is supported in OS/2 as a Microsoft 2-button mouse; in a DOS session the mouse will behave as you expect, but on the desktop, there might be different and more limited functions. The IBM CUA guidelines for the user interface contain no information on using 3-button mice.

Several intermittent problems have been reported by users of 50 MHz AT-bus systems, where the mouse gets out of synchronization. To avoid further problems, you should shut down and restart your system if this happens to you.

Other Pointing Devices and Touch Screens

Touch-sensitive screens are popular for certain applications, especially when a program requires that infrequent computer users make complex menu or on-screen choices. They can make that choice by pointing to the object on the screen that they want to choose. In some touch-screen displays, a clear pressure-sensitive film covers the screen, while others use a matrix of infrared LEDs and sensors around the outer edges of the screen to detect the touch.

If you have a touch-sensitive screen such as the IBM 8516 Touch Display attached to your computer, OS/2 supports a combined mouse and touch screen device driver. The entries in your CONFIG.SYS file for this should be:

```
DEVICE=C:\OS2\PDITOU0x.SYS CODE=TOUC021D.BIN
INIT=TOUCH.INI

DEVICE=C:\OS2\TOUCH.SYS TYPE=PDITOU$

RUN=C:\OS2\CALIBRATE.EXE-C C:\OS2CALIBRAT.DAT

DEVICE=C:\OS2\MOUSE.SYS TYPE=PDIMOU$
```

where x is either 1 or 2, depending on the bus used in your computer, TOUC021D.BIN is the microcode binary file for the touch device, and TOUCH.INI is a text file that contains default parameter settings.

The RUN=CALIBRAT.EXE statement activates the Calibration program, which downloads calibration information into the touch screen device each time OS/2 is started, and allows for the calibration of the touch device at initial setup.

To recalibrate a touch device, type the following at the OS/2 command prompt:

```
C:

CD \OS2

CALIBRAT –U
```

The –U option updates the existing CALIBRAT.DAT file with revised calibration information.

Setting Interrupt Request Levels on an ISA Computer

In the PC architecture, the main processor does not accept interrupts from hardware devices directly; instead, interrupts are routed to an Intel 8259A Programmable Interrupt Controller (PIC) chip. This chip responds to each hardware interrupt, assigns a priority, and forwards it to the main processor. Each hardware device is attached or "jumpered" into inputs known as Interrupt Requests, often abbreviated to IRQs.

On an ISA or Micro Channel computer, two 8259A PICs are tied together. That is, one of the interrupt lines (line 2) accepts input from the other 8259A chip. This gives a total of 15 interrupts, with interrupt 2 usually described as the *cascade*. Table 11.5 lists the standard IRQ assignments.

TABLE 11.5: Standard ISA Computer IRQ Assignments

IRQ LEVEL	ASSOCIATED DEVICE
0	System Timer
1	Keyboard
2	Secondary Interrupt Controller (Cascade)
3	COM2 (Serial Communications Port 2)
4	COM1 (Serial Communications Port 1)
5	LPT2 (Parallel Port 2)
6	Floppy Disk
7	LPT1 (Parallel Port 1)
8	Real-time Clock
9	Reserved
10	Reserved
11	Reserved
12	Reserved
13	Math Coprocessor
14	Hard Disk
15	Reserved

IRQ levels described as Reserved in Table 11.5 do not have standard assignments. If you have only one parallel port and you want to use COM3 or COM4, you can use IRQ 5; just remember that this IRQ is now in use if you ever install another parallel adapter or a Sound Blaster card that may be set up with IRQ 5 as the initial default setting.

MS-DOS printing does not typically use the interrupt for the parallel port, but OS/2 does use it in support of multitasking operations, and this too can expose problems; it is quite common to find that the interrupt feature on the parallel port doesn't actually work. In MS-DOS this was never a problem, but in OS/2 your printing will be erratic or may not work at all.

N O T E

IRQ lines *can* be shared on a Micro Channel computer as long as the adapter card is designed for micro-channel architecture, and has been configured properly with the Reference Disk.

Non-standard adapters are notorious for causing problems often identified as IRQ conflicts, in which two devices are attempting to use the same IRQ. This may never have been a problem under MS-DOS where the two devices were never used at the same time, but in a multitasking environment like OS/2, many more combinations are possible. If you use multiple serial adapter cards, there is a much greater chance that you will try to access them at the same time with OS/2 than there ever was with MS-DOS; careful configuration can help avoid these problems.

Using COM Ports on ISA/EISA Computers

By default, OS/2 supports two serial communications ports, COM1 and COM2. Computers that use the ISA/EISA bus (clones that use the AT bus) can handle two more ports, COM3 and COM4. The problem is that there has never been any formal definition of the I/O port addresses and IRQ lines associated with ports 3 and 4. A convention has emerged that places the port address for COM3 at 03E8 and the address for COM4 at 02E8; check the documentation that came with your serial port adapter card to be sure of the addresses and IRQ numbers.

In OS/2 COM ports do not have to be assigned sequentially; you can specify COM4 and not specify COM3, however, to avoid confusing DOS, you can assign ports that do not actually have physical adapters attached.

NOTE

The port address for COM1 is 3F8 and the port address for COM2 is 2F8. Another potential trouble source is having several hardware adapters trying to share the same I/O port address; all the adapters in your system must use unique port addresses.

To enable COM3 and COM4 on an ISA/EISA computer, use the DEVICE=COM.SYS command as follows:

    DEVICE=C:\OS2\COM.SYS (n, xxx, i)

where:

- *n* is the number of the COM port, either 3 or 4
- *xxx* is the I/O port address, either 03E8 or 02E8
- *i* is the IRQ or interrupt request level

To specify that COM3 is at address 03E8 on IRQ 5, and COM4 is at address 02E8 using IRQ 10, add the following entries to CONFIG.SYS:

    DEVICE=C:\OS2\COM.SYS (3,03E8,5) (4,02E8)

Solving Communications Problems

OS/2 can detect that an interrupt line is shared and will not allow its simultaneous use. If two applications attempt to access serial ports using the same IRQ at the same time, OS/2 will prevent the second application from accessing the port, and will return an error message to this effect.

MS-DOS, on the other hand, may not recover so elegantly, and will probably just suspend, waiting for the port to open.

When the DOS setting COM_DIRECT_ACCESS is set to On, DOS programs use VCOM.SYS to access the communications ports directly. However, buffering is not available when using VCOM.SYS, and sometimes characters may be lost, causing problems for some programs. To avoid this, set COM_DIRECT_ACCESS to On for most DOS programs.

The DOS setting COM_SELECT allows a DOS application to select and use a communications port, and nonselected ports are then hidden from the program. Some programs, such as Laplink Pro, take over all the available communications ports. To run Laplink Pro and another application that uses a communications port at the same time, set COM_SELECT to All to avoid conflict.

Configuring Parallel Ports

Parallel port adapter cards are usually configured with jumpers or dip switches on the card itself. Table 11.6 shows the normal IRQ and I/O port addresses used for parallel ports with OS/2.

TABLE 11.6:   Parallel Port Addresses and IRQ Levels

PORT	ADDRESS	ISA IRQ	EISA IRQ	MICRO CHANNEL IRQ
LPT1	3BC	IRQ 7	IRQ 5 or 7	IRQ 7
LPT2	378	IRQ 7	IRQ 5 or 7	IRQ 7
LPT3	278	IRQ 5	IRQ 5 or 7	IRQ 7

If you have a PS/2 computer capable of direct memory access to parallel ports, such as the PS/2 model 56, 57, 80-A21, 80-A31, 90 or 95, OS/2 will automatically take advantage of this feature as long as the parallel-port arbitration level is set to SHARED7 (enabled). If the parallel-port arbitration is set to disabled, use the Reference Disk to change the system configuration.

A Word about Cables

Some peripheral cables may cause problems if they do not meet normal length or shielding requirements, and some manufacturers try to shave costs by not wiring all of the connectors inside a cable. This may not have been a problem in the past when using MS-DOS or Windows, because MS-DOS does not use all the connections; however, OS/2 uses some interface signals that MS-DOS does not.

Cable length can be a problem with parallel port cables; they should not be extended to longer than 6 feet (or 2 meters) without adding an amplifier or line driver to boost the signal. Serial cables, however, can be much longer than this without any significant loss of signal quality.

Configuring a Scanner

If you see an error message telling you that you cannot use your HP Scanner on your ISA computer, change the switch settings on the scanner adapter to 1010.

On a PS/2 computer, use the Reference Disk to set the adapter to hexadecimal ROM addresses C8000–CBFFF and input/output addresses 268–26F.

In both ISA and PS/2 computers, make sure that the DOS setting EMS_FRAME_LOCATION is set to Auto.

Fax Support

OS/2 provides support for certain Group Three fax modems, and OS/2 version 2.1 also contains Fax/PM, a desktop application for sending, receiving and managing single-page faxes. See Chapter 4 for more on using Fax/PM.

N O T E To use the Fax/PM application, you must first install Serial Support using the OS/2 installation program or the Selective Install object in the System Setup folder on the desktop.

OS/2 does not support fax boards and applications that require more than 1000 interrupts per second (9600 baud, or greater). The following fax boards and programs produce timing problems that may prevent reliable operation: ATI ETC, Cardinal FAX, Smartfax, and Twincomm 24/96.

If you use an Intel SatisFAXtion fax modem, use the fax board in a single DOS session; if you load the application into several DOS sessions, the fax may stop transmitting when it is reset by another session starting. Use the DOS setting DOS_DEVICE to load the device driver command for your fax modem to set up this session as a fax session.

Almost all fax adapters also contain regular modems. If your modem works properly, but the **fax** modem doesn't work in a DOS session, the serial device driver **VCOM.SYS** may be inducing timing problems into the commands that are used to manage the fax and are not part of normal asynchronous communications.

As a first step, change the DOS setting COM_DIRECT_ACCESS to On; this may allow your fax adapter to function properly, but may cause other effects too. You can also try removing the VCOM.SYS device driver from CONFIG.SYS, but you may suffer from lower baud rates, and some programs, including Prodigy, will not run without it.

On an ISA computer, you can set the fax modem up as COM3 or COM4 using the commands in CONFIG.SYS described earlier, then set up the switches on the fax modem to reflect these settings, and do all your faxing from a single DOS session.

In the end, it may be that the real answer to this problem is to purchase an OS/2-based fax with its associated software.

PART IV

Becoming an OS/2 Power User

CHAPTERS

OS/2 OS/2 OS/2

OS/2 OS/2 OS/2 OS/2 OS/2 OS/2 OS/2 OS/2 OS/2 OS/2

OS/2 OS/2 OS/2

12

Working from the Command Line

FOR many users, the OS/2 desktop described in the early chapters of this book represents the ultimate in ease of use. For others, the command line is the key to unleashing the power of the operating system. In this chapter, I'll describe many of the commands you can use from the OS/2 command lines, and show you, with examples, how you can get the most out of OS/2.

The sections that follow present OS/2 commands alphabetical order, with a command description, the syntax, examples, and special usage notes where appropriate. Users migrating to OS/2 from DOS should check these notes for any significant differences between an OS/2 DOS session command and the equivalent MS-DOS command.

Most of the commands described in this chapter are available in both OS/2 sessions and DOS sessions, although a few are specific to one operating environment or the other. Table 12.1 lists all the OS/2 commands, and indicates where differences exist between usage at the OS/2 command line, the OS/2 DOS-session command line, and the MS-DOS command line.

TABLE 12.1: OS/2 Command Comparison Chart

COMMAND NAME	OS/2	OS/2 DOS	MS-DOS
ANSI	a	n/a	n/a
APPEND	n/a	a	sd
ASSIGN	n/a	a	nsd
ATTRIB	n/a	a	nsd
BACKUP	a	n/a	nsd
BOOT	a	nsd	n/a
BREAK	a	nsd	nsd
CD (or CHDIR)	a	nsd	nsd

TABLE 12.1: OS/2 Command Comparison Chart (Continued)

COMMAND NAME	OS/2	OS/2 DOS	MS-DOS
CHCP	a	nsd	nsd
CHKDSK	a	nsd	sd
CLS	a	nsd	nsd
CMD	a	n/a	n/a
COMMAND	n/a	a	sd
COMP	a	nsd	sd
COPY	a	nsd	sd
CREATEDD	a	n/a	n/a
DATE	a	nsd	nsd
DDINSTAL	a	n/a	n/a
DEBUG	a	nsd	nsd
DEL (or ERASE)	a	nsd	nsd
DETACH	a	n/a	n/a
DIR	a	sd	sd
DISKCOMP	a	nsd	sd
DISKCOPY	a	nsd	sd
DPATH	a	n/a	n/a
DOSKEY	n/a	a	nsd
EAUTIL	a	nsd	n/a
EXIT	a	nsd	nsd
FDISK	a	n/a	sd
FDISKPM	a	n/a	n/a
FIND	a	nsd	nsd
FORMAT	a	nsd	sd
FSACCESS	a	a	n/a
GRAFTABL	n/a	a	sd

TABLE 12.1: OS/2 Command Comparison Chart (Continued)

COMMAND NAME	OS/2	OS/2 DOS	MS-DOS
HELP	a	sd	sd
JOIN	n/a	a	nsd
KEYB	a	n/a	n/a
KEYS	a	n/a	n/a
LABEL	a	nsd	nsd
MAKEINI	a	n/a	n/a
MD (or MKDIR)	a	nsd	nsd
MEM	n/a	a	a
MODE	a	sd	sd
MORE	a	nsd	nsd
MOVE	a	n/a	n/a
PATCH	a	n/a	n/a
PATH	a	nsd	nsd
PICVIEW	a	n/a	n/a
PMREXX	a	n/a	n/a
PRINT	a	sd	sd
PROMPT	a	nsd	nsd
PSTAT	a	n/a	n/a
RD (or RMDIR)	a	nsd	nsd
RECOVER	a	nsd	sd
REN (or RENAME)	a	nsd	nsd
REPLACE	a	nsd	nsd
RESTORE	a	n/a	nsd
SET	a	nsd	nsd
SETBOOT	a	n/a	n/a

TABLE 12.1: OS/2 Command Comparison Chart (Continued)

COMMAND NAME	OS/2	OS/2 DOS	MS-DOS
SORT	a	nsd	nsd
SPOOL	a	n/a	n/a
START	a	nsd	n/a
SUBST	n/a	a	nsd
SYSLEVEL	a	n/a	n/a
SYSLOG	a	n/a	n/a
TIME	a	nsd	nsd
TREE	a	nsd	nsd
TYPE	a	nsd	nsd
UNDELETE	a	nsd	nsd
UNPACK	a	nsd	n/a
VER	a	nsd	nsd
VERIFY	a	nsd	nsd
VIEW	a	n/a	n/a
VMDISK	n/a	a	n/a
VOL	a	nsd	nsd
XCOPY	a	sd	sd

Legend: a = available; n/a = not available; sd = significantly different; nsd = not significantly different.

I have divided the commands into several functional groups, and describe them in this chapter under the following main headings:

- Command Processing
- Program Management Commands
- Disk Management Commands

- System Customization and Control Commands
- Batch File Commands

Chapter 3 presents the commands used in file and directory management. The commands associated with international settings are included in Chapter 11, and those used for diagnosing OS/2 problems are described in Chapter 14.

Understanding the OS/2 and DOS Command Prompts

To access the OS/2 or DOS command lines from the desktop, double-click the OS/2 System icon on the desktop, and then double-click the Command Prompts folder. You will see several icons in this folder, including:

- DOS Window
- DOS Full Screen
- OS/2 Window
- OS/2 Full Screen

You can run DOS or OS/2 command sessions either inside a window on the desktop or as a full-screen session. A DOS session in OS/2 looks and behaves much like MS-DOS; most of the commands used in MS-DOS are available, and there are a few new ones. If you have used the MS-DOS command prompt in the past, you will have no trouble adapting to a DOS session under OS/2, or to using the OS/2 command prompt. Just type the commands you want to use directly at the command prompt, including any optional switches or filenames you want to use with the command.

N O T E

OS/2 is a multitasking operating system, so you can start several different DOS sessions all running at the same time; the system limit is well over 100. Refer to Chapter 6 for more information on starting and using multiple DOS sessions.

To close a windowed session and return to the desktop, double-click on the icon in the top left corner of the window. In a full screen session, press Ctrl+Esc to switch back to the desktop, or type EXIT at the system prompt to close the session.

Stacking Commands

Ever since OS/2 version 1.0 was released in 1987, OS/2 has supported *command stacking*, or the ability to specify several commands on the command line. This allows you to enter several commands all at the same time, and then go away and do something else as they execute.

To stack two commands, use the ampersand character (&), as in this simple example:

DIR C: & DIR D:

This sequence displays a listing of the contents of drive C followed by the contents of drive D.

If you use two ampersand symbols (&&) together, OS/2 will only execute the second command if the first command succeeds. Consider a slightly more complex example:

COPY C:\MYFILE.TXT B: && DEL C:\MYFILE.TXT

In this case, MYFILE.TXT will only be erased from drive C after it is copied successfully onto drive B.

Finally, you might want an operation to occur if a previous operation fails; include two vertical bars (||) on the command line for this. If you have a program that makes a noise, called SOUND, you can run this program to alert you to the fact that an operation has failed:

COPY C:\MYFILE.TXT B: || SOUND

You can combine these command stackers into quite complex operations:

COPY C:\MYFILE.TXT B: && DEL C:\MYFILE.TXT || SOUND

In this example, MYFILE.TXT will be copied from drive C to drive B, and if the copy is successful, the file will be erased from drive C. If the copy fails, you will hear the noise contained in SOUND instead.

If you want to process more complex sequences than the examples given here, you should probably write batch files to automate your operations, rather than stacking commands at the command prompt.

Understanding Redirection

Being able to redirect a command's input or output is one of the things that gives the command line so much power. The concept of redirection (along with the programming structure that makes redirection work) was borrowed from the Unix operating system. Usually, OS/2 receives information from the *standard input device,* the keyboard, and sends output to the *standard output device,* which is the screen. However, you can make OS/2 redirect its output to another device or even to a file. OS/2 considers device names and file names functionally equivalent, so you can use them interchangeably with commands that require you to specify a source or destination name.

The three symbols used when redirecting input or output are:

>   Sends the output of a command to the device name or file name given after the symbol; if a file of this name already exists, it will be overwritten.

>>   Adds, or *appends*, the output of a command to the end of an existing file, or creates a new file if the specified file does not exist.

<   Directs input to a command from the source specified after the symbol.

Redirecting Output

When you type the DIR command at the command prompt, a listing of the contents of the current directory are shown on the screen. You can use redirection to send this listing to your printer instead by typing:

    DIR > PRN

where PRN is the device name for the printer.

To send the output from the DIR command to a file, type:

    DIR > *filename*

where *filename* can be any legal filename you want to use. This command sequence creates the file if it does not already exist, or overwrites an existing file with this name with the listing from the DIR command. You will not see anything shown on the screen, since you have redirected all output from this command into the file.

If the file already exists and you want to add the output from the DIR command to the end of the file rather than overwrite the file, use this form instead:

    DIR >> *filename*

Redirecting output to a file comes in handy in a variety of situations. For example, if you are in a hurry, you can collect output from a lengthy process into a file that you can examine at your leisure. Alternatively, when you do not want to modify the data but need to see a copy of it at some point, you can send the output directly to your printer.

Redirecting Input

You probably won't need to redirect input as often as you redirect output, but there are several circumstances when programmers find it useful. When you redirect input, it must come from a file rather than from the keyboard. You can redirect input from a file to any OS/2 command that needs input, but you cannot use it to provide parameters or switches to a command.

A common use for redirecting input is to speed up the operation of an interactive process that stops its execution to wait for a keystroke from the keyboard before continuing. To indicate that the keystrokes are coming from a file rather than from the keyboard, use the redirection symbol with a file name, as follows:

command < file name

For example, the following short batch file deletes all the files from a directory you specify at the command prompt, then removes the directory itself. The name of the directory you specify is loaded into the replaceable parameter %1, and is used by the DEL command and by the RD command also.

```
DEL %1 <YES.DAT
RD %1
```

When you use this kind of delete sequence, the operating system asks if you are sure you want to delete all the files, and waits for you to type a Y from the keyboard. The same thing happens with this batch file too, except that the file YES.DAT contains the Y character, followed by a carriage return. This means that the Delete command receives its input (the Y character followed by a carriage return) from the YES.DAT file rather than from the keyboard as normal; the Delete command can't tell the difference.

Using Error Redirection

There is a third standard device known as the *standard error device* in addition to the standard input device and the standard output device previously described. When OS/2 generates an error message, the message is displayed on this standard error device. You can use redirection to send these error messages to a file, so that you can look at them later. Why might you want to do this? Programmers are the most frequent users of this technique, particularly if they expect an operation to generate a large number of mostly trivial errors, far too many to fit onto a single screen. They redirect the error text into a file and then sort though the messages later on, when the operation is complete.

Using Pipes and Filters

Another concept borrowed from Unix is that of the *pipe*. A pipe sends the output of one command to another command for processing. You create a pipe using the | symbol, the vertical bar. To send the output from COMMAND1 to COMMAND2 for processing as input, enter:

COMMAND1 | COMMAND2

You can combine several commands together to create complex operations using a pipe, and pipes are often used with a special kind of command known as a *filter*. A filter is a program that takes the output from one command and modifies that output in some way.

There are three commands, available from both the OS/2 and the DOS command prompts, that function as filters: MORE, SORT, and FIND. These commands are described in detail in Chapter 3.

An example of a filter appears in the discussion of the PSTAT command, and is worth duplicating here. PSTAT can produce long and complex screen output, and to make the command display the information one screen at a time so you can read it, pipe the output though the MORE filter, as follows:

PSTAT | MORE

When you are ready to view the next screenful of information, just press ↵.

Command-Processing Commands

This section describes the OS/2 BOOT command used to switch between the OS/2 and MS-DOS operating systems when OS/2 is set up with the boot manager, and the COMMAND and CMD commands used to manage the OS/2 or DOS-session command processors. You can also use KEYS or DOSKEY to manage and manipulate everything you have entered at the command line during the current session. This way, you can avoid typing the same command over and over, and so save yourself some time.

N O T E In the syntax descriptions presented throughout this chapter, required parameters are shown in bold, while optional parameters that modify or change the behavior of the command are shown in *italic*.

BOOT

The BOOT command switches between the OS/2 and the MS-DOS operating systems when they are both installed on the same hard disk drive, drive C.

Here's the syntax:

BOOT *switches*

The BOOT command is available from an OS/2 session command prompt, from an OS/2 DOS session command prompt, or from an MS-DOS command prompt, and can be used if:

- A version of MS-DOS later than version 3.2 (later versions of MS-DOS are recommended for more complete OS/2 compatibility) was resident on drive C before OS/2 was installed.

- Drive C was not reformatted during the OS/2 installation.

- The HPFS was not installed on drive C.

Before running the BOOT command, be sure to complete all system operations and end all application programs; otherwise data may be lost.

Switches

/OS2   Changes to the OS/2 operating system from MS-DOS.

/DOS   Changes to the MS-DOS operating system from OS/2 or from an OS/2 DOS session.

S O L U T I O N

You can also change from OS/2 to MS-DOS directly from the desktop, without going to the command line. Double-click the OS/2 System folder, then double-click the Command Prompts folder. You will see an icon labeled Dual Boot inside the Command Prompts folder. Double-click on this icon, and a window opens asking:

> SYS1714: Warning! Make sure all your programs have completed or data will be lost when the system is restarted.
>
> You requested to start DOS from drive C:
> Your system will be reset. Do you want to continue (Y/N)?

Type a Y followed by the Enter key to continue to boot MS-DOS from drive C, or enter N to abort the process and return to the desktop.

Examples   To change to MS-DOS from OS/2, type:

    BOOT /DOS

from either the OS/2 command prompt or the DOS prompt of an OS/2 DOS session.

To switch to OS/2 from MS-DOS, type the following from the OS2 directory:

    BOOT /OS2

N O T E   When you next turn your computer on, the operating system (OS/2 or MS-DOS) that was running immediately before you turned it off is automatically reloaded.

CMD

CMD starts a new OS/2 command processor running from the OS/2 command prompt. The command processor is the command-line interface that accepts and processes commands, loads and runs programs, and writes out error messages as necessary. To return to the original command processor, use the EXIT command.

Here's the syntax:

CMD *drive:path /switches*

Switches If you plan to use multiple switches with CMD, use /Q or /S before you use /K or /C.

/Q	Starts a new command processor in an echo off mode.
/S	Starts a new command processor and tells it to ignore any break characters (Ctrl+C).
/K "*string*"	Passes the contents of *string* to CMD.EXE, but does not return to the original command processor when the command contained in *string* is complete.
/C "*string*"	Passes the contents of *string* to CMD.EXE, and returns to the original command processor when the command contained in *string* is complete.

Examples To start a new command processor in echo off mode, type

CMD /Q

To start a new command processor, pass it a set of commands, and stay in the new environment, type

CMD /K "TYPE MYFILE.TXT"

NOTE If you change any of the environment variables for the new command processor, these variables are available only to the new command processor; when you return to the original command processor, any changes are lost.

COMMAND

COMMAND starts a new DOS command processor running from the DOS prompt. The command processor is the command-line interface that accepts and processes commands, loads and runs programs, and writes out error messages as necessary. To return to the original command processor, use the EXIT command.

Here's the syntax:

COMMAND *drive: path /switches*

COMMAND used with no parameters starts a new command processor. The existing environment variables are duplicated for this new command processor, but if you change any of these settings, they are lost when you return to the original command processor. COMMAND expects to find the file containing the DOS command processor, COMMAND.COM, in a directory called C:\OS2\MDOS. If the file is located elsewhere, use the appropriate path information.

Switches

/E:*nn*	Specifies the new size of the DOS environment. The range for a valid environment size extends from 160 bytes to 32,768 bytes, and is always rounded up to the nearest multiple of 16.
/P	Makes this new copy of the DOS command processor permanent until you restart OS/2 again.
/K *string*	Passes the contents of *string* to the new command processor, but does not return to the original command processor when the command contained in *string* is complete.
/C *string*	Passes the contents of *string* to the new command processor, and returns to the original command processor when the command contained in *string* is complete.

Examples   To start a new permanent DOS command processor, type:

COMMAND /P

If you want to enlarge the DOS environment space, type:

COMMAND /E: 4096

To start a new command processor, run a command, and then return to the original command processor, type:

COMMAND /C TYPE MYFILE.TXT

To repeat the previous example, but remain in the new DOS command processor, type:

COMMAND /K TYPE MYFILE.TXT

N O T E

If you use the SET command to change any of the environment variables for the new command processor, these variables are available only to the new command processor; when you return to the original command processor, any changes are lost.

This version of COMMAND does not include the MS-DOS switch & /MSG that stores all error messages in memory. If you want to boot from a floppy disk, you'll need to keep a disk containing COMMAND.COM in drive A.

DOSKEY

The DOSKEY command installs the DOSKEY program that lets you recall and edit the DOS command line, as well as create and run small DOS command-line macros.

Here's the syntax:

DOSKEY /switches macroname=text

DOSKEY is a small terminate-and-stay resident program that gives you more flexibility to edit the DOS command line and work with macros. If you invoke DOSKEY with no parameters, the program loads using its default settings. DOSKEY saves everything you type at the command line, mistakes as well as legal commands.

DOSKEY uses the following keys to recall a command:

Up arrow	Recalls the previous DOS command.
Down arrow	Recalls the next DOS command.
Page up	Recalls the oldest DOS command in this session.
Page down	Recalls the most recent DOS command in this session.

To edit the command line, use these DOSKEY editing keys:

Left arrow	Moves the cursor one character to the left.
Right arrow	Moves the cursor one character to the right.
Ctrl+Left arrow	Moves the cursor one word to the left.
Ctrl+Right arrow	Moves the cursor one word to the right.
Home	Moves the cursor to the beginning of the line.
End	Moves the cursor to the end of the line.
Esc	Clears the command from the screen.
F1	Copies one character from the memory buffer to the command line.
F2	Searches forward though the memory buffer for the next key you type after F2.
F3	Copies the contents of the memory buffer to the command line.
F4	Deletes characters from the memory buffer, from the first character up to the character you type after F4.

F5	Copies the current command line into the memory buffer, clearing the command line in the process.
F6	Adds an end-of-file character (Ctrl+Z) to the end of the current command line.
F7	Displays all the commands stored in the memory buffer, along with their associated sequence numbers.
Alt+F7	Deletes all the commands stored in the memory buffer.
F8	Searches memory for a command. Type F8, then type the beginning of the command, then type F8 again.
F9	Asks for a sequence number and displays the command associated with that number.
Alt+F10	Deletes all the macro definitions.

When creating a macro, you can use the following commands:

$b	Sends macro output to a command. Equivalent to the pipe (|) redirection symbol. See the heading "Understanding Redirection" in this chapter for more information on this topic.
$g	Redirects output to a device rather than sending the output to the screen. Equivalent to the normal redirection symbol (>).
gg	Adds output at the end of a file rather than overwriting the file. Equivalent to the normal symbols for appending redirected output (>>).
$l	Redirects input. Equivalent to (<).
$t	Separates commands in a macro.

$$ Specifies the dollar sign (should you ever wish to use one in a macro).

$1 through $9

Placeholder symbols used to allow you to specify different information on the command line each time you run the macro. The $1 character in a DOSKEY macro is similar in function to the %1 character in a batch program.

$*

Holds all the command-line information you specify when you run your macro. Everything you type on the command line after the macro name is substituted for the $* in the macro.

None of these macro-creating commands are case sensitive; you can use $g or $G as you wish.

Switches

/REINSTALL

Installs a new copy of the DOSKEY program, even if a copy is currently installed, and empties the memory buffer.

/BUFSIZE=*nnn*

Specifies the size of the memory buffer. The default size of *nnn* is 512 bytes, the minimum size is 256 bytes.

/H

Displays a list of the commands stored in memory.

/M

Displays a list of all the DOSKEY macros.

/OVERSTRIKE

Specifies that any new text you type will replace existing text. /OVERSTRIKE is the default setting. Cannot be used with /INSERT.

| /INSERT | Specifies that any new text you type will be inserted into the existing text. Cannot be used with /OVERSTRIKE. |
| macroname=text | Creates a macro that processes one or more DOS commands. *macroname* specifies the name of the macro, while *text* represents the commands you want to use in the macro |

Examples   To load DOSKEY for the first time, type:

DOSKEY

You can now use any of the command-editing commands as described above; use the up arrow to recall the previous command, or page up to see the first command of this DOSKEY session.

If you want to create a macro called WP that will start your copy of WordPerfect from the /WP52 directory, type:

DOSKEY WP = CD\WP52$tWP.EXE

To run the WP macro, type **WP** and WordPerfect will start running.

N O T E

Because all DOSKEY macros are stored in memory rather than on disk, they are lost when you turn your computer off. Also, you cannot invoke a macro from inside a batch program.

The OS/2 equivalent to DOSKEY is the KEYS command, described later in this section.

EXIT

The EXIT command ends or closes the current command processor and returns to the previous command processor or to the desktop if no previous session exists.

Here's the syntax:

EXIT

Examples   If you want to leave the current OS/2 or DOS session, type:

EXIT

If you are running an application program, you must close the program before invoking EXIT.

KEYS

The KEYS command lets you retrieve and edit commands previously issued from the OS/2 command prompt.

Here's the syntax:

KEYS *switches*

Use the command with no parameters to see the current status of the KEYS command.

When KEYS is turned on you can use the following editing commands:

Esc	Clears the command line, and returns the cursor to the command prompt
Home	Moves the cursor to the beginning of the command line
End	Moves the cursor to the end of the command line
Ins	Toggles insert mode on and off
Del	Deletes characters
Left arrow	Moves the cursor one character to the left
Right arrow	Moves the cursor one character to the right
Up arrow	Displays the previous command
Down arrow	Displays the next command
Ctrl+Left arrow	Moves the cursor to the beginning of a word
Ctrl+Right arrow	Moves the cursor to the beginning of the next word

| Ctrl+End | Deletes from the cursor to the end of the line |
| Ctrl+Home | Deletes from the beginning of the line to the cursor |

There are several editing commands you can use only when KEYS is off. Function keys F1 through F5 work the same way that the same function keys work at the DOS command line.

Esc	Clears the command line and cancels the command
F1	Copies one character from the last command
F2	Displays all the characters in the last command up to the character you type
F3	Repeats the last command
F4	Deletes all the characters in the last command up to but not including the character you type
F5	Copies the current command into the buffer and clears the command line

The DOS equivalent of the KEYS command is the DOSKEY command, described earlier in this section.

Switches

ON	Turns command-line editing on
OFF	Turns command-line editing off
LIST	Displays a list of the commands entered during this session, up to a maximum of 64K characters.

Examples   To see the current status of KEYS, type:

KEYS

To tell OS/2 to store commands typed at the command prompt, use:

KEYS ON

If you want to list the contents of the KEYS memory area, use:

KEYS LIST

and finally, use:

KEYS OFF

to stop recording commands at the command line.

N O T E   If you enter KEYS ON, you disable ANSI extended keyboard support in OS/2 sessions.

Program-Management Commands

This section details all the commands used to control the operating environment. APPEND tells programs how to find data files not located in the current directory; DEBUG is an old MS-DOS utility used to troubleshoot or patch executable files; DETACH and START are two commands used when starting programs, and PMREXX brings special capabilities to the REXX programming language (described in detail in Chapter 16).

APPEND

APPEND tells DOS programs where to find data files that are not in the current directory. APPEND is similar to the PATH command, except that PATH refers only to executable files, and the APPEND command refers to all files.

Here's the syntax:

APPEND *dir 1; dlr2; /switches*

APPEND can be used from the command line or added to your AUTOEXEC.BAT file. The first time you use APPEND, it acts as an OS/2 external command, and you may have to specify drive and path information to locate the command. After APPEND is loaded, it becomes an internal command; the drive and path information are no longer needed. You can append as many directories as you can specify in 128 characters.

Switches

dir1; dir2	Specifies the drives and directories to be appended. You can specify more than one directory; separate them by a semicolon.
/PATH:ON	The default setting; allows APPEND to search for data files that include drive or path or both drive and path in their names.
/PATH:OFF	Prevents APPEND from searching for data files that include both drive and/or path in their names. If you use /PATH:OFF and then type a drive or a path, APPEND will not search for the file; if you type just the file name, APPEND will find the file.
/E	Stores the specified search path in the OS/2 environment space, so that the information can be accessed by other application programs. You can only use /E the first time you use APPEND in a DOS session.

If you use this command without a parameter, the current APPEND directory list is displayed on the screen, and if you type APPEND ; you cancel the current APPEND setting.

Examples   To tell all DOS programs to look for data files in the C:\FILES directory and the D:\DATA directory, type:

    APPEND C:\FILES;D:\DATA

DEBUG

The DEBUG command lets you display, test, and debug executable files from the DOS command line.

Here's the syntax:

DEBUG *drive: path filename*

Here, *drive: path filename* specifies the name of the executable file that you want to debug.

When you use the DEBUG command, you enter the DOS debug environment and the command prompt changes to a dash. Type a question mark to see a list of all the commands available in the debug environment, as follows:

?	Lists all the commands available in DEBUG
A	Assembles 8086/8087/8088 assembly-language mnemonics
C	Compares two areas of memory
D	Displays the contents of an area of memory as hexadecimal and ASCII values
E	Enters data into memory starting at a specific address
F	Fills an area of memory with a specific value
G	Runs the executable file that is in memory
H	Performs hexadecimal arithmetic on two numbers
I	Inputs and displays a one-byte value from a port at the specified address
L	Loads a program file or a specified number of disk sectors from a program file into memory
M	Moves the contents of an area of memory
N	Specifies a file for use with the L or W commands
O	Sends a one-byte value to the specified output port
P	Executes a program, subroutine, loop, or interrupt
Q	Quits DEBUG

R	Displays or changes the contents of registers
S	Searches an area of memory for a specific pattern of byte values
T	Enters trace mode and single-steps though a specified number of instructions one at a time, displaying the contents of all registers
U	Unassembles bytes and displays the appropriate source statements
W	Writes the current file or a specified number of disk sectors from memory to disk
XA	Allocates the specified number of 16K pages into expanded memory
XD	Deallocates expanded memory
XM	Maps expanded memory pages
XS	Displays the status of expanded memory

Examples To access DEBUG, type:

DEBUG

at the DOS command prompt.

NOTE   Debugging a program is not an everyday task for most users; it is a job best left to programmers. Also, most modern computer language compilers have much more capable and advanced debugging aids available to them than the DEBUG command.

DETACH

The DETACH command starts an OS/2 program and immediately detaches it from its command processor and runs the program in the background. The command processor continues to run in the foreground.

Here's the syntax:

DETACH *command*

The *command* parameter can be any OS/2 program or command that does not need input from the keyboard or mouse and does not output anything to the screen. Any program started with DETACH must be able to operate without the services of the command processor.

Examples To run a batch program called MYFILE.CMD in the background, while the OS/2 command processor continues to run in the foreground, type:

DETACH MYFILE.CMD

PMREXX

The PMREXX command provides a windowed environment used to display output from REXX procedures, and to accept input to them.

Here's the syntax:

PMREXX *path\filename arguments*

Where *path\filename* specifies the name of the .CMD file to be displayed, and *arguments* specifies the arguments used in the REXX program.

REXX is a complex programming language built into OS/2, and you can use REXX to create procedures you can use instead of batch programs. See chapter 16 for more on REXX.

When you start PMREXX you add several important features to REXX, including:

- a window to display the output from REXX procedures

- an input window for REXX procedures

- a browsing, scrolling, and clipboard capability for REXX

- a set of fonts for use in the output window

- a window used for testing REXX procedures with the REXXTRY.CMD program

Examples To display the current PATH statement in a CON-FIG.SYS file referenced by the REXX program MYPROG.CMD, type:

```
PMREXX MYPROG PATH
```

START

The START command starts an OS/2 program in another OS/2 session. Here's the syntax:

START *"program"* /switches **command** *command inputs*

Type this command with no switches to start a new OS/2 session. To load a program in a new OS/2 session, use START followed by a name enclosed in quotes (no longer than 60 characters), and the appropriate switches. This name will be displayed in the OS/2 window list and at the top of the program window. The *command* parameter can specify any OS/2 command, batch program, or application program, and *command inputs* represents any arguments needed for the *command*.

Switches

N O T E	Several of the START switches are mutually exclusive. Choose one switch from the group /K, /C, and /N, one from /F and /B, one from the group /FS, /WIN, /PM, /DOS, and one from /MAX and /MIN.

/K	Starts the program using CMD.EXE and keeps the session running when the program ends.
/C	Starts the program using CMD.EXE and closes the session when the program ends.

/N	Starts the program directly without invoking CMD.EXE. You cannot use this switch to start a batch file or an internal OS/2 command. Do not enclose the program title in quotation marks.
/F	Starts the program running in the foreground.
/B	Starts the program running in the background.
/PGM *"name"*	Interprets the *"name"* string as containing the name of the program.
/FS	Indicates that the application is a full screen DOS or OS/2 application that must run in a separate session.
/WIN	Indicates that the application is an OS/2 application that runs within an OS/2 or DOS window.
/PM	Indicates that the application is a Program Manager application.
/DOS	Starts the program as a DOS program.
/MAX	Asks that a windowed application start in a maximized window.
/MIN	Asks that a windowed application start as an icon in a minimized state.
/I	Forces the new session to inherit the environment variables established by SET commands in the CONFIG.SYS file, instead of the CMD.EXE environment variables of the current session.

Examples   To begin a new OS/2 session from the OS/2 command prompt, type:

    START

To begin a new DOS session from the DOS command prompt, use:

    START /DOS

Disk Management Commands

This section lists the disk management commands available in OS/2, including ASSIGN, used to redirect disk operations; CHKDSK, for looking at important disk information; EAUTIL, used to manage a file's extended attributes; FDISK and FDISKPM, for managing hard-disk partitions; FSACCESS, used to access the OS/2 file system from a DOS session; JOIN, which connects a drive to a directory on another drive; LABEL, used to look at or change a disk's volume label; MEM, which details memory usage; SUBST, used to access a drive and path using only a drive letter; UNPACK, which expands packed files; VERIFY, used to set data verification; VMDISK, which creates an image file of a DOS boot disk, and VOL, used to display the disk volume label.

ASSIGN

ASSIGN redirects disk operations to a drive other than the specified drive. This command is most often used with older application programs that only use drives A and B; ASSIGN does not work on a hard disk.

Here's the syntax:

    ASSIGN drive1 = drive2 /switches

With the ASSIGN command, *drive1* specifies the drive that will not be used when ASSIGN is in effect; all references to this drive are redirected to *drive2*. *drive2* specifies the drive that will be used when ASSIGN is in effect; all references to *drive1* are sent to this drive. Do not include a colon with either drive letter.

Switches

/S   Displays the current drive reassignments.

Examples   To assign all requests for drive B to drive C, type:

ASSIGN B=C

or

ASSIGN B C

The equal sign may be replaced by a space.

If you want to see if drive assignments are active, type:

ASSIGN /S

To reset all drives back to their original assignments, use ASSIGN with no switches.

N O T E   The following commands do not work on ASSIGNed drives: CHKDSK, DISKCOMP, DISKCOPY, FORMAT, JOIN, LABEL, PRINT, RECOVER, RESTORE, SUBST.

The /S switch lists the same drive reassignment information that the MS-DOS /STATUS switch provides.

CHKDSK

The CHKDSK command produces a status report on your files and directories, and is available from both the OS/2 and the DOS-session command lines. When used with the appropriate switch, CHKDSK can fix certain file-related problems. CHKDSK also displays the disk volume label and volume serial number.

Here's the syntax:

CHKDSK *drive: path filename /switches*

If you use CHKDSK without parameters, you will analyze your current drive; specify a drive letter if you want to analyze a different drive. CHKDSK reports the following:

- the type of file system in use, FAT or HPFS
- the disk volume label
- the disk volume serial number
- the total formatted disk space, in bytes
- the amount of space occupied by hidden files, in bytes
- the number of hidden files
- the amount of space occupied by directories, in bytes
- the number of directories
- the amount of space occupied by user files, in bytes
- the number of user files
- the amount of space occupied by extended attributes, in bytes
- the remaining available disk space, in bytes
- the size of the disk allocation unit, in bytes
- the total number of disk allocation units on the disk
- the number of available disk allocation units

If you run CHKDSK in a DOS session, you will also see:

- the total amount of conventional memory available to the DOS session, in bytes
- the conventional memory available for application programs, in bytes

CHKDSK can also fix certain disk errors known as lost clusters; see Chapter 14 for more on this.

Switches   The following switches are available for use on both FAT and HPFS disks.

/F   Tells CHKDSK to fix any errors found. This switch cannot be used when analyzing the hard disk that you use to start OS/2, nor can it be used onthe disk that contains the CHKDSK program. If you have to run CHKDSK on your boot disk, you must first reboot your system using your original OS/2 Installation disk. When the logo panel appears, replace the Installation disk with disk 1, and press Enter to continue. When the *Welcome to OS/2* screen appears, press the Escape key, and insert the floppy disk that contains CHKDSK. Now run CHKDSK and specify drive C as the drive for analysis. You can also create an OS/2 boot disk for this purpose rather than use your original distribution disks; See Chapter 14 for details.

/V   Displays all files along with appropriate path information for the specified drive. This switch creates a very long file listing, usually only of interest to system managers or to people concerned with software inventories.

The following switches are available only when using the HPFS.

/C   Recovers files only if the file system was in an inconsistent state when the computer was first started, and files remain open. This might happen if the power failed during a disk operation before all the files could be closed.

/F   Specifies that one of four recovery levels be used
          (if no recovery number is specified, F:2 is used as
          the default) :

    /F:0   Tells CHKDSK to analyze the file system,
            and display the results, but not make any
            repairs.

    /F:1   Tells CHKDSK to resolve any inconsistent
            file-system structures.

    /F:2   Tells CHKDSK to resolve any inconsistent
            file-system structures, and to scan the rest of
            the disk space in use to recover any
            recognizable directory or file elements not
            referenced by the file system.

    /F:3   Includes the /F:2 level recovery options, and
            also tells CHKDSK to scan the whole disk
            partition, looking for recognizable file system
            elements.

Examples   To make a listing of all the files on a disk, including appropriate path information, type:

    CHKDSK /V

Type the following to see a status report on drive C and fix any errors encountered:

    CHKDSK C: /F

With the HPFS, CHKDSK defaults to the /F level of repair. If you want to use the /F:3 level, type:

    CHKDSK /F:3

N O T E

Remember that CHKDSK can only give accurate results when the disk being analyzed is not being used or actively written to by another session or application program. In a DOS session, you cannot use CHKDSK on drives that have an ASSIGN, APPEND, JOIN, or SUBST command still in effect. Also, CHKDSK cannot be used on network drives; if you are using a Novell network, use the Novell CHKVOL command.

There are also two limitations when using CHKDSK with the HPFS: (1) you cannot use a filename with CHKDSK when using the HPFS; and (2) if CHKDSK finds lost clusters under the HPFS, they are treated differently. When lost clusters are found and the /F switch was specified, CHKDSK creates a new directory called \FOUND.nnn below the root directory, and places all directories, files, and extended attributes in this directory. The *nnn* directory extension represents a unique three-digit number so that each \FOUND directory name is unique. CHKDSK uses the FILEnnnn.CHK format for recoved files and the DIRnnnn.CHK format for recovered directories.

EAUTIL

The EAUTIL command lets you detach and save extended attributes from a file so that the file can be used by an application that does not recognize these attributes. When the application is finished, you can use EAUTIL to reattach the extended attributes. EAUTIL is available from both OS/2 and DOS-session command prompts.

Here's the syntax:

EAUTIL ***datafile*** *holdfile* /*switches*

Not all application programs running under OS/2 understand how to use a file's extended attributes, so EAUTIL offers a method of splitting these attributes off from the file and saving them in a safe place. You can then use EAUTIL to rejoin them to the original file when the application program is finished. This prevents the extended attributes from being erased or lost by accident. You can use the DIR command with the /R switch to see if your files include extended attributes.

The *datafile* parameter specifies the file whose extended attributes will be split off and stored in the file specified by the *holdfile* parameter. If no *holdfile* is specified, EAUTIL creates a hold file with the same name as the data file and places it in a new subdirectory of the current directory called /EAS.

Switches

/S — Separates extended attributes from a file and stores them in a hold file

/R — Replaces the extended attributes in the hold file with those from the data file

/J — Reconnects the extended attributes in the hold file to the data file

/O — Overwrites or deletes the extended attributes in the data file with the extended attributes from the hold file

/M — Merges the extended attributes from the hold file with those in the data file

/P — Copies extended attributes to or from a data file or a hold file without deleting the original copy of the extended attributes

Examples   If you want to split the extended attributes from MY-FILE.TXT and save them in the default hold file called MYFILE.TXT in the new subdirectory created by EAUTIL called /EAS, type:

EAUTIL MYFILE.TXT /S

To reattach the extended attributes to MYFILE.TXT, type

EAUTIL MYFILE.TXT EAS\MYFILE.TXT /J

FDISK

The FDISK command lets you create or delete a primary hard disk partition, or a logical drive in an extended hard disk partition. This is a potentially dangerous command and must be used with care; FDISK is only available from the OS/2 command prompt.

Here's the syntax:

FDISK */switches /options*

If you type FDISK with no switches, the menu-driven portion of the program opens to guide you through hard disk partition configuration. This mode of operation is much easier to use if you are unfamiliar with FDISK, but you can also work with FDISK directly from the command line, specifying switches and switch options as needed.

Remember that the switch must appear in the command line before the appropriate limiting option.

All hard disks are divided up into partitions. A partition can be defined as that part of a disk that belongs to a particular operating system, and it may, in fact occupy the whole disk. Although a hard disk can be divided into several primary partitions and/or one extended partition, the first hard disk on a system must have a primary partition. An extended partition can be further subdivided into smaller logical drives for convenience.

Switches

/QUERY	Displays a list of all the partitions on the hard disk, as well as the unpartitioned free space.
/CREATE: *name*	Creates a primary partition or logical drive in an extended partition with the optional *name*. Specify the type of partition to create using the /VTYPE:*n* option described below.
/DELETE	Deletes a logical drive or partition.

/SETNAME:*name*	Establishes a *name* for primary partitions or logical drives, and makes them bootable from the Boot Manager; if *name* is not specified, then the partition will not be bootable.
/SETACCESS	Makes a primary DOS partition accessible. Once this is done, all other primary DOS partitions on the same drive become inaccessible.
/STARTABLE	Specifies a partition as startable.
/FILE:*filename*	Processes FDISK commands contained in the batch file called *filename*.

The following options are used to limit the scope of the switches described above:

/switch/NAME:*name*	Specifies the name of a partition. This option can be used with all FDISK switches except /FILE and /SETACCESS.
/switch/DISK:*n*	Specifies the number of the hard disk. This option can be used with all FDISK switches except /FILE.
/switch/FSTYPE:*x*	Specifies the file system type of the partition. Type *x* can represent DOS, FAT, IFS, FREE, or other. This option cannot be used with the /FILE or /SETACCESS switches.

/switch/START:*m*	Specifies the partition starting location, where *m* can be *t* for the top of the partition, or *b* for the bottom. /START cannot be used with /FILE.
/switch/SIZE:*m*	Specifies the size of the partition in MB. This option cannot be used with the /FILE switch.
/switch/VTYPE:*n*	Specifies the type of the partition, where *n* can be:

0	unusable space
1	primary partition
2	logical drive
3	display free space

/VTYPE can be used with all FDISK switches except /FILE, /SETACCESS, or /STARTABLE.

/switch/BOOTABLE:*s*	Indicates the bootable status of the partition; *s* is 0 for a non-bootable partition, or 1 for a bootable partition. The /BOOTABLE option can be used with all FDISK switches except /FILE.
/BOOTMGR	Indicates that the switch is intended for the Boot Manager partition

Examples To see a display of the partitions on your system, type:

FDISK /QUERY

To create a new logical drive in an extended partition on drive 1 with the name MYDRIVE, type:

    FDISK /CREATE:MYDRIVE /VTYPE:2 /DISK:1

and to delete the logical drive called MYDRIVE, use the following:

    FDISK /DELETE /NAME:MYDRIVE

NOTE FDISK cannot be run in an OS/2 DOS session, and cannot work with drives with current ASSIGN, JOIN, or SUBST commands.

FDISKPM

The FDISKPM command is the graphical equivalent of the FDISK command; it lets you create or delete a primary hard disk partition, or a logical drive in an extended hard disk partition.

Here's the syntax:

    FDISKPM

The FDISKPM command opens an OS/2 mouse- and window-based program that helps you manage the hard disk partitioning process using selections from the Options menu. You can use selections from this menu to:

- install the Boot Manager partition
- create or delete a primary partition or a logical drive
- add or change a partition name
- set startup values such as the default partition
- remove a partition from the Boot Manager menu
- set a primary partition as installable
- specify a primary partition to be a startable partition

FSACCESS

The FSACCESS command accesses a drive using the OS/2 file system during a specific DOS session. For FSACCESS to work, the device driver FSFILTER must be installed as the first DEVICE = statement in your CONFIG.SYS file, and you can't remap the current drive. See Chapter 13 for more information on FSACCESS and CONFIG.SYS.

Once FSFILTER is installed, there are three main ways you can use FSACCESS, as follows:

FSACCESS *DOSdriveletter*

where *DOSdriveletter* specifies a particular local drive letter. The following colon is optional.

FSACCESS *DOSdriveletter – DOSdriveletter*

The minus sign and second drive letter indicates an inclusive range of drive letters.

FSACCESS *DOSdriveletter = OS/2driveletter*

In this case the equal sign maps a local DOS drive letter to an OS/2 drive letter. Again the following colon is optional.

In most circumstances, your DOS drive letters are assigned the same drive letters for OS/2 drives. To check the current mappings, use the FSACCESS command with no parameters. To change the mapping, use the FSACCESS command and the appropriate drive letter. To indicate that a drive should not be mapped, use an exclamation point before the drive letter.

Examples   To give a DOS drive access to the OS/2 file system, type:

FSACCESS J:

All references to drive J will now be sent to the OS/2 file system. Use the minus sign to include a range of drives:

FSACCESS J: – M:

You can use an equal sign to map a DOS drive to a different OS/2 drive, if you type:

FSACCESS C: = E:

Use an exclamation point to tell OS/2 not to allow a drive access to the OS/2 file system, as follows:

FSACCESS !J:

To remove a mapping, use:

FSACCESS "J:

JOIN

The JOIN command connects the directory structure on a disk drive to a specific directory on a different drive. You can only JOIN a drive at the root directory, and in a DOS session.

Here's the syntax:

JOIN *drive1: drive2:\path* */switches*

The JOIN command allows programs that were written to access a particular drive to access a directory instead.

drive1 represents the drive that you want to connect to a directory on a different drive, while *drive2:\path* represents an empty directory in the root of the second drive; if this directory does not exist, OS/2 creates it for you.

While a drive is joined, it is no longer recognized by the operating system, and cannot be accessed directly; if you try, you will see an error message.

To see a list of the currently joined drives on your system, use JOIN with no parameters.

Switches

/D   Cancels a JOIN

Examples   To join drive B to the path C:\DRIVEB, and access drive B using the \DRIVEB subdirectory, type:

JOIN B: C:\DRIVEB

and to cancel the join, use:

JOIN B: /D

NOTE You cannot JOIN the current drive, and you cannot use the following commands on joined drives: ASSIGN, BACKUP, CHKDSK, DISKCOMP, DISKCOPY, FORMAT, LABEL, RECOVER, RESTORE.

LABEL

The LABEL command lets you attach or change the short text description of a disk known as the volume label. LABEL is available from both OS/2 and DOS-session command prompts.

Here's the syntax:

LABEL *drive: text*

The *drive* parameter specifies the drive letter that contains the disk you want to label; if you don't specify a drive letter, the LABEL command defaults to the current drive.

The *text* specifies the text label you want to attach to this disk, up to 11 characters. You can use spaces between words in the label text, but leading spaces will be ignored. You cannot use punctuation characters in a volume label.

Use the LABEL command with no parameters to display the current volume label.

Examples   To look at the volume label on drive C, type:

LABEL C:

The operating system will then prompt you to enter a new volume label, or to press ↵ to leave the volume label unchanged.

To change the volume label on drive C to the text BIG_DISK, type:

LABEL C: BIG_DISK

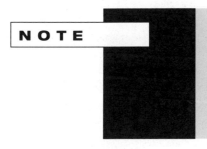

NOTE

You can also add a volume label to a disk if you format the disk using the FORMAT command /V switch.

The LABEL command does not work on drives that have an ASSIGN, JOIN, or SUBST command in effect, and LABEL does not work on network drives.

MEM

The MEM command lists the amount of free and used memory in the current DOS session.

Here's the syntax:

MEM */switches*

The MEM command lists all the memory available to the current DOS session, including high, expanded, and extended memory (unlike the CHKDSK command, which only lists information on conventional memory). MEM is also faster than CHKDSK because it only reports on memory and does not have to check disk information.

Use MEM with no switches to see a short summary display of memory availability, as Figure 12.1 shows.

Switches　You can only use one MEM switch at a time; you cannot combine switches.

/PROGRAM	Displays the programs loaded into memory. This switch can be abbreviated to /P.
/DEBUG	Displays the memory and status of programs and device drivers. This switch can be abbreviated to /D.
/CLASSIFY	Displays the status of programs loaded into conventional and upper memory. This switch can be abbreviated to /C.

FIGURE 12.1

MEM display
contained in a DOS
session window

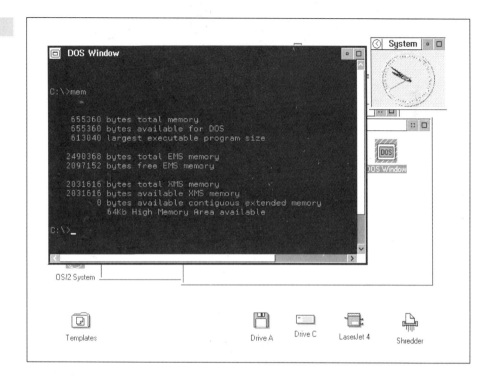

Examples To see a display of the programs loaded into memory and the status of conventional, expanded, and extended memory, use:

MEM /P

SUBST

The SUBST command substitutes a drive letter for a complete drive and path name in a DOS session to simplify access to long and complex paths. Here's the syntax:

SUBST *newdrive: existing drive:\path /switches*

Drive and path combinations can often get very long and complex. SUBST offers a way around this problem by using a drive letter instead of a long complex path. In the SUBST command, *newdrive:* specifies the drive letter you want to use instead of the *existing drive:\path* path. The *newdrive:* must be an unused drive letter; you cannot use a drive letter that already exists on your system.

Type SUBST with no parameters to see a list of the currently substituted drives.

Switches

/D   Removes a drive and path substitution

Examples   To substitute the drive letter H in a DOS session for the path C:\OS2\PROGS\MYPROGS, type:

    SUBST H: C:\OS2\PROGS\MYPROGS

Now you can type:

    DIR H:

instead of the cumbersome:

    DIR C:\OS2\PROGS\MYPROGS

N O T E   The following commands do not work in DOS sessions on drives that have a SUBST command in effect: BACKUP, CHKDSK, DISKCOMP, DISKCOPY, FORMAT, LABEL, RECOVER, RESTORE.

UNPACK

The UNPACK command decompresses compressed files, and copies files from the OS/2 Installation disks. Compressed files have an @ character as the last character of their file-name extension. UNPACK is available from both OS/2 and DOS-session command prompts.

The UNPACK command uses two different syntaxes:

    UNPACK *sourcedrive:\path***filename** *targetdrive:\path /switches* or

> UNPACK *sourcedrive:\path**filename** /SHOW*

To copy a compressed file, specify its drive, path, and filename, then specify the drive and path where you want to copy the file, adding switches as needed.

Alternatively, because a packed file can actually contain several other files, you can use the /SHOW option to list all the files contained inside a packed file.

Switches

/V	Verifies that the unpacked files were written to disk correctly. This option will make UNPACK run slightly slower as the check is performed for each file.
/F	Tells UNPACK not to unpack files with HPFS extended attributes if the target file system cannot support extended attributes.
/N:*filename*	Specifies that one particular file be unpacked from a packed file containing multiple compressed files.
/SHOW	Lists the target path and file name information for all the compressed files contained inside a packed file.

Examples   To unpack all the files contained inside the file called BIGFILE.CO@ in drive A into the OS2 directory on drive C, type

> UNPACK A:BIGFILE.CO@ C:\OS2

To display the path and filename information for all the compressed files contained inside BIGFILE.CO@, type:

> UNPACK A:BIGFILE.CO@ /SHOW

N O T E

It is not necessary to supply an output filename when using UNPACK. UNPACK uses the names, dates, times, and attributes of the original uncompressed files. UNPACK can also copy regular (non-compressed) files in addition to packed files, and so can be used to process a disk containing a combination of packed and unpacked files.

VERIFY

The VERIFY command confirms that files written to a disk have been written correctly, and is available from both OS/2 and DOS-session command prompts.

Here's the syntax:

VERIFY ON

Turns verification on, and:

VERIFY OFF

turns it off again. This is the default setting.

Examples   To turn on disk-write verification, type:

VERIFY ON

When VERIFY is turned on, you will receive an error message if a write error is detected. To suspend disk-write verification, type:

VERIFY OFF

Type the command with no parameters to check the current status.

VMDISK

The VMDISK command creates a file that contains the image of a DOS boot disk. You can then use this file to create a DOS session.

Here's the syntax:

VMDISK *sourcedrive:* targetdrive:\path*filename*

In the VMDISK command, *sourcedrive:* specifies the floppy disk drive where the DOS startup disk is located, and *targetdrive:\path\filename* represents the image file. You must specify a file name for the image file. Also, the target drive must have more available space than the source drive.

Examples To create an image file of an MS-DOS startup disk in the root directory of drive C, place the startup disk in drive B, and type:

    VMDISK B: C:\MSDOS.IMG

See Chapter 6 for more information on running specific versions of MS-DOS on your system.

VOL

The VOL command displays the disk volume label and volume serial number if they exist, and is available from both OS/2 and DOS-session command prompts.

Here's the syntax:

    VOL *drive: driven:*

Type this command with no parameters to see information for the current drive.

In a DOS session, you can only see information for one drive at a time. Under OS/2, you can see information on multiple drives.

Examples To display volume label and volume serial number information for the current drive, type:

    VOL

In an OS/2 session, you can use several drive designations with one VOL command, as follows:

    VOL A: B: C:

and see information on all three drives.

Commands for System Customization and Control

This section covers commands available from the OS/2 command line for customizing elements of your computer and operating system. ANSI is used to allow extended display and keyboard support; CLS clears the screen; DATE is used to set the system date; and DDINSTAL helps to install device drivers. HELP provides help information. MODE is a complex command used to control how various hardware devices work. PROMPT allows you to customize the system prompt. PSTAT provides detailed system information. SPOOL is used to control printing; TIME sets the system time; and VER displays the version level of the operating system.

ANSI

ANSI enables or disables extended display and keyboard support for OS/2 programs; most OS/2 programs do not need this special support.

Here's the syntax:

```
ANSI ON
ANSI OFF
```

ANSI enables or disables the processing of ANSI control sequences in an OS/2 session. ANSI control sequences usually begin with an escape character, and they are used to redefine keys on the keyboard, control the cursor, or change the display color attributes.

If you use this command without a parameter, the current ANSI status is displayed. Specify ANSI ON to enable extended display and keyboard support. This is also the default setting. Specify ANSI OFF to disable this support.

The KEYS ON command, used to control and edit the command line, always disables ANSI extended keyboard support.

CLS

The CLS command clears the command interpreter screen or window except for the system prompt and the cursor. They are rewritten on the first line of the screen or window. CLS is available from both OS/2 and DOS-session command prompts.

The CLS command is simplicity itself to use; just type:

CLS

at the command prompt.

DATE

The DATE command displays or resets the system clock. Special circuitry inside your computer automatically keeps track of the date, even when the computer is turned off, so it is not usually necessary to reset the date, even at the end of the month or the end of the year. DATE is available from both OS/2 and DOS-session command prompts.

Here's the syntax:

DATE *mm-dd-yy*

The month is specified by *mm*, and must be a number between 1 and 12. The day is specified by *dd*, and must be between 1 and 31. Years, *yy*, are entered using the numbers from 00 to 99, where 00 to 79 represent the years from 2000 to 2079.

You can use a slash (/), a period (.), or a dash (-) as the separating character between entries.

Examples To set the system clock to August 1, 1993, type:

DATE 08-01-93

If you want to see the current system date, type:

DATE

You can then either type in a new date or press ↵ to return to the operating system without changing the date.

DDINSTAL

The DDINSTAL command lets you install new device drivers after the operating system has been installed. DDINSTAL is available from the OS/2 command prompt only.

Here's the syntax:

DDINSTAL *drive:\ path*

Enter this command without parameters to open the Device Driver Install program on the desktop. This program, described in Chapter 2, guides you through a step-by-step procedure for installing new device drivers that come with a Device Support Disk. Such disks contain a Device Driver Profile (DDP) file that controls the driver installation process; DDINSTAL uses information found in this file to copy the correct statements into your CONFIG.SYS file, and to copy all of the support files into the right directories on your hard disk. After DDINSTAL has loaded the device drivers, press Ctrl+Alt+Delete to restart your system.

HELP

The HELP command provides several ways to get help information when you are at the DOS or OS/2 command prompts.

Here's the syntax:

HELP *switches*

Some DOS commands display a short help screen if you add the /? switch after the command at the DOS prompt. For example, to see a help screen on the switches available with the DIR command, type:

DIR /?

If you type HELP without switches at the OS/2 or DOS prompts, you will see a list of commands you can use to switch between sessions and get help on different topics.

Switches

ON	Turns on the help line at the top of the screen.
OFF	Turns off the help line at the top of the screen.

message number	Requests help on a specific system error number. You do not have to type the message prefix or the leading zeros.
book	Identifies the book or .INF file you want to search for information. If you do not specify a name, HELP searches the *OS/2 Command Reference* by default.
topic	Identifies the topic you want information on.

Examples   To turn the help line on, type:

HELP ON

and to turn it off again, type:

HELP OFF

This command only refers to the help line; all other help features will continue to work normally.

A very common error in OS/2 is *SYS0002: The system cannot find the file specified*. To see a longer explanation of what this message means, type:

HELP 2

You do not have to type all the characters that precede the actual message number. For information on common OS/2 errors, see Chapter 14.

MODE

The MODE command lets you configure peripherals attached to your computer system. The command can be used with different types of peripheral device, and takes different switches depending on the circumstances. MODE is available from both OS/2 and DOS-session command prompts.

For the sake of clarity, this entry presents the MODE command's functions in separate subentries.

N O T E

As impressive as these MODE commands look, you probably won't need to use many of them for two reasons: (1) Modern software takes care of many of these settings for you from inside the application. Communications programs set up the serial ports for your modem, and the OS/2 printer driver settings prepare your printer for use by your word processor. (2) Some of the functions, for example, the display mode settings, are much better handled from the desktop with either System Setup or Color Palette.

MODE (Communications)

This form of the MODE command sets asynchronous communications parameters used with modems or serial printers for DOS and OS/2 sessions.

Here's the syntax:

MODE ***COMn baud***, *parity, databits, stopbits, P, handshake*

Before using the MODE command to establish communication port settings, make sure that the appropriate device driver is loaded in CONFIG.SYS.

COMn   Specifies the number of the serial port from COM1: through COM8:.

baud   Sets the baud rate. If the port does not support direct memory access (DMA), choose from 110, 150, 300, 600, 1200, 1800, 2400, 3600, 4800, 7200, 9600, 19200, 38400, and 57600. For ports that do support DMA, choose from 300, 600, 1200, 2400, 4800, 9600, 19200, 38400, 57600, 76800, 115200, 138240, 172800, 230400, or 345600. If you do not specify a rate, the default of 1200 will be used. You do not have to type all of the trailing zeros for the high baud rates; 96 and 9600 are both interpreted as 9600 by the MODE command.

parity	Specifies the parity. Select N (none), O (odd), E (even), M (mark), or S (space). The default is E.
databits	Specifies the number of data bits in each word. Choose from 5, 6, 7, or 8. The default is 7.
stopbits	Specifies the number of stop bits. Choose from 1, 1.5, or 2. The default is 2 when the baud rate is 110, otherwise the default is 1. When *stopbits* is set to 1.5, the only valid entry for *databits* is 5.
P	Specifies a 30-second timeout for DOS programs that write directly to the hardware. This parameter is only available in DOS sessions.

In an OS/2 session, the MODE command can also set several additional parameters designated by the *handshake* option in the syntax line shown above. Many of these parameters allow you to control low-level communications hardware functions, as follows:

TO	Specifies the type of timeout. TO=ON allows for an infinite timeout; TO=OFF, the default, allows for a 60-second timeout.
XON	XON=ON sets automatic transmit flow control; the default is XON=OFF.
IDSR	IDSR=ON sets input handshaking using data set ready (DSR), the default. IDSR=OFF turns off data set ready handshaking.
ODSR	ODSR=ON sets output handshaking using data set ready (DSR), the default. ODSR=OFF turns off data set ready handshaking.

OCTS	OCTS=ON sets output handshaking using clear to send (CTS), the default. OCTS=OFF turns off clear to send handshaking.
DTR	DTR=ON sets data terminal ready (DTR), the default. DTR=OFF prevents DTR, and DTR=HS allows input handshaking using DTR.
RTS	RTS=ON sets request to send (RTS), the default. RTS=OFF prevents RTS, RTS=HS allows input handshaking using RTS, and RTS=TOG allows RTS toggling in transmit mode.
BUFFER	Sets extended hardware buffering. Choose from ON, OFF, and AUTO.
ENHANCED	Enables or disables enhanced mode support provided by the hardware on the communications port. In enhanced mode, processing is performed in either first-in, first-out (FIFO) mode, or direct memory access (DMA) mode.
RXDMA	Controls the DMA receive operations and can be set to AUTO, OFF, or ON.
TXDMA	Controls the DMA transmit operations and can be set to AUTO, ON, or OFF.

Examples   To see the status of the asynchronous COM 1 port, type:

MODE COM1:

To set COM1: baud rate, parity, data bits and stop bits, use:

MODE COM1: 9600, N, 8, 1

separating each parameter by a comma.

If you don't want to reset all the parameters, use a comma in place of the default you want to keep:

MODE COM1:9600,,,,,

MODE (Video)

The MODE command can also control the video output to one or more monitors.

Here's the syntax:

MODE *CON# display, rows*

CON#	Specifies the display number, either CON1 or CON2. This parameter is required if more than one display monitor is installed.
display	Sets the display mode: 40, 80, or 132 columns; BW40, BW80, BW132 for black & white monitors; CO40, CO80, or CO132 for color monitors; and MONO for monochrome monitors. The 132-character width is only supported by the XGA video adapter.
rows	Sets the number of rows, either 25, 43 or 50 depending on the video adapter installed in your computer.

Examples   To set a color 80 column by 43 row display on display number 1:

MODE CON1 CO80, 43

Always separate the *display* parameter from the *rows* parameter by a comma.

MODE (Printer)

The MODE command can set parallel printer parameters.

Here's the syntax:

MODE **number** *characters, lines, P*

number	Specifies the printer number, LPT1, LPT2, or LPT3. PRN is also an acceptable entry for this parameter. MODE also supports LPT4 through LPT9 for network printers.

characters	Sets the number of characters per line, either 80 (the default) or 132.
lines	Sets the number of lines per vertical inch, either 6 (the default), or 8.
P	Tells the MODE command to continue sending output to the printer even if a timeout occurs.

Examples   To set up your printer as LPT1 with 132 characters across the page, and 6 lines per inch, type:

    MODE LPT1 132,6

Always separate the *characters* parameter from the *lines* parameter by a comma.

MODE (Disk Write Verification)

The MODE command also turns on or off disk write verification. Here's the syntax:

    MODE **DSKT** VER=state

Where *state* is either ON or OFF.

Examples   To turn disk write verification on, type:

    MODE DSKT VER=ON

> ## S E C R E T
>
> This function of the MODE command is different from the VERIFY command in that MODE DSKT checks write operations only to floppy disks, while VERIFY checks write operations to both hard and floppy disks on a per-session basis.

PROMPT

The PROMPT command changes the system command prompt, and is available from both OS/2 and DOS-session command prompts.

Here's the syntax:

PROMPT *text*

Typing PROMPT without a parameter resets the prompt to the appropriate default. OS/2 and DOS system prompts are independent; changing one does not change the other.

The default OS/2 command prompt is the name of the current directory contained in square brackets. For example, if the OS2 directory on drive C is your current directory, your prompt will look like this:

[C:\OS2]

The default DOS system prompt is the current drive letter and directory, followed by the > symbol. If you are in the OS2 directory on drive C, your command prompt will look like this:

C:\OS2>

You can specify a custom system prompt, consisting of any text you want, and the operating system will display it as the system prompt. You can create a prompt by typing:

SET PROMPT = *your prompt*

at the command prompt, or, if you always use the same system prompt, you can establish it using CONFIG.SYS.

The PROMPT command can contain any of the following special characters when preceded by a $ sign:

COMMAND	SPECIAL CHARACTER
A	& symbol
B	| symbol
C	(symbol
D	Current date
E	An escape character (ASCII 27)
F	) symbol

COMMAND	SPECIAL CHARACTER
G	> symbol
H	Backspace
I	The help line
L	< symbol
N	Current drive letter
P	Current directory of the default drive
Q	= symbol
R	Return code or error level
S	Space
T	Current system time
V	The operating system version number
_ (Underscore)	Adds carriage-return and line-feed characters for a multiple-line prompt
$	$ symbol

Examples To set the system prompt to display *Good Morning* followed by the name of the current directory, type:

PROMPT Good Morning $P

A common DOS prompt includes the name of the current directory, followed by the > symbol. To set this prompt, type:

PROMPT PG

N O T E

If you use PROMPT $V in a DOS session to display the operating system version number, the OS/2 version number is displayed; the DOS version number is never displayed.

PSTAT

The PSTAT command gives you information on OS/2 processes, threads, priority levels, system semaphores, shared memory, and dynamic library links.

Here's the syntax:

PSTAT */switches*

Use the PSTAT command with no switches to see information about current processes and threads, system semaphores, shared memory, and dynamic link libraries.

Switches

/C   Displays current process and thread information, including, for each process, the process ID number, parent process ID number, session ID number, and process name. For each thread, the following is displayed: thread ID number, state, priority, and block ID number.

/S   Displays semaphore information for each thread, including process module name and ID number, session ID number, index number, number of references, number of requests, flag number, and semaphore name.

/L   Displays a list of the dynamic link libraries for each process, including process module name and ID number, session ID number, and library list.

/M   Displays shared memory information for each process, including handle number, selector number, number of references, and shared memory name.

/P:*id*   Displays information about the specified process, including process ID number, parent process ID number, session ID number, process module name, a list of dynamic link libraries, and shared memory name. It also shows the following information for each thread: thread ID number, priority number, and status, block ID, and owned semaphore information.

Examples   To display information on the current processes and threads in your system, type

    PSTAT /C

If you want to look at semaphore information for each thread, type:

    PSTAT /S

To see information about a particular process, determine the process ID number using:

    PSTAT /C

For example, if the ID number is 0002, use this number as follows:

    PSTAT /P:0002

> ### ▶ S O L U T I O N

Depending on the current state of your system, the PSTAT command can generate several screens full of information, so it is a good idea to make PSTAT display the information one screen at a time by adding a pipe to the MORE command, as follows:

    PSTAT /*switches* | MORE

This displays the PSTAT information one screen at a time, so that you can actually read the information.

Alternatively, you can redirect the output from the PSTAT command to a file so that you can read or process the information at a later time. See the heading "Understanding Redirection" in this chapter to learn how to do this.

SPOOL

The SPOOL command redirects printer output from one device to another, and can only be used from the OS/2 command prompt.

Here's the syntax:

SPOOL */switches*

The SPOOL command can redirect printer output from one parallel printer to another, or from a parallel printer to a serial printer. Use the command with no switches to start SPOOL running or to see the current status of SPOOL, and information on current printer assignments.

Switches

/D:*device*   Specifies the input device used by application programs for printing. Valid *device* names are LPT1 (the default name), LPT2, LPT3, and PRN. Serial COM# devices cannot be specified as input devices.

/O:*device*   Specifies the output print device. Valid *device* names are LPT1, LPT2, LPT3, and PRN, or COM1 through COM4. The default is the same as your choice for /D:*device*.

/Q   Displays current device redirections. The default setup has each input device assigned to the corresponding output device; LPT1 is directed to LPT1, LPT2 to LPT2, and so on.

Examples
To start the spooler, type:

SPOOL

If you want to redirect output from LPT1 to LPT3, use the following:

SPOOL /D:LPT1 /O:LPT3

NOTE

If you want to spool to a serial printer, you must add a DEVICE statement in your CONFIG.SYS file for the COM.SYS device driver. Use the MODE command to make sure the serial port is configured correctly for your serial printer.

Some DOS programs do not contain the appropriate instructions to work correctly with the spooler, and you may find that a print file will not be printed until you close the application program. To fix this problem and force printer output, press the Ctrl, Alt, and PrtScrn keys together. This causes the temporary spool file to close and print.

TIME

The TIME command displays or resets the system time. Special circuitry inside your computer automatically keeps track of the time, even when the computer is turned off, so it is not usually necessary to reset the time. The TIME command is available from both OS/2 and DOS-session command prompts.

Here's the syntax:

TIME *hh:mm:ss:cc*

In the TIME command *hh* specifies the hours, from 0 to 23; *mm* specifies the minutes, from 0 to 59; *ss* specifies the seconds, from 0 to 59; *cc* specifies the hundredths of seconds, from 0 to 99. Hours, minutes, seconds and hundredths are usually separated by periods or colons. You can use the COUNTRY command in your CONFIG.SYS file to change to different separator characters.

Use the TIME command with no parameters to see a display of the current system time on your computer.

Examples   To see the current system time on your computer, type:

TIME

Type the following to reset the time to 6 P.M.:

    TIME 18:00

VER

The VER command displays the OS/2 operating system version number from either the OS/2 or the DOS-session command prompt.

Here's the syntax:

    VER

Although this command is available at both the OS/2 and DOS command prompts, it always displays the OS/2 version number; the DOS version number is never displayed.

Batch File Commands

This section describes all the commands you can use in your batch files. A batch file is just an ASCII text file containing a list of commands. Each line in the batch file contains one command along with any switches that might be required, in just the same form that you would use at the command line. Batch files can automate complex or little-used commands, and can make life much easier.

Use the Enhanced Editor to create your batch file in an OS/2 session or use the EDIT program in a DOS session. You can use any name you like for your batch file, but the file name extension for an OS/2 session batch file must be .CMD, and the extension for a DOS session batch file must be .BAT.

When you type the name of the batch file at the command prompt, the operating system opens the file and executes the commands that it finds just as if you had typed them from the keyboard.

OS/2 also includes the Restructured Extended Executor (REXX) programming language, which is similar to the batch language, but is a fully-fledged programming language; see Chapter 16 for more information on writing programs using REXX.

@

Used at the beginning of a batch file line, @ suppresses the display of the commands that follow.

Here's the syntax:

@ command

Command lines that include the @ symbol are processed normally, but are not displayed. The @ symbol must be the first character on the line.

Examples   To turn off the display from the ECHO command, add the following line to your batch file:

@ECHO OFF

CALL

The CALL command invokes a second batch file from within the current batch file without ending the first one.

Here's the syntax:

CALL ***batchfile*** argument

In the CALL command *batchfile* is the name of the batch file you want to invoke, including drive and path information as needed, and *argument* is any specific information you want to pass to this second batch file.

The second batch file executes, and when it completes, control returns to the line in the original batch file immediately after the line that contained the CALL command.

Examples   To call a batch file called ADDRESS.CMD, add the following to your batch file:

CALL ADDRESS

In an OS/2 session a batch file may not call itself. In a DOS session it may; just make sure that the batch file ends itself eventually. Do not use piping or any kind of redirection with CALL.

ECHO

The ECHO command tells the operating system whether to display batch commands as they run. You can also use ECHO to display a text message on the screen.

Here's the syntax:

ECHO *state message*

The *state* parameter can be set to ON or OFF. ECHO ON is the default setting, and displays all commands as they run. ECHO OFF suppresses the display of commands, including the REM command. *message* can be any text, and is displayed regardless of the current setting of *state*.

Examples To display all the commands in a batch file as they are processed, add the following to the beginning of your batch file:

ECHO ON

To turn this output off, use the following instead:

ECHO OFF

ENDLOCAL

The ENDLOCAL command restores the drive, directory, and environment variables to their original condition before the SETLOCAL command was invoked.

Here's the syntax:

ENDLOCAL

Sometimes it is convenient to use different environment variables during the execution of a particular batch file. Use the SETLOCAL command at the beginning of the batch file to record the current setting of these important system variables. At the end of the batch file use ENDLOCAL to restore these original values back to the environment again. In this way, a batch file can run with its own environment variables without impacting the rest of the system.

Examples When using the SETLOCAL/ENDLOCAL pair of commands, be sure to place them before and after any environment variables are changed, as shown in the following example:

```
SETLOCAL
A:
PATH A:\;A:\ELVIS
CD \ELVIS
ROCKSTAR
ENDLOCAL
```

In this example, the SETLOCAL command saves the current settings for drive, current directory, PATH, and other information. Then the batch file makes drive A the current drive and \ELVIS the current directory, and it starts the program called ROCKSTAR. When this program finishes, the ENDLOCAL command restores the original drive, directory, and PATH information back to the environment.

EXTPROC

The EXTPROC command specifies that an external batch processor should be used to process a batch file, rather than the usual batch processor.

Here's the syntax:

EXTPROC *filename* arguments

If you ever want to replace the OS/2 batch processor with your own, you can do so using the EXTPROC command. The *filename* parameter specifies the name of the batch processor you want to use, and *arguments* details any extra information you want to pass to the batch processor.

Examples   To use the batch processor called MYPROC.EXE located in the MYFILES directory, add the following to your batch file:

EXTPROC C:\MYFILES\MYPROC.EXE

The EXTPROC command *must* be the first command in the batch file, because it is still processed by the regular OS/2 command processor; only the commands that follow will be processed by your batch processor.

FOR

The FOR command allows for the repetitive running of OS/2 commands.

Here's the syntax:

FOR *%%variable* IN *(set)* DO *command*

The FOR command creates a loop in a batch file that allows a single command to repeat on a series of file parameters, until all the parameters are exhausted. In the syntax above, *%%variable* is a symbol to be applied to each item in the *set*, and *command* is the OS/2 command you want to execute repeatedly.

Always enclose *set* in parentheses, and if *set* includes file names, you can use the wildcard characters * and ? if you wish.

Examples   To delete all the files in the C:\WRITE directory with the file-name extension of .BAK, add this to your batch file:

    FOR %%Y IN (*.BAK) DO DEL C:\WRITE\%%Y

You can also invoke the FOR command from the command prompt. In this case, just use one percent sign in the variable symbol, rather than two.

Piping and redirection are available with the FOR command only in OS/2 sessions, not in DOS sessions.

GOTO

The GOTO command transfers batch file control to a line beginning with a label rather than executing the next command in the file.

Here's the syntax:

    GOTO *label*

The GOTO command sends a batch program to a label, a unique string of 8 characters on a line by itself, preceded by a colon, where processing continues. The label can actually be longer than 8 characters (the processor will ignore the extras), but make sure the label is uniquely identifiable by the first 8 characters to avoid confusion with any other labels in the file.

GOTO is often used with IF or IF NOT so that the batch file can respond differently under different circumstances.

Examples   When the operating system encounters the statement

    GOTO :END

in a batch file, it jumps to the line

    :END

where batch file processing continues. If you try to GOTO a label that does not exist, OS/2 stops processing the batch file, and posts an error message. If you use a label without a GOTO, OS/2 ignores the label and continues processing.

IF

The IF command allows for the conditional processing of batch file commands.

There are several ways to use the IF command, to evaluate an error level, a string, or a filename:

IF ERRORLEVEL *n command*

This statement checks the status of *ERRORLEVEL n*, and is true if the previous program had an exit code of *n* or higher. When this is true, the *command* is executed; otherwise the *command* is ignored.

IF *string1==string2 command*

In this syntax, if the two strings are equal, the *command* is executed; otherwise the *command* is ignored. This comparison is case sensitive, so upper- and lowercase must match. The strings must not be blank.

IF EXIST *drive:\path\filename command*

In this syntax, if the *drive:\path\filename* exists, *command* is executed; if not, *command* is ignored. You can use the wildcard characters * and ? in the filename.

All of these syntax forms can be reversed by the inclusion of a NOT statement after the IF. For example, the first syntax shown above becomes:

IF NOT ERRORLEVEL *n command*

> ## SOLUTION

Several OS/2 commands return what is known as a *completion code*, or ER-RORLEVEL, when they complete an operation. If the operation completes successfully, they return an ERRORLEVEL of 0, but if an error occurs during their operation, the value of this code indicates the nature of the error.

You use the ERRORLEVEL code with an IF statement in your batch file, using the following form:

IF ERRORLEVEL *code command*

or

IF NOT ERRORLEVEL *code command*

where *code* is the returned completion code, and *command* is the operation you want to perform as a result of the IF statement being true.

By using ERRORLEVEL in your batch programs, you can decide what action you want to take when an error is encountered, and how you want the batch file to continue. See the description of the XCOPY command in Chapter 3 for another example of using ERRORLEVEL.

Examples   To test an ERRORLEVEL, and then branch to a label based on that ERRORLEVEL value, add the following lines to your batch file:

```
IF ERRORLEVEL 4 GOTO FOUR
IF ERRORLEVEL 3 GOTO THREE
IF ERRORLEVEL 2 GOTO TWO
IF ERRORLEVEL 1 GOTO ONE


:FOUR
ECHO NUMBER FOUR
GOTO END
:THREE
ECHO NUMBER THREE
GOTO END :TWO
ECHO NUMBER TWO
GOTO END
:ONE
ECHO ONE
GOTO END

:END
```

PAUSE

The PAUSE command suspends batch-file processing and displays this message:

Press any key when ready...

Also, using the PAUSE command is one way you can give the user of this batch file a convenient way out; if you don't like what is happening, you can press Ctrl+Break (or Ctrl+C) from the keyboard, and abort the batch file at that point. When you press Ctrl+Break, batch processing stops and you will see the message:

Terminate batch job (Y/N)?

Press Y to return to the command prompt; press N to continue processing the batch file.

Here's the syntax:

PAUSE *message*

You can use a *message* with the PAUSE command; it will only be displayed when ECHO is on.

Examples   To pause your batch file and display the message *Please change disks*, add the following to your batch file:

PAUSE Please change disks

REM

The REM command adds comments to a batch file or to your CONFIG.SYS file.

Here's the syntax:

REM *comments*

Use the REM command to annotate your batch files and your CONFIG.SYS file; a sequence of commands may be obvious to you now, but will that still be true a year from now? The non-executing *comments* can be any characters up to a maximum of 123, and they are displayed if ECHO is on. If ECHO is OFF they are not displayed.

You can also temporarily disable a complex entry in your CONFIG.SYS file if you place a REM statement in front of it. This avoids having to delete the entry, and possibly having to rebuild it later.

Examples   To display the title *This is a Batch File*, add the following to your batch file:

```
REM This is a Batch File
```

To suppress this output, use:

```
@REM This is a Batch File
```

To add three blank lines to a batch file to make it easier to read, add these lines:

```
REM
REM
REM
```

SETLOCAL

The SETLOCAL command saves the current drive, directory, and environment variables, and it lets the batch file establish its own variables. The original settings are restored by an ENDLOCAL command, or when the batch file ends.

Here's the syntax:

```
SETLOCAL
```

Sometimes it is convenient to use different environment variables during the execution of a particular batch file. Use the SETLOCAL command at the beginning of the batch file to record the current setting of these important system variables. At the end of the batch file, use ENDLOCAL to restore the original values to the environment. In this way, a batch file can run with its own environment variables without impacting the rest of the system.

Examples   When using the SETLOCAL/ENDLOCAL commands, be sure to place them before and after any lines that change environment variables, as shown in the following example:

```
SETLOCAL
A:
PATH A:\;A:\ELVIS
CD \ELVIS
ROCKSTAR
ENDLOCAL
```

In this example, the SETLOCAL command saves the current settings for drive, current directory, PATH, and other information. Then the batch file makes drive A the current drive and \ELVIS the current directory, and starts the program called ROCKSTAR. When this program finishes, the ENDLOCAL command restores the original drive, directory, and PATH information to the environment.

SHIFT

The SHIFT command allows you to use more than 10 replaceable parameters in a batch file.

Here's the syntax:

SHIFT

Batch files can handle up to 10 replaceable parameters, %0 through %9. If you use the SHIFT command, all parameters on the command line are moved one place to the left; the %1 parameter replaces the %0 parameter, %2 replaces %1, and so on. A new parameter is loaded into %9.

There is no reverse shift command, so after a SHIFT command, the original contents of %0 cannot be recovered.

Examples If %0 contains "fat," %1 contains "thin," %2 contains "beards," and %3 through %9 are empty, a SHIFT command produces the following:

%0   thin

%1   beards

and "fat" is lost.

OS/2 OS/2 OS/2

OS/2 OS/2 OS/2 OS/2 OS/2 OS/2 OS/2 OS/2

OS/2 OS/2 OS/2

13

Optimizing OS/2 Performance

AS an operating system, OS/2 is much more capable than any version of MS-DOS released to date, and to some users, that power can be intimidating and sometimes hard to appreciate. This chapter looks at several aspects of OS/2 operations from the inside, including how OS/2 organizes multitasking, how that scheme compares with other systems, and how you can use multitasking in your own work. We'll look at how OS/2 handles memory management, and how the availability of memory influences overall system performance.

In the second part of the chapter, I'll review methods you can use to optimize and tune the performance of your OS/2 system, including how to get the most from the HPFS and FAT disk caches. I'll end the chapter with a detailed look at OS/2's CONFIG.SYS file, and how you can use the configuration commands on your system.

OS/2 Multitasking Explained

One of the greatest benefits OS/2 brings to the desktop is multitasking, or the ability of the operating system to run many applications simultaneously. In OS/2, multitasking services are built into the operating system, and to appreciate how multitasking works, it is important to understand a little of the terminology.

Preemptive Versus Cooperative Multitasking

In previous chapters we have looked at the different elements that allow OS/2 to manage apparently conflicting demands made on the system, but how does it actually do it? There are two main theoretical methods used to implement multitasking, *preemptive* and *cooperative* multitasking. OS/2 uses preemptive multitasking while Microsoft Windows uses cooperative multitasking.

NOTE Another way of sharing computer resources is by using *context switching*; however, context switching is not the same as multitasking. Context switching lets you load several programs at the same time, but only the program in the foreground actually runs, the others are waiting for their turn to run; if you never switch to them, they will never run.

Preemptive Multitasking

In a preemptive multitasking system, the operating system controls not only when a process receives processor time, but also the amount of time it receives. A process runs until its time slice expires, and at that point it is preempted and another process gains access to the processor for its allocated time slice. Although a process can relinquish control before the time slice expires (for example, during I/O wait states), no process can execute for longer than its defined time period.

With preemptive multitasking, the application programmer is freed from the responsibility for releasing control periodically, and no single process can gain overall control of the operating system, even by accident.

Cooperative Multitasking

In a cooperative multitasking scheme, each application has to tell the operating system when it will relinquish processor time. Cooperative systems are relatively easy to design and program for, but they have several disadvantages, including:

- Just one badly-written program can hog the entire system, and by refusing to relinquish the processor, can cause serious problems for other programs running on the system.

- Application programmers must explicitly declare in their programs the point at which they will pass control back to the operating system.

Poorly implemented cooperative multitasking can produce a kind of stuttering effect on running applications, depending on how well (or badly) individual programs behave.

Sessions

A *session* is the top level of OS/2's multitasking structure, and in previous chapters we have worked with OS/2 sessions, DOS sessions (both VDM and VMB sessions), and WIN-OS/2 sessions. This is the most obvious manifestation of multitasking; you can start a copy of WordPerfect for OS/2 in one OS/2 session, then run your spreadsheet in another, and open a WIN-OS/2 session to run some Windows applications. In other words, sessions look like individual, separate MS-DOS computers, except that everything is happening under the control and coordination of OS/2 in a single PC.

Processes

A session consists of at least one *process*. In OS/2 terms there are really no such things as programs; they are known as processes instead. All EXE and COM files execute as processes, and one process can run one or more other processes. Indeed, all full-screen sessions contain two processes, CMD.EXE and the application running in that session. All processes are assigned unique Process Identification (PID) numbers, and OS/2 can manage support for up to 4095 processes.

Threads

The third level of multitasking is the *thread*. OS/2 applications always have at least one thread, but by using multiple threads, an application can itself appear to do several things at once. Typical OS/2 applications consist of many threads. Only one thread at a time can actually run, even if several threads are ready to run. Processor access is managed by the OS/2 system scheduler, and each thread is assigned a priority that determines when it will run. Threads can be in one of three states; running, ready to run, or blocked.

OS/2 provides support for up to 4095 threads, system-wide, for both the operating system and all applications, but the usual default is 64 if there is no THREADS command in CONFIG.SYS.

Time Slicing versus Scheduling

There are two ways of dividing processor time between competing applications, *time slicing*, and *scheduling*:

- **Time Slicing**. In simple time slicing, each application is allotted a specific period of time or number of time slices in which to execute. All programs are allotted the same number of time slices, and the operating system cannot respond dynamically to shifting load, changing application mix, or different priorities.

- **Scheduling**. In a scheduling system, a component of the operating system manages the available time slices dynamically, and this makes the operating system more responsive to changing circumstances.

You can use the following CONFIG.SYS commands to fine tune OS/2's multitasking:

- **THREADS** establishes the maximum number of threads available in the system.

- **TIMESLICE** establishes the minimum and maximum amounts of time allocated to processes.

- **PRIORITY** selects the priority calculation used to schedule regular-class threads.

- **MAXWAIT** establishes the length of time a process must wait before OS/2 assigns it a higher priority.

All these commands are covered in detail in the description of the OS/2 CONFIG.SYS file later in this chapter.

OS/2 implements a multilevel priority system to organize and schedule threads. Each thread is assigned its own execution priority, and high-priority threads that are ready to run are dispatched before low-priority threads that are ready to run. In OS/2, processes also have a priority level, but this does not influence which threads will run next; it acts as the default priority level for the threads in that process. There are four priority classes in OS/2:

- **Time Critical:** This class is used with threads that may lose data if they do not receive sufficient time from the operating system. Threads in this class will receive processor time within 6 microseconds (6 millionths of a second) of being ready to run.

- **Server:** This priority class is used in applications running on a file server that also runs local applications. Server priority threads receive time before regular threads, so that remote users do not suffer a performance degradation just because someone is running an application on the server itself.

- **Regular:** Most of the threads in OS/2 processes run at this normal priority level.

- **Idle:** Threads with an idle priority only run when nothing else is waiting to run at any of the other priority levels.

Each priority class is further divided into 32 priority levels; at any given priority level in a class, OS/2 allocates time slices to each thread in turn until the thread finishes, or a thread of a higher priority becomes ready to run. In this case, the running thread is preempted in favor of the higher priority thread.

OS/2 also uses *dynamic priority variation* to adjust or boost the priority of a thread based on its activity, to improve system performance and responsiveness. Three types of boost are used, as follows:

- **Foreground boost** is given to the thread that controls the user interface to make the system as responsive as possible.

- **I/O boost** helps increase ease I/O bottlenecks.

- **Starvation boost** is given to a thread that has not run for the value of the MAXWAIT parameter in CONFIG.SYS.

As you can appreciate from this discussion, OS/2's priority-based multitasking scheme is designed to make the system as flexible and responsive as possible in as many different circumstances as possible.

Interprocess Communications

Effective communication between processes is vital in a multitasking operating system to allow concurrent processes to operate together. OS/2 includes several methods of interprocess communication:

- **Shared Memory** is an area of memory in cooperative use by one or more processes.

- **Semaphores** are used to signal the beginning or end of an operation, and provide mutually exclusive ownership of some system resource, such as shared memory. OS/2 provides three kinds of semaphore:

  - **Event Semaphores** allow a thread to tell other threads that an event has occurred, and it is safe for them to resume execution.

  - **Mutual Exclusion (Mutex) Semaphores** protect system resources such as files, data, and peripherals from simultaneous access by several processes, allowing threads to serialize their access to resources.

  - **Multiple Wait (Muxwait) Semaphores** allow threads to wait for multiple events to occur or for multiple resources to become free.

- **Queues** are named, ordered lists of 32-bit elements used to pass information between threads of the same process or between different processes. Queue elements can be anything that will fit into 32 bits, including values, flags, and pointers to shared memory regions. The data in a queue can be accessed by priority, by FIFO (first-in-first-out), or by LIFO (last-in-first-out) methods.

- **Pipes** are named or unnamed buffers, used to pass data between processes. A process reads from or writes to a pipe as if the pipe were standard input or standard output. The data in a pipe is accessed using FIFO. Unnamed pipes are temporary files used between filter commands such as MORE and SORT, while named pipes are used in client-server programming, and allow related or unrelated processes on either the same or different computers to communicate with each other.

Taking Advantage of Multitasking

Now that we have described the elements that make up OS/2's multitasking environment, what sort of operations can you multitask? Some of the more familiar candidates are printing with the OS/2 spooler, sending and receiving files in the background, and copying or formatting disks. A frequent problem for users new to OS/2, especially those migrating from the MS-DOS world, is simply remembering that multitasking is always there whenever you want to use it.

Using Modems with OS/2

The Productivity folder on the desktop contains PM Terminal, a fully-featured communications program you can use for sending (or *uploading*) or receiving (or *downloading*) files to and from bulletin boards or other OS/2 users. There really isn't much to see on the screen as files are sent or received; there is very little user interaction with the program, and OS/2 will take care of providing the correct amount of processor time to see that communications are not interrupted. Even if you use your modem only occasionally, you will benefit from multitasking your communications sessions.

Formatting Disks and Copying Files in the Background

Formatting a disk is another task well suited to OS/2's multitasking environment. It used to be that you would sit and stare at the display as the floppy disk was formatted; the time it took was never long enough to really do anything else. OS/2 lets you format floppy disks in the background while you get on with something more interesting in the foreground.

You can open a command prompt session, start the format running, then switch back to another session and continue working. Alternatively, use the Format Disk option on the popup menu for the Drive A icon on the desktop if you prefer.

Making a duplicate copy of a floppy disk is another boring task well suited to background mode. Again, use either a command- prompt session, or use the Drive A icon on the desktop.

In the end, the range of applications you can multitask is limited only by the range of your applications, because OS/2 was designed to be a responsive, multitasking operating system right from the very beginning.

OS/2 Memory Management

MS-DOS and Windows users are all very familiar with the results of "RAM cram" on the PC; and programmers are tired of wrestling with the segment:offset memory addressing scheme when writing programs. Fortunately, OS/2 has sent both of these limitations the way of the dinosaur, by implementing a virtual memory scheme to banish the first, and a flat memory model to banish the second.

The Flat Memory Model

OS/2 is based on a flat memory model, where all memory is addressed as a single continuous area. Taking advantage of features of the Intel 80386 (and later) processors, OS/2 can address up to 4GB of *virtual memory*, consisting of both physical memory in the computer and an area of hard disk storage space that temporarily holds data that will not fit into memory. This flat memory model not only provides a significant performance boost, it also makes writing applications much more convenient, and allows application developers to port their programs to other microprocessor systems much more easily than did the segment:offset system.

Virtual Memory

Virtual memory consists of both the physical RAM present in your computer and a file on the hard disk known as the swap file. When OS/2 runs out of physical memory, it uses this disk space just as if it were RAM. Memory is managed in *pages* of 4K each using a *least-recently used* method; this means that the oldest unused pages are swapped to disk first. Pages of the swap file are reloaded back into memory as needed. This scheme makes it possible for applications to use more memory than is actually present in the computer. The MEMMAN command in CONFIG.SYS, described later in this chapter, enables or disables paging to and from the hard disk, while the SWAPPATH command specifies the location of the file on the hard disk.

> ## ▶ S O L U T I O N
>
> You specify the location of the swap file with the SWAPPATH command in CONFIG.SYS; this command is described in detail later in this chapter, but how do you decide *where* to put the swap file? If your system uses both FAT and HPFS hard disk partitions, make sure that the swap file is on the HPFS partition to take advantage of the increased speed available with the HPFS.
>
> If your other partitions have more free space than the default drive C, then use one of them for the swap file. If you have two hard disk controllers on your system, put the swap file on a disk managed by the least used controller to see the biggest performance gain. And never put the swap file on a networked drive.

The swap file is created at the time you install OS/2, and Table 13.1 shows the initial default size of the swap file depending on the amount of available memory.

The swap file is called SWAPPER.DAT and is located in the directory specified by the SWAPPATH command in CONFIG.SYS. Unless you have changed this on your system, you will find SWAPPER.DAT in the OS2\SYSTEM directory. SWAPPER.DAT changes size continually as you work, and as memory is paged in and out.

It is a good idea to look at the size of SWAPPER.DAT from time to time; a size of about 4MB is right for most modest installations. If your swap file grows and continues growing, this is a good indication that you can increase your system performance by adding more physical memory. However convenient paging to and from disk is, there is a performance penalty, and it is therefore vital to maximize the amount of memory available on your system. Even relatively modest increases can boost performance quite considerably.

TABLE 13.1: Swap File Size and Available Physical Memory

AVAILABLE MEMORY	INITIAL SWAP FILE SIZE
4MB	6144K
5MB	5120K
6MB	5120K
7MB	4096K
8MB	4096K
9MB	3072K
10MB	3072K
11MB	2048K
12MB	2048K

Tuning OS/2

For many users, the default settings established by OS/2 at installation time are the best settings to use, and on many systems these defaults are never changed. As we have seen in preceding chapters, there are many factors influencing system performance, but there is a big difference between making something work and making something work better.

NOTE One of the most common reasons you might change a system setting is in response to something that has changed on your system. Perhaps you have added a major new application, or a new adapter board in support of new hardware, or you have been hooked up to the network.

Before changing any system settings, think about what you are trying to achieve, and make sure that the goals you set are reasonable. Also, many system settings have a Default button you can use to reset everything back the way it was before you made the change; if there is no Default button, take a careful note of the original settings so you can reset them manually if you have to.

Tuning the OS/2 Disk Cache

When an application program needs information from the hard disk, it asks OS/2 to find it. OS/2 reads the data and passes it to the application program. If you are updating a large database, for example, this means that the same information is requested and read many times as you access the database. A *disk cache* is a program and an associated memory area that mediate between the hard disk controller and OS/2, and is usually installed by statements in CONFIG.SYS. Once the cache program is installed and the application requests information from the disk, the program first checks to see if the information is already in the cache memory. If it is, the program loads the data from the cache rather than from the hard disk, which, of course, is much faster. If the data is not in memory, the cache program reads the data from the disk, copies it into the cache memory for further reference, and then passes the data to OS/2 and to the application that made the original request.

➤ S O L U T I O N

How do you decide how big you can make the cache? Base your decision on the amount of memory available in your computer, not on the size of your hard disk. You should work out the normal operating requirements of your system, and then dedicate whatever remains to your cache. The cache is static; it does not change size dynamically as the swap file can. The bigger your cache, the more likely it is that the information needed is in memory, and the faster your system will perform.

If your applications, along with your DOS and WIN-OS/2 sessions normally take about 6MB, and you have 16MB of memory installed in your computer, you can use up to 10MB for your cache. That is a lot of space for your applications to read and write at nanosecond speed rather than at millisecond speed. If your application mix changes over time, be sure to re-evaluate the amount of memory set aside for the cache.

Because users constantly face choices between increasing speed and using more memory, disk cache programs usually have lots of options so that you can tailor the cache to your exact requirements. To decide how to do this, you must first examine both your computer hardware and the way in which you use your computer. Any memory set aside for the cache is memory that cannot be used for applications.

Because OS/2 supports different file systems, it also provides different cache programs; each designed for a specific file system. If you use the FAT system, you will work with the DISKCACHE command in CONFIG.SYS, but if you use the HPFS, you will use the CACHE command. The size of the cache is selected during OS/2 installation, based on the amount of memory installed in the computer, the size of the hard disk, and the file system you install.

NOTE The maximum size for the HPFS cache is 2MB, while the FAT file system cache can be up to 14MB.

Table 13.2 lists the various disk cache sizes.

When both FAT and HPFS are used on the same computer, the larger size is assigned to the file system with the most space. The default cache size for a computer with 4MB of memory is 128K, but as we will see in a moment, there are times when you might want to change this number.

TABLE 13.2: Disk Cache Sizes

SYSTEM MEMORY	CACHE SIZE	
	BOTH FAT AND HPFS	**EITHER FAT OR HPFS**
4MB	128K and 64K	128K
5MB	128K and 64K	128K
6MB	256K and 64K	256K
7MB	256K and 128K	256K
8MB	256K and 256K	384K
9MB	256K and 256K	384K
10MB to 16MB	512K and 512K	1MB
17MB to 32MB	1MB and MB	2MB

HPFS and CACHE

The CACHE command sets various parameters for HPFS caching, and is only available if you formatted a hard disk partition for use with the HPFS. The HPFS manages the disk cache memory in 2K blocks. If an application requests information that is not in the cache, the HPFS selects the least-recently used block, writes that block to disk if necessary, and then loads the requested data into this block. The file system can also take advantage of its knowledge of the contents of the cache blocks. Information that the file system suspects will not be needed is placed in blocks marked for immediate reuse.

> ### ► S E C R E T

If you just use the HPFS, comment out or remove the DISKCACHE statement from your CONFIG.SYS file. The presence of this statement allocates memory for the FAT cache, even if the FAT file system is not being used on your system. You can also do this if you have a FAT system, but don't use it very much.

> ### ► S E C R E T

HPFS disk structure is somewhat different from the FAT disk structure used in MS-DOS. Hard disks are divided into sectors, and the HPFS allocates sectors as follows. Disk sectors 0 to 15 are called the *Bootblock*, and they contain the volume name, volume ID, and the disk bootstrap loader program. Sector 16 is called the *SuperBlock* and it contains pointers to the free space bitmaps, the bad block list, the directory block band, and the root directory. Sector 17 is known as the *SpareBlock* and contains control information used as OS/2 runs. The rest of the disk is divided up into 8MB *bands*. Each band has a free space bitmap which indicates the free sectors inside the band. In the center of the disk is the *Directory Band*, which contains the information on files and directories on the disk. By placing it in the middle of the disk, you keep the amount of hard disk head movement needed to access the directory band to a minimum.

Near each file is a *File Node* or F-node, which stores control information about each file, including its length and the first 15 characters of its name, and which can describe a very small or a very large file. OS/2 uses a binary tree data structure to describe the file's locations on the disk, and this binary tree can be searched very much faster than the FAT's linked list.

The HPFS attempts to store files in large contiguous areas of disk space, and it keeps the file's control information as close to the file itself as it possibly can, which also helps to minimize hard disk head movements.

The HPFS also contains additional levels of caching that can speed up access to directories.

To change the parameters controlling the HPFS disk cache, specify the CACHE command as part of a RUN statement in CONFIG.SYS, or directly from the command prompt. The syntax for use in CONFIG.SYS is as follows:

    RUN=C:\OS2\CACHE.EXE /switches

You can type the CACHE command at a system prompt without parameters to see the current settings being used.

> ## S E C R E T

The HPFS looks at the size of the file being read, and, depending on the size of the cache (specified in CONFIG.SYS, and described later in this section), it will try to read the whole file at one time. The largest readable file size for each cache size is as follows:

CACHE SIZE	LARGEST READABLE FILE
128K	16K
256K	32K
512K	64K
1MB or more	128K

A cache of 1MB will load files of 128K or less in their entirety, which will dramatically improve performance. In fact, even in more modest systems, where the cache is small as 128K, files of up to 16K or less will be cached in one go.

The HPFS also provides an asynchronous read-ahead thread for sequentially accessed files. This loads the disk cache asynchronously, and improves system performance because the next record requested by the application is actually in the cache before the application asks for it to be loaded. Read-ahead is slightly different in OS/2 version 2.1, and has the capability to read data from physically discontinuous pages in a single operation. This is a hardware feature found on DMA devices such as SCSI adapters.

Switches

/LAZY:*state*

When set to OFF, specifies that data should be written to disk immediately; when set to ON, the default, specifies that data should be written to disk when the disk is idle. When /LAZY is set to ON, the disk controller can perform higher-priority actions first, and then complete any pending file writes when it is convenient; this makes applications appear to run much faster, because requests for reads are completed before writes are handled.

W A R N I N G   If you set the /LAZY switch to On, *always* select the desktop Shut Down option before turning off your computer. If you don't use Shut Down, you may lose any data still in the HPFS cache but not yet written out to disk.

/MAXAGE:*time*

Specifies the length of time, in milliseconds, before data is transferred to another cache level or to disk. The default is 5000.

/DISKIDLE:*time*

Specifies the length of time, in milliseconds, that the disk must be idle before it can receive data from cache memory. The default is 1000, and must be larger than the value specified for /BUFFERIDLE.

/BUFFERIDLE: *time*

Specifies the length of time, in milliseconds, that the cache can be idle before the information is written to disk. The default is 500.

Examples

To set the cache so that all cache information is immediately written out to disk, add the following line to your STARTUP.CMD file:

    C:\OS2\CACHE.EXE /LAZY:OFF

To make CACHE write data that has been in memory longer than 4000 milliseconds out to disk, add this entry to your CONFIG.SYS file:

    RUN=C:\OS2\CACHE.EXE /MAXAGE:4000

The /LAZY switch is available at the OS/2 command prompt; the other switches are only accessible though settings in CONFIG.SYS. If you reset /LAZY during an OS/2 session, and want to change it again without exiting the session, you must first use the DETACH command, as follows:

    DETACH CACHE /LAZY:*ON*

DETACH starts and then simultaneously detaches an OS/2 program from its command processor.

FAT and DISKCACHE

SECRET

IBM has added several important improvements to the FAT file system used in MS-DOS, while retaining complete compatibility; you may see the improved version referred to as SuperFAT. IBM has added 32-bit capabilities to increase speed, as well as a 16K read-ahead, lazy-writes, extended attributes, and a free-space bitmap which results in reduced allocation times.

The DISKCACHE command specifies the amount of memory to use for the FAT disk cache and for cache control information. Here's the syntax:

    DISKCACHE = *n,LW,T,AC:x*

In the DISKCACHE command, n specifies the size of the cache, from 64K to 14400K. This number represents amount of physical memory space occupied by information read from the disk. The default is 64K. T indicates the threshold size for the number of sectors that will be loaded into the cache, from 4 to 128. IBM recommends that you set the threshold to 32, unless the application you are using is particularly disk-intensive, and the supplier provides information on the block size required. LW, included by default, specifies that the cache contents are written to disk only during disk-idle time; leave this parameter out to make the cache write to disk immediately. The *AC:x* autocheck parameter specifies that the specified drive is checked using CHKDSK /F to make sure that the file system is intact. The drive letter can be any letter from C to Z; the letters A and B cannot be used because OS/2 knows that they represent floppy disk drives.

Examples

To set your FAT disk cache size to 64K, with a default threshold of 32, with lazy-write on, and to make AUTOCHECK check the D: FAT partition for errors, add the following to your CONFIG.SYS file:

```
DISKCACHE=64,LW,32,AC:D
```

Optimizing the WorkPlace Shell

There are a number of things you can do to help optimize the productivity of your desktop, including using the Startup folder and templates, being frugal with disk space, and paying attention to how you run applications on the desktop:

- **Startup Folder:** Any objects placed in the Startup folder will open automatically when you start OS/2. You can use a combination of the Startup folder and the CONFIG.SYS option SET RESTARTOBJECTS= to maintain a consistent startup, so that OS/2 begins in the same way every time you start your system.

Place important and frequently used applications in the Startup folder on the desktop, and then make sure that SET RESTARTOBJECTS is equal to STARTUPFOLDERSONLY. This setting ensures that only those objects placed in the Startup folder will run; any applications running when you last shut down will not start automatically unless they are also included in the Startup folder.

- **Templates:** Using existing templates and creating new ones can ease the burden of supporting many similar users. OS/2 contains many default templates, and these can be customized for different application needs.

- **Conserving Disk Space:** Once you are familiar with the operation of the desktop, you can recover valuable disk space by deleting the OS/2 Tutorial and perhaps one of the two editors bundled with the operating system. You will find the Tutorial file in OS2\HELP\TUTORIAL; it is called TUTORIAL.HLP. If you never play any of the games, then you can also consider removing them to save space. However, many OS/2 files have cryptic names that may not reveal their true function; if you are in doubt about a particular file's function, do not delete it!

- **Applications:** Running your applications in a full-screen session will almost always give better performance than a windowed session. This performance boost has to do with the amount of translating that OS/2 must perform when writing to the application in the window and when writing to the desktop.

You can also make your desktop easier to use by closing windows and folders when they are not in use; this just makes it easier to find things when you need them. You can also consider opening multiple desktops as described in Chapter 2, or adding your own frequently used options and selections to the desktop pop-up menu, which was also described in Chapter 2.

Tuning the DOS and WIN-OS/2 Environment

The VDM DOS settings were discussed in detail in Chapters 6 and 7. Two areas that can help improve system performance are memory allocation for DOS sessions, and the session mode.

- **Memory Allocation:** Memory allocation for DOS sessions can have a direct effect on overall OS/2 system performance. The default setting for XMS_MEMORY_LIMIT, EMS_MEMORY_-LIMIT, and DPMI_MEMORY_LIMIT for VDM sessions is 2MB each, and this may be overly generous for your DOS applications, many of which cannot use 1MB, much less 2MB. If your application does not use this much memory, change the appropriate setting to zero, and you may find that OS/2 reduces the amount of swapping as a result.

- **Session Mode:** Run DOS and WIN-OS/2 sessions in full-screen mode rather than as windows on the desktop. This may reduce the convenience of running applications side-by-side on the desktop, but the performance improvement you will see will surely outweigh this drawback. OS/2's workload is reduced considerably when it only has to handle one screen image in the foreground; for example, a WIN-OS/2 session uses a different palette from the desktop, and you can remove the need for any translation by running WIN-OS/2 full-screen.

Other DOS settings that may affect system performance are:

- **DOS_BACKGROUND_EXECUTION:** If your application cannot perform useful work when it is switched into the background, turn this setting Off, and your other applications will receive more processing time as a result. Do not turn this setting off if your program, such as a communications program, needs to process interrupts while in the background.

- **INT_DURING_IO:** This version 2.1 setting creates a second thread for an application to use for interrupt handling when the main thread is busy performing disk operations. Leave this setting Off unless your application is a game, uses MSCDEX, or is a multimedia application.

- **DOS_RMSIZE:** Many DOS sessions do not use the 640K allocated to VDM DOS sessions. Reducing this setting can lower the overhead associated with this session.

A Typical OS/2 CONFIG.SYS File Explained

The CONFIG.SYS file is a text file containing system-configuration information that OS/2 loads each time you start your computer. OS/2 reads the file all in one go, as the operating system loads, and then executes the commands contained in it. For the most part, the order in which a statement appears in the file is not particularly important, except when you load support for a specialized piece of hardware. In this case, you must make sure that the statement that loads the device is located before any statements that access that device.

You can use the following commands in a CONFIG.SYS file:

AUTOFAIL
BASEDEV
BUFFERS
CACHE
CODEPAGE
COUNTRY
DEVICE
DEVINFO

DEVICEHIGH

DISKCACHE

DOS

DPATH

FCBS

FILES

IFS

IOPL

KEYB

LASTDRIVE

LIBPATH

MAXWAIT

MEMMAN

PATH

PAUSEONERROR

PRINTMONBUFSIZE

PRIORITY

PRIORITY_DISK_IO

PROTECTONLY

PROMPT

PROTSHELL

REM

RMSIZE

RUN

SET

SWAPPATH

THREADS

TIMESLICE

TRACE

TRACEBUF

TRACEFMT

Those commands used to set up your disk cache were described earlier in this chapter, the commands that manage national-language support were described in Chapter 11, and the problem-determination commands are described in Chapter 14.

WARNING Be sure to make a copy of your current CONFIG.SYS file before you add new entries or change any of the existing ones. Create a new directory off the root directory called something that you will remember, such as BOOT or CONFIG, and copy your current CONFIG.SYS file into this directory. If things do not work out as you plan, or if you accidentally damage the file as you make your changes, you can always go back and reload this copy of the file and recover.

In OS/2, the CONFIG.SYS file is likely to contain 60 or 70 lines of entries, unlike the MS-DOS version which might contain 5 to 10 lines at the most. Many of the commands will be familiar to MS-DOS users, although they may have different options under OS/2. You can use the OS/2 Enhanced Editor to look at or change the entries in your CONFIG.SYS file, but remember that any changes you make will take effect only after you restart your computer. Listing 13.1 shows a typical CONFIG.SYS file for an 80486 computer with 8MB of memory, a 200MB hard disk, CD-ROM, sound card, and a VGA display adapter.

The sections that follow summarize the configuration commands not covered elsewhere, with descriptions, syntax, and, where appropriate, system tuning recommendations. The layout of the command-syntax information used in this chapter is the same as used in Chapter 12.

LISTING 13.1

A Typical CONFIG.SYS File

```
IFS=C:\OS2\HPFS.IFS  /CACHE:256 /CRECL:4
PROTSHELL=C:\OS2\PMSHELL.EXE
SET USER_INI=C:\OS2\OS2.INI
SET SYSTEM_INI=C:\OS2\OS2SYS.INI
SET OS2_SHELL=C:\OS2\CMD.EXE
SET AUTOSTART=PROGRAMS,TASKLIST,FOLDERS,CONNECTIONS
SET RUNWORKPLACE=C:\OS2\PMSHELL.EXE
SET COMSPEC=C:\OS2\CMD.EXE
LIBPATH=.;C:\OS2\DLL;C:\OS2\MDOS;C:\;C:\OS2\APPS\DLL;C:\MMOS2\DLL ;
SET PATH=C:\OS2;C:\OS2\SYSTEM;C:\OS2\MDOS\WINOS2;C:\OS2\INSTALL;C:\;
    C:\OS2\MDOS;C:\OS2\APPS;C:\MMOS2;
SET DPATH=C:\OS2;C:\OS2\SYSTEM;C:\OS2\MDOS\WINOS2;C:\OS2\INSTALL;C:\;
    C:\OS2\BITMAP;C:\OS2\MDOS;C:\OS2\APPS;C:\MMOS2\INSTALL;C:\MMOS2;
SET PROMPT=$i[$p]
SET HELP=C:\OS2\HELP;C:\OS2\HELP\TUTORIAL;C:\MMOS2\HELP;
SET GLOSSARY=C:\OS2\HELP\GLOSS;
SET IPF_KEYS=SBCS
PRIORITY_DISK_IO=YES
FILES=50
DEVICE=C:\OS2\DOS.SYS
DEVICE=C:\OS2\PMDD.SYS
BUFFERS=30
IOPL=YES
DISKCACHE=384,LW
MAXWAIT=3
MEMMAN=SWAP,PROTECT
SWAPPATH=C:\OS2\SYSTEM  2048
BREAK=OFF
THREADS=256
PRINTMONBUFSIZE=134,134,134
COUNTRY=001,C:\OS2\SYSTEM\COUNTRY.SYS
SET KEYS=ON
SET DELDIR=C:\DELETE,512
BASEDEV=PRINT01.SYS
BASEDEV=IBM1FLPY.ADD
BASEDEV=IBM1S506.ADD
BASEDEV=OS2DASD.DMD
SET BOOKSHELF=C:\OS2\BOOK;C:\TOOLKT20\BOOK;D:\BOOKS;
SET EPMPATH=C:\OS2\APPS
SET FAXPM=C:\OS2\APPS
PROTECTONLY=NO
SHELL=C:\OS2\MDOS\COMMAND.COM C:\OS2\MDOS /P
FCBS=16,8
RMSIZE=640
DEVICE=C:\OS2\MDOS\VEMM.SYS
DOS=LOW,NOUMB
DEVICE=C:\OS2\MDOS\VDPX.SYS
DEVICE=C:\OS2\MDOS\VXMS.SYS /UMB
```

LISTING 13.1

A Typical CONFIG.SYS
File (Continued)

```
DEVICE=C:\OS2\MDOS\VDPMI.SYS
DEVICE=C:\OS2\MDOS\VWIN.SYS
DEVICE=C:\OS2\MDOS\VCDROM.SYS
BASEDEV=OS2CDROM.DMD /Q
IFS=C:\OS2\CDFS.IFS /Q
BASEDEV=OS2SCSI.DMD
BASEDEV=FD8XX.ADD DEVICE=C:\OS2\MDOS\VMOUSE.SYS
DEVICE=C:\OS2\POINTDD.SYS
DEVICE=C:\OS2\MOUSE.SYS SERIAL=COM1
DEVICE=C:\OS2\COM.SYS
DEVICE=C:\OS2\MDOS\VCOM.SYS
CODEPAGE=437,850
DEVINFO=KBD,US,C:\OS2\KEYBOARD.DCP
SET AUTOSTART=PROGRAMS,TASKLIST,FOLDERS
SET EPATH=C:\OS2\APPS
SET BOOKMGR=D:\BOOKS;
SET READIBM=D:\BOOKS;
SET PROGREF20=GUIREF20.INF
SET PMREF=PMFUN.INF+PMGPI.INF+PMHOK.INF+PMMSG.INF
     +PMREL.INF+PMWIN.INF+PMWKP.INF
SET HELPNDX=EPMKWHLP.NDX
SET MMBASE=C:\MMOS2;
SET DSPPATH=C:\MMOS2\DSP;
DEVINFO=SCR,VGA,C:\OS2\VIOTBL.DCP
SET VIDEO_DEVICES=VIO_VGA
DEVICE=C:\OS2\MDOS\VSVGA.SYS
DEVICE=C:\MMOS2\SSMDD.SYS
DEVICE=C:\MMOS2\ADSHDD.SYS
SET VIO_VGA=DEVICE(BVHVGA)
DEVICE=C:\MMOS2\ACPADD2.SYS A
```

BASEDEV

The BASEDEV command installs a base device driver by specifying the complete file name of the device driver in CONFIG.SYS. Here's the syntax:

> BASEDEV *filename* arguments

where *filename* specifies the name and extension of the device driver file, and *arguments* specifies any additional information needed by the device driver.

As discussed in Part III, a device driver is a file that contains special code needed by the operating system to work with a specific piece of hardware. Device drivers are only loaded as needed, thus relieving the operating system of having to know about all possible hardware options. Base device drivers are those needed by OS/2 when the operating system is first started, and support devices such as hard disks, floppy disks, and printers. Installable device drivers used by DOS or OS/2 sessions are handled by the DEVICE command described later in this section.

Following are some of the commonly used base device drivers included with OS/2:

PRINT01.SYS	Supports local printers on non-Micro Channel computers
PRINT02.SYS	Supports local printers on Micro Channel computers
IBM1FLPY.ADD	Supports floppy disk drives on non-Micro Channel computers
IBM2FLPY.ADD	Supports floppy disk drives on Micro Channel computers
IBM1S506.ADD	Supports non-SCSI disk drives on non-Micro Channel computers
IBM2ADSK.ADD	Supports non-SCSI disk drives on Micro Channel computers
IBM2SCSI.ADD	Supports SCSI disk drives on Micro Channel computers
IBMINT13.I13	Supports other devices on non-Micro Channel computers
OS2DASD.DMD	Supports disk drives
OS2SCSI.DMD	Supports non-disk SCSI devices

NOTE

The BASEDEV command cannot contain drive or path information, because BASEDEV statements are processed before OS/2 can establish a path. All base device drivers must be located in either the root directory of the boot disk, or the C:\OS2 directory.

A typical non-Micro Channel computer might have the following statements in CONFIG.SYS:

```
BASEDEV=PRINT01.SYS

BASEDEV=IBM1FLPY.SYS

BASEDEV=IBM1S506.SYS

BASEDEV=OS2DASD.DMD
```

BASEDEV statements are not necessarily processed in the order in which they appear in CONFIG.SYS, but by file-name extension, in the following order:

- .SYS
- .BID
- .VSD
- .TSD
- .ADD
- .I13
- .FLT
- .DMD

Files with other extensions will not be loaded.

BREAK

The BREAK command tells DOS to check to see if the Ctrl+Break keys have been pressed before executing a program operation, and only affects DOS and WIN-OS/2 sessions. Here's the syntax:

```
BREAK =state
```

The *state* parameter can be either ON or OFF. If BREAK = ON, the operating system checks to see if you pressed the Ctrl+Break keys before executing any program requests. If BREAK = OFF, the operating system checks for the Ctrl+Break keys during keyboard and standard operations. As this setting can have an effect on system performance, you should normally leave it set to OFF. Type the BREAK command at the DOS prompt to display the current status.

BUFFERS

The BUFFERS command specifies the number of disk buffers available for direct disk writes. Buffers primarily work with direct I/O writes to FAT disk partitions, controlled by the IOPL command described in a moment. Here's the syntax:

BUFFERS = *n*

where *n* specifies the number of 512-byte buffers allocated when the operating system starts.

NOTE   The default setting for BUFFERS is 30, but you can use any number from 3 to 100; numbers outside this range force OS/2 to use the default.

A buffer is a method of temporary storage for information read from and written to disk. You can increase the speed of your system by increasing the BUFFERS specification in CONFIG.SYS, but as always, this is a trade-off; the more Buffers you specify, the less memory available for other uses.

If you don't use FAT but have an all-HPFS partition, set BUFFERS to 3.

DEVICE

The DEVICE command installs device drivers to support mice, touch pads, printers and other hardware. Here's the syntax:

DEVICE = *drive:\path**filename** /switches*

The *drive:\path\filename* parameter specifies the path and filename containing the device driver, while the */switches* vary in usage from device driver to device driver.

The following list describes the most common device drivers supplied with OS/2:

ANSI.SYS	Provides extended screen and keyboard support for DOS sessions.
COM.SYS	Allows OS/2 programs to use serial ports. If you have a PS/2, this driver is called COM02.SYS.
DOS.SYS	Provides support for virtual DOS sessions.
EGA.SYS	Supports EGA video adapters for DOS programs. This device driver does not take any parameters or switches.
EXTDSKDD.SYS	Supports external floppy disks.
LOG.SYS	Supports system error logging using the SYSLOG utility.
MOUSE.SYS	Provides mouse support. Additional parameters specify the type of mouse, such as TYPE=PDIMOU$ for a PS/2 mouse, or TYPE=PCMOU$ for a Logitech mouse.
PMDD.SYS	Supplies mouse-pointer support for OS/2 desktop sessions. This device driver does not take any parameters or switches.
POINTDD.SYS	Provides mouse support. This device driver does not take any parameters or switches.
TOUCH.SYS	Provides support for touch devices; see the heading "Other Pointing Devices and Touch Screens" in Chapter 11 for more information.

VCOM.SYS	Loads serial port support for DOS sessions.
VDISK.SYS	Provides virtual disk support.
VDPMI.SYS	Adds DPMI support to DOS sessions.
VEGA.SYS or VVGA.SYS	Loads EGA or VGA support to a DOS session.
VEMM.SYS	DOS expanded-memory manager.
VMOUSE.SYS	Loads mouse support for a DOS session.
VXMS.SYS	DOS extended-memory manager. Add the /UMB parameter at the end of the statement to enable upper memory block support in a DOS session.

Switches

Different device drivers use different switches. Those device drivers that have no switches are not shown in the following list.

The switches for ANSI.SYS are as follows:

/X	Allows keys with extended key values to be redefined as distinct keys.
/L	Maintains the same number of screen rows specified by the MODE command, and ignores the application program settings.
/K	Disables extended keyboard support.

The switches for COM.SYS are as follows:

n	Specifies the number of the COM port you are accessing.
a	Specifies the communications port address.
i	Specifies the IRQ.

See the section headed "Using COM Ports on ISA\EISA Computers" in Chapter 11 for more information.

The switches for EXTDSKDD.SYS are as follows:

/D:*d*   Specifies the physical drive number, from 0 to 255.

/T:*t*   Specifies the number of tracks per side, from 1 to 999; the default is 80.

/S:*s*   Specifies the number of sectors per track, from 1 to 99; the default is 9.

/H:*h*   Specifies the number of disk heads, from 1 to 99; the default is 2.

/f:*f*   Specifies the floppy disk drive type, as follows:

0	360K 5.25"
1	1.2MB 5.25"
2	720K 3.5"
7	1.44MB 3.5"
9	2.88MB 3.5"

The switches for LOG.SYS are as follows:

/E:*n*   Specifies the size of the error-log buffer; the minimum is 4K, the default is 8K, and the maximum is 64K.

/A:*n*   Specifies the size of the entry alert notification buffer; the minimum is 4K, there is no default, and the maximum is 64K.

/OFF   Disables error logging as soon as the device driver is loaded.

The switches for VDISK.SYS are as follows:

bytes   Sets the size of the virtual disk. The minimum is 16K, the default is 64K, and the maximum is 4096K.

sectors	Sets the sector size to 128, 256, 512, or 1024. The default is 128.
directories	Sets the number of directory entries. The minimum is 2, the default is 64, and the maximum is 1024.

The switches for VEMM.SYS are as follows:

n	Limits the amount of expanded memory available to each DOS session. The default is 4MB, and the maximum is 32MB.

Switches for VXMS.SYS are as follows:

/XXMLIMIT = *x,y*	Sets a system-wide memory maximum to *x*K (rounded to multiples of 4), and the per DOS session maximum of *y*K. The default values are /XMMLIMIT = 4096, 1024.
/HMAMIN = *n*	Sets the minimum request size for a high memory area request to succeed, from 0K to 63K. The default is 0.
/NUMHANDLES = n	Sets the number of handles per DOS session. The minimum is 0, the default 32, and the maximum 128.
/UMB	Creates upper memory blocks.
/NOUMB	Does not create upper memory blocks.

DEVICEHIGH

The DEVICEHIGH command loads a particular DOS device driver into an upper memory block. Here's the syntax:

DEVICEHIGH *SIZE=xx drive:\path***filename** *arguments*

In the DEVICEHIGH command, the SIZE=*xx* statement establishes the amount of upper memory required by the device driver, *drive:\path\filename* represents the name of the device driver, and *arguments* can be any optional parameters you want to pass to the device driver.

DOS

The DOS command specifies that the DOS operating system will be loaded into the high memory area (HMA), and whether DOS or an application program controls upper memory blocks (UMBs). Here's the syntax:

DOS = *place,blocks*

In the DOS command, *place* can be either HIGH to load the operating system kernel into the high memory area, or LOW to load the kernel into conventional memory. The *block* parameter can be set to UMB, in which case the operating system controls the allocation of upper memory blocks, or to NOUMB, which means that applications programs can allocate upper memory blocks but cannot be located there.

FCBS

The FCBS command establishes information about file-control-blocks for DOS sessions. Here's the syntax:

FCBS = *m,n*

In the FCBS command, *m* represents the number of file-control blocks DOS can open at once, and *n* represents the number of blocks that DOS cannot close to make room for new ones.

FCBS may be needed by older programs written to run on DOS 1, but is not much used by modern programs.

FILES

The FILES command specifies the maximum number of files that a DOS session can have open at the same time. Here's the syntax:

FILES = *nnn*

where *nnn* specifies the number of files, up to a maximum of 255. This setting has no effect on OS/2 sessions, which can have up to 64,000 files open at once.

IFS

The IFS (Installable File System) command installs a file system by specifying the drive, path, and file name of the file system program. Here's the syntax:

IFS = *drive:\path***filename** */switches*

The IFS command can be used to load the HPFS or the file system used on CD-ROMs.

Switches

/CACHE:*nn*	Specifies the amount of memory for installable file system disk caching; this switch has no effect on the FAT system performance.
/AUTOCHECK:*nnn*	Specifies the drive letters (without the colon) that you want to check using CHKDSK at system startup to determine if the file system is in an inconsistent state. If a disk system stops unexpectedly, extended attributes may become detached; CHKDSK will notify you of this, and can fix some simple problems.
/CRECL:*x*	Specifies the maximum record size for caching. The minimum is 2K, the default is 4K, and the maximum is 64K.

IOPL

The IOPL (Input/Output Privilege Level) command specifies whether any OS/2 processes can issue direct input/output statements, bypassing the normal OS/2 built-in protection against writing directly to disk. Here's the syntax:

IOPL = *state*

In the IOPL command, *state* can be set to NO, to prevent direct input/output statements, or to YES, to allow such statements.

Under MS-DOS, applications are allowed to use BIOS services to write directly to specific sectors on a disk, regardless of whether those sectors are already in use by another program. OS/2 prevents this from happening in order to protect the file system; unfortunately, a number of older OS/2 applications, such as Lotus 1-2-3/G and WordPerfect for OS/2, need IOPL set to YES. So that you can run several such programs on your system, and still maintain some degree of disk protection, a third option, *list*, lets you specify the names of the executable files to which you want to grant IOPL privileges. The IOPL entry would now look like this:

IOPL=123.EXE, WP.EXE

Remember to separate each executable file name from the next with a comma.

LASTDRIVE

The LASTDRIVE command establishes the maximum number of drives for a DOS session, and has no effect in an OS/2 session. Here's the syntax:

LASTDRIVE = *x*

The *x* parameter specifies a drive letter, from A to Z, and must reflect the number of physical drives you have installed on your system.

LH

The LH (LOADHIGH) command loads terminate-and-stay resident (TSR) programs into upper memory blocks (UMB) if they are available for a DOS session. Here's the syntax:

LH *drive:\path**filename** arguments*

The *drive:\path\filename* parameter specifies the drive, directory and file name for the TSR, and *arguments* adds any additional parameters needed for the TSR. If upper memory blocks are not available DOS will automatically load the TSR into conventional memory.

LIBPATH

The LIBPATH command establishes a path to identify the location of dynamic link libraries (DLL) for OS/2. Here's the syntax:

LIBPATH = *drive:\path*

The *drive:\path* parameter establishes the path information for LIBPATH. This setting is not part of the operating system environment information, and so is not established by the SET command; nor can you view the information using SET.

When you install OS/2, the Installation program adds the following line to your CONFIG.SYS file:

LIBPATH=.;C:\OS2\DLL;C:\OS2\MDOS;C:\OS2\APPS\DLL

MAXWAIT

The MAXWAIT command establishes the length of time that a process must wait before the system assigns a higher priority. Here's the syntax:

MAXWAIT = *x*

The *x* parameter is the number of seconds, from 1 to 255, that must elapse before the priority is increased. When this time limit is reached, OS/2 raises the thread's priority to give it a chance to be processed. The system default is three seconds, and there seems to be little to suggest that it be changed.

MEMMAN

The MEMMAN command controls OS/2's use of virtual memory. Here's the syntax:

MEMMAN = *parameters*

There are several groups of parameters you can use with this command. The first group has two states, SWAP or NOSWAP. These parameters control how OS/2 uses virtual memory and tell the operating system whether it can swap data to disk if it needs more RAM. SWAP allows segment swapping and storage compaction, and NOSWAP prevents it. SWAP is the system default, and, unless you are running critical applications that process large amounts of real-time data, there is no need to change it.

The second group also has two options, MOVE and NOMOVE; these options are provided for OS/2 version 1.3 compatibility. On a floppy disk, MOVE allows storage compaction and prevents segment swapping; on a hard disk both are allowed. NOMOVE prevents storage compaction and segment swapping.

The third setting, COMMIT, is new in OS/2 version 2.1, and is intended for use on unattended machines such as file servers. It forces the system to reserve space in the swap file for all committed memory allocations. This means that an application will receive an error code if it requests more space but none is available. If you use COMMIT, increase the initial size of the swap file with the INITIAL parameter in the SWAPPATH statement. The default is NO COMMIT.

▶ S O L U T I O N

In OS/2 version 2.0, it was theoretically possible for the swap file to grow to the limits of available disk space, and for the system to run out of virtual memory and stop! OS/2 2.1 has removed this possibility by providing a new MEMMAN switch, COMMIT.

When you use COMMIT, the *minfree* value specified for SWAPPATH now indicates the amount of swap file disk space that will *always* remain free on the partition. Previously, *minfree* specified the point at which OS/2 would post a message warning that disk resources were running low.

Finally, PROTECT enables certain APIs to allocate and use protected memory; only programmers will set this to NOPROTECT, everyone else should use the default, PROTECT.

PAUSEONERROR

The PAUSEONERROR command establishes whether CONFIG.SYS processing pauses or continues if an error is encountered. Here's the syntax:

PAUSEONERROR = *state*

The *state* parameter can be either YES, in which case the system pauses, posts a message on the screen, and asks you to press a key to continue. When set to NO, you will still see an error message, but it will fly off the screen before you have a chance to read it. Leave PAUSEONERROR set to YES.

NOTE   If there is no PAUSEONERROR statement in the CONFIG.SYS file, OS/2 assumes that PAUSEONERROR = YES.

PRIORITY

The PRIORITY command establishes the priority level for all regular-class threads. Here's the syntax:

PRIORITY = *state*

The *state* parameter can be set to DYNAMIC or to ABSOLUTE. DYNAMIC, the default setting, establishes a priority dependent on the availability of system resources, while ABSOLUTE sets a rigid priority system. If your application depends on critical timing (for example, perhaps it collects a large amount of real-time data), you should change this setting to ABSOLUTE to prevent OS/2 from changing the priority level of other tasks to make sure that they run.

PRIORITY_DISK_IO

The PRIORITY_DISK_IO command establishes hard-disk priority for foreground applications. Here's the syntax:

PRIORITY_DISK_IO = *state*

state can be either YES or NO. YES establishes that foreground applications have priority over background processes. This is the default state, and usually gives the best system performance. A setting of NO specifies that all applications have the same priority, and are treated equally with respect to disk access. If you are in the habit of running large, file-intensive programs like databases or large file downloads in the background, set this to NO, to give all applications equal access to the hard disk.

PRINTMONBUFSIZE

The PRINTMONBUFSIZE command establishes the size of the parallel port device driver buffer. Here's the syntax:

PRINTMONBUFSIZE = *x, y, z*

In this command, the *x*, *y*, and *z* parameters establish the size of the buffers for LPT1, LPT2, and LPT3, respectively. The minimum and default value is 134 bytes and the maximum is 2048 bytes; use a larger buffer size for a slower printer. If you decide to change just one buffer size, for example LPT2, you must specify all three in the command, as follows:

PRINTMONBUFSIZE=134,512,134

PROTECTONLY

The PROTECTONLY command allows you to customize your operating environment. Here's the syntax:

PROTECTONLY = *state*

In this command, *state* can be set to either YES or NO. When set to NO, the default, this selects both OS/2 and DOS environments. When set to YES, it selects OS/2 sessions only; DOS sessions are not available. The only time you might set this to YES might be if you are using a computer as a dedicated file server for a LAN, and you know you will never use the machine for application programs.

PROTSHELL

The PROTSHELL command loads the OS/2 user interface and command processor. PROTSHELL can also replace the default command processor with another command processor. Here's the syntax:

PROTSHELL *drive:\path***filename** *arguments*

The *drive:\path\filename* parameter specifies the name of the existing or replacement command processor file, and *arguments* represents any additional options needed for the command processor.

The standard OS/2 workplace shell user interface requires several configuration statements in CONFIG.SYS, as follows:

PROTSHELL=C:\OS2\PMSHELL.EXE

SET USER_INI=C:\OS2\OS2.INI

SET SYSTEM_INI=C:\OS2\OS2SYS.INI

SET OS2_SHELL=C:\OS2\CMD.EXE

SET AUTOSTART=PROGRAMS,TASKLIST,FOLDERS

To establish your own file, MYFACE.EXE, as the user interface, change the first of these lines as shown, then delete the SET AUTOSTART line above to disable the OS/2 Workplace Shell.

PROTSHELL=C:\OS2\MYFACE.EXE SET USER_INI=C:\OS2\OS2.INI

SET SYSTEM_INI=C:\OS2\OS2SYS.INI

SET OS2_SHELL=C:\OS2\CMD.EXE

RMSIZE

The RMSIZE command tells a DOS session how much conventional memory is available. Here's the syntax:

RMSIZE = *xxx*

In the RMSIZE command, the *xxx* parameter represents the amount of memory available to the DOS session, from 0 to 640, where each number is equivalent to 1024 bytes or 1K. If you specify a number greater than 640K, or greater than the total amount of physical memory available if it is less than 640K, then the operating system ignores this command and calculates its own default value.

SET

The SET command is used to establish many OS/2 environment settings. Environment variables represent the current settings for many commands that OS/2 uses during the normal course of operations. Here's the syntax:

SET *variablename=command*

where *variablename* specifies the name of the environment variable you want to create, change, or delete, and *command* specifies the current contents of the variable with a string of characters, a path name, or even a file name.

SET DPATH

The DPATH command sets a search path for application programs to locate data files outside the current directory. Here's the syntax:

SET DPATH = *drive:\path*

► S O L U T I O N

You can use the SET command in CONFIG.SYS to establish an environment variable, but you can also use SET from the command prompt to look at or change a value. Type SET at the command prompt without a parameter, and OS/2 displays all the current environment variables. You can use SET to specify a new value for an environment variable if you type:

SET *variablename=command*

from the command prompt; and if you specify *variablename=* with no following *command*, as in:

SET *variablename=*

the variable name and its value will be removed from the environment.

In the DPATH command *drive:\path* specifies the drive or drives and directories to be searched for data files. DPATH is an operating system environment variable, so that application programs can access this information and can act accordingly.

SET KEYS

The KEYS command was described in detail in Chapter 12. To use CONFIG.SYS to establish KEYS, add the following to your CONFIG.SYS file:

    SET KEYS=ON

SET PATH

The PATH command sets a search path for application programs to locate program files outside the current directory. Here's the syntax:

    SET PATH = *drive:\path*

In the PATH command *drive:\path* specifies the drive or drives and directories to be searched for program files. PATH information is included as an operating system environment variable so that application programs can access this information and can act accordingly.

NOTE The PATH command only locates executable files; in a DOS session, this includes files with the filename extensions of COM, BAT, or EXE. In an OS/2 session PATH also works with the CMD filename extension.

SET PROMPT

The PROMPT command was described in detail in Chapter 12. To establish a PROMPT setting in your CONFIG.SYS file, add the line:

    SET PROMPT=*your prompt*

OS/2 uses a number of SET commands to configure the operating system. These settings are listed next, and they can usually be left at their installation defaults.

SET AUTOSTART

Starts parts of the workplace shell according to the specified options. You can customize the desktop by removing one or more options, and thus limit users' access to programs. Here's the syntax:

    SET AUTOSTART= *options*

where *options* can be one or more of the following, separated by commas:

CONNECTIONS	Recreates the network connections used when you were last logged on.
FOLDERS	Opens all folders, including the desktop
PROGRAMS	Opens all programs
TASKLIST	Opens the Window List

SET BOOKSHELF

Specifies the location of on-line documents. This setting is used by the VIEW command described in Chapter 3. Here's the syntax:

    SET BOOKSHELF=*path*

where *path* specifies the location of the documents.

S O L U T I O N

If you have an HPFS partition, you can copy all the on-line documentation onto this drive, and then change the SET commands to reflect this new location. HPFS searches will be much faster than FAT searches.

SET COMSPEC

Specifies the name of the command processor to use for OS/2 window and full-screen sessions. Here's the syntax:

    SET COMSPEC=*path*

where *path* specifies the location of the command processor. The default is to use CMD.EXE, the OS/2 equivalent of the DOS COMMAND.COM command processor.

SET DELDIR

Specifies the location and the size of directories used to store deleted files; one such directory is specified for each logical drive on your system. Here's the syntax:

> SET DELDIR=*drive:\path, maxsize; drive2:\path, maxsize*

where *drive:\path* defines the name and path for the directory (the default is DELETE), and *maxsize* specifies the maximum size that this directory can achieve. When a file is deleted in OS/2 using DEL or ERASE, or is dragged to the Shredder object on the desktop, the file is copied into this directory just in case you ever want to recover it. See Chapter 14 for more on how this environment variable works in tandem with the UNDELETE command.

SET DIRCMD

Specifies how the DIR command behaves. Here's the syntax:

> SET DIRCMD=*switches*

where *switches* can be any of the DIR command switches described in Chapter 4.

► **S O L U T I O N**

You can use any combination of DIR switches you like with DIRCMD. For example, if you use SET DIRCMD=/OGN /A /N /L in your CONFIG.SYS file, when you type the DIR command at a command prompt, you will see your directories followed by your files, both sorted into alphabetical order, and with all hidden and system files displayed. The list will be shown in the HPFS format, and will be in lower-case.

There are many variations you can use to tailor the DIR listing to your liking. For example, use /OGE to change the sort order from alphabetical order by file name to alphabetical order by file type. This change will then group your files by type, which some people find much more valuable.

SET GLOSSARY

Specifies the location for the glossary included in OS/2's on-line documentation. Here's the syntax:

    SET GLOSSARY=*drive:\path*

where *drive:\path* indicates the directory. The default setting is the OS2\HELP\GLOSS directory on the drive used to boot the system.

SET HELP

Specifies the location of OS/2's on-line help information. Here's the syntax:

    SET HELP=*drive:\path*

where *drive:\path* indicates the directory. The default is the OS2\HELP directory.

SET OS2_SHELL

Specifies the location of the OS/2 command processor. Here's the syntax:

    SET OS2_SHELL=*drive:\path*

where *drive:\path* is the location and file to use.

SET RESTARTOBJECTS

Configures how OS/2 starts back up again after being shut down. Here's the syntax:

    SET RESTARTOBJECTS=*option*

where *option* can be one of the following:

YES	Starts all objects that were running at the time you last shut down the system, as well as all objects contained in the Startup folder. This is the default.
NO	Does not start all the objects that were running at the time you last shut down the system, and does not start the objects contained in the Startup folder.
STARTUP-FOLDERSONLY	Starts only those objects contained in the Startup folder.
REBOOTONLY	Only restarts programs if the workplace shell is restarting after a Ctrl+Alt+Del. You can use this option with any of the previous three options.

SET RUNWORKPLACE

Specifies the name and location of the primary graphical user interface. Here's the syntax:

    SET RUNWORKPLACE=*drive:\path*

where *drive:\path* specifies the location. The default is PMSHELL.EXE, which runs the familiar Workplace Shell interface.

SET SYSTEM_INI

Specifies the name of the .INI configuration file to be used for the operating system settings. Here's the syntax:

    SET SYSTEM_INI=*drive:\path*

This setting defaults to OS2SYS.INI, and you won't have to change it. OS2SYS.INI controls the desktop and the folders that should appear on the desktop. See Chapter 14 for information on how to repair this file if it is ever damaged.

SET USER_INI

Specifies the file used for user-specified configuration options on the desktop. Here's the syntax:

SET USER_INI=*drive:\path*

This file controls colors and fonts on the desktop, and applications can also store custom configuration information into this file. The default is OS2.INI, and there is more information in Chapter 14 on how to repair this file if it is ever damaged.

SETBOOT

The SETBOOT command lets you set up the Boot Manager for your hard disk. Here's the syntax:

SETBOOT */switches*

Switches

/T:*x*	Specifies the number of seconds that the Boot Manager menu will stay on the screen before the default system starts running. A value of 0 seconds bypasses this menu and starts the default system running immediately.
/T:NO	Leaves the Boot Manager menu on the screen until you make a selection.
/M:*m*	Specifies the mode for the startup menu:
	m = n for normal mode
	m = a for advanced mode
	Normal mode displays only the aliases of the partitions available for selection. Advanced mode adds extra information displayed in the Boot Manager.

/Q	Queries the current startup environment, and displays the default logical disk alias, timeout value, mode, and drive letter assignments for unattended operation.
/B	Performs an orderly shutdown of the system and then restarts the system again.
/X:*x*	Sets the system startup index to indicate the partition that the Boot Manager should start, where *x* is from 0 to 3.
/N:*name*	Establishes the partition or logical drive specified in *name* as the default operating system to be booted.

SHELL

The SHELL command loads and starts the DOS command processor, COMMAND.COM, or lets you replace the default command processor with your own. Here's the syntax:

SHELL = *drive:\path***filename** *arguments*

In the SHELL command, the *drive:\path\filename* parameter defines the file that contains the command processor. The default is COMMAND.COM, but you can use your own if you wish. The *arguments* parameter sets any optional switches for this command processor.

Switches

If you use COMMAND.COM, you can use the following switch:

/P	Keeps the command processor in memory

SWAPPATH

The SWAPPATH command specifies the size and location of the virtual memory swap file. Here's the syntax:

SWAPPATH = *drive:\path minfree initial*

The *drive:\path* parameter specifies the location of the swap file, named SWAPPER.DAT, and *minfree* specifies the minimum amount of space you want to have free on the drive after the creation of the swap file. This means that the swap file can only grow to a size that leaves this amount of space free on the drive. The *minfree* value is specified in K, and can be any size, from 512K to 32767K; the default is 2048K.

The last parameter, *initial*, is new in OS/2 version 2.1, and specifies the size of the swap file initially allocated by the operating system at installation (see Table 13.1). This size depends on the amount of actual memory present in the computer when OS/2 is installed.

N O T E

For swapping to take place, you must also have the command MEMMAN=SWAP in CONFIG.SYS.

▶ **S O L U T I O N**

In OS/2 version 2.0 the *minfree* parameter specified the threshold where, if the swap file grew too large, OS/2 generated the message:

> The partition with the SWAPPER.DAT file is full.
> Please close applications or free additional space on the partition.

This message is only useful if there is someone present to see it. If it's ignored, SWAPPER.DAT can grow to the limits of available disk space, and OS/2 will stop.

In OS/2 version 2.1 the possibility of the system stopping has been removed by a slight change in the way *minfree* works when used with the new COMMIT parameter used with MEMMAN. When the MEMMAN statement includes COMMIT, as follows:

> MEMMAN=SWAP,COMMIT

the *minfree* parameter now specifies the amount of disk space that will *always* remain free. If the swap file grows to the size specified by *minfree*, OS/2 returns an error code indicating that no more memory is available to the application requesting the memory.

THREADS

The THREADS command specifies the maximum number of independent threads an OS/2 session can create at one time. Here's the syntax:

THREADS = *xxx*

In OS/2, more than one thread can exist at the same time inside a single process or application program. The *xxx* parameter specifies the maximum number of threads that can exist in an OS/2 session, from 64 (128 in version 2.0) to 4096; the default is 256. A rule of thumb quoted by IBM for setting the value of THREADS is to count three threads per running application, and then add 60 extra.

TIMESLICE

The TIMESLICE command establishes the minimum and maximum amount of processor time allocated to threads and programs in both OS/2 and DOS sessions. Here's the syntax:

TIMESLICE *x, y*

The *x* parameter establishes the minimum time, in milliseconds, that a thread can be processed before it has to yield the processor to another thread of the same priority level. This value must be a whole number greater than or equal to 32. The *y* parameter is optional and specifies the maximum time that a thread can be processed, also in milliseconds. The *y* value must be greater than or equal to the *x* value, and less than 65536.

OS/2 OS/2 OS/2

OS/2 OS/2 OS/2 OS/2 OS/2 OS/2 OS/2 OS/2

OS/2 OS/2 OS/2 O

14

Troubleshooting OS/2

OS/2 is a robust operating system, designed to handle gracefully many of the circumstances that would bring either MS-DOS or Windows crashing to their knees. But still, computers are not entirely foolproof, and a time may arrive when you have problems. That's where this chapter comes in; it covers the reasons why certain problems may occur and describes some of the proven solutions you can use to correct these problems.

OS/2 offers several elegant problem-determination commands that are normally used only under the direction of an IBM Technical Support person, and we'll look at these commands in this chapter, as well as some of the more conventional problem-solving commands like UNDELETE, RECOVER, CHKDSK and MAKEINI.

You'll see how to make a disk that will let you boot from a floppy, and you'll learn about hard disk problems and the (relatively minor) threat from computer viruses to OS/2. The chapter ends with a review of OS/2 error messages.

Don't Press Ctrl+Alt+Del!

The first troubleshooting lesson everybody has to learn about OS/2 is that when you see a problem, you don't automatically reach for the keyboard, ready to give the three-fingered salute. Pressing Ctrl+Alt+Del will reboot the whole operating system. This may have been the only way out in the MS-DOS world, but OS/2 is much more capable and robust than MS-DOS.

The first step to take when you see a problem is to remind yourself of where you are in the operating system. Are you using the desktop, or a Windows application in WIN-OS/2, or are you running a DOS full-screen session? In most cases, you can open the Window List, or get to a point where you can open the Window List, and then just close the offending session.

If an OS/2 program has a problem, you may see a window open on the desktop displaying an error number, SYS3175, along with the message:

A program in this session encountered a problem and

cannot continue.

and two options. You can choose the End Program/Command/Operation check box and return to the desktop, which is the recommended course of action, or if you are curious, you can choose the Display Register Information check box and look at the state and contents of the processor's registers. If a program consistently gives problems, display both these screens and use the Print Screen key on the keyboard to make hard copies that you can send to the technical support department of the company that supplied the program.

Because OS/2 uses all the memory installed in the computer, instead of just some of it like most MS-DOS applications, OS/2 itself has been described as a great memory-testing program. If you see many system traps during installation, or during the first few days of operation, you might begin to suspect that OS/2 is using your memory in a way that it has never been used before, and you may have a genuine memory fault.

Using the OS/2 Problem-Determination Commands

There are several OS/2 programs and commands available to help troubleshoot the operating system. These commands have been available since the early OS/2 days, because the developers of OS/2 were quite aware of the time and effort that people can expend while attempting to track down subtle software problems. They designed these commands to make their job easier.

The built-in problem-determination features in OS/2 fall into four main categories:

- **System resource analysis:** You can display current information about processes and threads, as well as system revision-level information.

- **System dumping:** Using a dump, developers can make a disk image of the entire memory of a running system, for later analysis.

- **Error logging:** Events are logged into an error-log file, also for later analysis.

- **Event tracing:** Significant changes in the state of the operating system can be tracked and analyzed.

You can use the commands that fall into the first category to find out more about how your system works, and to become familiar with the terminology used with processes and threads. The commands in the last three categories should only be used at the request—and under the direction—of a qualified IBM Technical Support person, although it is always useful to know about these commands; both how successful they are in locating problems and also how they are used. These commands can have serious effects on system performance, and they are not designed for use by the mildly curious. To make sure that all these system analysis aids are copied on to your system during OS/2 installation, you should choose either the Install All Features or the Install Preselected Features option. If you choose the Select Features and Install option, you should then select the Serviceability and Diagnostic Aids option. To install these commands at a later date, you can use the Selective Install object in the System Setup folder; just check the Serviceability and Diagnostic Aids check box, and then click on the Install button.

System Resource Analysis

There are several commands in this category, all installed as a part of the normal OS/2 installation. The AUTOFAIL command is used inside CONFIG.SYS, while PSTAT and SYSLEVEL can be used from the OS/2 command prompt.

AUTOFAIL

The AUTOFAIL command specifies how certain information about errors encountered during CONFIG.SYS processing will be displayed.

To use AUTOFAIL, add the following line to your CONFIG.SYS file:

AUTOFAIL = *state*

The AUTOFAIL command *state* can be set to NO, the default, in which case a window will open to inform you about hard system errors, or to YES, in which case you will just see an error code. Hard system errors may require the system to be reconfigured before the operating system can run correctly.

PSTAT

The PSTAT command gives you complete information on processes, threads, priority levels, system semaphores, shared memory, and dynamic library links in your system. It is very useful for providing an overall view of system activity.

You can use PSTAT from the OS/2 command prompt with the following syntax:

PSTAT */switches*

Use the PSTAT command with no switches to see information about current processes and threads, system semaphores, shared memory, and dynamic link libraries. Figure 14.1 shows part of the output from PSTAT that deals with process and thread information.

FIGURE 14.1

Process and Thread
Information in a PSTAT
Report

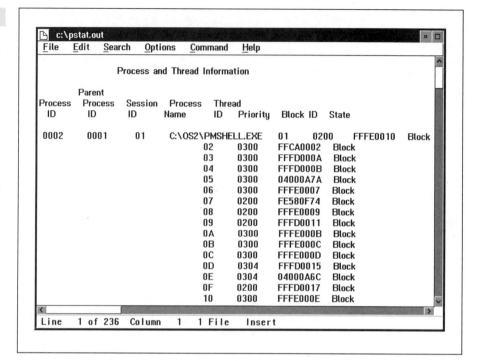

Switches

/C   Displays current process and thread information, including, for each process, the process ID number, parent process ID number, session ID number, and process name.

For each thread, the following is displayed: thread ID number, state, priority, and block ID number.

/S   Displays semaphore information for each thread, including process module name and ID number, session ID number, index number, number of references, number of requests, flag number, and semaphore name.

/L   Displays a list of the dynamic link libraries for each process, including process module name and ID number, session ID number, and library list.

/M   Displays shared memory information for each process, including handle number, selector number, number of references, and shared memory name.

/P:*id*   Displays information about the specified process, including process ID number, parent process ID number, session ID number, process module name, a list of dynamic link libraries, and shared memory name. For each thread, it also displays thread ID number, priority number and status, block ID, and owned semaphore information.

> # SOLUTION

Depending on the current state of your system, the PSTAT command can generate a large amount of information, several screens full, so it is a good idea to make PSTAT display the information one screen at a time by filtering its output through the MORE command, as follows:

PSTAT /*switches* | MORE

Alternatively, you can send the output from PSTAT to a file for later analysis by using:

PSTAT /*switches* > *filename*

Figure 14.1 was created by sending PSTAT output to a file called PSTAT.OUT which I then loaded into the OS/2 Enhanced Editor for review.

Examples

To display information on the current processes and threads in your system, type:

PSTAT /C

If you want to look at semaphore information for each thread, type:

PSTAT /S

To see information about a particular process, you must first determine the process ID number:

PSTAT /C

And then, for example if the ID number is 0002, use this number as follows:

PSTAT /P:0002

SYSLEVEL

The SYSLEVEL command displays service level information for the main parts of the OS/2 operating system.

Use SYSLEVEL from the OS/2 command prompt with the following syntax:

SYSLEVEL

The SYSLEVEL command displays the name of the directory that contains SYSLEVEL data, the name and revision level of the operating system, and the current and prior corrective service levels, as Figure 14.2 illustrates.

NOTE

A system dump is made as a troubleshooting aid when a problem is especially difficult to reproduce, and is only done at the request of a service technician or a technical support person. Once a system dump has been started, your only choices are to process the dump disks, or restart the system; you cannot abort the dump process.

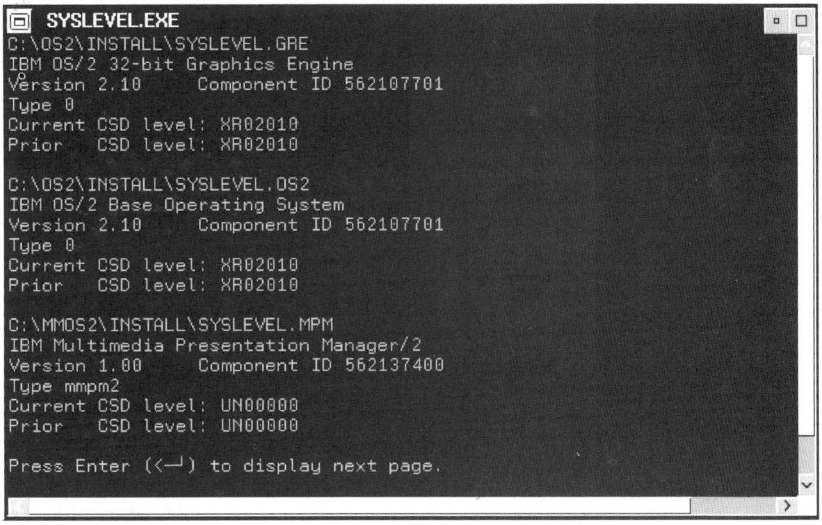

FIGURE 14.2

Output from the SYSLEVEL command shows the revision levels of the major system components

```
□ SYSLEVEL.EXE                                          ▫ □
C:\OS2\INSTALL\SYSLEVEL.GRE
IBM OS/2 32-bit Graphics Engine
Version 2.10     Component ID 562107701
Type 0
Current CSD level: XR02010
Prior   CSD level: XR02010

C:\OS2\INSTALL\SYSLEVEL.OS2
IBM OS/2 Base Operating System
Version 2.10     Component ID 562107701
Type 0
Current CSD level: XR02010
Prior   CSD level: XR02010

C:\MMOS2\INSTALL\SYSLEVEL.MPM
IBM Multimedia Presentation Manager/2
Version 1.00     Component ID 562137400
Type mmpm2
Current CSD level: UN00000
Prior   CSD level: UN00000

Press Enter (<┘) to display next page.
```

System Dumping

The system dump mechanism gives OS/2 support personnel the opportunity to capture and then examine the entire memory contents of a running system. A dump can be either asynchronous or synchronous:

- Asynchronous dumps are triggered when the user presses Ctrl+Alt+NumLock twice in quick succession, and are useful when analyzing problems associated with application programs or when the operating system hangs up. No special preparation is needed for an asynchronous dump.

- Synchronous dumps are triggered when OS/2 is appropriately configured and an application program undergoes a program trap that it chooses not to handle. To take a synchronous dump, you must add the statement TRAPDUMP=ON to your CONFIG.SYS file. This statement tells OS/2 to trigger a system dump if a Ring 3 trap occurs, and the program does not handle the trap.

N O T E

The Intel 80386/80486 processor architecture provides two broad classes of protection. One is the ability to separate tasks by giving each task a separate address space. The other protection mechanism operates within a task to protect operating-system memory objects and special processor registers from access by application programs.

Within a task, four execution privilege levels are defined, and the easiest way to visualize these levels is as four concentric circles; the innermost bull's eye is assigned privilege level 0 (the highest, or most privileged level), and the outermost circle is privilege level 3 (the lowest or least privileged level). Rings 0 and 2 are reserved for the operating system extensions, respectively. Ring 3 is not privileged and is therefore available to applications. This protection is achieved through the use of complex hardware and software contained in the processor's Memory Management Unit.

You should only add the TRAPDUMP statement to your CONFIG.SYS file when you are tracking down a specific problem. If you leave the statement installed when it is not needed and an unexpected Ring 3 trap occurs, an unnecessary system dump will be triggered, and once the dump process starts you can't stop it.

System dumps are written to a series of floppy disks, normally 1.44MB floppy disks. If your system contains 8MB of memory, and you are using 1.44MB dump disks, it will take six disks to dump the entire contents of memory. The first dump disk in a series must be created using the CREATEDD utility in OS/2.

CREATEDD formats the disk and adds two files, RASDMP.COM and DUMPDATA.001 to the disk; all the other disks used in the dump should be formatted using the OS/2 FORMAT command.

Once a dump starts, you are guided through the process step-by-step. First, you are asked to insert the disk made with CREATEDD. The system then loads the dump program from the floppy disk, and starts to copy the contents of memory onto the floppy. When this disk is full, you are prompted to insert a normally formatted floppy disk so that the process can continue. When all of memory has been dumped, you are asked to reinsert the first disk once again so that summary information can be written onto the disk. You cannot reuse a disk made by CREATEDD for another dump; you must run CREATEDD on the disk again before you can use it again.

When the dump is complete, send it off to your OS/2 technical support people for analysis.

Error Logging

Error-logging features are available to both the operating system and applications inside OS/2, and hardware and software errors are logged into a centralized error log file for later analysis by your Technical Support representative. There are three main components to the error logging system:

- **Error-logging device driver (LOG.SYS):** This device driver collects error-log information from the appropriate software modules, and forwards them to the error-logging process. There are three switches you can use with LOG.SYS:

/E:x	Specifies the size, in K, of the error-log buffer. The minimum is 4K, default is 8K, and the maximum is 64K.
/A:x	Specifies the size of the error-log device driver alert notification buffer; the minimum is 4K, the maximum is 64K, and there is no default.
/OFF	Turns off error logging as soon as the device driver is installed. Normally, error logging is on until you suspend it using the SYSLOG program.

- **Error-logging process (LOGDAEM.EXE):** The error logging process writes the entries into the error log file. Once the file reaches a user-specified limit, old entries in the file are overwritten to make room for the new entries. There are two switches for LOGDAEM.EXE:

/E:*filename*	Specifies the path and filename of the error-log file.
/W:*x*	Sets the size of the error-logging file. The default is 64K, and the minimum is 4K. If an error-log file does not yet exist, and you do not use the /W: switch, a 64K error-log file will be created.

- **Error-log formatter (SYSLOG.EXE):** The error-log formatter lets you look at and print the contents of the error log file.

To start the error-logging process running, you must add the following commands to your CONFIG.SYS file:

DEVICE = C:\OS2\LOG.SYS

RUN = C:\OS2\SYSTEM\LOGAEM.EXE

assuming your OS/2 system was installed on drive C.

When an error log file has been created on your system, you can use the SYSLOG command to look at the contents of the file. The syntax for SYSLOG is as follows:

SYSLOG *switches*

If you type SYSLOG with no parameters, the OS/2 Error Log Formatter opens, as in Figure 14.3, and you can use the menu selections in this program to manipulate the error log file, rather than using command-line switches.

SYSLOG saves error information into a file called LOG0001.DAT, unless you specify a different file name. The error log file is of a fixed size, so that at some point new entries will overwrite existing entries, starting with the oldest; this is known as "wrapping." You can use the entries in the File menu to perform the usual file-related operations, and you can use the Display Options selection from the Options menu to sort through the error log file if you are looking for a particular kind of error. The View menu contains options you can use to look at the error log file header information, as well as look at a summary of the information in the error log file.

FIGURE 14.3

SYSLOG, the Error Log Formatter, open on the LOG0001.DAT Error Log File

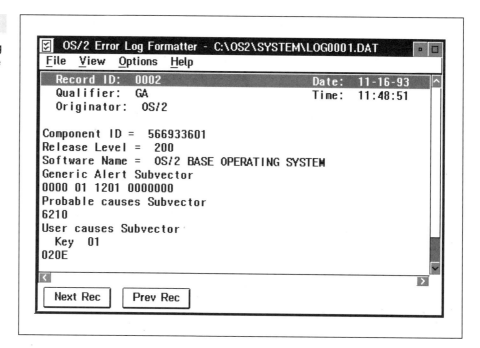

Switches

You can use the following command-line switches with SYSLOG:

/S	Suspends error logging.
/R	Restarts error logging.
/P:*filename*	Redirects error logging to the specified path and file name.
/W:*x*	Specifies the size of the error-log file; the default is 64K, the minimum is 4K.

Event Tracing

The final weapon in the OS/2 troubleshooting arsenal is event tracing. An event is any state that can be defined within a software module and that executes within a particular section of that module. Event tracing can have a considerable effect on overall system performance, and because of this, it is up to the user to specify the events to be traced. OS/2 supports two classes of function calls for event tracing:

- **Static tracepoints** are OS/2 function calls placed within a software module. Each static tracepoint is associated with a major and an optional minor trace code, and the user turns individual trace points on or off by specifying these major and minor trace codes.

- **Dynamic tracepoints** are defined within Trace Definition Files (TDF), and so are independent of the software module itself. Dynamic tracepoints can be defined for .EXE and for .DLL files, and the TDF associated with a file will have the same file name, but will have a file-name extension of .TDF.

To enable event tracing, add the following line to your CONFIG.SYS file:

TRACE=ON

TRACEBUF =*size*

where *size* is the size of the circular event buffer, in K. There is no automatic mechanism for logging events into an event file, unlike the facilities available for error logging.

To see what is happening in the trace buffer, use the TRACEFMT command from an OS/2 command prompt to open the OS/2 System Trace Formatter window. Every formatted event trace consists of three sections:

- A descriptive title identifying the event.

- A summary line containing major and minor trace codes, the PID of the process that caused the entry, and the time that the event was logged.

- One or more lines containing the actual event-specific parameters that were logged within the entry.

For more information on using event tracing, error logging or making a system dump, see your IBM technical representative.

Creating and Using an OS/2 Boot Disk

As we will see in the next few sections of this chapter, there are times when it is useful to be able to boot OS/2 from a floppy disk, especially if you are having problems accessing your hard disk, or something has gone awry with your desktop configuration files making the desktop difficult or impossible to use.

N O T E

If you think you may have to perform this operation more than once, use the DISKCOPY command to make exact copies of the installation disk and OS/2 disk #1. It is important that you use DISKCOPY so that hidden system information on the disk is copied; if you use the COPY command, this system information will not be transferred and the disks you make will not work.

One way to boot from a floppy disk is to boot up using your original OS/2 installation disk, then insert OS/2 floppy disk #1 when you are prompted for it. When you see the "Welcome to OS/2" text screen, you have the option of pressing Enter to continue with the installation, or pressing Escape to cancel the installation. Press Escape, and a moment later you will see an OS/2 command prompt on your screen. At this point, a general-purpose CONFIG.SYS file has been loaded, and you have access to the disk-partitioning program FDISK, as well as the internal OS/2 commands. As long as your hard disk is not damaged, you should be able to access it from this command prompt. As you are now running OS/2 from a disk in drive A, you can run the CHKDSK command on your hard disk (see the following section for more information on using CHKDSK), or use MAKEINI to rebuild your OS/2 system initialization files; however, for obvious reasons, you cannot use the familiar OS/2 desktop.

If you loaded OS/2 from a network, and you don't have access to the original OS/2 distribution disks, you can still create a recovery disk for yourself, by copying certain files onto a 1.44MB or 2.88MB 3.5" floppy disk. First, format a fresh floppy with OS/2 to ensure that the correct boot information is placed on the disk, then copy the file SYSINSTX.COM from the installation disk onto your hard disk and run it on the floppy by typing:

    SYSINSTX A:

Now copy the following files from the installation disk to your boot disk:

    OS2KRNLI

    OS2LDR

    OS2LDR.MSG

Rename the OS2KRNLI file as OS2KRNL, and copy these files from OS/2 disk #1 to your boot disk:

    SYSINST1.EXE

    KEYBOARD.DCP

Now copy the following files from C:\OS2\DLL to the boot disk:

    ANSICALL.DLL

    BKSCALLS.DLL

    BMSCALLS.DLL

    BVHINIT.DLL

    BVSCALLS.DLL

    DOSCALL1.DLL

    KBDCALLS.DLL

    MOUCALLS.DLL

    MSG.DLL

    NAMPIPES.DLL

    NLS.DLL

OS2CHAR.DLL

QUECALLS.DLL

SESMGR.DLL

VIOCALLS.DLL

and the following files from C:\OS2 to the boot disk:

CLOCK01.SYS

CMD.EXE

DOS.SYS

HPFS.IFS

IBM2FLPY.ADD

IBMINIT.I13

KBD01.SYS

OS2DASD.DMD

PRINT01.SYS

SCREEN01.SYS

Copy these files from the C:\OS2\SYSTEM directory:

COUNTRY.SYS

HARDERR.EXE

and the following file from C:\OS2\INSTALL:

SYSLEVEL.OS2

Use your favorite editor to create a file called ABIOS.SYS that contains nothing but a blank space on one line. This is to fool OS/2 into thinking that the file ABIOS.SYS is present. Next, create the CONFIG.SYS file show in Listing 14.1.

This CONFIG.SYS will support a basic system, and you can add other device drivers as you wish, for example a SCSI driver. The problem is that after you have copied all the files listed above onto your boot disk, there is less than 100K of spare space on a 1.44 MB floppy; enough space to add either FDISK or CHKDSK but unfortunately not enough for both.

LISTING 14.1

CONFIG.SYS for a
Boot Disk

```
IFS=HPFS.IFS /C:64
BUFFERS=32
IOPL=YES
MEMMAN=NOSWAP
PROTSHELL=SYSINST1.EXE
SET OS2_SHELL=CMD.EXE
DISKCACHE=64,LW
PROTECTONLY=YES
LIBPATH=.;A:\
PAUSEONERROR=NO
CODEPAGE=850
DEVINFO=KBD,US,KEYBOARD.DCP
DEVICE=A:\DOS.SYS
SET PATH=A:\
SET DPATH=.;A:\
SET KEYS ON
BASEDEV=IBM2FLPY.ADD
BASEDEV=IBMINIT.I13
BASEDEV=OS2DASD.DMD
BASEDEV=PRINTO2.SYS
```

Rebuilding a Damaged Desktop

OS/2 uses binary INI files (OS2.INI and OS2SYS.INI) for storing certain system and desktop configuration information, and because these files are binary files, you cannot edit them using the normal text editor as you would a Windows INI file. Several utility programs are available that you can use to look at and change the contents of these files, and one of the better programs in this class, INIMAINT, is included on the shareware disks packaged with this book.

WARNING

Do not back up the OS2.INI file before starting OS/2 for the first time; the file will not be complete.

The OS2.INI file contains system settings such as application program defaults, display options and file options, and the OS2SYS.INI file contains information on fonts and printer drivers. If your desktop is damaged, and the OS/2 INI files are corrupted, you can recreate them using the MAKEINI command. Also, if you see an OS/2 error message stating that your OS2.INI file is corrupted, you should use the MAKEINI command to recreate both INI files. MAKEINI will recover a corrupted desktop, but this process will also remove any customization you have made to the desktop since you installed OS/2 on your system.

> ## ► S O L U T I O N

To preserve the customization choices recorded in OS2.INI and OS2SYS.INI, You can create a small REXX program to make copies of these files. If you place this program in the startup folder, it will run every time you start your system. The following program maintains three copies of both the .INI files:

```
REM*****CREATE INI BACKUPS*****
C:
CD\OS2\INSTALL
REM*****COPY OS2.INI*****
COPY OS2INI.TWO OS2INI.THR
COPY OS2INI.ONE OS2INI.TWO
COPY OS2.INI OS2INI.ONE
REM*****COPY OS2SYS.INI*****
COPY OS2SYS.TWO OS2SYS.THR
COPY OS2SYS.ONE OS2SYS.TWO
COPY OS2SYS.INI OS2SYS.ONE
REM*****ALL DONE*****
```

First, boot up using an OS/2 boot disk or the original OS/2 Installation disk, and press the Escape key to get to a command prompt. Change to the OS2 directory and delete the OS2.INI and OS2SYS.INI files. In OS/2 version 2.0, you can go on to the next step, but in OS/2 version 2.1, these two files are now read-only files, and so you must use the ATTRIB command to reset the read-only bit before you can delete them, as follows:

ATTRIB –R OS2.INI

and

ATTRIB –R OS2SYS.INI

Then type:

MAKEINI OS2.INI INI.RC

followed by:

MAKEINI OS2SYS.INI INISYS.RC

to recreate the INI files. Next, delete the hidden system file WP ROOT. SF from the root directory. To make this file deletable, you must remove the hidden and system attributes. Use the ATTRIB command, as follows:

ATTRIB –H –S "WP ROOT. SF"

and then use the DEL command to delete the file. Now remove any floppy disks from drive A and press Ctrl+Alt+Del to reboot the computer from the usual startup drive. Your desktop will be reinstalled to its initial installation setup. As soon as the desktop is rebuilt on your system, use the Shut Down command and restart the system again.

Backing up the Desktop

It is a good idea to make backups of the two OS/2 system INI files from time to time. They only change when you alter the printer setup information or change something on the desktop, so you don't have to back them up every day. However, if you use the COPY, BACKUP, or XCOPY commands on these files with OS/2 version 2.0, you will be rewarded with the message:

SYS0032: The process cannot access the file because

it is being used by another process.

0 file(s) copied.

This is because the files are locked as soon as the desktop starts, then kept open at all times, and open files cannot be copied.

S O L U T I O N

If you have an IBM Internal Tape Backup Unit, a 6157 Streaming Tape, an IBM 4 mm or 8 mm tape drive, or an IBM 128MB Rewritable Optical disk drive, you can use version 1.35 (or later) of the SYTOS Plus File Backup Manager (part number 53G0927) to back up OS2.INI and OS2SYS.INI.

One way to solve this problem is to boot up using the OS/2 boot disk described above, then copy these two files, and when the copy is complete, reboot your computer. This is not a particularly elegant solution, and fortunately there is a better way. Add the following line to your CONFIG.SYS file:

```
RUN=C:\OS2\CMD.EXE /S XCOPY.EXE C:\OS2\OS2*.INI C:\OS2\*.IN1
```

Because CONFIG.SYS runs very early in the boot-up process, this RUN command can invoke an OS/2 command processor to make the XCOPY command copy the two files. Granted, you now have two copies of these files in the same directory, and they will be recopied each time you boot up your system, but you can now manually copy them to a floppy disk without having to reboot because these copies are not locked.

If you want to be doubly safe, you can add another RUN statement to CONFIG.SYS so that you end up with two copies of the INI files, each a generation apart:

```
RUN=C:\OS2\CMD.EXE /S XCOPY.EXE C:\OS2\OS2*.IN1 C:\OS2\*.IN2
RUN=C:\OS2\CMD.EXE /S XCOPY.EXE C:\OS2\OS2*.INI C:\OS2\*.IN1
```

This will allow you to go back one previous configuration; if this still isn't enough, add more RUN statements to your CONFIG.SYS file until you are happy. Just remember to enter the statements in reverse order so that the IN4 file is copied on to the IN5 file, before the IN3 file is copied on top of the IN4 file, and so on.

Backing up these files is much easier in OS/2 version 2.1; changes have been made to allow you to copy these files any time you like. To make a backup copy, assuming you installed OS/2 on drive C, place a floppy disk in drive A, and type:

    COPY OS2.INI A:

followed by:

    COPY OS2SYS.INI A:

and keep the floppy disk in a safe place. You can use the XCOPY command in place of COPY if you prefer.

Using the RECOVER Command

The RECOVER command recovers data from a file on a disk with bad sectors, or reconstructs all the files on a disk with a corrupted directory structure. You can use RECOVER to retrieve those portions of a file that can still be read, but it is important to remember that no data is recovered from the bad sectors themselves. RECOVER can only recover those portions of the file stored in the readable sectors on the disk; the other information is lost forever. For this reason, there is absolutely no point running the RECOVER command on program files; the program will never run correctly if a chunk of the file is missing. It is sometimes worth using RECOVER on long text files.

The RECOVER command is issued from the OS/2 command prompt with the following syntax:

RECOVER *drive:\path***filename**

OR

RECOVER ***drive:***

In the first syntax, *drive:* specifies the drive that contains the file you want to recover, and *path\filename* specifies the file you want to recover. The second syntax specifies that the entire drive be recovered.

RECOVER saves what information it can from the damaged files, and stores the results in consecutive files beginning with FILE0001.REC. Any HPFS extended attributes are saved in consecutively numbered files named EA0000.REC. When you recover the files, OS/2 rebuilds the structure of the disk from scratch. You now have to examine these files one by one to see what, if anything, can be salvaged.

Because the RECOVER command locks the disk it is working on so that no other processes can access the disk at the same time, you cannot recover the disk that contains the RECOVER command, or the boot disk used to start OS/2.

To recover files on the drive that you use to start OS/2, you must first boot using an OS/2 boot disk or the original OS/2 Installation disks.

If you are using the HPFS, make sure you use the RECOVER command from an OS/2 session so that any extended attributes will be saved properly.

Also, when RECOVER is run on a disk containing the HPFS, files are recovered, but not the entire disk. RECOVER initially attempts to use the original file name, but if this is impossible, it uses the convention FILE*nnnn*.REC. A damaged sector in the middle of a file will be filled with zeros in the recovered file to preserve the original file size.

The RECOVER command cannot work on drives with ASSIGN, JOIN, or SUBST commands in effect, and the command does not work on network drives.

Recovering Lost Folders on the Desktop

WARNING　　You should only use this technique if a particular folder is no longer accessible from the desktop.

The power and flexibility of the desktop make it possible to move a folder to a place from which you cannot access it any more. Technical support people tell apocryphal stories of users moving the OS/2 System folder into the Drives folder, closing the drives folder and being unable to access the System folder. Recovery just becomes a problem of organization; just remember that folders on the desktop are the same as subdirectories at the OS/2 command line.

NOTE　　In OS/2 version 2.0, the desktop directory was called C:\OS!2_2.0_D if you were using the FAT, or C:\OS2 2.0 Desktop if you were using the HPFS.

When you install OS/2, the desktop is represented by the directory C:\DESKTOP. If you list the contents of this directory, you will find that it contains several subdirectories, depending on your OS/2 installation choices:

TEMPLATE

MINIMIZE

INFORMAT

NETWORK

```
DOS_PROG

OS!2_SYS

WIN-OS!2

OS!2_PRO
```

These names are for the FAT file system. If you use the HPFS, you will see very similar names, but the names will be longer and less cryptic because the HPFS is not constrained by the FAT "8.3" naming convention. For example, the FAT INFORMAT directory is called Information in the HPFS.

Notice that some of these directory names match the names of the folders on your desktop. If you look at the subdirectories inside the OS!2_SYS directory, you will see several names that correspond to names in the System folder, including these:

```
DRIVES

STARTUP

SYSTEM_S

COMMAND_

GAMES

PRODUCTI
```

Again, these are FAT names; HPFS names will be longer; for example, SYSTEM_S becomes System Setup, and PRODUCTI becomes Productivity. If any of these folders get out of whack, you can use the MOVE command to put them back where they should be located. To move a displaced folder or directory, for example the GAMES folder, change to the directory that currently contains the GAMES folder, then type:

```
MOVE GAMES C:\DESKTOP\OS!2_SYS
```

to move this folder back to the desktop. If you use the HPFS, the command becomes:

```
MOVE GAMES C:\DESKTOP\OS!2 SYSTFM
```

Rebuilding the Command Prompts Folder

If you lose your Command Prompts folder, it becomes very difficult to start a DOS or OS/2 window session. Fortunately, it is a relatively simple procedure to recreate the Command Prompts folder on the desktop.

Open the Templates folder and drag the folder template to the desktop. Hold down the Alt key and click the left mouse button on this folder, and change its name to Command Prompts. Hold down the Alt key and press the mouse button when you are done. Now drag the Program template from the Template folder to your new Command Prompts folder, and change its icon name to DOS Window.

N O T E

Just use the right mouse button to drag the Program template to the new Command Prompts folder.

Open the DOS Window Settings notebook at the Program tab, and enter an asterisk (*) into the Path and File Name field. This tells OS/2 that you want to create a command prompt. In the Session tab, select the DOS Window, then double-click on the title-bar icon to close the Settings notebook. Repeat the process for an OS/2 Window, OS/2 Full Screen, and a DOS Full Screen. Then make another DOS Full Screen object, open the Settings notebook at the Session page, and click on the DOS Settings button. Select the DOS_STARTUP_DRIVE setting and enter A:. Then, change the name of this object to DOS From Drive A. The final step in the process is to make another DOS Full Screen Object, but this time, instead of typing an asterisk into the Path and File Name field, type WINOS2.COM, and change the name of the object to WIN-OS/2 Full Screen. It takes longer to describe this process than to actually do it; it might take you all of five minutes.

Recovering Deleted Files

OS/2 includes a feature that delays the permanent removal of files, giving you the chance to change your mind about deleting them. The files are not deleted immediately, but are copied to a special directory where they are held for a period of time. You can recover files from this directory by using the UNDELETE command.

But before you can use UNDELETE to recover deleted files, you must have a DELDIR command in your CONFIG.SYS file, as follows:

SET DELDIR = *drive1:\path, maxsize; drive2:\path, maxsize*

for each drive you want to protect. DELDIR establishes a directory for each of the specified drives, into which files are copied when you delete them.

S E C R E T

When you install OS/2, the SET DELDIR command shown above has a REM statement in front of it, effectively disabling it. Use the OS/2 Enhanced Editor to remove the REM from the line in CONFIG.SYS, save the file, shut down OS/2 and restart your system. You will now be able to use the undelete features of OS/2.

Files are only removed from this special directory on an as-needed basis, when the number of deleted files exceeds the maximum size of the directory, and they are removed in first-in, first-out sequence.

The syntax for the UNDELETE command is as follows:

UNDELETE *drive:\path\filename/switches*

You can use the UNDELETE command to recover the deleted file called *filename*. If you do not specify a filename, all the deleted files in the current directory will be restored.

Using UNDELETE is fine for recovering a few files deleted by accident, but is no substitute for a well thought out, comprehensive, backup system.

Switches

You can use the following switches with the UNDELETE command.

/L   Lists files that could be recovered but does not undelete any files.

/S   Includes all files in the specified directory and all subdirectories.

/A   Recovers all available deleted files without waiting for confirmation.

/F   Specifies that a file or files be permanently deleted so that they cannot be recovered.

Fixing Hard Disk Problems

The CHKDSK command is provided in OS/2 as a disk-analysis tool. When you run CHKDSK on a HPFS hard disk, you will see a report like this one:

The type of file system for the disk is HPFS

The HPFS file system program has been started

CHKDSK is searching for lost data

CHKDSK has searched 100% of the disk

xxxxx kilobytes total disk space

xxxxx kilobytes are in *xx* directories

xxxxx kilobytes are in *xx* user files

xxxxx kilobytes are in extended attributes

xxxxx kilobytes are reserved for system use

xxxxx kilobytes are available for use

In this display *system use* includes all sectors used by the HPFS for volume management, including node entries (which are similar to FAT entries), free-space bitmaps, hotfix sectors, and will represent a certain percentage of hard disk or volume size.

WARNING

On a dual-boot system, you should be careful if you use OS/2 and MS-DOS applications on the same file—for example, if you use an MS-DOS editor and the Enhanced Editor to look at or make changes to a text file. When OS/2 opens the file, it creates extended attributes that MS-DOS applications cannot understand or update. If you open the file with an MS-DOS editor, the extended attributes may no longer be associated properly with the original file; and as a result, CHKDSK will report extended attribute errors for the file.

When you include the /F switch, CHKDSK can also fix certain disk errors known as *lost clusters*. These are parts of files that the operating system did not save properly for some reason; they are unusable as lost clusters and they occupy valuable disk space. If CHKDSK finds lost clusters on your disk, it asks whether to convert them into files. If you answer Yes, CHKDSK converts the lost clusters into files so that you can examine their contents and delete them if they are not needed. The files created by CHKDSK are stored in the root directory of the disk and are named FILE*nnn*.CHK, where *nnn* is a number beginning at 0000. If errors occur in a file that contains extended attributes, CHKDSK recovers these lost clusters into files named EA*nnnn*.CHK. If you answer No, CHKDSK deletes the lost clusters without further ado.

If you want to run CHKDSK on the hard disk you normally use to start OS/2, you will have to boot using the boot disk described above, or use the original OS/2 Installation disks to get to a command prompt; you cannot run CHKDSK to fix hard disk problems on the disk that actually contains the CHKDSK program.

WARNING

If you use a file utility on either a FAT or an HPFS hard disk, check that it is OS/2-compatible before you use it. Even though the OS/2 FAT file system is compatible with the MS-DOS FAT system, it is not identical, and what works in the MS-DOS world may not work in the OS/2 FAT system.

GammaTech of Edmond, Oklahoma, offers a set of 32-bit utilities written specifically for OS/2 that handle all sorts of utility tasks. Contact them at PO Box 70, Edmond, OK 73083, telephone 405-359-1219 and fax 405-359-7391.

One problem that received much attention in the MS-DOS world in recent years that HPFS users do not have to worry about is file fragmentation. Many utility programs included in packages such as the Norton Utilities, PC Tools, the Mace Utilities were designed to defragment files by rewriting them into single contiguous areas of disk space. Files managed by the HPFS do not fragment to the point of causing any system delays.

A similar topic that has ceased to be a problem recently (and not just for HPFS users) is that of the hard disk interleave factor. *Interleaving* is the process of arranging the sectors on a hard disk track to optimize the data transfer rate. There was a period in the late 1980s when disk manufacturers wrongly configured many disks, and so utility programs were written to rearrange the interleave factor in an attempt to speed up hard disk operations.

Modern hard disks are aready interleaved to the point that they provide data rates that leave these older drives standing in the dust, so there is just no point in changing the interleave factor. In fact, some IDE drives can actually be damaged by changing the interleave factor.

Viruses and OS/2

► S O L U T I O N

McAfee Associates are the premier virus detecting company, and they provide shareware virus detection and eradication programs. Contact them using their bulletin board at 408-988-4004, fax at 408-970-9727, or phone at 408-988-3832, or on CompuServe through the McAfee Virus Help Forum (Go MCAFEE). You will also find their OS/2 virus detection programs on the disks included with this book.

Much is made in the MS-DOS and Windows world of computer viruses, and to date 865 different viruses have been identified, with a total of approximately 1561 different variants or strains. All these known viruses affect some combination of the hard disk partition table, the boot sector, and one or more executable files on the disk.

So far, no OS/2 specific viruses have been identified; however, it is possible that an MS-DOS or Windows virus could infect an OS/2 system. Because of the way OS/2 is designed, it is likely that such an infection would be confined to that specific session, and would not affect the whole system. Many viruses work by low-level disk accesses, and because OS/2 prohibits such access serious infection is highly unlikely. You should still take the usual precautions with floppy disks and refuse to use software of completely unknown origin.

OS/2 Service Paks and Bug Fixes

One of the major advantages of belonging to CompuServe or using the IBM National Support Center bulletin board is that you will see when Service Paks become available; they are often posted in their own IBM OS/2 forum on CompuServe. Service Paks contain a collection of fixes in a form you can apply to your system. They are made available through the normal IBM channels, and you can also download using a modem and communications software. They are often quite large, and so can take a long time to download; for example, a Service Pak released for OS/2 2.0 during 1992 contained fifteen 1.44MB floppy disks.

If you work with IBM in tracking down and fixing a specific problem, they may provide a patch and ask you to install it on your system. A patch is a method of changing program code by editing it from the keyboard, rather than recompiling and redistributing the whole operating system. And yes, the command you use for this purpose is called PATCH.

PATCH

The PATCH command lets you make IBM-supplied changes or patches to existing software. Most people will never need to use this command. You should only use it when you understand *exactly* what you are doing when you change the contents of an executable file. It only takes one error to make a program completely unusable.

Use the following syntax with the PATCH command:

PATCH *path*filename /A

where *path\\filename* specifies the name and path of the file you want to patch. If you are implementing an IBM-supplied patch, add the /A switch and the patch will be applied and verified automatically. If you do not specify the /A switch, PATCH guides you through the whole process interactively. First you are asked to provide a hexadecimal offset to indicate where the patch should be made. PATCH displays the contents of the

16 bytes associated with that location, with the cursor positioned on the first byte. You can enter one or two hexadecimal digits to change the contents of this byte, or use the space bar to leave this byte unchanged and move on to the next byte. Patching continues until you press the Enter key; then OS/2 asks if you want to continue. Press Y (yes) to continue, and PATCH prompts you for another offset. When all the patches have been entered, OS/2 displays them on your screen and asks if they should be applied. If you answer Yes, they are written to the disk file in the order in which they were entered.

If you answer No, you can correct any mistakes before continuing.

Switches

The following PATCH switch is available:

/A   Tells the PATCH command to patch the file automatically; if /A is omitted, the file will be patched interactively.

Examples

To apply an IBM-supplied patch to the file OS2PROG.EXE, type:

PATCH OS2PROG.EXE /A

Remember, all offsets and patches must be entered in hexadecimal.

OS/2 Error Messages

When you type something at an OS/2 command prompt that the operating system does not understand, you will see an error message on the screen:

SYS 1041: The name specified is not recognized as an

internal or external command, operable program or batch file.

This is a much more helpful message than MS-DOS's terse equivalent:

Bad command or filename

Under other circumstances OS/2 is even more helpful. If you use an OS/2 window session, and try to copy a file onto a write-protected disk, you will see an error window open on the desktop. The error is described in plain English at the top of the window, and there are three check boxes you can use to tell OS/2 what to do next to recover from the error.

There are literally hundreds of error messages in OS/2, and if the message text does not adequately describe the error conditions and what you can do to correct the situation, you can ask for further help on the message by typing HELP followed by the error number. For example, to see more on the SYS1041 message, type:

HELP 1041

and you will see the text shown in Figure 14.4. This additional information is available from both OS/2 and DOS-session command prompts.

One kind of error message you can't do much about is when an internal processing error halts the whole OS/2 operating system and you see a screen full of hexadecimal numbers referring to a trap 000d, as in Listing 14.2

Fortunately, this kind of halt error is extremely rare. It may occur when something goes badly wrong with your hard disk or system memory; a

FIGURE 14.4

Additional help information is available

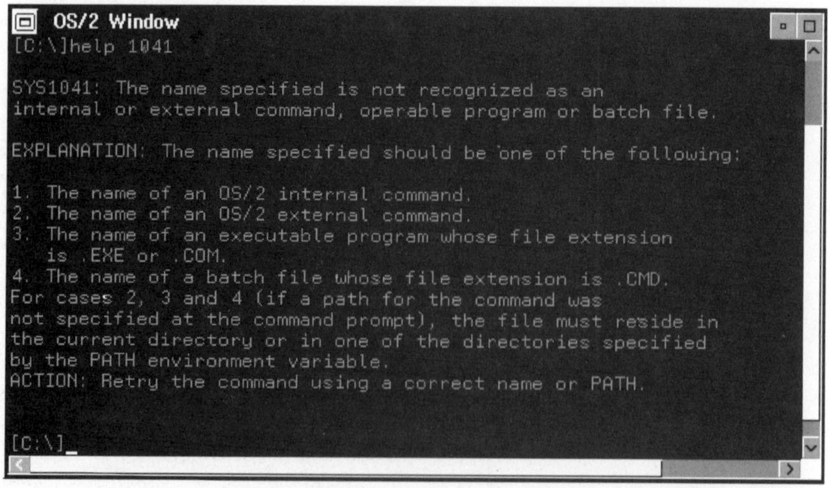

LISTING 14.2

An example of an
Internal Processing Error

```
TRAP 000d    ERRCD=0e60 ERACC=**** ERLIM=********

EAX=7d350104 EBX=00000362 ECX=ff080000 EDX=ffe20e60

ESI=7d230362 EDI=0000037e EPB=00035e3a FLG=00012202

CS:EIP=0148:00000e24 CSACC=009b CSLIM=0000854a

SS:ESP=0030:00005e30 SSACC=1097 SSLIM=00004f4f

DS=0400      DSACC=0093   DSLIM=000070c0    CR0=8001001b

ES=0158      ESACC=c093   ESLIM=ffffffff    CR2=fff8abd0

FS=03b8      FSACC=0093   FSLIM=00000023

GS=0000      GSACC=****   GSLIM=********



The system detected an internal processing

error at location ##0160:fff60967 - 000d:9967.

60000, 9084


048600b4

Internal revision *.***, 93/04/01


The system is stopped.  Record the location number

of the error and contact your service representative.
```

memory hardware parity error can trigger a trap. Record the salient information (that is, the error's location) so that you can pass it on to your IBM technical representative, and then power down and restart your computer. Pressing the reset button or using Ctrl+Alt+Del will probably not be sufficient to restart your system again.

PART V

Advanced OS/2 Topics

CHAPTERS

OS/2 OS/2 OS/2

OS/2 OS/2 OS/2 OS/2 OS/2 OS/2 OS/2 OS/2

OS/2 OS/2 OS/2 O

15

Networking and OS/2

OS/2 OS/2 OS/2 OS/2 OS/2 OS/2 OS/2 OS/2 OS/2 OS/

ONE of the largest growth areas in computing is the connection of individual PCs into local area networks, or LANs. LANs are providing the basis for important business applications, often based on client-server technology, and in many corporate environments the LAN is seen as a replacement for the mainframe, particularly as proprietary systems such as databases are replaced by industry-standard SQL (structured query language) databases.

As companies continue to assess their data-processing needs, there is much talk of *downsizing*, that is, converting applications from mainframes to run on networks of smaller computers, often PCs. A more accurate term might be *rightsizing* instead. A collection of appropriately configured PCs, networked together, can provide more than 10 times the power for the same cost as a mainframe supporting remote terminals.

Networks allow many users to share resources such as file servers, printers, and communications hardware, and can be connected using three main arrangements or *topologies*: a bus, a star, or a ring. Connections can be made using coaxial cable, twisted-pair wiring, or even (at least partially) without wires, and many different protocols have been developed over the years to allow computers to communicate.

This chapter primarily addresses the network administrator, although the network user will also find much of interest. We'll look at using your OS/2 system with networks in general, before concentrating on one of the industry's most popular network operating systems, Novell NetWare. We'll review several other network systems, and we'll look at OS/2-to-mainframe connection methods in the context of distributed SQL database applications.

Using OS/2 with a Network

N O T E

OS/2 supports all major network connections except AppleTalk (LocalTalk) and ARCnet; you can access these two protocols by means of a bridge into the network in which OS/2 is being used.

OS/2 has many key networking features already built into the operating system, and it uses an add-on software package called a *requester* to access a specific network. A requester is software loaded into OS/2 on the workstation that requests services from the network.

S E C R E T

You don't have to stop at one requester; you can load more than one requester at a time if you have to access more than one type of network; for example, you could load both a Novell NetWare requester and an IBM LAN Server requester.

Requesters use varying amounts of memory depending on the network you are attached to, but the general OS/2 rule "the more memory, the better" certainly applies here, too. You should plan to install at least 8MB of memory on a networked OS/2 workstation.

OS/2 makes accessing the network and using network resources as simple as possible. A folder on the desktop provides access to the network, and once you have logged into the network, you can access network drives, files, and network printers as though they were local.

N O T E   See Chapter 9 for more information on printing from a network.

All the usual desktop object-manipulation techniques are available. Once you've placed network resources on the desktop (or in any folder), you can open those objects, move, copy, and drag-and-drop them, create shadows of them, and change their settings. You can even associate an application on the network with a data file on your workstation or on the file server; the only restriction is that you must have the appropriate read/write permission for the file or drive.

OS/2 and Novell NetWare both support a special kind of communications protocol known as *Named Pipes*. A Named Pipe is a software connection between a client and a server, and the protocol includes a relatively easy-to-use API that lets programmers create inter-program communications using routines very similar to those used in normal operations for disk-file opening, reading, and writing.

Accessing Novell NetWare

Given Novell NetWare's preeminent position as the leader in PC network operating systems, it was vitally important that OS/2 be able to function as a workstation in a NetWare environment.

S O L U T I O N

You can order the OS/2 NetWare Requester from either Novell or IBM; there is a small charge. To order from IBM, call 800-3IBMOS2 and ask for the NetWare Workstation Kit for OS/2. To order from Novell, call 800-UPDATE1 and ask for the NetWare Requester for OS/2 2.

The OS/2 workstation must have a supported network interface card, as well as the appropriate device driver for the board. Interface cards are available from Novell, IBM, and other third-party vendors, and several are listed in Table 15.1. Micro Channel Architecture (MCA) and Industry-Standard Architecture (ISA) boards are available.

Supported network adapters include Ethernet, IBM PC Network, Token-Ring, and 3174 Peer Communications Network. The vast majority of connections used with OS/2 will be either Ethernet or Token-Ring.

TABLE 15.1: Network Interface Cards supported by OS/2 Requester

INTERFACE CARD	NETWORK TYPE	WORKSTATION BUS TYPE	LINK DRIVER NAME
3COM 3C523	Ethernet	MCA	3C523.SYS
3COM 3C501	Ethernet	ISA	3C501.SYS
3COM 3C505	Ethernet	ISA	3C505.SYS
IBM Token Ring Adapter	Token Ring	MCA/ISA	TOKEN.SYS
IBM PC Network Adapter II and IIA	Ethernet	MCA/ISA	PCN2L.SYS
Novell NE/2	Ethernet	MCA	NE2.SYS
Novell NE/2-32	Ethernet	MCA	NE2-32.SYS
Novell NE1000	Ethernet	ISA	NE1000.SYS
Novell NE2000	Ethernet	ISA	NE2000.SYS
Novell NE2100	Ethernet	ISA	NE2100.SYS

You prepare the file server and the OS/2 workstation in two separate steps that you can perform relatively independently, although you obviously must complete both steps before you can log on to the network from the workstation. We'll look at preparing the workstation first.

Preparing the OS/2 Workstation

NOTE The NetWare Workstation Kit supports NetWare version 2.2, NetWare version 3.11, and NetWare for AIX, and its documentation assumes that you have an understanding of basic networking terms and concepts.

Once you have obtained a copy of the OS/2 NetWare Requester, installation is straightforward. Insert the Requester disk into a floppy disk drive, open the Drives object in the OS/2 System folder on the desktop, and double-click on the Install object. Alternatively, you can go to an OS/2 command prompt, make the floppy drive the current drive, and type INSTALL.

Either way, the NetWare Requester for OS/2 Installation Utility window opens on the desktop. The Help menu in this window works as you would expect, and there is additional information accessible from the ReadMe! menu. ReadMe! lets you review any text files containing information about this version of the Requester package. It is always wise to check these text files for late-breaking news that may not have made it into the written documentation. Select the Requester on Workstation option from the Installation menu to begin the installation process.

NOTE To configure a previously installed requester, use This Workstation from the Configuration menu.

In the next dialog box, enter the path information where you want to install the requester, and confirm the Source Drive from which you plan to load it. The default directory is C:\NETWARE.

You will then see three installation options in the Requester Installation window:

- **Edit CONFIG.SYS and Copy Files** is the option that most people will choose. It copies all the appropriate files into the directory you specified on your hard disk, and then makes additions to your CONFIG.SYS file to support the selections you make during the installation process.

- **Only Edit CONFIG.SYS** changes your CONFIG.SYS, but does not copy the requester files onto your hard disk.

- **Only Copy Files** just copies the files onto your hard disk.

Next, the Select Options for CONFIG.SYS window shown in Figure 15.1 opens, so you can choose the networking elements your applications need from the following:

- **Network Interface Card Driver** lets you choose the name of the device driver associated with your network adapter. If you want to install a third-party driver not shipped with the requester, click in the LAN Driver text field and enter the file name of the driver. A dialog box opens so you can enter the appropriate drive letter.

- **SPX Support for OS/2 Sessions**. Click on this box if you want to use network printing, Named Pipes, or applications that use the SPX protocol.

- **NetBIOS Emulation for OS/2 Sessions**. Check this box if your applications use the NetBIOS protocol. Don't choose this option if you are already running NetBIOS on this workstation.

- **NetWare Support for DOS and Windows Applications**. Check this option if you want to access the network from a DOS or WIN-OS/2 session running in a VDM.

FIGURE 15.1

The Select Options For
CONFIG.SYS window

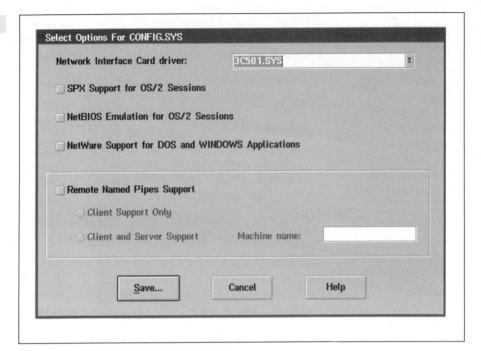

If you want to use Named Pipes, you will have to check the Remote
Named Pipes Support check box, and then choose between Client Support Only and Client and Server Support. If you choose Server, enter a
server name of up to 16 characters.

Make your selections and then click on the Save button; then choose the
Copy button to start transferring files onto your hard disk. To complete
the requester installation on your system, use Shut Down from the
desktop, and then restart your system again. This ensures that the
changed CONFIG.SYS file is used. You will see several additional startup
messages on your screen as you restart your system; they are just the
load messages from the requester and are quite normal.

Looking at CONFIG.SYS

Listing 15.1 shows the part of a typical CONFIG.SYS file that is prepared
by the requester installation program. These entries are specific to both a
particular workstation and a particular file server; however, if all your

```
REM
DEVICE=C:\NETWARE\LSL.SYS
RUN=C:\NETWARE\DDAEMON.EXE
DEVICE=C:\NETWARE\3C523.SYS
DEVICE=C:\NETWARE\IPX.SYS
REM DEVICE=C:\NETWARE\SPX.SYS
REM RUN=C:\NETWARE\SPDAEMON.EXE
REM DEVICE=C:\NETWARE\NMPIPE.SYS
REM DEVICE=C:\NETWARE\NPSERVER.SYS
REM RUN=C:\NETWARE\NPDAEMON.EXE np_servername
DEVICE=C:\NETWARE\NWREQ.SYS
IFS=C:\NETWARE\NWIFS.IFS
RUN=C:\NETWARE\NWDAEMON.EXE
REM DEVICE=C:\NETWARE\NETBIOS.SYS
REM RUN=C:\NETWARE\NBDAEMON.EXE
DEVICE=C:\NETWARE\VIPX.SYS
DEVICE=C:\NETWARE\NWSPOOL.EXE
REM
```

workstations use exactly the same network adapter card, and you only
have one file server, the same CONFIG.SYS entries will work on all
workstations on the network. Some options may not be used on your system, and these options will be preceded by a REM statement so that they
cannot be accessed. If at some point in the future, you want to change
your configuration, use This Workstation from the Configuration menu in
the requester installation program.

As there are only a few statements in this part of an OS/2 CONFIG.SYS
file, we can look at each statement individually:

- **DEVICE=C:\NETWARE\LSL.SYS** loads the Link Support
  Layer driver required by Novell's Open Datalink Interface (ODI)
  model. This device driver must be active for the requester to work,
  and it must be loaded before any other NetWare driver.

- **RUN=C:\NETWARE\DDAEMON.EXE** runs a small daemon
  program, which also must be active for the requester to run. A
  daemon is a background program that runs unattended, without
  user interaction, collecting information or performing system administrative tasks. Another example of an OS/2 daemon is the
  LOGDAEM error-logging process described in Chapter 14.

- **DEVICE=C:\NETWARE\3C523.SYS** loads a small device driver specific to the network interface card installed in your workstation; this example is for the 3Com 3C523 Ethernet adapter; if you have a Token-Ring adapter, this entry will be C:\NETWARE\TOKEN.SYS. Manufacturers of the network adapters provide this software customized for the specific model of adapter card, and it interacts with the Link Support Layer driver described above.

- **DEVICE=C:\NETWARE\IPX.SYS** loads support for the Novell IPX (Internet Packet Exchange) communications protocol, used to move data between the workstation and the file server. IPX packets are encapsulated and carried by the packets used in Ethernet and similar data frames used in Token-Ring networks.

- **DEVICE=C:\NETWARE\SPX.SYS** loads support for the Novell SPX (Sequenced Packet Exchange) communications protocol. SPX adds an enhanced set of commands implemented on top of IPX, and includes guaranteed packet delivery.

- **RUN=C:\NETWARE\SPDAEMON.EXE** runs an SPX daemon process.

- **DEVICE=C:\NETWARE\NMPIPE.SYS** loads the OS/2 support needed for the workstation to operate as a Named Pipes client.

- **DEVICE=C:\NETWARE\NPSERVER.SYS** loads the support needed for the workstation to operate as a Named Pipes server. Both DEVICE=C:\NETWARE\NMPIPE.SYS and DEVICE=C:\NETWARE\NPSERVER.SYS must appear in CONFIG.SYS to enable Named Pipes server support.

- **RUN=C:\NETWARE\NPDAEMON.EXE** *np_servername* runs the Named Pipes daemon, and includes the name of the file server as a parameter.

- **DEVICE=C:\NETWARE\NWREQ.SYS** loads the actual requester module. This line should follow lines that include support for IPX, SPX, or Named Pipes, because the requester should be loaded after these lower-level networking elements.

- **IFS=C:\NETWARE\NWIFS.IFS** loads support for the installable file system for the network, so that the workstation can access the network file server or servers in the same way as it can access local disks.

- **RUN=C:\NETWARE\NWDAEMON.EXE** loads the daemon process for the requester. This statement must appear after the

  IFS=C:\NETWARE\NWIFS.IFS

  statement in CONFIG.SYS.

- **DEVICE=C:\NETWARE\NETBIOS.SYS** loads support for NetBIOS. NetBIOS (Network Basic Input/Output System) is a layer of software originally developed by IBM and Sytek to establish communications between workstation on a network. Today, many vendors either provide a version of NetBIOS to interface with their hardware or to emulate its communications services in their network products.

- **RUN=C:\NETWARE\NBDAEMON.EXE** loads the NetBIOS daemon.

- **DEVICE=C:\NETWARE\VIPX.SYS** loads support for the multiple virtual DOS machine environment and must be present if you want to run the NetWare DOS-based utilities such as PRINTCON and SYSCON.

- **DEVICE=C:\NETWARE\SPOOL.EXE** loads the network spooler, needed if you want to print to the NetWare network printer queue.

To make sure that your OS/2 sessions find the OS/2 versions of the NetWare utilities before they find the MS-DOS versions (they both have the same filenames), you should change your path so that it includes *drive*:\PUBLIC\OS2 at the beginning of the path statement, where *drive* is the file server drive letter.

In an OS/2 DOS session, you want the opposite to happen; you want to access the DOS versions rather than the OS/2 versions. Add a similar path statement into the file you are using as the AUTOEXEC.BAT startup file for the session. See the description of the new OS/2 version 2.1 DOS setting DOS_AUTOEXEC in Chapter 6 for information on how to configure an OS/2 DOS session.

Adding OS/2 Name Space Support

NetWare supports workstations based on MS-DOS as its default, and so file names on the file server are in the usual 8.3 format. In order to use HPFS long file names, you must load OS/2's module that provides name-space support onto the file server.

NOTE — Loading OS/2 name-space support does consume more file-server RAM than that used in servers supporting only MS-DOS.

Starting from the : prompt on the NetWare file server, load the OS/2 name-space support module by typing:

LOAD OS2.NAM

Then type:

ADD NAME SPACE OS2 TO VOLUME *name*

where *name* is the name of the file server volume to which you want to add name space support. You do not need a final colon when specifying the volume name. The process runs for about 15 minutes in most cases, and when it finishes, you should shut down the file server and reboot the network operating system.

NetWare also uses a text file called NET.CFG to configure communications options for the connection to the network. This file is created and managed automatically, and so there is no need to change any of the settings in the file.

Logging Into the Network

Once you've prepared the workstations by installing the requester, you can log into the network either from the desktop or from a command prompt. When you restart your workstation after installing the requester, you will see a new folder on the desktop called NetWare, containing two objects, labeled NetWare Utilities and NetWare. Open the NetWare folder and you will see listed all the file servers on your network. If you double-click on one of the file server icons, a dialog box opens asking for your user name and password. Log into the network as usual, and you will see icons for all the network resources accessible from that file server. Each folder icon represents a volume on the network, and each printer icon represents a network print queue. You can open any of these objects, but what you see will depend on your user level and the security privileges you were assigned by the network administrator. If you open a printer icon, you will see the list of jobs waiting to be printed, and if you open a server folder, you will see the usual display of files and subfolders.

As discussed in Chapter 2, you can create shadows of any of these objects on the desktop so that they are easier to access. If you try to access a network shadow before you have logged in to the network, a dialog box opens automatically to allow to log in.

The only disadvantage to logging into the network in this way is that you cannot execute any login scripts or commands at the same time. However, you can use scripts when you log in from a command prompt. When you log in using MS-DOS, the LOGIN command asks for your user name and password, and then runs any login scripts created by the SYSCON utility. OS/2 can operate in the same way, but only after a little work. Login scripts are not shared between MS-DOS and OS/2, and so one account may need two different login scripts. The following limitations apply to OS/2 login scripts:

- The COMSPEC setting does not work, so be sure to set this in CONFIG.SYS.

- The EXIT *filename* command does not work, and so to get around this you should have the user log in from a command file that calls LOGIN, and then calls another command file after LOGIN completes.

- The SET command sets the environment variables only for the login itself, and not for the other OS/2 sessions. You can get around this if you set the necessary environment variables using CONFIG.SYS.

- MAP INS does not work, so you should use the SET command to change path information.

NOTE The MAP command works; only the MAP INS command does not.

Run the OS/2 version of SYSCON in an OS/2 windowed session to create an OS/2 login script; you cannot use the MS-DOS version of SYSCON. If you work in a networked environment where OS/2 and MS-DOS workstations are both common, be prepared for some level of confusion.

Using the OS/2 NetWare Tools

If you open the other folder inside the NetWare folder on the desktop, you can access NetWare Tools. Using NetWare Tools, you can save your network configuration into a file, and then use that file to log into the network automatically every time you start your computer. To do this, create a shadow of the NetWare Tools object in your Startup folder, then open the shadow's Settings notebook at the first tab, and enter the name of the file you just created into the Parameters field, including complete path information. Once this is done, NetWare Tools will automatically log you in to the network every time you boot up your computer.

You can also use NetWare Tools to perform the following jobs:

- Send messages to other users.
- Display a list of all users logged in to the network.
- Manage printer queues.
- Log in to and out of servers.
- Map drives to network volumes.

SOLUTION

If you want to load the OS/2 versions of the NetWare utilities, programs such as FILER and SYSCON, you will need approximately 3MB of free space on the file server. You must install NetWare support on your workstation first so that you can access the network before you can load these utilities onto the file server. To load the utilities, start the requester installation program as described in the section headed "Preparing the OS/2 Workstation" above, but this time choose the Utilities on Server option from the Installation menu. You will be prompted to swap floppy disks from time to time as necessary to complete this installation.

When you double-click on the NetWare Tools icon, you will initially see the Disk Drives window, listing all your disk drives, and whether they represent local drives or mapped network drives. You can switch between the three main tool options, Drives, Printer Ports, and Servers, with the Tools menu in this window. When you do switch to a new tool, its menu appears on the menu bar. You can also select User Lists to detail all the users on a particular file server, or to send a message to one or all of the users currently logged on to the network.

The Drives menu contains selections you can use to map a drive or remove a drive mapping, as well as list all the drive letters, and list those drives currently mapped.

To access the Printer Ports tools, open the Tools menu, and choose Printer Ports. Double-click on one of the ports listed in the Printer Ports window to change the network settings for the chosen queue, including the network queue name, and whether a banner is printed along with your print job. To look at the print jobs waiting in the queue, select the queue, and then choose the View Queue option from the Printers menu.

To open the Servers tool, use the Servers option from the Tools menu, and you will see a list of all the file servers attached to the network. Using this menu, you can change a password, look at the users logged in to a file server, or log out from existing connections.

Virtual DOS Machines and Network Resources

Every VDM on an OS/2 workstation that is running the OS/2 Requester can choose to have either global or private network resources. Global is the default for all VDM sessions for DOS and WIN-OS/2, and is the easiest way to manage your network accesses. In a VDM using global resources, almost all of the network device drivers are located outside the VDM. This means that much more memory is available to a VDM than when using the network with native MS-DOS. A session using global resources inherits all network settings from the OS/2 parent, including drive mappings and port assignments. A session with private resources must load and manage its own network settings.

Accessing other Local Area Networks

While Novell may lay claim to almost 70 percent of the network operating system installations, it has formidable competition from other network operating system suppliers. OS/2 can be attached as a workstation to a Banyan VINES or a LAN Manager network.

When attached as a workstation to one of these networks, OS/2 can take advantage of many of the system-level features described in Chapter 1, such as preemptive multitasking, task scheduling, and access to large amounts of memory.

Banyan System's VINES

Banyan System's VINES (VIrtual NEtworking Software) is a network operating system more closely aligned with the world of minicomputers, and it delivers the features and complexity often associated with mini-computer software. VINES is a series of applications running over a special version of UNIX System V, designed to run on computers with multiple processors.

OS/2 support is provided through a package called VINES Support for OS/2, available from Banyan Systems. An installation program called Vclient copies the appropriate files from the distribution disks to a directory on the OS/2 workstation hard disk and alters the CONFIG.SYS file accordingly. You start the VINES requester by running a program called Ban, and you can automate this process if you add Ban to your Startup folder.

LAN Manager

LAN Manager for Microsoft uses an enhanced version of OS/2 as the underlying network file-server operating system. LAN Manager will support many types of workstations, including MS-DOS, OS/2, UNIX, and Macintosh through the following protocols:

- NetBEUI
- AsynchBEUI
- IPX
- TCP/IP
- AppleTalk

These protocols let you integrate MS-DOS, OS/2, UNIX, and Macintosh workstations together; one of the most important current requirements for networks is that they support multiple platforms in a way that is completely transparent to the user.

AsynchBEUI is Microsoft's asynchronous implementation of NetBIOS, and is used for remote access with a modem, a dial-up telephone line, and a serial port connection. It supports communication rates from 2400 to 14400 bits per second, and in the area of asynchronous communications OS/2 as a client excels with LAN Manager. Running AsynchBEUI under MS-DOS can seem torture, but with OS/2's advanced task scheduling and preemptive multitasking you can run multiple tasks while using AsynchBEUI.

An OS/2 workstation can also monitor the print queue for LAN Manager and AppleTalk print jobs, as well as use the LAN Manager's serial ports for communications.

OS/2 LAN Server

NOTE OS/2 is used as the basis for two network products, LAN Manager from Microsoft, and OS/2 LAN Server from IBM. Confusingly, IBM also has a product called LAN Manager, but it is a Token-Ring system management and diagnostics package.

OS/2 LAN Server is IBM's top-of-the-line PC LAN operating system, and as its name implies LAN Server runs on top of OS/2, taking advantage of OS/2's advanced features. LAN Server supports OS/2-, MS-DOS-, and Windows-based workstations using Token-Ring, Ethernet, and IBM PC Network adapter cards for microchannel architecture or ISA computers.

Using LAN Server on the Network File Server

NOTE LAN Server is available in Canadian French, English, UK English, Finnish, French, German, Italian, Norwegian, Spanish, and Swedish.

Besides the network features you would expect, such as network resource sharing, system security, and administrative and accounting functions, LAN Server also supplies several advanced network features:

- **Multiple Adapters:** An OS/2 LAN server or an OS/2 workstation can support up to four network adapters at a time, but certain restrictions apply to some combinations. If a workstation has multiple adapters, these adapters cannot be on the same network, or provide access to networks connected by bridges. Multiple adapter support allows a workstation to communicate only with the networks that it is connected to; it does not pass network requests from one type of network to another as a bridge would. IBM and Novell have removed all the obstacles in both LAN Server and NetWare to allow peaceful coexistence of the two network environments. If you need to access both of these networks, IBM or Novell can supply a document called COEXIST.TXT that describes this cooperative support.

- **Domains:** A *domain* is a server or a set of servers, including all the attached network workstations, that can operate as a single logical system. The network administrator establishes domains, and designates one of the servers in each domain as the domain controller. The domain controller manages the resources within the domain; if a domain has only one server, then that server is also the domain controller.

- **386 HPFS:** The HPFS provides extremely fast access to very large disk volumes, and optimizes performance in the server environment where a large number of files are open simultaneously. The 386-specific, server-aware version of the HPFS is format-compatible with the HPFS under OS/2, and existing partitions using the HPFS need not be reformatted when LAN Server is installed.

- **Coprocessor Support:** IBM has indicated a direction for LAN Server that will include support for a coprocessor environment to allow parallel execution.

- **Fault Tolerance for Fixed Disk.** Fault Tolerance for Fixed Disk, usually known simply as Fault Tolerance, adds the capability to handle disk hardware problems without losing data or significantly affecting overall system performance. The techniques used include disk mirroring and disk duplexing as well as monitoring of disk performance, alerting, and error logging.

- **Disk Mirroring** is the duplication of the information held on one disk drive on another, separate disk drive. If one drive experiences problems, the data is read from the other. In disk mirroring both drives may use the same hard-disk controller.

- **Disk Duplexing** is an advanced type of disk mirroring where both hard disks must use separate hard disk controllers. Disk duplexing provides additional protection against faulty controllers.

Fault Tolerance supports as many as 11 mirrored drives, and it uses an advanced disk device driver designed for SCSI, ESDI, and ST506 drives. If you want to use a different type of drive, consult your hardware documentation to make sure that fault-tolerant software is supported.

NOTE Even if you install and use Fault Tolerance, you must still adhere to a planned sequence of disk backups. Fault Tolerance is designed to protect the system against a single disk failure, but not against multiple disk failures.

- **Uninterruptable Power Supply (UPS) support** provides protection against loss of data during power failures. When power is interrupted, users of active sessions are informed of the imminent shutdown, and the server is shut down in an orderly way.

The LAN Server package includes software for the server, and requester software for OS/2, DOS, and Windows workstations, as well as complete documentation; see Appendix B for details of the documentation.

Using OS/2 Workstations with LAN Server

The primary type of workstation on a LAN Server network is the OS/2 workstation, and this workstation can access all OS/2 and MS-DOS applications on a LAN Server network. OS/2 workstations add capability not possible with an MS-DOS workstation, such as access to Named Pipes and system administration. Named pipes, described earlier in this chapter, are built into OS/2. System administration tasks can only be performed from an OS/2 workstation or directly from the file server; they cannot be performed from an MS-DOS workstation. You can also log into the LAN Server network using a modem if you do so from an OS/2 workstation.

Extended Services for OS/2

There are two OS/2 Extended Services products:

- IBM Extended Services for OS/2
- IBM Extended Services with Database Server for OS/2

Both products contain Database Manager and Communications Manager, but the Extended Services with Database Server adds:

- Database server support
- A distributed database client application enabler for use on MS-DOS, Windows, and OS/2 workstations.

Database Manager, based on the relational database model, allows users to create, update, and access databases using static or dynamic Structured Query Language (SQL). We'll hear more about SQL in the next section. Other Database Manager features include backup and restore, roll-forward recovery to rebuild crashed databases, date/time arithmetic, and user-defined collating sequences.

Communications Manager adds services that your workstation can use to communicate and share resources with a host computer over LANs, Systems Network Architecture (SNA) and X.25 networks. You can write or use applications written to the following API standards:

- Asynchronous Communications Device Interface (ACDI)
- Advanced Program-to-Program Communications (APPC)
- Emulator High-Level Language Application Programming Interface (EHLLAPI)
- SAA Common Programming Interface for Communications (CPI Communications)
- Server-Requester Programming Interface (SRPI)
- X.25 API
- NetBIOS and IEEE 802.2 APIs
- Conventional LU Application (LUA) API
- Common Services API
- System Management API
- Programmable Configuration API

Communications Manager supports a variety of connection types, including coaxial, twin-axial, switched and nonswitched SDLC, asynchronous, X.25, and LANs.

The OS/2-to-Mainframe Connection

In the past, commercial computing often used a traditional hierarchical architecture with nonprogrammable "dumb" terminals attached to a mainframe or a minicomputer. The database was always on the machine running the application.

> ## ▶ S O L U T I O N
>
> How is client/server architecture different from a LAN, and what benefits does it bring? LANs usually focus on sharing resources system-wide; files and peripherals can be shared easily over the network. In a client/server environment, the emphasis is on processor sharing and application cooperation. This allows a mix-and-match approach you can use to select the right processor for the job, whether it be a PC, a minicomputer, or a mainframe. Very often the client portion is located on a PC and the server on a larger system. The server accepts processing requests from the client and processes them. An example of a server might be a large DB2 application running on the host system.
>
> Typically, client\server reduces network load, because only relatively small amounts of data are moved backwards and forwards. This is in sharp contrast to the typical PC-based LAN applications, where entire files must be transmitted between the workstation and the file server.

A *client/server* architecture replaces this hierarchical structure by dividing the application into two (or more) separate processes, a front-end client and a back-end server. These processes may be on the same or on different machines, connected by a LAN or by some other connection method. The client component, itself a stand-alone PC, provides the user with power for running applications and is usually optimized for user interaction. The server component, which can be a PC, a minicomputer, or a mainframe, and can be local or remote, provides the data management, administration and system security features, and information sharing.

Database applications are one of the most common uses of client\server architecture, particularly with distributed Structured Query Language (SQL, usually pronounced "sequel"). SQL is a standard, and is relatively easy to implement. It is robust, powerful, and easy to learn.

SOLUTION

CICS (Customer Information Control System) is available for OS/2. CICS allows one program to communicate with another anywhere in the system; the client program calls the server program just as if it were local, and all the routing is handled by CICS.

A SQL *statement* is a request sent by the client application to the server, and you can group several related requests together into a *transaction*. SQL is often implemented in two main ways:

- **Static SQL** statements are coded into application programs, and as a result do not change. These SQL statements are processed by a precompiler before being bound into the application.

- **Dynamic SQL** statements are interactive, and can be changed as needed. If you normally access SQL from a command line, you are using the dynamic version. Dynamic SQL may be slower than static, but it is obviously much more flexible.

The OS/2 Database Manager, part of the add-on product Extended Services for OS/2, provides both client and server parts, as well as providing access to larger database systems, often removing the need for a minicomputer.

There are several ways to implement and manage OS/2-to-mainframe connections.

- **DDCS/2** (Distributed Database Connection Services/2) provides transparent, direct access from database clients such as OS/2 Database Manager to DB2 running under MVS, to SQL/DS running under VM, as well as to the AS/400 SQL database. DDCS/2 is based on IBM's Distributed Relational Database Architecture, and allows applications to access and update a database just as if it were stored locally.

- **APPC** (Advanced Program-to-Program Communication) is IBM's peer-to-peer communications protocol, and allows two programs on separate computers to engage in a conversation in a Systems Network Architecture (SNA) environment.

- **EHLLAPI** (Emulator High-Level Language Application Programming Interface) is a Communications Manager API that allows programmers and users to access existing 3270 terminal and AS/400 5250 workstation applications. Communications Manager is also part of Extended Services for OS/2.

See the heading "OS/2 LAN Server" earlier in this section for more information on connection and protocol types available in OS/2.

The UNIX Connection

The benefits of using the UNIX operating system have been well stated elsewhere, and I will not duplicate that discussion here. UNIX has become widely available, on many popular workstations and minicomputers, and from many different vendors. Work done at Berkeley with the Berkeley Standard Distribution (BSD) added an implementation of the popular TCP/IP protocols. TCP/IP stands for Transmission Control Protocol/Internet Protocol, and was developed at the Department of Defense as a mechanism for linking dissimilar computers. It has been adopted widely by corporations, universities and other institutions in the UNIX world.

TCP/IP support under OS/2 is provided by a program called TCP/IP for OS/2. This program can connect to, and share information with, many different UNIX servers from several vendors including IBM's own AIX. TCP/IP for OS/2 supports the following capabilities:

- Remote login
- Terminal emulation
- File server, file sharing and file transfer functions
- Security functions
- Network management
- Security functions
- Remote printing
- Electronic mail

Support is also provided for Sun Microsystem's Network File System (NFS), RPC (Remote Procedure Call), and X-Windows. TCP/IP for OS/2 can communicate over Token Ring, IEEE 802.3, and Ethernet connections.

N O T E

RPC is a set of software tools developed by a group of manufacturers, designed to assist developers creating distributed applications. These software tools automatically generate the code needed for both sides of the program (client and server), and so let the programmer concentrate on the application rather than be burdened by implementation details.

OS/2 OS/2 OS/2

OS/2 OS/2 OS/2 OS/2 OS/2 OS/2 OS/2 OS/2 OS/2

OS/2 OS/2 OS/2 O

16

Programming
with REXX

OS/2 OS/2 OS/2 OS/2 OS/2 OS/2 OS/2 OS/2 OS/2 OS/

REXX, the REstructured eXtended eXecutor language, has been available for a long time in the mainframe world, and is now included as a part of the OS/2 operating system. REXX is an easy-to-use structured programming language, simple enough for new programmers to understand, while at the same time providing the advanced features that more experienced programmers demand. REXX uses English-like words rather than the sometimes terse syntax of the C or C++ programming languages. Authors have written entire books about using REXX; it is a large subject. This chapter must be more modest in scope, and will serve as an introduction to REXX programming for users who have some programming experience with another language.

REXX is a general-purpose language, well suited to solving programming problems in environments where the REXX interpreter is available, such as OS/2, VM, and MVS. Short programs that solve immediate problems outside the range or scope of the OS/2 batch language (described in Chapter 12) can be written easily in REXX with the minimum of overhead, yet REXX also allows programmers to construct large, complex programs too. If your program must run in all circumstances, including those where the REXX environment may be unavailable, then you must use one of the other generally-available OS/2 programming languages such as the C language.

Getting Started with REXX

In Chapter 12 we looked at the batch programming commands available in OS/2; the REXX language is a much more powerful tool that you can use to automate repetitive or complex tasks. Following are some of the most important features that REXX offers the programmer:

- **Easy-to-use syntax:** REXX is easy to learn and use because it uses many English-like words as part of its syntax, rather than the harder-to-understand abbreviations used by other popular programming languages.

- **OS/2 Commands:** You can add OS/2 commands into your REXX programs.

- **Free Format:** There are few rules about format, or how you lay out your program. You can write a single instruction on a line or you can cram multiple instructions onto a line; and instructions can be entered in uppercase, lowercase, or as mixed case; it all depends on your own personal style. In many ways, it is best to use one instruction (known as an *expression*) on each line, but if you want an expression to span more than one line, end the line with a comma to indicate that it continues. If you want to use more than one expression on a line, separate one from the other with a semicolon. There is no line numbering in REXX.

- **Interpreted language:** REXX is an interpreted language rather than a compiled language. In an interpreted language, each line in the source file is read and then executed, just like a batch file. Thus you can detect and correct programming errors quickly and easily. In a compiled language, the source code must be compiled into a machine-readable form before it can be run.

- **Extensive list of Commands and Functions:** REXX provides a comprehensive list of commands and functions. You can even use one of the REXX functions (RexxFuncAdd) to add your own commands to the REXX language command set.

- **Data as strings:** To simplify the processing of variables, REXX handles all data as strings of either characters or numbers. This means that you don't have to predefine variables or arrays specifically as strings or as numbers of a particular size. Strong typing, a mechanism used in C and Pascal by which the values that a variable can hold are tightly constrained, is not present in REXX.

- **Parsing:** REXX includes commands and functions for processing character strings to allow programs to read and manage individual characters, numbers, and mixed input.

- **Debugging aids:** When a REXX program encounters an error, the error messages tend to be easy-to-understand English messages, and the REXX language itself contains useful built-in debugging commands.

REXX programs can only run in an OS/2 session, and must have the file-name extension CMD. As with batch files, you omit the extension when you type the file name to start the procedure. Each REXX program must begin with a comment line that starts (in the first column of the first line) with the characters /* and ends with */.

The Information folder on the desktop contains the REXX Information object, which, when you open it, displays the OS/2 Procedures Language 2/REXX document. This document lists all the commands and functions available in the language, along with syntax and usage notes, so that information will not be repeated here.

N O T E

For more information on using REXX, see the *Procedures Language/2 REXX User's Guide* (part number 10G6269) or the *Procedures Language/2 REXX Reference* (part number 10G6268), both available from IBM as individual documents or as parts of the OS/2 Technical Library. See Appendix B for more information on the OS/2 Technical Library.

REXX programs are text files, just like batch files, that you create, edit, and save using a text editor such as the OS/2 System Editor or the Enhanced Editor (both found in the Productivity folder, and both described in Chapter 4). Once you have created the file, you can run it by typing the file name at any OS/2 command prompt. When the program completes, you return to the command prompt once again.

Using REXXTRY

REXXTRY is a REXX program, located in the OS2 directory, that you can run in an OS/2 session to test REXX instructions and look at the results. If you run REXXTRY with no parameters or with a question mark on the command line, it will display a short description of itself. You can study REXXTRY.CMD as a good example of a structured program, and it contains many comments that explain what is happening throughout the program.

REXXTRY is also useful if you want to execute a REXX procedure just once, because it is quicker and easier than creating, editing, and running a CMD file. Type the REXX command at the command prompt, and it will be executed immediately. For example, type:

    REXXTRY CALL SHOW

to see a list of the user variables provided by REXXTRY. To use REXXTRY as a simple command-line calculator, use the SAY command:

    REXXTRY SAY 100-73

and press Enter to see the result. You can think of REXXTRY as a one-time interactive version of the REXX interpreter.

Using PMREXX

Another useful REXX tool is the PMREXX program, which brings REXX to the desktop. PMREXX invokes a windowed environment in which you can display the output from any REXX program, as well as a single-line input field for input to the REXX program or to any command called by the REXX procedure. PMREXX adds the following features to REXX:

- A window to display the output from a REXX program

- An input field to a REXX program

- A browsing and scrolling window

- A selection of fonts to use in the output window

Figure 16.1 shows the output from the REXXTRY program displayed in the PMREXX window. It was produced by typing:

    PMREXX REXXTRY

at an OS/2 command prompt and then typing

    CALL TELL

in the resulting PMREXX window's Input box.

Use the selections in the File menu to save PMREXX output or exit from PMREXX. The Edit menu contains selections you can use to copy to the clipboard, paste from the clipboard to the input box, clear marked text from either the Input box or the output window, and select all the lines in the output window. The Options menu allows you to restart the REXX interpreter, turn on the interactive trace mode, and select a font for the output window. Use the Action menu to halt the current REXX program, trace the next instruction, repeat the last instructions, and turn trace mode off.

FIGURE 16.1

PMREXX Displaying the
REXXTRY Program
Output

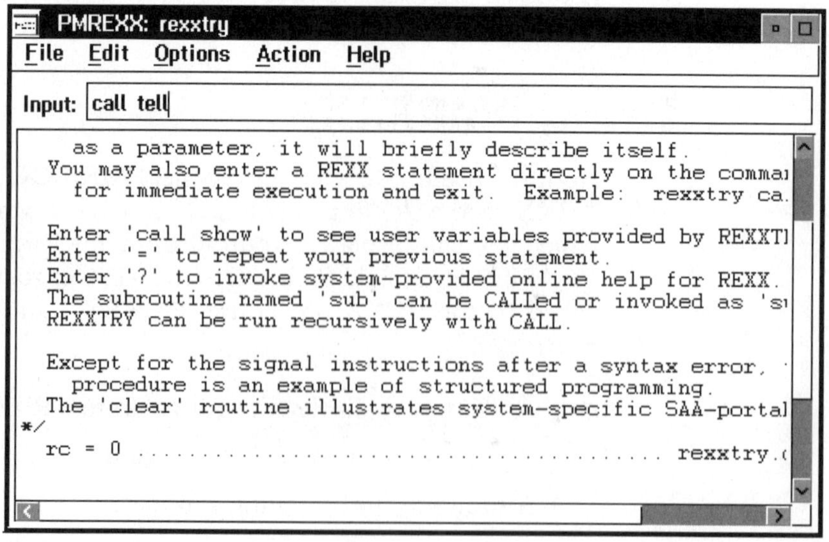

REXX Programming Language Elements

A REXX program can contain any or all of the following elements:

- Comments
- Keywords
- Strings
- Variables
- Assignments
- Expressions
- OS/2 Commands
- Labels
- Functions

In the sections that follow, we'll look at each of these elements in turn, and we'll look at some simple examples of how you might use some of them.

Comments

All REXX programs must begin with a comment line that starts in the first column of the first line in the program. If you don't include this comment, OS/2 assumes that the file is an ordinary batch file, and starts processing the contents of the file. When OS/2 encounters the first REXX expression in this file, you will see an OS/2 SYS1041 error, indicating that OS/2 does not recognize the expression as an internal or external command, program, or batch file. The initial comment line can be as short as

```
/**/
```

but comments are a very useful way to tell someone else, who may not be a programmer, what your program is doing. And because some REXX programs can be long and complex, thorough commenting can be just as useful a reminder of exactly what the program is doing if you need to modify your own program in a year's time. Use comments to annotate your programs, and use lots of them. A comment line might look like the following:

```
/*  This program predicts the winning numbers in the  */
/*  lottery and was written in September of 1993       */
/*  It predicted its first set of winning numbers      */
/*  two weeks after it was finished                    */
```

In the REXX interpreter, /* indicates the beginning of a comment, and */ indicates the end of a comment; the interpreter ignores anything between these two symbols. This means that comments can follow the instructions they annotate on the same line, or they can extend across line boundaries.

Keywords

Keywords are names reserved in the REXX language for specific instructions, such as control statements (IF, DO,), input and output instructions (SAY, PULL), and other operations (EXIT, TRACE). Keywords are used in specific circumstances, and you shouldn't use them as variable names.

See the online REXX Information for a complete list of the keywords used in REXX.

Using Variables

All programs must be able to work with data whose value is unknown at the time the program is written, and so programming languages use *variables* as placeholders for this varying data. Inside a REXX program a variable is known by a unique name, and is always referred to by that name. The name can be as short as a single character or as long as 250 characters. The following limitations apply:

- The first character must be A–Z, a–z, !, ?, or _; REXX translates lowercase initial letters to uppercase before using variables.

- The other characters in the variable name can be A–Z, a–z, !, ?, _, ., or 0–9. The period has a special significance, and turns a simple variable into a compound variable.

As a rule, you should give variables names that describe the data they represent and that are easy to tell apart (longer names are easier to remember than shorter ones). Don't use variable names that are the same as OS/2 commands or reserved REXX keywords. Finally, use a variable for one purpose only; do not use the same variable for two different purposes in the same REXX program.

Assignments

An assignment tells the REXX program to place a value in a variable. The simplest assignment uses the equal sign as in:

    Name = *value*

where Name is the name you gave to the variable, and *value* is the value you want it to hold. To set Name to a value of zero, use:

    Name = 0

To assign a string to Name, use:

    Name = "PETER"

When you assign a value to a variable, you can also use a simple calculation:

    Total = Total + Delta

Use the SAY instruction to display the contents of a variable on the screen, as in:

    SAY What

S E C R E T

In some languages, using a SAY instruction with a variable that has no current value will generate an error. In REXX, the default value of a variable is its own name, converted into uppercase letters. If your program contains the statement:

SAY Farquharson

and the variable Farquharson has no value, you will see:

FARQUHARSON

on your screen instead.

Using Expressions

An *expression* is a math operation that you want the program to calculate. It can be as simple as adding two numbers together, or it can be much more complex. An expression consists of *terms*, the data used in the calculation, and *operators*, the computations that are performed.

N O T E

You should try to keep expressions relatively simple and well commented, so that you, and other users, can still understand your intentions a year from now.

Expressions can be made up of the following REXX terms:

- **Numbers:** Numbers are constants contained in strings that REXX can calculate.

- **Strings:** Strings are text within matched pairs of quotation marks.

- **Variables:** Variables hold data that may change from one run of the program to the next.

- **Function calls:** Function calls are special calculations. They fall into two types; those built into REXX and those you add yourself. More on function calls later in this chapter.

NOTE For the rules on arithmetic precedence, see "Performing Arithmetic" later in this chapter.

The most common operators in REXX are used for arithmetic and to join or *concatenate* two strings into a single string:

- **Addition:** Use the + sign to add two or more numbers together.

- **Subtraction:** Use the – sign to subtract one number from another.

- **Multiplication:** The * character multiplies two numbers together, and ** raises a number to the specified power.

- **Division:** There are three ways of performing division in REXX:

  - Use / to perform normal division, where the result may contain a decimal number.

  - Use % to derive the integer result of a division. For example, to determine the integer result of 10 divided by 3, use 10 % 3. The answer is 3, and REXX ignores the remainder.

  - Use // to determine the remainder, or modulus, after a division. For example, to determine the remainder after 10 is divided by 3, use 10 // 3, and the result is 1.

- **Concatenation:** Concatenation joins two or more strings together to make one string, and can be performed as follows:

  - If you leave one or more blanks between the strings, they will be separated on the screen by a single space.

  - If you leave no blanks between the strings, REXX uses *abuttal*, displaying the strings with no separating space. REXX must be able to distinguish between the strings for abuttal to work.

- If you use the concatenation operator *vbar,* which is represented by two vertical bars (two ASCII 124 characters), there will be no separating blanks.

Concatenation works with numeric strings as well as with character data. (This technique is used when you are assembling a number constructed from several different input sources and avoids having to do the arithmetic needed to establish the thousands, hundreds, tens, and ones needed to assemble the number correctly. It is possible because REXX uses strings rather than the more usual data types such as integer or real, found in other languages.) If you use the vbar operator inside parentheses, you can force REXX to concatenate two numeric strings before performing another operation, such as division, on the result. For example, (10||5)/5 yields an answer of 21; the 10 and 5 are concatenated to 105 before the division by 5 occurs. Without the parentheses, REXX would have performed the division first, 5/5 (result 1), and then the concatenation for a final result of 101.

OS/2 Commands

N O T E

There are two main ways you can add an OS/2 command into your REXX program. You can explicitly "hard code" the text of the command, which is exact but inflexible, or you can use a REXX expression to assemble the command. This latter method is well suited to accepting input from the user or from another REXX program; you'll find an example of it in Listing 16.1 at the end of this chapter.

The REXX interpreter processes your program one element at a time, and if the element is not a keyword instruction, a variable assignment, a label, or a null operation, REXX evaluates the element as an expression and passes the resulting string to OS/2. In other words, whatever the REXX interpreter cannot process, it evaluates, and then passes any result to the OS/2 command processor. If the resulting string is a valid OS/2 command, OS/2 processes it just as though you had typed it at the command prompt and pressed Enter.

This means that you can invoke OS/2 commands, such as TYPE, PRINT, and COPY, from inside your REXX program.

The command is also echoed on the screen, but you can suppress this echoing if you find it distracting, by using an ECHO OFF statement in your program. This instruction turns off all echoing for the rest of the program; to suppress echoing for a single command, place an @ character in front of the command.

N O T E The CALL instruction can access an internal subroutine present in the current REXX program, another REXX program, or a built-in REXX function. See "Labels" later in this chapter for more on subroutines.

To make REXX invoke another REXX program, use the CALL instruction, as in:

    CALL myfile

REXX recognizes the CALL keyword, and processes the file as you would expect. To invoke a non-REXX CMD file, you have to use the OS/2 CALL command instead, as in:

    "CALL myfile2"

The quotation marks identify the line as a string rather than an instruction the REXX interpreter can process. So REXX evaluates the expression and passes the string to the OS/2 command processor, which in turn invokes the OS/2 CALL command.

Program Control Structures

REXX provides three sets of instructions you can use to make decisions based on conditions determined by your program as it runs: IF...THEN...ELSE, for conditional branching; SELECT, which is a switch statement; and keywords for several types of DO looping. To perform more complex evaluations, you can nest these instructions, one inside another. The structured programmers among us will note immediately that REXX does not provide a GOTO instruction.

Conditional Branching with IF...THEN...ELSE

The IF statement is used to make a decision based on the value of an expression. This expression must evaluate to either true (1) or false (0). The general form is as follows:

IF *expression* THEN *statement*

If the *expression* is true, the *statement* following THEN will be processed next, and if it is not true, the program will continue processing with the next statement. You can also use an optional third element, the ELSE clause, to handle a second processing path for more complex cases:

IF *expression*

THEN *statement*

ELSE *statement*

For example:

/* stay in bed on Sunday */

IF day = "Sunday" THEN SAY "You can stay in bed today"

ELSE SAY "Get up and go to work, lazybones"

The IF statement is a very common and easy-to-use program-control structure; you will find yourself using it over and over again in your programming.

Using SELECT for Conditional Branching

The IF...THEN...ELSE conditional statement limits you to two choices, but the SELECT instruction lets you choose from any number of different branches; it is the multiple choice instruction. SELECT has the form:

SELECT

WHEN *expression1* THEN *instruction1*

WHEN *expression2* THEN *instruction2*

WHEN *expression3* THEN *instruction3*

OTHERWISE

instruction

instruction

END

REXX begins by looking at *expression1*; if it is true, then *instruction1* is processed, and the program exits from the control structure and continues processing with the next statement following the END instruction. If *expression1* is false, REXX looks at *expression2*. If it is true, *instruction2* is processed, and the program continues with the next statement following END. If *expression1*, *expression2*, and *expression3* are all false, then processing continues with the instruction following OTHERWISE. You can consider OTHERWISE to be the SELECT equivalent of the IF statement's ELSE clause, and if there is any possibility that all the WHEN statements could be false, you must use an OTHERWISE clause.

Looping with DO

The loop is an essential part of any programming language, and is a way to make a program repeat a set of instructions a certain number of times. You can loop:

- A specific number of times
- Until a condition becomes true
- As long as a condition remains true
- Forever

and in REXX all these different kinds of loops can be programmed using the DO instruction in one of the following forms.

DO *count* This basic form of DO executes the instructions in the control structure the number of times specified by *count*. For example:

```
/* Display the message 5 times */
DO 5
    SAY "Hello OS/2 world"
END
```

NOTE

The only way to exit the structure without satisfying *count* is by using the optional LEAVE instruction.

You can also control the way the loop runs, as follows:

```
/* Loop Counter */
count =1
DO I = 1 to 10 by count
    SAY I
END
```

This example writes the numbers from 1 to 10 on the screen.

DO WHILE Sometimes the number of times a program will need to process a loop will depend on the data the program is processing at the time. The next two loop structures, DO WHILE and DO UNTIL, both test whether an expression is true. The two structures may look similar, but there is an important difference. DO WHILE tests the condition *before* executing the following command, and DO UNTIL does so *after* checking; this means that the DO WHILE command may never execute, but the DO UNTIL command always executes at least once. Here's the DO WHILE syntax:

```
DO WHILE expression
    instruction
    instruction
END
```

as long as *expression* is true, the *instructions* will be repeated. As soon as *expression* is false, REXX exits the structure.

DO UNTIL You may want to loop an unknown number of times (but more than once), until a specific condition becomes true, and you can use DO UNTIL for this purpose:

DO UNTIL *expression*

   instruction

   instruction

END

The instructions are executed once, before expression is tested. As long as *expression* is false, the *instructions* will be repeated. As soon as *expression* is true, REXX exits the structure.

DO FOREVER The simplest way of creating a loop is to use DO FOREVER, which, as its name suggests, creates an endless loop. By adding a LEAVE instruction, you can create an exit point:

DO FOREVER

   SAY i=i+1

   IF i=6 THEN LEAVE

END

You can use an endless loop to wait for a specific time, and then perform a specific operation. The TIME() function returns a variety of different kinds of values, including hours since midnight, minutes since midnight, and the current time in the usual hh:mm:ss format that you can use in your programming.

Labels

A *label* marks the beginning of a subroutine in REXX, and can be any word followed by a colon, as long as there is no space between the word and the colon, and the word is not enclosed in quotation marks.

In REXX a subroutine is accessed by the CALL command, and ended by the RETURN command when control is passed back to the original calling expression. Here is a short example:

```
IF panic = "yes" THEN CALL error
    EXIT



error:
    SAY "Captain, don't ask me what's holding her together"
    RETURN
```

Performing Arithmetic

In REXX, numbers can be integers, decimal fractions, or signed numbers, and can be expressed in conventional or exponential notation. Calculations are performed to nine significant digits, if necessary.

Expressions are normally evaluated from left to right, and the normal rules of algebra apply. If you use parentheses in an equation, the REXX interpreter evaluates the contents of the parentheses first. The precedence used in REXX expressions (in decreasing order) is as follows:

- Prefix operators
- Power
- Multiply and divide
- Add and subtract
- Concatenation (with or without blanks)
- Logical AND
- Logical OR

Use the NUMERIC instruction if you want to change the way in which arithmetic is done in a REXX program. The instruction has three forms:

- **NUMERIC DIGITS** *expression*   Controls the precision with which arithmetic operations are performed. The default is 9, and any value contained in *expression* must be a positive integer larger than the current setting for NUMERIC FUZZ. There is no upper limit, but keep in mind that very high precision will consume a great deal of processor time. Use the default unless you have a very good reason to change it. You can examine the current setting of NUMERIC DIGITS with the DIGITS() function.

- **NUMERIC FORM**   May be either SCIENTIFIC, the default, in which only one, nonzero digit appears before the decimal point, or ENGINEERING, in which case the power of ten is always a multiple of three.

- **NUMERIC FUZZ** *expression*   Controls the number of digits, at full precision, that are ignored during a numeric comparison. If *expression* is omitted, the default is 0 digits; otherwise, *expression* must be a positive whole number smaller than the current NUMERIC DIGITS setting.

This next small program calculates the value of 2 raised to the power 1000, with the appropriate precision:

```
/* Raise 2 to the power 1000  */

NUMERIC DIGITS 1000

SAY "The exact result of raising 2 to the power 1000 is "

answer = 2**1000

SAY answer
```

The result of this program is shown in Figure 16.2.

In this example, if you omit the step that assigns the result to the variable answer, and run the program with SAY 2**1000 instead, you may see an OS/2 error SYS1041. This is because the result of this calculation exceeds the normal length of the OS/2 command-line buffer.

FIGURE 16.2

The Result of Raising 2 to the Power 1000

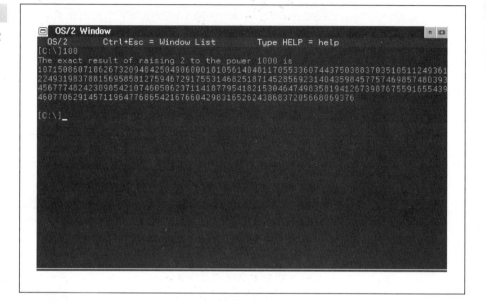

Using Boolean Operators

REXX also provides logical or Boolean operators to help evaluate a condition and then perform a task based on what it finds:

- **Comparison:** REXX lets you compare values and make a decision based on the result. For example, IF A > B THEN *instruction* is a common comparison. The result of a comparison expression is either *true* (1) or *false* (0). Table 16.1 lists the REXX comparison operators.

- **NOT operator (\):** The NOT operator, when placed in front of an expression, changes its value from *true* to *false* or from *false* to *true*. For example, SAY \(10 = 10) displays a value of 0 for false.

- **AND operator (&):** The AND operator lets you evaluate two expressions as if they were one. If both expressions are true, the AND operation returns a value of 1 for true. If either expression is false, the returned value is equivalent to false.

TABLE 16.1: Comparison Operators in REXX

OPERATOR	MEANING
=	Equal to
<> or \=	Not equal to
>	Greater than
\>	Not greater than
<	Less than
\<	Not less than

- **Inclusive OR operator (|).** An inclusive OR combines comparisons so that the whole expression evaluates to true (1) if any of the comparisons are true.

- **Exclusive OR operator (&&).** An exclusive OR combines comparisons so that the whole expression evaluates to true if one (and only one) of the comparisons is true.

Comparison operators can be combined; for example, >= stands for *greater than or equal to.*

Working with Strings

The way that REXX handles numbers is a good example of its flexibility. Most computer languages impose lots of rules to differentiate between character data and numbers. In REXX a number is just a string that can be calculated.

A string is any set of characters contained inside either double or single quotation marks; you can use either kind, but the beginning and ending marks must always match. An example:

'To the curious incident of the dog in the night-time'

If you want to use an apostrophe inside a string, just use double quotation marks to delimit the string:

"Quick Watson, the game's afoot"

PROGRAMMING WITH REXX

To prompt the user of your program for input, or to add instructions on the screen, use SAY followed by the expression you want to use. For example:

```
SAY "It was the best of times"
```

causes *It was the best of times* to appear on the screen. If the string is too long to fit conveniently on one line of your REXX program, use a comma at the end of the line to indicate that it continues:

```
SAY  "It was the best of times,"
"   it was the worst of times."
```

This continuation comma is replaced by a space when the string is displayed:

```
It was the best of times, it was the worst of times.
```

You can also add expressions to SAY:

```
SAY 5 * 10 "= Fifty"
```

displays *50 = Fifty* on the screen.

When SAY is used to ask the user a question, PULL is then used to collect the answer. When PULL is processed by the REXX interpreter, the program pauses for the user to enter information and press Enter. PULL then converts the information to uppercase, and assigns the answer to the appropriate variable. The input to the variable is converted to uppercase (if it is character data rather than numerical) to simplify the programming problems associated with detecting differences in case. Looking for a *Y* or an *N* is a lot simpler than looking for *Y* or *y* or *N* or *n*, when decoding the answer to a yes/no question.

When you start your REXX program, you type the program name at an OS/2 command prompt. You can also pass arguments to your program at the same time by using the ARG command. ARG processes command arguments in exactly the same way that PULL processes keyboard input, except that the first argument typed, the program name, is always ignored.

You cannot use a period by itself as a variable name, but you can use it with the PULL instruction to discard input information. For example:

```
PULL . . finalvar .,
```

throws away the first two words entered, assigns the third to *finalvar*, and discards all subsequent input.

S O L U T I O N

To make sure the user has entered the right number of words or numbers, create an extra variable and test that it is empty while you also test that the last word the user is expected to type is *not* empty. For example, the program fragment that follows accepts three numbers as input:

```
/* Testing how many numbers entered  */
    DO UNTIL done
        SAY "Please enter three numbers"
        PULL firstnum secondnum thirdnum test
        SELECT
            WHEN thirdnum = "" THEN SAY "Enter another"
            WHEN test \= "" THEN SAY "Too many numbers"
            OTHERWISE done = 1
        END
    END
```

REXX Functions

To implement more complex computations, REXX includes a rich set of over 60 built-in functions, covering areas such as:

- Numeric operations
- File input
- File output
- Word-oriented string manipulation
- Character-oriented string manipulation
- OS/2-specific system operations

Unlike a keyword, a function always returns a value; a keyword performs an operation and does not return a value. A function consists of the function name followed, without spaces, by parentheses containing the function's argument—the value that you want the function to work with. The argument can be a number, a variable, a string or one or more expressions. The value that a function computes is known as the *return value*.

For example, the MAX() function returns the largest number in a list of numbers:

```
MAX(10,20,30,40)
```

This expression returns a value of 40 that you can then use in subsequent calculations. MAX accepts up to 20 numbers, and you can nest calls to MAX if you need to process more than 20 at a time, as follows:

```
MAX(1,2,3,4,5,6,7,8,9,10,...15,16,17,18,19,MAX(20,21))
```

See the online REXX Information for a complete list of the functions contained in REXX.

Debugging Your REXX Programs

Two kinds of errors can occur when a program is run. Most common is a syntax error in the way the program is written; perhaps quotation marks are mismatched, or an IF statement does not have a matching THEN. When an error like this occurs, you will see a REXX error message such as:

```
REX0006: Error 6 running program, line n: Unmatched "/*" or
quote
```

where *program* is the complete path information for the REXX program you are running, and *n* is the number of the line in the program where the error was detected. To see more information on this error, type:

```
HELP REX0006
```

and you will see several lines of explanation that should help you to track down the syntax error.

The second type of error occurs when an OS/2 command fails; perhaps the COPY command cannot find a file, or the target disk is full. When you write your program, you must try to anticipate what might happen if a command fails to run as you intend.

When a command is issued from a REXX program, the command interpreter receives a return code, which is stored in a special REXX variable called RC (for return code). You can test the value of this variable in your program; if it is zero, all is well and the command ran as anticipated. IF RC is not zero, it usually means something went wrong. The following fragment illustrates one way you might implement this kind of code:

```
/* Return Code Trap */

SAY "Enter a file name: "

PULL filename

COPY filename B:

    IF rc = 0  THEN SAY "File copied successfully"

    ELSE SAY "Error occurred copying the file"
```

If your program does not perform as you expect, you can add the TRACE instruction to your program and display how REXX evaluates your program as it runs. You can examine this output, and then make the appropriate changes. The most common forms of TRACE are:

- **TRACE Normal**. This is the default setting, and any failing command is traced after execution.

- **TRACE Off**. Allows you to turn tracing off for a section of a program. By using a combination of TRACE Normal and TRACE Off, you can selectively trace your program's execution.

- **TRACE All**. All program elements are displayed before being executed.

- **TRACE Intermediates**. All program elements are displayed before execution, and any intermediate results calculated by expressions are also traced.

- **TRACE Results**. All program elements are displayed before execution, and final results calculated by expressions are displayed. Values assigned during PULL, PARSE, and ARG instructions are also displayed. This is by far the most popular option for TRACE as it shows the information that is most useful for general program debugging.

NOTE

Although you can enter the TRACE option word in full, only the first uppercase letter is actually used, so you can abbreviate if you wish.

Every element in your program will be traced, and the output you see on the screen will depend on the TRACE option you selected. Formatting on the screen follows the level of indentation used in the program, and any results are indented an extra two spaces and enclosed in double quotation marks so that leading and following space characters will always be apparent.

You can stop most REXX programs by pressing the Ctrl and Break keys at the same time; REXX will recognize Ctrl+Break when it completes the current instruction. Sometimes, you may have to follow Ctrl+Break with an Enter keystroke. If you still can't stop the REXX program, press Alt+Esc to open the Window List, select the current session, and use Close from its pop-up menu.

Some Example REXX Programs

To end this chapter, we'll look at a few short REXX programs that illustrate some of the points we have covered so far. Listing 16.1 is a program that makes a backup copy of a file to a floppy disk. This program also demonstrates a method of using the RC (return code) variable to detect errors on execution.

LISTING 16.1

A REXX file-backup
program

```
/* A REXX file backup program */

/* accepts a file name and extension from the command line */

ARG filename"."ext

/* if no file name was entered at the command line, ask for one  */

IF filename = "" THEN
        DO
        SAY "Please enter a filename: "
        PULL filename"."ext
        END

/* if no extension was entered, then use BKP */

IF ext = "" THEN
        ext = "BKP"

/* ask for a drive letter, and do not accept numbers */

DO UNTIL DATATYPE(drlet) = "CHAR"
        SAY "Please enter a drive letter (without a colon): "
        PULL drlet
        IF DATATYPE(drlet) = "NUM" THEN SAY "That was a number"
END

/* concatenate the drive letter and a colon together */

drlet = drlet || ":"

/* do a DIR to make sure that the file exists */

"DIR" filename"."ext

/* if the file doesn't exist, display message and exit gracefully */

IF rc <> 0 THEN
        DO
        SAY "File not backed up."
        SAY "Program ended"
        EXIT
        END
```

LISTING 16.1

A REXX file-backup
program (Continued)

```
/* if the file exists, copy it to the specified drive */

        ELSE DO
        end  /* Do */
        SAY "Backing up " filename"."ext
        "COPY" filename"."ext drlet
        SAY "Backup Complete"
        SAY "Program is ending"
        EXIT
        END
```

Let's look at the program in detail. First, the ARG statement accepts a file name and extension from the command line, and if one is not specified, the program asks for a file name. If a name is entered but no extension, the extension is automatically set to BKP. Next the program uses a DO UNTIL loop to ask for a drive letter, and uses the DATATYPE() function to test whether a letter or number was entered. If a number was entered, the DO UNTIL is not true, so the question is repeated. Then the drive letter and a colon character (:) are concatenated to make a valid drive name; an alternative would have been to ask the user to enter a drive letter and colon together, but that would complicate the DATATYPE() function call. A DIR command is performed next to make sure that the file exists; if it does not, the program displays a message and exits. If the file exists, it is copied to the specified drive.

There are many ways you could make this program more foolproof, such as checking that the drive letter entered is either A or B, that there are no files on the target drive, and so on.

Listing 16.2 demonstrates string comparison techniques, and uses a SELECT WHEN OTHERWISE program control structure.

This program will also rank letters that you enter as well as numbers; remember that all data is treated as a string in REXX, so it is completely reasonable that one string is greater in value than another.

LISTING 16.2

A REXX program that compares two numbers

```
/* A REXX program that compares two numbers */
/* entered by the user                      */

/* ask for the numbers */

SAY "Please enter a number"
PULL number1

SAY "Please enter a second number"
PULL number2

/* Use a SELECT structure to sort the numbers */

SELECT
        WHEN number1 = number2 THEN
                SAY "These numbers are the same "
        WHEN number1 > number2 THEN
                SAY "The first number is larger than the second"
        OTHERWISE
                SAY "The second number is larger than the first"
END
```

Listing 16.3 demonstrates how you can use the CALL command to invoke a REXX subroutine, and also includes a TRACE statement so you can watch the program as it works. To see the program run without invoking the TRACE instruction, place /* before and */ after the instruction and restore the file.

By isolating frequently used pieces of code in subroutines, you avoid repeating that code unnecessarily. A good use for a subroutine is code that asks a yes/no question and then returns the answer to the main program.

Finally, Listing 16.4 shows how to control input from the user with the DATATYPE() function to get the kind of input you want, character or numeric. This function accepts a string as an argument, and returns either NUM if the string contains a number, or CHAR if the string contains character data. Notice that the program can decipher mixed input (type *888* and see what happens), spaces, and no input at all if you just press the Enter key in response to the "Please enter a number" prompt.

LISTING 16.3

A REXX program using
a CALL instruction
and a subroutine

```rexx
/* A REXX program using a CALL instruction and a subroutine */

/* turn on TRACE Results */

TRACE R

/* This is the main program */

SAY "This is the main program "

/* Set up parameters for the DO loop */

start = 1
increment = 1
maximum = 10
DO count = start TO maximum BY increment
        CALL subroutine
        SAY "Back in the main program again"
        SAY "Result is " answer
END
EXIT

/* This is the subroutine */

subroutine:
SAY "You are now in the subroutine "
answer = count * 10
RETURN
```

LISTING 16.4

A REXX program to
illustrate the DATATYPE()
function

```rexx
/* A REXX program to illustrate the DATATYPE() function */


/* Start the DO UNTIL loop */

DO UNTIL DATATYPE(number) = "NUM"
        SAY "Please enter a number "
        PULL number
        IF DATATYPE(number) = "CHAR" THEN
                SAY "Ooops, that was not a number. Try again"
END

SAY "The number you typed was " number
```

You can take this idea further by modifying this program to use another form of the DATATYPE() function:

DATATYPE(*string, type*)

where *string* is the string you want to test, and *type* refers to the kind of data in the *string*. When *type* is specified, this function returns a 1 if the string matches the type, otherwise it returns a 0. You can use any one of the following *types*, and each one can be abbreviated to the letter shown in parentheses; alphanumeric (A), binary (B), lowercase (L), mixed case (M), number (N), symbol (S), uppercase (U), whole number (W), or hexadecimal (X).

This chapter introduced the REXX language, and you should now be able to start inventing and writing your own REXX programs. To find out more about REXX, see the REXX Information object in the Information folder, or see the OS/2 Technical Library entry in Appendix B.

PART VI

The Best of OS/2 Shareware

Shareware and Copyright

Installing the Applications

Desktop Applications

Command-Line Utilities

THIS final part of OS/2 Secrets and Solutions contains descriptions of the OS/2 application programs found on the two companion disks that accompany this book. These programs fall into two broad categories:

- Desktop applications that bring new and enhanced capabilities to OS/2.

- OS/2 command-line utilities that do just one thing, but do it very well and usually do it very quickly.

Many of the programs come with several other associated files, usually ASCII text files containing documentation or contact and licensing information. This information is in addition to the often comprehensive online help information you can access from the desktop programs. These files are included on the companion disks in their entirety, and you can review them individually with your favorite text editor. They may have names such as ORDER.DOC, SHARE.TXT, REGISTER.DOC, or any permutation of README, including README.DOC, READ.ME, README.1ST, and so on. These documentation files, along with the online help information that many of the programs provide, explain the programs in their authors' own words; I have not edited this information.

Shareware and Copyright

Most of the OS/2 applications on these disks are shareware, although some of them are demonstration versions of commercial products. Any distinction between the two is getting harder and harder to make, because shareware programs these days have all the polish you would expect in a full-blown commercial product.

Shareware is not a kind of program but a method of software distribution. Software distributed as shareware gives you the chance to try the product before you pay anything—if you don't like the program, then there is nothing to pay. If you try a program and find that it fits your needs, then you are expected to register your copy. Individual software developers take different approaches on this issue; some politely ask you to forward a small sum to cover support and distribution costs, while others use more complex programming techniques to offer the program for a trial period after which it will no longer operate.

► SOLUTION

The Association of Shareware Professionals (ASP) was formed in 1987 to support shareware as an alternative to more traditional methods of software marketing and distribution. If you are a software developer and are interested in finding out more, contact:

The Executive Director
Association of Shareware Professionals,
545 Grover Road, Muskegon, MI 49442-9427

or send a message to CompuServe ID 72050,1433. Membership fees are very reasonable; $50 for the first year, $75 thereafter.

Each of the programs on the companion disks has its own license agreement and terms of use, usually defined as part of the documentation, although in some cases, you will find this information in a separate file.

Once you register the program, you are often entitled to additional benefits, which will vary from company to company, but may include:

• A license to use the program on one computer.

• The chance to upgrade to the latest version of the program.

- Technical support from the software developer. This may also include access to the developer's own bulletin board.

- A complete printed manual for the latest version of the software.

In all cases, registration of shareware encourages the developers to continue supporting their existing programs and to work to develop new applications.

It is important to remember that copyright laws apply to shareware in the same way that they apply to commercial software, and that copyright owners retain all rights to their product. In some cases, shareware developers may relinquish certain rights so that their software can be distributed freely in a variety of forms. For example, certain shareware authors require written permission before a commercial CD-ROM manufacturer can copy their shareware.

All the programs, associated files, and documentation included on the companion disks to this book are distributed with the written permission of the program authors, and are supplied as is, with no warranties of any kind.

Installing the Applications

NOTE

The disks that accompany this book are 5.25" floppy disks. Instructions for obtaining 3.5" disks can be found on the disk envelope inside the back cover. The installation process for 3.5" disks is exactly the same as for 5.25" floppy disks.

Both disks that accompany this book are in compressed form, and the expanded size of all the included files is approximately 5MB. To install the programs, you must have that much free disk space available. Place the first floppy disk in a disk drive, change to that drive, and run the Install program from an OS/2 command prompt, specifying the drive letter of your hard disk as the first parameter. For example, to install the programs on drive C, place Disk #1 in drive A, and type:

```
A:
INSTALL1 C:
```

Similarly, to install the programs contained on Disk #2, use the IN-STALL2 program from an OS/2 command prompt. These two batch files manage the copying and decompressing of all the application programs onto your hard disk. After running both installation programs, you will find two directories called SYBEX1 and SYBEX2 on your hard disk. They contain a separate subdirectory for each of the applications.

If you want to install one of these applications individually, you must first create a target directory on your hard disk, then copy the compressed file into that directory, and use the LH/2 program to uncompress it. You will find a working version of LH/2 on both of the companion disks.

The documentation that accompanies each application gives details on installation and configuration options specific to each program. Follow these instructions for best results.

Desktop Applications

The applications in this first section all run as Presentation Manager programs on the OS/2 desktop, and include an archive viewer, games, and several productivity applications you can use in your day-to-day work with OS/2. Several of these programs are fully-featured, powerful applications that offer the user access to complex functions, so you should consult the program's documentation files or online help for details. The accompanying documentation may also describe any special setup requirements that the program might have, or any assumptions that the programmer has made about the structure of your system and the locations of certain files.

In the sections that follow, I'll give a brief overview of what each program can do. If you're interested, you can complete your investigation of the program on your own.

Archive Viewer

AV (Archive Viewer) is a desktop program you can use to look at archive files made with one of the popular file compression programs like LH/2 or PKZIP.

You can tailor the program to your own computing environment with the Config button in the main AV window. Here you can specify the directory in which you want to place extracted files, as well as the names of the programs that you want to use with AV, including your favorite text editor. If you click on the Cvt button in the main AV window, you can look at or change the archiving programs available on your system. All this configuration information is stored in a text file called ARCHIVER.BB2.

AV lets you view, edit, extract, or delete files from an archive. You can even run an extracted program file, but this could be dangerous as many programs require configuration files or DLLs to run properly.

BlackJack

BlackJack for OS/2 is a desktop version of the popular card game. As blackjack is played in several slightly different ways, you can choose your preferred house rules from Atlantic City, Las Vegas, or Reno, and as you change between these sets of rules, the game setup in the center of the main BlackJack window changes also. Good luck!

Chron

Chron is a scheduling program that you can use to start programs running at specific times. A LAN supervisor might use it to start a file server back-up program in the middle of the night when network traffic is at a minimum, or to rebuild a database when users are not accessing that data. You can also use Chron as a reminder program for meetings or other regularly scheduled events.

The first time you run Chron, a window opens so you can specify the name of the file where you want to store scheduled events. When Chron is running, you will see two windows on the desktop. The smaller, titled Chron–Event Dispatcher, contains the current time and date, and the number of pending events. Use the selections from the Event and Options menus in this window to create and manage the events you want to schedule, and to establish the default settings for the program. The larger window, called Chron–Posted Events, contains all the scheduled messages from scheduled events, and you can even copy this information to the OS/2 clipboard.

ClipEdit

The ClipEdit program lets you view, print, modify, and save the contents of the OS/2 clipboard. The main ClipEdit window is divided into three sections:

- The Format list box at the top left of the window lists the format of the information on the clipboard.

- The Details box shows the size of the information in the clipboard.

- The Display area shows as much of the information on the clipboard as can fit in this area.

Use the options in the File menu to load or save information to or from the clipboard, and to print the clipboard's contents. The Clipboard–Edit menu lets you look at, edit, or clear the contents of the clipboard, while the Options menu lets you change the colors used by ClipEdit. Bitmap–Options lets you choose whether to size a graphical image, and the Help menu provides the usual help facilities.

DiskStat

DiskStat displays information for a specified disk drive in a window on the desktop. Information displayed includes:

- Drive letter and volume label
- Name of the file system installed on the disk

- Disk size in bytes
- Amount of free space on the disk, in bytes
- Amount of space used as a percentage of the whole
- Current size of the swap file, as long as the swap file is on the specified disk

Click on the title bar icon to access the Overall summary window. This shows how long DiskStat has been operating on your system and how the free space amount and percentage of disk space used have changed. You can also access the help system through this menu.

Galleria

Galleria is a well-written and carefully thought-out program for capturing and managing bitmapped images. You can print, load, crop, resize, and rotate an image, as well as convert it to monochrome or to gray-scale using Galleria, and you can capture screen images using the companion program, Galleria/CM.

Galleria supports the following bitmap formats for file import or export:

- OS/2 version 1.x bitmap
- OS/2 version 2.x bitmap
- Microsoft Windows 3.x bitmap
- Encapsulated PostScript (EPS)
- CompuServe Graphics Interchange Format (GIF)
- Digital Research (IMG)
- Apple MacPaint
- OS/2 metafile
- Microsoft Paint
- Kodak Photo CD

- PCX bitmap
- TGA
- TIF
- WPG

Figure VI.1 shows a bitmapped image displayed in Galleria.

FIGURE VI.1

A Bitmap displayed in Galleria

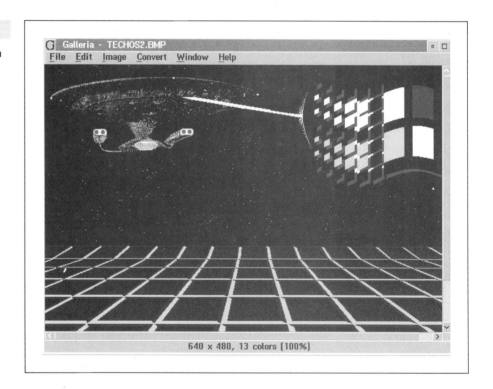

Besides the online help information, Galleria provides two OS/2 .INF files, GALLERIA.INF and GALLERCM.INF; you can look at these files using the VIEW command from an OS/2 command prompt.

INIMAINT (INI File Maintainence)

The INIMAINT program is a desktop application you can use to display and edit the information contained in OS/2's INI files. Because these INI files are binary files, they cannot be accessed by a normal text editor, but must be read by a program that understands their internal organization.

Looking at the contents of your INI files is a harmless enough pastime, but INIMAINT also gives you the option of changing entries, and that can be extremely dangerous unless you know exactly what you are doing. Before making *any* changes to your INI files, *always make and save a back-up copy first.*

One of the text files that accompanies INIMAINT, called INIFILE.TXT, contains a good description of how OS/2 uses INI files.

Lst/PM

Lst/PM is a 32-bit desktop application for viewing files as text in either ASCII or EBCDIC (Extended Binary Coded Decimal Interchange Code, a coding scheme developed by IBM and used on all IBM minicomputers and mainframes), or in hexadecimal notation. You can install Lst/PM on your desktop, and then drag and drop a selected file onto the program's icon for viewing, or you can start the program from an OS/2 command prompt and specify the file name as an optional parameter. You can also drop a file into Lst/PM's window while it is running, and the file will be loaded and displayed. You can search through the file backwards or forwards looking for text or for a regular expression, and you can make the search case-sensitive or not, as you wish. You also have complete control over fonts and colors, whether the contents of the file are displayed as text, text with line numbers, or in hexadecimal; you can even choose the code page you want to use. Figure VI.2 shows part of a text file displayed in hexadecimal form in Lst/PM.

Lst/PM is well documented and includes an OS/2 .INF file that you can read using the OS/2 VIEW command, as follows:

```
VIEW LSTPM
```

This command opens the OS/2 Information Presentation Facility on the desktop so you can view the contents of LSTPM.INF.

FIGURE VI.2

Part of a Text File
Displayed in
Hexadecimal in Lst/PM

Mah Jongg Solitaire

Mah Jongg Solitaire is a very attractive desktop game played with the standard set of 144 Mah Jongg tiles, stacked from 1 to 5 tiles high in the form of a dragon. The game proceeds as you select matching pairs of tiles from this dragon until there are no tiles left. You must choose identical tiles, with two exceptions; a season tile can be matched with any other season, and flower tiles can be matched with each other without regard for color. Figure VI.3 shows the arrangement of the tiles before the game begins.

FIGURE VI.3

The Mah Jongg
Solitaire Dragon at
the Start of a Game

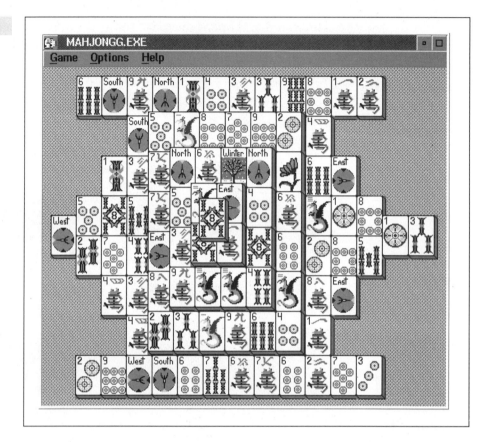

A tile can only be removed if:

- There are no tiles on top of it, and

- The tile is not blocked to the left or the right with tiles stacked at
  the same height.

Continue to select and remove pairs of tiles, until no more matches
remain visible, in which case you lose the game, or until all the tiles have
been removed, which means you win the game. Right-click on a tile to see
how many tiles of that type remain in the game. If you right-click
anywhere in the window away from the tiles, the program will tell you how
many tiles remain and how many possible tile matches there are. If you

thought that the flying-card display at the completion of a Microsoft Windows Solitaire game was impressive, just wait until you win your first game of Mah Jongg!

NA (Numerical Assistant)

NA (Numerical Assistant) is a desktop scientific calculator that also allows equation-based editing. The program features a one-line display, a row of function buttons for help, editing and cursor control, and a set of calculator-like buttons for mathematic or scientific data entry. The function buttons, below the one-line display and above the calculator keys, are used as follows, from left to right:

- **Shift+Del:** Cuts the selected information from the display to the clipboard.

- **Ctrl+Insert:** Copies the selected information from the display to the clipboard.

- **Shift+Insert:** Pastes the contents of the clipboard into the display at the current insertion point, replacing any existing text.

- **Alt+Backspace:** Undoes changes made in the display. Also known as the Oops button.

- **Left:** Moves the display cursor to the left.

- **Right:** Moves the display cursor to the right.

- **Insert:** Toggles the data entry mode from overstrike to insert.

- **Del:** Deletes the current selection in the display.

- **F1:** Opens the help system.

Enter numbers or functions by clicking on the appropriate key, and you will see the information in the one-line display at the top of the window. If you make a mistake, a message box opens, informing you of a syntax error, or other error such as an attempt to divide by zero.

PM Color Configuration (SYSCOLS)

This program lets you change any of the 41 colors used on the desktop. The color template called Different demonstrates what the desktop might look like if each configurable element were a different color. The program includes over 30 sample color templates, and additional templates can be created or modified. You can set colors temporarily, or save them permanently in OS/2's INI file. Try as many as you like; select a template from the Color Templates list in the main SYSCOLS window, click on the Set button, and the window elements will change color right before your eyes. Just remember that the Reset button will always restore your palette to the settings in effect before you started SYSCOLS running, so if you don't like Viking or Sunset, you can go back to your original boring old settings.

System Shutdown Plus

System Shutdown Plus is a small desktop application that installs an icon on the desktop you can use to shut down your system. Instead of using the desktop pop-up menu, you just double-click on this icon, and your system will be shut down in an orderly way.

Command-Line Utilities

The programs described in this final section can all be run from an OS/2 command prompt, rather than from the desktop. They all do just one thing, but they do it very well, and often very quickly. The programs are included for those OS/2 users who think that the command line is where the power of an operating system can be fully realized.

DELPATH

DELPATH is a very powerful program that lets you delete an entire directory, including all subdirectories, and all files contained in these subdirectories, including the normally protected system, hidden, and read-only files.

This capability is particularly useful in a LAN environment, where the network supervisor may decide to prune off entire branches of the directory structure. Deleting all the files from each directory and then removing each directory individually can take a lot of time, particularly when you consider the possible number of directories involved.

To delete all the files and directories in the VICTIM directory, including all files in all subdirectories, type:

```
DELPATH C:\VICTIM
```

DELPATH is a very powerful, and therefore potentially dangerous program; be careful not to delete the wrong directory. A confirmation message is always displayed to emphasize exactly which files and directories are about to be deleted, and as individual files are deleted, their names are displayed on the screen.

FSHL

FSHL is a shell program that adds considerable power to the OS/2 command line, including aliases and macros for commonly used or difficult-to-remember commands, extended command-line recall and editing capabilities, extended command set and batch language, and a provision for the user to add their own extensions, all without removing access to any of the basic OS/2 command-line features. For devotees of the OS/2 command line, this program is a must.

Documentation for FSHL is both extensive and well written, and when you register your copy, you can access Oberon Software's bulletin board for free technical support.

LH/2

LH/2 is a 32-bit OS/2 version of the popular LHARC file compression and decompression program popular in the MS-DOS world. It is based on the Lempel-Ziv-Huffman compression method developed by Haruhiko Okumura and Haruyasu Yoshizaki. With this latest version of the program, version 2.20, all previous restriction on use, including commercial use, have been removed by the author, Peter Fitzsimmons of A:Ware Incorporated; and the program is now in the public domain.

This program is included on the companion disks for your own use, and is also used as the compression and decompression mechanism when the files on these disks are transferred to your hard disk.

LH/2 supports OS/2's long file names, and file extended attributes, and when decompressed onto your hard disk, includes an OS/2 .INF file that you can read using the OS/2 VIEW command, as follows:

    VIEW LH2

This command opens the OS/2 Information Presentation Facility on the desktop so you can view the contents of LH2.INF.

The syntax for LH/2 is as follows:

    LH *command archive file1 file2 /switches*

where *command* specifies the LH/2 mode, *archive* is the name of the compressed file you are creating, *file1 file2* are the names of the files you want to compress, and */switches* are optional switches used to modify LH/2.

LH/2 commands can be one of the following:

A	Creates an archive or adds files to an existing archive.
M	Moves files to an existing archive. Once the archive is complete, the original files will be deleted.
L	Lists information about the files contained in an archive.
X	Extracts files from an archive.

T	Tests an archive by extracting the files to the NUL device.
D	Deletes specific files from an archive.

and you can use the following LH/2 switches:

/V	Turns on verbose mode when used with the L command.
/A	Maintains file attributes (archive, hidden, system, and read-only attributes) when used with the A, M, or X commands.
/S	Saves or restores subdirectory information. If the directory does not exist when you decompress the archive, you will be prompted to create the directory. The /O switch will suppress this prompt.
/O	Suppresses all prompts; when used with the X command, this option will overwrite existing files without prompting.
/I	Ignores extended attributes when used with A, M, or X.
/E	Saves or restores empty directories and directory extended attributes, when used with A, M, or X.
/M	Stores only those files that have the archive attribute set, when used with the A or M commands.
/H	Provides command-line help information.

KILLEM

KILLEM is a 32-bit command-line application that kills processes by name, or by a decimal process identification number provided by the OS/2 PSTAT command. For example, if you run a program by typing:

```
PROGRAM
```

or

RUN PROGRAM

from the command prompt, you would type:

KILL PROGRAM

to kill it.

OS2SCAN (Virus Scan)

OS2SCAN, written by the experts at McAfee Associates, searches your OS/2 system for computer viruses in memory, the partition table, boot sector and in data and program files on your disks. Viruses in a VDM cannot be detected in memory by OS2SCAN, so make sure to close all DOS and WIN-OS/2 sessions on your system before using OS2SCAN, so that any viruses lurking in memory cannot reinfect your files after OS2SCAN has run.

This version of the program detects 865 viruses, or up to 1561 if you count all the virus variants. For a complete list of known viruses, check out the companion text file, VIRLIST.TXT.

Infected files can be deleted safely by using the OS2SCAN /D switch at the command line, or with the OS2CLEAN virus removal program, described in the next section.

NOTE   If you are a network administrator, you can download NETSCAN for OS/2, or the NET SHIELD antivirus NLM for NetWare 3.11 from the MCAFEE forum on CompuServe (GO MCAFEE), or from McAfee and Associates's own 25-line bulletin board at 408-988-4004.

OS2SCAN uses three methods to detect unknown or new viruses. First, validation codes are checked, looking for the changes made by a virus to files or to system areas. Second, Generic and Family virus detectors look for viruses that are variants of existing, known viruses, and finally, external virus signatures can be inserted into the OS2SCAN database.

Before using OS2SCAN for the first time, check it by running the companion validation program, OS2VAL. For information on OS2VAL, see the text file OS2VAL.DOC. The validation results for OS2SCAN should be as follows:

> FILE NAME: OS2SCAN.EXE
>
> > SIZE: 178,352
> >
> > DATE: 12-09-1992
>
> FILE AUTHENTICATION
>
> > Check Method 1: 78A3
> >
> > Check Method 2: 10CA

OS2SCAN also runs a self-check when it runs, and if it has been modified in any way, you will see a warning message, and you should stop using the program immediately.

OS2CLEAN (Virus Removal)

OS2CLEAN removes all viruses detected by the previous program, OS2SCAN, and in most cases, can repair the infected areas of the system, restoring them to their original state. If the file is infected with a less common virus, OS2CLEAN will display a warning message asking the user whether it should overwrite and delete the infected file. You cannot recover files erased in this way.

Before using OS2CLEAN for the first time, check it by running the companion validation program, OS2VAL. For information on OS2VAL, see the text file OS2VAL.DOC. The validation results for OS2CLEAN should be as follows:

> FILE NAME: OS2CLEAN.EXE
>
> > SIZE: 268,112
> >
> > DATE: 02-26-1993
>
> FILE AUTHENTICATION
>
> > Check Method 1: 64BB
> >
> > Check Method 2: 03E2

OS2CLEAN also runs a self-check when it runs, and if it has been modified in any way, you will see a warning message, and you should stop using the program immediately.

When OS2SCAN detects a virus on your system, it creates an identification code (enclosed inside square brackets), specific to the virus, that you must use with OS2CLEAN to remove the virus from your system. For example, the ID code for the Jerusalem virus is [Jeru], and this code must be used with OS2CLEAN, in the following form:

    OS2CLEAN [Jeru]

The square brackets must be included.

TE/2

TE/2 (Terminal Emulator/2) is a communications and terminal emulation program that supports the following communications protocols:

- X-Modem
- 1K-X-Modem
- Y-Modem
- Y-Modem-G
- Z-Modem
- ASCII

and the following terminal emulations:

- ANSI
- Extended ANSI
- VT100
- IBM 3101
- TTY

TE/2 has a built-in script language, and its default line parameters can manage multiple 200-entry dialing directories. It also allows automatic redialing and round-robin queue dialing.

WHEREIS

WHEREIS is a small, fast, command-line file finder. To see a list of the available program options, just type:

WHEREIS

at a command prompt. To start a search, type:

WHEREIS *file name*

at a command prompt, and all your hard disks will be searched for the specified file. To restrict the search to a single drive, include the drive letter on the command line:

WHEREIS *drive:file name*

and to restrict the search to a specific directory, use:

WHEREIS *drive:\path\file name*

where *drive* is a valid driver letter, and *path* is any directory path. If you omit the drive letter, WHEREIS searches the current drive. To start the search from the current drive and current directory, use:

WHEREIS .*file name*

and to specify disks for the search, use:

WHEREIS *file name//drive letters*

where *drive letters* represent the drives you want to search. For example, to search drives F and G for the file LVS.EXE, use:

WHEREIS LVS.EXE //FG

You can toggle the running directory display if you type D during a search; turning this display off can speed up a search by a huge amount. The /S option is useful if you want to send output from WHEREIS to your printer, because this switch turns off all the progress messages the program generates as it runs.

The /P option pauses the program, and you can exit from the program by pressing the Escape key.

Also included with WHEREIS you will find an additional program called PGMPATH, which searches the path for the specified EXE or CMD file name and returns the fully qualified path.

OS/2 OS/2 OS/2

OS/2 OS/2 OS/2 OS/2 OS/2 OS/2 OS/2 OS/2 OS/2

OS/2 OS/2 OS/2 O

Installing OS/2

THE OS/2 installation process is extremely flexible; you can install OS/2 from almost any type of media—floppy disks, CD-ROM, local area network, or another hard disk—and the installation process can be controlled by the user from the keyboard or left unattended and controlled by a text response file. In this appendix we'll look at all these options and cover some topics you should consider before installing OS/2 on your system.

OS/2 is available in three slightly different forms:

- **Full Package:** This version is for users who do not have a previous operating system installed on their computer, and is available on CD-ROM, and on both sizes of floppy disk.

- **Upgrade Package:** This version is for users who currently have a version of OS/2 installed or who are users of MS-DOS and/or Windows. If the installlation program does not find an existing operating system, this version will not install. The package is available as 3.5" or 5.25" floppy disks.

- **Preload Package:** This version of OS/2 is preloaded onto selected IBM PS/2 and OEM computers before they are shipped. If the package does not include backup OS/2 floppy disks, make sure you find out how you can get these disks, and also what they will cost you; in the event of an accident, you cannot reinstall OS/2 without them.

Table A.1 lists the number of floppy disks included in the OS/2 version 2.1 package.

If you buy OS/2 version 2.1 on a CD-ROM, you will find two floppy disks included in the package. These disks are equivalent to the first two floppy disks in the diskette-based product, the installation disk and the first

TABLE A.1: OS/2 Version 2.1 Floppy Disk Count

SYSTEM ELEMENT	3.5" DISKS	5.25" DISKS
Install	1	1
Operating System	19	22
Printer Drivers	5	6
Display Drivers	2	2
MMPM/2	2	4

operating system disk, and are used to boot the computer when you first start the installation process. Installing from a CD-ROM is by far the easiest method; if OS/2 supports your CD-ROM and adapter (see Chapter 8 for details), you should use this method.

Installation Overview

N O T E

See Chapter 11 for information on installing and configuring the multimedia package, MMPM/2, bundled with OS/2 version 2.1.

There are several decisions that you must make before you start the OS/2 installation process: how you want to install OS/2 (as the only operating system, alongside an existing version of MS-DOS, or as one of several operating systems); which file system you want to use; and which parts of the whole OS/2 system you want to install. In Chapter 8, Table 8.1 shows how much memory various parts of the OS/2 system will use, and Table 8.2 lists the memory requirements of some typical mainstream applications. Table 8.4 lists the amount of free hard disk space you will need available to install the optional portions of the OS/2 system. Installation decisions must be based on how you plan to use OS/2, and that in turn will affect the amount of space that OS/2 takes up on your system.

Installing OS/2 as the Only Operating System

When you install OS/2 as the only operating system on your hard disk, you can install it either on a new unused hard disk, or as an upgrade to an earlier version of OS/2. For an upgrade the installation program will update the appropriate OS/2 system files, but will not affect your application programs or data files. With OS/2 as the only operating system on your hard disk, you can run OS/2 applications, most Microsoft Windows applications, and most MS-DOS applications.

Installing OS/2 Alongside an Existing Version of MS-DOS

Another installation option is to add OS/2 to a system that already has a version of MS-DOS installed on it. This gives you the option of switching between MS-DOS and OS/2 should you need to; some poorly written MS-DOS programs do not run well under OS/2. With this option, you can run OS/2 applications, DOS and Microsoft Windows applications under OS/2 software emulation, and MS-DOS applications using the native version of MS-DOS.

The disadvantage of this flexibility is that you have to reboot the computer when you change from OS/2 to MS-DOS. The OS/2 Dual Boot handles this for you, and you can switch from one operating system to the other from either the DOS or the OS/2 command line by using the BOOT command (see Chapter 13 for more information on this and other commands), or from the OS/2 desktop by selecting the Dual Boot icon from the Command Prompts folder.

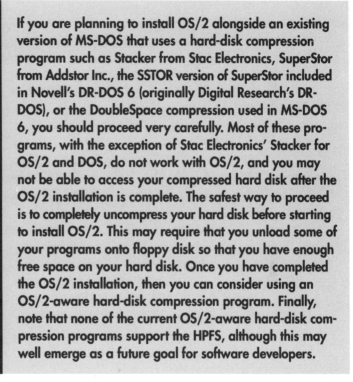

WARNING

If you are planning to install OS/2 alongside an existing version of MS-DOS that uses a hard-disk compression program such as Stacker from Stac Electronics, SuperStor from Addstor Inc., the SSTOR version of SuperStor included in Novell's DR-DOS 6 (originally Digital Research's DR-DOS), or the DoubleSpace compression used in MS-DOS 6, you should proceed very carefully. Most of these programs, with the exception of Stac Electronics' Stacker for OS/2 and DOS, do not work with OS/2, and you may not be able to access your compressed hard disk after the OS/2 installation is complete. The safest way to proceed is to completely uncompress your hard disk before starting to install OS/2. This may require that you unload some of your programs onto floppy disk so that you have enough free space on your hard disk. Once you have completed the OS/2 installation, then you can consider using an OS/2-aware hard-disk compression program. Finally, note that none of the current OS/2-aware hard-disk compression programs support the HPFS, although this may well emerge as a future goal for software developers.

To use Dual Boot you must make additions to your DOS AUTOEXEC.BAT and CONFIG.SYS files before you start to install OS/2. Add the following lines to AUTOEXEC.BAT:

```
SET COMSPEC=C:\DOS\COMMAND.COM

PATH C:\DOS

APPEND=C:\DOS

COPY C:\DOS\COMMAND.COM C:\ >NUL
```

If you are using DOS 5 or later, be sure to add these commands before the C:\DOS\DOSSHELL command.

Add this line to your CONFIG.SYS file:

```
SHELL=C:\DOS\COMMAND.COM /P
```

These changes are required because the OS/2 installation program will delete the MS-DOS file COMMAND.COM from the root directory when OS/2 is installed, and the MS-DOS system needs to know where to find the command processor. Finally, make sure that CONFIG.SYS and AUTOEXEC.BAT are the only files in your root directory. Then install any MS-DOS or Microsoft Windows application programs you want to add to your system, and you are ready to start the OS/2 installation program.

Installing OS/2 as One of Several Operating Systems

This installation option gives you the most flexibility. The OS/2 Boot Manager lets you install several operating systems on your hard disk, and when you start your computer running, a menu asks you to choose the operating system you want to run. This kind of setup is particularly useful for programmers and application developers who have to use several different operating environments.

Installing the Boot Manager is considered to be an advanced procedure because you may have to reformat and repartition your hard disk with FDISK, depending on its original structure. If you have just one partition that occupies the whole hard disk, you must reformat the disk and repartition it into multiple partitions, including a 1MB partition for the Boot Manager, and up to three other partitions for the other operating systems you plan to install. Reformatting the hard disk will destroy all the data stored on it, so be prepared to make a complete backup before you start the OS/2 installation.

You should carefully plan how you will divide up your hard disk before you start the installation. You can divide your hard disk into four primary partitions or into three primary partitions and one extended partition. Boot Manager requires its own 1MB primary partition, which leaves three other primary partitions that could hold three operating systems. There are several limitations on where you can install MS-DOS; version 3.3 must be in a primary partition within the first 32MB on the first hard disk, and later versions of MS-DOS must be installed in a primary partition on the first hard disk. See Table 8.3 for details of operating system hard disk space requirements.

To take advantage of Boot Manager, you need to install the Boot Manager in its own partition, as described under "Advanced Installation Options" later in this appendix.

Deciding on a File System: HPFS or FAT?

Another choice you must make is which OS/2 file system you want to use, the FAT or the HPFS. FAT is a good choice for hard disks of up to 60MB in size, but if your disk is larger, choose the HPFS because it provides much better performance on large disks than is possible with the FAT system.

The advantages and disadvantages of using FAT and HPFS are described in detail in Chapter 13.

 **WARNING** If you ever plan to boot your computer with a version of MS-DOS from a floppy disk, remember that MS-DOS cannot access a HPFS hard disk; you should use the FAT instead.

Installing OS/2

Once you have decided whether to install OS/2 as the only operating system, with the Dual Boot option, or with the Boot Manager, you have backed up any existing hard disk data that you want to keep, and you have chosen a file system, you are ready to start installing OS/2. If you are installing from floppy disks, be prepared for the process to take about an hour; installing from a CD-ROM is much faster.

NOTE

If you are installing OS/2 from a CD-ROM, you boot the Install floppy disk, and change to the second floppy disk when prompted. Then the rest of the installation takes place directly from the CD-ROM; there is no more disk swapping.

To start the OS/2 installation program, place the floppy disk marked "Installation Diskette" in drive A and reboot the computer. OS/2 can only be installed from drive A; if you have the wrong disk size, you will have to return to the dealer to get the correct size. If you have both 3.5" and 5.25" floppy disk drives on your computer, and the wrong one is set up as drive A, you can consider changing over the floppy disk drive cable connectors. However, if you do this, remember to change the CMOS parameters so that your computer also knows about the change.

You are prompted by screen messages to remove and replace floppy disks as needed during the installation process. As information is displayed on the screen, you can either accept it or change it; accepting and using the standard defaults will work in almost all circumstances. The first six floppy disks are used to prepare (and, if necessary, partition) the hard disk, install the Dual Boot or Boot Manager options if required, and load the code needed to drive the graphical user interface. When the basic installation is complete, you will be asked to reboot the computer, and when you do you will see the OS/2 Installation and Setup window on the screen. This window contains the following choices:

- **Learn how to use a mouse** starts the mouse tutorial. If you've never used a mouse before installing OS/2, you can run this program now to get some practice. This may make it easier to use the installation program. The mouse tutorial is also part of the larger OS/2 tutorial on the desktop.

- **Install preselected features** installs the basic operating system and a selection of the operating system utilities.

- **Install all features** loads the complete operating system, including all utilities and games onto your system, using the default settings.

- **Select features and install** lets you choose the operating system components to install. This option opens the OS/2 Setup and Installation window, which looks and works exactly like the Selective Install object described in Chapter 2. In OS/2 version 2.1, you install and configure your mouse, serial port support, the primary and secondary displays, the country and keyboard settings, and CD-ROM, SCSI adapter, and printer support. Figure A.1 shows the OS/2 Setup and Installation window for OS/2 version 2.1.

The available free space on your hard disk, and the amount of space that each of these options will occupy, are shown on the screen to help you decide which option to choose. Use the ↓ key to highlight your selection, then press the Enter key. With the mouse, click on the selection you want, then click OK. Choose the installation option that best meets your needs from the choices offered in this window. If you do not install certain features now but later find that you need them, you can add them to your

FIGURE A.1

The OS/2 Setup and Installation window for OS/2 version 2.1

System Configuration

Use the mouse or the spacebar to place a check mark in the box next to each option you would like to change, and then press OK.

System
- Mouse
  Serial Pointing Device

- Serial Device Support
  - Install Support
  - Do Not Install Support

- Primary Display
  Video Graphics Array [VGA]
- Secondary Display
  None

Locale
- Country
  United States
- Keyboard
  United States

Currently Installed Peripherals
- CD-ROM Device Support
  Toshiba 3301,3401
- SCSI Adapter Support
  Future Domain 845,850,860,8;
- Printer
  LASERJET.HP LaserJet III

OK   Help

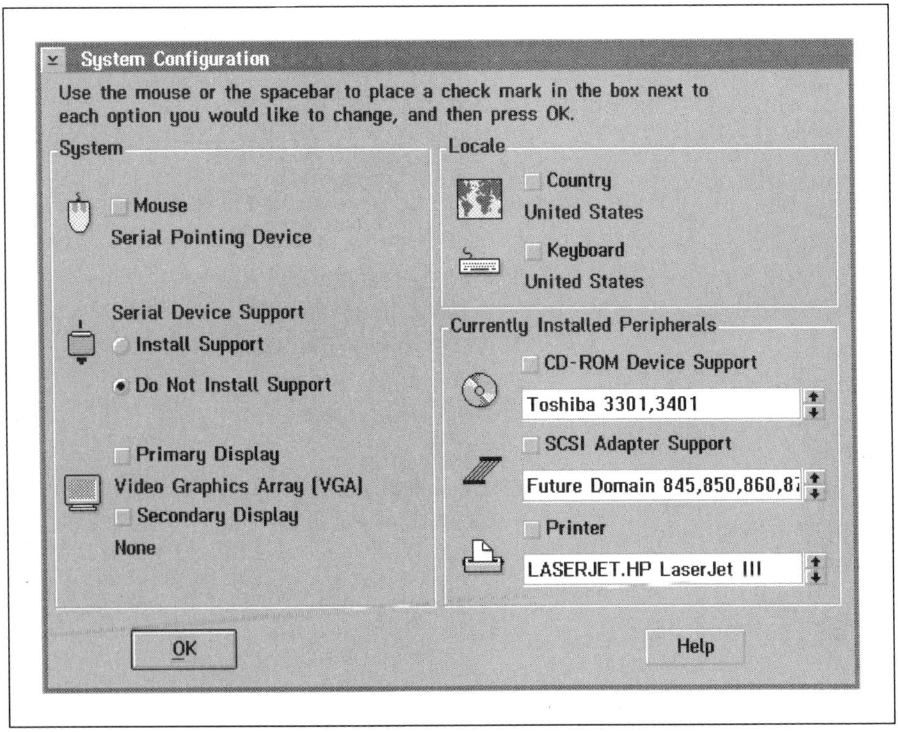

system by using Selective Install from the System Setup folder as described in Chapter 2.

If you choose the Select Features and Install option, another window opens so you can specify the operating system elements you want to install, as Figure A.2 shows.

Initially, all the features will be checked to indicate that all elements will be installed. To the right of each entry, you will see the amount of disk space (in MB) that each option will require. Several options allow you to make additional choices, and you access these choices using the More button. To prevent an element from being installed, click on the appropriate check box with the left mouse button. When your choices are complete, click on the Install button to continue.

FIGURE A.2

Select the Optional Elements you want to Install

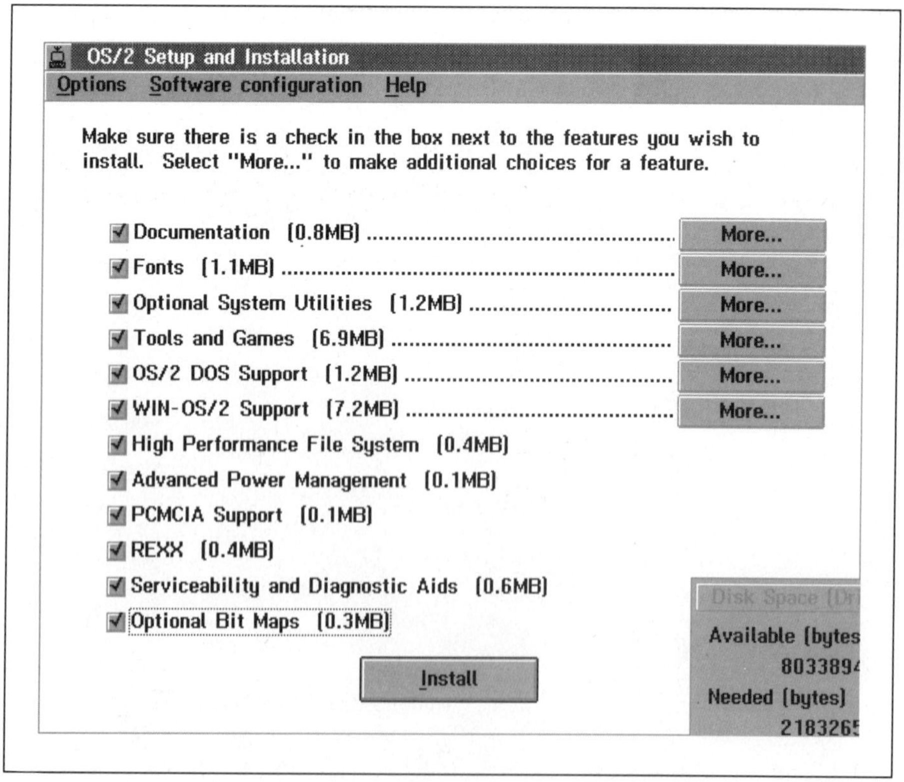

If you are installing from floppy disk, you will be prompted to swap disks as the installation process continues. A progress indicator display shows the name of the file currently being installed, and the percentage of the information on the current disk that has been copied. The Find Programs window lets you migrate your MS-DOS or Microsoft Windows applications to the OS/2 environment. This process is exactly the same as that performed by the Migrate Applications object described in Chapter 2, and the same database of application file names is used to recognize your applications. If the migration program does not find all your applications, use the Add button to search for and then migrate additional applications. The programs found during the migration process are grouped into desktop folders called OS/2 Programs, DOS Programs, or Windows Programs depending on their type, and any applications that you added are located in separate folders called Additional OS/2 Programs, Additional DOS Programs, or Additional Windows Programs. If you add more programs after the OS/2 installation is complete, use the Migrate Applications object in the System Setup folder on the desktop to move them to the right folder.

Once your applications are migrated, you can give the OK to let the installation program migrate your CONFIG.SYS and AUTO-EXEC.BAT files. If you prefer, you can choose to change these files manually, and add any specialized settings that you need on your system. You can also choose between keeping your existing Windows desktop settings and installing a default Windows desktop.

> ## S E C R E T

As the installation program proceeds, entries that describe its progress are added to a text file called INSTALL.LOG located in the OS2\INSTALL directory. You can look at this file using your favorite text editor, and you will see entries like the following:

INSTALL.LOG

Installing Operating System/2.
Model = FC
Submodel = 01

```
Non-ABIOS machine
Bus Architecture: |0|
Disk Type: |0|
Greater than 20MB primary partition exists.
Copying files C:\CONFIG.SYS -> C:\CONFIG.BAK
Copying files C:\AUTOEXEC.BAT -> C:\AUTOEXEC.BAK
Making directory C:\OS2
Making directory C:\OS2\DLL
Making directory C:\OS2\DLL\FAXPM
Making directory C:\OS2\DLL\DISPLAY
Making directory C:\OS2\HELP
Making directory C:\OS2\INSTALL
Making directory C:\OS2\SYSTEM
Making directory C:\OS2\SYSTEM\TRACE
Making directory C:\OS2\BOOK
Making directory C:\OS2\MDOS
Making directory C:\OS2
Making directory C:\OS2\MDOS
Making directory C:\OS2\MDOS\WINOS2
Making directory C:\OS2\MDOS\WINOS2\SYSTEM
Making directory C:\OS2\BITMAP
Making directory C:\OS2\APPS
Making directory C:\OS2\APPS\DLL
Making directory C:\OS2\HELP\GLOSS
Making directory C:\OS2\HELP\TUTORIAL
Making directory C:\OS2\DRIVERS
Copying files A:\UNPACK.EXE -> C:\OS2\UNPACK.EXE
Dual Boot installed.
DISK 2
C:\OS2\CHKDSK.COM
C:\OS2\FORMAT.COM
C:\OS2\INSTALL\UHPFS.DLL
```

Headings appear throughout INSTALL.LOG for each installation disk processed, followed by the full path names of the files copied from each floppy disk. You will also see progress marker comments, indicating that a specific point in the installation process has been reached. These comments include "System files are being copied to the fixed disk," and "System file transfer is complete." If any installation steps failed, you will see entries such as "No Dual Boot installed."

When you have completed the OS/2 installation, restart your computer. The first time you start OS/2, the operating system must create many of the important system configuration files needed to build the desktop, and this process can take a while, so be patient. You will see the OS/2 logo screen appear, and then the desktop and the OS/2 tutorial will be displayed on your screen. Click on the Next button or press Enter to start the tutorial. If you'd rather skip the tutorial, click on the Exit button to go directly to the OS/2 desktop. You will find the following objects on the default desktop:

- OS/2 System folder
- Master Help Index
- Information folder
- Start Here folder
- Minimized Window Viewer
- Templates folder
- Printer
- Shredder
- Drive A

as well as folders for your OS/2, DOS, and Windows applications. As soon as the desktop is complete, and all hard-disk activity has ceased, right-click on a blank area of the desktop to open the pop-up menu, and select Shut Down. Do this before you start any applications programs. After the system shuts down, reboot, and start using your system. Congratulations, you made it.

Advanced Installation Options

There are several more advanced methods you can use to install OS/2, depending on your computing environment. The first of these, installing OS/2 with the Boot Manager, allows you to maintain several operating systems on the same hard disk. You can also install OS/2 from a hard disk, use a text *response file* containing defined keywords to communicate with the installation program rather than accepting user input from the keyboard, or install OS/2 from a local area network. These three methods can become very important if you are faced with the task of installing OS/2 on a large number of different systems.

Installing OS/2 with the Boot Manager

When you start the OS/2 installation, if you are installing on a blank hard disk, you will see the Installation Drive Selection screen offering you the following choices:

1. Accept Predefined Installation Partition

2. Specify Your Own Installation Partition

but if you are installing onto an existing system, the choices will be slightly different:

1. Accept the drive

2. Specify a Different Drive or Partition

In either case, select option 2 to display the partitions on your system in the FDISK screen.

W A R N I N G

Any time you change anything concerning the partition table, and that is exactly what installing the Boot Manager does, *always back up your hard disk first* if you have data or programs that you want to save. Changing the size of a partition deletes all the information about that partition.

There must be enough room on your disk to support the partitions that you need; if your disk has just one partition that occupies the complete disk, you must delete that partition first. Select Install Boot Manager from the Options menu, and specify whether you want it at the beginning (the recommended position) or the end of your hard disk. After you have created the Boot Manager partition, create the other partitions that you will need for your other operating systems. Highlight the partition that you want to use for OS/2, press Enter to open the FDISK Options menu, select Add to Boot Manager Menu, and press the Enter key. Type the name you want to use with this partition or logical drive, and press Enter once again.

Open the Options menu again, and this time select Set Installable, to indicate that this partition will be used for OS/2. If you plan to install other operating systems on your hard disk, use Set Startup Values from the Options menu to set the length of time that the Boot Manager menu will be displayed when you start your system (you can change this later using the SETBOOT command, which is covered in Chapter 12), and select whether you want to use the normal or the advanced Boot Manager menu. The only difference between these two menus is that the normal menu lists the names of the operating systems installed on your hard disk, while the advanced menu also lists additional partition information. Once you have set up your hard disk, you must save your changes; press F3, select Save and Exit, then press the Enter key.

Once all your partitions are established, you can resume installing OS/2, and this time, when the Installation Drive Selection screen is displayed, choose option 1: Accept the Drive. The installation of OS/2 now continues with the OS/2 Setup and Installation window described earlier in this chapter. Once the installation is complete, you can restore any programs or data files that you backed up before starting the installation process.

N O T E

If you have installed AIX, you can add it to the Boot Manager menu by opening the Drives object pop-up menu in the OS/2 System folder, then choosing Create Partitions. This opens the FDISKPM window on the desktop; now highlight the entry that contains AIX information, select Options from the menu bar, and choose Add to Boot Manager Menu. Type the name that you want to use with AIX and press Enter, then select Options again and choose Exit. Finally, use the Save button to save these changes. Now you will be able to start AIX from the Boot Manager startup menu.

You can install your other operating systems immediately after you complete the installation of OS/2, or you can do it later; the choice is yours. If you want to install another operating system in another primary partition, you need to indicate which partition you want to use. Open the OS/2 System folder on the desktop, open the Drives object pop-up menu, and select Create Partitions. This opens the FDISKPM window on the desktop (FDISKPM is described in Chapter 12). If the partition you want to use is not the active primary partition, highlight the partition you want to use, selection Options from the menu bar, select Set Installable, then select Options; this time choose Exit, then select the Save button. Now that the correct primary partition is selected, you can boot up the operating system you want to install. If you are asked whether to format the partition, you should do so.

Installing OS/2 from a Hard Disk

If you have an earlier version of OS/2 previously installed on your hard disk, and you have sufficient free hard disk space, you can actually install

OS/2 from your hard disk, and so cut down the amount of time an installation takes. This technique is particularly useful for installing from a network file server onto individual workstations, as described shortly. It involves creating image files of each of the installation floppy disks, and requires about 30MB of hard disk space that will not be used for any other purpose during the installation.

You need several special programs to perform this installation, and you will find them on Disk #7 of the OS/2 package. These programs are not loaded onto your system during a normal installation from floppy disk. They are compressed into a single file called CID, which stands for Configuration, Installation, and Distribution, and to unpack them from a floppy disk in drive A, use the following command from an OS/2 command prompt:

    UNPACK A:\CID

This command decompresses four files—SEIMAGE.EXE, SEDISK.EXE, SEINST.EXE, and SEMAINT.EXE—into the OS2\INSTALL directory on your hard disk.

You can unpack these four files into a different directory if you prefer, using the following syntax:

    UNPACK A:\CID C:*directory name*

and you can unpack the files one at a time using the /N: switch:

    UNPACK A:\CID C:*directory name* /N:*file name*

The SEMAINT and SEINST programs are included for use in future product implementations and will not be discussed further; SEIMAGE and SEDISK are the programs used in a hard-disk installation, and they perform the following tasks:

- **SEIMAGE** automates the creation of the directory structure needed by the installation process. SEIMAGE copies all the floppy disks in the OS/2 package into specific directories on your hard disk that share the same name as the original floppy disk volume label. For example, the contents of the first floppy disk, labeled DISK 0, will be copied into the DISK_0 subdirectory. Here's the syntax to use:

    SEIMAGE /S: *source drive* /T:*target drive*

where *source drive* is the floppy disk drive from which the original distribution disks will be read, and *target drive* is the complete path name of the directory on the hard disk. If you are reading the floppy disks from drive A and creating the disk images in the OS2SE21 directory on drive C, this command might look like the following:

SEIMAGE /S:A: /T:C:\OS2SE21

If you are using 3.5" disks, this command will create the following directory structure:

```
C:\
   C:\OS2SE21
      DISK_1
      DISK_2
      DISK_3
      DISK_4
      DISK_5
      •
      •
      •
      DISK_20
      PMDD_1
      PMDD_2
      PMDD_3
      PMDD_4
      PMDD_5
      DISP_1
      DISP_2
```

With 5.25" disks, there will be more directories because there are more 5.25" disks in the OS/2 package than there are 3.5" disks. SEIMAGE lists the names of all the files copied, and prompts you to change floppy disks as the process proceeds.

- **SEDISK** creates a slightly modified installation disk and disk #1 (often referred to as the Transport Disk) for the hard disk installation process, and requires two blank but formatted floppy disks. You must first use SEIMAGE to create the hard-disk images of these floppy disks before you use SEDISK to transfer these images to floppy disk. The SEDISK syntax is:

SEDISK /S:*source path* /T:*target drive*

where *source path* is the path for the floppy disk image directory, and *target drive* is the drive letter of the floppy disk drive you want to use. Continuing with the previous example, this command becomes:

SEDISK /S:C:\OS2SE21 /T:A:

Again, the program guides you through the floppy disk creation process, asking you to change floppy disks as needed.

WARNING Throughout this process, the floppy disks you create must match the original OS/2 distribution disks in both physical size and in formatted capacity; you cannot create 5.25" disks from 3.5" disks, nor can you create 3.5" disks from 5.25" originals.

Once the disk images are prepared and you have created the two floppy disks, there is just one more task you must complete before starting the installation. Listing A.1 shows a typical CONFIG.SYS file, created on the Transport disk by SEDISK. Check through the file to make sure that all the appropriate device drivers you might need are invoked; if you created the floppy disk images on an HPFS hard disk, copy the file UHPFS.DLL from the C:\OS2SE21\DISK_2 directory to the Transport disk, so that the installation process can access the HPFS disk.

You should also check the SET OS2_SHELL statement to make sure it points to the installation program SYSINST1.EXE, as follows:

SET OS2_SHELL=C:\OS2SE21\DISK_1\SYSINST2.EXE C:\OS2SE21

SET SOURCEPATH=C:\OS2SE21

SYSINST2.EXE is the standard OS/2 installation program, and when it receives the drive letter and path information for the floppy disk images, will perform a normal dialog-driven installation from that drive. The installation program searches the OS/2 environment space for the setting of

LISTING A.1

A typical CONFIG.SYS file created by SEDISK.

```
buffers=32
iopl=yes
memman=noswap
protshell=sysinst1.exe
REM set os2_shell=cmd.exe
set os2_shell=c:\os2se21\disk_1\sysinst2.exe c:\os2se21
set source_path=c:\os2se21
diskcache=64,LW
protectonly=yes
libpath=.;\;\os2\dll;
ifs=hpfs.ifs /c:64
pauseonerror=no
codepage=850
devinfo=kbd,us,keyboard.dcp
devinfo=scr,ega,vtbl850.dcp
device=\dos.sys
REM set path=\;\os2;\os2\system;\os2\install
set path=\;\os2;\os2\system;\os2\install;c:\os2se21
set dpath=\;\os2;\os2\system;\os2\install
set keys=on
basedev=print01.sys
basedev=ibm1flpy.add
basedev=ibm1s506.add
basedev=ibm2flpy.add
basedev=ibm2adsk.add
basedev=ibm2m57.add
basedev=ibm2scsi.add
basedev=ibmint13.i13
basedev=os2dasd.dmd
device=\testcfg.sys
```

the SourcePath variable, and this should also be set to the directory containing the disk images; the path statement in CONFIG.SYS should also include this same information, as follows:

```
PATH=\;\OS2;\OS2\SYSTEM;OS2\INSTALL;C:\OS2SE21
```

When these changes are complete, you are ready to make the installation from the disk images on drive C. Insert the installation disk created by SEDISK in drive A, and boot your computer; when prompted, remove this floppy disk and insert the Transport Disk. From this point, the rest of the installation is performed using the floppy disk images on your hard disk, and runs just like a normal installation, except that this method is much faster.

If you're installing OS/2 onto network workstations, your users will use the Installation and Transport disks to install the image files from the server drive onto their hard drives, as described in "Completing the Installation from a File Server."

Preparing a Response File to Install OS/2

So far we have described dialog-driven installations, in which the user provides input from the keyboard to confirm configuration choices, but you can also install OS/2 using a text-based *response file* and a different installation program. Instead of requiring users to enter information from the keyboard, you can configure the response file ahead of time with the correct entries, and install OS/2 with virtually no operator interaction. Except for a progress indicator display, no windows open during this type of installation. This method is especially suited to a corporate environment where a large number of systems must be installed. (The next section shows how to complete the installation onto network workstations.) You can even embed response files inside other response files; doing so allows you to create a generalized response file that will handle the bulk of all installations, and then use another response file to tailor an installation to specific user requirements. Because a response file is a text file, you can look at or change it using either of the OS/2 editors.

> ## SOLUTION

If your company decides to use remote installation methods to install OS/2, locate a copy of the IBM Redbook *OS/2 Remote Installation and Maintenance*, part number GG24-3780. This manual, prepared by IBM's International Technical Support Centers, contains information on installing

OS/2 using a response file as well as information on installing OS/2 from IBM's LAN Server, Novell NetWare, and TCP/IP-based local area networks.

> The document also contains a 3.5" floppy disk with many examples of REXX procedures and C-language source code for several useful programs. You should also obtain copies of the following related IBM documents:
>
> - *IBM Network Transport Services/2 Redirected Installation and Configuration Guide*, part number S96F-8488.
>
> - *Automated Installation for CID Enabled Services LAN Server V3.0 and Network Transport Services/2*, part number GG24-3781.
>
> - *Automated Installation for CID Enabled OS/2*, part number GG24-3783.

Response files contain the following entries:

- **Comment lines** document what the response file is doing; comment lines begin with an asterisk (*) and are ignored. All blank lines are also ignored.

- **Response lines** define the keywords and keyword values that the installation program will use in constructing the installation. Over 50 keywords are available; they range from AlternateAdapter, which specifies the secondary adapter for two-display systems, to Windowed WIN-OS/2, which specifies whether Windows applications should run in windowed or full-screen sessions on the desktop. A typical entry might look something like:

KEYWORD = *parameter, parameter, parameter*

For example, the keyword ToolAndGames specifies which productivity applications and games will be installed. A value of 0 installs none of them, a value of 1 installs all of them, and by using other numbers, separated by commas, you can install specific programs. The entry

ToolsAndGames= 2, 4, 7

installs the Enhanced Editor (2), PM Terminal (4), and Solitaire—Klondike (7). The IBM Redbook *OS/2 Remote Installation and Maintenance* lists all the keywords and provides examples of how to use them.

Keywords can appear in the response file in any order, but it makes sense to group them by function; if a keyword occurs twice in a file, only the last one found is used.

An example response file called SAMPLE.RSP is loaded into the OS2\INSTALL directory, and can be unpacked directly from floppy disk #7 using the following command:

```
UNPACK A:\REQUIRED /N:SAMPLE.RSP
```

or unpacked from the directory DISK_7 using this command:

```
UNPACK C:\OS2SE21\DISK_7\REQUIRED C:\OS2\INSTALL
   /N:SAMPLE.RSP
```

Part of SAMPLE.RSP is shown in Listing A.2.

The program RSPINST, which can also be unpacked from the RE-QUIRED file on floppy disk#7, is used to process a response file. RSPINST accepts a single parameter, the name of the response file you want to use; all the entries contained in the response file are processed before the installation actually begins. RSPINST also creates an installation log file that you can review once the installation is complete.

Once the response file is prepared, you must also create the appropriate Transport Disk needed to make the connections across the LAN; this is usually done by redirecting source drives.

Completing the Installation from a File Server

Redirected source drives are used to manage a remote installation. The optimum situation is one in which a central server contains the floppy disk images, and is accessible from all the workstations requiring an installation. This ensures a consistent approach to installing OS/2 on a large number of workstations.

LISTING A.2:

Part of the SAMPLE.RSP response file.

```
*************************************************************
*                                                           *
* Advance Power Management                                  *
*                                                           *
*   Specifies whether or not to install APM.                *
*                                                           *
*   Valid Parms:                                            *
*                                                           *
*      0=Don't install (DEFAULT)                            *
*      1=Autodetect (DEFAULT)                               *
*      2=Install                                            *
*                                                           *
*************************************************************


APM=1


*************************************************************
*                                                           *
* AlternateAdapter                                          *
*                                                           *
*  Specifies secondary adapter for two display systems.     *
* This should be a lower or equal resolution display since  *
* the highest resolution display will be primary for PM.    *
*                                                           *
*   Valid Parms:                                            *
*                                                           *
*      0=None (DEFAULT)                                      *
*      1=Other than following (DDINSTAL will handle)        *
*      2=Monochrome/Printer Adapter                         *
*      3=Color Graphics Adapter                             *
*      4=Enhanced Graphics Adapter                          *
*      5=PS/2 Display Adapter                               *
*      6=Video Graphics Adapter                             *
*      7=8514/A Adapter                                     *
*      8=XGA Adapter                                        *
*      9=SVGA Adapter                                       *
*                                                           *
*************************************************************


AlternateAdapter=0


*************************************************************
*                                                           *
* BaseFileSystem                                            *
*                                                           *
```

LISTING A.2:

Part of the SAMPLE.RSP
response file.
(Continued)

```
*   Specifies which file system should be used to format     *
*   the install partition                                    *
*                                                            *
*   Valid Parms:                                             *
*                                                            *
*      1=HPFS (DEFAULT)                                       *
*      2=FAT                                                  *
*                                                            *
**************************************************************

BaseFileSystem=1

**************************************************************
*                                                            *
* CDROM                                                      *
*                                                            *
*   Specifies which, if any, CD ROM devices you wish to      *
*   install support for.                                     *
*                                                            *
*   Valid Parms:                                             *
*                                                            *
*      0 = None                                              *
*      1 = Autodetect                                        *
*      2=CDTechnology T3301                                   *
*      3=HitachiCDR-1650,1750,3650                            *
*      4=HitachiCDR-3750                                      *
*      5=IBMCD-ROM I                                          *
*      6=IBMCD-ROM II                                         *
*      7=NEC25,36,37,72,73,74,82,83,84                        *
*      8=PanasonicCR-501,LK-MC501S                            *
*      9=SonyCDU-541,561,6211,7211                            *
*      10=SonyCDU-6111                                        *
*      11=TexelDM-3021,5021                                   *
*      12=TexelDM-3024,5024                                   *
*      13=Toshiba3201                                         *
*      14=Toshiba3301,3401                                    *
*      15=OTHER                                               *
*                                                            *
**************************************************************

CDROM=1
```

The process itself is largely independent of the underlying network, and can be performed on the following types of network:

- Novell NetWare
- IBM LAN Server
- IBM TCP/IP for OS/2 on OS/2, AIX, or UNIX systems

First create a set of floppy disk images as described in the previous section, then make Installation and Transport Disks. Your users will boot using these two floppy disks, then establish a connection to the server, and complete the installation from the floppy disk images contained on the server. This can be a dialog-driven installation, or the process can be automated with an appropriate response file. If you use a response file, change the CONFIG.SYS file on the Transport Disk to use the response file installation program RSPINST.EXE rather than the normal installation program, SYSINST2.EXE.

Once again, the topics that have been covered in this section are considered to be advanced procedures, and should only be attempted by knowledgeable system administrators armed with all the appropriate backup documentation.

Recovering from Installation Problems

NOTE Make sure that the system configuration parameters stored in CMOS are set correctly for your computer. Several installation problems have been tracked down to wrongly specified floppy disk drives.

If OS/2 refuses to run, make sure the computer is on the list of qualified machines in Chapter 8, or contact the supplier for information. Here are some other things that you can check:

- If possible, look at the README file that came with the operating system for any late-breaking news on compatibility issues.

- Check local bulletin boards, CompuServe, or the IBM National Support Center bulletin board for the latest news in device drivers and for up-to-the-minute information.

- Check that the computer has at least 4MB of memory installed.

- Make sure that the computer is an 80386 or 80486 (or better) processor. If the machine uses an 80386, check that it has a stepping level of D0 or later.

- Make sure that there is sufficient free space on the hard disk for the swap file to grow.

See Appendix B for more information on the toll-free telephone numbers you can use to contact IBM Technical Support with details of your problem.

If the installation started but did not complete, reboot the computer using the first two floppy disks, the installation disk and the first operating system disk, and when you see the blue screen, press the Escape key instead of continuing with the installation. This puts you at an OS/2 command prompt. Place an empty floppy disk in drive A, change to the OS2\INSTALL directory, and copy the INSTALL.LOG file onto the floppy disk. You will now be able to review this text file on another computer, and perhaps determine the cause of the failure.

OS/2 OS/2 OS/2

OS/2 OS/2 OS/2 OS/2 OS/2 OS/2 OS/2 OS/2 OS/2

OS/2 OS/2 OS/2 OS/2 O

OS/2 Resources

THIS appendix lists many of the varied sources of technical information (some formal and some less formal) available for the OS/2 operating system, including IBM technical support, IBM publications, bulletin boards, magazines, and periodicals.

IBM Technical Support

You are automatically entitled to 60 days of free technical support for questions on installing and using OS/2 via the OS/2 Support Line. Mail in your registration form, or call the OS/2 Support Line at 800-237-5511, and you will be assigned a registration number to use for further support. The 60-day time window begins on the date of the first call, not the OS/2 purchase date. At the end of 60 days, you can continue support if you wish, but there is a charge associated with continuing this service.

If you find a bug in OS/2, and report it through the official service support channels, and the problem is confirmed by IBM, an Authorized Program Activity Report (APAR) is generated. Each APAR is assigned a unique number so that it can be tracked, and at some point a fix will be available and the APAR will be "closed" in IBM jargon. Not all APARs are closed, however; some are described as "working as defined," while others may be designated as "SUG," suggested for inclusion in a future release, or as "DOC," indicating that the program documentation was in error. Eventually, APARs make their way into Corrective Service Diskettes, or CSDs, and then into the next release of the product. CSDs are accumulative; that is, you only need to install the most recent CSD to bring your system up to date from any previous level. Use the SYSLEVEL command at the OS/2 system prompt to see your current and previous version number and CSD level. CSDs can be ordered by anyone with an IBM customer number, and can be downloaded from the IBM National Support Center BBS, from the OS/2 forums on CompuServe, or from the IBM OS/2 BBS. If you've just bought version 2.1, you can assume that your system is up-to-date; if you're using version 2.0, you should order the current CSD.

If IBM Central Service cannot provide the appropriate level of defect support during the first three months of your license, they will, as a last resort, refund you the purchase price of OS/2.

If you install OS/2 on a PC that's not on the compatibility list shown in Chapter 8, and you run into problems, are you out of luck? No. Call the IBM Defect Center at 800-237-5511 and explain the problem you are experiencing. If they cannot develop a workaround or resolve the problem to everyone's satisfaction within 90 days, they will refund you the purchase price of OS/2 as a gesture of goodwill.

The OS/2 Support Line is not available to users of the OS/2 Extended Edition or LAN Server; contact your vendor for more information on technical support.

OS/2 Standard Edition Documentation

The following publications are included with the OS/2 operating system:

- *Installation Guide* (84F8486) describes the basics of installing OS/2.

- *Getting Started* (84F8465) contains an overview of OS/2 and its main features.

- *Migrating to the OS/2 Workplace Shell* (42G0239) covers the similarities and differences between the OS/2 workplace shell, Windows, and OS/2 version 1.3.

- *Using the Operating System* (42G0238) describes the object-oriented approach used in the OS/2 graphical user interface.

- *OS/2 Compatibility Information* (41G8276) is a small booklet that describes the kinds of programs likely to cause problems in OS/2.

- *Adobe Type Manager for WIN-OS/2* (41G8275) describes using the Adobe Type Manager in WIN-OS/2.

- *OS/2 Quick Reference* (42G0231) is a handy six-sided card containing information on installing OS/2 and performing everyday tasks from the desktop.

- *OS/2 Electronic Device Driver Distribution Mechanism* (10G5961) describes how to download device drivers from the IBM National Support Center bulletin board (described in detail later in this appendix).

Also included are the usual software license registration, special offer, and change-of-address forms.

The following OS/2 publications are available separately:

- *IBM OS/2 Command Reference* (10G6313) contains the same information as the online OS/2 Command Reference.

- *Keyboards and Code Pages* (10G6312) lists information about keyboard layouts, code-page tables, and specific accented characters.

- *OS/2 Workplace Shell Video* (41G5097) contains information that helps you to make the transition to the workplace shell.

- *OS/2 2.0 Using Bidirectional Support* (41G8688) describes using bidirectional functions.

- *IBM Extended Services for OS/2 Information and Planning Guide* (3260161) provides information on planning and use of OS/2 Extended Services, including the Communications Manager, the Database Manager, and the Query Manager.

- *IBM LAN Server Version 2.0 Information and Planning Guide* (3260162) provides an overview of all the main features of LAN Server.

These publications can be ordered from:

IBM Corporation
PO Box 2009
Racine, WI 53401

or by calling 800-426-7282 (414-633-8108 in Alaska).

You can also order:

- *OS/2 Application Solutions*, a cross-referenced directory of applications that lists more than 1400 listings worldwide, and includes applications certified for OS/2 LAN Server.

from 800-READ-OS2.

IBM OS/2 Red Books

Several important documents are available as Red Books, so called because of their red covers, produced by IBM International Technical Support Centers. Red Books are intended for system engineers, technical support personnel, and IBM dealers. The following Red Books are available:

- *OS/2 Version 2: Remote Installation and Maintenance* (GG24-3780) describes installing and maintaining OS/2 using redirected input/output on LAN-based client/server systems and response file techniques.

- *OS/2 Version 2*, vol. 1: *Control Program* (GG24-3730) covers the functions provided by the OS/2 Control Program.

- *OS/2 Version 2*, vol. 2: *DOS and Windows Environment* (GG24-3731) details the virtual DOS machine and virtual machine boot internals, as well as covering WIN-OS/2.

- *OS/2 Version 2*, vol. 3: *Presentation Manager and Workplace Shell* (GG24-3732) covers Presentation Manager features.

- *OS/2 Version 2*, vol. 4: *Application Development* (GG-24-3774) is aimed at developers interested in using object-oriented design and progranmming constructs under OS/2.

- *OS/2 Version 2*, vol. 5: *Print Subsystem* (GG24-3775) covers printing and managing the spooler.

- *OS/2 Version 2.1 Update Redbook* (GG24-3948) covers the differences between OS/2 version 2.0 and version 2.1.

OS/2 RESOURCES

You can also order the entire set of OS/2 Version 2 Red Books as the *OS/2 Version 2 Technical Compendium*, GBOF-2254.

Other Red Books that cover OS/2 and operating system extensions are also available, including:

- *Automated Installation for CID-Enabled OS/2* (GG24-3783).
- *Automated Installation for CID-Enabled Extended Services, LAN Server, and Network Transport Services/2* (GG24-3781).
- *LAN Server 2: New Functions and Features* (GG24-3875).
- *NetWare from IBM: Network Protocols and Standards* (GG24-3890).
- *Extended Services for OS/2 Database Manager; New Features* (GG24-3794).
- *Developing a CUA Workplace Application* (GG24-3580).
- *Evaluation of OS/2 Application Development Tools* (ZZ81-0295).
- *Practical Introduction to Object-Oriented Programming* (GG24-3641).
- *Migrating from a DOS/Windows Environment to OS/2* (GG24-3822).
- *Multimedia Application Enablers and PS/2 Ultimedia* (GG24-3749).
- *IBM Personal System/2 Multimedia Fundamentals* (GG24-3653).

Red Books are also made available on disk in .INF format, suitable for use with the OS/2 VIEW command.

► S O L U T I O N

You can order IBM documents by fax or by telephone. If you want to order by fax, include the following information:

- Your IBM Customer Number, if you have one.
- The part numbers for the publications you want to order.

- Your credit card type (VISA, MasterCard, or Diners Club), card number, expiration date, and your name as it appears on the card.

- Your name, telephone number, fax number, and the shipping address you want the documents sent to.

Send your fax to 800-284-4721, toll-free in the USA.

To order by telephone, collect all the information listed above, and then call 800-879-2755 to reach the automated IBM Software Manufacturing and Delivery facility. When the phone is answered, select option 1, and follow the directions. You can place telephone orders from 6:30 A.M. to 6:00 P.M. mountain standard time.

OS/2 Extended Services Documentation

The OS/2 Extended Services software runs on top of the standard edition of OS/2, and includes the Communications Manager, the Database Manager, and the Query Manager. A separate product, IBM Extended Services with Database Server for OS/2, also includes those three components, as well as a database server capability and a distributed feature, offering a database client application enabler for use on DOS, Windows, and OS/2 workstations.

The following documentation is shipped with both of these Extended Services products:

- *Product Supplement Information* (04G1009) collects together information not found in the other publications, and should be read before installing Extended Services.

- *Start Here* (04G1000) contains task-oriented road maps, a product overview, and a bibliography of related IBM publications.

- *Workstation Installation Guide* (04G1008) describes how to install or remove the basic components of OS/2 Extended Services.

- *Query Manager User's Guide* (04G1010) is aimed at users who will use the Query Manager to perform Database Manager tasks.

- *Query Manager Exercises* (04G1011) includes exercises to introduce the functions contained in the Query Manager.

- *Structured Query Language (SQL) Reference* (04G1012) is a guide for programmers who want to develop database applications that use SQL to access a database.

- *Guide to Database Manager* (04G1013) includes theoretical information about how the Database Manager works, rather than listing the steps needed to complete an operation.

- *Hardware and Software Reference* (04G1014) is a planning tool for users of OS/2 Extended Services.

- *Communications Manager User's Guide* (04G1015) provides the information a user needs to perform tasks using the Communications Manager.

- *Communications Manager Additional Functions Installation Guide and Reference* (96F8312) describes additional device drivers used when networking in DOS partitions under OS/2 version 2.0.

- *Productivity Aids* (96F8313) details the utilities provided with the Communications Manager.

- *Messages and Error Recovery* (04G1017) lists all the Extended Services error messages.

- *Keyboard Layouts* (04G1018) describes the functions performed by keyboards when the Communications Manager is installed.

- *Glossary* (04G1019) provides a description of the technical terms used throughout the Extended Services.

The following publications are also available with the Extended Services with Database Server:

- *LAN Support Program* (04G1115) is aimed at the network administrator, and describes how to configure the LAN support program.

- *Guide to Database Manager Client Application Enablers* (04G1114) is designed for network administrators who install and maintain database client application enablers on networked workstations.

Also included with these products are the usual software license registration, special offer, and change-of-address forms.

The following publication is available separately:

- *Extended Services for OS/2 Information and Planning Guide* (G326-0161) provides information useful to anyone planning to use or implement Extended Services.

OS/2 LAN Server Documentation

OS/2 LAN Server is a local area network program that provides OS/2 LAN Server, OS/2 LAN Requestor, and DOS Requestor. OS/2 LAN Server provides network resource sharing of files, disks, printers, and other devices; OS/2 LAN Requestor and DOS LAN Requestor allow OS/2 and DOS users, respectively, to use network resources.

The following documentation is shipped with OS/2 LAN Server:

- *Network Administrator Reference*, vol. I (04G1032), vol. II (04G1033), and vol. III (04G1034) cover network planning and installation, performance tuning, and network administrator tasks, respectively.

- *Network Administrator Reference Supplement for OS/2* (41G8776) describes the differences between this and previous versions of OS/2, and how these differences affect OS/2 LAN Server.

- *User's Quick Reference* (04G1035) describes how to use the OS/2 Requestor and the OS/2 operating system to perform everyday network tasks.

- *DOS LAN Requestor User's Quick Reference* (04G1037) describes how to use the DOS LAN Requestor part of OS/2 LAN Server to perform everyday network tasks.

- *Productivity Aids* (41G8758) quickly describes the bundled OS/2 LAN Server productivity programs.

- *Migration Handbook* (04G1044) describes the tasks involved when migrating from PC LAN Program 1.3 (or earlier), or IBM OS/2 LAN Server 1.0 (or later), to OS/2 LAN Server Version 2.0.

- *DOS LAN Requestor Windows User's Guide* (04G1038) describes how to configure and use DOS LAN Requestor Windows.

- *LAN Support Program User's Guide* (04G1039) is aimed at the network administrator, and describes how to configure the LAN support program.

- *Problem Determination Reference* vol. I (04G1144), vol. II (41G8774), and vol. III (41G8775) cover problem determination, LAN alerts, and LAN error messages, respectively.

- *Master Index* (41G8773) is a master index for all the publications listed above in the OS/2 LAN Server library.

Also included with the OS/2 LAN Server are the usual software license registration, special offer, and change-of-address forms.

The following publication is available separately:

- *LAN Server Version 2 Information and Planning Guide* (G326-0162) provides information useful to anyone planning to use or implement LAN Server 2.

Extended Services Administrator's Kit

An IBM Extended Services Administrator's kit is also available. This kit includes the documentation needed to perform all the administrative tasks associated with planning and implementing a multiple-workstation or host-connected environment. The kit encompasses DOS 3.3 and later versions, OS/2 2.0 Standard Edition, OS/2 Extended Services, OS/2 Extended Services with Database Server, OS/2 LAN Server, and more; and it includes the following publications:

- *Network Administration Guide* (04G1001) is aimed at those people who will plan, install, configure and maintain any combination of the software described in the previous paragraph.

- *Communications Manager Configuration Guide* (04G1002) is aimed at people who will install or configure Communications Manager.

- *Programmable Configuration Reference* (04G1003) covers Communications Manager configuration files and how to use the REXX programming language to write configuration programs.

- *Host Connection Reference* (04G1004) is aimed at the IBM System/370 and IBM AS/400 programmer using Virtual Telecommunications Access Method (VTAM) and Network Control Program (NCP) listings.

- *Guide to User Profile Management* (04G1112) describes the access control system used for logging onto workstations and accessing protected network resources.

- *LAN Adapter and Protocol Support Configuration Guide* (04G1113) covers workstation configuration for connection to several different networks.

- *Example Scenarios* (04G1005) describes how to plan, install, and configure 14 different network communications connections, including workstations, printers, and other LANS.

- *Problem Determination Guide for the Service Coordinator* (04G1006) helps the service coordinator identify problems that users cannot resolve using the online information available to them.

- *Programming Services and Advanced Problem Determination for Communications* (04G1007) describes the advanced facilities available to troubleshoot communications using the Communications Manager.

- *Communications Manager System Management Programming Reference* (04G1116) is for anyone who wants to set up an OS/2 workstation as part of an Advanced Peer-to-Peer Networking (APPN) network using OS/2 Extended Services.

The kit also includes a package of worksheets, part number 04G1111.

IBM's HelpWare

IBM has established HelpWare as part of the PS/2 marketing effort, and several of the toll-free numbers are aimed at OS/2 users.

- **Help Center:** Call 800-PS2-2227 (800-426-4238 TDD/ASCII) with a PS/2 or OS/2 question.

- **OS/2 Information Line:** Call 800-342-6672 for OS/2-specific information.

- **OS/2 Support Line:** Call 800-237-5511 with specific OS/2 installation, system setup, or usage questions.

- **OS/2 Bulletin Board:** Call 800-547-1283 for registration information for the OS/2 bulletin board.

- **OS/2 Application Assistance Center:** Call 800-547-1283 for expert application programming assistance, and technical workshop information.

There is a fee for many of these services.

> ## SOLUTION
>
> You can receive up-to-the-minute information on IBM products by fax through IBM's computerized fax machine and voice response unit. Information is available on products that range from large systems to PCs, operating system and application software, IBM services, and other general information.
>
> Call 800-IBM-4FAX or 800-426-4329 to select the product information document, brochure, or specification sheet you are interested in, and it will be sent to your fax machine. This service is available round-the-clock, seven days a week, and best of all, there is no charge for this service.

IBM National Support Center Bulletin Board

IBM's National Support Center bulletin board (NSC) is available to OS/2 licensees and users on a toll-call basis, but with no charge to access the bulletin board. The bulletin board features product conferences on PC and PS/2 products, as well as MS-DOS and OS/2 subjects, and OS/2 device drivers in a format suitable for downloading.

N O T E The IBM NSC bulletin board runs on an OS/2 LAN Server version 1.3 Token-Ring network.

To connect to the bulletin board, you need:

- A modem capable of 1200 baud, or better.
- A communications program (such as PM Terminal) that supports the XMODEM file transfer protocol.
- Communications parameters in your communications program set to eight data bits, one stop bit, and no parity.

The bulletin board can be reached by dialing one of the following numbers:

- 404-835-6600 for the first available modem.
- 404-835-6296 reaches the first available Hayes Ultra modem.
- 404-835-5300 dials the first USR V.32bis modem.
- 404-835-5578 reaches the first available IBM 7855 Model 10 modem.

NOTE

In Canada, the Canadian Software Support Center also supports several OS/2 bulletin boards, as follows. In Vancouver dial 604-664-6464; in Toronto, dial 416-946-4244, or 416-946-4255; and in Montreal, dial 514-938-3122.

Even though there are 40 lines available, this bulletin board can get very busy during normal hours, so be prepared to dial several times, or try to dial during the early morning or very late at night.

The following File Directories are available on this bulletin board:

1. IBM Hardware Announcements
2. IBM Software Announcements
3. Upgrade Forms
4. Corrective Service Software
5. Bulletin Text Files
6. PC User Group Text Files
7. Miscellaneous Files
8. System Specific Files
9. Printer Specific Files
10. OS/2 Utilities
11. OS/2 Programming
12. OS/2 Graphics and Music
13. OS/2 Entertainment
14. OS/2 Communications Files
15. OS/2 Text Files
16. OS/2 Applications
17. OS/2 Device Drivers
18. OS/2 Bulletin Board

19. DOS Utilities

20. DOS Programming

21. DOS Graphics and Music

22. DOS Entertainment

23. DOS Communications Files

24. DOS Text Processing

25. DOS Applications

26. DOS Bulletin Board

27. Reference and Adapter Diskettes

28. Disability Enabling Text Files

29. Reserved

30. Reserved

31. Reserved

32. Network Support Files

33. NetWare 2.2 Update Files

34. NetWare 3.11 Update Files

U. Upload Directory

P. Private User Files

S. SysOp Private Files

IBM OS/2 Bulletin Board

A special IBM bulletin board is available for OS/2 users. For information about registering and accessing this bulletin board, call 800-547-1283. To locate an IBM OS/2 bulletin board in your area, call 609-596-1267. This automatic service asks for your telephone area code and responds with the phone numbers of bulletin boards in your area.

The bulletin board provides conferences and forums, customer-to-customer messaging, technical support, news, announcements, and software in a form suitable for downloading.

OS/2 RESOURCES

The following topics are generally available:

- OS/2 Installation
- OS/2 Base Commands and Functions
- Workplace Shell
- OS/2 Virtual DOS Machine Support
- OS/2 Windows Support
- OS/2 Applications
- OS/2 Beginner's Forum
- Printing Under OS/2
- OS/2 Publications Help
- OS/2 General Question and Answer
- OS/2 Arena
- OS/2 and Presentation Manager Programming
- IBM WorkFrame/2
- IBM Developer's Toolkit for OS/2
- IBM C Set/2 Compiler
- Procedures Language/2 REXX
- Extended Services—Communications Manager
- Extended Services—Database Manager
- IBM LAN Server for OS/2
- NetWare Requester for OS/2
- IS THERE?
- IBM Mini Applications for OS/2
- Games
- Hardware Vendor Boards and Systems for OS/2
- OS/2 2.0 Enhanced Editor
- TCP/IP for OS/2 and DOS

- Comments and Suggestions on OS/2 BBS
- Comments and Suggestions on OS/2 Electronic Search
- ForBrowse—OS/2 BBS Offline Forum Viewer
- LAN Systems Beta Testing

Additional topics are added as required for specific beta testing programs, and other needs.

IBM OS/2 Customer Classes

For the latest IBM customer class schedules, or to enroll in these classes, call 800-IBM-8322. Recently added classes include:

- Introduction to OS/2 Version 2 Programming
- Introduction to DOS for OS/2
- OS/2 Version 2.0 Facilities and Installation Workshop
- Advanced Programming Techniques for OS/2 version 2.0
- ENFIN/2 Object-Oriented Development for OS/2
- OS/2 Version 1 to Version 2 Programming Migration

IBM also offers "private" classes, for specific customers requesting a particular class. For information on these classes, call 800-462-2468. There is a charge for all classes.

IBM Field Television Network Broadcasts and Tapes

From time to time, IBM broadcasts topics of interest via satellite using the IBM Field Television Network (FTN). Anyone who wants to can watch these programs live by tuning a dish antenna to Satellite SBS-5, at 123 degrees West longitude, horizontal polarity, transponder 9, 12.117 GHz frequency, and 6.8 MHz audio subchannel. These broadcasts are also taped, and VHS tapes can be ordered by calling 800-282-0226, or by writing to:

IBM Technical Coordinator Program
IBM Corporation 40-A2-04
One East Kirkwood Boulevard
Roanoak, TX 76299-0015

A charge is made for videotapes.

OS/2 Technical Library

The OS/2 Technical Library is aimed at professional software developers. The following documents make up the OS/2 Technical Library:

- *Application Design Guide* (10G6260) describes specific aspects of programming in the OS/2 environment, and is a companion volume to the *OS/2 Programming Guide*, vols. I, II, and III.

- *Programming Guide*, vol. I (10G6261), vol. II (10G6494), and vol. III (10G6495), includes examples and code fragments for common programming tasks such as windowing, graphics, file management, and the print system and spooling.

- *Presentation Manager Programming Reference*, vol. I (10G6264), vol. II (10G6265), and vol. III (10G6272), covers programming the Presentation Manager interface.

- *Control Program Programming Reference* (10G6263) is a detailed technical reference to the base operating system functions with the DOS prefix.

- *System Object Model Guide and Reference* (10G6309) describes the OS/2 System Object Model (SOM) and explains how C programmers can write programs using SOM.

- *Systems Application Architecture Common User Access Guide to Interface Design* (SC34-4289) describes the theory behind user interface design.

- *Systems Application Architecture Common User Access Advanced Interface Design Reference* (SC34-4290) provides an alphabetical list of the interface components detailed in the CUA definition.

- *Presentation Driver Reference* (10G6267) describes OS/2 presentation drivers.

- *Physical Device Driver Reference* (10G6266) covers the operation and definition of physical device drivers.

- *Virtual Device Driver Reference* (10G6310) details information needed to write virtual device drivers.

- *Information Presentation Facility Guide and Reference* (10G6262) describes the Information Presentation Facility (IPF) used to design and develop online documents and help facilities.

- *Procedures Language 2/REXX User's Guide* (10G6269) describes how to use the Restructured Extended Executor language, REXX.

- *Procedures Language 2/REXX Reference* (10G6268) is a reference to all REXX functions, error numbers, and error messages.

You can order the complete OS/2 Technical Library as a single package, by specifying part number 10G3356, or you can order each book individually. Call 1-800-IBM-PCTB (1-800-465-7282) to place your order in the USA; in Alaska call 1-414-633-8108, and in Canada call 1-800-465-1234. You can also order these books from an IBM authorized dealer or representative.

The following single volume is also available:

- *National Language Design Guide*, vol. 1: *Designing Enabled Products, Rules and Guidelines* (SE09-8001) explains rules and guidelines aimed at helping developers produce applications enabled for national-language support.

Multimedia Presentation Manager/2 Technical Library

The MMPM/2 Technical Library is addressed to software developers interested in producing MMPM/2 multimedia applications for OS/2. You will find the following documents in the MMPM/2 Technical Library:

- *Getting Started* (41G8306) describes installing and configuring MMPM/2.

- *OS/2 Multimedia Advantage* (41G2923) describes the advantages of using OS/2 and MMPM/2 as a multimedia platform.

- *Programming Guide* (41G2919) provides information on multimedia programming systems and interfaces.

- *Sample Programs Workbook* (41G2921) contains information on multimedia programming along with extensive sample code you can use in your own applications.

- *Programming Reference* (41G2920) gives detailed information on multimedia functions, messages, and data structures.

- *CUA Guide to Multimedia User Interface Design* (41G2922) helps designers of multimedia products develop a consistent user interface.

The complete MMPM/2 Technical Library is available as part number 41G3321.

OS/2 Application Development Tools

IBM has provided a complete set of 32-bit programming tools in support of OS/2, including:

- C Set/2 is an ANSI-standard 32-bit optimizing C compiler that exploits the power and speed of the 80386 and 80486 processors.
      The compiler is provided with a complete set of run-time libraries, and an interactive, source-level debugger. C Set/2 is available on 3.5" disks (10G2996) or 5.25" disks (10G3293).

NOTE   The C Developer's WorkSet/2 contains both the C Set/2 compiler and the Developer's Workbench for OS/2, and is available in 3.5" disks (10G2995) or 5.25" disks (10G3663).

- Developer's Toolkit for OS/2 contains tools for developing an on-line help system, creating dialog boxes, and for modifying fonts and icons, and is available in 3.5" disks (10G3355) or 5.25" disks (10G4335).

- WorkFrame/2 is a graphical user interface designed to simplify application development, and to integrate your choice of development tools, including those from MS-DOS and Windows. The WorkFrame/2 is available on 3.5" disks (10G2994), or on 5.25" disks (10G3292).

For more information call 800-342-6672; in Canada call 800-465-7999.

Other OS/2 software development tools, including 32-bit C and C++ compilers, are also available from Borland and from Zortech.

The IBM Developer Assistance Program

IBM's Developer Assistance Program (DAP) provides technical information and assistance to qualified software developers creating OS/2 products for retail sale. Participants in the program receive the following benefits:

- **Technical Support:** Support via the IBMLink bulletin board.

- **Defect Support:** A toll-free number for reporting defects and requesting the latest Corrective Service Disks.

- **Software Discounts:** Discounts on selected OS/2 products ordered from IBM.

- **Hardware Rebate:** A rebate on selected PS/2 products purchased from IBM authorized dealers.

- **PS/2 Loan Program:** A loan program for certain IBM PS/2 hardware.

- **Application Migration Workshops:** Information on technical workshops to help developers migrate their applications to OS/2.

- *IBM OS/2 Developer*: Free subscription to this quarterly technical magazine and other technical mailings.

To qualify for entry into the Developer Assistance Program, IBM requires that you meet the following qualifications:

- You develop OS/2 products.

- The products are being actively marketed now.

- Your company is a US company, or a US subsidiary of a foreign company.

If your product is not yet ready for marketing, you can submit a nonconfidential business plan showing development plans and schedules.

IBM reserves the right to accept or reject an application to the DAP, and there is no charge for enrollment. For an application form, contact:

IBM Corporation
Software Developer Support
PO Box 1328
Boca Raton, FL 33429-1328

or call 407-443-2000. Dial 407-982-6408 to receive a sign-up form by fax, or type GO OS2DAP on CompuServe and complete the electronic version of the sign-up form.

The IBM Independent Vendor (IV) League

IBM provides free marketing and technical assistance to qualified independent vendors who provide products or services for OS/2. IV League members include consultants and authors, training companies, book publishers, and companies developing OS/2 courseware. Contact the IV League at the following address for more information:

IBM Corporation
150 Kettletown Road,
Southbury, CT 06488

The IV League Catalog, available free by calling 800-342-6672, details the products and services available from the independent vendors.

OS/2 Special Interest Groups

Many PC User Groups have Special Interest Groups (SIGs) specializing in OS/2 applications and development. Contact the group in your area for meeting times and locations.

SOLUTION

Any local retail computer store or bulletin board should know where and when your nearest PC User Group meets each month. If you draw a blank, call the User Group Locator Line at (914) 876-6678 and enter your ZIP code, state abbreviation, or telephone area code to find the nearest group.

The Association of PC User Groups (APCUG) is a nonprofit affiliation of local PC User's Groups, dedicated to fostering communications between personal computer user groups, and acting as an information network between user groups and software publishers and hardware manufacturers. You can contact them at:

APCUG
1730 M Street N.W., Suite 700
Washington, DC 20036

CompuServe and the OS/2 Forums

NOTE   Golden CommPass, an OS/2 CompuServe access program, is available from Creative Systems Programming Corp, PO Box 961, Mount Laurel, NJ 08054-0961, phone 609-234-1500, fax 609-234-1920, CompuServe ID 71511,151.

CompuServe is one of the largest online information services, and provides an incredible array of information, communication, electronic mail, and entertainment services. For CompuServe membership information, call 800-848-8199. CompuServe has several hundred forums, or special interest groups, and each forum offers three main services:

- The Message Board allows you to swap ideas and experiences with other forum members. You can read messages left by other forum members, and post messages of your own.

- Libraries contain files that you can download to your computer. These files may be text files or program files, and may have been compressed by the popular compression program PKZIP. If the file name extension is .ZIP, the file has been compressed, and you must use the decompression program PKUNZIP to return the file to its normal form so you can read or run it.

- Conference Rooms allow you to interact online with other forum members.

N O T E   You can contact PKware, the distributors of PKZIP, at 9025 N. Deerwood Drive, Brown Deer, WI 53223, phone 414-354-8699, fax 414-354-8559.

When you log onto CompuServe, you can enter a forum immediately if you type *GO forum*, where *forum* is the name of the forum you want to visit. At this writing, there are several OS/2 forums on CompuServe:

- IBM OS/2 User's Forum
- IBM OS/2 Support Forum
- IBM OS/2 Developer's 1 Forum
- IBM OS/2 Developer's 2 Forum

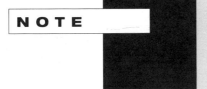

N O T E   Occasionally, you may encounter another forum, ServicePak, that just contains updated OS/2 system files in a form suitable for downloading and installing on your computer.

The last library in each OS/2 forum is called IBM Files, and it contains two important entries that summarize all the files in all the libraries in that particular forum. For example, the file USRSUM.ZIP contains a one-line summary of all the files in all the libraries in the IBM OS/2 Users Forum. This file is updated on the first of each month. The companion file USRNEW.ZIP contains a one-line summary of all the new files added to all the libraries in the forum since the beginning of the month. You can retrieve these index files and peruse them at your leisure rather than on-line (saving time and money), then download just the files you are interested in reading or using. Each individual library also contains a short summary file listing the entries in the library. The four summary files are called USRSUM.ZIP, SUPSUM.ZIP, DF1SUM.ZIP, and DF2SUM.ZIP.

The update files are called USRNEW.ZIP, SUPNEW.ZIP, DF1-NEW.ZIP, and DF2NEW.ZIP. The individual library summary files are named for the forum, then the library number. For example, the OS/2 User's Forum Library 5 is the Documentation Library, and its summary file is called USRL5.SUM.

Other useful files found on many online services include OS/2 Tips and Techniques (usually called OS2TNT), and OS/2 Frequently Asked Questions, (usually called OS2FAQ). These files are text files and answer many of the common questions on OS/2.

IBM OS/2 User's Forum

The IBM OS/2 User's Forum on CompuServe is for new users of the operating system, and includes the following libraries:

1. OS/2 Public Image
2. 1.x General Questions and Answers
3. OS/2 and Hardware
4. Application Questions
5. Documentation
6. New User Questions
7. Suggestions
8. IBM Marketing
9. TEAM OS/2
10. Moving to OS/2DF1
11. RouteXpander/2
12. Open Forum
13. Fun and Games
14. IBM Files

IBM OS/2 Support Forum

The IBM OS/2 Support Forum on CompuServe is aimed at the general user of OS/2 and includes the following libraries:

1. General Questions
2. Install Questions
3. Hardware—I/O Media
4. Hardware—Platform
5. Hardware—Displays
6. Hardware—Printers
7. Hardware—Miscellaneous
8. WPS/SOM Questions
9. ES/LS Questions
10. REXX Language Questions
11. DOS Application Questions
12. Windows Application Questions
13. OS/2 Application Questions
14. Communications Application Questions
15. Open Forum
16. Beta Program '92
17. IBM Files

IBM OS/2 Developer's 1 Forum

The IBM OS/2 Developer's 1 Forum on CompuServe is aimed at the professional software developer, and includes the following libraries:

1. Base OS APIs

2. PM APIs

3. Object Technology

4. IBM C SET/2 IPMD

5. IBM C++

6. REXX/Other Languages

7. Development Tools

8. Debugging

8. Thunking 16 <–> 32

10. OS Migration

11. Device Driver Development

12. MMPM/2—Multimedia

13. DMK/2—Mirrors

14. Open Forum

15. Product Suggestions

16. IBM Files

IBM OS/2 Developer's 2 Forum

The IBM OS/2 Developer's 2 Forum is also aimed at the professional software developer, and includes the following libraries:

1. Communications Manager

2. Database Manager

3. LAN Server

4. NTS/2—Transport

5. TCP/IP

6. CID Enablement

7. PEN Software

8. Installer and DA/2

9. SPM/2—Performance

10. LAN NetView

11. DCE—OSF/DCE on OS/2

12. Developer CD-ROM

13. OS/2 Developer Magazine

14. Open Forum

15. Product Suggestions

16. IBM Files

Prodigy and OS/2

Prodigy, a joint venture of IBM and Sears-Roebuck, is another popular online information system that offers conferences on many different topics. For information on OS/2, Prodigy subscribers should "jump" to Computer Club and select a topic. At the moment, there are two topics containing OS/2 discussions; Windows and OS/2, and Operating Systems.

Call the voice line 800-PRODIGY (800-776-8277) for information about membership and monthly charges.

OS/2 Bulletin Boards Around the World

There are many bulletin boards across the USA and around the world that specialize in OS/2 and OS/2 applications. Table B.1 lists some of the bulletin boards in the USA, and Table B.2 lists bulletin boards from the rest of the world.

TABLE B.1: OS/2 Bulletin Boards (BBS) in the USA

TELEPHONE NUMBER	BBS NAME
203-483-0348 (CT)	Fernwood BBS
213-494-6168 (CA)	BLUEzz BBS
214-578-8774 (TX)	Megasys BBS
215-879-3310 (CA)	Optical Illusion BBS
301-680-7792 (MD)	Midlantic BBS
302-477-0236 (DL)	Delaware Valley OS/2 User's Group BBS
314-554-9313 (MI)	Gateway/2 OS/2 BBS
404-471-1549 (GA)	Information Overload BBS
408-259-2223 (CA)	AmsLang and OS/2
503-883-8197 (OR)	Multi-Net BBS
510-657-7948 (CA)	Bay Area OS/2 BBS
619-558-9475 (CA)	OS/2 Connection BBS
702-399-0486 (NV)	Communitel OS/2 BBS
703-323-7654 (VA)	System's Exchange
703-385-4325 (VA)	OS/2 Shareware BBS
703-560-5616 (VA)	Life's Like That
707-895-4042 (IL)	Greater Chicago Area Online
713-437-2859 (TX)	Soldier's Bored BBS
714-963-8517 (CA)	Omega-point BBS
817-485-8042 (TX)	Ruck's Place/2 CBCS
818-706-9805 (CA)	Magnum BBS
904-682-1620 (FL)	Wizard's Opus BBS
904-739-2445 (FL)	OS2 Exchange
908-382-5671 (NJ)	The Monster BBS
908-506-0472 (NJ)	The Dog's Breakfast
919-226-6984 (NC)	Programmer's Oasis BBS

TABLE B.2: OS/2 Bulletin Boards (BBS) Around the World

TELEPHONE NUMBER	BBS NAME
31-4752-6200 (Netherlands)	INFOBOARD
32-3-3850748 (Belgium)	Moving Sound OS/2
32-3-3872021 (Belgium)	OS/2 Mania Belgium
33-1-6409-0460 (France)	OS/2 Mania BBS
34-1-519-4645 (Spain)	Icaro BBS
41-41-538607 (Switzerland)	Mics OS/2 Paradise
41-61-9412204 (Switzerland)	PC-Info
44-4545-633197 (Great Britain)	MonuSci CBCS (OS/2 User Group)
45-98451070 (Denmark)	OS/2 Task & FrontDoor
47-83-33003 (Norway)	PerlePorten
49-7331-69116 (Germany)	CheckPoint OS/2
49-201-210744 (Germany)	IBM Mailbox
49-6183-74270 (Germany)	OS/2 Express
49-243-9279222 (Germany)	OS/2 Point
49-6196-27799 (Germany)	PC Softbox OS/2
514-374-9422 (Canada)	Logistique BBS
54-1-742-3674 (Argentina)	OS/2 and Sound BBS
61-2-234-2466 (Australia)	OS/2 Sidney BBS
61-2-875-1296 (Australia)	Programmer's BBS
61-6-259-1244 (Australia)	PC User's Group
61-7-398-3759 (Australia)	OZ-Share OS/2 BBS
65-274-0577 (Singapore)	OS/2 Centre

To access one of these bulletin boards, start out with your system configured for 2400 baud, eight data bits, one stop bit, and no parity. Many of the bulletin boards can operate at much higher baud rates, and many use modems with built-in error-correction, but these communications settings will get you started.

OS/2 Magazines, Periodicals, and Newsletters

OS/2 Developer
PO Box 1079
Skokie, IL 60076-9772
800-WANT-OS2 in the USA, or 708-647-5960 internationally.

A quarterly magazine, formerly called the *Personal Systems Developer*, published by IBM.

IBM Personal Systems Technical Solutions
c/o The TDA Group
PO Box 1360
Los Altos, CA 94023-1360
800-551-2832 in the USA, or 415-948-3140 internationally.
The fax number is 415-948-4280.

A quarterly magazine published by the TDA Group.

OS/2 Monthly
JDS Publishing
PO Box 4351
Highland Park, NJ 08904
800-365-2642

An independent OS/2 monthly magazine from JDS Publishing.

Inside OS/2
The Cobb Group
Louisville KY 40232
502-491-1900
800-223-8720

A monthly OS/2 newsletter from the Cobb Group.

OS/2 Professional
IF Computer Media, Inc
6129 Executive Blvd,
Rockville, MD 20852
301-770-7303; fax 301-770-2327

A bimonthly magazine mailed to qualified users of OS/2.

INDEX

Note: Page numbers in **boldface** are a major source of information on a topic; page numbers in *italics* are references to figures.

J

P

Q

SYBEX

FREE BROCHURE!

Complete this form today, and we'll send you a full-color brochure of Sybex bestsellers.

Please supply the name of the Sybex book purchased.

_____

How would you rate it?

_____ Excellent   _____ Very Good   _____ Average   _____ Poor

Why did you select this particular book?

_____ Recommended to me by a friend

_____ Recommended to me by store personnel

_____ Saw an advertisement in _____

_____ Author's reputation

_____ Saw in Sybex catalog

_____ Required textbook

_____ Sybex reputation

_____ Read book review in _____

_____ In-store display

_____ Other _____

Where did you buy it?

_____ Bookstore

_____ Computer Store or Software Store

_____ Catalog (name: _____)

_____ Direct from Sybex

_____ Other: _____

Did you buy this book with your personal funds?

_____ Yes   _____ No

About how many computer books do you buy each year?

_____ 1-3   _____ 3-5   _____ 5-7   _____ 7-9   _____ 10+

About how many Sybex books do you own?

_____ 1-3   _____ 3-5   _____ 5-7   _____ 7-9   _____ 10+

Please indicate your level of experience with the software covered in this book:

_____ Beginner   _____ Intermediate   _____ Advanced

Which types of software packages do you use regularly?

_____ Accounting	_____ Databases	_____ Networks
_____ Amiga	_____ Desktop Publishing	_____ Operating Systems
_____ Apple/Mac	_____ File Utilities	_____ Spreadsheets
_____ CAD	_____ Money Management	_____ Word Processing
_____ Communications	_____ Languages	_____ Other _____

(please specify)

Which of the following best describes your job title?

_____ Administrative/Secretarial   _____ President/CEO

_____ Director   _____ Manager/Supervisor

_____ Engineer/Technician   _____ Other _____

(please specify)

Comments on the weaknesses/strengths of this book: _____

_____

_____

_____

_____

Name _____

Street _____

City/State/Zip _____

Phone _____

PLEASE FOLD, SEAL, AND MAIL TO SYBEX

SYBEX INC.
Department M
2021 CHALLENGER DR.
ALAMEDA, CALIFORNIA USA
94501

SYBEX

SEAL